EMPIRE AND POPULAR CULTURE

EMPIRE AND POPULAR CULTURE

Edited by John Griffiths

Volume I

LONDON AND NEW YORK

First published 2022
by Routledge
2 Park Square, Milton Park, Abingdon, Oxon OX14 4RN

and by Routledge
605 Third Avenue, New York, NY 10158

Routledge is an imprint of the Taylor & Francis Group, an informa business

© 2022 selection and editorial matter, John Griffiths; individual owners retain copyright in their own material.

The right of John Griffiths to be identified as the author of the editorial material, and of the authors for their individual chapters, has been asserted in accordance with sections 77 and 78 of the Copyright, Designs and Patents Act 1988.

All rights reserved. No part of this book may be reprinted or reproduced or utilised in any form or by any electronic, mechanical, or other means, now known or hereafter invented, including photocopying and recording, or in any information storage or retrieval system, without permission in writing from the publishers.

Trademark notice: Product or corporate names may be trademarks or registered trademarks, and are used only for identification and explanation without intent to infringe.

British Library Cataloguing-in-Publication Data
A catalogue record for this book is available from the British Library

Library of Congress Cataloging-in-Publication Data
Names: Griffiths, John, 1966– editor.
Title: Empire and popular culture / edited by John Griffiths.
Description: London ; New York, NY : Routledge, Taylor & Francis
   Group, 2021– | Includes bibliographical references and index. |
   Contents:Volume 1 — |
Identifiers: LCCN 2021020136 (print) | LCCN 2021020137 (ebook) |
   ISBN 9781138495043 (hardback) | ISBN 9781351024822 (ebook)
Subjects: LCSH: Imperialism in popular culture—Great Britain—
   History—Sources. | Popular culture—Great Britain—History—Sources. |
   Propaganda, British—History—Sources. | Great Britain—In popular
   culture—Sources. | Great Britain—Colonies—History—Sources. |
   Great Britain—History—Sources.
Classification: LCC DA115 .E66 2021 (print) | LCC DA115 (ebook) |
   DDC 306.0941—dc23
LC record available at https://lccn.loc.gov/2021020136
LC ebook record available at https://lccn.loc.gov/2021020137

ISBN: 978-1-138-49504-3 (hbk)
ISBN: 978-1-351-02482-2 (ebk)

DOI: 10.4324/9781351024822

Typeset in Times New Roman
by Apex CoVantage, LLC

CONTENTS

General Introduction: The British Empire in Domestic
Popular Culture   1

Introduction: Youth and education: class, gender and the
making of the imperial citizen 1880–1940   25

1   St. Cyprian's, Eastbourne: 'St. Cyprian's Preparatory
School, Eastbourne', in *War Office Times and Naval
Review*, 1st May 1910, pp. 24–26.   49

2   The training of an English gentleman in the public
schools: Rev. J.E.C. Welldon, 'The Training of the English
Gentleman in the Public Schools', in *The Nineteenth
Century and After*, Vol. 60, No. 355 (1906), pp. 396–418.   53

3   Rev. J.E.C. Welldon, 'The Imperial Aspects of Education',
in *Proceedings of the Royal Colonial Institute*, Vol. 26
(1894–95), pp. 322–347.   69

4   The national life: Rev. J.E.C. Welldon, 'The National Life',
in *Fire Upon the Altar: Sermons Preached to Harrow Boys,
Second Series, 1887–1890* (London: Percival and Co.,
1891), pp. 228–239.   89

5   Eton and the Empire: G. Drage, *Eton and the Empire: An
Address* (Eton: Ingleton Drake, 1890).   94

6   'The Corps', in *The Harrovian*, 2nd June 1900, pp. 46–47.
Reproduced with kind permission of Harrow School Archives.   106

CONTENTS

7   'In Memoriam: William Joseph Myers 1858–1899', in *Eton College Chronicle*, 20th December 1899, pp. 763–764.   110

8   Military training: Rev. J. P. Way, 'Military Training', in *The Public Schools From Within: A Collection of Essays on Public School Education, Written Chiefly by School Masters* (London: Sampson, Low, Marston & Company, 1906), pp. 208–217.   115

9   'With the Scottish Yeomanry in May', in *The Lorettonian*, 27th October 1900, p. 1. Reproduced with kind permission of Loretto School Archive.   122

10 H. B. Gray, 'To the Parents of England's Sons', in *The Public Schools and the Empire* (London: William & Norgate, 1913), pp. 1–26.   126

11 'Public School Boys Empire Tour', in *The Times Educational Supplement*, 18th August 1931, p. 321.   140

12 A visit to the Boer camp – Diyatalawa, Ceylon: 'A Visit to a Boer Camp'.   142

13 The duties and privileges of imperial citizenship: 'The Duties and Privileges of Imperial Citizenship'.   145

14 J. Grant, 'The last day of Khartoum', in *Cassell's History of the War in the Soudan Vol. II* (London: Cassell, 1885–1886), pp. 148–158.   150

15 Richard Danes, *Cassell's Illustrated History the Boer War* (London: Cassell, 1902), pp. 1–24.   157

16 S. R. Gardiner, *A Student's History of England From the Earliest Times to 1885* (London: Longmans and Co., 1892), pp. 952–955.   176

17 E. Salmon, *The Story of the Empire* (London: George Newnes, 1902), pp. 154–163.   179

CONTENTS

18	Victoria and her colonies: J.M.D. Meiklejohn and M.J.C. Meiklejohn, *A School History of England* (London: Alfred Holden, 1902), pp. 449–463.	184
19	C.R.L. Fletcher and R. Kipling, *A School History of England* (Oxford: Clarendon, 1911), pp. 240–241.	195
20	Twenty-second story. – the growth of the Empire: Lesson 43. – In the East: *The Patriotic Historical Reader Book V: Thirty Stories and Biographies from 1688–1897* (London: William Collins, 1898), pp. 208–216.	198
21	*Instructive Stories from English History, Holborn Series Historical Reader* (London: Educational Supply Association, 1900), pp. 135–144.	203
22	*The Young Briton's History Reader* (Glasgow: Collins, 1904), pp. 88–93.	209
23	'The first English colonies, or the work of Raleigh and his friends', in *Macmillan's New History Readers: Senior* (London: Macmillan and Co., 1902), pp. 158–165.	211
24	*Chambers New Geographical Readers, Book VI, British Colonies and Dependencies* (London: W. & R. Chambers, 1898), pp. 31–40; 76–77; 100–103.	216
25	R. Finch, FRGS, *The Kingsway Book of Geography Stories* (London: Evans Brothers Ltd, 1919), pp. 76–82; 152–157; 195–199.	222
26	E.C.T. Horniblow, *Lands and Life: Human Geographies, People and Children of Wonderful Lands* (London: Grant Educational Co., 1930–35). Extract taken from the 1944 edition. pp. 7–19; 103–108.	233
27	*Collins' Wide World Geography Reader: The British Empire* (London: William Collins, 1901–23), pp. 83–87.	237
28	B. G. Hardingham, *Round the Globe: The Foundations of Geography* 1 (London: Thomas Nelson and Sons, 1934), pp. 5–13; 73–86; 113–129.	242

CONTENTS

29 School drill: 'School Drill', in *The Globe,* 15th July 1889, p. 1. — 251

30 'Lads' Drill Association', in *Volunteer Service Gazette,* 19th June 1903, p. 530. — 253

31 'The Duty and Discipline Movement', in *The Times,* 5th November 1913, p. 6. — 256

32 'Celebration of Empire Day in Schools', in *The Scotsman,* 28th June 1938, p. 7. — 258

33 'Empire Day in Cheltenham', in *The Cheltenham Ladies' College Magazine* (Autumn 1907), pp. 260–264. Reproduced with kind permission of Cheltenham Ladies' College Archive. — 260

34 Empire Day pageant at Perth: 'Empire Day Pageant' in *Dundee Evening Telegraph and Post,* 24th May 1921, p. 1. — 265

35 'Children's Empire Day Broadcast' in *The Daily Independent,* 25th May 1936, p. 11. — 267

36 'The King's Empire Day Broadcast', in *The Evening News,* 25th May 1940, p. 2. — 269

37 The empire and the League of Nations: their real meaning and ideals: C. Norwood. — 271

38 *The Report of the Inter-Departmental Committee on Physical Deterioration* (London: HMSO, 1905), pp. 13–17. — 276

39 Morris dances: Mr Cecil Sharp's lecture at Queen's Hall. — 284

40 The masque of the children of the Empire: G. T. Kimmins. — 286

41 'The Union Jack', in *The Teacher's Treasury* (London: Home Library Book Co., Vol. 2, 1926), pp. 49–62. — 296

42 The British Empire League: meeting in Leamington. — 304

43 'The League of Empire', *The Gazette,* 2nd December 1905, p. 5. — 309

CONTENTS

44	Lord Balfour and the Victoria League: closer union of British subjects.	311
45	The teaching of geography from an imperial point of view, and the use which could and should be made of visual instruction.	314
46	Board of Education, *Handbook of Suggestions* (London: HMSO, 1937), pp. 416–419.	322
47	H. Martens and E. H. Carter, *Histories. Book IV. The Modern Age* (Oxford: Basil Blackwell, 11th Edition, 1952). First published 1931. pp. 183–189; 320–322.	325
48	A wonderful escape: 'A Wonderful Escape'.	331
49	Bound in Benin: A story of the massacre.	345
50	Froth: Rev. E. C. Dawson, 'Froth'.	358
51	Through Peril to Fortune: The Strange Adventures of Two Young Britons in the Heart of Africa.	362
52	'David Livingstone: Missionary and Explorer', in *Young England*, Vol. 34 (1912–13), pp. 219–223; 263–296.	367
53	The Four Adventurers: No. 1. – the initiation: 'The Four Adventurers', in *Chums*, Annual for 1927–1928, pp. 396–398.	379
54	'Hindu Women', in *The Girl's Own Paper* (1881), pp. 118–119.	385
55	On the purchase of outfits for India and the colonies: 'On the Purchase of Outfits for India and the Colonies', in *The Girl's Own Paper* (1889), pp. 68–69.	390
56	A girl in the bush: A. R. Buckland, 'A Girl in the Bush', in *Empire Annual for Girls* (London: RTS, 1910), pp. 283–291.	395
57	*The Boys' Brigade Gazette*.	402

CONTENTS

58 Patriotism; or, our duties as citizens: Camp fire yarn. – no. 26. Our empire: how it grew – how it must be held: Robert Baden-Powell, *Scouting for Boys*: *A Handbook for Instruction in Good Citizenship* (London: Pearson, 7th Edition, 1915, reprinted 2004), pp. 273–281.   447

59 How India develops character: R. Baden-Powell, *Indian Memories: Recollections of Soldiering, Sport, Etc.* (London: Herbert Jenkins), pp. 106–122.   455

60 Camp fire yarn. No. 33: Our Empire: Agnes Baden-Powell, *How Girls Can Help to Build Up the Empire: The Handbook for Girl Guides* (London: Thomas Nelson, 1912), pp. 405–412.   465

Index   471

GENERAL INTRODUCTION

The British Empire in Domestic Popular Culture

The Nation and the Empire

The author Salman Rushdie once commented that 'the trouble with the English is that their history happened overseas, so they don't know what it means'.[1] The volumes presented here contemplate this observation and are published in the midst of what has been denoted as the 'statue wars' that have broken out on both the university campus and in social media over the last few years.[2] The war is essentially about the place the British Empire should hold in popular memory, its representation in public space and the way in which it is taught within the academy. It also occurs in the context of a call to 'decolonise the curriculum' in terms of the history taught to both school children and university students.[3] In 2015 the 'Rhodes Must Fall' campaign emerged on the campus of the University of Cape Town, when Chumani Maxwele, a scholarship student studying political science, picked up a bucket of horse manure from the kerbside and threw it over the statue of Cecil Rhodes, a statue that had stood on the campus precinct since its unveiling in 1934. Marion Walgate, wife of the architect Charles Walgate had designed the new Cape Town Campus, sculpting the bronze figure. The campaign to remove the statue originated in the 1950s, as Afrikaner students saw Rhodes as a figure of imperialism, and holder of concomitant racist views. Rhodes had perceived the Afrikaners to be less than British and had therefore begun the process of segregation that led to the more overt Apartheid policy of the second half of the twentieth century. Subsequently, protestors targeted statues of Jan Smuts, twice-Prime Minister of South Africa and Maria Barnard Fuller, the first woman to gain a degree at the university. By 2016, the movement had become a transnational phenomenon, reaching both North America and Britain. At Oxford, the movement also targeted a statue of Rhodes, located on the face of Oriel College. The statue remained in place, despite calls for its removal, as donors threatened to withdraw their contributions to the university if removed. The Rhodes Must Fall' campaign can be viewed from multiple perspectives.[4] It illustrates the revival of student politics after an extended period of dormancy and the rise of a post-colonial anger at the continued representation in public space of imperial figures from the European past that signify older imperial attitudes of racism and oppression. The movement triggered a debate across the wider popular media as to whether imperial figures who held values now distasteful to the twenty-first century citizen should be removed from public space. In Bristol, the 'Countering Colston' movement similarly attempted to have the statue of slave trader and public benefactor Edward Colston removed from the city. The journalist Afua Hirsch suggested the removal of Nelson from his column in Trafalgar Square, given his support for slavery – a call rejected by the military historian Max Hastings.[5] The call for Nelson's removal was but one aspect of the post-colonial approach to empire, which since the 1970s had grown as an academic perspective. Its agenda was to hear the 'subaltern speak', that is to say those at the wrong end of the colonialism of the European power of the nineteenth century. It drew attention to the shameful episodes in the imperial past and to the inveterate racism within it.

However, there has been a push-back to this approach. Historian Dominic Sandbrook for example, argued that this stance on the imperial past would see the removal of many artistic representations of figures from public space, who had played significant roles in the trajectory of Britain's history. Almost all historical figures fell short of modern ethical standards he argued.[6] In this new scholarly 'war of empire', writers such as Niall Ferguson and latterly Jeremy Black have also defended the British Empire, arguing that there were worse empires than the British in history. Britain was 'more liberal culturally economically socially and politically that the other major European powers" and argues that presentism has begun to dictate the treatment of the past, and to treat 'contemporary attitudes to empire . . . as if Britain . . . could have been abstracted from the age, and should be judged accordingly is unhelpful and ahistorical'. Andrew Roberts gave the book a glowing recommendation, noting that a reading of Black's book would have significant effect on the reader. Thus, 'the shame you've been taught to feel about your forefathers work will be transformed into a genuine and lasting sense of pride'.[7] This book, not surprisingly earned the scorn of post-colonialists.[8]

The rather polarised debate that has unfolded over the past few years is a very clear of example of post-colonialism 'in action'. It also indirectly draws attention to the ways in which Britain's imperial history infused domestic culture since at least the mid-nineteenth century. Yet, post-colonialists argue, it was only ever the oppressors who were commemorated at the expense of the oppressed. Thus 'decolonial workers in the academy have for years sought to bring the marginalised to the centre-stage of scholarly labour; to memorialise and elevate their perspectives, histories and struggles, which would be otherwise be lost in the throes of oppression'.[9] Contemporaneously, there has arisen a debate as to whether other statues located in public space, should be removed, as historical figures who have previously been unquestionably venerated are now noted to have held a racist view. Among such figures are those of Horatio Nelson (a supporter of slavery) and Winston Churchill, (an opponent of Indian Home Rule), their statues located in prominent public space, within the British Capital, in Trafalgar Square and Westminster Square respectively.[10]

The current controversy regarding these representations of imperial figures in domestic space has added a new dimension to the debate on the connections between empire and domestic culture that have been taking place since the beginning of the new century. Consideration of the impact of the British Empire on domestic culture has attracted significant attention over the last thirty years. Before then however, imperial history had remained rather an isolated field of historical inquiry, dominated by political and diplomatic perspectives that focused on both Britain's first and second Empires. Historians only intermittently suggested that the overseas Empire impacted domestic culture or national identity. In his volume *The Story of the Empire*, one of twelve volumes published to coincide with the staging of the 1924 British Empire Exhibition Sir Charles Lucas briefly alluded to the fact that 'Except in the sense of literally adding thousands and millions of square miles to the shores of Great Britain, it has infinitely enlarged the Old Country's borders and changed its conditions. Without the Empire, Great Britain would be a shrunken island with a different, a narrower life'.[11] Later in the century the place of Empire in the domestic context was alluded to by Alan Sandison when he noted that it 'would be wrong to minimise the upsurge of strong imperialist feeling that occurred in the last thirty years of the nineteenth century'.[12] However, it was more common to simply ignore the domestic impact of Empire. The eight volume *Cambridge History of the British Empire* published between 1929 and 1961 was a series that looked outwards to the Empire without any consideration of the Empire's domestic impact.[13] As the leading editor of the series in its early phases, J.H. Rose held the post of Vere Harmsworth Professor Imperial and Naval History at Cambridge. He had published biographies of William Pitt the Younger and Napoleon that had a primarily political perspective, typical of the predominant perspective in that era. As the series concluded, Britain had largely divested itself of its empire replacing it by the looser structure of Commonwealth.

By the mid-1960s, the phrase 'history from below' entered the history discipline, denoting a shift towards the exploration of social history and with an emphasis on the working class experience. Despite this shift, as it was constituted imperial history remained rather unaffected by this new direction within the academy. As Douglas Peers noted in his survey of the field of imperial history in the 1960s and 1970s:

> This was also a time when social history was in the ascendant, and its emphasis on history from below initially found little that was compatible in a discipline such as imperial history that had been pre-occupied with the thoughts and actions of a pro-consular elite.[14]

Indeed, looking back at the articles published in the early years of the *Journal of Imperial and Commonwealth History*, which first appeared in 1972, it is noticeable that most authors were focusing on the diplomacy of Empire, rather

3

than its social history, and rarely its impact 'at home'. The contributions contained in the very first issue for example, focused upon Lord Salisbury, Mr. Chamberlain and South Africa 1895–9, the Imperial Conferences of 1923 and 1937 and trade relations between Australia and New Zealand. A special issue in 1974 focused on the partition of Africa, but there was no consideration of the partition's domestic role. Imperial historians had appeared to take the attitude that, if approached from a social perspective, Empire was ubiquitous and all-pervading within Britain's national borders – so it was stating the obvious to note its impact. If, by contrast, they came to the field via a more political-diplomatic route, they preferred to study the process by which imperial rule was established and maintained, largely through the lens of high governance, (a la Robinson and Gallagher) which ignored the social and cultural dimensions of the Empire in its localised form. An understanding of the ways in which historians perceived 'Empire's impact' in the decade between 1969 and 1979 is gained by reading historians such as Max Beloff, Jan Morris or Peter Calvocoressi.

For Beloff, writing in 1969, 'the British were not an imperially minded people', four years later Jan Morris claimed that, 'The oddest thing about that gigantic compendium of oddities, the British Empire was this; that for most of its time few people found it very interesting' and added 'only a small minority were certain what it was'.[15] In the later 1970s, Calvocoressi also believed that the loss of its empire 'had not one opines, cut deep; and the reason is that having an empire did not cut deep either. It did not transform the British way of life'.[16] He added that 'Empire was external to the lives of most British people. The British Empire was more apparent to foreigners than to the British themselves'.[17] This may have been wishful thinking. Paul Gilroy rather maintained that, 'once the history of Empire became a source of discomfort, shame and perplexity, its complexities and ambiguities were readily set aside. Rather than work through those feelings . . . that unsettling history was . . . actively forgotten'.[18]

The rare explorations of popular responses to imperial wars within Britain published at this time such as Richard Price's oft-cited 1972 monograph, *An Imperial War and the British Working Class*, a study of working class reactions to the Second South African War of 1899–1902, were highly sceptical that jingoism or even an interest in Empire had infused the working classes. He argued against the notion of war enthusiasm within working class institutions. They were he argued, largely indifferent to the war. Price added the caveat however, that it was 'fruitless to try to establish that the working classes were either for or against imperialism'.[19] A commonly asked question at working class meetings was 'What use is the British Empire to me?'[20] This book was oft-cited within the academy to deny the idea that Empire played any kind of role in working class life, yet it remained a rather isolated study for the rest of that decade. Price published no further work on empire for over three decades.[21] He explained his change in direction, towards researching domestic social and labour history as due to the history of empire being 'methodologically uninteresting' and that 'its close association with British imperialism made it politically dubious'.[22] Indeed, both Bernard Porter and Thomas Metcalf who were beginning their careers as imperial historians in the 1950s and 1960s, note that studying imperialism became in Porter's words, 'deeply unfashionable in the last forty years of the twentieth century'.[23] Dane Kennedy has more recently confirmed that in the 1970s imperial history seemed to be stuck in an 'intellectual and methodological time warp'.[24] He goes further to suggest that the most innovative research on Empire came from those who were located in fields of history not designated as 'imperial history'. Metcalf supports this view, recalling that with the collapse of the empire 'imperial history went fast out of favour'.[25] Porter also recalled that imperial history was taught, 'but only in ghettoes of its own . . . separate from mainstream British history and usually by imperialists, which made more radical domestic historians want to keep their distance'.[26] Occasional forays were still made but perhaps significantly but remained unpublished in monograph format In the mid-1970s Michael Blanch's research on the effect of both nationalistic and imperialistic culture in the city of Birmingham found that imperial propaganda did have a considerable effect on that city's working class, that partially explained the rush to the colours in 1914. Blanch took a wider perspective than Price by focusing on the years 1899–1914. In this period, arguably the years in which imperial propaganda was at its height, youth had been indoctrinated at school in the values of Empire, through the efforts of those such as Lord Meath who had introduced Empire Day on the date of Queen Victoria' Birthday. It was particularly marked in the context of the school calendar. Organisations such as the Boy Scouts and the Church Lads' Brigade were also imperially orientated.[27] Also in the mid to later 1970s, some left-leaning historians were captivated by the notion of a labour aristocracy, who it was thought, had been effectively bribed by the profits of empire and detached themselves from rank and file workers. This had meant that a serious challenge of capitalism had never materialised since the later nineteenth century. Among the contributors were John Foster, Robbie Gray and Geoff Crossick.[28] The potential for elements of the working class to be indoctrinated with popular imperialist attitudes was not denied by Gray. The lines between patriotism and imperialism were rather blurred. It was a complex issue and Gray believed it needed fuller study at that stage.

As Stuart Ward noted, we may well ask how the point was reached in the mid-1980s whereby Imperial history had become so detached from domestic history as to warrant resuscitation, or to use David Fieldhouse's phrase the process of 'putting of humpty dumpty back together again'.[29] Ward notes that before 1914, many school texts abounded in which commentary and description of Empire and, to use Raphael Samuel's' phrase 'a kind of ultimate fulfilment of the country's historic mission', was outlined.[30] For Ward, the answer is found in the relatively quick process of Britain's divestment of its overseas Empire in the two decades following the conclusion of the Second World War and the rise of a globalised culture which eradicated the imperial memory and as he puts it 'nurtured the idea that metropolitan societies were hermetically sealed from their dissolving empire'.[31] Even before this, during the inter-war period, the legacy of high Victorian imperialism had arguably been somewhat tempered by more pacifist and internationalist outlooks. Symbols of this internationalism symbolise were the League of Nations, created at the conclusion of the First World War. This idea is however, questioned by John MacKenzie, who believes that imperial sentiment was strongly inculcated within the British population until the 1950s.[32] Nevertheless, in the 1920s the forceful aggressive imperialist rhetoric of the pre-1914 age was somewhat transformed into a new language based on 'protectorates', 'protected states' and 'mandates'. Another force at work across the century as Nicholas Owen has also noted, was the school of 'Critics of Empire' that he charts across several decades of the twentieth century, who objected to Empire on moral grounds. These critics ranged from figures such as J.A. Hobson at the beginning of the century, elements within the Fabian Society, the Union of Democratic Control, the Movement for Colonial Freedom and the British Communist Party. The ending of Empire transmuted into growing protest within Britain at the Apartheid policy adopted in Southern Africa at the end of the 1940s. Sporting boycotts were in place in the 1960s and 1970s. Apartheids roots were attributed to the legacy of 'imperial white rule' first established by Cecil Rhodes and others of the later Victorian generation.

Indeed, by the 1950s many believed that imperialism was retrogressive and to be out of time. In essays published shortly after his death in 1950, the Austrian political economist Joseph Schumpeter summarised what he saw as a phenomenon that had reached its end. He described imperialism as the work of pre-industrial and aristocratic 'atavism'. 'War may [he noted] call them [imperialistic forces] back to life, even lead to a more closely-knit organization, one that appears more aggressive to the outside. But it cannot alter the basis of social and political structure. Even in England, imperialism will remain a plaything of politics for a long time to come. But in terms of practical politics there is no room left for it there'.[33] Elsewhere he argued that Imperialism was 'atavistic in character' a surviving feature from earlier ages that could not survive the arrival of modernity.[34] Perry Anderson challenged this interpretation in his essay *Origins of the Present Crisis* that appeared in 1964 in the *New Left Review*. Here, Anderson analysed the causes of what he saw as Britain's backwardness in social, political and economic terms. The article appeared in the context of the perception of a Britain that was ossified and declining, with traditional industries stagnating, an out of touch Edwardian styled government and a vanishing empire, a nation without a role. Empire had played its part in this. Taking issue with Schumpeter, he argued that in fact the merging of aristocratic and middle class cause in the nineteenth century had given imperialism and empire a new lease of life. Even in the 1960s as Britain divested itself of Empire, governance and leadership, in the final years of the long Conservative rule in Britain 1951–1963, was still 'aristocratic, amateur and normatively agrarian'.[35] Having the 'largest empire of any in history', Anderson argued that, 'it is clear that the existence, maintenance and constant celebration of the Empire affected all classes and institutions in Britain; it could not have done otherwise'.[36] He added that, 'general internalization of the presentations and motifs of Empire undoubtedly occurred and imperialism made a lasting imprint on English (British?) life'.[37] Anderson made some qualification to this by noting that, 'This did not necessarily mean that the working class became in a direct sense committed to imperialism'.[38] The primary effect of Empire on the working class he argued, was to deflect them 'from undistracted confrontation with the class exploiting it'.[39]

The notion of comparative indifference to the Empire on the part of the majority of the British population was implied in Robinson and Gallagher's seminal text *Africa and the Victorians* (1961). Whilst the later nineteenth century might be seen as the apogee of imperial enthusiasm, Robinson and Gallagher argued that in fact desire for more Empire was muted in the later Victorian period. Moreover, foreign policy they noted, was not made by the man on the street. 'When it came to acting there [Africa] they [Whitehall policy makers] did so more in fear of the nation's criticism than in hope of its approval'.[40] It has to be said however, that as the focus of the book was the 'official mind' based in Whitehall, the authors gave little consideration to public opinion outside of the corridors of power.

In the later 1960s, Eric Hobsbawn published his study titled *Industry and Empire* that attempted to make connections between the growth of the Empire and the origins of the industrial revolution. 'Behind our Industrial Revolution there lies this concentration on the colonial and the underdeveloped markets overseas, the successful battle to deny them to anyone else'.[41] As this book was published in *Pelican Economic History Britain* however, cultural dimensions were largely absent from his narrative. In fact, from this point on, the next fifteen years saw very few attempts by historians to make connection between the domestic sphere and the empire. As Britain looked towards Europe for its future, imperial identity was cast off. A small indication of how the British regarded empire is gained by reference to the filmic output of British cinema in the 1960s. At the beginning of the decade the nobility and romance of empire was on screen in David Lean's epic *Lawrence of Arabia*, (1962) but by the decades end the empire was presented a farce in *Carry on Up the Khyber* (1968). Perhaps indicative of the situation in the 1970s is that some of the most notable works that had empire as a theme were those written from a post-colonial perspective. Edward Said's classic text *Orientalism* first appeared in 1978, a text that accused Western scholarship of portraying negative stereotypes about the East. Western scholars of the East constructed an essentially binary divide between the West, which saw itself as masculine, psychologically strong and rational with a feminine, weak and irrational East. The West was modern, the East was static, trapped in time. The influence of this book was most distinctly felt in the field of literary and cultural studies. Some historians resisted the arguments made in Said's text, arguing that it collapsed all sources into a one dimensional whole and did not distinguish between the various zones of the East.[42]

At approximately the same time, many studies of a sociological hue that explored the experience of black and Asian migrants to Britain in the post 1945 era began to appear, drawing attention to the institutional and personal racism that these migrants experienced. The Centre for Contemporary Cultural Studies (CCCS) was established at the University of Birmingham in 1964 and by the 1970s under the directorship of the Jamaican-born British Marxist sociologist Stuart Hall, published studies of the alienation of black youth (either migrants or sons and daughters of migrants) in later 1970s Britain. One the most notable publications the CCCS oversaw was *The Empire Strikes Back: Race and Racism in 1970s Britain*, a work co-authored by Paul Gilroy, Valerie Amos, Hazel Carby and Pratibha Parmar. Further into the 1980s, Gilroy's subsequent book *There Ain't No Black in the Union Jack* appeared in 1987. It remains a classic sociological text, in which the author accused politicians of the period of refusing to take race seriously.

Whilst sociological studies of contemporary race issues in Britain grew significantly in the 1980s, historical studies of the impact of the Empire on domestic space remained rather thin. When David Fieldhouse surveyed the condition of imperial history in the mid-1980s, he noted that the years since 1960 had not been conducive to the interaction of imperial history with domestic history. 'Decolonisation' he noted, 'and the fact that these metropolitan states were then able to survive and prosper without their enveloping empires, destroyed the teleological concept of an imperial destiny'.[43] Andrew Thompson agreed with this view, noting that at this time 'empire was still something widely judged to have happened overseas and to have been mostly marginal to the lives of the British people. In so far as British historians acknowledged imperialism, it was usually as an unpleasant "aberration" that was "corrected" by decolonisation, which reinstated a normal course of national development'.[44] It was at this point however that the situation began to shift somewhat. In 1984, John MacKenzie published the first monograph in what would become the long running series titled *Studies in Imperialism*, (1984–present) under the auspices of Manchester University Press. *Propaganda and Empire: The Manipulation of British Public Opinion 1880–1960*, began the long road to reconnecting the two realms of history, followed in 1986 by MacKenzie's edited collection *Imperialism and Popular Culture*. The appearance of this series is ascribed to the revival of an interest in Empire provoked partly by the Falkland crisis of 1982, Stuart Ward believes that MacKenzie had this war in mind when he published his 1984 study.[45] His conclusion makes a clear parallel between later Victorian colonial wars and that of the Falkland episode, when he noted 'The values and beliefs of the imperial world view settled like a sediment in the consciousness of the British people, to be stirred again by a brief, renewed challenge in the late twentieth century'.[46] In the later 1980s, further titles in this series began to investigate aspects of popular culture such as J.A. Mangan's collection on *Benefits Bestowed: Education and British Imperialism* (1988), Jeffrey Richards' *Imperialism and Juvenile Literature* (1989) and J.S. Bratton et al's *Acts of Supremacy: The British empire and the Stage, 1890–1930* (1991). Yet at the beginning of the 1990s Shula Marks lamented that much imperial history was still produced by 'white middle aged, middle class, male scholars, divorced . . . from the concerns of women's history [and] social history'.[47] Despite the appearance of these collections, or perhaps because of them, some senior figures nevertheless remained either ambiguous or sceptical regarding the impact that the Empire had on British domestic culture. Writing in the *Times Literary Supplement* in 1993, the imperial historian P. J. Marshall argued that 'The history of the Britain and the history of the British Empire cannot easily be separated'[48] yet he also acknowledged that evidence of a strong consciousness of Empire amongst working men that their standard of living depended on Empire is 'elusive to find'.[49] The majority of those who emigrated in the later nineteenth century, he notes, did not travel to zones of the Empire but rather North America. 'The showy high imperialism of the late nineteenth century (he argued), 'can be demonstrated to have been superficial and ephemeral in its impact. But that is only a small part of the story. Two centuries of involvement in empire by wide sections of the British people inevitably took less exotic and less easily distinguishable forms, but the depth and extent of this involvement cannot be in doubt'.[50] Writing again on the topic three years later, Marshall was rather more assertive when he stated that the Empire 'shaped British people's views of their national identity'.[51] There is rather more evidence, he conceded, for the influence on the middle classes than the working class, sections of the former of whom, were educated for the purpose of administrating the empire. At approximately the same moment Linda Colley, reviewing Edward Said's *Culture and Imperialism* published in 1993, noted the author's tendency to 'overstate the cultural hold of empire on the imperial powers' since 'empire simply did not loom all that large in the minds of most men and women back in Europe'.[52] This was at odds with the perspective of someone such as Benita Parry who was convinced that 'at home the fact of empire was registered not only in political debate [. . .] but entered the social fabric, intellectual discourse and the life of the imagination'.[53]

By the later 1990s, such dismissal of the impact of the Empire on domestic metropolitan cultures was rectified to some extent. In her study of congregational missions to the Empire in the nineteenth century, Susan Thorne for example, noted that British historians 'had yet to explore in any systematic way colonialism's imprint on metropolitan language, institutions and practices'.[54] She believed moreover that:

> Here in other regards, we appear to have acquiesced in the conventional wisdom that influence flows down the hills of power, that imperialism is a one-way street on which the traffic in people, practices, institutions, and ideas moved always out from all-determining European centers to

appropriating if not supine peripheries. Social historians have been particularly remiss in this regard. Until very recently most social histories of Britain in this period were written without significant reference to the empire's existence.[55]

Thorne rather argues that whilst the number of Britons who actually went to the Empire was quite small, many Britons were nevertheless, subjected to the influence of Empire by various institutional mechanisms. These included institutions such as the Royal Geographical Society, the African Civilisation Society and her focus, missionary societies. Additional mechanisms for the education of citizens included the child's school curriculum, popular fiction, the stage and later the cinema screen, together with sporting encounters with teams who originated in other zones of the Empire. There were also significant number of people who had been born in the Empire who lived in Britain by 1900. Further studies of the various ways empire was reflected in domestic culture were published, invariably by North American based historians such as Antoinette Burton, Mrinalini Sinha, Anne McLintock and Anne Coombs. In the introduction to their edited collection *Tensions of Empire*, Anna Stoler and Frederick Cooper argued that 'Europe was made by its imperial projects, as much as colonial encounters were shaped by conflicts within Europe itself'.[56] This work, which was categorised as the 'new imperial history', tended to support the maximalist thesis. Nevertheless, significant interventions in the debate on the influence of empire, by Burton and subsequently Hopkins noted the recalcitrance of many historians within the academy to acknowledge the role of empire, instead, keeping the nation hermetically sealed from its influence in their work.[57] Burton rather claimed that 'The conviction that the nation and the empire was crucially joined was typical of both imperial apologia and popular perceptions in this (later nineteenth and early twentieth century) period'.[58] She has also added that this imperial ideology 'contained a cult of nation that made Britain and its citizens at home of primary concern in the ostensibly "external" imperial enterprise'.[59] The claims of the aforesaid works, Burton noted, seem to pose 'some kind of threat to national security' by conservative elements within the academy. Burton was particularly puzzled by the criticism of Said's work by John MacKenzie who by this criticism tended to present himself as a rather conservative historian. In his role as editor of the 'Imperial Studies project he had done more than anyone to promote connections between the domestic and the empire'.[60] As the new century arrived, it appeared two distinct camps had developed, one writing history with the empire left out, the other deconstructing national boundaries and allowing the empire in.

The later 1990s saw some attempt to consider the ways in which Empire influenced the domestic with the appearance of the *Oxford History of the British Empire*, initially in five volumes, (1998–9) under the general editorship of the North American scholar William Roger Louis. A parallel series on more specialised topics are still appearing at the time of writing (2004–present). In contrast to its Cambridge predecessor, included within these volumes were explorations of the impact of the Empire at home. In the third and fourth volumes edited by Andrew Porter (Volume III) William Roger Louis and Judith M. Brown (Volume IV) which dealt with the British Empire in the nineteenth and twentieth centuries respectively, John MacKenzie contributed chapters on the impact of Empire in a national context.

The initial five-volume series was largely welcomed with certain reservations. Andrew Thompson, reviewing the fourth volume that focused on the twentieth century applauded John MacKenzie's contribution to it, but believed that the 'motives for imperial propaganda were not adequately explored' by the author nor the ways in which inter-war imperial propaganda was received by the wider public. How, he asked 'do we disentangle the patriotic, pecuniary and philanthropic impulses of those involved?'[61] Reviewing the third volume on the nineteenth century. Tom Brooking noted that in comparison with the earlier Cambridge Series it was 'much less celebratory' and 'not at all whiggish'.[62] He applauded the chapters that acknowledged Empire as a 'two-way' process, which had been notably lacking in the Cambridge series. Canadian historian Phillip Buckner's review of all five volumes also welcomed the project as being far more nuanced than its Cambridge predecessor. However, he did note that overall, the authors seemed to 'underestimate the impact of empire in shaping domestic institutions and life'[63] In the Oxford volumes, 'the flow of people, ideas and culture is viewed not entirely but largely as a one–way flow'.[64] Buckner also noted contradictions in the argument made by authors such as Nicholas Owen in volume IV, focusing on the twentieth century, who suggested that 'most workers' were 'indifferent or apathetic to questions of Empire' whilst supplying evidence to suggest they were not. John MacKenzie in the same volume (IV) argued for an 'Indian Summer in the popular culture of Empire' between the two World Wars of the twentieth century, which he thought left the reader rather baffled.[65] Bernard Porter felt the volumes had little to say about British public opinion on the Empire.[66] This sentiment was echoed by Dane Kennedy who thought that the overall thrust of the volumes reinforced 'the view that the imperial experience was essentially unilateral, with Britain imposing its will on large parts of the world without itself undergoing any significant transformation'.[67] Since the first five volumes appeared, a further number of companion volumes that focus on specific themes have been published in this series. They might be viewed as a partial admission that so much was missed out of the initial cluster of volumes, although it is disingenuous to expect that they could have explored so many areas of empire activity in what were essentially overviews for the relatively uninitiated scholar seeking to enhance their understanding of the British Empire. Among the topics focused upon in the companion works were missionary activity, gender, architecture and a lengthier treatment of the twentieth century, first explored in Volume IV, edited by Andrew Thompson titled, *Britain's Experience of Empire in the Twentieth Century.* John MacKenzie's *Studies in Imperialism* has at the time of writing a current total of 164 monographs. At least twenty-five of these have focused on some aspect of the cultural impact of Empire on Britain herself.[68] Fascination with the domestic impact was particularly noted in the first half-decade of the series. Since then the series has become far more diverse, extending to other European nations' experience and even in recent years the empires accumulated by nations who were within the British Empire themselves.[69] One may have assumed that given the momentum generated by such a sizeable output any objections that were once posed by Colley or less forcefully by P.J. Marshall in the 1990s, would be overwhelmed and the ubiquity of empire accepted. However, the appearance of Bernard Porter's *The Absent-Minded Imperialists: Empire, Society, and Culture in Britain* in 2004 for a time at least, proved to be a significant disruptor to this viewpoint, which argued against the notion of imperial saturation in the domestic context.

The Awareness of Empire: Bernard Porter's Absent-Minded Imperialists and his Critics

In turning to the domestic impact of Empire at century's beginning, historians were now engaging, perhaps at times indirectly, with the question as to how far empire enjoyed popular support from those who were not in the employment of the State, or any of those organisations by which imperial rule was established after 1830. It was a return to studying Robinson and Gallagher's 'man or woman on the street'. Finally, empire's impact on popular culture was now being acknowledged as a topic for serious academic discussion. In this sense, it might be that the social history of the 1960s known in some contexts as reclaiming 'history from below' was making a rather belated entry into the field of imperial studies and the social and the imperial appeared to be being reunited. However, a significant disruption to this notion was marked by the publication of Porter's 2004 monograph. Across thirteen chapters, Porter produced a sceptical survey of the awareness by the majority of British people about the empire. The propaganda that was the focus for MacKenzie's 1984 study that began the *Studies in Imperialism* series, was for Porter just that. It was because people thought so little about the empire that more propaganda was needed to bring it home to the British. The book was reviewed sympathetically by some – Stephen Howe, John Darwin and Ian Phimister for example, all thought the work was a stimulating entry to the debate[70]. Far more negative reviews were submitted by Antoinette Burton and John MacKenzie.[71] Burton thought many of the examples that Porter used actually served to demonstrate the theory that he was seeking to deny, that is to say the ubiquity of empire in domestic culture. Burton noted that 'one cannot help but ask how (and why) readers at Oxford University Press allowed such a plethora of overblown and unsubstantiated statements to pass'. She added that it was not a book 'that is worth arguing either with or about'. So too, John Mackenzie was rather unimpressed by the work, perhaps understandably, as Porter had rather mockingly used the terms 'Mackenzi-ites' and

'Saidists' to critique those who believed that empire infused domestic culture. His evidence was 'selective and partial'. The book contained 'many silences'. Stuart Ward found the treatment of empire somewhat limited too, noting 'To the extent that popular forms of imperial culture can be shown to be determined by non-imperial influences (and by Porter's definition these can range from liberalism to paternalism, evangelicalism–even patriotism) they can be properly discounted as signs of the influence of empire on metropolitan Britain'. A further discussion between Porter and MacKenzie took place in the *Journal of Imperial and Commonwealth History* some four years after Porter's book was published.[72] Reflecting on its hostile reception in some quarters especially in North America, Porter pondered that this might have been partly explained by the under appreciation or even misunderstanding of class in Britain. The working class were effectively shut out of the empire – they played no role in policy decisions that were the work of a small elite cadre of civil servants and politicians based in Westminster; it had no impact on their daily lives. One of MacKenzie's issues with *Absent Minded Imperialists* was that the author had not appreciated the nature of the evidence in front of him. Thus, as far a theatre and empire was concerned, Porter argues that empire did not constitute a major theme as far as the stage of the nineteenth century was concerned. MacKenzie argued however, that many stage-plays that contained empire themes, gave no indication of containing such if judged simply by their titles. Better detective work was needed. A similar debate as to the role of empire in literature has taken place, with Porter criticising as what he sees as Said's overemphasis on imperial and empire connections in notable nineteenth century fiction produced by the likes of Jane Austen for example.[73] Richard Price, returning to a historical field he had rather long abandoned, believed Porter's empiricism was 'not quite enough'. He noted that 'Porter is willing to admit that empire cannot be ruled out as a component of British culture. But one gets the sense that his hammering of the new imperial history left him with no energy to explain how he might envisage the linkages'.[74] In the fifteen or so years since Porter's book appeared we may consider what impact it had within the academy. Before doing so however we may note the treatment of empire outside it. On television for example, the veteran journalist Jeremy Paxman presented a five-part series on the BBC titled *Empire* which was broadcast in 2012, that received rather mixed reviews. The series was anticipated by a book titled, *Empire: What Ruling the World Did to the British*. The subtitle was rather misleading, as the book was largely devoted to the how the British built its empire and focused on the role of what we now see as the immoral actions of some rather dubious characters in the nation's imperial history. Paxman concluded his survey by noting that the British empire was:

> essentially a project which belonged to the ruling class', [yet] the whole imperial experience shaped the British, as much as it shaped the places to which they took their flag, determining not merely how they looked

at the world but how they saw themselves, helping to define the Englishman and woman, [note his reluctance to include the Scots or Irish] setting the tone of the education system, restructuring the armed forces, broadening (and narrowing) the horizons of their statesmen, consolidating the monarchy and creating a worldwide diaspora.[75]

Another significant contributor to history on television by the mid-2010s was the British-Nigerian historian, David Olusoga. Olusogoa, now Professor of Public History at the University of Manchester, has set out to reclaim the lost or forgotten contribution of black British people to history. Based on his book *Black and British: A Forgotten History*, Olusoga has presented a BBC series of the same name, and another titled *Britain's Forgotten Slave Owners*, which drew on the findings of the ESRC funded research project directed by Catherine Hall, Keith McClelland and Nick Draper, based at University College London.[76] The latter demonstrated how the wealth generated by the slave trade and slave ownership had been redirected into other areas of the British 'cultural' economy in the 1830 and 1840s. Some of the wealth found its way into what became the nation's leading cultural and educational institutions, in some instances provoking internal inquires.[77] Reflecting on his work as a historian, Olusoga noted that:

> There is a tendency to imagine there was some period when Britain was not connected to the outside world. That if you go back far enough, you will find this England where everyone sat around under oak trees with no connection to the outside world. What this history shows is there is no mythical England to get back to – there is no Britain to get back to before 'they' got here.[78]

Such 'public' history chimes with calls within the academy to 'decolonise the curriculum' and recognise diversity on the university campus.[79] Interconnection has been insisted upon by Catherine Hall and her collaborators in books such *At Home With Empire* (2006) and in more recent work, where it is stressed that 'The histories of colonisers and colonised were inextricably linked: a proper understanding of both domestic and colonial histories on grasping the connections between the two. In the much-quoted terminology, metropole and colony must be analysed in the same frame'.[80] By way of a conclusion we might therefore ponder the 'journey' that the debate on empire's impact has travelled over the last fifty years. It has generally followed a trajectory of initial scepticism (in the 1960s and 1970s) as to the connection, to a point (post-2000) where few would deny the connection between the home and empire. Both Stuart Ward and John Darwin however, make the salient points in their foreword and afterword to a recent festschrift to John MacKenzie's career. In the words of Ward, 'we can no longer reduce public perceptions of empire to a balance sheet of indifference versus wholesale endorsement, or indeed arrive at any generalised verdict on popular imperialism that can be applied confidently to any given time frame'.[81] Similarly, Darwin echoes this in something of a volte face from his earlier admiration of Porter's book, by stating that 'we are now well past the point at which the essential complementarity of what once appeared two very different historiographical traditions should be widely acknowledged'.[82] It is clear that a legacy of the MacKenzie project is that the minimalist viewpoint will no longer hold paramountcy. Over the last twenty years it has been clearly established by a cluster of historians that the cities of Britain were infused with empire; a phenomenon that was hitherto relatively unappreciated.[83] Writing in the current century, historians such as Stephen Miller and Brad Beaven have attempted to move on from the work of Richard Price's aforementioned study of the South African War to show *how* imperialism was inculcated. Miller, focusing on volunteers for the South African War, focuses on a largely middle-class or even upper-class body of men, who joined either the City Imperial Volunteers, or the Imperial Yeomanry, argues that imperial values were successfully transmitted via educational institutions. Beaven by contrast, argues that such values were filtered through several civic institutions down to the working class. In doing so, the emphasis on empire could vary significantly between cities such as Leeds, Coventry and Portsmouth.[84]

Sources, Empire and Popular Culture

This collection consists of four volumes that focus on the impact of empire on British popular culture over the century 1850–1939. They are not presented as in any sense a 'celebration' of empire. However, in refusing to present these documents within a celebratory framework, is important not move to the opposite extreme of abandoning historical perspective and trying to judge these fragments of the past by reference to our twenty-first first century values. As Bernard Porter has noted 'imperialism was not a simple straight forward thing... not just a case of applied racism – but varied, complex and changeable and certainly uneven in its impact both abroad and at home'.[85] Clearly factions within British society across the period covered here did celebrate imperial events, such as jubilees, victories in war, or imperial occasions such as Empire Day. So too, both remorse and sadness were shown by contemporaries in relation to events such as the Indian Mutiny, or famines within the empire. Some of the documents use language in ways we would not adopt in at the current time, but we cannot airbrush this from the archive and de-historicise the past. Indeed, we need to keep in mind, as Andrew Thompson has noted, that the empire was 'not a single entity' but 'a very diverse collection of colonies'.[86] When Westminster politicians talked of 'empire' it invariably alluded to the white settler colonies, rather than India or Africa. This period witnessed the expansion of the 'second British Empire', which was largely located to the East of Egypt, (the expansion in the sub-continent the 'Raj' after 1857), the acquisition of more Australian colonies and its nearest neighbour New Zealand in the 1830s and 1840s, and more African colonies by the end of her life.

These gains went some way to replacing the 'first' Empire of the seventeenth and eighteenth centuries that was largely a phenomenon located in the Western hemisphere, (in North America and the Caribbean) and was based on the Slave Trade. The first volume is titled *Gender, Youth, Education and Empire* and considers the impact of Empire in the realms of schooling, youth organisations and adult organisations.

As several historians have noted, empire became a more significant feature of education, in the later nineteenth century, and more children were now attending some form of elementary education where school readers introduced pupils to the story of empire. On the death of Victoria in 1901, Reginald Brabazon the 12th Earl of Meath designated her birthday 'Empire Day', which became, by the outbreak of the First World War, a feature of the school calendar for the next thirty years. The Victoria notion of 'separate spheres' still carried heft when it came to the differences in the ways men and women experienced Empire at home. This is reflected in the kinds of activities that an organisation such as the Victoria League, founded in 1901 undertook, compared with the learned geographical societies such as the Royal Geographical Society (RGS) founded in 1830, or The Royal Colonial Institute (1870), that were largely male preserves in the later nineteenth century, or the defensively orientated organisations such as the Navy League, founded in 1895. The Navy League issued the *Navy League Journal*, which as John MacKenzie notes 'included a women's page'.[87] The proscribing of women's presumed interests to a few pages within the journal says much about the ways these leagues and society more widely, imposed roles on the genders in the later Victoria era. The exploration of the dark continent of Africa was seen as a playground for the imperial school-boy, where male fantasies of adventure, fuelled by popular literature in the period after 1870 could be fulfilled. Some women did migrate as single women to the settler communities of Australia, South Africa, New Zealand and Canada in particular, to work as teachers, or governesses or surrogate parents. Their letters sent back to British based relatives reveal their experiences of living the settler life. The second volume is titled *Empire and Popular Culture*. Here, documents that reflect how Empire was projected in popular culture, be it on stage and screen, or at exhibitions, or zoos. The documents in this section reveal attitudes to race and black presence in popular culture. Persons of colour appeared as entertainers in the Victorian era, on the stage, or on the sports field, they also were subjected to the western 'gaze' at exhibitions of the later 1800s too. Migration is also included here, with documents included that advertised empire and letters that related the migrants experience. Volume II also includes documents that reflect the ways in which empire was exhibited, be it through formal exhibitions, through public statues or portraits of imperial figures. The National Portrait Gallery was opened in 1856, and by 1896, it occupied a building that adjoined the National Gallery that had opened 1824. Ironically, the collections for the National Gallery were partly financed by money derived from the slave trade.[88] The Scottish Portrait Gallery opened in Edinburgh in 1882. Exhibiting empire became very popular by the late nineteenth century. There was a distinct shift in the later century to broaden exhibitions to cater for a desire for entertainment as well a fulfilling an educative function. This perhaps reflected the presence of larger numbers of the working class, who were now consuming commercialised leisure. Exhibitions were increasingly a provincial phenomenon as well as a metropolitan. Zoological gardens were opened displaying animals that inhabited zones of empire and further brought the empire 'home' to British people. So too, documents are included in this volume which were created by the various empire leagues formed in the later nineteenth and early twentieth centuries. In the third volume, the documents focus upon sport, religion and the wider popular culture of British society. Included here are documents relating to the empire on the stage and on the screen, in crowd-pleasing pyrotechnical displays and individually viewed panoramas of empire through a stereoscope. Volume III focuses on personal and collective identities in relation to popular culture, whilst Volume IV contains documents relating to the presentation of Empire in popular newspapers and journals, Empire in literature, in art and design.

The Collection

The collection includes sources that reflect aspects of the empire 'at home' in British popular culture c.1850–1939. This period approximates to the creation of the second British empire, created in a period that witnessed the abolition of the slave trade and slavery. The period under consideration is notable for a communications 'revolution', in term of print culture and new technologies that were pioneered, most obviously the camera and the photograph. By the 1920s, the role of the picture palace was being established in the lives of the majority of British people. Graphical representations of empire were placed in popular weekly publications from the 1840s. Among the most significant titles were those such as the *Illustrated London News*, *The Graphic* and *The Sketch* among others. The provincial press grew apace in the second half of that century too.[89] As more working class people obtained at least a rudimentary education in the 1870s and 1880s, they were able to read journalistic descriptions of the empire.[90] The rail network also enabled citizens to journey to cities to view exhibitions and attend imperial pageants in London.[91] So, whilst the majority of British people did not travel to the empire, they could get a reasonably accurate sense of the wider British world and the peoples who inhabited it. There is no comparable publication to these volumes. Most collections hitherto published have focused on the high politics of empire rather than the popular. David Fieldhouse, who held the Vere Harmsworth Professorship at the University of Cambridge (1981–1992), compiled several volumes which focused on the constitutional evolution of the empire. However, as a noted economic historian he did not consider the social perspective. Similarly, a major series which published primary sources focusing on the end of empire was overseen by A.J. Stockwell between the mid-1990s and the mid-2000s. They also took a largely constitutional perspective. From a more 'popular' perspective, Ashley Jackson and David Tomkins' *Illustrating Empire: A Visual History of British Imperialism* (2011) was exclusively based on the collections held in the John Johnson ephemera collection, located within Oxford's Bodelian library. The documents included in these four volumes are considered 'rare' in that the sources are held by only a comparatively few libraries around the world. Others can only be obtained by a scholar who can access a university library with inter-loan facilities. Alternatively, the documents are located behind paywalls that can only be freely accessed by a researcher visiting the library in person. The documents are reproduced exactly as they originally appeared, the only changes being to the typography. Where an extract of a longer document is included this is indicated by the symbol [. . .].

The debate regarding the maximalist or minimalist presence of empire in the lives of British people at home will need to be considered in the light of these sources. Indeed, it is hoped they might be used by students who are required to form an opinion on this subject. Of course, the scholar might also want to point to relevant 'silences' in relation to the empire at home to counter-balance the maximalist viewpoint. Some of the documents included here are published in order to give the student the opportunity to question the 'maximalist' account which stresses the ubiquity of empire at home. A recurring issue in the use of historical sources is of course that the majority were generated not by the working class themselves but by the more educated middle class in their roles as either educators, as teachers or the curators of museums, stagers of exhibitions or conveyors of news – editors of journalists for the daily and weekly press, or perhaps as commercial providers of entertainment for that class. It is a difficult exercise to explore quite what the receivers of imperial news or education actually made of it. So the documents are presented with a necessary caveat that, whilst there is evidence for the dissemination of empire in a variety of areas of popular culture in the century 1850–1939, we cannot say with any certainty that this was in response to any kind of demand or appetite for such knowledge. Bernard Porter is sceptical and would no doubt argue that much of the evidence that is presented here is simply propaganda presented to the wider population in order to gain support for the empire as popular democracy evolved after 1870. The volumes offer some brief comments before presenting each document which gives some indication as to the origin and context of the document and the purposes for which it was produced. The documents are not therefore meant to prove one way or another whether the majority of British people supported or rejected empire as a phenomenon, but rather to show the ways that it was indeed present in middle-class and working class lives. They can be used in conjunction with the extensive bibliography provided to arrive at their own opinions as to the maximalist and minimalist debate that has generated substantial attention since the new century began.

Notes

1. Quoted in H. K. Bhaba, 'DissemiNation: Time, Narrative, and the Margins of the Modern Nation', in H. Bhabha (ed.), *Nation and Narration* (New Yok: Routledge, 1990), p. 317.
2. For a consideration of the Black Lives Matter movement and the removal of the symbols of Empire in British cities see Richard Evans's discussion in R. Evans 'The History Wars' in *New Statesman*, 17th June 2020. Located at https://www.newstatesman.com/international/2020/06/history-wars Accessed 21st January 2021.
3. For a discussion of the wider movement see G. K. Bhambra, D. Gebrial & K. Nisancioglu (eds.), *Decolonising the University* (London: Pluto Press, 2018).
4. Some thoughts are also provided in S. Dubow, 'Rhodes Must Fall, Brexit and Circuits of Knowledge and Influence' in S. Ward & A. Rasch, (eds.), *Embers of Empire in Brexit Britain* (London: Bloomsbury, 2019), pp. 111–120. He notes the rather different results of the protest in Cape Town and Oxford.
5. See for example https://www.standard.co.uk/news/london/historian-call-to-pull-down-nelsons-column-the-height-of-cultural-vandalism-a3618441.html. Accessed 12 December 2019 For Hastings response seehttps://www.dailymail.co.uk/news/article-4818232/Removing-Nelson-column-nonsense-Max-Hastings.html. Accessed 12 December 2019 Dominic Sandbrook is of the same general view see https://www.dailymail.co.uk/news/article-4453488/amp/Will-tear-Churchill-Gandhi-Mandela-too.htmlhttps://www.dailymail.co.uk/news/article-4453488/amp/Will-tear-Churchill-Gandhi-Mandela-too.html Accessed 19 December 2019.
6. See https://www.dailymail.co.uk/news/article-4453488/amp/Will-tear-Churchill-Gandhi-Mandela-too.htmlhttps://www.dailymail.co.uk/news/article-4453488/amp/Will-tear-Churchill-Gandhi-Mandela-too.html Accessed 19 December 2019. A book which anticipated the Rhodes Must fall campaign by at least a decade was Paul Gilroy's *After Empire Melancholia or Convivial Culture?* (London: Routledge, 2004).
7. This is taken from Roberts' comment on the dust jacket of Black's book. I write this introduction from the campus of a New Zealand university. For the last 45 years by means of the Waitangi Tribunal established in 1975, this has been a nation that has tried to address the grievances of Māori generated by the legacy of the first British Empire –its breaches of trust regarding the original Treaty of Waitangi. Experiencing the legacy of empire at first hand does cause me to feel rather uncomfortable with Roberts' viewpoint.
8. J. Black, *Imperial legacies: The British Empire Around The World* (New York: Encounter, 2016). It was contemptuously described as 'a whitewash for Britain's imperial atrocities' in *The Guardian* by Kim Wagner. See https://www.theguardian.com/books/2019/aug/10/imperial-legacies-jeremy-black-review-empire-multiculturalism Accessed 27 February 2020.
9. D. Gebrial, 'Rhodes Must Fall: Oxford and Movements for Change', in G. K. Bhambra, D. Gebrial & K. Nisancioglu (eds.), *Decolonising the University* (London: Pluto Press, 2018), p. 19.
10. For a discussion of the events of 2020 see Richard Evans op. cit.
11. C. Lucas, *The Story of the Empire* (London: W. Collins and Sons 1924), p. 276.
12. A. Sandison, *The Wheel of Empire: A Study of the Imperial Idea in Some Late Nineteenth and Early Twentieth Century Fiction* (Macmillan: New York 1967), p. 3.
13. Noted by Douglas Peers in his chapter 'Britain and Empire' in C. Williams, (ed.), *A Companion to Nineteenth Century Britain* (Oxford: Blackwell, 2007), p. 67.
14. D. Peers, 'Is Humpty Dumpty Back Together Again? The Revival of Imperial History and the *Oxford History of the British Empire*', in *Journal of World History* Vol 13:2 (2002), p. 452.

15 M. Beloff, *Imperial Sunset Volume 1: Britain's Liberal Empire* (London: Methuen, 1969), p., 19; J. Morris 'Popularisation of Imperial History: The Empire on Television', in *Journal of Imperial and Commonwealth History* Vol 1:1 (1972), p. 113. Morris was reviewing the BBC's 13-part series *The British Empire: Echoes of Britannia's Rule* first broadcast in 1972. It had not evidently captured the public interest. I own these observations to a reading of Stuart Ward's 'The Moving Frontier of MacKenzie's Empire', which is the foreword to S. Barczwki & M. Farr, (eds.), *The MacKenzie Moment and Imperial History: Essays in Honour of John M. MacKenzie* (Basingstoke: Palgrave, 2019), pp. 15–22.

16 P. Calvocoressi, *The British Experience 1945–1975* (Harmondsworth, Penguin, 1978), p. 244.

17 Ibid., p. 245. I owe the observations regarding the treatment of empire by historians in the 1960s and 1970s to a reading of Stuart Ward's foreword to the recently published MacKenzie festschrift.

18 P. Gilroy, *After Empire: Melancholia or Convivial Culture?* (Abingdon: Routledge, 2004), p. 98.

19 R. Price, *An Imperial War and the British Working Class: Working Class Attitudes Reactions to the Boer War* (London: Routledge, 1972), p. 238.

20 Ibid., p. 239.

21 For Price's reflections on his career see R. Price, 'Empire and Class: The Making of a History Boy', in A. Burton & D. Kennedy, *How Empire Shaped Us* (London: Bloomsbury, 2016), pp. 49–58.

22 Ibid., p. 56.

23 B. Porter, *The Absent Minded Imperialists: Empire Society and Culture in Britain*, (Oxford: Oxford University Press, 2004), p. 4.

24 D. Kennedy, *The Imperial History Wars: Debating the British Empire* (London: Bloomsbury Academic, 2018), p. 133.

25 Thomas R. Metcalf, 'From Empire to India and Back: A Career in History' in A. Burton & D. Kennedy (eds.) *How Empire Shaped Us* (London: Bloomsbury, 2016), p. 17.

26 Ibid., p. 4.

27 M.D. Blanch, 'Nation, Empire and the Birmingham Working Class', unpublished PhD thesis, University of Birmingham, 1975.

28 See J. Foster, *Class Struggle and the Industrial Revolution: Early Industrial Capitalism in Three English Towns* (London: Weidenfeld & Nicholson, 1974); G. Crossick, 'The Labour Aristocracy and its Values: A Study of Mid Victorian Kentish London' in *Victorian Studies*, Vol 19: 3 (1976), pp. 301–328; R. Gray, *The Labour Aristocracy in Victorian Edinburgh* (Oxford: Clarendon, 1976); R. Gray, *The Aristocracy of Labour in Nineteenth–Century Britain c. 1850–1914* (London: Macmillan, 1981), p. 56.

29 D. Fieldhouse, 'Can Humpty-Dumpty be put together again? Imperial history in the 1980s' in *Journal of Imperial and Commonwealth History*, Vol. 12:2 (1984), pp. 9–23.

30 The comment of Raphael Samuel cited in S. Ward, 'The MacKensian Moment in Retrospect (or how one hundred volumes bloomed)' in A. Thompson (ed.), *Writing Imperial Histories* (Manchester: Manchester University Press, 2014), p. 32.

31 Ward, 'The MacKensian Moment', p. 32.

32 J.M. MacKenzie, *Propaganda and Empire: The Manipulation of British Public Opinion 1880–1960*, (Manchester: Manchester University Press, 1984), p. 256.

33 J.A Schumpeter, *Imperialism and Social Classes* (ed.), P. M. Sweezy (New York: Augustus Kelley, 1951), pp. 29–30.

34 Ibid., p. 84. An argument can be made for Empire as a modernising force - at least as far as the role of the white settler colonies are concerned. In New Zealand for example, women were given the vote in 1893, much sooner than their British counterparts, and

as a subsequent Dominion of empire it introduced a welfare state (by Michael Savage's Labour government of 193), several years before the Attlee administration in Britain followed suit. As a result, the soubriquet 'Better Britain' and 'social laboratory' have been used by some historians to describe the furthest flung zone of Empire. See for example for 'Better Britain' see J. Belich, *Paradise Reforged: A History of the New Zealanders from the 1880s to the Year 2000* (London: Penguin, 2001); for welfarism see L. Bryder and J. Stewart, '"Some Abstract Socialistic Ideal or Principle": British Reactions to New Zealand's 1938 Social Security Act', in *Britain and the World*, Vol 8:1 (2015), pp. 51–75.

35 P. Anderson, 'The Origins of the Present Crisis' republished in *English Questions* (London: Verso, 1992), p. 24.
36 Ibid, pp. 23–24.
37 Ibid., p. 25.
38 Ibid., p. 25.
39 Ibid., p. 26.
40 R. Robinson and J. Gallagher, *Africa and the Victorians: The Official Mind of Imperialism* (London: Macmillan, 1961), pp. 23–24. In the USA the book was published with the subtitle 'the climax of imperialism in the dark continent'.
41 E.J. Hobsbawn, *Industry and Empire* (Harmondsworth: Penguin, 1968), p. 54.
42 For a historical rebuttal of Said's approach see J.M. MacKenzie, *Orientalism: History, Theory and the Arts* (Manchester: Manchester University Press, 1995). Mackenzie was unhappy that the post-colonial approach was generally blind to shifts in thinking across time and that Orientalism as defined by Said, did not accommodate the possible admiration of Western scholars for the Orient.
43 Fieldhouse, 'Can Humpty-Dumpty be put together again? Imperial history in the 1980s', p. 14.
44 A. Thompson, 'Introduction' to his edited collection, *Writing Imperial Histories*, p. 1. Thompson is now one of the general editors of the 'Studies of Imperialism' series. It is fair to say he is more sceptical than his predecessor as to the saturation of imperial culture in the domestic.
45 More recently, MacKenzie himself has confirmed that the Falklands did indeed play a role in the book's appearance. As he notes in the early 1980s 'the popular imperialism of the nineteenth century seemed to be recreated before my very eyes. A colonial war, involving a group of almost forgotten islands off the coast of Argentina broke out. The press and all other media became obsessed, tabloids in a manner as jingoistic as 1878, 1884/5,1898 or any other climacterics of an earlier imperialism' See J. M. MacKenzie 'Empire From Above and Below', in A. Burton & D. Kennedy, (eds.), *How Empire Shaped Us* (London: Bloomsbury, 2016), pp. 41–42.
46 MacKenzie, *Propaganda and Empire*, p. 258.
47 S. Marks, 'History, the Nation and Empire: Sniping from the Periphery', in *History Workshop* 29 (1990), p. 112. Antoinette Burton also argued for the place of empire in the study of domestic British history in 1994. See also 'A. Burton, 'Rule of Thumb: British History and "Imperial Culture", in nineteenth and twentieth century Britain' in *Women's History Review*, Vol 3:4 (1994), pp. 483–50.
48 P.J. Marshall, 'No Fatal Impact? The Elusive History of Imperial Britain', in *Times Literary Supplement*, 12th March 1993, p. 8.
49 Ibid., p. 9.
50 Ibid., p. 10.
51 P.J. Marshall 'The World Shaped by Empire' in *The Cambridge Illustrated History of the British Empire* (Cambridge: Cambridge University Press, 1996), p. 10. Also his chapter within the same volume titled 'Imperial Britain', pp. 318–337.
52 L. Colley, 'The Imperial Embrace', in *The Yale Review*, Vol. 81:4, (1993), p. 96.

53 B. Parry, 'Overlapping Territories: and Intertwined Histories: Edwards Said's Post-Colonial Cosmopolitanism', in M. Spinker (ed.) *Edward Said: A Critical Reader*, (Oxford: Blackwell, 1992), p. 24.
54 S. Thorne, *Congregational Missions and the Making of an Imperial Culture in Nineteenth Century England* (Stanford: Stanford University Press, 1999), p. 3.
55 Ibid., p. 3. This chimed with other historical opinion in the 1990s, voiced by such authors as Vron Ware, Mrinalini Sinha and Antoinette Burton. See V. Ware, *Beyond The Pale: White Women, Racism and History* (London: Verso, 1992); M. Sinha, *Colonial Masculinity: The 'Manly Englishman' and the 'Effeminate Bengali' in the Late Nineteenth Century* (Manchester: Manchester University Press, 1995); A. Burton, *Burdens of History: British Feminists, Indian Women and Imperial Culture* (Chapel Hill: University of North Carolina, 1994); Idem, *At the Heart of the Empire: Indians and the Colonial Encounter* (Berkeley: University of California Press, 1998);
56 F. Cooper & A.L. Stoler (eds.), *Tensions of Empire: Colonial Encounters in a Bourgeois World* (Los Angeles: University of California Press, 1997), p. 1.
57 A. Burton, 'Who Needs the Nation? Interrogating British History', in *Journal of Historical Sociology*, Vol. 10:3 (1997), pp. 227–248; A.G. Hopkins,' Back to the Future: From National History to Imperial History', in *Past and Present*, 164, (1999), pp. 198–243.
58 Burton, *Burden of History*, p. 34.
59 Ibid., p. 37.
60 For MacKenzie's career and some of its apparent contradictions, see C. Leonardi, 'The Power of Culture and the Cultures of Power: John MacKenzie and the Study of Imperialism', in Thompson (ed.), *Writing Imperial Histories*, pp. 57–60.
61 A. Thompson, 'Is Humpty Dumpty Together Again? Imperial History and the Oxford History of the British Empire', in *Twentieth Century British History*, Vol. 12:4 (2001), p. 523.
62 T. Brooking, Review of Andrew Porter (ed.), 'The Oxford History of the British Empire Vol. III', The Nineteenth Century' in *Political Science*, Vol 53:1, (2001), p. 69.
63 P. Buckner, 'Was there a "British", Empire? The Oxford History of the British Empire from a Canadian Perspective', in *Acadiensis: Journal of the History of the Atlantic Region*, Vol 32:1 (2002), p. 126.
64 Ibid., p. 126.
65 Ibid., p. 114.
66 B. Porter 'An Awfully Big Colonial Adventure: The Stupendous Variety of Empire – and its Historians', in *Times Literary Supplement*, 14th January 2000, pp. 4–5.
67 Kennedy, *Imperial History Wars*, p. 34.
68 I have created the full inventory by adding to the list supplied by Andrew Thompson in his 2014 book *Writing Imperial Histories* that lists all works published up to 2013, to those published since then which are listed on Manchester University Press's web site dedicated to the series located at https://manchesteruniversitypress.co.uk/series/studies-in-imperialism/ Accessed 1st June 2020.
69 See K. Pickles and C. Colbourne, *New Zealand's Empire* (Manchester: Manchester University press, 2016).
70 See J. Darwin, 'Bored by the Raj', in *Times Literary Supplement*, 18th February 2005, pp. 5–6; S. Howe, *The Independent* 14th January 2005, p. 27; I. Phimister, Review of Absent Minded Imperialists, in *English Historical Review*,Vol.120 (2005), pp. 1061–1063.
71 A. Burton, Review of Absent Minded Imperialists in *Victorian Studies* Vol 4: 4, (2005), pp. 626–628; J. MacKenzie, Review of Absent Minded Imperialists in *Round Table*, 94 (2005), pp. 280–283.

72 B. Porter, 'Further Thoughts in Imperial Absent Mindedness', in *Journal of Imperial and Commonwealth History*, Vol 36: 1, (2008), pp. 101–117; J. MacKenzie, "'Comfort' and Conviction: A Response to Bernard Porter', in *Journal of Imperial and Commonwealth History* 36:4 (2008), pp. 659–668.
73 See E. Said, 'Jane Austen and Empire', in T. Eagleton (ed.) *Raymond Williams: Critical Perspectives*, (Cambridge: Polity Press, 1989), pp. 150–164; for Bernard Porter's response see *Absent Mined Imperialists*, p. 139.
74 R. Price, 'One Big Thing? Britain Its Empire and Their Imperial Culture', in *Journal of British Studies*, Vol. 45 (2006), p. 620.
75 J. Paxman, *Empire: What Ruling the World Did to the British* (London: Viking, 2011), pp. 283–284.
76 There have to date been two major publications arising from the project. C. Hall, N. Draper, Keith McClelland, K. Donington and Rachel Lang, *Legacies of British Slave-Ownership: Colonial Slavery and the Formation of Victorian Britain.* Cambridge: CUP, 2014; C. Hall, N. Draper and K. McClelland (eds.), *Emancipation and the remaking of the British Imperial world. (*Manchester: Manchester University Press, 2014).
77 For example at the University of Glasgow, see https://en.wikipedia.org/wiki/Centre_for_the_Study_of_the_Legacies_of_British_Slave-ownership Accessed 6th February 2020.
78 https://www.radiotimes.com/news/2016-11-09/david-olusoga-is-the-new-face-of-bbc-history-but-as-a-boy-he-was-driven-out-of-his-home-by-racists/ Accessed 7th February 2020.
79 See for example 'Decolonising the Curriculum: What's All the Fuss About?' Located at https://www.soas.ac.uk/blogs/study/decolonising-curriculum-whats-the-fuss/ Accessed 6 February 2020.
80 C. Hall, et al, *Emancipation and the remaking of the British Imperial world,* p. 2.
81 S. Ward, 'Foreword', to S. Barczwki & M. Farr, (eds.), *The MacKenzie Moment and Imperial History*, p. 22
82 J. Darwin, 'Afterword' to S. Barczwki & M. Farr, (eds.), *The MacKenzie Moment and Imperial History*, p. 403.
83 J. M. Mackenzie '"The Second City of Empire": Glasgow Imperial Municipality', in F. Driver & D. Gilbert (eds.), *Imperial Cities*: (Manchester: Manchester University Press, 1999); S. Haggerty, A. Webster, & N. J. White (eds.) *The Empire in One City? Liverpool's Inconvenient Imperial Past* (Manchester, Manchester University Press, 2008); M. Taylor, (ed.), *Southampton: Gateway to the British Empire* (London: I.B. Tauris, 2007); B. Beaven, *Visions of Empire: Patriotism, Popular Culture and the City 1870–1939* (Manchester: Manchester University Press, 2012).
84 See Beaven, *Visions of Empire;* S.M. Miller, *Volunteers on the Veld: Britain's Citizen Soldiers and the South African War 1899–1902*, (Norman: Oklahoma Press, 2007). For a review of the latter see S. Badsey, 'Review of Volunteers on the Veld' in *Victorian Studies* Vol. 51:3, (2009), pp. 543–544
85 B. Porter, 'An Imperial Nation? Recent Works on the British empire at home', in *Round Table,* Vol. 96. No 389 (2007), pp. 225–226.
86 A. S. Thompson, 'The Language of Imperialism and the Meanings of Empire: Imperial Discourse in British Politics 1895–1914', in *Journal of British Studies*, Vol. 36, (1997) p. 150.
87 MacKenzie, *Propaganda and Empire*, p. 154.
88 T. Standage *The Victorian Internet: The Remarkable Story of the Telegraph and the Nineteenth Century's Online Pioneers* (London: Wiedenfeld and Nicholson, 1999).
89 A. Jones 'The Press and the Printed Word,' in C. Williams (ed.) A Companion to Nineteenth Century Britain (London: Blackwell, 2007), P.W. Sinnema, *Dynamics of the Pictured Page: Representing the Nation in The Illustrated London News*. (Aldershot:

Ashgate, 1998). A. Hobbs, *A Fleet Street in Every Town: The Provincial Press in England 1855–1900* (Cambridge: Open Book Publishers, 2018), A. Morrison-Low, *Photography L A Victorian Sensation* (London: NMSE publishing 2015).
90 See for example, A. Griffiths, *The New Journalism, the New Imperialism and the Fiction of Empire 1870–1900*, (Basingstoke: Palgrave, 2015).
91 J. Simmons, *The Victorian Railway* (London: Thames and Hudson, 2009).

INTRODUCTION

Youth and education: class, gender and the making of the imperial citizen, 1880–1940

The 'maximalist' versus 'minimalist' debate outlined in the general introduction has encompassed discussion of the place of the Empire in the educational syllabus, and indeed in the wider culture of the schools that pupils drawn from the upper, middle and working classes experienced in the period after 1870. At the same time, extra-curricular leisure-time activities located beyond the school gates were also provided for this age group, in the form of youth movements, and the juvenile literature consumed, promoted and inculcated imperial values. Despite his scepticism regarding the role of Empire in the domestic sphere, Bernard Porter does concede that Empire began to figure more significantly in the years after 1880, because he believes that at this point, there was concern to secure the Empire from the threats of other European powers, such as a resurgent Third French Republic looking for national glory after defeat to the Prussians in 1870–71, and a new Imperial Germany, under the direction of Otto von Bismarck, emerging from the same war as a victor. Tensions in foreign policy continued in the longer history of the 'great game' between Russia and Britain in central Asia. The documents presented here do tend to confirm that larger numbers of British citizens were provided with more information about the Empire after 1880, in ways that had not been so prevalent before this date. This was the era of what has been designated the 'New' Imperialism, and in the British context, the partition of Africa was the first phase of imperial expansion to occur after the introduction of compulsory education and the widening of the vote to include more of the working class in participatory democracy. From the 1870s onwards more children were to obtain a basic education, which in the last quarter of the 19th century began to provide at least a rudimentary understanding of British imperial history and the geography of the Empire. The first section of this introduction analyses the development of the British educational system, explaining the value system upon which it was built, before then turning to the place of the British Empire in the school system and wider imperial influences on school culture.

To begin, we may usefully refer to the features of the British educational system that Michael Katz provided, based on his close reading of educational reports created during the late 19th and the 20th centuries, containing the key assumptions at the heart of the British educational system as it evolved after 1870. Katz noted that the educational system was based on the duty to impart a liberal education, and that there was a distinction between education and vocational instruction. It was also the duty of the school to offer training in character, with such training taking the form of moral and religious instruction. The curriculum was not to be too narrow, and what Katz described as the 'corporate' aspects of the school were as important as the academic. The individual teacher was seen as most important. Education was undertaken to benefit the British economy and British society, but it would also serve the individual. The school was to be run as efficiently as possible without wasting money, and the education system reflected the values and stratifications within that society. As a social institution, the school's function was to play a passive, not revolutionary, role.[1]

British society was indeed permeated with a sense of class by the mid-19th century, and class structures largely dictated the nature of the educational system that was created in the 1870s. The class-based nature of the educational system was reflected and reinforced by the fact that three separate commissions dealt with educational reforms in relation to the three classes in the 1850s and 1860s. The Clarendon Commission (1861–64) investigated the state of the public schools, which catered to the upper classes, the Taunton Commission (1864–68) was tasked with investigating the private endowed schools of the middle class and the Newcastle Commission (1858–61) reported on the 'sketchy system of schools only indifferently attended' by the working class.[2] Elite schooling for the wealthy had taken place in what were until the late 1860s known as charity schools. Originally these were schools which taught a limited number of poor scholars, but by the mid-19th century they were increasingly a second home to the children of the upper and upper middle classes. Seven were known as 'public schools', as a result of the 1868 Public Schools Act. The seven in question were Charterhouse, Eton, Harrow, Rugby, Shrewsbury, Westminster and Winchester. Before boys entered such an institution, they had invariably attended a preparatory school. As Donald Leinster-Mackay noted, 'The emergence of the preparatory school and the public school coincided . . . with the gradual increase in awareness of the British Empire amongst the British middle classes'.[3] The preparatory and public schools became the locations for the training of the gentlemen who would administer the Empire (see documents 1–11). In preparation for this, the child would spend most of the year away from home, isolated from family, thus providing some kind of grounding for the future imperial administrator who spent months, if not years, away from the mother country. Indeed, many of the boys were sons of fathers who worked in the Empire. Rifle shooting was a feature of many preparatory schools, whilst some of the public schools such as Eton developed a volunteer corps. By the early 1900s, at the time of the Second South African War, Geoffrey Best notes that cadet and rifle corps existed in many public schools, with an annual camp being staged at the military town of Aldershot, Hampshire[4] (see document 6). Drill was a central element in this militaristic culture. The 'old boys' of the public schools were invariably mentioned on the pages of the school magazine if they were involved in military manoeuvres in imperial wars. These schools invariably appointed a headmaster who was an ordained member of the clergy, and who proclaimed the virtue of, and need to defend, the British Empire. Edmond Warre, the headmaster of Eton College between 1884–1905, was, for example, the personal chaplain to Queen Victoria (1885–1901), and was succeeded in this role by J.E.C. Welldon, headmaster of Harrow (see documents 2–4). Both were keen sportsmen. Scotland's educational system used the term 'boarding school' rather than 'public school' but these schools nevertheless adopted the house system used by the English public schools. Among the leading Scottish schools were Fettes College, established in 1870, Merchiston, Loretto, Trinity College and Glenalmond. Lay headmasters such as Dr. Hely Hutchinson Almond of Loretto School, Edinburgh, whilst non-ordained, also delivered sermons to the schoolboys[5]. Almond gave what became known as the 'Waterloo Sermon' or 'The Divine Government of Nations' at a date located in the school calendar between the anniversaries of the Battle of Waterloo and Victoria's accession. It unashamedly celebrated 'jingoism, bigotry and racism', and Mangan concludes, 'in short "Lorettonianism" was the essence of imperial education'.[6]

The connection between the public school and the British Empire became a strong one after 1890, for as Cowper notes, 'The expansion and the maintenance of the Empire created a need to staff it with soldiers and administrators – in fact an "officer class"'. Mangan has added,

> The English public schoolboy . . . ran the British Empire. He was ruler and guardian, and not infrequently its farmer and its missionary . . . the schools were training grounds of generations of committed imperialists pledged to the survival of the empire upon which proverbially the sun never set.[7]

The relationship between the public schools and Empire was, however, rather more complex than some historians portray. The historian of public schools T. W. Bamford noted that whilst they provided a large percentage of the Indian Civil Service, in the 'white' settler zones of Empire, the public-school man was, by contrast, 'unwanted, ridiculed, even rejected'.[8] Schools such as Haileybury and Eton were leading providers of the civil servants and officers who administered and policed the Raj.

It may appear incongruous to include a study of elite schools in volumes which primarily focus on the impact of Empire on Britain's popular culture. One important reason for doing so, however, is that the kind of spirit developed in the public schools – that is to say, values of duty, patriotism, athleticism and Christianity (often combined to form 'muscular Christianity') – were subsequently to filter down to a popular level, included, for example, within the outlook of youth organisations of the later Victorian era and also included in school readers that were used in the context of working-class education, and popular youth magazines and works of fiction that romanticised the Empire for the young. Robert

INTRODUCTION

Baden-Powell, the founder of the scout movement, had attended Rose Hill Preparatory School, Tunbridge Wells, and Charterhouse public school, as it was moved from London to Godalming in the 1870s, and the essence of the scout movement was, of course, derived from Baden-Powell's military career, which involved time spent in both India and Africa and culminated in his participation in the South African War (1899–1902).[9] A. P. Thornton usefully summarised this when he noted that '"the public school spirit" became one of the most potent of the imperial elixirs'.[10] As a result of setbacks incurred during the South African War, there was some considerable criticism levelled at the public schools for their failure to provide the kind of education needed to maintain the Empire, for example a perceived disregard for science and technology.[11] The criticism corresponded with a growing call for national efficiency which peaked in the mid-Edwardian years.[12] The coverage of Empire topics in the magazines of elite schools was at its most noticeable before 1914. In the years after the end of the First World War, the coverage became more muted. In 1925, the *Eton College Chronicle* reported the marking of Empire Day by the Slough and District Scouts, which included 200 Etonians.

Before moving on, it should be noted that imperial awareness was not limited to the schools for young men. A perusal of the *Cheltenham Ladies' College Magazine* reveals that amongst the articles contained therein were those such as 'A Report on the South African War' (1900), an obituary of African explorer Mary Kingsley (1900), 'A Visit to a Boer Camp' (1902) and 'Nursing in the Indian Army' (1902). A student essay titled 'The Duties and Privileges of Imperial Citizenship' (1907), noted, 'The aim of the Empire is to extend to all more ignorant races . . . the benefits of Christianity, civilisation and education and to withstand injustice and oppression' (see document 13). A description of Empire Day in Cheltenham was also included in the Autumn 1907 issue (see document 33). By the 1920s and 1930s the coverage of Empire issues had become relatively muted, reflecting the more internationalist spirit of the decades between the two global wars. The Empire Day address to the school was reproduced in Autumn 1920, although Empire Day was not recorded any further in the magazine after this year. By the mid-1920s the magazine carried an article by Cyril Norwood, headmaster of Marlborough School, entitled 'The Empire and the League of Nations: Their Real Meaning and Ideals' (see document 37), in which he noted, 'The highest English patriotism, and the truest Imperialism to-day is to support that cause and those ideals for which the League of Nations stands'.[13] Perhaps it is significant that the first issue of the new series carried an article about Czechoslovakia. Yet Empire did not completely vanish as a topic in the magazine. In the Spring 1928 issue, articles were included on the subjects of a 'Trip to Cairo', 'University Life in New Zealand' and another, by 14-year-old Helen Hennings, on 'The Coming of the White Man'.

Another type of schooling in 19th-century Britain could be experienced in a grammar school. The Scottish equivalent of these schools was known as a 'high school' or 'academy'. Traditionally, these schools had focused on the teaching of Latin. In 1755, for example, Samuel Johnson's dictionary defined a grammar school as a school 'in which the learned languages are grammatically taught'. As a result of middle-class formation in the early 19th century, the curriculum was widened to include other subjects, such as arithmetic and English. In 1869, by the terms of the Endowed Schools Act, the 782 grammar schools that existed in England became more academic, and in effect tried to emulate the public schools in the way they taught their pupils. There remained the question of the education of the working class. In the mid-Victorian decades, provision for working-class education consisted of a rather patchy voluntary system, with the churches playing a significant role in this provision. Among the types of schools which offered some kind of education to the poor were branch schools, dame schools, industrial schools, ragged schools, national schools and Sunday schools. The term 'schooling' for the poor was perhaps more appropriately denoted as a mixture of care for the very poor and training for the majority of them. As Gillian Gear has noted, 'The founders of certified industrial schools were not the first people to see the possible benefits of teaching practical skills to children. Refuges, ragged schools, Poor Law schools and other similar institutions had included industrial work and training in their timetable. The intention was to make the children useful citizens, and subjects considered to be "useful" included gardening for boys and domestic economy for girls'.[14] Dame schools were by definition run by women, and had a long history stretching back to at least the 16th century. They had a poor reputation and often constituted simply a form of day care for the young. Two organisations formed in the early 19th century proved to be the leading education providers for working-class children until the 1870 Education Act reformed the system. The National Society of Promoting the Education of the Poor in the Principles of the Established Church and British and Foreign School Society schools were provided by the Church of England and the Non-Conformists, respectively, in 1808 and 1811. Both adopted the 'monotorial' system of teaching, whereby older pupils would assist in the teaching of younger pupils, enabling an economical deployment of adult teachers. In his pamphlet written in 1859, the Reverend John Fitzwygram noted the difficulty of educating the poor. He noted that many more pupils attended a dame school than a national school. Most pupils who left a dame school could 'scarcely read nor write by the time they are twelve or thirteen' whilst 'in a good National School the children, owing to the improved appliances for teaching, have usually acquired those arts by the time they are *ten* years old'.[15] Once a child had acquired these basic skills, the parent invariably took the child out of school. The attitude to wider scholarship on the part of mid-Victorian working-class parents was summarised thus:

> To other branches of instruction, such as history, grammar, geography, they are for the most part quite indifferent – ignorant of such things themselves, and conscious that they have done very well *without* such knowledge, they do not desire it for their children, nor are they disposed to make any great sacrifices to obtain it. When therefore their children

come to be about ten years old, and are tolerably proficient in reading and writing (as they of course would be at a good school, though at a *bad* school they would have to stay till eleven or twelve before they would be equally advanced) the parents naturally ask themselves, what is the use of Johnny and Polly staying at school any longer? they are now good enough scholars for labourers' children, and the five or six shillings a week which they could earn at work, would be a great help to us. On this ground it is quickly decided that Johnny and Polly shall make themselves useful.[16]

Thus, it is undeniable that as the educational historian J. M. Goldstrom has noted, 'The Victorians [. . .] saw it as their duty to provide "appropriate" education for the different classes and working class schools could never be mistaken for anything but establishments for the lower orders'.[17]

Fitzwygram believed that a balance between industrial training and non-vocational academic study should be achieved in the school. To that end he advocated that schools purchase from the National Schools depository located in Westminster copies of such books as *Geography of the Colonies* and *An Outline of English History*.[18] Another book Fitzwygram suggested be used in the classroom was Bishop George Davys' *Plain and Short History of England for Children*. Davys had been the tutor to Queen Victoria in her childhood and subsequently became Bishop of Peterborough. It was a book which took the form of a series of letters from a father to his son. Davys presented English history as the history of the monarchy, and the evolution of the Empire did not garner much consideration. In the chapter charting the reign of George III, brief mention of the careers of Robert Clive and Captain Cook was made. The generally low awareness of history and geography before 1870 was confirmed in the inquiry into the state of education in Wales published in the 1840s by a commission chaired by James Kay Shuttleworth. The resulting report noted that out of a sample of 12,510 pupils, a comparatively low number studied geography (1,320) and an even smaller number English history (598).[19]

The notion of providing an education for those at the bottom of the social pyramid was novel and far from universally appreciated in 1870. In the 'voluntary' era, from 1830–1870, for example, J. S. Hurt notes that gradations between sections of the working class were noted to exist: 'The children of the poorest classes – the "residuum" the "street arabs" the dangerous and perishing classes [. . .] were virtually untouched by the existing state aided voluntary schools managed by the religious societies'.[20] Whilst sections amongst the politically radical began to advocate universal education for the working class, a more common notion amongst the upper and middle class was that it was pointless to try and educate those who were destined to undertake monotonous labour. Education would only lead to that class questioning its place in society and ultimately a rebellion. Yet, it was rather ironically to prevent a rebellion in what was arguably the first component of the British Empire – Ireland – that the first experiment in state funding was undertaken. The Irish were provided with schools that were Protestant and English-speaking from the 16th century onwards. Another important way-marker identified by Sturt was the introduction of the New Poor Law in 1834 which retained education within its system.[21] The New Poor Law was also an example of the state operating at local level. The climate of opinion regarding the role of the state began to change in the 1860s, as the idea of a second reform act became reality, reaching fruition in 1867. Sections of the working class could now exercise their constitutional right to vote. In order that suffrage be used to best effect, it was thought that education should be provided. As a more collectivist spirit prevailed in Britain in the 1860s, the previously ingrained idea that the state should leave education to private, voluntary philanthropic bodies also evaporated. An important force here was that of the emerging creed of municipal socialism, espoused most notably by the man who would in the 1870s become the mayor of Birmingham, Joseph Chamberlain. In 1867 Chamberlain had, in conjunction with Jesse Collings, founded the Birmingham Education League. Collings had witnessed at first hand the American school system, free and non-sectarian, and thought a similar system should be introduced in Britain. After his pamphlet *An Outline of the American School System* was published in 1868, the National Education League was established to lobby for an American-style system to be introduced across England and Wales.

Another factor in the rise of working-class elementary education was the Victorian notion of 'citizenship'. To play a role as an 'active' citizen in Victorian society required an education. In elite schools, culture was imparted by means of classes in history and geography, but less so in the elementary schools of England. In the context of the elementary school, any notion of imperial citizenship was conveyed in classes aimed at either improving comprehension and understanding or in classes in moral instruction. In 1870 under the terms of W. E. Forster's Elementary Education Act, elementary schools were introduced, which would educate the working-class child from the ages of 5 to 13. Six 'standards' were introduced under the revised code of regulations in 1872, with a Standard VII subsequently added, under the terms of the Elementary Code of 1882.[22] Each of them focused on the ability to read, write and calculate (or 'reading, 'riting and 'rithmetic', the proverbial three Rs). At the outset, Standard I was the most basic, whilst Standard VI was the most advanced. Depending on the requirements of the local board in any given area of the country, a child could leave school once he or she had attained the designated minimum standard. This usually meant a child's attainment of between Standard IV and VI. The child could leave school at the age of 10 if they had acquired this set standard. The highest of the standards, Standard VI, required the child to read fluently and with expression, to write a letter or construct an essay, paraphrase, and demonstrate arithmetic ability with regard to proportions and fractions.

The equivalent of Forster's Elementary Education Act was introduced in Scotland two years later. Here, not only was elementary education more comprehensively introduced than in England, but some measure of secondary education was

INTRODUCTION

provided. The act also supressed the Scottish Gaelic language and established English as the primary language of instruction in the classroom. Under the terms of a second Elementary Education Act (the Mundella Act), introduced by the newly returned Liberal ministry in 1880, a child was compelled to attend a school. Thus, the years between the 1880s and the outbreak of the First World War represented the first phase of mass education and, as some historians have argued, the creation of the concept of 'childhood'. This era coincided with what has been denoted as a 'new' phase of British imperialism, most significantly witnessing the partition of Africa by Britain and other European powers; this was the first imperial project to take place in the context of a newly created 'mass' democracy. Secondary education for the working-class child was in its early phase; indeed the nature of such education for the 'adolescent' was debated by the Bryce Commission in 1894, resulting in its report of the following year. In the 1880s and 1890s this education took a number of forms. The first was the technical school, which as its name implies, offered largely vocational education. Nevertheless, the school retained arts subjects in its curriculum. The other form of embryonic secondary education before the First World War was the higher elementary school. This offered the capable older child the opportunity to continue with their studies to the age of 15. At the end of the First World War, Herbert Fisher's Education Act introduced compulsory education to the age of 14. This was an important stage in the development of secondary education. Pupils would, in this era, remain at the same school from the age of 5 to 14.

In terms of the focus of these volumes, we now turn to the issue of the place of Empire in the school in the years after 1880 and how historians have debated this issue in the recent past. How far did 'Empire' encroach upon the school syllabus and the wider school culture? Of the two primary subjects that lent themselves most obviously to the project of imperial education, historians have noted that it was the subject of geography, rather than history, which commanded a significant place in terms of content on the curriculum before the 1890s. By 1899 only 25 per cent of schools taught history, as compared with 75 per cent that taught geography.[23] Geography made more headway in securing a place in the classroom than history because it was generally perceived to be a more practical subject for younger children to understand, it stimulated more interest and, from a teaching perspective, it was easier for a child to pass an exam in this subject. It has been noted that geography textbooks often encouraged the idea of emigration to the settler zones such as Australia, Canada and New Zealand in particular, thus aligning education with state objectives in the later 19th century. It was also boosted by organisations such as the Royal Geographical Society, which had been established in 1830. It was significant in establishing geography as an 'academically respectable subject'.[24] By contrast, the Historical Association was established only at the later date of 1906. History as a subject had gained an initial foothold on the school timetable under the terms of the Elementary Code of 1875. Subsequently, directions were issued to H.M. inspectors to encourage interest in British colonial history in 1878 and 1885, together with the suggestion made in the elementary school code of 1882 that geography for Standard VI pupils should include the study of Britain's colonies and dependencies. In 1890 another code introduced an alternative syllabus for upper standards in geography that required a knowledge of Britain's imperial link and the history syllabus was also now to include colonial history.[25] As Yeandle has noted however, in 1898 'only 5,133 schools across England out of a sum number of nearly 50,000 chose to teach history'.[26] Since the 1870s, however, a new imperialist fervour had been building, growing by means of Disraelian rhetoric, that linked social reform to the Empire. The works of Sir John Seeley in the 1880s and the fiction of Henty and Kipling in the 1890s also reflected and partially fuelled this appetite for Empire. So, too, did the appearance of new journalism in the form of the *Daily Mail* (1896–) and the *Pall Mall Gazette* (1865). Under the editorship of Stead between 1883 and 1889, the *Pall Mall Gazette* included significant coverage of Britain's 'new' imperialism.

The Golden and Diamond Jubilees of Victoria in 1887 and 1897 also ramped imperial enthusiasm to new heights. This first era of imperial zeal arguably reached its height during the South African War with the 'orgy of Mafeking night' and the Khaki election of 1900. The years immediately following the war were in many respects a period of reflection as to how education could play a role in sustaining the Empire. The national efficiency movement played a significant role in this introspective examination that was a feature of the first decade of the 20th century. It was also partly as a result of this new idea of producing citizens in tune with national objectives in the early Edwardian era that a small group of educationalists began to have an impact in the field of history teaching. Collectively they were known as 'Herbartians'. The group consisted of figures such as Frank Hayward; John Findlay, Professor of History at Victoria University of Manchester; his colleague Catherine Dodd, the first female member of staff at Manchester; and John Adams, First Principal of the Institute of Education at University College London in 1909. 'Herbartian' referred to those who followed the pedagogy of Johann Herbart (1776–1841), who had advocated education for citizenship. History teaching, it was felt, should use historical examples to demonstrate moral character.[27] As Dodd claimed in her treatment of Herbartian theory:

> History, taken in its broadest sense includes all the studies in the Humanistic group, and it is placed first in the scheme of instruction, because it is considered of primary importance in moulding the character and in stimulating interest.[28]

The influence of this group can be seen in the extracts taken from school readers included in this volume (documents 20–23), which attempted to mould character in the child by the inclusion of heroic deeds of Empire.

The preparatory schools had a Harrow History Prize for which boys could be entered by the mid-1880s, and the history of Empire was amongst the historical topics taught.[29] Before this period, Bamford notes that of the 26–30 hours of classes scheduled in a given week of the term, approximately 18–19 would be devoted to study of the classics with relevant history and geography. Evidently lessons did begin in modern imperial history, which might explain the series of rather hefty tomes that were published by the Cassell publishing house, founded in 1848. The Edinburgh novelist James Grant wrote *British Battles on Land and Sea* (1873), which included imperial battles, and followed this up with the *Illustrated History of India* (published in 1876–77), and the *History of the War in the Soudan* (1885–86). Richard Danes subsequently wrote the *Illustrated History of the Boer War* (1903). Grant's *History of India* had been published to mark the first visit of the Prince of Wales to India and was still topical when Victoria was given the title 'Empress of India'. It was reissued when the second Afghan war broke out, in 1878, and again in 1885, when there was conflict between Britain and Russia over the Afghan frontier, and yet again when the Prince of Wales' eldest son visited India in 1889.[30] Each of these volumes ran to more than 1,000 pages (see documents 14–15). Thus 'Empire' evidently provided publishing houses with a new market. In the era of the 'new' imperialism, other publishers saw opportunities for either single volumes or new series. Just one example was the series called *Short Lives of Men with a Mission*, published by James Nisbet of London, that included a volume on Henry Stanley and David Livingstone (1890). Copies may have been acquired by elite schools' libraries. Samuel Rawson Gardiner's *Student's History of England: From the Earliest Times to 1885* (1891), included coverage of British India, and noted the expansion of British influence into both southern Africa and Australasia (see document 16). He tended to take a paternal attitude towards India. The lesson to be learnt from the mutiny, he concluded, was that it was 'better to leave evils untouched for a while than to risk the overthrow of a system of government which on the whole, works beneficially'.[31] Edward Salmon's *The Story of the Empire* appeared in 1902 (see document 17). The author was a member of the Royal Colonial Institute and the editor of its journal *United Empire*. The book was published in the series called the Library of Useful Stories. Salmon described the publication as 'not intended as a textbook' but rather 'a swiftly moving panorama,' as if the Empire were viewed from a moving train.[32] The tone that the author struck regarding native peoples of the Empire also showed rather more humility and less bombast than other comments found at the time of the mutiny. The history of India between the mutiny and the death of Victoria was described as one of 'consolidation and progress'.[33] However, the events of 1857 had taught both the Indians and the British lessons. It had taught the British the folly of deceiving the Indians in matters affecting religion.[34] In the decades following the Treaty of Waitangi (1840s), the New Zealand Māori were, in Salmon's words, 'more sinned against than sinning', and the wars of the 1860s were largely due to the 'Briton's inability to understand native customs and native ideas'.[35] In fact, Salmon asked, what had people in Britain made of the first 20 years of Queen Victoria's reign which saw so much colonial violence? He suggested that many episodes in the story of the Empire be described as 'humane rascality'.[36] The trajectory of humility was not necessarily linear. More explicitly racist in its views was Rudyard Kipling and Charles Fletcher's *A School History of England* (1911), which was viewed with suspicion by its Oxford University publisher Clarendon for its racist depiction of the Irish and the West Indian[37] (see document 19).

A. F. Pollard's *The British Empire: Its Past, Its Present and Its Future* (1909) and Edward Hawke's *The British Empire and Its History* (1911), published by John Murray, were titles overseen by imperial loyalty societies such as the Royal Colonial Institute (renamed the Royal Empire Society in 1928) and the League of Empire. A. J. Herbertson's *Survey of the British Empire* for Clarendon, Oxford, was published in 1914 and W. H. Woodward's *Short History of the Expansion of the British Empire* was published by Cambridge University Press in 1915. State schools were in some instances rather wary of using such books produced by imperial leagues, given that they represented a form of propaganda.

As more working-class men were included within the constitutional pale by means of the Second and Third Reform Acts of 1867 and 1884–85, educationalists thought it prudent that working-class schoolchildren be taught notions of civic, national and imperial duty, loyalty, ingenuity and bravery. In the promotion of such learning from history and geography, children attending elementary schools were presented with what were termed history or geography 'readers'. These were commonly acquired by schools in the later 19th century. Up until the 1890s, John MacKenzie has noted, readers were invariably compendiums that amassed the 'facts' of Empire, but after that they were published with the intention of instilling imperial patriotism and citizenship. Reader book sales outnumbered textbooks by a ratio of 10 to 1. Indeed, the readers were cheaper than textbooks and the leading publishing houses, such as Longman, Cassell, Chambers and Macmillan, made large sums from schools' acquisition of such readers. The reader was primarily aimed at developing a child's reading and comprehension, rather than his or her historical or geographical understanding. It was publications such as these, therefore, rather than history or geography textbooks, that were the prime vehicle for the imperial education that a child received in the local-authority-run school. School 'readers' had first appeared as early as the 1860s, one of the earliest being W. F. Collier's *History of the British Empire*, published as a Nelson School Reader in 1866. Collier's reader took a monarchical approach to the subject, moving through each reign from earliest times.

By the later 19th century there were those both within and without the education sector who advocated school as a place to promote the notion of local, national and imperial 'citizenship'. Quite what this word meant changed over time and the understanding of 'citizenship' passed through a number of phases between 1870 and 1939. Initially, in the decades between 1860 and 1880, the concept was used in relation to urbanisation, as large industrial cities grew and local authorities wished the individual to develop a sense of civic loyalty. This was then supplemented when the era of the new imperialism arrived after 1880 as nationhood and Empire were combined. It was necessary for all classes to think of themselves as imperial citizens, and as members of a race which had an imperial destiny. Because Britain had acquired an extensive empire, as had the Romans in an earlier epoch, an individual would need to be aware of being a citizen of an imperial nation. Those educated at elite schools might possibly play a role as colonial administrators, whilst middle-class children might become part of the administrative machinery that managed the industrial cities that competed for the title 'second city of Empire'. However, it was less likely that the working-class child would play any such role.

What exactly was the purpose of offering working-class children an education in the history and geography of the British Empire? To understand why the Empire's history and geography was taught to 'the masses', we need to appreciate the point made by Stephen Heathorn that there was little or no distinction in this period between the notion of citizenship in a domestic or imperial context. Empire was seen as a natural extension of the nation in this era. That is to say, figures known for their role in domestic history and those who had played a role in creating empire were equally significant in the context of classroom history teaching. 'The discursive construction of a fiery imperial-nationalist "Englishness" was certainly present in the elementary classroom', Heathorn notes, 'but this had as much to do with the projection of what was deemed an appropriate domestic social identity for the lower rungs of society as it did with promotion of the imperialist project overseas'.[38] We might also note that despite the Empire being deemed a 'British' venture, that is to say, a partnership between the English and the Scots and to a lesser extent the Welsh, and including figures who had originated north and west of the English border, the 'readers' were invariably marketed as English history.[39] This was to some extent conflation. However, Heathorn explains that in the later 19th and early 20th centuries, characteristics such as virility, heroism, justice and glory were the 'very foundation of nation and empire' and 'tended to be phrased as attributes of Englishness'.[40] Indeed, the formation of the United Kingdom was invariably regarded as the first 'imperial' project for the English, before they journeyed overseas. Virtually all the readers espoused a Whig/Liberal view of history as the 'onward march' of English liberty. In this respect they were essentially simplified versions of histories that had been published in the second half of the 19th century by leading Oxbridge historians of the period, such as J. R. Green's *History of the English People* (in four volumes, 1878–1880), J. A. Froude's *England and Her Colonies* (1886), J. R. Seeley's *The Expansion of England* (1883), E. A. Freeman's *History of the Norman Conquest* (six volumes, 1867–1879) and William Stubbs' *Constitutional History of England* (three volumes, 1891–1898).[41] The scholar of Caribbean slavery Eric Williams noted that Stubbs 'never said a word at any time about slavery, whether medieval or modern'.[42] As can be seen from the readers, children were taught to understand that the English had, since the time of Anglo-Saxon arrival, been a seafaring island people, and had, since at least the time of the Crusades, been involved in spreading Christianity to the 'heathens'. Both of these sentiments were present in the 'new' imperialism of the era 1880–1914. Heroic figures from various stages of English history, such as Sidney, Wellington, Nelson, Livingstone (a Scot) and Gordon, invariably appeared in the readers, as in the words of Yeandle they 'legitimated England (Britain) as the ultimate object of loyalty'.[43]

In addition to the work of Heathorn and Yeandle, research undertaken by Chancellor, Glendenning and Castle has noted the racial bias in many of the readers in their depiction of the various races who inhabited the British Empire.[44] Valerie Chancellor examined both readers and textbooks, and noted that Indian and African peoples were less kindly treated than Europeans. Yeandle notes that native Indians were invariably described as 'weak', 'cruel', 'effeminate', 'debauched', 'despotic', 'treacherous' or 'cold blooded'.[45] In her study of the representation of race in children's books, Kathryn Castle noted that invariably the 'crimes associated with figures such as Robert Clive or Warren Hastings were reduced to misdemeanours'.[46] In the Macmillan reader presented here (document 23), written for senior pupils, the author noted that Hastings was of the 'first rank of statesmen' and that 'the great work begun by Clive and Hastings has been continued by brave solders and notable statemen. It is true that India has been won by the sword, but England has given peace and prosperity to the three hundred million of that vast dependency.' In reflecting on the Indian Mutiny of the 1850s, the author noted, 'Every effort is made to govern India with wisdom and justice'. The *Holborn Series Historical Reader* (document 21) followed its description of the mutiny with a description of the awarding of the Victoria Cross which was given to 'many noble fellows' for their 'heroic conduct'. The school readers gave less coverage to Africa, although General Gordon's exploits in the Sudan were invariably described and the word 'heroic' usually appeared. In the *Young Briton's History Reader* (document 22) a chapter is devoted to David Livingstone. The child is told that the Africans 'knew nothing about true God' and that 'most of them were fierce and cruel'. Many of the readers omitted any discussion of the slave trade. Heathorn notes that comments about the trade were only ever made in relation to its abolition. This comment is accurate for the readers considered here. The *Young Briton's Reader* is the only one of the four readers included here to contain a chapter on 'Setting Free the Slaves', and the author struck what for the period was quite a regretful note when he noted, 'Our forefathers had not the same feeling for their fellow-men as we have'. A further comment noted that 'it is our proud boast that no one can be a slave under the British flag'.

With regard to geographical readers, these also provided the pupil with some narrative relating to the origins of British rule in both India and Africa. *The Chambers New Geographical Reader* of 1898 (document 24) justified British rule of India because Britain had 'nobly performed her duty to her great dependency', and it continued to boast that Britain had 'provided settled government, irrigated the land, constructed canals, railways and provided education'. The observation that there had been 'desperate conflicts with the Sikhs' did not disrupt the overall narrative that British rule of India had been benevolent and progressive. As Tesea Ploszajska has noted, several of the geographical readers aimed at the younger child adopted the fairy tale as a method of conveying a sense of the zones of the world where the British had established rule.[47] Examples are provided here from titles such as the *Kingsway Book of Geography Stories* (1919) by R. J. Finch (document 25). The introduction noted, 'All children love stories. That is why the story method provides the best introduction to a new subject'. Part I, billed as 'The Wonderful Room', contained 12 stories that follow the character of Peter to distant lands that are inhabited by what Finch called 'strange people' such as Zulus. Peter visits, among other zones, imperially governed territories such as Africa, the South Seas and Australia. In Part II, called 'Stories of Other Lands', another set of stories includes India, Canada, the West Indies and Egypt. An example from the 1930s is also provided (see document 26). It is taken from the first of the publications that were collectively titled *Lands and Life: Human Geographies* (1930–1935) authored by Edmund Horniblow. The first was titled 'People and Children of Wonderful Lands' and took the child on a tour of the world, taking in both imperial and nonimperial zones. Such descriptions of ethnic peoples are now seen as pejorative but of their time. The extracts here are from the 14th impression, by which time some of the more overtly racist descriptions had been edited out. Another example is B. G. Hardingham's *Round the Globe,* published in the Foundations of Geography series in 1934 (document 28), in which Australia is described as 'Never-Never Land'. The word 'strange' occurs twice in the first three paragraphs of the description of the continent. It is also used to describe the appearance of non-Anglo peoples such as Arabs. In post-modern parlance this is an example of the young child being conditioned to see black people as 'the other'. The other kind of geographical textbook tended to be a rather duller affair and were akin to almanacs consisting of 'facts' about the various components of the Empire. The description of black Africans or 'Kaffirs', as they were described in the later 19th century, was subject to change. In the *Chambers New Geographical Reader*, they are described as a 'warlike people' who 'do not take willingly to labour'.[48] When the *Collins Wide World Geography* readers appeared between 1901 and 1923, however, the image was now reversed: black Africans were described as 'good natured and friendly'[49] (see document 27).

Given that most working-class children were unlikely to visit the wider Empire, the purpose of education about the Empire in the state schools related to the aim of developing the child's character and morality. This can be illustrated by referring to some of the teaching manuals published in the later 19th and early 20th centuries, which suggested how to bring to life a particular subject in the school curriculum and how history and geography could create good 'citizens'. In their discussion of classroom management, for example, Collar and Crook asserted that the purpose of the teaching of history was four-fold. Firstly, it imparted information; secondly, it helped to train the memory; thirdly, it developed the imagination; and fourthly, it provided moral training.[50] History could, they believed, offer examples of 'perseverance' (Robert the Bruce or Richard Cobden), industry (ironmaster Thomas Foley, economist and physician William Petty or inventor William Strutt), devotion to duty (the Duke of Wellington or Cuthbert Collingwood of the Royal Navy), 'energy' (Governor-General of India Warren Hastings), philanthropy (the 'liberators of the slaves' such as Wilberforce) and 'living within one's means' (Charles Napier or John Jervis, first Earl of St. Vincent).[51] When the ship H.M.S. *Birkenhead* wrecked, in February 1852, soldiers sacrificed their lives to let women and children board lifeboats, and this was held up as a historical example of fortitude and chivalry.[52] Most significantly, however, the manual advocated history as instilling patriotism. The authors were sceptical that studying history could teach judgement, as they believed that pupils tended to simply follow the viewpoint provided by the teacher. Similarly, David Salmon had also identified patriotism and the inculcation of morals as being at the heart of history teaching in his manual *The Art of Teaching*, first published in 1898.[53] Writing in 1910, M. W. Keatinge, Reader in Education at the University of Oxford and an influential figure in the field of teacher training, voiced his frustration at the way history was taught in schools. He noted that despite history becoming ubiquitous in school curricula since the new century had begun, a 'lamentable ignorance is everywhere to be found'. He thought that simply reading from a textbook did not excite the child and he was generally critical of the idea that the primary objective of the study of history was to recite 'facts' about the past that had been memorised from texts. He rather thought that the subject could develop judgement in the child and that in a 'modern self-conscious democracy', it was essential for the individual to acquire such judgement.[54]

Beyond formal subject teaching

In addition to the advocacy of empire by writers such as these, there were other means by which Britain's overseas influence was promoted in the classroom and in the child's home. By the 1890s the threat to the British Empire was becoming more explicit, as it found rivals in France, Germany and Russia. As Dan Gorman has noted, 'The concept of citizenship was much on the lips of British imperial thinkers and activists in the late Victorian and Edwardian eras, the result of both an increased sense of military and economic competition and domestic pressures for greater social economic and political equality'.[55] A range of imperial societies were formed in this period to foster goodwill across the Empire, urge Empire unity, and facilitate teacher exchange. In 1902, Lord Meath (Reginald Brabazon), a Tory Imperialist and a leading advocate for imperial education, began to promote Queen Victoria's birthday, the 24th May, as 'Empire Day'. Before this he had endeavoured to have the Union flag raised in schools to foster patriotism, but had not succeeded in this project.[56] He successfully founded the Lads' Drill Association in 1899, which merged with the National Service League (NSL) in 1906. The NSL was effectively a movement which campaigned for peace-time conscription. However, it was ultimately unsuccessful in achieving its aims. Drill had been introduced into the school curriculum in 1895 and in some regions of Britain as early as the mid-1880s. Despite the misgivings of some headmasters, it became, as Anne Bloomfield notes, 'an accepted and acceptable part of British formal education'.[57] Meath's third project, Empire Day (see documents 32–37) was not to be officially recognised by the British state until 1916, but was being voluntarily acknowledged in some schools from 1904. In some parts of the Empire, such as Canada, this day had already been observed as 'Victoria Day' from the time of the Diamond Jubilee, in 1897. Empire Day was seen by Meath as a 'Christmas Day' for the Empire.[58] Schoolchildren would sing patriotic songs like 'Jerusalem' and 'God Save the Queen'. They might hear speeches that celebrated the Empire, perhaps given by teachers or school governors, and be presented with tales of British exploits in the Empire. The stories the children heard often celebrated figures such as Clive of India, Wolfe of Quebec or perhaps Gordon of Khartoum. Local dignitaries invariably played some role on Empire Day. In the early 20th century Meath also began what was projected as a five-volume study of the British Empire, titled *Our Empire Past and Present*. By the outbreak of the First World War, a fifth project, known as the Duty and Discipline movement, had been founded (see document 31) that aimed at removing slackness, indifference and indiscipline from the youth.[59] Imperial and militaristic practices of this kind were condemned in some quarters. An article in the *Journal of Education* noted that drilling could prepare ground for the introduction of a school cadet corps with 'sham fights, processions, waving of flags and singing of doggerel verse'.[60] Time was also scheduled in the school week for lessons in moral education which might promote 'quasi-nationalistic and imperialistic morals including the teaching of loyalty and patriotism duty and courage', particularly at Standards IV–VII.[61] In terms of being taught about the Empire, Blanch notes that in the later 19th century, 'Britain was seen as a great civilising Alma Mater, spreading freedom and justice to barbaric Africa and Australasia'.[62]

In some instances, there was recalcitrance on the part of individual teachers and some Labour councils to observe Empire Day, as they perceived the celebration of Empire as ethically questionable. London County Council School Inspector F. H. Hayward, noted above as a proponent of J. F. Herbart, observed that before the First World War, Empire Day had amounted to little more than 'bellicose celebration of England plus some lunatic waving of the Union Jack by alleged representatives of Ireland, South Africa, and India, countries which have done or are doing their best to get rid of that flag altogether'.[63] He further noted that in the 1920s and 1930s some teachers had turned the day into a civic celebration or affiliated the day to 'the League of Nations idea'. Children certainly looked forward to the afternoon events, because they left the confines of the classroom and made their way to local parks or other public venues where marches, maypole dances, concerts and parties took place. The children often wore fancy dress to reflect some aspect of the Empire. Yet, in contrast with its observance in the wider Empire, it has been shown that Empire Day took on a different meaning in the various regions of England. Empire Day was invariably adapted by local authorities to local conditions.[64] Whatever form it took, however, Empire Day remained on the school calendar until the 1950s. In December 1932, the BBC first began to broadcast a king's message to the Empire, and by the outbreak of the Second World War, a broadcast was made at mid-year. Empire-themed programmes with speeches from the Prime Minster or senior imperial figures became more established. Listening to the wireless was, of course, a home-based activity and this tended to reduce the 'public' nature of the day.

Lord Meath was supported in his efforts to introduce Empire Day observance into the school calendar by organisations that had developed in the later 19th and early 20th centuries to promote the Empire. Notable examples were the British Empire League, which had been founded in 1895 as a successor to the Imperial Federation League. Its founders were Lord Avebury (John Lubbock), a banker, philanthropist and Liberal politician (1834–1913), Lord Roberts, Military Commander of the British army (1832–1914) and Lord Strathcona (Donald Smith), a Scots-Canadian businessman who was a founder of Anglo-Persian Oil (1820–1914).[65] The League of the Empire, founded in 1901, also aimed to promote Empire unity with a special emphasis on imperially oriented education. By 1904 this league had 70 branches in Britain.[66] It enjoyed the support of the colonial office, agents-general and the Board of Education. Strathcona was also involved in the creation of this league. Others who offered support included the Canadian educator George Parkin, Canadian-born Gilbert Parker, a member of the British parliament, and Canon Lyttelton, headmaster of Haileybury College. The League of the Empire was founded to facilitate imperial education and to allow teacher exchange schemes between components of the Empire. The Imperial Union of Teachers, founded by Elizabeth Ord Marshall, developed as a sub-organisation of the League of Empire in 1913. The Victoria League was founded in 1901, and was, in its first phase at least, a largely female organisation, founded with the aim of facilitating an exchange of information, hospitality and cooperation between women in the components of the Empire[67] (see documents 42–44).

In the wake of the South African War, the concern that British youth was not fit enough to wage war was reflected in the notion of physical deterioration. *The Report of the Inter-Departmental Committee on Physical Deterioration* was published in 1904 (see document 38). The report found that 37 per cent of recruits to the army were not fit enough. The reasons for poor health originated in the living conditions found within British cities and towns and a poor diet for the working class. Given that the intellectual climate of the period included the notions of eugenics and racial superiority, this report caused significant concern and led to the improvement of meals for children in schools in order to prevent undernourishment

Dance was also utilised in the service of Empire. Cecil Sharp (1859–1924) led a revival of folk songs and dance. He founded the English Folk Dance Society in 1911. The impetus for this revival was the desire, as Bloomfield notes, to assert 'England as the centre of the Empire embracing and disseminating its own culture'.[68] The document included here titled *The Masque of the Children of the Empire* dates from 1909. The masque was the creation of Grace Kimmins, who became a leading advocate of child welfare, particularly for the disabled child. She established a Guild of Play and wrote 'a series of patriotic books detailing songs and dances drawn from the English and imperial past'.[69] Kimmins was based at the Bermondsey settlement, a poor district of south London. Another play with an imperial theme that could be performed by school children during the 1920s and 1930s was Enid Blyton's *The Union Jack*, published within her three-volume work titled *The Teacher's Treasury*. This publication sat alongside other texts she produced that were used in schools during the 1920s and 1930s, such as *Modern Teaching* (1928) and *Pictorial Knowledge* (1930) (see documents 39–41).

In the aftermath of the First World War, the imperial societies were challenged by the establishment of the League of Nations and the League of Nations Union (LNU) in an emerging spirit of internationalism. There were calls from some quarters (most obviously the LNU) and educationalists to reform the teaching of history and geography to reduce the implicit celebration of Empire and the battles that had taken place to establish British rule and the veneration of militaristic figures in school textbooks. Celia Evans and Helen Madeley both argued for such a 'recasting' of history and geography to emphasise the similarities between peoples of the world, rather than differences, and the recasting of military values transmitted to children. These arguments were subsequently adopted by the Board of Education in the 1930s (see document 46). Historians of internationalism have noted that efforts to reform the content of history and geography teaching met with some success. As Ken Osborne notes, 'History teaching often took on a proleague tone in North America, South America, Britain and the British dominions ... though without diminishing the emphasis given to the teaching of national and imperial themes'.[70] Some sign of this tempering of patriotism and militarism is seen in the text written by Henry Martens and E. H. Carter titled *Histories,* which first appeared in the early 1930s (see document 47). The authors noted in the preface to the fourth book, which covered the 'Modern Age', that the numerous wars of the era had been treated 'only in their essentials' so as to make room for farmers, scientists and inventors. Chapter 5 of the book concerned the league's work in the years 1919–1939.

Juvenile magazines, juvenile organisations: masculinity, femininity and empire

In the final section of this first volume, a selection of publications aimed at the child for perusal out of school hours are presented (see documents 48–55). As child literacy rates rose as a result of compulsory schooling, a corresponding growth was witnessed in the realm of literature for young boys and girls. In response to the perception of a threat to Empire from other nations and a wish to instil character into working-class youth, a number of organisations were created to instil self-discipline and respect, Christianity and drill. They created various publications as a response to the 'penny dreadfuls' of the period that offered youth sensational stories often featuring highwaymen or urban legends like 'Spring Heeled Jack'. One of the first publications to challenge this kind of storytelling was the *Boys' Own Paper (BOP)*, published by the Religious Tract Society (RTS) in 1879. The founding values of this publication and others that followed was the belief that the youth would read them and absorb Christian moral values. Patrick Dunae notes that in its early phase the *BOP* stressed the missionary aspect of Empire, not a surprising fact, given that the clergymen who had founded the RTS in 1799 had four years earlier founded the London Missionary Society. The paper and its companion the *Boys' Own Annual* promoted the British Empire, particularly in their first decade. Among those who wrote for the paper were Arthur Conan Doyle, R. M. Ballantyne, Jules Verne and G. M. Henty. Alfred Harmondsworth, who also funded a stable of youth publication in the later nineteenth century noted that his stable of publications aimed to eradicate 'the miserable literary rubbish, in which murderers, thieves and other criminals are raised to the position of heroes'.[71] The *BOP* reflected Britain's position as a leading imperial power and its descriptions of the races of Empire invariably included pejorative language. By 1900 the *BOP* was being challenged by other titles, such as those published by Edward Brett. Additional titles included *The Boys of the Empire*, published by Andrew Melrose and edited by Howard Spicer, and described by Dunae as the 'high water mark of juvenile imperialism'.[72] G. A. Henty's *The Union Jack*, and *Young England: An Illustrated Magazine for Boys Throughout the English Speaking World,* which first appeared in 1880, were published by the London Sunday School Union and also included articles by Empire enthusiasts.[73] By the later 19th and early 20th centuries, another crop of youth publications had appeared, among which were *Chums* (1892); *Pluck* (the full title of this publication was *Stories of Pluck: a high class weekly library of adventure at home and abroad, on land and sea* (1894); *Union Jack* (1894); *Gem* (1907); and *The Magnet* (1908). Charles Hamilton (known as Frank Richards) wrote the Greyfriars stories for *The Magnet*. All these magazines included adventures set in the Empire. Schoolboys made a trip to the Congo in issues 190 to 192 of *Gem*. Tom Merry brings a cannibal back to St. Jim's school. *The Magnet* included stories such as 'Colonial Chums' in issue 479 (1917); 'Harry Wharton and Co. in Africa' in issue 770 (1922); 'King Bunter of the Congo' in 772 (1922); 'The Foe from Africa!' in 863 (1924); 'The Nabob's Double' in 961 (1926); 'Harry Wharton and Co. in India' in 965 (1926) and 'Harry Wharton and Co. in Egypt' in 1279 (1932).

Chums was linked to the scout movement and eventually supported the British Boy Scouts (BBS), a breakaway faction of Baden-Powell's Boy Scouts movement. The BBS organisation objected to Baden-Powell's militaristic culture and it formed the National Peace Scouts in 1910. Whilst as Jeffrey Richards notes, the notion of what constituted imperialism changed across the years 1880–1939, ranging from evangelistic sentiment to more militaristic notions through to a more pacifist sentiment after 1918, what remained constant was the concept of manliness based on a notion of 'muscular Christianity'.[74] Kelly Boyd has added that 'manliness and imperialism were integrally bound up with one another in the boys' story papers'.[75]

Whilst most of these publications were aimed at the young boy, there were also publications for the young girl. One of the most notable was the *Girl's Own Paper (GOP)* which first appeared in 1880. It was a companion to the *BOP*. The *GOP* was edited by Charles Peters for its first 28 years and was aimed at the middle-class woman who may have had a university education. It combined the values of the 'new woman' of the 1890s with more traditional virtues of womanhood. The paper promoted the idea of women's independence and that they might journey to the Empire, and it also recorded the impact of Empire in a domestic setting, for example Indian cuisine in the kitchen. Michelle Smith has noted that the pages of the *GOP* contained advertisements for imperial products, thus creating the female 'imperial' consumer, information about the Empire in the form of fictionalised and non-fictionalised articles and the encouragement of girls to emigrate to the Empire as governesses, nurses or missionaries. A perusal of the index to the *GOP* shows that many non-fiction accounts of Empire life were published, among which were 'Girl Life in India' (1885), 'Christmas Day in India' (1887), 'In India with Medical Missionaries' (1891), 'The Colonies and Dependencies of Great Britain' (1883, 1886), 'At the Seaside in the West Indies' (1895), 'Life in the Colonies' (1891), 'From Aden to Sydney' (1891), 'Life on a Transvaal Salt Farm' (1898), 'An English Girl in South Africa' (1900), 'The Boer Vrouw' (1901), 'Camping in the New Zealand Bush' (1908), 'Canadian Girls in Camp' (1931), 'Housekeeping in Bechuanaland' (1927), 'The Loveliness of British Guiana' (1923) and 'Christmas Day in Australia' (1931). In 1924, the magazine ran an article about the British Empire Exhibition being staged that year. Smith concludes that the magazine represented 'several important intersections where gender and imperialism co-exist'.[76]

Three of the most notable youth organisations to be founded in the later 19th and early 20th centuries were the Boys' Brigade, the Boy Scouts and the Girl Guides (see documents 56–59). The Boys' Brigade was founded by Sir William Alexander Smith in 1883 and it rapidly became a movement of Empire, being established in New Zealand in 1886, Canada in 1889, South Africa in 1889 and Australia in 1890. It was founded on values of Christian manliness and semi-military discipline and thus provided the nation with youths who were capable of serving the British Empire. It anticipated the formation of the Boy Scouts by using the ideas of Robert Baden-Powell. The camp was a feature of both organisations. Baden-Powell was a notable imperial figure. He had served in India in the 1870s, in Natal province in the 1880s, fighting against the Zulu, and also fought in the Ashanti Wars on the Gold Coast. He subsequently played a role in the defence of Mafeking in the siege of 1899. He wrote several pamphlets on the art of scouting and reconnaissance. As John Ahier has noted, 'One imperial interest in the primitive people of other lands was in the way they were indeed elemental creatures, instinctive, and clever. . . . Many of the exercises of the Boy Scout movement were devoted to an emulation by youth of such primitive activities'.[77] This movement also reproduced itself across the Empire. Moreover, the scout movement, whilst becoming more international in its outlook in the 1920s, still had a strong link to emigration to the Empire.[78] A section of Baden-Powell's book *Indian Memories*, published in 1915, is reproduced here. In it he reflects on how Empire shaped his life. Baden-Powell's sister Agnes was asked to create a separate girls' organisation to be called the 'Girl Guides', which formed in 1910. Extracts from the book *How Girls Can Help to Build Up the Empire: The Handbook for Girl Guides* (1912) is included here. John Springhall described these kind of youth movements as 'conservative and conformist' – organisations that actively resisted change in British society.[79]

Notes

1. M. Katz, 'From Bryce to Newsom: Assumptions of British Educational Reports 1895–1963' in *International Review of Education*, Vol. 11:3 (1963), pp. 289–290.
2. N. Middleton, 'The Education Act of 1870 as the Start of the Modern Concept of the Child' in *British Journal of Education Studies* (1970), p. 169.
3. D. Leinster-Mackay, 'The Nineteenth-Century English Preparatory School: Cradle and Creche of Empire?' in J. A. Mangan (ed.), *Benefits Bestowed? Education and British Imperialism* (Manchester: Manchester University Press, 1988), p. 59.
4. G. Best, 'Militarism and the Public School' in B. Simon and I. Bradley (eds.), *The Victorian Public School: Studies in the Development of Educational Institution* (Dublin: Gill and Macmillan, 1975), pp. 134–136.
5. J. A. Mangan, 'Hely Hutchinson Almond: Iconoclast, Anglophile, and Imperialist' in *Scottish Journal of Physical Education*, Vol. 12:3 (1984), p. 40; Best, 'Militarism and the Victorian Public School', p. 142.
6. Mangan, 'Hely Hutchinson Almond'; G. Best, 'Militarism and the Victorian Public School', p. 142.
7. J. A. Mangan, 'Images of Empire in the Later Victorian Public School' in *Journal of Educational Administration and History*, Vol. 12:1 (1980), p. 31.
8. T. W. Bamford, *The Rise of the Public Schools: A Study of Boys' Public Boarding Schools in England and Wales* (London: Thomas Nelson, 1967), p. 241.
9. A. Warren, 'Powell, Robert Stephenson Smyth-Baden, 1857–1941' in *Oxford Dictionary of National Biography*. http://doi.org/10.1093/ref:ondb/30520. Accessed 21 February 2021.
10. A. P. Thornton, *The Imperial Idea and Its Enemies: A Study in British Power* (Basingstoke, UK: Macmillan, 1959), p. 90.
11. H. E. Cowper, "British Education, Public and Private, and the British Empire 1800–1930" (Unpublished PhD Thesis, University of Edinburgh, 1979).
12. For the rise of national efficiency and its impact on the education system, see L. Simpson, 'Imperialism, National Efficiency and Education 1900–1905' in *Journal of Educational Administration History*, Vol. 16:1 (1984), pp. 28–35; also Idem, 'Education, Imperialism and National Efficiency in England 1895–1905' (unpublished PhD thesis, University of Glasgow, 1979).
13. The *Cheltenham Ladies College Magazine No VII New Series Autumn 1925*, p. 78. For a detailed examination of the growth of internationalism see D. Gorman, *The Emergence of International Society in the 1920s* (Cambridge: Cambridge University Press, 2012).
14. G. Gear, 'Industrial Schools in England: 1857–1933: "Moral Hospitals" or "Oppressive Institutions"?' (PhD thesis, University of London, 1999), p. 116 (unpublished).
15. Rev J. Fitzwygram, *Hints for the Improvement of Village Schools and the Introduction of Industrial Work* (London: Joseph Masters, 1859), p. 5.
16. Ibid., p. 5.
17. J. M. Goldstrom, 'The Content of Education and the Socialization of the Working-Class Child' in P. McCann (ed.), *Popular Education and Socialization in the Nineteenth Century* (London: Methuen), pp. 106–107.
18. For an advertisement for these books see *Staffordshire Advertiser*, 2nd December 1865, p. 2.
19. J. P. Kay Shuttleworth, *Reports of the Commissioners of Inquiry into the State of Education in Wales*, Vol. 1 (London: William Clowes, 1847), p. 56.
20. J. Hurt, *Elementary Schooling and the Working Class 1860–1918* (London: Routledge, 1979), p. 4.
21. M. Sturt, *The Education of the People: A History of Primary Education in England and Wales in the Nineteenth Century*. See especially chapter 4, 'The Beginnings of State Control', pp. 62–93.

22 P. Gordon and D. Lawton, *Curriculum Change in the Nineteenth and Twentieth Centuries* (London: Hodder and Stoughton, 1978), p. 15.
23 J. M. MacKenzie, *Propaganda and Empire: The Manipulation of British Public Opinion 1880–1960* (Manchester: Manchester University Press, 1984), p. 176.
24 W. E. Marsden, '"All in a Good Cause": Geography, History and the Politicization of the Curriculum in Nineteenth and Twentieth Century England' in *Journal of Curriculum Studies*, Vol. 21:6 (1989), p. 513. *Idem*, 'The Royal Geographical Society and Geography in Secondary Schools' in M. H. Price (ed.), *The Development of the Secondary Curriculum* (Oxford: Routledge, 1986), pp. 182–213.
25 See P. Horn, 'English Elementary Education and the Growth of the Imperial Ideal, 1880–1914' in J.A. Mangan (ed.), *'Benefits Bestowed?' Education and British Imperialism* (Manchester: Manchester University Press), pp. 40–41; F. Glendenning, 'The Evolution of History Teaching in British and French Schools in the Nineteenth and Twentieth Centuries with Special Reference to Attitudes to Race and Colonial History in History Schoolbooks' (PhD thesis, University of Keele, 1975), p. 23 (unpublished).
26 P. Yeandle, *Citizenship, Nation, Empire: The Politics of History Teaching in England, 1870–1930* (Manchester: University of Manchester Press, 2015).
27 For Herbart's influence see R. J. W. Selleck, *The New Education: The English Background 1870–1914* (Melbourne: Isaac Pitman, 1968), pp. 227–272; and more recently Yeandle, *Citizenship, Nation, Empire*, pp. 34–42.
28 C. Dodd, *Introduction to the Herbartian Principles of Teaching* (London: Sonnenschein, 1906), pp. 35–36; see also A. Robertson, 'Catherine Dodd and Innovation in Teacher Training' in *Bulletin of Education*, Vol. 47 (1991), pp. 32–41.
29 Leinster-Mackay, 'The Nineteenth Century English Preparatory School', p. 63.
30 S. Nowell-Smith, *The House of Cassell, 1848–1958* (London: Cassell, 1958), p. 102.
31 S. R. Gardiner, *A Student's History of England: From the Earliest Times to 1885* (London: Longman, 1892), p. 954.
32 E. Salmon, *The Story of the Empire* (London: George Newnes, 1902), p. 5.
33 Ibid., p. 162.
34 Ibid., p. 153.
35 Ibid., p. 148.
36 Ibid., p. 157.
37 V. Chancellor, *History for their Masters: Opinion in the English History Textbook* (Bath: Adams and Dart, 1970), p. 121.
38 S. Heathorn, '"Us Remember that We Too Are English": Constructions of Citizenship and National Identity in English Elementary School Reading Books 1880–1914' in *Victorian Studies*, Vol. 38:3 (1995), p. 396.
39 For a survey of the incorporation of Scottish with Britishness and popular imperialism see, for example, R. J. Finlay, 'The Rise and Fall of Popular Imperialism in Scotland 1850–1950' in *Scottish Geographical Magazine*, Vol. 113:1 (1997), pp. 13–21; D. S. Forsyth, 'Empire and Union: Imperial and National Identity in Nineteenth Century Scotland' in *Scottish Geographical Magazine*, Vol. 13:1 (1997), pp. 6–12. For the identity of 'Britishness', see L. Coley, *Britons: Forging the Nation 1707–1837* (New Haven, CT: Yale University Press, 1992).
40 S. Heathorn, *For Home, Country and Race: Constructing Gender, Class and Englishness in the Elementary School 1880–1914* (Toronto: University of Toronto Press, 1999), p. 95. For an example of a history textbook that took this approach, see for example, J. Hight, *The English as a Colonising Nation* (Christchurch: Whitcombe & Tombs, 1905) and more recently, K. Tidrick, *Empire and the English Character* (London: I. B. Tauris, 1992). For an analysis of the relationship between the four component parts of the United Kingdom as it was constituted in the period 1800–1921, see H. Kearney, *The British Isles: A History of Four Nations* (Cambridge: Cambridge University Press, 1989).

INTRODUCTION

41 Heathorn, *For Home Country and Race*, pp. 44–47.
42 Cited in P. Fryer, *Black People in the British Empire: An Introduction* (London: Pluto Press, 1988), p. 75. See also comments by K. Castle, *Britannia's Children: Reading Colonialism Through Children's Books and Magazines* (Manchester: Manchester University Press, 1996), p. 5.
43 Yeandle, *Citizenship, Nation, Empire*, p. 112.
44 Chancellor, *History for Their Masters*.
45 Ibid., p. 109.
46 Castle, *Britannia's Children*, p. 18.
47 See T. S. Ploszajska, 'Geographical Education, Empire and Citizenship' (PhD thesis, University of London, 1996), especially pp. 67–97 (unpublished).
48 *Chambers's New Geographical Readers Book VI: British Colonies and Dependencies* (London: W. & R. Chambers, 1898), p. 76.
49 *Collins' Wide World Geography Reader Book VIII: The British Empire* (London: William Collins, 1901–23), p. 72.
50 G. Collar and C. Crook, *School Management and the Methods of Instruction* (New York: Macmillan, 1905), pp. 181–185.
51 Ibid., p. 183.
52 The sinking of the *Birkenhead* gave rise to the chivalric expression 'women and children first', and it was also subsequently commemorated as '*Birkenhead* Drill' in Rudyard Kipling's 1893 poem titled 'Soldier an' Sailor Too'.
53 D. Salmon, *The Art of Teaching* (Longmans Green and Co.: London, 1898), pp. 212–214.
54 M. Keatinge, *Studies in the Teaching of History* (London: A. & C. Black, 1910), p. 5. For Maurice Keatinge's obituary, see *The Times*, 24th April 1935, p. 12.
55 D. Gorman, *Imperial Citizenship: Empire and the Question of Belonging* (Manchester: Manchester University Press, 2006), p. 2.
56 R. Betts, 'A Campaign for Patriotism the Elementary School Curriculum: Lord Meath 1892–1916' in *History of Education Bulletin*, Vol. 46 (1990), pp. 38–45.
57 A. Bloomfield, 'Drill and Dance as Symbols of Imperialism' in Mangan (ed.), *Benefits Bestowed*, p. 81.
58 For a useful overview of Empire Day and the ways in which it became politically disputed in Britain, see J. English, 'Empire Day in Britain 1904–1958' in *Historical Journal*, Vol. 49:1 (2006), pp. 247–276.
59 J. O. Springhall, 'Lord Meath, Youth and Empire' in *Journal of Contemporary History*, Vol 5:4 (1970), p. 104.
60 'Military Drill in Schools' *Journal of Education*, December 1900, p. 748; cited in M. D. Blanch, *Nation, Empire and the Birmingham Working Class, 1899–1914* (unpublished PhD thesis, University of Birmingham, 1975), p. 51.
61 Ibid., p. 54.
62 Ibid., p. 59.
63 F. H. Hayward, *An Educational Failure: A School Inspector's Story* (London: Duckworth, 1938), p. 305. For a study of Hayward, see N. Bhimani, 'F. H. Hayward (1872–1954): A Forgotten Educationalist or an Educational Failure?' (Unpublished MA thesis, University of London, 2015).
64 B. Beaven, *Visions of Empire, Patriotism, Popular Culture and the City 1870–1939* (Manchester: Manchester University Press, 2012), pp. 152–172.
65 For the founding of the British Empire League, see *The Times*, 4th December 1896, p. 7.
66 For the League of Empire, see *Berwickshire News and General Advertiser*, 16th February 1904, p. 5.
67 For imperial propaganda societies in the era 1880–1940, see MacKenzie, *Propaganda and Empire*, pp. 148–171; M. Hendley, *Organized Patriotism and the Crucible of War:*

Popular Imperialism in Britain, 1914–1932 (Montreal: McGill–Queen's University Press, 2012); E. Riedi, 'Women, Gender and the Promotion of Empire: The Victoria League, 1901–1914' in *Historical Journal*, Vol. 45:3 (2002), pp. 569–599.
68 Bloomfield, 'Drill and Dance', p. 87.
69 S. Koven, 'Kimmins [nee Hannam], Dame Grace Thryza, 1870–1954' in *Oxford Dictionary of National Biography*. www.oxforddnb.com/view/10.1093/ref:odnb/9780198614128.001.0001/odnb-9780198614128-e-34315. Accessed 21 February 2021.
70 K. Osborne, 'Creating the "International Mind": The League of Nations Attempts to Reform History Teaching 1920–1939' in *History of Education Quarterly*, Vol. 56:2 (2016), p. 236.
71 J. Springhall, '"Healthy Papers for Manly Boys": Imperial and Race in the Harmsworth Halfpenny Boys' Papers of the 1890s and 1900s' in J. Richards (ed.), *Imperialism and Juvenile Literature* (Manchester: Manchester University Press, 1989), pp. 110–111.
72 P. Dunae, 'Boys' Literature and the Idea of Empire 1870–1914', in *Victorian Studies*, Vol 24:1 (1980).
73 For a useful overview of boys' papers in the era 1870–1914, see P. Dunae, 'Literature and the Idea of Empire, 1870–1914' in *Victorian Studies*, Vol. 24:1 (1980), pp. 105–121.
74 Richards, 'Introduction' to *Imperialism and Juvenile Literature*, p. 5.
75 K. Boyd, *Manliness and the Boys' Story Paper in Britain; A Cultural History 1855–1940* (Basingstoke: Palgrave, 2003), p. 125.
76 M. J. Smith, *Empire in British Girls' Literature and Culture: Imperial Girls 1880–1915* (Basingstoke: Palgrave, 2011), p. 58.
77 J. Ahier, *Industry, Children and the Nation: An Analysis of National Identity in School Textbooks* (London: Falmer Press, 1988), pp. 170–171.
78 Some 5,000 Scouts emigrated to the Dominions in the 1920s. A. Warren, 'Citizens of the Empire: Baden-Powell, Scouts and Guides and an Imperial Ideal' in J. M. MacKenzie (ed.), *Imperialism and Popular Culture* (Manchester: Manchester University Press, 1986), p. 246.
79 J. Springhall, *Youth Empire and Society: British Youth Movements 1883–1940* (London: Croom Helm, 1977), p. 18.

1

ST. CYPRIAN'S, EASTBOURNE

Principal: Mr. L. C. VAUGHAN WILKES, M.A.

'St. Cyprian's Preparatory School, Eastbourne', in *War Office Times and Naval Review*, 1st May 1910, pp. 24–26.

St. Cyprian's was founded in 1899 by Lewis Vaughan Wilkes and his wife Cicely Comyn. The school was a fairly typical preparatory school of its type for the period, promoting the notion of 'muscular Christianity', which had been established as a school culture at Thomas Arnold's Rugby School in the mid-19th century and placed much emphasis on developing self-reliance and character in young boys. Boys attended the school until the age of 13. These were known as prep schools because they prepared the boys for entrance to the English public schools. These schools grew in number in the later 19th century, as the numbers of parents working overseas in the Empire grew and many chose to place their sons in prep schools. The school submitted itself annually to an independent academic assessment, conducted by the historian and fellow of All Souls College, Oxford, Charles Grant Robertson. Two features were of note at the school. The first was that it was located close to the South Downs, giving boys a chance to run wild, study natural history, take walks, enjoy picnics, ride and even play golf on the adjacent links. The second was the character of Mrs Wilkes (known as 'Mum'). A figure of great influence in the school, Mrs Wilkes was an advocate of teaching history and saw the Harrow History Prize as an opportunity to bring the subject into the classics-dominated curriculum. Mrs Wilkes also taught English, and stimulated generations of writers with her emphasis on clear, high-quality writing. In addition to Mrs Wilkes, a major influence was the second master R. L. Sillar, who joined the school staff soon after it opened. Sillar was interested in natural history and had shooting skills, and he is revered in several old boys' accounts.

> "Knowledge, the wing with which we fly to Heaven."
> – Shakespeare.

One would imagine that the choice of a Preparatory School by officers for their sons or wards would not be a difficult task. As a matter of fact, however, this is not the case, as a conscientious parent speedily realises. The value of many educational establishments admirably conducted in all other respects is seriously impaired by the system of large, unwieldy classes, or by a lack of that individual attention to the moulding of character, which is the root-basis of all permanently successful educational effort. It is proposed in the following notes to deal briefly with the work of a school for the sons of gentlemen, the Head of which is not content merely to educate those boys entrusted to his care in the narrow scholastic sense in the acquirement of knowledge usually taught at these establishments, but attaches equal importance to the formation of character at the most plastic stage of a boy's life. This is, after all, simply a recognition of the fact that education, like a well-cut diamond, has many facets. The work of the school in question, St. Cyprian's, Eastbourne, has been of a satisfying character and the record below may possibly help those hesitating between two opinions in the Selection of a School to come to a right decision in the matter. That decision is obviously of a momentous character not to be hastily arrived at, for on it the career of a boy, whether for weal or woe, often depends. We propose to deal with the matter under the respective headings of: –

1. – The District and the School.
2. – The Principal and the Work of the School.
3. – The Play and Recreations of the School.
4. – The Outcome.

The district and the school

Eastbourne is one of the most healthy and select watering places of England. The school is in many respects unique. It was built under the direct instructions to the architect by Mr. Vaughan Wilkes himself. It stands within a few minutes' walk of the sea in eight acres of ground, on the borders of the famous Downs, in the open country, and faces south-west and west. There is a fine view of the sea from the bedrooms. There is not such a school, in fact, on the South Coast. It is of handsome appearance and ideal for comfort and convenience within, being in every way adaptable for its special purpose. The classrooms, of which there are from eight to ten, are light and cheerful, and, like all the other rooms, are lofty and spacious. There is a fine dining hall, entrance hall with billiard table and boys' library, a play room 52 ft. long, which is also used as a gymnasium, a cycle house, swimming baths, and large lavatories and dressing rooms for cricket and football. The swimming baths are so arranged that when required they can be boarded over and the space utilised for private theatricals, etc. There is a capitally equipped carpenter's shop with a competent residential carpenter to give tuition. The dormitories have the windows carried up flush to the ceiling, thus providing plenty of light and ventilation, and there are separate rooms for the elder scholars. There is a Chapel for the Sunday services, which are conducted by the School Chaplain, the Rev. F. Atkinson, M.A. (Oxon). There is a perfect water supply, and the sanitary arrangements are of the best and latest type.

The principal and the work of the school

The Principal is peculiarly qualified by experience and attainments for the control of a high-class school. He was formerly Classical Scholar of Hertford College, and has had many years' successful Preparatory School work. He is assisted by no fewer than seven resident Masters; and Mr. R. L. Sillar, M.A. (of Shrewsbury School and Worcester College, Oxford) – an old friend and colleague of Mr. Wilkes, who has had many years' experience in one of the leading preparatory schools – has become a permanent and valued member of the staff. The correct acquirement of modern languages – grammatical, idiomatic, and conversational – is a strong feature of school life at St. Cyprian's, the ordinary parrot-like stereotyped methods of learning French and German being vigorously eschewed. All boys learn French, but German and higher Mathematics are taught as an alternative to Greek for boys on the modern side. The correct acquirement of French and German has proved invaluable at the Public Schools for Sandhurst and Woolwich and at Osborne by boys who have passed through the School. Cramming in any form is avoided, but promising pupils are prepared with the idea of taking scholarships at the Public Schools or of gaining admission to the Royal Navy. The aim of the Principal is to give the boys a thorough grounding and a sound knowledge of elementary subjects, to interest them in their work, to furnish them with that mental and moral equipment suitable for the sons of gentlemen, and which shall enable them to successfully engage in the perennial Battle of Life, whether in the professional or any other career, to which their destiny calls them. There is a *camaraderie* prevalent throughout St. Cyprian's which is an important factor in the excellent work carried on there. The Principal wisely prefers to rely on a boy's word of honour rather than to impose burdensome restrictions on every movement, and the confidence implied thereby has been justified, for a high standard of honour prevails at the school. A boy, after he has left a school of this kind and entered on the wider life of the Public School or Osborne, looks back with affectionate regret at his Preparatory School days, and never forgets the lessons of manliness, adherance to truth, generous emulation, self-control, love of work, not for its prizes merely, but for the work itself inculcated thereat. Every well-conducted Preparatory School should have a magazine of its own – it is a wonderful incentive to *esprit de corps*. "The St. Cyprian's Chronicle" is an excellent magazine.

The play and recreations of the school

There is no lack of healthy recreations and games at St. Cyprian's. We are glad to note that the rule of the school is that, as the spirit and discipline of games form an important part of a boy's education, games are compulsory. And not only so, but the Masters cordially co-operate. There are capital fields for Cricket, Football, and Tennis. It is not surprising to find that the health record of St. Cyprian's is extremely good. There is an excellent series of games and recreations available, the purest air and the most equable climate in England, cheerful surroundings, a generous and judicious dietary, unceasing maternal care by the Principal's wife – everything, in truth, that can render school life attractive and profitable, both morally and physically, for the boys. The boys take a keen interest in their miniature Rifle Range, and there are various prizes and challenge trophies for which they compete. No fewer than four teams of eight entered for the Challenge Shields in the Preparatory School Rifle Association competition in March, which was shot under N.R.A. rules, the average age of the fourth eight being 11 years 9 months. The first eight are at the present time holders of the St. Andrew's Shield at 100 yards, and were second out of sixteen teams at the 50 yards' range. Six members of the eight hold the first class certificate signed by Lord Roberts, awarded for a score of 130 points out of a possible 150 in ten consecutive shots.

The physical and mental training in vogue at St. Cyprian's is not to be excelled. Our Special Scholastic Commissioner, who visited the school a few days back was particularly struck by the healthy and bright appearance of the boys. Mr. Wilkes, we may here mention, takes sole charge, when required, of Anglo-Indians, and some fifty sons of officers stationed abroad have passed through his hands with satisfactory results. The school has an exceptional health record. There is a sanatorium wing consisting of a sick room, a convalescent room, and a nurse's bedroom, and is cut off from the main building by a passage with two doors, and has a separate staircase leading direct into the garden. In this way perfect isolation is ensured. Happily the healthy life of the boys, the care taken of them by Mrs. Wilkes, aided by a competent Matron, who is also a trained nurse, and the excellent environment have combined to keep disease or serious ailments away from the school.

An interesting feature is the attention paid to swimming. Every boy is taught to swim and dive in the fine fresh water swimming bath of the School; all the boys bathe in the sea during the warm weather, and annual swimming races and diving competitions are held in the Devonshire Park Baths.

The outcome

The result of all this care, this excellent organisation and systematised up-to-date training is, as might be expected, admirable. The fruits of the St. Cyprian's methods are of excellent savour, and we have before us a remarkable list of references – most of them people of rank and distinction – including many parents or relatives of present and past pupils who unreservedly testify in this direction. We are pleased to note the names of many officers of rank in this list. A perusal of it should decide those seeking a select school for their sons or wards to test the educational advantages available at St. Cyprian's, Eastbourne.

2

THE TRAINING OF AN ENGLISH GENTLEMAN IN THE PUBLIC SCHOOLS[1]

From: Rev. J.E.C. Welldon, 'The Training of the English Gentleman in the Public Schools', in *The Nineteenth Century and After*, Vol. 60, No. 355 (1906), pp. 396–418.

James Welldon (1854–1937) was appointed master of Dulwich College in 1883. He had been educated at Eton and King's College, Cambridge. In the short time he held this position he did much for the college, including the creation of the school song, 'Pueri Alleynienses'. He resigned his post in July 1885 to take up the position of headmaster of Harrow School, which he held from 1885 to 1898. He was disliked by many of the masters as autocratic but held in high esteem by the boys. At Harrow he also accepted a number of clerical positions. He was honorary chaplain to Queen Victoria from 1888 to 1892, and Chaplain in Ordinary from 1892 to 1898. He was the Hulsean Lecturer at Cambridge in 1897. (These were lectures established by an endowment made by John Hulse, a clergyman.) In 1898, Welldon became a Doctor of Divinity. The documents included here demonstrate the promotion of Empire from the school chapel, and within the Harrow School culture such as the playing field, with the promotion of a cult of athleticism too. In addition we can see Welldon's connection to the Royal Colonial Institute, at which document 3 was delivered, on the topic of imperial education.

THE first part of my duty, and the pleasantest, is to offer you, sir, my sincere thanks for your kindness in suggesting that I should give a lecture before this large audience, and, still more, in consenting to preside at it. For the title of the lecture the responsibility must rest upon yourself, or upon my old friend Mr. Inagaki, who introduced me to you. But to me it can be only a high privilege, if by any words of mine upon English education – a subject, as you have said, not unfamiliar to me – I can help, in however small a degree, to strengthen the sympathy between your country and my own. For there is an *entente cordiale* in arts as well as in arms; and it may be that the community of intellectual and moral ideals, if it can be realised, will prove in the end not the least potent factor of a lasting international alliance.

I do not know, indeed, that we in England are apt to dwell so much upon the ambition of becoming gentlemen as others may be who look at the English educational system from outside. The true gentleman is one who speaks and thinks as little as possible about gentility. The character of a gentleman is silently formed; it is the product of many subtle and almost secret influences; and never, perhaps, is it so perfect as when it is unconscious. Yet Tennyson, the poet who is the typical exponent of so much that is truest and highest in modern English thought, says of the friend whom his love has immortalised that

> he bore without abuse
> The grand old name of gentleman;

and what that friend was, all English youths, more or less, aspire to be.

You tell me, sir, that there is something in an English gentleman which has touched the imagination of Japan. If I am not wrong, the Japanese students some time ago formed a society in the University of Cambridge, for the sole purpose of studying the character of an English gentleman. It does not perhaps altogether lend itself to imitation, except upon English soil and in the circumstances of English life. But you rightly hold that, such as it is, it is largely moulded by the public schools and the universities, and you wish me to speak chiefly of them. They are noble institutions, but they are not perfect. If it were necessary to criticise them in a single sentence I should say that they have generally proved more successful in the discipline of the character than in the cultivation of the intellect. But it remains true that the British Empire in its magnitude and importance is, and has long been, a commanding fact in human history; that, with many faults and not a few stains, it has yet been singularly successful in producing administrators of high character and capacity; and that most of them, or many, have traced the secret of their lives to the lessons which they learnt, or perhaps more truly to the spirit which they acquired, when they were still young, in the schools and colleges of Great Britain. A famous English statesman, Mr. Canning, once used these words: 'Foreigners often ask by what means an uninterrupted succession of men, qualified more or less eminently for the performance of parliamentary and official duties, is secured. First, I answer (with the prejudices perhaps of Eton and Oxford) that we owe it to our system of public schools and universities. From these institutions is derived (in the language of the prayer of our collegiate churches) "a due supply of men fitted to serve their country in Church and State." It is in her public schools and universities that the youth of England are, by a discipline which shallow judgments have sometimes attempted to undervalue, prepared for the duties of public life.'

It is not possible for me, within the limits of a single lecture, to examine in much detail the English type or types of scholastic and academical education. Neither the universities nor the public schools are all of one kind. Some universities are ancient, others are modern. In the former the students reside, for a shorter or longer portion of the year, away from their homes in small societies which are called colleges, or, if not in colleges, still under the special care of authorities belonging to the university. In the latter they generally live at home; the university is a local institution, and its office is not so much social or moral or spiritual as purely intellectual. But, even where universities are national, and students come to them from all parts of the United Kingdom, and, indeed, of the Empire, they may be widely different, as Oxford and Cambridge differ from the Scotch universities. I may pretty safely assume, however, that when the training of an English gentleman is in question, it is the universities of Oxford and Cambridge which are recognised as exercising a paramount influence among universities upon the national character; and it happens that these are the universities which are best known to me.

Similarly the public schools may be divided into several classes, but chiefly into two. These are day schools, where the boys live at home with their parents, and spend only certain hours, but no more, a day under the immediate control of their masters. But the best-known schools are boarding schools; in these the boys live away from their homes for the greater part of the year, congregated in houses, as undergraduates are in colleges, and guided and governed, in all the various aspects of their lives, by masters who do for them what would in natural or normal circumstances be done by their parents. There are also schools in which the boys are partly boarders and partly day boys. One who has been concerned, as I have been, with schools of different kinds will not be disposed to argue that all the advantage lies with any one kind. But it is the boarding schools which are the peculiarly characteristic features of the English educational system. They do not, as the day schools do, find a close parallel in the schools of other European countries. Every such public school, indeed, has an individuality of its own. The Government exercises, or has exercised, so slight a control upon the schools that they have developed, for good or for evil, each upon its own special lines. The pupils of each school are distinguished by certain broad qualities which unite them, despite all differences of rank and age, to one another, and part them off from the pupils of all other schools. An Etonian, a Harrovian, a Wykehamist, a Rugbeian – each represents a certain type of character. My own experience of the great boarding schools has been principally drawn from two, but these are perhaps the greatest of them all – Eton and Harrow; in one I lived as a boy, in the other as a master; and as no other schools have done more, or perhaps so much, for the formation of the character exhibited now for several centuries by the statesmen, administrators, and reformers, the men of action and, although in less degree, the men of thought, who have created or dignified the Empire, you will forgive me if I derive my remarks, not indeed solely, but chiefly, from these two schools.

Between the universities, indeed, and the public schools, no comparison is possible. The universities enjoy an intellectual distinction to which the schools make no pretence. Oxford and Cambridge have been for centuries the homes of famous discoverers, scholars, and teachers, whose names are household words wherever learning is held in honour throughout the world. But it is not improbable that there is nobody in this room who can recall the name of any English schoolmaster, living or dead, unless it be that of Dr. Arnold, the headmaster of Rugby, whose portrait is drawn in the pages of *Tom Brown's Schooldays*, or possibly that of Mr. Thring, the headmaster of Uppingham, who had the honour, I think, of educating his Excellency the British Ambassador, Sir Claude Macdonald. But upon the character of English gentlemen the influence of the public schools seems to be even greater than that of the universities. There are several reasons why it should be so. Practically the whole governing class of Englishmen is educated in the public schools. But it is only a fraction of public school boys who matriculate at the universities. A boy spends four or five years, and those the most impressionable years of his life, from thirteen to eighteen or nineteen, at his public school. If he goes to the university, the years which he spends there are usually not more than three. Again, while he passes only half of each year as a resident at his university, the other half being vacation, when he may be, and generally is, away from college, he passes two-thirds of each year during his school life at his public school. Still more important is the fact that a boy at school is subject to a personal authority closer and stronger than any which he experiences in his university or his college.

Thus it is, probably, that Englishmen have in general felt a deeper affection for their schools than for their universities. I do not forget that a good many notable men, like Lord Macaulay, have been warmly attached throughout life to their colleges at Oxford or Cambridge. Such men have, often, not passed through public schools. But the history of the great English public schools is replete with instances of the affectionate and even passionate feeling shown by illustrious Englishmen for the places in which they had spent the golden days of boyhood. Gray's *Ode on a Distant Prospect of Eton College*; Byron's *Lines Written Beneath an Elm in the Churchyard at Harrow*, are known to all students of English literature. But will you let me cite what has always seemed to me the most beautiful example of patriotic devotion to a school? The Marquis Wellesley, the elder brother of the great Duke of Wellington, received his education at Eton. He became there almost the ideal of a scholar and a gentleman. After a life of noble service to the State in various offices, he attained that supreme position in the British Empire, the Governor-Generalship of India. But he never forgot his old school. From the banks of the Ganges he would correspond, upon points of classical learning, with his tutor at Eton. To serve Eton was the ambition – the inspiration – of his life. He prayed to be buried at Eton; and there, in the college chapel, he lies now at rest, and upon his monument are graven the exquisite Latin verses which he wrote for his own epitaph in the desire of expressing his sense of indebtedness to the school which had wrought its spell upon his life.

If, then, in this lecture I seem to dwell more upon the public schools than upon the universities, as formative influences in the character of an English gentleman, the reason is not only that I know them better and have spent a longer time in them; it is that I believe them to have played a larger historical part in making English gentlemen to be such as they are. But as touching the formation of character there is no broad difference between the universities and the public schools; they aim at the same end, and they seek to attain it by much the same means; they are largely interdependent; and the youth who passes from school to college, although he enters upon a liberty which has hitherto been strange to him, is conscious of no such moral shock as would necessarily occur if his new life were wholly alien from the old.

It is true, alike of a university and of a public school, that he who is admitted to one or the other becomes at once a member of a society. He does not stand alone. He occupies a position in which his actions affect others, and the actions of others affect him. He becomes participant, as others are, not only in the credit, but, if need be, in the misfortune or disgrace of the body to which he and they belong. So, too, his own conduct in turn affects that body. If he does well, his good deeds reflect honour upon his university or his school. But if he commits any flagrant violation of the moral law upon which the society depends, then his punishment is to be struck off the roll of membership, to be degraded or expelled, and to go out into the world as one who has proved himself unworthy of incorporation in a community of honourable gentlemen. There is a well-known story that Dr. Arnold, on an occasion when some gross evil had displayed itself at Rugby, and he had been compelled to send away several boys, exclaimed in the presence of all the school: 'It is *not* necessary that this should be a school of three hundred, or one hundred, or of fifty boys; but it *is* necessary that it should be a school of Christian gentlemen.' By my own experience I know how keenly boys, and their parents too, feel the pain of their enforced removal from the society of a public school. Yes, and I know, too, what pains they will sometimes take in after life to regain the honourable position from which they have fallen in the eyes of the school.

As regards the training of an English gentleman, you will not, I think, feel surprise if I put as the first lesson to be learnt at a public school – obedience. The philosopher Aristotle remarked long ago that no one can be qualified to command but he who has already been taught to obey. To be equally capable of exercising authority and of submitting to it was the ancient Greek educational ideal. A good schoolmaster, like a wise parent, expects absolute, unhesitating obedience from the child. He issues his orders; he does not, and in the nature of the case he cannot, explain his reasons. If he argues with his pupils, he is lost. I am not sure that this principle of action is good for the master. But beyond doubt it is good for the pupil. It inculcates that sovereign consciousness of duty which elevates public life. 'England expects' – or, as the better original word was, 'confides' – 'that every man will do his duty,' was, as you know, Nelson's signal at Trafalgar. The English boy learns at school, the English undergraduate learns at college, that, when once the path of duty is seen to be plain, he must choose it unquestionably and unhesitatingly, he must never shirk it, must never depart from it, but, at all costs, must follow it to the end. I do not say this lesson is not equally well taught elsewhere than in the public schools of England. It is a principle magnificently illustrated in the recent history of your own nation. I say only that English gentlemen learn it, and learn it in the universities, and still more in the public schools.

> Theirs not to make reply,
> Theirs not to reason why,
> Theirs but to do and die;
> Into the valley of Death
> Rode the Six Hundred.

The first element in all noble character, and therefore in the character of an English gentleman, is obedience.

When a boy goes to school in England, he comes under the influence of his masters and also of his schoolfellows. It is this double influence which shapes his character. Nor is the same double influence wanting in the university; but there it is somewhat less powerful.

As a rule, it is characteristic of English education that, while a boy or a youth in his intellectual training passes freely from one teacher to another, from one lecturer to another, there is one person who is charged with his moral training throughout the whole period of his life at school or at college. That person is often, but not always, called a tutor. It is his business to study his pupil's idiosyncrasy, to watch and to guide him, to draw out what is best in him, and, if need be, to protect him against misunderstanding and punishment. The tutor in a public school enjoys a unique responsibility. He stands in relation to a boy's whole composite nature – to his body and mind and spirit. He looks after his physical, intellectual, moral, and spiritual welfare. He is to him, or is supposed to be, all that a parent, when the boy is at home, may be and ought to be. No profession, perhaps, makes a larger demand upon tact or insight or sympathy; for there is no profession in which a good and virtuous man may do so much harm, by mere faults of judgment, as the educational.

The schoolmaster begins, as I have said, by exacting obedience. But he will never be a first-rate schoolmaster if he stops there. Not authority alone, but sympathy, is the secret of his success. He must study individual character. He must not treat all natures alike. He must know when to draw in the reins of discipline, and when to relax them. He must aim at winning not only the obedience but the loyalty of his pupils. And the great agent in the creation of a loyal temper is trust. To read boys' letters, to listen to their conversation, to practise what is called *espionage* upon their movements would in English eyes be an unpardonable offence. I have heard of a schoolmaster who was suspected – wrongly, I hope and believe – of trying to watch his pupils at play through a telescope, but it was long before they forgave him. There is a curious unwritten code of honour determining the proper relation of masters and boys in the public schools. For example, a master must not question one boy about others, nor must he question a boy about himself, or, if he asks a boy whether he has done a thing or not, he must not punish him for doing it; he must not (unless in certain extreme instances) use the evidence of servants against boys; for all such behaviour would undermine confidence. He must be just; boys will pardon rudeness and harshness, but never injustice; a master may be a 'beast,' as was said of one of the most famous of English schoolmasters, and if he is 'a just beast' he will be honoured and admired; but let him once make favourites, let him treat one boy with greater partiality than others, and he will never win – he will never deserve to win – respect. Above all, he must accept a boy's word. If a boy says that a thing is so, it is so; the master unhesitatingly believes him. It is better, far better, that a boy, who is base enough to tell a lie, should now and then escape punishment than that there should be an atmosphere of distrust between master and boys. The public opinion of a school emphatically condemns the boy who tells a lie. It responds at once to a master's generous trust in a boy's word. Dean Stanley, the biographer of Dr. Arnold, relates how he would stop boys from trying to prove the truth of their words, telling them, 'If you say so, that is quite enough – *of course* I believe your word;' and he adds, 'There grew up in consequence a general feeling that "it was a shame to tell Arnold a lie – he always believes one."'

It is impossible to overrate the moral value of the assumption, freely and not unreasonably made in the public schools, that an English gentleman will never tell a lie. If 'the word of an Englishman' possesses, as I think it does (and long may it possess!), a signal value all the world over, if it is readily trusted, just because the speaker is an Englishman, by the various races of mankind within and beyond the limits of the British Empire, the honour attaching to that word is in some sense the product of the education which Englishmen receive in their public schools and universities.

I have said that a master must be just. Justice is the quality most highly admired by boys in masters. English boys are strangely indignant at any real or supposed injustice which is done to them. But when they are justly treated, then, if they do wrong and are found out by legitimate means in doing it, they not only consent but expect to be punished. It is probably known to you that in the public schools the punishment is sometimes corporal. I do not defend such punishment; neither do I deprecate it. It is a recognised part of English education. To English thought the humiliation seems to lie not in the punishment, but in the wrong-doing which deserves it. Perhaps one who has inflicted this kind of punishment as often as I have is not altogether an unprejudiced judge of it. But about corporal punishment in England, two curious facts lie beyond dispute. One is that, while the working class and the lower middle class dislike and resent it, and will not in general allow their children to undergo it, the aristocracy tolerate it without complaint. The time is coming, one might assert paradoxically, when it will be impossible to flog anybody but the son of a peer. And the other fact is that public school boys have often felt a special affection for the masters who have punished them most. In Westminster Abbey stand side by side the tombs of a master and his pupil. The master was Dr. Busby, who was headmaster of Westminster School for so long a time as fifty-eight years. Nobody ever flogged so many boys as he. The pupil was the theologian, Dr. South. It is told – I am not sure the story is true – that, when

South came as a small boy to Westminster, Busby greeted him with the ominous words: 'I see great talents in that sulky little boy, and my rod shall bring them out.' If so, he was no doubt as good as his word. But when South lay upon his deathbed, it was his last prayer to be buried at his old master's feet; and the master and the pupil now rest side by side.

I have been trying to show you how an English educator seeks to affect the lives and the characters of his pupils. He may make many mistakes. But in intention he aims at the two noblest ends which can be anywhere or at any time proposed to human effort – the encouragement of virtue, and the diffusion of knowledge. His influence is largely personal. It is what he is, rather than what he teaches, that tells upon the young. Such as he is, they naturally tend to be. But the object of his whole teaching and his whole example, whether at school or in the university, is to make them feel that they are members of a great society, and that a society constituted upon an indissoluble moral basis; in a word, it is to impress upon them the dignity of learning, but the yet higher dignity of character.

But it is probable that, in the formation of character, a boy's schoolfellows exercise a stronger influence than any teachers; for they create the public opinion which is, as it were, the atmosphere of his life, and public opinion is the greatest force in the world of school. The rules which boys make for each other, even in matters so unimportant as dress, are often more stringent than any rules which masters make for them. One of the greatest difficulties in the education of the young is to inculcate an originality which will not be afraid to depart from the conventional standard of right and wrong. Originality is not always good, nor is convention necessarily bad; but without originality there can be no progress.

Public opinion, as it exists among the youth of England in schools and colleges, is not, indeed, free from curious eccentricities or limitations; but upon the whole it is sound, and it is strong. At all events, it sustains the ideal to which English gentlemen aspire.

If an English schoolboy could be asked what is the moral quality which he appreciates most highly, whether in masters or boys, he would probably answer that while in masters it is justice (as I have already suggested), in boys it is courage. English boys admire one who is brave. But it is physical courage which chiefly evokes their admiration. They hold that a young Englishman should do his duty gallantly, however unwelcome it may be, should bear pain unflinchingly, should volunteer for difficult and dangerous service, and should face the hardships of life with a smile. They are impatient, nay, contemptuous of the signs of emotion, especially of tears. They honour 'pluck,' as it is called. Such a story as that Nelson in his boyhood said, 'What is fear? I never saw fear,' inspires their enthusiasm. They hate cowardice – *i.e.* physical cowardice. I wish it were possible to say that they equally hate what Milton calls 'the cowardice of doing wrong.'

Then there is among English boys, and not less among young Englishmen generally, a binding sense of honour. 'Honour' is a word which comes home to English hearts. Sometimes when I have been upon my travels I have inquired if the Oriental languages possessed an equivalent word for 'honour.' Your own word

Bushido comes nearest to it. It would not become me, as a stranger in Japan, to examine the precise moral significance of a word so delicate as *Bushido*. But the English 'honour' implies, among other things, that a person must speak the truth, that he must not take advantage of his neighbour's ignorance or weakness, that he must think less of himself than of his cause, and that he must avoid, as if it were a stain upon his shield, whatever is or tends to be mean, low, shabby, or ungentlemanly. In nothing perhaps is the character of a gentleman more strikingly seen than in his sensitive shrinking from a breach of trust. You will not mind my referring again to the illustrious name of Nelson. When he was a boy his father sent him on horseback to school at some distance from his home, telling him and his brother, as there was deep snow upon the ground, that he would leave it to their honour to go on or come back. The road was difficult and dangerous, but Nelson refused to turn back. 'We must go on,' he said. 'Remember, brother, it was left to our honour.'

A man's sense of honour, the consciousness of his obligation to do all and more than all that can be rightly expected of him, is a conspicuous feature in noble English character. It is the distinguishing mark of a gentleman. To violate it is, in common parlance, 'bad form.'

You will not think I claim this feature for my countrymen alone. It may be as prominent in Japan as in Great Britain. All I say is, that without the absolute personal trustworthiness, without the chivalrous code of honour which raises acts of grace or courtesy into duties, no people nor any individual can attain the supreme beauty and dignity of the moral life.

The universities and the public schools render yet another service to the nation by fostering a broad sympathetic spirit among different classes. They are the most democratic places in the world; they are almost wholly free from snobbishness. In them a youth is taken for what he is worth in himself, without regard to rank, or wealth, or antecedents. The spirit prevailing in them is liberal and tolerant. Nor is it possible that boys or men, differing in social position or political sympathy or religious opinion, should be educated side by side in the same school and boarding-house, or in the same college, without learning something of the conciliation, the 'give and take,' the spirit of compromise, the disposition to look for points of agreement amidst divergences, which are among the best features of English public life. For a salutary lesson, such as the young need ever to learn, as it touches one side of gentlemanly conduct, is how to get on, not only with those with whom one agrees, but with those from whom one differs; and the universities and public schools, by their catholic spirit, emphasise that lesson.

There is something more. Not tolerance only, but generosity, is an attribute of high character. The young are naturally generous. They are free from malice and rancour. They take pleasure in each other's successes; even the vanquished can freely congratulate the victors. Time was when the public schools were defaced by cruelty, as *Tom Brown's Schooldays* shows. But they are changed, or are fast changing. In my thirteen years at Harrow, I was never once called upon to deal with a serious case of bullying. Towards physical infirmity, if it be nobly borne, boys are sympathetic. They appreciate the high temper which bravely fights against difficulties. Weakness, especially in womanhood, constitutes an irresistible claim upon their help. The age of chivalry is not dead. The appeal to the generous instincts of youth never fails.

It may be that the character of a gentleman is not often seen in its perfection. So Thackeray says; but he recognises what it is. 'Which of us can point out many such in his circle – men whose aims are generous, whose truth is constant, and not only constant in its kind, but elevated in its degree; whose want of meanness makes them simple; who can look the world honestly in the face, with an equal manly sympathy for the great and the small?'

At all events, to produce the character of a gentleman is the object set before the universities and public schools in England. Nor can that character wholly fail, where courage, honour, and a tolerant and generous spirit are freely preached and not infrequently displayed.

The influence of boys upon other boys is great, as I have said, but never is it so great as when the older and higher boys are entrusted with a disciplinary power over their schoolfellows. Such boys are known as prefects, or præpostors, or monitors. They are few in number (perhaps a dozen or twenty at the most in a school of six hundred boys), but they are the intellectual and moral *élite* of the school. They enjoy certain privileges, and in return for them they are held to be largely responsible for the good order and the good conduct of the junior boys. They render a service of conspicuous value. For where trustfulness is the law of school life, there must be wrong incidents which a master does not and cannot know, and which it is better that he should not know; but the boys know them, and if they are disposed and empowered to put them down, their authority is more potent than his. My experience has shown me that, where a healthy confidential relation exists between a master and his leading boys, he need not fear the prevalence – I do not mean that he can feel safe against the occasional existence – of the most dangerous moral evils in a school. It is clear, too, that the prefectorial, or præpostorial, or monitorial system (call it by what name one may), through the delicate relation in which the leading boys stand alike to their masters and to their schoolfellows, is peculiarly fitted to prepare them for the honourable exercise of the governing function in manhood.

The life of a university or of a public school naturally divides itself into two parts; it comprises the hours of instruction and the hours of recreation, or, in other words, lessons and games. You will not, I hope, suspect me of forgetting the superior dignity which intrinsically attaches to the cultivation of the mind over any possible graces of the body. Upon this superiority it is the educator's duty to dwell in season and out of season. But I am speaking of the character of a gentleman; and when the athletic games of English youth are considered in their reference not to physical energy but to moral worth, it would seem that they possess an even higher value than intellectual studies. For learning, however excellent in itself, does not afford much necessary scope for such virtues as promptitude, resource, honour, co-operation, and unselfishness; but these are the soul of English games.

Of the intellectual education given in the universities and public schools I need perhaps say no more than that it is mainly linguistic and scientific. To either part of it a proper value belongs. In the study of science – if, indeed, science be taken to mean not only the so-called natural sciences, or the investigation of the properties and resources of the physical world, but, as it strictly should mean, all forms of exact observation and reflection – the young mind is taught to appreciate the nature of truth, to distinguish fact from theory, and to realise – as is, indeed, the primary condition of knowledge – what can and what cannot be said to be proved. But the fault of exact science as an educational instrument is that it is exact; it largely deals with certainties rather than probabilities, it can establish its results beyond dispute. And this is true of mathematics pre-eminently, but in a less degree of all the experimental sciences. But human life is not made up of certainties. Such questions as arise in it can seldom, if ever, be settled absolutely; they demand the balance of opposing considerations, and if the balance upon the whole inclines one way, it might easily, in the majority of cases, incline the other. The reason why language is perhaps the supreme instrument of culture, why it disciplines the mind, as nothing else can, for the purposes of life, is that, as being itself a human product, it offers problems which are not absolutely determinable, but evoke and exercise the same balanced judgment as is needed in the daily affairs of life.

But both elements, the linguistic and the scientific, find a natural place in education; both tend to the strengthening and quickening of the mental faculties; and the best educator is he who makes the truest proportionate use of them. And if, apart from the actual training of the intellect, he can stamp upon his pupils' hearts the deep conviction that it is the attainment or even the pursuit, and not the reward, of knowledge which is man's true glory, if he can bring home to them the immensity of the triumphs which have been won for all mankind by the humble, patient, self-sacrificing labours of a number of devoted students, who have loved truth as a pearl of great price, and in the search for it have gladly borne neglect, reproach, contumely, persecution, and even death, he will send them out into the world with a largeness of view and a breadth of sympathy which are the attributes, as they are the guarantees, of noble character.

But it is here, I think, that in the training of an English gentleman, whether at school or at college, the games are more important than the studies. You will understand that I speak of the games, not as physical exercises, but as moral disciplines. At all events, there is in English education nothing on the intellectual side which distinguishes it from the education of other Western countries; but on the athletic side there is something that is unique.

It has often struck me that the English language is a witness of the interest and importance attaching to sport or sports in English life; for the language is full of phrases and figures drawn from games. I do not know how far foreigners, in learning the English language, appreciate them; but the following will serve as illustrations.

To 'play up,' to 'play the game,' to 'play an uphill game,' to 'pull together,' to 'play with a straight bat,' to 'follow up,' to 'be in at the death,' 'fair play,' 'foul play,' 'a sportsmanlike spirit,' 'the game is never lost till it is won' – these and a score of other expressions which might be quoted are freely taken from the games and sports of English life.

It would ill become me to decide how far the interest in games, which is common in England, extends to Japan. Since I have been here, I have watched a game of football, or something like a game of football, being played in one of your public parks. And when I was in India it occurred to me more than once that the throng of natives who would look on at a game of cricket, and still more of football, in the Maidan at Calcutta, whether the players were Englishmen or Indians, held out the hope of a new bond of sympathy between the governing class and the governed in the Indian Empire.

Let me try to indicate some of the lessons which the youth of England learn from their games; for not in the public schools only, but in the universities, the games, and especially cricket, football, and rowing, excite much interest – more, it is sometimes thought, than is suitable to places of education.

Among these lessons the first is fairness. So essential is it, that in public life if a person does what is not altogether straight or upright, he is said 'not to play the game.' For to games a gentlemanly spirit is essential. No game can be properly played if the players condescend to sharp practice, if they take advantage one of another, if they condescend to underhand tricks, or even if they insist upon the letter, as against the spirit, of the rules under which the game is played. Cheating at cards is said to be the one offence which is never pardoned in English society. But in all games unfairness is unpardonable. It is destructive of the confidence upon which games depend. It is fatal to honourable sport. And the absolute fairness required of the players in games is equally requisite in the umpires. They, too, must be above suspicion. It must not enter into the heads of the friendly antagonists who compete for victory in the games that an umpire could ever give a decision which is not strictly conscientious, or that his decision, when it is given, is open to dispute. The implicit obedience to the umpire in games is not the least salutary lesson which boys and young men learn by playing them. It prepares them for the obedience which they must yield in after life to the umpires who preside over great assemblies, and notably to the Speaker of the House of Commons. There is some reason, it is said, to fear that members of the House of Commons are in danger of forgetting the spirit of fair play; I do not indeed know that it is so; but I do know that as little as cricket or football can the game of politics be properly played, if the honourable temper characteristic of it is wanting. It is impossible to frame such rules as will prevent persons who are not gentlemen from doing ungentlemanly things. But if public men in England should ever need to be taught again what is the true temper of conducting affairs both public and private, they may learn it from the games as played, where it is customary to play them with the smallest alloy of cheating or gambling, in the public schools and universities. That temper has lately been called by a distinguished athlete, Mr. C. B. Fry, the English *Bushido*. I do not doubt – nay, I know – that you in Japan appreciate and exemplify it. You have acquired it by other – perhaps better – means than we have. But Englishmen, to whom it is as the breath of their nostrils, have to a great extent discovered its secret and its value through their games.

May I not add, ere I leave this part of my subject, that, if there is one lesson which the world needs to learn, and for all I know may learn fully or partly in the present century, it is how great the blessing would be if civilised nations would come to treat each other with the candour, the good faith, the generous confidence with which gentlemen treat each other in private life?

Again, the games which Englishmen play are schools of nerve. It is not perhaps necessary to assure you that my countrymen, in spite of their many acknowledged virtues, which I am not likely to deny or to depreciate, are not the most modest race in the world. They tell you that 'Englishmen never know when they are beaten,' as though no other race had ever stood up against heavy odds. In the light of recent events you may surely dispute the palm of valour with any nation. Yet games serve a useful purpose in England, as training the nerves. Young Englishmen are taught in them not to lose head or heart. It has often been a pleasure to me to see how boys of seventeen or eighteen years or even younger, who had lived lives far away from the glare of publicity, would take their places with quiet modesty to represent the school at cricket before a crowd numbering fifteen or twenty thousand people, and would then go back, as if it were the most natural thing in the world, to their old simple obscure routine of scholastic duties. The spirit which 'plays an uphill game' to the last, and sometimes 'pulls the match out of the fire,' as the phrase is, in circumstances apparently hopeless, is a splendid feature of character. There are thrilling moments in games – moments when everything turns upon the resolution of one player – and there are such moments in war, or politics, or human life. It may well be hoped that he who has not failed in the one will not fail in the others; for the power of quick decision is one of the greatest human acquirements. According to my experience of life, it is often more important that a decision should be made than that the decision so made should be the best possible. 'Opportunity,' as the proverb says, 'is bald at the back of her head.' To seize the fleeting opportunity when it comes, and to make the best use of it, is a lesson of high value in life. For lost chances seldom recur; and mistakes, even single mistakes, are hard, and perhaps impossible, to retrieve, as in life, so also in games. It is thus too that games are a useful discipline for life.

But there are other and still higher lessons to be learnt in games. The spirit of subordination and co-operation, the complete authority, the ready obedience, the self-respect and self-sacrifice of the playing-field enter largely into life. If a boy will yield up his coveted place in the Eleven to one whom he recognises as a better player than himself, or if he will throw away the chance of personal distinction in order that another may distinguish himself, if he shows modesty in success or fortitude in defeat – has he not learnt something which will help him to be a nobler citizen? There is no cricketer worthy of the name, be he boy or man, who does not think more of the Eleven than of himself, and who would not be glad to sacrifice himself if he could so win the victory for his side. Nay, the true sportsman, the true gentleman, will be careful, at whatever cost, to let others have the credit rather than himself. He will, if need be, take the second place, and not the first, as that noble English soldier, Sir James Outram, did in the Indian Mutiny, when he generously surrendered to his junior officer, Sir Henry Havelock, the honour of relieving Lucknow, and himself served in a civil capacity under him.

All these are qualities, and others like them, tending to produce what I may perhaps claim as a characteristic of the British race – the power of government; for it is a quality which the race has exhibited in relation to subject peoples at many periods of English history in the many regions of the world where the flag of England flies. From India alone it were possible to draw a hundred instances. Englishmen in India have not perhaps won the affection of the native population. They have been trusted, but they have not always been liked. Yet they have evinced a high administrative capacity. There are parts of India where two or three Englishmen by their mere presence maintain order through vast tracts of country. Their rule is as beneficial as it is efficacious. I remember visiting a part of Rajpootana where one official – a youth whose years cannot much have exceeded twenty-five – was administering famine relief single-handed to a million of starving people; his superiors had died or were invalided, and he stood alone face to face with such a task. But he did not falter, he did not fail, he saved the people from death.

If my country owes a peculiar debt of gratitude to any of her sons, it is to those officials, whether military or civil, who in far parts of the world have, often in spite of neglect, and sometimes of discouragement, sustained the honour of the Empire. I do not think I say too much if I profess that one who has received the education of an English gentleman will not wholly fail, however tight the place may be in which he finds himself, however serious the difficulties to be overcome. When he is put down in the face of duty, he will not lose heart or head, he will know what to do, and he will do it. It is this reserve power lying hidden in the British race which is, I think, the hope of the Empire.

But let me come back once more to the universities and the public schools.

There is a certain sympathy, not the less influential because indefinable, a sort of Freemasonry (if I may use a telling English expression) among all the members of the same school or college, or even the same university. To have been educated at Oxford or Cambridge, and still more at Eton or Harrow, is a bond of union with all who have been educated there. All the world over, Oxford and Cambridge men, Etonians and Harrovians, are knit together by strong and sacred memories. It has been my fortune in various distant parts of the world to attend dinners and meetings connected with the public schools of which I am a member; and if ever a man living far from home finds himself in difficult circumstances, he may turn for sympathy and help, with an almost certain hope of receiving it, to men to whom he can address an appeal in the name of their common *Alma Mater*.

It has sometimes happened that the old association of school or college has been a strength to Englishmen charged with an onerous and even perilous responsibility. Not many years ago, in the most troublous days of Ireland, that unfortunate country which seems to be at once nearest to and farthest from the heart of the British Empire, the three men who were called to bear the chief burden of

Irish administration had all been schoolfellows at Harrow. In still more recent days, the Viceroy, or Governor-General, of India, and the Governors of Bombay and Madras, were men who had all received their education, not only in the same school, but, I think, at the same time in the same house at Eton.

Can it be wrong for me, then, at this point, to insist upon the friendships of school and college as forming not only a charm no less enduring than delightful in the personal life, but a strong element in the elevation of character? Nobody who has spent a part of his life at school or college will fail to appreciate afterwards what he owes to noble friendships there begun. He will know something at least of the admiring gratitude which led a distinguished Englishman long ago to desire that he might be simply described in his epitaph as having been 'the friend of Sir Philip Sidney.'

It is difficult for me, in addressing any but a British audience, to express in adequate words how the varied associations of school life tend to create what I can only call a feeling of School patriotism. The thought of the school becomes an inspiring motive in life. As the descendant of a noble family, so the member of a famous school is lifted above himself by his inherited associations. He shrinks from all that is lowering, he aspires to all that is honest and of good report, for the sake of the school which he loves. It is well then that in the public schools, and to some extent also in the colleges at the universities, the sense of historical continuity should be constantly brought before the minds of the young. There is perhaps an annual commemoration of benefactors. Eminent members of the school, when they come back to the place of their education, are welcomed with signal honour. When one of them attains a high distinction, a holiday is granted to his successors in the school. When one of them passes to his rest, his memory is honoured by the tolling of the school bell or by some reference to his life in the chapel or the speech-room.

Let me illustrate this obligation of nobility – this ennobling influence of school-life upon Englishmen – by reference to one of those songs which, in not a few schools, but pre-eminently at Harrow, have been written and set to music, to serve like national airs in inspiring or quickening lofty sentiments. At Harrow, when the boys are called over, each of them as he passes the master signifies his presence by the simple words, 'Here, sir.' One of my late colleagues, a richly gifted master, who is now lost to the school, has chosen these words as the motto of a song in which the boys are taught that, whenever duty calls them, be it to effort, or suffering, or even to death, they must not flinch, but must meet it, gladly and cheerfully, with the familiar words of their school-life, 'Here, sir,' on their lips. It was in such a spirit as this that the young Etonian soldier at Laing's Nek in Natal, breathing the prayer *Floreat Etona*, 'May Eton flourish!' laid down his life.

And now I can bring this lengthy lecture to an end.

Education, whether in Great Britain or in Japan, is all preparatory to after-life. The test of an educational system is not what the pupils are, or how they acquit themselves at fifteen or nineteen or twenty-two or twenty-five years of age, but how they behave as men in private and public affairs. So to discipline them that they may do well in the battle of life is the end of all teaching. Apart, then, from the general linguistic and scientific curriculum of the schools and universities there are various subjects, such as the history of the nation, the growth of the Empire, the worth of imperial sentiment, the relation of labour and capital, the sense of public duty, and even the art of public speaking, which are or ought to be studied by all Englishmen. In late years there has been an effort to quicken the sense of civic duty by familiarising the young in some degree with the aspects of practical philanthropy. Many public schools and colleges have instituted missions – *i.e.* centres of philanthropic and spiritual activity – in crowded cities. On Harrow Hill a memorial tablet reminds successive generations of boys that at the particular spot where it is placed a great Harrovian, the Earl of Shaftesbury, when he had but recently ceased to be a Harrow boy, conceived the idea of devoting his life to the amelioration of the conditions under which the working classes lived and laboured. And so it becomes natural to remark, although I can only just suggest before this audience, that the life of English youth, whether in colleges or in schools, is constantly hallowed by religion. The chapel is the soul of the life. There the boys in a public school meet regularly for worship; there they listen to words of encouragement and exhortation from the masters, from the headmaster especially; there they look upon the memorials of their school-fellows who, in the long history of the school, have done noble service, and perhaps have laid down their lives for their country. For all English education is actuated by the Spirit of Him of whom an ancient English poet has said, that He was

The first true gentleman that ever breathed.

So I have tried to give you a sketch of English education, if only on one of its sides. Great Britain and Japan have many things in common. There have been points of resemblance in their history. There will be yet other such points, if I mistake not, in their destiny. Some of the problems which we have partly solved still await their solution here. I hope you will approach them in the spirit of that imitative originality which chooses the good and leaves what is faulty and wrong. It is a happy fortune in the world to be associated with institutions which are either very old or very new. The civilised world to-day looks with admiration on your achievements. It dreams your dreams with you. For my part, I cannot but cherish the confident hope that the alliance between your country and mine will tend more and more to that end which seems to be the ultimate goal of human history – viz. the intellectual, moral, and at last the spiritual fusion of the races of the East and of the West.

Note

1 An address delivered in Tokio (Tokyo) on the 12th of April, 1906, at the instance of the Minister of Education in Japan, Mr. Makino, who himself took the chair. It ought perhaps to be said that, as the address was not read from manuscript, it is here not verbally but substantially reproduced; and I have inserted in it two or three passages which were omitted, in order to save time, in the delivery.

3

REV. J.E.C. WELLDON, 'THE IMPERIAL ASPECTS OF EDUCATION', IN *PROCEEDINGS OF THE ROYAL COLONIAL INSTITUTE*, VOL. 26 (1894–95), PP. 322–347

James Welldon (1854–1937) was appointed master of Dulwich College in 1883. He had been educated at Eton and King's College, Cambridge. In the short time he held this position he did much for the college, including the creation of the school song, 'Pueri Alleynienses'. He resigned his post in July 1885 to take up the position of headmaster of Harrow School, which he held from 1885 to 1898. He was disliked by many of the masters as autocratic but held in high esteem by the boys. At Harrow he also accepted a number of clerical positions. He was honorary chaplain to Queen Victoria from 1888 to 1892, and Chaplain in Ordinary from 1892 to 1898. He was the Hulsean Lecturer at Cambridge in 1897. (These were lectures established by an endowment made by John Hulse, a clergyman.) In 1898, Welldon became a Doctor of Divinity. The documents included here demonstrate the promotion of Empire from the school chapel, and within the Harrow School culture such as the playing field, with the promotion of a cult of athleticism too. In addition we can see Welldon's connection to the Royal Colonial Institute, at which document 3 was delivered, on the topic of imperial education.

The imperial aspects of education

It is my first duty to offer my respectful thanks to the members of the Council of the Royal Colonial Institute for the honour they have paid to myself and to Harrow by asking me to deliver an address upon the imperial aspects of education. And may I not, in thanking the Council, refer in their name, as in my own, with deep regret, to the memory of one who was a member of the Council when I undertook this address, and indeed invited me to undertake it, and who is now no more, one whose gentle and accomplished mind was ever set upon binding the parts of the Empire in closer and closer union – my respected neighbour, my valued friend, Mr. de Labilliere?

I am not aware that the subject of education has until now been brought directly before this Institute. No doubt a great many of the questions which have been discussed here possessed, and were felt to possess, an educational interest. But it has not been shown that an imperial people might be trained and disciplined in a sense of their imperial responsibilities. Yet it will hardly be denied that education, as it relates to the whole conduct of human life, whether public or private, must in a sense relate to the administration of an empire. The Roman Empire of Augustus is perhaps the only parallel in strength and beneficence to the modern British Empire, and Virgil has stamped the character of its citizens in some noble lines which breathe the spirit of a high imperial dignity.

> Excudent alii spirantia mollius æra,
> Credo equidem, vivos ducent de marmore voltus,
> Orabunt causas melius, cælique meatus
> Describent radio et surgentia sidera dicent:
> Tu regere imperio populos, Romane, memento;
> Hæ tibi erunt artes; pacisque imponere morem,
> Parcere subiectis et debellare superbos.

The lines are pagan – they are even savage: but they are imperial lines. They exhibit the Romans as content to leave to other nations the accomplishments of art, science, philosophy, and rhetoric, if only conquest and command were their own prerogatives, and it is felt that a nation which could produce such poetry was alone capable of raising such an empire.

In English history there is a coincidence of dates which serves to bring out in strong relief the connection between educational advance and imperial power. Two reigns, both queenly reigns, may be said to mark, the one the beginning, the other the consummation of the British Empire. The first is the reign of Queen Elizabeth; the second is the reign of Queen Victoria. It is, of course, well known to me, as to you all, that to the Elizabethan era belongs, strictly speaking, the foundation of one Colony only, the earliest of all British Colonies, and, I am afraid, the most unfortunate, Newfoundland, and, I ought perhaps to add, the discovery of Virginia, which still bears the name of the "imperial votaress," the "fair vestal thronèd by the west," though the earliest Colonists of Virginia all came home again, and it was not settled until the reign of James I. So far and in that sense the British Empire is a creation later than the reign of Elizabeth. But that reign was the birthday of the colonial spirit, if not of the Colonies – of the imperial spirit, if not of the Empire. The names of Willoughby and Chancellor, the heroes of the north-east passage, and of Frobisher and Davies, the heroes of the north-west passage to the Indies; of Hawkins, whose love of adventure was intensified, but not disgraced, by his love of money; of Drake and Cavendish, both circumnavigators of the globe, at whose bold feats the Inquisition itself turned pale; of Sir Humphrey Gilbert, who in his frigate, the "Squirrel," of ten tons, was wrecked on his way home from Newfoundland, and crying "We are as near Heaven by sea as by land," went down into the wild waves; and, last and greatest of all, the very impersonation of the spirit of the time – statesman, courtier, scholar, explorer, captain, knight-errant – Gilbert's brilliant and erratic half-brother, Sir Walter Raleigh. They did not found many great Colonies, these bold mariners; they left them for the generation that followed; but it was their daring, their adventures, and the tales they told of wonderful far-off countries which excited the hopes and ambitions of the men who in the seventeenth century became the founders of the British Empire in the west. What a difference lies between the line which Shakespeare puts into Valentine's lips in the "Two Gentlemen of Verona," "Home-keeping youth have ever homely wits," and the sinister meaning habitually associated with such words as "vagrant" and "vagabond"! I venture to assert, too, that the striking episode of the Armada is not correctly understood as a struggle between a Catholic and a Protestant power for religious supremacy; it is also, and indeed still more, a war to the death between the two great conquering and colonising states for the empire of the New World. Thus the seventeenth century is as truly the child of the sixteenth as is the eighteenth of the seventeenth. And as it is in the tales of Drake's and Raleigh's followers that the historian sees the germs of the great associations, such as the Virginia Company and the East India Company, which carried the flag of England to the ends of the world, so he will look for the motive which sent Drake and Raleigh on their long voyages, to the Reformation and the Revival of Learning, the two co-ordinate stirrings and strivings of the human heart and intellect which made England in the sixteenth century sublime. For it is only when great deeds are done that great thoughts are possible, as the names of Shakespeare and Milton and Byron among others prove.

But if the Elizabethan era marks the beginning, it is not less true that the Victorian era marks the consummation of the British Empire. The seventeenth century may be said to be the age of individual explorers, the eighteenth of commercial companies, the nineteenth of the State. I do not so much mean that the acquisitions made in the last fifty years have never been equalled or surpassed in English history. New Zealand, Hong Kong, the Punjab, British Columbia, Queensland, Burmah, South Africa, are great possessions. But the foundation of the British Empire in India, the conquest of Acadie and Canada, the names of Clive and Warren Hastings and Wolfe, stand out in still brighter colours. It is not the expansion of Empire, it is the spirit of Empire, which is the characteristic of the reign of Queen Victoria. When the Queen ascended the throne, it was doubtful among statesmen and administrators whether the Colonies and Dependencies were not more justly regarded as burdens or encumbrances than as jewels in her crown, nor had the idea of welding them into a vast whole dawned on men's minds. When the Queen dies – may the day be far distant! – she will bequeath an empire to her successor not only immeasurably greater in extent and population than it was at the beginning of her reign, but knit together by innumerable ties of interest, and sentiment, and devotion. The late Sir John Seeley's celebrated book, "The Expansion of England," is one of the signs, as it was one of the causes, of the new spirit. The British Kingdom has become the British Empire. The English-speaking peoples of the world and their subjects and allies – I do not forget or exclude the population of the United States – are become conscious of a high imperial destiny.

But while this is so, it falls within the proper scope of my paper to remind you that the two great reigns of Elizabeth and Victoria mark the chief epochs, not only of empire but of education. There were anticipations of colonial enterprise before Elizabeth; but they were no more than the shadows of coming glory. The illustrious foundations of Winchester and Eton, among the public schools of England, are pre-Elizabethan; they were the precursors of all the more modern schools. But the strange thing is that the age of Elizabeth was one active and progressive era in education, the age of Victoria has been another; and between them little or no advance was made. The seventeenth and eighteenth centuries held no educational place as compared with the sixteenth and the nineteenth. In the year 1572 Sir Francis Drake started on his first famous voyage round the world. In that same year the founder of Harrow began his work of building up his school as an educational institution upon the strength of the charter which he had obtained the year before from Queen Elizabeth. Like other founders of schools John Lyon seems to have conceived the idea of a wider than a purely local foundation; for in the statutes of the school it is provided that "The schoolmaster may receive over and above the youth of the inhabitants within this parish, so many foreigners as the whole may be well taught and applied, and the place can conveniently contain, and of these foreigners he may take such stipend and wages as he can get." That is what I am doing to-day.

If in this paper I refer to the public schools particularly, you will forgive me; for I shall speak of what I know. No English institutions are more characteristic of England. Talleyrand is reported to have said in his sarcastic way that the English Public School educational system was the best in the world – and that it was detestable, *et cela est détestable*. The Public Schools have many faults, and to be engaged in administering one of them is to know pretty well what the faults are; but they are so well adapted to the English nature, they possess such a hold upon the affections and interests of the English people, that no criticism, however well it may be descried, is apparently capable of injuring their prosperity. It has happened to me to live for a good time abroad in continental places of education; and I say unhesitatingly, and I know you will agree with me, that the sentiment of an English Public School man for his school is unknown and unimagined elsewhere. Where will you find such tender lifelong devotion to a school as Lord Wellesley's to Eton? Read his letters written when he was Governor-General of India to his old tutor; or still more the felicitous and pathetic Latin verses which he composed as his own epitaph, desiring to be buried, as he was at last, in the chapel of Eton College; what tribute in the world is there more honourable to the writer, more honourable to the school whose son he was? Or look at Byron's desire that his daughter Allegra might rest in death within the church where he had worshipped as a boy at Harrow. Who but a Public School boy would come home, like Bruce the Harrovian traveller, from Abyssinia in time to dine with his schoolfellows at Harrow; who would rush into battle, like that young officer at Tel-el-Kebir with the cry of *Floreat Etona* on his lips? The feeling so exemplified is remarkable, and all the more so because it cannot be pretended that the Public Schools which have inspired the most devoted affection have been always the places of highest culture or most refined delicacy. I can hardly be expected to approve of the remark which Bacon in his "Advancement of Learning" quotes from Cicero about Cato, that "his excellencies were his own, his defects came from the schoolmaster." But I remember how Mr. Carlyle in a familiar passage of his "Life of John Sterling" says he had observed in his friends educated at Eton that it was not the things which the masters commanded, but the things which they forbade, that had done the boys' character so much good. I cannot perhaps go the whole way with Mr. Carlyle; but it is only too sad a truth that schoolmasters have been in the past strangely blind and dull to the promise of their pupils, and have often thought little and hoped little of those who became the bright glories of their schools. It will be well if the schoolmasters of the future shall take a wider view of education. For after all it is not so much the lessons learnt in class that constitute education; it is the habits formed in a great and generous community. "What is the education of the generality of the world?" exclaims Burke on his impeachment of the great proconsul, whose faults as well as virtues were so vastly successful in extending the scope and celebrity of the British Empire. "Reading a parcel of books? No. Restraint of discipline, emulation, examples of virtue and of justice, form the education of the world."

I take my stand upon these words. You will forgive me if I speak warmly as one whose life is given to the education of the young. What is education? What should be the aim that every teacher sets before himself? It is not a narrow or circumscribed view. It is large and spacious and profound. It is in Milton's stately phrase, so to train his pupils that they may "perform justly, skilfully, and magnanimously all the offices both private and public of peace and war." That is "a compleat and generous education," that and nothing less. Speaking in my own name (for I have no right to speak for others), I do not care to turn out scholars and mathematicians, or indeed, I do care, but I care far more to turn out governors, administrators, generals, philanthropists, statesmen. It is a grave error to judge the work of any teacher by the results which his pupils attain when they are twelve years old and go to school, or when they are nineteen and leave school, or when they are twenty-two and leave the university. Let me be judged, if judged at all, upon the large field of national or international affairs. If it can be said with truth of the English schools and universities that year after year, generation after generation, century after century, they send forth men not without faults, not without limitations of knowledge or culture, not always guiltless perhaps of false quantities, as the Duke of Wellington himself was not guiltless nor immaculate perhaps in spelling, as the Duke of Wellington was not immaculate; but men of vigour, tact, courage, and integrity, men who are brave and chivalrous and true, men who in the words of the academical prayer are "duly qualified to serve God both in church and state," then they can afford to smile at criticisms or can listen to them without shame or self-reproach. That is the object which the educator of to-day may set before himself; that is the service which he can render to his country.

In this view of education it is natural to ask, what are the qualities of Englishmen which have enabled them not only to win but to retain their mighty Empire? I say to "retain" as well as to "win;" for the thought which will occur to any historical student as extraordinary is not that the Empire should have been lost or won by the inhabitants of the little British Isles – a people once regarded as being cut off from civilisation, *penitus toto divisos orbe Britannos* – but that the process of building it up should have lasted for three centuries, and should even now, after so long a time, show no signs of coming to an end. Other nations besides the British have possessed foreign empires. "The British Empire," says Sir John Seeley, "is the only considerable survivor of a family of great Empires which arose out of the contact of the western states of Europe with the New World so suddenly laid open by Vasco da Gama and Columbus." There was a Spanish Empire once; there was a Portuguese Empire; there was a French Empire; there was a Dutch Empire. Some of them, conspicuously the Portuguese and Dutch Empires, like the Phœnician and the Greek in antiquity, were the creations of small states. But all have perished or decayed. Those which remain are but the shadows of their past selves. A glance at the map of the British Empire shows how many places which are now integral parts of the Empire bear or once bore names significant of some other dominant power than the British. How much history is contained in such old names as Acadie, Van Diemen's Land, Louisiana, New Amsterdam! But the colonising genius of Englishmen has been not less remarkable in its duration than in its extent. It is greater now than it ever was; it will apparently be far greater than it now is. To take one instance only: the Suez Canal was a French work; but eighty per cent. of the tonnage which passes through it belongs to Great Britain.

What are the qualities which have produced this striking result? In other words, what are the qualities by which the English, as an imperial people, have shown themselves superior to other nations?

I will mention four.

It is possible that I shall be misunderstood, and it is almost certain that I shall be criticised, if I say that England owes her Empire far more to her *sports* than to her studies. The duty of a conscientious schoolmaster is sometimes supposed to lie in looking askance upon the athletic games of his pupils. I disdain that conscientious hypocrisy. It is the instinct of sport which has played a great part in creating the British Empire. I do not deny that the appreciation of games, among the young especially, may become excessive. It may not be the best use of money to spend thousands of pounds upon telegraphing from the Antipodes the details of a cricket match between England and Australia. The *Spectator* newspaper has called cricket a "very tedious game." It is not half so tedious as the *Spectator*. It may not be the best expenditure of time that some fifty thousand people should visit the Crystal Palace to see the final football match for the Association Challenge Cup. But these are the interests which have made England a strong and dominant power; nor can anyone who has lived in a French *lycée* or a German *gymnasium* help being thankful for the healthy, vigorous, athletic tastes of the English nation. It is not long since I was at Harrow, looking on at a football match, and a lady said to me, "What do you think of this, Mr. Welldon?" I said, "It is to this that we owe the British Empire." Englishmen are not superior to Frenchmen or Germans in brains or industry or the science and apparatus of war; but they are superior in the health and temper which games impart. That the battle of Waterloo was won in the playing-fields of Eton is a saying which has passed into a proverb. But I do not think I am wrong in saying that the sport, the pluck, the resolution, and the strength which have within the last few weeks animated the little garrison at Chitral and the gallant force that has accomplished their deliverance are effectively acquired in the cricket-fields and football-fields of the great public schools, and in the games of which they are the habitual scenes. For it is not the physical value of athletic games that is the highest. The pluck, the energy, the perseverance, the good temper, the self-control, the discipline, the co-operation, the *esprit de corps*, which merit success in cricket or football, are the very qualities which win the day in peace or war. The men who possessed these qualities, not sedate and faultless citizens, but men of will, spirit, and chivalry, are the men who conquered at Plassey and Quebec. In the history of the British Empire it is written that England has owed her sovereignty to her sports.

But above athletic vigour stands the quality of which Englishmen, and especially English Public School men, stand pre-eminent. I will call it *readiness*. It can indeed be scarcely defined in a single word. It means courage, it means self-reliance, it means the power of seizing opportunities, it means resource. But whatever it is, it is characteristic of the English race. I remember asking the most distinguished of living travellers what he had found to be the secret of success in life, and his answering that it was not so much intellectual ability as promptitude in taking advantage of opportunities. That is, I believe, the hereditary gift of Englishmen. It is fostered by the English public schools. When I look at the lines of my own pupils, I sometimes say to myself, "These boys are not remarkably clever or remarkably cultivated, but if you take any one of them and put him down in difficult circumstances and tell him to make the best of them, the chances are that he will not greatly fail." There are few facts more striking than the latent reserve power of the English race. It is not in the few men whose names are familiar as household words, it is the far greater number of men who, if they were called upon to face an emergency, would face it successfully, that the strength of England consists. Wonderful in history has been the manner in which Englishmen have risen above disasters, nay, not seldom, have turned them into blessings. The same century saw the loss of the United States and the conquests of Canada and India. The original English settlement in Australia followed only five years later upon the Peace of Versailles, by which England recognised the independence of the United States of America. There lie but a few years between the mutiny of the Nore and Nelson's victories at the Nile and Trafalgar. Again and again have Englishmen, left to themselves, been better and greater than their government. It has been well said, "If the work done by the English nation has, in the end, proved to be of better quality and more lasting character than that of other peoples, if the English succeeded in India, while the Portuguese failed, if British America has prospered, while Spanish America has not, if the United States grew and developed out of all proportion to the French colony in Canada, one great reason for the difference seems to be, that the members of the English-speaking race, as compared with other races, have, throughout its history, both at home and abroad, relied, not so much on their government, as on themselves." The men who made the Empire had faith in England and in themselves; and they needed no other faith, except in God. They did not theorise about the work which had to be done, they did not talk about it, but they set to work doggedly, irresistibly, "pegging away," as President Lincoln said, and, in spite of many failures, they did it. It was so with the founders of the British Empire in India. It has been so with that remarkable group of men who might all, I suppose, have been driven out of Cairo in a single omnibus, Lord Cromer and his colleagues, the regenerators of Egypt. It is so with Mr. Rhodes. There is no need to eulogise or criticise his career. I do not defend all Mr. Rhodes's actions; they do not need defence. A great career is not free from shadows; they only throw up its brilliancy. But I say he is the kind of man who has made the Empire. I say he is an example of what an Englishman can do who has confidence in himself, and who wins the confidence of others. You see how the British Empire in India was built up by seeing how the British Empire in South Africa is being built up to-day. And, unless I am mistaken, you learn two lessons from the scenes that are being enacted before your eyes. One is, that the worst method of choosing men for great administrative and imperial positions is by counting up marks obtained in a literary examination. And the other is that a great man, if he is to do a great work, must have a free hand. If the telegraph had existed in the days of Clive and Warren Hastings, there would have been no British Empire in India. Mr. Rhodes owes his success, not to himself alone, but to his freedom from the control of Downing Street. The imperial government is unequal, as it always has been, to the task of creating an Empire. The Empire is the work of bold, courageous, and invincible spirits, who knew when their chances came and took advantage of them, and who chose, for themselves and for their country, not to be "little Englanders" but great Englanders, imperial Englishmen.

Do not let it be thought, however, that in estimating the greatness of England and of the British Empire I forget the value of *character*. It is the supreme ruling quality of Englishmen. They owe more to their morals than to their arms. I think every year that one lives one feels more strongly the supremacy of high and noble character. It is the habit to say to my boys when they are leaving school: "I do not much care that you shall have gifts or powers or riches or good fortune; but if you have character – if it is known of you that no temptation on earth would divert you by a hair's breadth from the strict path of honour, then there is nothing too hard for you in life." The word of an Englishman – the honour of an Englishman – what a treasure that is! Englishmen are not the most attractive people in the world. They are often proud, intolerant, unsociable, they are apt to ride roughshod over other's feelings, which they call prejudices. But upon the whole, with many defects, they have won the confidence of mankind. I was very much struck in reading that excellent book "Where Three Empires Meet" with the following passage: "Those who knew Russian Turkestan will tell us that even there, should a dispute occur – over some trade transaction, for instance – between two natives, they, having no confidence in their own magistrates and not much faith in Russian incorruptibility, will ask any English traveller who may be by to act as arbitrator on the case, his word being of higher authority than the decision of tribunals." That is striking testimony, and if it be true, what higher service can a schoolmaster or any teacher render to education than by pointing out to his pupils how much they advance the cause of the Empire by unswerving honesty, how great an injury they may do it, if by any act of theirs they lower the name and fame of England? and how can he better impress the lesson upon them than by holding up before their eyes the examples of the men *sans peur et sans reproche* who made the Empire, such as Wellington, Havelock, Dalhousie, the Lawrences, Livingstone, and Gordon?

And is it wrong to add that the British Empire has depended not upon these qualities only of which I have spoken, but upon *religion*? It is true enough that the religious character of Englishmen has been stained at different times by grievous faults. But deep down in their hearts has been the fear of God. I believe it has been the secret of their success. I will say no more about it. But Sir John Seeley's words are worth remembering. "I always hold," he says, "that religion is the great state-building principle. These Colonies" – he is speaking of the Colonies of North America – "could create a new state because they were already a church, since the church, so at least I hold, is the soul of the state; where there is a church a state grows up in time; but if you find a state which is not also in some sense a church, you find a state which is not long for this world."

Such are the qualities, as I conceive, upon which the British Empire has been based – physical strength, promptitude, self-reliance, character, religion. And if so, it follows that one whose life is spent in training citizens for the service of the Empire will think only or chiefly of these things. But an Empire based upon these qualities will inspire him and will help him to inspire others with certain sentiments. Will you let me try to say what those sentiments are?

He who would give his pupils what I have called an imperial education will profoundly believe in the imperial destiny of the British race. I do not know if patriotism has at all times been the special feature of the English race. Bishop Warburton, writing in the middle of the last century, speaks of "that antiquated forgotten virtue called the love of our country." It is not so now. Patriotism is not the spirit of one party in the State, but of all parties. I am not ashamed to say, as a teacher of the young, that I share it to the full. I believe, and I want my pupils to believe, that the British race is the best in all the world. It is the race which has most succeeded in combining liberty with law, religion with freedom, self-respect with respect for other races. I believe that it is called by Providence to play a paramount part in the history of nations. I believe in my heart that the best thing which can happen to the uncivilised peoples of the world is that they should come more and more under the influence of Great Britain. It is much to say, but it is not more than Milton said when he used the proud words, "When God is decreeing to begin some new and great period in His church, even to the reforming of the

Reformation itself, what does He then but reveal Himself to His servants, and, as His manner is, first to His Englishmen!"

To be a patriot is not the same thing as to be a Jingo. But a man cannot be an honorary citizen of all nations any more than he can be in Wilberforce's phrase, "an honorary member of all religions." And if a man thinks other nations as good as his own, it is not that he loves all nations, but he does not love any.

It is clear then that whatever fosters the spirit of a just patriotism is of national value. Patriotism is an unmixed good when it is not the first sentiment in the mind but the second; in other words, when it is subordinated to the fear of God.

I think that it is the duty of a teacher to bring before his pupils, and not once in a way only, but habitually, the magnitude and dignity of the British Empire. The history and geography of the Empire will become in his hands powerful educational instruments. He will show, by a series of illustrative maps, such as are found, e.g. in Mr. Lucas's book on the "Historical Geography of the British Colonies," by what steps the dominion of Great Britain was spread over the world. The insular position of Great Britain, separating it naturally from continental politics, will be appreciated at its true value. The scientific study of geography begins with Hakluyt, and he was a contemporary of the Elizabethan explorers. The geographical extent of the Empire, its population, its commerce, its variety of resources, its shipping, its policy, will fall into place. What a revelation it is when the young mind apprehends that the British Empire to-day includes some 350,000,000 of human beings, that its annual imports and exports amount to £1,000,000,000, and that it covers one-sixth part of the habitable globe! Lectures or addresses, such as Mr. Parkin has often delivered on behalf of Imperial Federation, arrest and impress the minds of youthful hearers. Nor can it be wrong to point out that the chief failures of British enterprise have, unlike those of other nations, been frequently blessings in after-time. The Revocation of the Edict of Nantes served only to cripple the resources of France and to enrich other nations, England especially, at her expense. But the enforced or voluntary expatriation of the Puritans gave England, or the English-speaking race, the dominion of a new world. Queen Mary said that when she died the name of Calais would be found written on her heart; but it was the loss of all direct interest in the great continental wars that set England free for the foundation of her Colonial Empire. When Lord Palmerston in the famous Dom Pacifico speech quoted the formula *Civis Romanus sum*, as typical of the protecting power by which an English citizen was encircled all the world over, his words possessed an even deeper and wider meaning than he knew.

But it is not in treaties and conventions, it is in the sympathies of race, of language and of religion, that the strength of Empire lies. And more and more the English race is realising its unity. It is becoming compacted in great confederations – the United States of America, the Dominion of Canada, the Indian Empire, which are already established realities, and the confederations of Australia and of South Africa, which are tending towards realisation. That there are difficulties, especially of tariff and taxation, in the way of formal union, I know well; perhaps such union in itself is not desirable. But it may at least be said that the task of imperial representation is not greater or stranger than the task of representative government itself seemed to antiquity. Aristotle, in his "Politics," could not conceive of a State in which the citizens should be unable all to hear the voice of the same herald. And if the one difficulty has been overcome, so may the others be, not, indeed, at once, or for many years, but at last.

For, if the Empire is ever extending in magnitude, the means of communication between its parts extend still more rapidly. It is greater, far greater than it was, but for practical purposes it is smaller. The telegraph kills time. The steam engine kills distance. The ocean is no longer the great dissevering, but the great uniting power. And if Burke thought that the Atlantic Ocean forbade, and must for ever forbid, any confederation of the Old World and the New, he thought so in an age when Rome was farther from London than New York is now.

It is not easy to calculate the educational effects of the evergrowing passion for foreign travel upon the English-speaking world at home and abroad. What is certain is that the passion exists and is likely to grow. A journey round the world is no more now than the continental *grand tour* was in Lord Chesterfield's time. Travel has itself become a part of education. It is safe to predict that a time is coming when a man who has not made himself to some extent acquainted with the English colonies and dependencies abroad, will seem disqualified for a high position in public life at home.

I do not deny that foreign travel has its dangers. Faraday held that no man could travel much and be religious. There is no doubt a danger that a man, by acclimatising himself, as it were, in all countries, may lose the distinctive features, which are frequently the most valuable, of his own. The society of Paris is on a large scale, the society of Simla or Cairo on a small, a witness to this danger. Yet it is only by travelling that Englishmen can learn to appreciate the full strength and glory of the British Empire. As Mr. Rudyard Kipling says in his splendid poem, "The English Flag:"

What should they know of England who only England know?

But to have sailed through the Suez Canal, to have crossed the great continent of the West by the Canadian Pacific Railway, to have stood in the bazaars of Cairo or Calcutta, to have entered the harbour of Sydney, to have seen the stir and stress of commercial life in Cape Town, is to understand what the present and the future have in store. It must be remembered, too, that among the English-speaking Colonies in years to come, there will be generations of men and women who have never known the old country as their fathers and their fathers' fathers knew it, who have no special feeling for it or interest in it, who never think of it as home. Between them and us the communion which foreign travel affords may come to be of even higher value than it now is. It will aid in intensifying sympathy. The time has come already when the Australian Colonies can voluntarily ally their arms with ours in the Soudan. The time is coming, I think, when the whole

English-speaking world, not excluding the people of the United States, would forbid, and by their united action prevent, any grievous loss or injury to England.

For, whatever may happen, there is one bond of union which unites and must unite the English-speaking world. It is the English language itself. That language is the heritage of all who live beneath the flag of England. The future has few certainties or none; but if there be any, one is that, if ever there is a universal language – a language spoken or understood among all members of the human family – it will be English. The language of Shakespeare and Milton will control the world. Already its influence is infinitely wider and more powerful than was ever the influence of Greek under Alexander the Great, or of Latin under Augustus. My friend Mr. George Curzon, who is so brilliant an example of the results attained by bringing a trained intelligence to bear by personal direct experience upon questions of foreign policy, says of it: –

> Already spoken in every store from Yokohama to Rangoon; already taught in the military and naval colleges of China, and in the schools of Japan and of Siam; already employed on the telegraphic services of Japan, China, and Korea, and stamped upon the silver coins that issue from the mints of Osaka and Canton; already used by Chinamen themselves as a means of communication between subjects from different provinces of their mighty Empire – it is destined with absolute certainty to be the language of the far East. Its sounds will go out into all lands, and its words unto the ends of the world.

The wide extension of the English language, as it brings the far parts of the world into greater sympathy with the modes of life and thought in England, will help not a little to the happy determination of a large and difficult question. That question is whether it is within the power of a democracy to govern an Empire. That democracy makes imperial government difficult no one will deny who knows what democracy is or what government is. Thucydides, who could not have conceived of democracy in its present wide acceptation, seems to have held that the democracy of Athens would fail as an imperial power. And I think it may be said that in modern times the statesmen whose faith in the future of the Empire has been lowest are they who possessed the least faith in the democracy which they saw and feared to be inevitable.

For my own part, I entertain a brighter hope. If I distrust the democracy at all, it is its discretion which I distrust, and not its disposition. I think the sympathies of the democracy will be found, and all the more as it advances in culture and information, to lie on the side of duty, honour, and generosity.

At all events it is the part of education to foster and promote such a spirit. The history of India suggests that duty. It may be that the means by which the British Empire in India was won lie open to censure. But history presents no full parallel to the spirit in which it is administered. For in India Government exists in the strictest sense for the benefit, not of the governors, but of the governed. It has enriched 250 millions of people with the unexampled riches of peace, and law, and order. What the issue may be rests in other Hands than ours. The unforeseen will happen in the future as in the past. It is enough if the work that is given us to do is done in a responsible and righteous temper.

The case of India affords an inspiring lesson to the educator. But other examples are not wanting. They show how rapidly progress is made, when the conscience, first of individuals, then of the nation, has been touched. Among those examples the case of the slave trade stands pre-eminent. The Assiento contract by which the English nation obtained the exclusive right of importing negro slaves into the Spanish West Indies, was signed between England and Spain in 1713. Nearly eighty years later, in 1791, Mr. Wesley wrote from his deathbed to Mr. Wilberforce the celebrated letter in which he said: "Unless the Divine power has raised you up to be as *Athanasius contra mundum,* I see not how you can go through your glorious enterprise, in opposing that execrable villainy which is the scandal of religion, of England, and of human nature. Unless God has raised you up for this very thing you will be worn out by the opposition of men and devils; but if God be for you, who can be against you? Are all of them together stronger than God? Oh, be not weary of well-doing. Go on in the name of God, and in the power of His might, till even American slavery, the vilest that ever saw the sun, shall vanish away before it." That was on February 24, 1791. Look on sixteen years – sixteen years to a day – it is the day when the Bill for the Abolition of the Slave Trade passed the House of Commons – and it is told in the "Life of Wilberforce," that when Sir Samuel Romilly, the Solicitor-General, "entreated the young Members of Parliament to let this day's event be a lesson to them, how much the rewards of virtue exceeded those of ambition; and then contrasted the feelings of the Emperor of the French, in all his greatness, with those of that honoured man, who would this day lay his head upon his pillow and remember that the Slave Trade was no more; the whole House surprised into a forgetfulness of its ordinary habits, burst into acclamations of applause."

The history of the awakening national conscience in respect of the slave trade does not stand alone. The protest of Wilberforce and Clarkson against the traffic in slaves was repeated in the protest of Archbishop Whately and others against the system of transporting convicts. From the birth of that system to its death is a period of only eighty years. The first batch of convicts was sent to New South Wales in 1787; the last batch was sent to Western Australia in 1867. So rapidly, so completely can public opinion be changed by the action of enlightened citizens! And the spirit of equity and charity which animated these noble and philanthropic men was afterwards the spirit of those who, as Bishop Selwyn and Bishop Colenso, advocated the claims of the native populations upon the English conscience, or of Livingstone in his lifelong, immortal crusade against "the open sore" of Africa.

These are the instances which elevate and ennoble English history. That they have been self-denying and sometimes costly is their merit. The Imperial Parliament voted in 1834 the sum of twenty millions sterling as compensation to the slave-owners. By that vote Parliament enacted two great principles which it may be well to bear in memory for all time, viz. (1) that a nation possesses a conscience, and is called to a duty – a nation as well as an individual; and (2) that in the discharge of its duty it must avoid, as far as possible, inflicting loss upon individuals.

One last lesson there is which the study of the British Empire suggests, and the student of imperial politics will enforce upon his pupils. It is the lesson of Imperial unity.

The Empire is one. The English-speaking world is one. Amidst a thousand differences of place, climate, resources, life, culture, religion, and politics, it is in essential tone and character one. The men who founded it, the men who upheld it, have been animated by the same spirit, and have aspired to the same exalted aim. In the large life of the British Empire questions of domestic policy, however important in themselves, decline and vanish. What is "one man one vote," what is Local Veto, what is Welsh Disestablishment, what even is the resolution which shall sweep away the House of Lords, in comparison with those vast national and international interests which claim the thoughts and ambitions of all imperial Englishmen? They have evoked, and they evoke to-day, a wealth of patriotism, of self-sacrifice, of enthusiasm, which the ears of men and statesmen at home are too often slow to appreciate. By great deeds and true, by splendid efforts, by noble deaths and yet more noble lives, the British Empire has been consolidated, and stands:

> Tantæ molis erat Romanam condere gentem,

And it is there that the unity of the race is felt and realised. There it is that Englishmen, Scotchmen, Welshmen, Irishmen too, have learnt or have not forgotten their unity; or if they forget it at home, they learn it anew abroad.

It is needless, or it would take too long, to quote here the famous passage in which Sheil, in his speech on the Irish Municipal Bill, repudiated the allegation made, or supposed to have been made, by Lord Lyndhurst, that the Irish were "aliens." But his appeal to Sir Henry Hardinge is in point: –

> Tell me, for you were there (at Waterloo) . . . tell me, for you must needs remember – on that day when the destinies of mankind were trembling in the balance – while death fell in showers – when the artillery of France was levelled with a precision of the most deadly science – when her legions, incited by the voice and inspired by the example of their mighty leader, rushed again and again to the onset – tell me if, for an instant, when to hesitate for an instant was to be lost, the "aliens" blenched?. . . . The blood of England, Scotland, and Ireland flowed in the same stream and drenched the same field. When the chill morning dawned, their dead lay cold and stark together – in the same deep pit their bodies were deposited – the green corn of spring is now breaking from their commingled

dust – the dew falls from heaven upon their "union" in the grave. Partakers in every peril – in the glory shall we not be permitted to participate? and shall we be told, as a requital, that we are estranged from the noble country for whose salvation our life-blood was poured out?

I pray God that this spirit may continue. So long as it is permitted me to play a part, however humble it may be, in education, it will be my effort to impress it upon my boys. Others will impress it with more vigour and success than I. But it is the one lesson worth teaching and worth learning. The boys of to-day are the statesmen and administrators of to-morrow. In their hands is the future of the British Empire. May they prove themselves not unworthy of their solemn charge! May they scorn the idea of tarnishing or diminishing the Empire which their forefathers won! May they augment, consolidate, and exalt it! May it be given them to cherish great ideas, to make great efforts, and to win great victories! That is my prayer.

> We sailed wherever ship could sail,
> We founded many a mighty state;
> Pray God our greatness may not fail
> Through craven fear of being great!

Discussion

Professor J. A. LIEBMANN (Cape Colony): I feel particularly proud at having been requested to offer a few remarks on the most eloquent paper that our worthy lecturer, the eminent scholar and learned divine, the Head Master of Harrow, has just addressed to us. It is a paper that in my opinion is pregnant with so many points of interest that a whole volume of essays could be written upon it. What the opinion of others may be I do not know, but, as one who has lived a number of years in the Cape Colony, I may be allowed to remark that a great many of us, who call ourselves Colonists, will be delighted to note the truly Imperial point of view from which the lecturer has treated his subject. The pith of the lecture perhaps may be put in these words, "That it should be the duty of you 'who live at home at ease' to educate your sons and your daughters to their Imperial responsibilities." In order to do so, you should not have, as the lecturer remarked, hazy notions of what Empire means. It was, I believe, the humorist Max O'Rell who remarked that the English schoolboy's knowledge of France was confined to the fact that it was a country which produced the French irregular verbs. In order that you should know what Empire means, you should have more than a hazy idea about the glorious birthright that it is each Englishman's privilege to inherit. I believe I am correct in saying that the Council of this Institute has frequently drawn attention to the national importance of education in matters of geography, history, climate, and the commercial resources of this mighty Empire, and one of our Fellows, the Rev. W. P. Greswell, who used to be a lecturer in my own college, has published a book on the part of the world that, at the present, is occupying a good deal of attention – South Africa. You have a Geographical Association for the furtherance of knowledge concerning the Empire by improving the teaching of geography in schools. I regret in reading over one of the reports of the Council to find remarks to the effect, that the knowledge of geography as at present existing is very unsatisfactory and far inferior to that possessed by boys in foreign schools. As an Englishman myself I regret to say we are extremely bad copyists. English copies of French plays are as a rule execrable. We try to copy the German "Pickelhaube" and produce an abortion, but there is one thing in which we might follow our Teutonic cousins, and that is the matter of thoroughness in study – the study of the geography of their own country. When I speak of *our* own country I do not mean the little mud bank in the Atlantic. I mean the Empire as a whole. We dwellers beyond the sea are your own kith and kin, people united by language, race, religion, and by the great characteristics that Mr. Welldon has referred to – sport, readiness of character, promptitude and self-reliance. I take it you can only get to know what Empire means by educating your sons and daughters to thoroughly understand what a glorious birthright is theirs. May I mention a few amusing points which date back not very long ago, proving the grossest ignorance about the Colonial possessions? They are all of South Africa. It was reported at the time of the discovery of the diamond fields by a leading London paper, that it was the customary habit of nurse girls of Cape Town to wheel their little charges in their perambulators on Saturday afternoons, for the purpose of getting the fresh air, along the banks of the Orange River. It has been stated that during the Boer war the Admiralty ordered one of the gunboats to go up the coast of Natal as near as could be and shell Potchefstroom, in the Transvaal. It is on record that a request had been made for an extra chaplain in King William's Town, a town in the eastern province of Cape Colony. A reverend gentleman got up in Convocation and said that he saw absolutely no necessity for another chaplain, because we had one at Grahamstown and another at Natal, and surely the two could arrange between themselves to ride over on alternate Sundays and take the services required. I think the best thanks are due to Mr. Welldon, not only of those present, but of the Fellows of this Institute beyond the seas, who will have the opportunity of reading the eloquent words with which the lecturer has charmed us. They have not had the opportunity of enjoying the studied eloquence of his address, but they will be able to gather from the report the force of character, broadness of views, warmth of colouring, depth of sentiment, and largeness of sympathy with which he has clothed his words, pointed the moral, and adorned the tale.

Judge PROWSE (Newfoundland): It was a very happy thought on the part of the Council of this Society to invite a schoolmaster to address the Royal Colonial Institute on this important subject, and in choosing Mr. Welldon they selected the best known and most distinguished schoolmaster in England. The Head Master of Harrow fills a very high position, a post of honour and power. There is this peculiarity about the position of a great English head master. They won't let him remain a schoolmaster for long, they are always wanting to put wings on him, to make a bishop of him. Well, I think a great schoolmaster, a man set on high as Mr. Welldon is at Harrow-on-the-Hill, is a much greater man and a more important man than a bishop. What bishop in this century has filled such a large place in the public mind of England as Arnold, the great educator? What bishop is there at the present time who will be noted in the history of our century? Well, perhaps you will say the archbishop; if so, it is mainly through his son. There is no country where a great schoolmaster fills so high a social position, or is so honoured, and so deservedly honoured, as in England. This lecture was badly wanted. We want to know, and all the school children in England should know, more about the Empire. There is much room for improvement. A grocer's shop in England is to-day a study in the commercial geography of the Empire. We know, I am thankful to say, more than our forefathers about the greater England beyond the seas. There used to be a joke about the Duke of Newcastle running off in a hurry to tell King George he had discovered that Cape Breton was an island. This is an attractive subject, but, before an English audience, there should be, and there is only one subject near my heart, and that is not the Empire but the part of the Empire I belong to. That is the only part of supreme interest to me. I am an Englishman, of course, and I look upon the unity of the Empire as a great object. You could not have a greater object. It may seem an impudent thing for me to attempt to instruct a schoolmaster, but let me tell Mr. Welldon he is very much astray with regard to the formation of the British Empire. The British Empire was formed by individual effort, by the efforts of humble west country fishermen. They laid the foundation of the Empire. They began in Iceland and carried on the work in Newfoundland, and the history of Newfoundland and the foundation of the Empire goes back a hundred years before Mr. Welldon began. For that I have the highest authority, the authority of one of the greatest men the Empire ever produced, Sir Walter Raleigh. You believe in the unity of the Empire, and, as I have said, you could not have a greater object. But just now there is one little hitch in regard to the unity of the Empire. The Empire can only be united by its large detached pieces coming together in Australia, West Indies, Africa. But there is another part, North America. It should be united. I do not want to tell any official secrets, but I think, in the present condition of affairs, if North America is not united, it will be a scandal. On whom the blame will fall I do not say, and I do not know; but if this movement towards the unity of the Empire is a failure, it will be a grave disaster.

Mr. G. R. Parkin, M.A.: It has been to me a matter of deep interest to see and hear the Head Master of Harrow here to-night. It is about four years ago – I mention this to explain to you what seems to me the full meaning of his presence to-night – that he led me into that noble speech-room at Harrow before 600 of his boys. He told me they had an hour off from studies, and they looked upon this lecture-hour as a part of their recreation. As I had several large maps on the wall it rather troubled me, because it looked very much like a geographical lesson, so I had to fall back on my wits to awaken their interest. So I said: "Boys, this looks like a geographical lesson, and I have been a schoolmaster myself twenty years, but before you give up all hope of some evening's recreation let me mention something to you." And I told them of a banquet that had just been held. The Lord Mayor had been entertaining Her Majesty's Ministers. In his opening speech, the Lord Mayor – the man who was at the head of the mightiest city in the world – mentioned that he was an old Harrow boy. Lord Knutsford, then at the head of the whole of our vast Colonial system; Mr. Stanhope, who was managing the army that secured this great Empire, and Lord George Hamilton, at the head of the navy, all got up and said they too were old Harrow boys. I said: "If Harrow is going to do this, the sooner you get out your big maps and study them the better." With this view of their relation to the subject, you can imagine that the boys were interested as I tried to picture to them what the Empire was. I never had an audience that listened with more fixed attention. I mention this to emphasise what it means to have at the head of one of our great public schools, which trains our ruling classes, and turns out statesmen in such large proportions, a man who is so disposed to spread and elevate this great Imperial idea. More than that, in much visiting of the great public schools, I have been convinced there is no greater turning point with regard to the future of the Empire than catching the mind and enthusiasm of these boys, because out of these schools spring, in the main, the future rulers of the Empire, and to influence them in the right direction is of supreme importance. For these reasons this Institute is right in welcoming with the greatest enthusiasm a speech such as we have heard to-night. Mr. Welldon made one very striking and searching remark. If, he said, "the telegraph had existed in the great days of the foundations of this Empire, we might not have had the Empire that we have." What does that mean? It means that we have an Empire in which the supreme governing power is decided entirely by the votes of people influenced by the local issues that prevail in these islands; that had these local issues and had party spirit had their full sway and their immediate influence in those days, the great Viceroys whom we sent out might not have had that free hand in building up the Empire that they had. Hence, if we are to maintain a great Empire we must adapt our minds to new conditions, and take care that, no matter how rapidly the telegraph works, we shall have such an educated opinion at home equal to the greater responsibilities thrown upon it. This lays an important duty on all of us, and not least on the heads of our great public schools, for if they will only teach this lesson to their boys – who are likely to be the leaders of the democracy – that they must rise above mere party faction, that they must not only have large Imperial instincts themselves, but must go down to the masses and appeal to them on broad natural grounds, we shall have gone a long way towards showing that a great democracy can also be a ruling Empire for good throughout the world. One point I would like to mention in this audience, where there is a large proportion of ladies and gentlemen who come from the Colonies. A previous speaker dwelt with emphasis on the necessity of the people of this country studying the geography of our vast Empire. I want to say to my fellow-colonists that that is another side to this question. How shall I express it? Mr. Cecil Rhodes has been mentioned. It was once mentioned to him, I am told, that one of the great Colonies of the Empire had given up the study of British history on account of questions arising in local politics. His remark was that "it was enough to damn the soul of any Colony." I ask you to carry home the thought which lies behind that expression. Any Colony which allows itself, collectively or individually, to break the link of those great national traditions which they possess as a right, is losing the greatest power and stimulus and means of elevating itself that any young community ever possessed. I wish that every Colonist would spend quite as much energy in his Colony urging people to study and imbue themselves with the great and glorious traditions of English freedom and liberty, as they do in ridiculing Englishmen for their ignorance of Colonial geography and history. It has been remarked by a previous speaker, as a matter of regret, that great English head masters are constantly being lifted into the position of bishops and archbishops. When, as I suppose will be the case some day, the gentleman who has addressed us enters into such a higher position he will find himself face to face with what is wanted quite as much as anything else – a statesmanship in the Christian Church which will organise the enormous forces which this Empire can wield in the way of moral influence, and of bringing the moral impact of this country to bear with full force on those connected with it. This is another vast question, and Mr. Welldon will find there also abundant employment for the Imperial spirit shown in his address to-night. A distinguished thinker has remarked that the most probable dissolvent of this Empire will be ignorance. To those who feel this, it must be an immense satisfaction to have heard the Head Master of Harrow speak as he has spoken to-night, for it shows that ignorance is not likely to prevail in one great centre of English education.

Mr. G. R. GODSON referred to the improper pronunciation of the Latin and Greek languages as at present taught in English schools, and considered it to be the duty of the heads of schools to rectify their teaching in this respect; and also that, the principle of half a loaf being better than none, the decimal system should be adopted up to such time as the duodecimal system could be taken in hand. The English climate assisted Englishmen in the way of educating them to sudden changes and various sorts of climates, it being of such a variable nature, and thus giving them an advantage over other nationalities in this respect.

The CHAIRMAN: In rising to ask you to accord your most cordial thanks to Mr. Welldon, I shall not say more than a word or two. I am sure you will all agree with me that we have listened to a most interesting and instructive lecture, and that we have had a very interesting and instructive discussion. I congratulate you, and I congratulate Mr. Welldon, on the audience he has had to hear him. I congratulate him also on the distinguished persons amongst us. We have Sir Thomas Fowell Buxton, the Governor-Elect of South Australia, and I am sure I shall not be transcending my powers and functions if I say we offer him our sincere congratulations on his appointment, that we welcome him here to-night, and that we wish him God-speed on his journey and a useful and happy period of administration in that great Colony. We have also here my old friend, Sir Robert Herbert, from whom I have learnt not a few things, and whom I always look upon with great awe, wondering how it is possible for one human being to know so much about so vast a subject as the British Empire and yet remain in tolerably good health. Mr.

Welldon has pointed out one fact, a very evident fact, that never occurred to me before, that the two great periods of Colonial extension and consolidation have taken place under the reigns of two Queens. I hope that noticeable fact may have a soothing effect on some of those products of modernity who seem to think that somehow the mere male creature has acquired a too great preponderance in the affairs of the world. I have no doubt in creating the Empire men had something to do with it. The lecturer laid a great stress, and rightly so, on the points in our national character that have enabled us to create this great Empire. As a matter of fact, the men who created the Empire had not the slightest idea of what they were doing. They did not so because they wanted to create an Empire, but because they could not help themselves. They did it from self-interest, and the national characteristics in them compelled them to do it in a masterful way, and in a way that has been successful. These characteristics he described as honesty, self-reliance, and a sense of duty and courage. I believe it is mainly summed up in the word courage. I do not mean ordinary physical courage, which I have no doubt is pretty evenly shared out amongst all races of men, but the higher form of courage which enables men to take responsibility, to act in difficult circumstances, perhaps quite alone; the kind of courage which enables a man with a mere handful of supporters to administer an enormous population and affairs like those of our Indian Empire. It is that, and also, I believe, our honesty. Foreign nations are apt to describe us as being perfidious in our foreign politics. My own impression is that what they look upon as the effect of extreme cunning is really the effect of exceeding simplicity of character. We do things perfectly simply, and they think we have a very deep motive for it when we have none at all; however, there can be no doubt the great fact that an Englishman's word can be relied upon has done more for us with the native races in all parts of the world than perhaps any other characteristic. I will not detain you with any further criticism of this most admirable paper, and will now ask you to return your most cordial thanks to the Lecturer.

The Rev, J. E. C. WELLDON: I am sure it is not necessary for me to say more than a very few words of thanks, for I have already addressed this meeting at almost excessive length, and it is necessary, moreover, for me to return to my sphere of labour, for I shall be in school to-morrow at a time perhaps when everybody here will be in bed. I simply undertook to read the paper because I was asked to read it, and I have done my best. It only remains to ask you to pass a cordial vote of thanks to the noble lord who has taken the chair to-night.

4

THE NATIONAL LIFE

From: Rev. J.E.C. Welldon, 'The National Life', in *Fire Upon the Altar: Sermons Preached to Harrow Boys, Second Series, 1887–1890* (London: Percival and Co., 1891), pp. 228–239.

James Welldon (1854–1937) was appointed master of Dulwich College in 1883. He had been educated at Eton and King's College, Cambridge. In the short time he held this position he did much for the college, including the creation of the school song, 'Pueri Alleynienses'. He resigned his post in July 1885 to take up the position of headmaster of Harrow School, which he held from 1885 to 1898. He was disliked by many of the masters as autocratic but held in high esteem by the boys. At Harrow he also accepted a number of clerical positions. He was honorary chaplain to Queen Victoria from 1888 to 1892, and Chaplain in Ordinary from 1892 to 1898. He was the Hulsean Lecturer at Cambridge in 1897. (These were lectures established by an endowment made by John Hulse, a clergyman.) In 1898, Welldon became a Doctor of Divinity. The documents included here demonstrate the promotion of Empire from the school chapel, and within the Harrow School culture such as the playing field, with the promotion of a cult of athleticism too. In addition we can see Welldon's connection to the Royal Colonial Institute, at which document 3 was delivered, on the topic of imperial education.

"Before Him shall be gathered all nations."
St. Matthew xxv. 32.

THE judgment of God, to which the Advent season points, is twofold. It is a judgment of individuals. "We must all appear," each for himself, "before the judgment seat of Christ;" each of us will stand then face to face with his Maker; each will see the revelation of his own heart's secrets; each will answer to the dreadful inquisition; each will receive the inexorable doom. But it is also, I think, a judgment of the nations. It shall visit the life which we lead not by ourselves but in community; it shall determine whether we as a nation, like other nations, have proved worthy or unworthy of the benedictions which God, Who rules the peoples of the world, has shed upon us. "Before Him," *i.e.* before Christ at His Advent, "shall be gathered all nations;" every one a grand total of individuals, but every one, too, an individual in itself.

There is a solemnizing as well as an ennobling power in this reflexion. It emphasizes the deep responsibility of the corporate national life. It enlarges and expands the sentiment of moral obligation, until we cease to think what we must do each by himself, and think what we may all do as members of a great society. For nobody, I think, can read the Bible, however cursorily, without appreciating the strength of its testimony to the facts of the national life. The Old Testament is the history of a nation – not of a chosen individual, but of a chosen people. The promise given to the patriarch Abraham assured him that in his seed should the nations of the earth be blessed. It was the appointed work of Moses and Aaron to emancipate and consolidate a nation. All through the Jewish history the individual lives of judges, psalmists, and prophets are merged in the full stream of nationality. In that eventful history it is, I say, not a person nor a succession of persons, but it is a people which is selected by God, distinguished from other peoples and consecrated to His service; and that people, after being richly privileged, after lapsing into sin, after spurning its opportunities of self-reform, after submitting to its sentence of condemnation, is a witness, though an unwilling witness, at this hour to the reality and the responsibility of the national life. Nor were sadder words ever spoken upon earth than those in which the Saviour Christ, on the eve of His Passion, pronounced with tears that the elect nation of God had forfeited its election. "And when He was come near, He beheld the city, and wept over it, saying, If thou hadst known, even thou, at least in this thy day, the things which belong unto thy peace! but now they are hid from thine eyes."

Is not England, too, a nation, an elect nation of God? Has she not a proud imperial duty and destiny? Are there not "things which belong unto her peace;" and is it possible that they may some day be "hid from her eyes"? Let us draw out these thoughts a little in detail.

Every nation has a life, a character, a conscience. It may be composed, as in England herself, of diverse elements; but it fuses them into a corporate whole. It is distinguished from all other nations by certain physical, social, and moral attributes. How different is one nation from another – the English from the French, the French from the German, the German from the Italian or the Spanish! How hard it is – does not the story of England and Ireland prove this? – for one nation, however approximate in position, to enter into complete sympathy with another! Yet, widely as the nations are separated, there is none which is incapable of arousing and sustaining the enthusiastic sentiment which is known as patriotism. Men do great deeds and bear great sufferings for their country. Is there one of us to-night who does not thrill at the inspiring thought of English nationality; one of us, man or boy,

> "With soul so dead,
> Who never to himself hath said,
> This is my own, my native land"?

Is there one who does not believe with immutable faith in the God-given mission of the English people; one who does not reflect with personal satisfaction upon that strange, chequered web of struggles, passions, hopes, ambitions, failures, victories, and reverses that make the ancient tale of English history; one who does not feel a glow within his soul at the strong, self-conscious language of the poet[1] –

> "This England never did, nor never shall,
> Lie at the proud foot of a conqueror.
> . . . .
> Come the three corners of the world in arms,
> And we shall shock them. Nought shall make us rue,
> If England to itself do rest but true"?

And why is this? Because a nation is a living thing; it is born and dies; it is susceptible of a common sorrow or joy, a common shame or glory. Have not these last days brought home to many hearts the consciousness of a national sentiment? Has it not been with a feeling of humiliation – of common national humiliation – that we have read of deeds done by countrymen of ours in the far dark land of Africa, where no eye looked on them but the one Omniscient Eye, which they forgot – deeds which have jeopardized the English character of humanity, which have shown that deep in the human heart lies still unredeemed such a savagery as would dishonour very savages, and which have demonstrated that nothing – nothing on earth save the fear of God – can be a guarantee of honour, of clemency, or of decency, when the force of public opinion is removed? And at such a time, when the national heart was saddened and ashamed, has it not been as with a glow of national pride that we have seen the gallant crew, officers and men, of an English war-ship,[2] at the sudden, awful call of doom, go down quietly, thinking not of themselves, obeying and obeyed, without disorder or dismay, into the grave of the unfathomable deep?

Such is the common sentiment of English nationality; such is the sentiment which makes the many one. But if it be so, then I ask you, What are the things which "belong unto" a nation's "peace"? What shall we try to do and to be as Englishmen, if we would serve and save our country?

Other nations, other powers, have had their day. They have been disciplined by suffering and purified by adversity; they have risen to the dignity of great vocations; then they have failed and declined, and are dead. Who can stand upon the Acropolis or the Capitol, who can call to mind the historical associations of which these hills have been the witnesses and the centres, and not ask himself if the fate of other nations – not less glorious in their day, or dignified, than England – will be the fate of the English nation as well?

Let me mention three characteristics, as they seem to me, of a permanent national life.

1. The first is a *national faith*.

"The fear of God," says Mr. Froude, in his latest book, the *Life of Lord Beaconsfield* – "the fear of God made England, and no great nation was ever made by any other fear." It is a true and profound saying. It does not mean that all the citizens of a community will embrace one theory of religion; that may be desirable, but experience proves it to be impossible. It does not mean that they will consent, even on rare and solemn occasions, to unite in common offices of worship. It does not mean, or it does not necessarily mean, that they will connect the body politic, by the method known as Establishment, with a Church or a plurality of Churches. But it does mean that the nation, not as individuals only, but as a body, will live in the faith and fear of God, will own and submit itself to His providence, will recognize the operation of His laws, will believe in its responsibility to His judgment, will prefer righteousness to expediency and justice to gain, and in its corporate actions, whenever it is called upon to pursue a common policy, will try, however imperfectly, to accomplish the purposes of His All-Holy Will.

2. The second element of a nation's weal may be said, I think, to be a *national morality*.

For a nation, like an individual, has a conscience. It has its sense of right and wrong. It may be stirred to a conception of duty. It may choose the path of virtue, or may refuse it. Nor is there any service which a statesman can render to his country so sublime as that of enlightening and energizing its conscience.

What is the history of all philanthropic movements issuing from a people's heart? Some one man, perhaps, wakes up to the sense of an evil which the world, until his day, has taken for granted; he is laughed at, then abused, called fanatical; his peace of mind is wrested from him; he stands alone; it may be that he, too, has his Calvary, like his Master. But at last the great heart of the nation is touched. It owns the wrong; it will consent to it no more. Then at last the battle is won. It was so in those awakenings of the national conscience which are known in history as the Puritan and Methodist Reformations. It was so in that awakening which issued under Clarkson and Wilberforce in the abolition of the Slave Trade. It is so now, or will soon be so, in the mighty causes of peace, of temperance, of purity. There is such a question which looms before the nation to-day. The demand that public men shall not offend the national conscience by private immorality is a new demand – it marks a positive advance of moral sentiment – but it is essentially a sound and valid demand. It is a protest for righteousness and virtue. It is a refusal to subordinate morals to politics. It is a witness that as civilization itself ultimately rests, and must rest, on the domestic life, so it is the interest, the supreme interest, not of one party only in the State, but of all parties, to sustain that life in the fulness of sanctity and honour.

3. But there remains the third and last element of the nation's life – *national duty*.

A nation must regard itself as having a mission. It must not live, any more than an individual, to itself. It must believe and must profess that it is summoned to a duty – a God-given duty. Is not this, too, a sense which belongs to us as Englishmen? Who can forget the stately words in which Milton expresses his faith in the privileged destiny of England: "When God is decreeing to begin some new and great period in His Church, even to the reforming of the Reformation itself, what does He then but reveal Himself to His servants, and, *as His manner is, first to His Englishmen?*"

There is a duty, then, which lies upon England. It is a high, a terrible duty. It is to set forth, before the eyes of men and nations, an example of elevated morality in life, in commerce, and in politics. It is to shed the rays of a pure and enlightened religion upon all dark regions of the earth. It is to exhibit the harmony of knowledge and faith, of progress and reverence, of science and conscience. It is to prove that above all qualities of art and learning, above the gifts and graces of life, stands the inalienable quality of character. It is to assert by example and precept that it is the duty, as of an individual so of a nation, to bow itself in its corporate capacity with deep and awful obedience before the throne of the Eternal God.

This is the mission, if I mistake it not, of England. It is for this that God has given us the richest heritage, the amplest empire, the language most widely spoken among men. May He grant us to be not unworthy of our prerogatives! May He fill us with the spirit of duty and sanctity! And at the last day, when "before Him shall be gathered all nations," may He reward us as a nation with His blessing!

Notes

1 Shakespeare.
2 HMS *Serpent*.

5

ETON AND THE EMPIRE

From: G. Drage, *Eton and the Empire: An Address* (Eton: Ingleton Drake, 1890).

Geoffrey Drage (1860–1955) was an English writer and Conservative politician who had an interest in the affairs of the poor and sat on London County Council. He had attended Eton and Christ Church College, Oxford. In this address, written in an age of high imperialism, Drage asserts and celebrates the benefits of British rule. He claims that British rule in India had prevented every kind of oppression, tyranny and wrong. He believed boys in the English schools should know more about the Empire. Drage had no time for the Manchester school of the 19th century which eschewed any further imperial acquisition and he notes the strong connection between Eton and senior positions in the British army and navy. Drage wrote and spoke on a range of imperial problems of the period, including: The Grievance of British Subjects in the Transvaal; The Real Causes of the War; Differences Between Liberal and Conservative Imperialism; the Colonial Conference of 1902; and the Imperial Conference of 1911.

Speaking in this place and to such an audience I need not trouble myself to enumerate the different divisions of the British Empire or the wars and individual acts of heroism which led to their acquisition. There is no part of that empire, vast though it be, on which some Eton boy has not left his mark for good, there is no part where some Eton boy has not cheerfully laid down his life for his country and his Queen, and the whole empire in its present extent is in large measure a monument to the courage, the patriotism, and the statesmanship of an Eton boy, William Pitt, the great Lord Chatham. But the task to which I shall address myself this evening is that of shewing to the present generation the mainsprings of the constitution under which the empire grew, and the part that schools like ours have played in the past and must play in the future, if that empire is not to be counted among the things that have ceased to be.

The English constitution, that is the whole body of law written and unwritten which regulates the central and local government of this country, assumes as inherent in the breast of the citizen three public virtues, which have till the present century been the guiding stars of the English nation. English institutions are founded on loyalty, piety and patriotism. The last two expressions speak for themselves, the first needs further definition. Loyalty is obedience where it is noble, that is where it involves self-denial! It is in fact self-denying obedience to superiors and to that which is in England supreme, the law of the land. It finds its expression in the local self-government for which England is famous, as English piety finds its expression in the national church, and English patriotism in the national militia, in the which every Englishman was and should be bound to serve. The history of English public law is the history of the development of the Church, the militia, and local self-government! On these three columns is raised the superstructure of parliament, in which those who lead in the Church, the militia, and local self-government, assist in ruling the state which they have first learnt to serve. Political rights are the result of political duties duly performed. The sovereign is supreme because the sovereign is at the same time the first servant of the state. In the eighteenth century political philosophers seeing how well England was governed attributed the fact to the parliament. They imagined parliament to be the creator instead of the creature of English political institutions. Hence in the nineteenth century parliaments have been introduced into almost all civilised countries, unfortunately without the solid basis to which they owe the whole of their value. The decline of parliamentary government in England has been very largely due to the decline of the institutions on the vitality of which it depends. The first step which the regenerators of England will take will not be to reform parliament, but to reform the national Church, the national militia and the national system of local self-government.

The natural tendency of the individual man is undoubtedly at all times to be selfish and to heap up money. In order to have more leisure for this object the tendency of the present age has been to pay others to perform those public duties which a man is bound by our English law to perform himself contrary to his private interests. But money payments cannot take the place of unpaid personal services in every department of local self-government, of unpaid personal services in every department of religious and charitable work, and above all of unpaid personal services in the defence of the country. These are the duties which the legislator has in the past and must in the future compel and by compulsion accustom those who have the privilege of being British citizens to perform. By the performance of these duties alone can the different classes of the state be brought to see that they have but one true interest, the conscientious administration and defence under the Queen and with God's help of the greatest empire that the world has ever seen.

I do not pause to ask what are the benefits that English rule has conferred upon mankind in the past. I do not lay stress upon the fact that it was England that broke the power of Spain under Queen Elizabeth and saved the world from a universal tyranny of body and soul, or on the fact that from that time to this her arm has always been raised in the cause of liberty, of justice and of truth. But I *do* point out to you that for the last century in the great continent of Africa, which we are gradually making our own, England is the only country which has never failed to turn an attentive ear to the cries of the down-trodden and oppressed, and for that purpose, she has poured out not only treasure but the blood of the noblest of her sons like water. I *do* lay stress upon the fact that it is our rule in India and our rule alone, which stands between countless millions and every kind of oppression, tyranny, and wrong. It has been my lot in many a foreign country to enter and examine schools and to find how well each scholar knew what parts of the English Empire should be torn from it by his own country, and to wonder with bitterness how many English boys would so much as know the names of the places mentioned. And it was my fortune in a Russian school, on asking what India was, to be told that it was a country oppressed by the British and that it is the mission of Holy Russia to liberate it. I want to know whether every boy in this school is aware that in the words of a famous living German statesman, "If we lose Shakespere and Milton and every other writer that has ever made our name illustrious throughout the world, the justice and ability with which we have administered India will be an imperishable memorial to our nation." If such is the opinion of a foreigner, what should be the opinion of an Englishman? Is there any sacrifice public or private so great, that it should not cheerfully be made in order not only to maintain but also to extend as far as possible the only empire known to history, of which the rulers may proudly say, "we have loved righteousness and hated iniquity, and we have striven to do justice to all men without respect of persons."

There has long been in this country a body of political philosophers called the Manchester school, on whose honesty I cast no doubt, who have held that it is the duty of this nation to decline any further burdens and responsibility; there has been and still is a growing party which makes light of the heroic virtues which have planted the Union Jack in every country and in every clime. We have much wealth laid up for many years, we are to be content to enjoy it, and give up the duties which that wealth imposes on us. Worst of all they have expressed a doubt whether love for the fatherland is a virtue, and whether we should not be ashamed instead of proud of our country, and this idea creeps slowly forward like the fatal horse of Troy.

> Illa subit mediæque minans illabitur urbi,
> O patria, O divum, domus Ilium atque inclyta bello
> Moenia Dardanidum.

It is then at such a time as this well worth considering what our history has been, what our country is; and I think that from such study no one of you will arise without a firm determination not to betray the glorious inheritance we have received from our ancestors. It was founded on self-respect, it was built up by self-denial, it has been crowned by self-sacrifice. But, says our philosopher of the Manchester school, self-denial is not the real principle of life, it is an enlightened selfishness, such as will lead England to cast off her colonies as a tree sheds her fruit when it is ripe. I tell you, NO! Selfishness is selfishness still, the greatest crime, the foulest blot on human or on national character. What is more I tell you that it is your duty at whatever cost to stand by your countrymen wherever they may be, so long as they are within their lawful rights. What is more you are to watch over them as a mother watches over her children, and not to allow anyone to come between you and them. What is more

I tell you your colonies *will* not be cast off. They have done their duty by you in the past. Witness the Soudan expedition! and will do so in the future whether you like it or not. You may have heard people talk of colonial disloyalty. Now it is my profound conviction, and I speak well weighing the words I use and after seeing nearly every person of any weight in the colonial world, that, should this country be in any difficulty, and should there be any men unwilling to come forward, by Heaven they had better learn how to mind the children for, if they don't come, the women will.

There remains the last great bolt that our philosopher has to hurl. All nations have decayed why should not ours? Athens and Sparta, Carthage and Rome, Florence and Pisa, are down. Their places know them no more. We have reached our zenith, we too must fall! Sir, I know full well that the time will come when this poor frame shall be laid to rest, "earth to earth, ashes to ashes, dust to dust." I know full well and it is my greatest sorrow that the time will come when sacred Troy shall fall and Priam and the folk of Priam with his good ashen spear.

ἔσσεται ἦμαρ ὅταν ποτ' ὀλώλη Ἴλιος ἵρη,
καὶ Πρίαμος καὶ λάος εὐμμελίου Πριάμοιο.

But with God's help it shall not be in my time, nor shall it be please God while one stone is left upon another in this ancient school of ours.

Here then I must speak of Eton, and for more reasons than one I feel that word; fail me. I see around me men whose names are household words wherever Eton is known; men, who while boys built up the reputation, which the school at this moment enjoys in the contemporary world, for athletics, for scholarship, for manly and chivalrous behaviour, in every word and deed, and who are now devoting the best years of their lives to bringing up another generation to follow in their footsteps. I ask myself who am I that I should speak of the school in the presence of those who have borne the burden and heat of the day, and I beg them to believe that it is with the deepest sense of my own unfitness that I stand here tonight in the faint hope that I may point out some principles underlying their practice, which may escape the notice of those in the midst of the fray, but which strike a student who has seen most of the systems of the world.

What then is Eton? I have often wondered that in this age of political philosophers no one has ever been struck by the fact that schoolboy life at a public school is as nearly as possible that under a model republic. Here as far as I know and as far as I may speak from my own experience, there is true liberty to those who can use it, true equality to those who deserve it, and true fraternity to those who are congenial. Neither birth nor wealth nor favour can raise one boy above another in the eyes of the school, but merit and merit alone at play or work. That is one thing of which you cannot be too jealous; the name and success of the school depends upon it. But what I have often been asked by foreign professors and foreign statesmen, what is the groundwork of your schoolboys self-respect, on which alone a schoolmaster or the best of school traditions can build. For I assure you that at this moment an Englishman who deserves the name, stalks abroad through Europe like a Spartan through the fields of Greece in her degenerate days, or like Achilles through the meadows of asphodel, and every one says "Great Heavens, why are not our boys like that?" Now I am afraid that compared to foreign boys the average Eton boy, of my time at any rate, could only be described as ignorant. What is it then that sets the ignorant above the learned and gives them a repose and a dignity, which all the knowledge contained in the Encyclopædia Britannica fails to do? I have often said that a boy goes to Eton knowing nothing, or next to nothing, according to foreign standards, but he takes with him an ideal of his mother and his sister, and you may crunch the soul out of the feeblest child among you before he will allow you to take the name of his mother or his sister in vain. Sir, that is a boy's religion; and a boy's religion no less than a man's is not what he says but what he does. The Palladium of this country, whatever cynics and philosophers may say to the contrary, is its respect for its womankind. It is never mentioned, for, as I have said, a man and above all an Englishman never speaks of what he believes and trusts. Mind, respect for women is the first and best criterion of a gentleman, and it is an almost certain mark of a brave man. At any rate I can only tell you as one who has knocked about a good deal in most parts of the globe that, if I am to be in a fix, give me behind me a man who has no woman's ruin on his conscience. For that is, as far as I have seen, the thing which most troubles a man, however brave, when he thinks the game is up and fear paints on his face the sickly yellow that old Homer rightly attributes to the panic-stricken.

It is just as though, while you are here at school, any one of you Sixth Form were to forget the responsibility which the traditions of this place lay on you with regard to the smaller boys or the weighty maxim of the poet Juvenal,

>   Maxima debetur puero reverentia.

or the still more awful threat of the most merciful lawgiver that the world has ever known. "It were better for him that a millstone were hanged about his neck and he cast into the sea than that he should offend one of these little ones." Such sins I tell you αἰσχύνην ὁμολογουμένην φέρουσι, such sins bear with them the most terrible punishment in this world and you can only pray that in the next world the Lord of all power and might will have mercy upon such offenders, for in this world man and their consciences will have none.

But of such things there is here no danger. What I do think we ran a risk of forgetting in my time was that life is not all one gigantic game and that schoolwork is something more than an unpleasant incident in the day's pleasure. I have no doubt, from the magnificent buildings and institutions that have been erected since my time, that this has all been altered, and probably I ought now to be standing up for games and leisure, in both of which I am a profound believer. At any rate there is one department out of school, in which I am inclined to think from what I have seen elsewhere we did not spend time enough, and that is school singing. Recollect that while the playing fields are the best training for the body, and the schoolroom for the mind, there remains the loftiest side of your nature, by which you grasp the pathetic and the sublime, and which can only be properly cultivated by the practise of music. Recollect also that no music is so elevating and inspiring as that which is used in the service of the Church. Such words I feel I am illqualified to speak. These facts have been urged on you before and will be urged on you again by others gifted with far greater eloquence and erudition than I can bring to bear on this noble theme. I know that it is part of our national reserve, and a very wholesome reserve it is, that such subjects should not be so much as mentioned by laymen, but I cannot help emphasizing with all the force in my power the fact that we should all of us in my time have been much better men, if we had taken more interest in the services in Chapel. At any rate I will speak for myself. Repetition and reiteration of the same sentences, however noble, make them tame, and it is not till many years after he has left school that a man discovers that except the Bible the grandest English prose is contained in the Book of Common Prayer. And now that I have mentioned the Bible I do not hesitate to say that I think there is a sheepish dislike among all schoolboys of reading the Bible. It seems to be mollycoddlish and soft. Now the Bible has strengthened and consoled far greater and nobler men of our race than you or I are likely to be, and we may be sure that to read it will not make us any less creditable to our school or country.

If I lay stress on these considerations, it is because they were the only things I can find fault with looking back at my time here. It behoves you, if these things are still so, now if ever to set them right. The eyes of all English-speaking not to mention foreign schools are turned upon you. Every new state wishes to have its Eton and Winchester and, if it may be, to improve on the models in the old country. It is your duty to maintain the school in her proud position as the first in the whole world.

Such in fact is my view of Eton as it is. If I am asked what Eton has been, I reply "Si monumentum requiris, circumspice." Chapel and Upper School alone will shew what your predecessors have done. Their works form the noble Liturgy that Eton has rendered to the state on earth, their words spoken or written form the Litany she offers to God in heaven. Equal them we cannot, but we can strive to see that we do not fall further behind them than we can help.

It is while you are here that you have the best chance of rivalling those that have gone before you by throwing yourselves heartily and unsparingly into every kind of game and work. But it is when you leave school and choose your career in after life that difficulties thicken, and I wish now to point out among the well-worn tracks some newer paths to which you may perhaps feel inclined to turn your steps, and do not forget that coming from this place you will be expected to prove capable of leading wherever you may go.

The army and navy have always been favourite professions here, and I will not enlarge on the charm and romance that attaches to them, but I will remind each one who thinks of them that, with his regiment and his ship, he acquires a new responsibility, a new dignity, and new traditions that he must maintain, and, further, that the enthusiasm, which he must carry from here, must be such as will render him proof against any of the slights that superiors and above all permanent officials have from time immemorial in this country thought it their business to lay upon young officers. In this there is nothing new, nor is there any new thing that I can say to you about the noble and self-denying profession – with which I am told my family has been connected for more than two centuries and of which I am immeasurably proud – the profession of medicine. Those, whose talents call them in that direction, I may remind that they bind themselves for life to a mistress, who allows no holiday, who has no gratitude, and who shews them the ignoblest, as well as the noblest, sides of human character. One reward indeed they have, that, when all is done, when they have earned their bread and educated their children, they can look back and say with certainty, "We have appreciably lessened the sum total of human misery," and this is more than a barrister can say with certainty of his profession, whatever charms the law may have for her votaries, among whom I reckon myself.

But the careers, to which I particularly call your attention, are those of education, engineering, and of trade. With regard to the first, I point out to you that it is your business to use every effort to place the masses, who now exercise the vote and control the destinies of the country, in a position to use that vote for the benefit of the whole empire. It is of the utmost importance that those, who bring up the younger generation of the lower orders, should be before all things gentlemen, and I use the term in the highest sense. What is wanted there, as elsewhere for the young, is not a cram knowledge of all the "osophies," the "ologies," and the "onomies," but a certain ἦθος as Aristotle calls it, a tone and a code of honour such as is obtained here, however faulty the schoolboy code may appear to the complete philosopher. They must above all be brought up to respect their parents, a virtue which is dying out, and to respect themselves and their womankind. These are things which cannot be lectured into any one. It is merely by coming into contact with manly persons, who act on such ideas, that children adopt them. Such a profession will take many of you from luxurious homes to spend your lives among the poorest of the poor in the haunts of misery and of vice. Reward on earth you will have none; your friends will look on you as Quixotic, your enemies, if you have any, as mad. But here, if anywhere, the ancient motto "noblesse oblige" applies, and I say to you that of all the ways in which you can render service to this country at this moment, the most certain, if the least striking, is that of the qualifying for and serving in the humble career of a master in a schoolboard school. And I may add that it is in respect of our popular education that we have most to learn from our cousins in America and our countrymen in the Colonies.

For the adventurous spirits, of whom there are no doubt many here, there are untold new worlds in the realms of travel and of science. Africa is still practically unexplored. Two or three expeditions have made their way across the great dark continent, and many a young Englishman has already lost his life in hunting tours, undertaken to gratifying his mere love of sport. If half the time and energy, which has in the last twenty years been applied by Eton men alone to sport, had been turned in the footsteps of Rajah Brook of Sarawak, this country would be able to reckon many an island in the eastern seas, and many a province in the southern continent, among the presents she has received from this school. Besides devoting your attention to bringing new countries under the Union Jack, there are great careers for the mining and civil engineer, in those which have already been subdued. It is not on conquest but on administration that we rest our right to rule. In this, as in trade, of which I would next speak to you, recollect that if you would be happy as well as successful men you must have some idea beyond that of your own purely selfish interests. Take to yourselves, you who engage in these professions, the idea of making some corner of the world more English, that is more thoroughly subject to the ideals by which we live, and you will find with that idea before you, perils and difficulties which seemed insurmountable, illnesses and the petty miseries of life which seem insupportable, will disappear from your path like the dew from off the grass before the sun.

I mentioned trade as a profession, and I cannot help calling your attention to the fact that there is no such atrocious snobbery as that of being ashamed of trade. Great heavens, this nation lives by trade, and yet I have just heard of a fifth-rate grandson of a third-rate Peer at one of the Universities, whose only claim to consideration is that his grandfather made money as a grocer or a huckster, persuaded his set to cut a man – an undergraduate – engaged in trade, whose shoes he was not fit to black. Pride of race is quite as contemptible as pride of wealth. The only criterion is that which holds in this school. What has the man done? What can he do? If it were only because trade follows the flag and the flag follows the trade, we should be proud of it. But trade, as trade, is in this country ennobled by the spirit of enterprise, of adventure, and of sport, just as the handicrafts are now again being illuminated by the spirit of art.

Those of you then, who will in time join the ranks of our merchant princes, must remember that you join a body with great traditions, and never forget that any transaction, of which you do not in your heart of hearts approve, casts a slur on the probity of your compeers in trade as well as on your own house. At this moment the name of English merchants is in the commercial world of Europe synonymous with princely dealings on a large scale. Try to heighten and not to blur that reputation.

There are two more callings to which I must now direct your attention. No! there are three. I had almost forgotten that of the diplomatist. For him I am sure as for the lawyer, of whom I made such slight mention, the most important consideration is to keep the lamp of truth burning brightly in his soul. Be sure that the old maxim that "An Ambassador is sent to lie abroad for the good of his country," does not hold good for an Englishman. Your word as Englishmen is worth a thousand times more to you than any petty temporary advantages deceit may seem to give you.

But of the two professions now left to you besides letters – and for me the pen includes the pencil – on which I shall not touch, because "Poeta nascitur non fit," I will take the least difficult first.

If the future of this country is not to be shrouded in the deepest gloom, there must be some among my hearers, on whom the mantle of Pitt and Fox will fall in earlier or in later years. But beware how you lightly commit yourselves to the career of a statesman. Above all, recollect that John Bull, with his material common sense demands that a statesman should have a stake in the country. It is idle to cite great names to him. "Those," he stolidly replies, "are exceptions, and who are you?" Poverty, as the Russian proverb says, is not a crime but it is twice as bad, and I say, let the poor man weigh well before he launch forth on a career, in which he can only become poorer. It may be that the day will come, when some of the nearest to him shall stand in need of money, the dross which he now despises to earn, and he in the bitterness of his heart shall wish to sell body and soul for their sakes and all in vain. I tell you that the bitterness of that moment is worse than the bitterness of death, and that the death of the best beloved relation in the world.

But this I only say in warning for I cannot convey to you with what anxiety, and yet with what confidence the eyes of all old Etonians are turned upon this school. From among you there must come forth some great ones to steer this country through the coming storms. In this great task all can help, to this all must turn their eyes, and if any word of mine written or spoken shall make any single one of you more manly, more honourable, more chivalrous, I feel that I shall not have lived in vain. But to that young soul among you who shall take up the great task of guiding the destinies of the old country or that of one of her children across the seas, when he emigrates, to him I say above all "BE SILENT." If you feel you can do somewhat, keep your own counsel even from your dearest friend.

I am no model for any boy among you, but perhaps my experience may be of use to you. Eleven years ago I left this school with the idea not of doing anything myself, but of amassing knowledge for the use of the most perfect character that has fallen across my path. Five years I toiled, travelling from time to time for the object I had in view, and then it fell to my lot to see the life, on which my hopes were staked, fade from before my eyes. Five years more I spent in silence, toiling and travelling, following out the plan I promised him, who alone knew of it, not to give up and raised to him a memorial which I believe is not unknown among you. I mention these facts because I know that nothing but silence would have carried me the little way I have gone, and if I have broken silence now, it is because from among you must come the man whom I have failed to find elsewhere. And when I say, "be silent" I do not mean that there is any question here of tragic airs, and an assumption of terrible purposes and tremendous aspirations after an unknown something. You must go through the world without sighs and gloomy faces, but recollect, if you have trouble, the Spanish proverb – "He who sings terrifies his woes." No! work harder, play harder, ride harder in the holidays, polish your intellect to the utmost of your abilities, elevate your character by noble thoughts, noble music, noble deeds. Don Quixote says with truth, "Every man is the son of his own works." You have in this place your whole future in your hands. Every lie, every mean act, every nasty book makes your character at every step more treacherous, more mean, more nasty. Every straightforward, every generous, every noble act makes such acts easier and more natural to you. There is nothing more terrible for a man than to find that in his character which he has made himself, lies the chief obstacle to the good he is anxious to do.

I am not here to talk politics, but I will point out to you, before I turn to my last great subject, that it is the duty of every one of you to take an active interest and an active part in the government of the country. I have no sympathy for the finnikin milksop spirit which is afraid to lose its refinement in the turmoil of politics. Believe me, if your refinement is worth anything, it will stand that test, and what is more it will refine others. A man, who is so exquisitely frail that he requires to stand apart from the vulgar herd on the pedestal we reserve for our womankind, is not only useless but he is a reproach to our sex. In every English speaking country you have the same duties as here, and in every English speaking country you will find two great parties. The one takes for its motto law, the other takes for its motto liberty. The former stands on guard to see that liberty does not degenerate into license, the latter that law should not harden into tyranny. Both sides have noble watchwords, both have noble traditions and a noble history. I do not attempt to influence your choice, but when that choice is made, which will be long after you have left this school, let your decision be final. Above all, which ever side you take at home or in the Colonies, try at all times to sympathise with the hopes and the fears and especially with all that is lofty in the ideals of other English speaking countries. Put away from you that John Bull spirit which induces us both as a nation and individually to tell the most unpleasant truths with the most tactless and brutal candour to our nearest and dearest relations. That brutality has its good side, a hatred of exhibiting feeling. I have often seen in distant places partings, which were destined to be permanent, between English families on the one hand and foreign families on the other. The foreign boy embraces his mamma frequently and weeps copiously. The English boy stands apart looking ineffably sulky, and says "Don't paw me." But he is aware, and his mother is aware, that he does not wish her to break down, for his own heart is breaking too, and there would be, what he most detests, a scene, and he knows that nothing but his truculent attitude will prevent it. On the other hand this brutality has its bad side. The unnecessary repulsion of the yearning for affection, which blood relationship must produce, is naturally returned with interest, and leads to the bitter feeling which our foes try to foment between ourselves and our American cousins. But they are in fact as proud of us as we are of them, and that is no light word. I tell you that there are among the rising generation over there thousands and thousands of chivalrous warm-hearted men and women who will eagerly grasp the right hand of fellowship, if you only hold it out to them. That you will do with most dignity when the storm which has so long threatened our country has broken.

I rejoice that before it breaks America has begun to build a fleet, for you know as well as I do that, if in the midst of that storm a hostile fleet should attack her shores, a large part of our fleet, which is already insufficient for the defence of ourselves and our colonies, would surely be detached at whatever cost to protect them. When that storm does break I need not say to you here "Strike home." If you fall, you know that Eton will send forth still better men to fill your places. Recollect –

> Stat sua cuique dies breve et irreparabile tempus
> Omnibus est vitae, sed famam extendere factis
> Hoc virtutis opus.

There remains but one calling more. It is the highest of all on earth, and one of which I am unable, as I am unqualified to speak, that is the calling of the Church. Not many months ago an eloquent person called upon me, and desired me to direct the attention of a colonial government, to a certain abuse not unconnected with religion. I answered that it would ill-become a young Englishman who was travelling to learn, to criticise colonial statesmen, and could do the country no good, and my friend replied with a burst of enthusiasm, that I ought to live "ad majorem Dei gloriam." Sir, I am, I deeply regret it, unable to take that higher standpoint, it is enough for me as I told my friend, to break my lance, if it may be, "ad majorem Angliæ gloriam," and to leave to higher natures, the highest human office. But I am here to night to point out to you the better path, and, if I told you to be silent, should you feel a vocation for the service of our country, how much more shall I tell you to be silent if you feel a vocation for the service of Him "Who maketh the clouds his chariots; Who walketh upon the wings of the wind." In these days of morbid sentiment, of morbid self-examination, of morbid confession, of morbid fears for one's miserable self you cannot be too careful to avoid gush, to maintain a manly reserve in this the highest sphere, and to keep the "mens sana in corpore sano." Here above all keep silence even from good words. Learn the evils mental, moral, and religious, from which your country suffers, and if there be among you, as I know there are, characters as noble, loyal, and chivalrous as that of Galahad, blameless in thought and word and deed, to them in this place, if anywhere, shall come at this the darkest hour of our national religion the call which came to Samuel, and with that call strength from on High and words like those, which were spoken by the Lord to Gideon in the day of woe. "Go in this thy might, for thou shalt deliver the land of Israel. Have not I sent thee."

Strive to be ready when the call shall come, to whatever duty, to whatever sacrifice, in whatever part of Her Majesty's dominions. For you shall leave father and mother and wife, and children for your Queen, your country or your faith. You shall conquer and rule others as you have learnt to conquer and rule yourselves. You shall go out unhesitatingly into the uttermost parts of the earth, and you shall return, however insignificant your errand may seem, with your shield or upon it.

You shall do your duty as Eton men. And may the God of our ancestors, in whom you and I believe, prosper the work of your hands. Go forth in His name and in the name of St. Mary, the patron saint of this College. Go forth and shew yourselves worthy of this high mission. So shall all English speaking men of after times join in our glorious anthem – "Floreat Etona." May Eton flourish – Aye, and she *shall* flourish!

6

'THE CORPS', IN *THE HARROVIAN*, 2ND JUNE 1900, PP. 46–47

Reproduced with kind permission of Harrow School Archives

This extract, taken from an issue of the Harrow School magazine of 1900, notes the increasing compulsion introduced by the headmaster for boys over 15 years old to enter the rifle corps in the context of the South African War, thus reinforcing the connection between the school and Empire. The Harrow Corps cadet force was connected to the wider movement that originated in 1859, and was an affiliate of the Middlesex Regiment. By the 1890s there were approximately 50 volunteer units in London alone. In the Corps, boys were taught military skills such as riding and fencing as well as gunmanship. One notable member of the Harrow rifle corps was Winston Churchill, who had entered the Corps in May 1888. Other public schools are noted as increasing the number of pupils in the rifle corps at the time of the South African War. The volunteer force had a membership of some 207,000 in 1900.

The corps

AT the beginning of the term the Head-master announced to the School his intention, which had been indeed no secret last term, of placing all boys in the School over the age of fifteen years in the Rifle Corps. Exceptions were to be made where absolutely necessary, but speaking generally, his desire was that every Harrovian should pass through the Corps. This plan was, he explained, to have come into effect this term, but there were difficulties which are not indeed unsurmountable, but cannot be got over in a hurry. It would be impossible to drill a corps of 400 or 500 on any existing ground; a proper parade ground – level and dry – would have to be prepared. The existing armoury would be altogether too small. Finally, since the great aim of the volunteer movement is to turn out men not only drilled and disciplined, but fairly trained shots, the present range is useless. Apart from its inaccessible position, it is so small that no more than fifteen or sixteen boys can shoot in the course of an afternoon. It would be impossible for the whole Corps to have more than one shoot each in the course of a term.

The difficulties, then, are local and financial, It is delightful to live on the apex of a hill, but practically inconvenient when flat ground is required; it is convenient to be near town, but a nuisance to have town so near us that land is almost prohibitive in price. The task of getting over the difficulties is not easy.

A parade ground no doubt might be made in the Northwick fields. That is some distance for those who are at the south end of the town. It would give a short time for the half-hour morning drill, if that is to be over by ten. The difficulty if serious might be met by making first school end at 8–30 instead of 8–45. Many schools think that an hour's work before breakfast is enough. Money would be wanted, but increased numbers in the School Corps will provide more money.

An armoury might be built; or it might be placed in the cloisters, if they were enclosed. But the Schoolyard is somewhat out of the way if the parade ground is to be in the Northwick fields. We suggest that when – an indefinite temporal clause – when the Governors build some more school-rooms, the old Music School, now used by Mr. Sankey as a form room, might be enlarged and converted into an armoury. Its position is convenient. Another scheme is to have no armoury. This is followed by some schools, the rifles being kept in each house hall, properly racked, and an attendant being sent round to clean them. There is something to be said for this plan. A row of well-kept rifles is an ornament.

These devices do not however offer any solution of the range question. To earn the Government efficient grant the Corps must shoot. And this on the present range is almost impossible; while to demand a new range seems to be crying for the moon.

Under these circumstances, the new scheme is necessarily hung up for a time. Perhaps the most satisfactory feature of the situation is the great increase in the number of our recruits this term; were the present rate to become the regular one, and were those once in the Corps to remain in it for the rest of their School career, there would be practically no need for any form of compulsion. The Corps would soon number over 400, which would be as large a percentage of the School as would be desirable. We see no reason why this result should not be attained; and it is certain that there is no way in which volunteering can so well be made popular in the country as by the Public Schools taking it up. And even if our present range does not permit us to turn all of our recruits into passable shots, yet there is much to be said for the discipline of drill, not necessarily of the most formal kind, but of the sort that makes men familiar with command, ready to obey, confident in their comrades by dint of an early training. Shooting is much; but it is not everything. It was not shooting that sent the Light division up the breach at Cuidad Rodrigo, for they went with unloaded muskets, trusting to their bayonets; it was courage, hardened by discipline. It's a far cry from a Peninsular veteran to a school boy volunteer, you say; yes, but it has not proved far from our own schoolrooms to Talana Hill, and Belmont, and the Boer trenches at Magersfontein.

While the new scheme was under consideration, it occurred to us that it would be interesting to find out something of what other schools were doing under the impulse of the same wave of military feeling which was stirring us. Accordingly some of the greater schools were asked whether there was any marked spontaneous increase in numbers and interest in their Cadet Corps, and whether there was any scheme of compulsion in existence, or in contemplation. We summarise the answers received.

At CHELTENHAM there is no very marked increase attributable to the war. The Corps has been steadily growing for the last three years. No definite scheme is in contemplation for increasing the numbers, nor is there any idea of making membership compulsory.

Much the same report comes from CLIFTON, which also has a corps whose numbers have steadily risen since 1894. No alterations are in view. The masters, however, shew an increased interest.

MARLBOROUGH on the contrary observe a marked increase, somewhere about 20 per cent., but the Marlborough Corps, with its present numbers is 180, somewhat under the average size of the larger public schools. No scheme of compulsion is contemplated, and it is noteworthy that there are no extra inducements. The Morris Tube range has been thrown open to the School, and those who are good enough are allowed to go to the Rifle Range whether members of the Corps or not. The Lower School has a course of Physical Drill on Army lines, quite apart from the Corps. The Captain of the Corps adds that in his opinion a scheme of compulsion to do two years' service in a volunteer corps between the age of 17 and 23, applying all through the country, would be a sound measure, and we may perhaps infer that he would approve of a compulsory scheme in the School.

ETON reports a very large and quite spontaneous increase, many boys of 18 coming in for their last school year. A hundred recruits above the average joined; the establishment has been raised from four companies to five. A number of masters have joined. No compulsion would be attempted unless in line with a large scheme applying to the Public Schools generally.

At RUGBY nearly all the members of the School inclined to things military were members before the war, so there is no perceptible increase in numbers, though there is a keener interest. The corps numbers 250 out of 570 boys. There is no scheme to increase the numbers whether compulsorily or otherwise.

WELLINGTON reports no increase in numbers or interest; and no scheme in contemplation to bring about an increase.

At WINCHESTER there has been some spontaneous movement towards the Cadet Corps, which was already sufficiently big, there has been a very marked growth (50 per cent.) in the numbers of enrolled men, and the whole establishment numbers 260. A scheme of compulsion for those over 15½ or 16, and no admittance for those under, would perhaps be looked on with favour.

From this we may gather that in the multitude of counsels there is wisdom – somewhere – but no remarkable unanimity of action. Meanwhile our own corps has been smitten with a severe blow from fortune. Gallantly, as we know, that Captain Searle and his officers are striving to do all that can be done, and loyally as the rank and file will aid them, the loss of Captain Johnson is very great. A catastrophe has been avoided. Our loss is temporary only. Captain Johnson is to return to us, when his service with his regiment to which he is recalled is over. This then is not the occasion to try to express the gratitude, which all who are interested in the corps feel towards him for his work, first as Adjutant, and afterwards as Captain in command. Yet none the less the momentary consternation at the thought that he might be in that most inappropriated phrase "going for good," serves to shew how valuable his work has been, and we may be glad that in the Head-master's phrase, "When the gates of the temple of Janus are closed, the gates of Harrow will still remain open."

7

'IN MEMORIAM: WILLIAM JOSEPH MYERS 1858–1899', IN *ETON COLLEGE CHRONICLE*, 20TH DECEMBER 1899, PP. 763–764.

This memoriam for William Joseph Myers featured on the pages of the Eton College magazine. Major William Joseph Myers of the 7th Battalion of the King's Rifle Corps was killed in action near Ladysmith on 30th October 1899. He was born in 1858 and was educated at Eton. He joined the 16th Foot in May 1878 and then transferred to the 60th Rifles in 1879 where he was promoted to the rank of captain. Moving to the King's Royal Rifle Corps, he became a major in 1899. An acting adjutant of the 4th Eton Volunteer Corps, Myers served in the Zulu campaign, in the Sudan and the Hazara (1888) and Miranzai (1891) expeditions, which were part of the North West Frontier Campaigns in India and Afghanistan. Myers fell in the first phase of the South African War.

Major W. J. Myers

MANY are the losses which we at Eton have already to deplore, both as individuals and as a community, from the war in South Africa; many a true son of Eton has shed his blood for his country, and Etonians are there in their hundreds, as is fitting, to do their utmost for England in her need. But the greatest loss that could have befallen Eton came upon us as a sudden blow in the first days of the war. Before the middle of this Half, at the beginning of which he had been in our midst, Major Myers had fallen at the battle of Farquhar's Farm, killed on the spot by a bullet through the head. Nothing could have brought home to us with more startling effect the stern reality of the war: the one soldier who was a familiar figure to every one here, and for whom very many had a warm regard and affection, was killed within three days of his reaching the front. His leaving us for the war had cost him a great effort: he was obviously and genuinely torn in two directions; but the impulse which led him to his death was too strong to be overcome even by his devotion to Eton. The letters which he wrote on board ship, and from Cape Town and Pietermaritzburg, are full of touching proofs of this devotion, and of his consideration for others: advice as to Field Days, arrangements in case his return should be delayed, are combined with such phrases as "Eton is never out of my thoughts," "There will be very many Etonians out here when the force is complete, and I am sure we shall all remember *Floreat Etona*." These last words were written from Pietermaritzburg on October 26, when he had already heard of the death of

Colonel Gunning and Captain Pechell, and other officers of the 1st Battalion of the King's Royal Rifle Corps, to which he had been attached: he was just on the point of starting for the front. In the absence of letters from Ladysmith, it is impossible here to give a detailed account of the action at Farquhar's Farm on October 30 in which he fell; but it seems that his Battalion was in the thickest of the fighting on the right front, and that there, as elsewhere in the early battles of the war, our officers were singled out by the deadly aim of the Boer marksmen. We are told that when he fell, two brother officers, Lieut. Marsden, and Lieut. H. C. Johnson, formerly at Mr. Mozley's, bent over him to see if they could give any help; while they were doing so, Johnson was hit in the shoulder by a bullet. Marsden bound up Johnson's wound for him, and immediately after was shot through the head. So there lay these two gallant officers of the 60th, in death not divided. We cannot but believe that it was the death of all others that he would have chosen.

The E. C. R. V. Adjutancy

When Major Godsal retired, after seventeen years' loyal service as Adjutant of the E.C.R.V., it was obviously not easy for any successor to take up the work which had been so ably and energetically done by him. Major Myers, on joining us in February, 1898, at once stepped easily and naturally into the ways of the place, making friends of old and young without an effort, doing his duty brightly, and in harmony with the best traditions of Eton. It seemed to all his friends that he had found work which exactly suited him, and he and they looked forward to many happy years spent in teaching the rudiments of soldiering to Eton boys. Those who were in Camp at Aldershot in the Summer of 1898 will always retain a vivid memory of him. The life of Camp, as those know who have tried it, enables firm friendships to be struck up in a few hours, and many were those who came away from that Camp with the feeling that they had found a friend who took interest in them as individuals, who would remember them and their peculiarities and tastes, which he had taken trouble to discover, and would not let them drop, but keep up the friendship. Whether as old Etonians or as members of the School, they were sure of a hearty welcome, and of ready sympathy from him: and how much this meant to them they hardly knew, till they suddenly realised, with intense grief, that they were to see him no more in this life.

Memoir

WILLIAM JOSEPH MYERS was born on August 4, 1858, in London, near Primrose Hill; but his parents, soon after his birth, succeeded to the family property in Hertfordshire, and it is there that his boyhood was spent. After being at a private school at Brighton, and also one at Great Malvern, he came to Eton in 1871, and spent four happy years there as a member of the Rev. C. Wolley-Dod's house, the present Lower Master being his Tutor. On leaving in 1875, he went to a coach at Ehrenbreitstein on the Rhine. After a short preparation he passed into Sandhurst, and in due course obtained his commission in the King's Royal Rifle Corps, in which he served for 16 years, leaving it with the rank of Captain in 1894, and joining the Herts Militia in 1897. He served in the Zulu Campaign of 1879, and as A. D. C. in the Sudan in 1885–86. He also took part in the Miranzai, Hazara, and Isazai expeditions of 1891–92. Besides his profession, in which he took a keen and active part, two great interests absorbed his life. He was an ideally devoted son to his mother, left a widow: and it has been said by those who knew him best, that after his mother's death, Eton seemed in some sort to supply her place in his heart, and to that *Alma Mater* he came, prepared to lavish something of the same personal devotion and service as had made him the best of sons to his mother.

His other great interest was in the collection of antiquities. From his boyhood he had developed strong musical and artistic tastes, and the means and opportunities for indulging and cultivating them occurred to him during the early years of his military service. As a collector of antiquities, he turned his attention to whatever was beautiful and artistic or of historical interest in whatever part of the globe he chanced to find himself, and he thus allowed himself a wide scope within which to gratify this particular passion. As a schoolboy he turned his attention to stamps, and he continued to interest himself in, and to add to this collection, up to the last. When serving in S. Africa at the time of the Zulu War he made a considerable collection of Zulu arms, implements, and trophies of all descriptions, and from this time dates the commencement of his career as a serious collector. The most precious trophy that he brought back with him from S. Africa at that time was the pen which signed the treaty of Ulundi, at which occurrence he was present. In 1882, he was ordered to Egypt, and there he found himself in the centre of all that was most attractive to his nature, and during the five years that he spent there, he devoted all his energies to Egyptian research, and succeeded in forming the nucleus of his magnificent collection of antiquities. He has since several times visited Egypt in a private capacity, and on each occasion his collection has gained considerable additions. While in Egypt he turned his attention among other things to old velvets, brocades, embroideries, and carpets, of Asia Minor and Persian origin, of which he amassed large quantities.

In 1889 his military duties took him to Gibraltar, and the following year to India, where he continued to collect steadily.

When on leave most of his time was spent in travelling: and wherever his footsteps led him, he managed to acquire tangible evidence of his wanderings in the shape of antique and artistic additions to his collection. Latterly he interested himself much in old prints and furniture, of which he made a considerable collection. His military duties, combined with his passion for travel, led him into many parts of the world. He went as a soldier to South Africa, Egypt, India, Gibraltar, and Cyprus. Egypt he explored extensively. He travelled over, more or less, the whole of India, far into Kashmir and Thibet, into Burmah, through Persia, Turkey, Asia Minor, and Central Asia; and on one occasion he spent his leave in visiting the West Indies and Panama, and rode across the Andes, unearthing, even there, old embroideries, &c., at the churches and monasteries that he visited on his road. In Europe he travelled a great deal, Italy, Spain, and Russia being countries which interested him much: while his passion for music led him often to Germany and other parts of the Continent. A musical festival, a notable operatic production, or any ceremony of special interest, he would travel long distances to attend; he was more than once present at the Passion Play at Oberammergau. Wherever, in fact, there was good music to be listened to, or any thing artistic or interesting to be seen, thither he would direct his steps, if it were in any way possible for him to do so. His artistic tastes were reflected throughout his life in his every word and action.

His entire collection is bequeathed to his old School, where, with the countless books that he lavished on the Library, the windows in the Lower Chapel, and the beautiful Drill Hall, we may well say of him *Si monumentum quæris, circumspice.* To say more of his truly boundless generosity to his School would, we know, offend that taste and delicacy which made him the least ostentatious of givers.

Memorial service

A singularly impressive Memorial Service in connection with the death of Major Myers was held on Tuesday, the 7th November, in the Upper Chapel. The Corps paraded at 1 p.m. and marched to Chapel through School Yard. Full dress was worn, the officers having a band of crape on the left arm. As they went, the band played *The Last Stand.* Almost the entire Corps attended, and there were few seats vacant in Chapel. While the congregation were taking their places Dr. Lloyd played *Beethoven's Funeral March on the Death of a Hero,* after which the Volunteers entered, and lined the central aisle from end to end in a double row. Helmets were removed on entering the building. The friends and relations of Major Myers, among whom were Miss Myers, Mrs. Vandeleur, Mr. and Mrs. Robert Taylor, Mrs. Dudley Myers, Mr. W. H. Myers, M.P., Rev. Charles Myers, Colonel Bruce Fellows, C.B., Mr. Wedderburn, Q. C., Rev. Herbert O. F. Whittingstall, had been previously conducted to their places, and Dr. Lloyd played a part of *Schubert's Marche Solennelle,* while the procession was entering. The Burial Sentences were then sung to *Croft's* music, and the Psalm (xxxix) to a double chant in F Sharp *minor* by *Sir J. Barnby.*

The Provost then read the lesson, and *Spohr's* anthem, '*Blest are the departed,*' was sung. The rest of the service, omitting the prayer of Committal, was read by the Head Master, and before the conclusion, the hymn '*O God, our help in ages past,*' was sung by the entire congregation with very solemn effect.

The *Dead March in Saul* was then played, the congregation standing. While the Volunteers marched out *Rachmaninoff's Prelude* in C Sharp *minor* was given, and finally, as the congregation dispersed, the *Marche Funébre et Chant Séraphique* by *Guilmant.*

Memorial to Major Myers

Two meetings of Officers and Non-Commissioned Officers were held in the Drill Hall to discuss the question of a Memorial. The proposal which seemed to commend itself to the majority was the placing of a window in Lower Chapel, as Major Myers had, himself, given two windows, and was known to be most anxious that the whole set should be completed.

The senior Volunteer in each House was directed to consult with the rank and file, and to invite promises of subscriptions: in a very short time the boys in the Corps promised some £180, and as in the meantime it became known that Major Myers, in his will, had left to the Head Master a sum of money for the completion of two more windows, the second meeting decided almost unanimously to devote the subscriptions to a work which was so obviously near his heart.

The sum required for the window will be about £270; and it was also decided to put up a Memorial Tablet in the Drill Hall, and to send any surplus that there might be to the Riflemen's Aid Society, for the benefit of the King's Royal Rifle Corps and the Rifle Brigade. The Officers and the Permanent Staff have promised about £90.

Any Old Etonians who served under Major Myers, and would like to join in, are hereby invited to send contributions to the Commanding Officer.

Major Myers' brother and sisters have most kindly and generously offered to present each member of the E.C.R.V. with a portrait, reproduced by Photogravure. Those members who are leaving are requested to leave their addresses at the Orderly Room.

8

MILITARY TRAINING

By the Rev. J. P. Way, D.D.

From: Rev. J. P. Way, 'Military Training', in *The Public Schools From Within: A Collection of Essays on Public School Education, Written Chiefly by School Masters* (London: Sampson, Low, Marston & Company, 1906), pp. 208–217.

Dr. John Pearce Way was headmaster of Rossall School, 1896–1908. The school was founded in 1844 by Rev. St Vincent Beechey, as a sister school to Marlborough College, for the sons of clergymen and others. It was listed in the top 30 public schools in the later 19th century. This chapter, taken from a collection published in the Edwardian era, observes the militaristic culture that was part of the public school ethos. Approximately 100 old boys served in the South African War, with 17 dying in active service. In the First World War, 297 old boys lost their lives. In the document, Way showed reasons why a militaristic culture was necessary – amongst which were to eliminate hooliganism, to instill self-discipline, promote a healthy body and protect the Empire. Way stressed the defensive nature of military training. Militaristic culture became a feature of both elite and non-elite schools of the period and was also a feature of the youth movements of the later Victorian and the Edwardian years. Way also notes that compulsory military training introduced in Germany had also improved industrial efficiency.

ENGLAND loves peace, and rightly. Yet to love peace overmuch is to provoke war. The humorous press delights to represent John Bull in its cartoons as a rotund and comfortable personality, evidently quite unfit to run a race or wrestle for his life. He wears old-fashioned dress, he fingers a well-filled purse, and looks altogether a tempting prize for any highwayman. The picture is all too true. A true joke is no joke. It represents a really serious state of affairs, when one remembers that the "law of the jungle" still holds sway, despite our boasted civilisation. If England wishes to maintain her own, she needs to grapple more vigorously with the problem of defence. She needs to train every citizen to be ready to take his share in the defence of his country against a real danger, the greatest she has ever had to face.

A military training on a far larger scale than she has ever before attempted is absolutely needed. It is a matter of life and death. We are apt to think our shores impregnable. This is not so certain as once we imagined. Vessels go thirty miles an hour nowadays. Our rivals at any rate have thought the invasion of England a matter worth serious discussion; *academically*, of course, at present. But, even if the coast of England can be kept inviolate, and our fleet can maintain the command of the sea, and our food supply be assured, the size of the British Empire provides many vulnerable points. Our Empire is continental as well as insular. Lord Roberts in his impressive speech before the London Chamber of Commerce, in August, 1905, has made quite clear the terrible risk we run. Even international rivalry in trade is itself a great danger. Very soon, with the growth of population, it may become a struggle for the necessaries of life. It is quite evident that the Empire needs the personal service of its own sons. It is a matter of vital importance that some universal system of military training should be established in England. If not compulsory, it must at least be comprehensive.

To some this seems a terrible thing. Yet military training in itself is a good thing. Experience has shewn that it is a blessing and not a curse, especially to that portion of the community which would otherwise grow up untrained and undisciplined. There is plenty of testimony as to this. Organisations, such as the Church Lads' Brigade, have deliberately selected military training as a missionary agent, and found it of immense value. The public conscience has been concerned of late with the supposed signs of physical degeneration. Military training is one of the best remedies. Those who have seen its effect know well how astonishing an improvement in the physique of ill-grown and weedy boys is the result of only two or three months physical training. If Englishmen are to hold their own in the competition of the nations, a healthy body is the first requisite.

Again, there is the "hooliganism," which has caused grave concern. Those who have tried to devise a specific to cope with this disease have found the military system invaluable. In a very short time it gives habits of discipline, cleanliness, and self-respect. It is ten thousand times better than imprisonment or the cat o' nine tails.

Even when it comes to practising a craft, the military training has shewn its value. Sir Joseph Whitworth once said that the labour of a man who had gone through a course of military training was worth 1/6 a week more than that of the untrained man. The training gives promptitude, attention, and capacity for joining in combined action. The great manufacturers on the continent, such as Krupp, have borne the same testimony. Here, the conscription, which we dread above all things, has done much for the continental nations by improving physique and instilling habits of punctuality, readiness to take trouble, and respect for authority. It has even been utilized to provide a spur for the idleness of boyhood.

If conscription has all these advantages, how much greater advantages will there be in a voluntary system which shall be equally thorough and equally comprehensive! A sense of individual responsibility will grow, a spirit of self-sacrifice be fostered. The voluntary submission to a sound military training, as a duty, for the good of one's country, and the defence of those near and dear, may indeed be said to lay a sound foundation for the finest type of Christian manliness.

It is difficult to say when an organised system of volunteer service for National Defence was first adopted in this country. As early as the time of Henry VIII. a charter was granted to the Volunteer Corps, which is now known as the Honourable Artillery Company of London. John Milton's name was once upon its roll. Our modern system owes its origin to the warlike attitude of France under Napoleon III. The application of steam to ships of war had made invasion easier than it was before. Then came the Orsini Plot. A supposed accomplice was tried in the English Courts and acquitted. There followed such a manifestation of feeling in France that it was thought high time for England to look to her defences. On May 9th, 1859, the "Times" newspaper published some stirring verses by the poet Tennyson, beginning: –

There is a sound of thunder afar,
Storm in the South that darkens the day!

with the refrain at the end of each verse: –

Riflemen, Riflemen, Riflemen, form!

Three days afterwards General Peel, Secretary of War, issued a circular letter to the Lords Lieutenant of the Counties authorising the formation of Volunteer Corps. In a few months a force of over one hundred thousand volunteers was raised.

Along with this a similar movement began in the schools. It so happened that Rossall School was the first to enrol a corps. Her School Corps was enrolled on February 1st, 1860, and two Cadet Companies established in connection with it, during the Headmastership of the Rev. W. A. Osborne. The first Captain was the late Mr. Hector Croad, formerly Clerk to the London School Board. To him the establishment of the Corps was mainly due. It is said that the Government of the day was at first disinclined to put rifles into the hands of school boys. The Duke of Devonshire (then Marquis of Hartington) showed more foresight. He persuaded them that the rifle in the hands of school boys would be more dangerous to the enemy than to the boy. As a matter of fact many of the soldiers of the great Napoleon were only fifteen years old when they began their service; and, in later years, the excellence of the shooting at Wimbledon, Bisley and elsewhere has proved over and over again that it is quite easy to make a school boy into a good shot.

The Rossall Corps was enrolled under the name of the 65th Lancashire, and was attached to the battalion under the command of the Marquis of Hartington. The boys had to cross the waters of Morecambe Bay two or three times a term to drill with their battalion, and might almost be described as a species of Marine Light Infantry.

If in this honourable rivalry Rossall had the good fortune to be first to enrol a corps, Eton, Harrow, Marlborough, and Winchester all raised corps much about the same time – certainly in the same year. These five schools, then, may be said to have led the way in a movement which now, under the auspices of the Earl of Meath and our great soldier patriot, Earl Roberts, seems likely to provide England with a practicable solution of the compulsory service difficulty. Though every other nation adopts the system except ourselves and the United States, conscription is a name of ill savour to an Englishman. To us the idea of compulsion in such a matter is unbearable. Yet compulsion by our own elected Parliament is far better than the compulsion of a victorious enemy; and it cannot be denied that to remain unarmed is to invite attack.

In England things move slowly – too slowly in the face of danger. Yet, if the nation hangs back, the schools seem to be going on. So far, the military training in the schools has been mainly confined to those schools which maintain a corps and, in these schools, to those who are energetic and patriotic enough to join the corps. Now, however, a new departure has taken place. At Bradfield and Rossall, and possibly other schools, the elements of military drill have been taught for some years past to the rest of the school, the civilians outside the corps. The custom is spreading, and under the influence of the recent appeal made by Lord Roberts, some twenty or thirty schools now drill all their boys. Some schools are more fortunate than others. Some, for instance, have as many as three ex-army sergeants permanently retained – the School Sergeant, the Sergeant in charge of the Gymnasium or Baths, and a third, the Sergeant of the Cadet Corps. With these it is possible to give the civilian contingent a drilling which is quite first rate. The employment of Army Sergeants in various capacities about a school is to be recommended on a great many grounds. They are the pick of the army, and could easily replace some of the civilians already employed. As for the drilling, it certainly does the boys much good. It gives them an upright carriage, expands the chest, removes the slouch, and trains them to be attentive to the word of command and quick in obeying it. The drill is not found to interfere either with school work or with school games. Half-an-hour's drill twice a week throughout the year is found to be quite sufficient to teach a squad the elements. An elaborate system of drill is not deemed necessary. If more is required, more time can be given, still without interfering with work or games. This may, however, be more difficult at day schools, where work does not begin till 9 a.m., and boys have to spend time travelling to and fro between school and home. Still, it is hoped it will not be long before a military training will be a recognised part of all school training. There will then be less need of conscription. Every boy in the elementary schools, and also in the secondary schools, including the larger public schools, will have received a military training which is both physically and morally beneficial. Thus will be provided, against the hour of need, a great citizen army, an army destined for defence not for aggression. It will embrace nearly all the manhood of England.

More, however, is needed than drill. We have to be practical. Drill is little good without shooting. Good shooting, even without drill, was found all too effective in the Boer War. Though it is a great thing that universal drill has become the custom in so many schools, it is infinitely more important that some practice in shooting should be made part of the routine of every school. This is already the case at Uppingham, Harrow, Rossall, Glenalmond, Repton, and Dover. It is no new idea. History tells of a time when the practice of archery was encouraged by Act of Parliament even in the schools, as the Shooting Fields at Eton and the Butts at Harrow bear witness. Neglect, be it noted, was punishable by a fine.

It is greatly to be desired that more schools would encourage rifle practice. There have been difficulties in the way. It has been wished, for instance, to preserve the shooting as one of the privileges of the Cadet Corps. Then there has been the cost of the ammunition, the difficulty of finding a range close at hand, or of providing enough butts on the range to render it possible to pass, perhaps, several hundred boys through their shooting course in the limited time available. It has, however, been discovered that practice with a miniature rifle at a miniature target with miniature bullets at thirty yards range is almost as good a training for a boy as the practice with the full sized rifle. These small rifles are of two classes – air rifles and powder rifles. Where the miniature air rifle is used, the cost of the rifle, and of the ammunition, and the labour required for cleaning, are reduced to a minimum. The rifles in which powder is used require more cleaning, and the ammunition costs more. It is a great advantage that the miniature rifle is only useful at short range. Little space is needed. The element of danger is all but eliminated. It is possible to put several ranges side by side, with a partition between each if necessary. If the civilians use the miniature rifle, the use of the full-sized rifle can be retained as the privilege of the Cadet Corps.

Some day, perhaps, the Board of Education will require all this as an essential part of every English boy's physical education. The Government will then, it is hoped, find rifles and ammunition; and, above all, will use their great powers to compel the provision of ranges. This is of vital importance. Meanwhile, the Volunteer Cadet Corps are invaluable to the nation. Everything should be done to encourage them. Privileges may well be reserved for those whose patriotism is willing to take so much trouble and incur so much expense. At all schools they alone are given the right to wear the King's uniform. They alone have the privilege of attending field days. These are generally held in some attractive piece of country, and provide the corps with an outing, which is a useful experience, and certainly a very enjoyable holiday. In some schools, as at Rossall, the members of the corps have also the privilege of the use of the baths as a drill hall in winter time. The water is turned off, and the bath boarded over with a stout platform supported by trestles. Here the winter hours are enlivened by spirited competitions between the various houses in physical drill and squad drill. It is an interesting sight to see the boy sergeants of the houses, each in their turn, march and countermarch their squads backwards and forwards across the drill hall at the word of command, unravelling difficult situations, and managing the whole squad as if it were a single individual. The use of the rifle range is also confined to the corps. Few schools are fortunate enough to have a private range. There must be a good many districts throughout the length and breadth of England where the provision of more ranges would greatly help the movement.

But if good shooting is the most important element in our defensive organisation, good scouting is also equally important, especially in a nation which has to make the most of the small army at its command. In old days the "thin red line" showed itself a match for serried masses containing many times its numbers. Good scouting and great skill in the art of taking cover can still multiply indefinitely the fighting power of our small army. Why should not scouting be practised more than it is at the public schools, and also the art of signalling? General Baden-Powell's little book gives many interesting hints. A scouting match might be made much more amusing than a paper chase, and become an intellectual exercise as good as a game at chess. Many schools have close at hand great commons, or woods, or moors, where scouting could be developed into a healthy sport, every whit as fascinating as even the much-loved cricket. It would exercise the brains as well as the bodies. If every English youth, in the course of his school training, were made a first-rate scout as well as a dead shot, he would be the better for it, and we should hear little talk of invading England. Peace would be assured, always provided it were known that there was a full supply of rifles and ammunition for our citizen defenders, and all the other supplies which the experts know are so sorely needed.

Some have thought that, if a whole school receives military training, difficulties may possibly arise between the civilian headmaster and the militant member of his staff who commands the school in the field. There should not be more danger of this than in any well-regulated state. Apart from the loyalty and good feeling which may be looked for in the English public schoolmaster, it should be remembered that the headmaster himself appoints the captain of the school rifle corps. The War Office have always taken care to show that they fully recognise the importance of preserving the headmaster's position as head of the school.

A point of really great importance is the higher training of the officers. Here is the greatest need and the greatest difficulty. A battle line nowadays has to be "far flung." Highly trained intelligence is needed more than ever. Special training must be provided for those who are to be officers. At school boys can have a certain amount of practice as officers, either with or without a commission. They can also be trained in the subjects of instruction prescribed for the Army Examination. A thorough general education has been given them. The rest presumably must be a matter of special training after the school days are over.

It would be a great help to the public school movement if more open encouragement were given by the military authorities; and if more opportunities for combined field days were arranged. Much is already done for the schools in the south, but little for the schools in the north.

It will be clear, it is hoped, that the necessity of military training on a universal scale is only urged in view of the many dangers which are acknowledged by all. It is not aggression, but defence which we desire. A war of aggression is nothing better than robbery and murder on a gigantic scale. The defence of hearth and home, the defence of freedom, the safeguarding of the supply of the necessaries of life are all part of our inalienable right as a nation. By proper precautions we may stave off the horrors of war; and military training, so far from disturbing the peace, may preserve it, till at last we ring in "the thousand years of peace," and "the thousand wars of old" are gone, never to return.

9

'WITH THE SCOTTISH YEOMANRY IN MAY'

The Lorettonian, 27th October 1900, p. 1. Reproduced with kind permission of Loretto School Archive

This document is the first page of the Loretto School magazine, The Lorettonian. *It reports the activities of the Scottish Yeomanry in the South African War. Loretto School was founded in 1827, in Musselburgh, East Lothian, Scotland. The headmaster of the school between 1862 and 1903 was Dr Hely Hutchinson Almond (1832–1903), who, as John Mangan has noted, was a supporter of English elitist education and the belief in Anglo-Saxon imperial burden, as well as a keen advocate of sport and the Empire. To be ready to govern the Empire, the schoolboy needed to be imbued with the Sparto-Christian ideal. Indeed, the school became a leading 'nursery' for rugby players and Almond was a significant figure in the founding of the Scottish Football Union in 1873. A connection was forged here between athleticism and Empire. Former pupils of the school trained as missionaries, soldiers, teachers and administrators in the Empire. The extract here is news of the Scottish Yeomanry engaged in operations in the South African War. The Scottish Horse was raised by the Marquess of Tullibardine on the request of Lord Kitchener and saw action in Western Transvaal.*

With the Scottish Yeomanry in May

GREAT was our state of excitement on Monday, May 7, when "Regimental Orders" for the day included the statement that we were to proceed without delay up country, for we were then at Worcester, only 100 miles from Cape Town. Each Company required a separate train, for we had now our full complement of horses. The horses were closely packed in trucks, most of which were covered. We ourselves were put in seven to a compartment. As luck would have it we were fortunate enough to comandeer three seat cushions from a first-class carriage of a passenger train that happened to pass through the station. I must say a good word for the Cape Government Railway. Though we were seven to a third-class compartment yet we all managed to get a full stretch at night: the backs of each seat could be raised, and also near the ceiling above each seat there was a berth. The seventh man slept on the floor on one of the cushions. At De Aar the stationmaster had received orders to arrest the culprit who had commandeered the cushions, and after this we only managed to reserve one of them for the man on the floor.

We arrived at Kimberley on the second night after leaving Worcester. Just before reaching our destination we had passed through that most interesting country between Gras Pan and Magersfontein – a flat country with lines of kopjes here and there, and plenty of broken-down fences. Next morning we unloaded stores and horses, leading the latter to Newton Camp. Next morning we had to load up all our stores again. What labour might have been saved had we only been allowed to proceed straight up, but such is army regulation, commonly known as red tape. Still our stay in Kimberley was interesting, for it enabled us to see some of the siege fortifications. We were pointed out the fort from which Long Cecil belched and thundered. The town itself bore few traces of the siege. One of the striking features of the place were the donkey-waggons, waggons led by 14, 16, 18, and even as many as 28 donkeys.

Our journey to Warrenton was in open trucks, enjoyable but for the dust and sand. Next day, Sunday, May 13, we had a bathing parade in the Vaal, which we left even dirtier than we found it. Report said that Boers had been buried in the river, but we never came across any. On Monday the Regiment, with the exception of about 80 of us whose horses were sick, moved across the river to Fourteen Streams, in order to make an early start on Tuesday with General Hunter. We were getting pretty sick of idling here; for all we had to do was to ride the horses down to water at the Vaal, 1½ miles off, three times a day, till one of our party suggested that he should buy a gee and rejoin his squadron. In answer to this he was informed that in all probability the camp would be attacked that night. Our excitement was still more raised when we saw the armoured train patrolling the station. Moreover to us was entrusted the guardianship of "Bobs," the well-known 9·3 inch gun. About 9 P.M. one of our picquets returned in a great state of perturbation and alarm. He had seen a lion. The sergeant of the guard thereupon sallied out with him, and gradually approaching the beast of terror, they saw it was a donkey grazing. Perhaps it was the same fear of lion which kept the Boers away, for they never came though we were quite ready for them for several days.

Meanwhile General Hunter's column headed by the Scottish Yeomanry, had entered Christiana unopposed. This was the first Transvaal town that fell into British hands, the march to it being made to ward off a probable attack on the Mafeking relief column.

On Sunday, May 20, about 30 of us were told off to proceed to Kimberley for remounts. We travelled down in an armoured train which patrols the line. This train had been in action at the Modder River, but had never suffered severely. The plates of iron were ⅝ of an inch thick. The truck which we were in had a Maxim at one end, and a certain number of men have this truck as their temporary home. On Monday, Kimberley celebrated the relief of Mafeking, the whole town being ablaze with red, white, and blue, and khaki. Next day we got our 100 remounts, which we entrained in 15 minutes. On the following morning we got out at Taungs, but found that the Yeomanry had gone on to Vryburg. Close to the station was a large native village, consisting of round mud huts with thatched conical roofs. The native chief, Malada, was on view at the station. He has at his beck and call 20,000 natives. He seemed a fine old man, but looked rather comical in buff breeches and leggings, an overcoat with very broad yellow facings, like a clergyman's stole, and an ordinary cloth tweed cap on his head. After a day's delay in waiting for our saddles, we proceeded with our remounts but only got 10 miles before dusk. The country we passed through was well studded with large fields of mealies. There were ant-hills in this region of a kind that resembled sticks planted in the ground. They have a hollow chimney down the centre. The common kind found everywhere in South Africa look like large round red sandstone boulders, and are almost as hard, making excellent cover for the Tommy. On dismounting, we formed our horses into rings, heads inwards. We would have been off by 3 A.M. the next day, except for the fact that one man spent an hour looking for his rifle and bridle. We started at 4 minus the rifle.

By this time our horses were getting very thirsty, for, with some few exceptions, they had had very little water since leaving Kimberley. It is little wonder then, that on approaching a pan on our march, a general rush was made despite the warning of our Captain. This was followed by general confusion, and this again by general mud; some of the horses found themselves up to the neck in mire. They were all extricated after a time, but some of us in our efforts to release them, had exchanged our khaki uniform for a grey one. All along our march we were watched by Boers, and a Sergeant who had happened to get behind heard several bullets whizz by.

We reached Brussels siding in the evening, picking up a large portion of the division, with whom we marched next day to Vryburg.

Here we found that the 17th and 19th Squadrons had already gone, and early next morning we, the 18th and 20th Squads, set out with General Barton. We were to do his cavalry work, forming a screen in front and guarding the flanks. We had also to visit any suspicious farms which we passed on the way.

Our troop had orders to go to a certain farmer and take off his cattle and rifle, but no sooner had we done this than we were ordered to restore the said cattle and rifle – an old and useless Snider.

We halted, as if for the night, after doing 20 miles; but as soon as we had picqueted our horses (in strict geometrical straight lines) and had our dinners, a new order came out and we had to do another 6 miles – fancy the poor Tommy on foot! The column we were with was about 1½ miles long. We had a considerable amount of artillery, including the battery which Lieut. Roberts lost his life to save. Our next march was one of 18 miles, to a place not far from Kraai-Pan, which is about 30 miles south of Mafeking. We constantly passed farms in this region, which seems healthy, lying as it does about 8000 feet above sea level. These Boer farms are usually placed in some slight hollow where the ground gives good opportunity for a pan to be made which shall collect the rain water of the surrounding district. The houses are made and roofed with sun dried bricks, and have always a garden and a well. No farm would be complete without its fowl. These, when roasted with onions, make an excellent supper on the lonely veldt, but to be thoroughly enjoyed, need the only really true sauce – hunger.

The nights were by this time getting extremely cold (June 21 is mid-winter), though the days were warm and sunny. However, with blanket, horse rug, overcoat, and Mackintosh sheet, we did fairly well. Our saddles with a helmet on top made an excellent pillow. Some few of us had pneumatic pillows, and what a luxury they were. Our feet we put into our saddle bags, and our bed was complete. It was certainly rather disagreeable to feel the ice that formed on our Mackintosh sheets grating under our chins.

However, here ends the month of May. My story is complete, for, while the column marched east to Lichtenburg, I trained south to Kimberley the victim of that soldiers' scourge – enteric.

9230, I.Y.

10
H. B. GRAY, 'TO THE PARENTS OF ENGLAND'S SONS', IN *THE PUBLIC SCHOOLS AND THE EMPIRE* (LONDON: WILLIAM & NORGATE, 1913), PP. 1–26.

Written just before the onset of the First World War, this is the first chapter of Herbert Branston Gray's book The Public Schools and the Empire. *Gray (1851–1929) sounded a warning note that the nation may become too complacent in possessing an empire. Gray was a scholar at Winchester College and Queen's College, Oxford; chairman of the Headmaster's Conference in 1900; and headmaster of Bradfield College, in Berkshire, and Louth School, in Lincolnshire. Whilst at Bradfield he organised the staging of the Greek play Alcestis. He was ordained in 1877. His text represents something of a warning to parents of the public-school boy. Gray had been a keen athlete, but he objected to what he saw as the overemphasis on sport. His objection was that it developed a passive spectatorship or, as he put it, an 'abnormal craze for vicarious sport' and a parochial patriotism, which negated a national or imperial patriotism. He also noted that the press were giving more coverage in their papers to sport than to imperial news. He thought that the awareness of Empire should be raised on the domestic front. Gray wrote several other works, among which was* Eclipse or Empire? *(1916) in which he argued that the First World War would change the nature of the Empire and urged a greater awareness about the Empire on the part of the Englishman. He noted that most of the significant inventions during the period 1880–1914 had not originated in Britain but rather in the USA, often by British men residing in the USA, and therefore the nation was no longer amongst the world powers and would be eclipsed. He thought the Empire should become an organic whole, with an imperial parliament based at Westminster. This in fact did not materialize in the 1920s, as the Dominions became more powerful in their own right.*

To the parents of England's sons

"To see ourselves as others see us," though it may not imply a reference to the highest of all Courts of Appeal, yet sums up in a phrase the whole philosophy of a just self-esteem and of our proper conduct towards the world at large. But it is a philosophy which, from the combined effect of racial instinct, of peculiar geographical and climatic features, and of the consequent course of his history, the Englishman has been of all men the most slow to grasp.

On the force of the first-named ingredient in the composition of national character it might seem at first sight neither safe nor profitable to dwell. The question, however, may at least be ventured – Is racial instinct generally, and that particular blend in man-making which goes by the somewhat loose and inaccurate name of Anglo-Saxon, an ultimate factor baffling further analysis? If not, how far has that blend been modified by climatic, geographical, and other physical conditions? The various answers which have been given to these questions tend to show that critics are by no means in complete agreement on the problem. It is therefore one upon which it would be perhaps presumptuous for a plain man to dogmatise.

Unfortunately, however, for the Englishman's success in arriving at a just estimate of his own qualifications as seen by the eyes of foreign critics, such a philosophic reserve has never been the prevailing note of public utterances in this country. On the contrary, Press, Platform, and Pulpit have been loud and confident about our national virtues. Even when the march of events has forced the admission of a certain native sluggishness in adapting ourselves to new circumstances and new ideas – in other words, when we have "muddled through," – there has always been an underlying note of complacent reassurance as to the innate racial genius of the Englishman for world-government. Comparative silence, however, reigns as to the part played in our past history by the geographical position of these islands, their climate, their natural features, and their mineral resources in having helped to bring us into the front rank among the nations of the world.

Even the carefully balanced opportunism of a leading daily journal, when well launched on this inspiring theme, gives place to a glowing optimism, and we digest alternately with our morning toast its sonorous periods about "Britain's Inalienable Imperial Destiny." Some veteran warrior, like an old war-horse scenting from afar the smell of battle, with convictions ripened by long service in his country's cause, may have censured us in trumpet tones for our national apathy, urging our unpreparedness for the stern arbitrament of war, the necessity for some form of national service, and the near peril of imperial disaster. Our *Morning Oracle*, while it bestows a chastened praise on the hero's forceful personality, dismisses in a breath his grave and measured warning, and hastens to lull the national conscience into its normal repose by adding in a tone of lofty complacency:

"It is a welcome sign that we are gradually awakening to a greater sense of public duty," etc., etc.[1] With equally unconscious dignity might the Sanhedrim have reassured itself when the legions of Titus were battering at the walls of Jerusalem!

Meanwhile our Public Orators, and pre-eminently those of unimpeachable rank and dignity, join in the chorus of self-satisfaction, and in tones of impressive challenge call on the God of History to bear witness that He has inspired the Anglo-Saxon race with a unique genius and an unquestionable commission "to replenish the earth and subdue it," or, as it has more graphically been phrased, "to paint the map of the Globe red" – though in the process, by the by, the brush has not infrequently been steeped in blood.[2]

Nor have the Churches been silent. Our ecclesiastical directors seem insularly oblivious of the fact that all nations, at all times and in all causes, have invoked the Lord God of Sabaoth to go forth with their righteous armies. Even in the twentieth century our liturgies still continue to encourage the belief that the Omnipotence that rules the stars in their courses recognises the Englishman as His own appointed instrument for organising this particular planet. Are not the faithful instructed to pray, as though we had ever been a gentle and unassuming race, that He would "abate the pride, assuage the malice, and confound the devices" of any other people with whom, justly or unjustly, we may happen to be at war? Meanwhile the Pulpit thunders out, in the name of "this Christian Empire," denunciations about the Congo and the Peruvian atrocities, although our social conscience has only just been awakened to the fact that there is a White Slave traffic in our own land.

In spite, therefore, of solitary voices crying in the wilderness, from all responsible quarters proceeds apace the great conspiracy of national self-adulation. All classes of the community become thereby hypnotised into apathy. Meanwhile the silent army of those sons of toil, who tramp daily in their millions over the bridges that span their workshops and their homes, have their ears dulled by the soft platitudes of Editors, Politicians, and Priests. Perhaps those ears will never be unstopped until they are startled from slumber some morning by bolts from a lurid sky, when bridge and office and homestead may alike be dissolved "in one red burial blent."

Warning voices, indeed, are not lacking. From time to time astute thinkers venture to remind us that the phenomenal achievements of science in the last half-century may have impaired the value of those natural advantages which in the past have helped in great part to make England what she is to-day. They point out that even our one vital asset of insularity has been already seriously discounted, and that the engirdling belt of silver sea may be rendered of no saving value in the near future by

"airy navies grappling in the central blue."

But such prophets deliver their message to unheeding ears. Sometimes, indeed, they are treated with the disdain that Cassandra encountered, without deserving any of the demerit that attached to the unguarded career of that luckless heroine. And yet their only offence appears to consist in discharging a national duty by giving logical and cogent expression to unpalatable truths.

The fact is that, from whatever cause, we are as a people incapable of deductive reasoning, and impatient of general principles. We therefore lack, alike in our external and internal relations, the power of forecast, which mainly depends on the grasp of general principles. We abhor abstractions as pedantic; we pin our faith to the isolated facts immediately before our eyes; we disdain ideas: we thank God that, if we are a nation of shopkeepers, at least we are not, as other men are, "a nation of —— professors."[3]

This sluggishness to apprehend fresh ideas and to appropriate new methods of life and movement, until they have been dinned into the popular consciousness by the stern logic of facts, becomes, in the sphere of national security, a defect of paramount and vital concern. But it is by no means confined to that sphere. The same mental immobility is recognisable in other activities which make for social well-being and progress. This may be illustrated by countless instances drawn from English customs and habits. It takes a long time for new ideas to permeate the public mind. Prejudice against change is everywhere. "What was good enough for our fathers is good enough for us" is the rallying cry. Thus those who are scarcely now on the threshold of middle age can remember the time when the introduction of the motor car into the British Islands was regarded with grave mistrust, and while our neighbours across the Channel were already careering at high speed along the roads of the Riviera, the speed of the new machine was in England still, by law, limited to little more than a snail's pace, and the monster's approach was signalled by a man bearing a danger flag.

Again, it is notorious that even at the moment of writing the construction and organisation by the British Government of aeroplanes and dirigible airships as weapons of war have been far outstripped in time and in number by their rivals on the Continent.

Even in commerce, where, owing to our geographical advantages, we once held premier place, the American and the German are quick to respond to the calls of their customers for incessant improvements in machinery, and are bold to fling out-of-date patterns on the scrap-heap. The British manufacturer, on the other hand, turns a cold shoulder to demands for modifications of existing material, and falls back on the principle of "take it or leave it."

But it is chiefly when lightning-like rapidity in being the first on the field of battle, with equipment and organisation, "ready to the last gaiter button," is of overwhelming consequence, that we seem to have failed to take advantage of the object-lessons afforded by the spectacle of stricken nations and by our own late hair-breadth escape from imperial disaster. It was not very flattering to our national self-esteem that it took nearly three years to subdue a small race of farmers. But when three days may suffice to decide the fate of the Empire, small breathing space is left for recovery from a knock-down blow and to "come out on the top" at the end. At such times of crisis our inveterate lack of prescience in realising the vital correspondence between idea and fact may prove a failing fraught with national peril and perhaps irretrievable disaster.

The same incapacity for, and suspicion of, general principles is observable in our political attitude. The ordinary Englishman takes his stand on "the impregnable rock of the constitution." He rebukes every wave of new ideas as if it were going to eat away the foundations, instead of making principles his foothold, and modifying the Constitution thereby. The feeling of the British Public towards domestic politics has indeed been wittily described as "a spasm of pain recurring once in every four or five years."

A similar attitude of mind is observable in our foreign sympathies and antipathies. We are all things by turns, and nothing long. It is hardly surprising, then, that our friends across the water rail against "perfidious Albion," and that Continental critics sneer at our national mode of thought and morals as a "tissue of organised hypocrisies." Both indictments are partly superficial, and neither is wholly true. Our incapacity for ascending to general ideas, and acting on them, is chiefly to blame, and earns us a name for bad faith. The hypocrisy may be unconscious; but, because it is latent, and arises rather from mental than moral defect, it is none the less hypocrisy.

And so in all matters of national concern, instead of realising some universal principle such as "He who is unready is lost," and translating that principle into action, we fall back on some supposed "ultimate factor" such as "The stubbornness and integrity of the English race," "The backbone of Old England," "The practical certainty that our grit will pull us through in the end," and other quack phrases dear to the insular mind. Verily it has been said by them of old time: *Quem Deus vult perdere, prius dementat.* This is a true saying. The Englishman's native powers of reasoning seem to have been undermined by the chronic intoxication of money-making, and led astray by claptrap. In spite of clear warnings, the whole nation sits still with folded hands and does nothing, oblivious of the extreme probability that trouble, when it is due, will come upon us like a thief in the night, that "the day of our ordeal may be at hand," and that to be unprepared is to court national and imperial dissolution.

Essentially self-satisfied and immobile, we buoy ourselves up with the retrospect of a glorious past. We hug the conviction that "with our own right hand and with our mighty arm have we gotten to ourselves the victory." We appear blissfully unconscious of the adage *Tempora mutantur, nos et mutamur in illis,* while our music-halls ring with the perpetual pæans of emancipated carpet-knights:

"We don't want to fight, but, – by Jingo – !"

How largely and from what causes the national character has deteriorated from models and standards which prevailed in more spacious days it is fairly easy to determine. Granted that a cheap pessimism which easily finds material at its command becomes barren and irritating if it cannot suggest a remedy, nevertheless it is undeniable that the plethora of money, and the luxury and self-indulgence that money brings, are among the chief causes of our national deterioration and national self-deception. The trouble is, that those who do not despair of the future of the British Empire, but yet see clearly the flaws and gaps in the joints of her armour, are heard with impatience when they deliver drastic warnings and suggest unpalatable remedies.

And why are the remedies unpalatable? Simply because they conflict with the exigencies of an absorbing commercialism, and still more obtrusively with the existing standards of comfort and morals which prevail in the national life. So, like the preacher of old, the prophets of our time are ridiculed and dubbed faddists or alarmists, and the community at large, as in the days before the flood, go on buying and selling, eating and drinking, until – .

And yet is it not a commonplace of history that nations have their periods of progress, supremacy, decay, and fall? The deciphered monuments of prehistoric centuries lay bare for our study the ruins of suddenly vanished empires; and, however much we may turn our eyes from the handwriting on the wall, the modern world of to-day thrusts upon them pictures of sick and dying peoples.

It is not a little disquieting to the thinker to reflect that many of the social and political phenomena of our own time reproduce with painful exactness the conditions of these dead Empires which have left little more than a name behind them, and have perished out of human memory, as though they had never, in the dim days of the past, been gigantic factors in the evolution of the human race.

But the mirror of truth is held before our eyes most convincingly when in it is pictured the later history of that great people whose world-government was summed up in *Pax Romana*. The luminous pages of Gibbon, which reveal the signs preceding the dissolution of the greatest Empire which the world (up to that date) had ever seen, cannot fail to startle the student with the ominous resemblances between the social and political phenomena of those days and of our own.

Therein are chronicled all the same evils which beset England to-day; the same decay of agriculture following the aggregation of landed estates in a few hands;[4] the same predominance of town over country life; the same deterioration of physique[5] and general health; the same growth of luxury and desire for bodily comfort; the same increasing distaste for the burdens of married life; the same decline in the birth-rate;[6] the same excessive taxation; the same subservience to class distinctions; the same want of balance in religious thought; the same extravagance in religious ceremonials; the same decadence in public morals; the same reaction towards morbid and monstrous superstitions;[7] the same substitution of State gratuities for parental duties; the same love of display in social life; the same demand for unearned bread; the same lust for gladiatorial exhibitions of athletic skill;[8] the same decreasing sense of national responsibility and self-sacrificing patriotism.

An insistence on each and all of these disquieting features would be beyond the scope and province of the particular problem on which we are engaged – the problem of higher education. But I must not allow myself to forget that these introductory chapters are addressed to English parents on behalf of England's sons. A word, therefore, in passing may not be out of season with regard to the two last-named symptoms, inasmuch as their influence is of very serious importance on the formation of youthful character.

The number of columns devoted, even in the most sober and dignified daily journals, to records of athletic prowess have increased more than a hundred per cent. in the last quarter of a century. The newspapers themselves are not to blame. Their business is to feel and register the popular pulse and to minister to the prevailing sentiments and preoccupations. Such a growth in the sporting columns of the Press may therefore not unfairly be regarded as an indication-measure of our national insanity, or, to put it more gently, of a lack of wholesome balance.

It is not, indeed, self-evident that this exploitation of professional athleticism, craze for record breaking, and deification of champion performers are coincident with, and indicative of, the decay of strenuous national vigour. On the contrary, it may even be maintained that a certain exultation in exploits of physical prowess reflects a sane and robust virility in the life of the people. A deeper analysis, however, tends to show that it is rather a manifestation in the race of that decadent spirit which takes delight in spectacular performances, in sitting still and watching others suffering or performing feats of activity, endurance, and danger of which it is itself incapable – in fact, a species of blood-lust for gladiatorial shows translated into the manners of a milder age. This explains the phenomenon of 100,000 people sitting and shouting, while twenty-two athletes go through astonishingly agile performances with head and arm and leg – "to make an English holiday."

The matter is deeply rooted. It springs from an increasing unwillingness of the man to do things himself, and an unwholesome desire to get things done for him by others.[9]

The Olympian Games in the palmy days of Greece differed alike in meaning and in result from these twentieth-century exhibitions. They formed an attempt to consolidate a nation by summoning the Pan-Hellenic world to take part in contests partly religious and partly patriotic. Their competitions symbolised a real national synthesis. Our provincial rivalries, on the other hand, stimulate a local patriotism to the detriment of the wider sentiment. The Greek contests, moreover, were the outcome of a noble education – a glorification of the *mens sana in corpore sano* – a display of vigorous manhood, to gain which all, and not an insignificant section, "endured hardness." But the difference of spirit between the two is best seen in the nature of the rewards set up as the aim of successful effort. The Hellenic athlete struggled to secure only the "corruptible crown" of bay, olive, and parsley. But the prize tables of the modern school or club must advertise a glittering show of pots and cups from the silversmith's counter to entice the candidate to display his skill and hardihood; while the services of the "muddied oafs" of municipal arenas are retained by local managers at salaries for which a Post-Office Clerk of ten years' standing would sigh in vain, and which would be far beyond the mundane visions of a hard-working Curate.

But if "one of their own poets," living in the days of a decadent Hellas, when the glow of the national spirit had in some measure passed and gone, could declare that "the race of athletes is ever a pestilential crew,"[10] a latter-day philosopher might more readily take leave to doubt whether the deification of professional gladiators in modern England is altogether a sign of national sanity.

And if it be thought that undue emphasis has been laid on this particular feature of the times, as compared with other equally disquieting social phenomena, perhaps a more sustained reflection will disarm such criticism.

Patriotism, as a factor in the national life, is bound up with the integrity of the Empire. But unlike some other virtues, it does not appear to be a plant of indefinite or infinite growth. What it gains in intensity it loses in extent. The parochial enthusiasm, which is expended on some internecine conflict between Puddletown-in-the-Vale and Hecklebury-on-the-Hill, drains away the loftier sentiments which might otherwise animate citizens with devotion to their country's weal, and keeps them in permanent indifference to the vast estate and interests of the Empire.

It is by no means, of course, asserted that this narrowness – this parochialism – of view is confined to devotees of an extravagant athleticism. On the contrary, it is characteristic of the English people as a whole. This insularity is traceable, indeed, in the proceedings of Parliament itself, where the astounding ignorance sometimes shown as to the sentiments prevailing in the Empire beyond the Seas seems the only possible explanation of the continual flouting of them in the Central Assembly.[11]

Nor can these reflections be altogether scouted as a fanciful piecing together of cause and effect. The page of history shows that, wherever there is an extravagantly developed local or provincial outlook, there is a corresponding lack of expansion towards a larger ideal. The record of that ancient civilisation to which allusion has been made points to this truth. The very intensity of local patriotism in Greece – an intensity created by her geographical conditions – and the inveterate rivalry between town and town, only temporarily quelled by the threat of foreign invasion, prevented Greece from ever becoming a homogeneous entity. The same disintegrating influence eventually brought about her subjugation beneath the feet of a more united race of conquerors.

But it may be asked how does all this concern the modern Englishman? Granted that there are certain curious similarities in the history of Rome and Greece on the one hand and of England on the other, it does not follow that the signs of decadence in the former are necessarily disquieting symptoms in the latter. History, it may be said, never wholly repeats herself. She moves in a trajectory, not in a circle. Moreover, the supposed signs of decay might in neither case be really symptomatic at all, but the ordinary concomitants of a civilisation which has reached a certain stage of development – it might, in fact, be a case not of *propter hoc*, but merely of *post hoc*. It may be argued again that Babylons, ancient and modern, have owed their fall to external catastrophes rather than to internal rottenness. Alaric with his Visigoths, Attila with his Huns, Gaiseric with his Vandals, rather than the Coliseum with a State-fed people and cheap gladiatorial shows, were the historical causes of the fall of the Roman Empire.

Finally, it may be maintained that there is something inherent in the British character – an inflexible stubbornness, which, notwithstanding errors of life and doctrine, "overcometh all things," which will enable us, in spite of insufficiency of mental education and national training, not only to muddle through, but to "come out on the top" at the end. Would not every citizen of Clapham Junction, fresh from the office stool or the football field, array himself with sling and musket, and doing desperate battle in the day of Armageddon, beat back the insolent invader from his suburban hearthstone? So run the incoherent ideas of many a believer in our insular inviolability.

As for the security of the Empire, is not our innate racial genius for world-government (as was gently intimated at the beginning) an ultimate factor behind which analysis cannot penetrate, and the reality of which the most perverse scepticism cannot dispute? What better inductive proof can be set forth than that which is presented by the spectacle of our young pro-consuls, some of them fresh from our public schools, ruling with discretion over provinces whose boundaries are more spacious than the whole geographical area of the British Islands? Surely in this matter of Empire-ruling there have been committed to Anglo-Saxon genius "the lively oracles of God."

To all which comforting contentions it may, perhaps, be replied that, if indeed there were some Divine pronouncement on this matter, if it were indisputably and scientifically certain that a Higher Power had given an inalienable commission in perpetuity to the English race to govern the world, why, then, nothing else would matter. No disturbing symptoms would henceforth plague us, the craze for luxury and comfort would not disquiet, declensions in the birth-rate would not alarm, increase in abnormalities and superstitions would cease to be ominous, while the decay of country life and the despairful cries of a starving proletariat might be looked upon as "an act of God," to afford opportunity for letting loose the purse-strings of charity. Moreover – and this is what really concerns the English parent and the present writer – it really would not matter one jot what sort of education the children of the ruling classes received – whether two ancient languages were their exclusive educational pabulum, or whether ten-year doses of these should be diluted with an infusion of French and German, a modicum of mathematics, a tincture of physics here, and a trace of chemistry there, or whether the classics were swept away with a ruthless hand – elegiacs, irregular verbs, and all – and the youthful mind kept instead constantly excited with all sorts of interesting experiments – whether, in fact, our sons were trained with Spartan rigour at Lycurgus House Academy, Peckham, or basked under the elm-trees on the banks of the Thames. All these things would not matter one jot. The English capacity for world-power would rise superior to such educational environments, and would send forth its sons, time without end, conquering and to conquer. Above all, and this might be a blessing without disguise, which some critics of these pages would doubtless be forward to grasp, the present book need never have been written.[12]

Unfortunately, however, there is an increasingly large class of sceptics who are beginning to doubt the solidity of the doctrine once delivered *Urbi et Orbi* of English infallibility in Imperial rule. They dare to deny the (slightly modified) Dogberry pronouncement that

"Reading and writing come by nature, but Empire by the Grace of God."

The candid and thoughtful traveller starting from his island home, encumbered with no parochial prejudices, observes that certain picked young men, and therefore *ex hypothesi* the most finished products of the public-school education, achieve creditable results, when called upon to govern the affairs of countries inhabited by people of inferior civilisation. He notices again that they do passably, if less conspicuously, well, when appointed to manage provinces populated by races which, though superior in abstract thought to the governing race, and not inferior in culture, have yet been for centuries held in subjection under British rule. The personal courage of such picked young men is undeniable, their integrity generally unimpeachable, their faculty for leadership respectably well developed.

But the traveller realises, as he moves from one British possession to another, that this area comprises only a portion – a large portion, it is true, but still only a portion, and that not the most vital portion – of the British Empire. He observes, when he leaves India and East and West Africa, and treads the shores of Australia and Canada, that there is a very different tale to tell. The truth is forced upon him very strongly, and at times very painfully, that the English boy, as he emerges from the crucible of the public-school laboratory, is generally a more conspicuous failure – especially at first – in those new and partially discovered Continents, than he has proved himself to be a conspicuous success in dealing with lower or more submissive races in the wilds of Africa or in the plains of India.

Our traveller finds that the public-school-trained youth often fails to realise that he is no longer going among races accustomed to obey, but that he has to encounter a people entirely free from subservience to rank or wealth, a people intolerant therefore of dictation or condescension, in whose lives, face to face with the rugosities involved in earning a livelihood, the distinction between class and class has for all practical purposes disappeared – stern-featured men who are continually fighting nature at the edge of a wilderness, and who will not brook the airs and affectations and languid graces and soft-hued tones which are appropriate enough in the lilies of the field, but inconvenient in the case of those who toil and spin.

Such a nation has "no use for" young men the majority of whom have not been taught in the days of youth any educational connection between mind and hand, except how to wield the willow or to kick a bladder, and who have been accustomed to look with the scorn of ignorance on manual training as being suitable only to the Helots or the Heathen.

And when our traveller sees posted up in conspicuous characters in thriving townships, increasing in population by leaps and bounds, where real men and real work of head and hand are urgently needed, the disappointing legend, "No English need apply," he begins to doubt after all whether the English innate racial genius for world government is quite so indubitably an ultimate factor as he has hitherto been led to believe. He begins to question with himself whether the education received in the great public schools has always been, or even now is, altogether in harmony with a capacity for world-government, or precisely what is required by men of the ruling classes to whom the nation is still looking anxiously for the exposition and realisation of Imperial statesmanship.

Such uneasy misgivings, gathered no longer from insular preconceptions but from the light of travelled experience, must needs give pause to the seeker after general truths, and bid him inquire further into the question suggested at the beginning of these pages: Has the imperial domination exercised by the British nation over such a huge portion of the earth's surface been due not to the innate capacity of the race so much as to the peculiar geographical, climatic, and other physical characteristics of these islands? Have not these natural advantages, combined with adverse conditions prevailing from time to time in the history of other peoples, rather than any extraordinary intrinsic qualities of her own, brought about her unexampled expansion as a world power?

And if, for the sake of argument, such a hypothesis be admitted to have some foundation in fact, further and more anxious questions will arise: Is the present condition of the world such as seems likely to perpetuate these accidents of fortune? Are we wise in relying on "native racial instinct" as the ultimate factor rather than as the "residuary element," which may or may not be capable of overriding the force of unfavourable external phenomena? Do we possess not merely the genius to conquer, but also the genius to consolidate? Have we got such a grasp of such comprehensive principles of world-government as will enable us in the long run to accomplish the tremendous task of assimilating and uniting under one head the peoples, nations, and languages of such vastly different types as are represented to-day in the huge expanse of the British Empire?

If we are once forced to admit that the tenure of that Empire may not be after all "Britain's inalienable destiny," but must henceforth depend on the foresight, sagacity, and adaptability of those who are sent out either to bear rule in, or to become citizens of, the outlying portions of the Empire, and if furthermore, as some prophets foretell, the capital of that Empire may at some not distant date be shifted from London to Toronto or Winnipeg, then we are forced to ask a still further question: Are we educating these future rulers and future world-citizens in our great schools and "seminaries of useful and religious learning" in the best possible way, so as to secure this foresight, this sagacity, and this adaptability; and if not, how shall we best modify or reform our existing institutions so as to bring about the desired result?

The present work is intended to be a small contribution towards the solution of this vital problem. It professes to be part of the gleanings of many years gathered by one who has had an almost life-long experience of great public schools. The ordinary Englishman, being a business man, is naturally impatient of listening to anyone who merely theorises. It may be well, therefore, at the outset to state the author's claim to be heard. This is his only reason for striking a personal note.

He began life by being a pupil and assistant master in two of the greatest and oldest public schools in England, with an academic interval spent at Oxford, where he graduated, after a classical training at school and college, as a classical scholar. He was then for a year headmaster of a first-grade grammar school in the north. Afterwards for thirty years he was responsible as Chairman of the Governing Body and headmaster for the development of a modern public school from its days of hesitating growth and partial atrophy to days of prosperous maturity. It was one of those interesting institutions which sprang up here and there all over the country in the mid-Victorian epoch – plants sown from different motives and for different culture – some of them blessed by royal showers, some of them nipped by biting financial winds or the frosts of unpopularity, but finally prospering, flowering, bearing fruit, and fertilising an educational waste.

The particular school, whose servant the writer was for three decades, owed its foundation to a man of forceful genius and inspiring personality, who, however, had "built better than he knew." The writer, therefore, was in a sense unfettered, except financially, in recreating the form, while preserving the spirit, of the original institution.

Some years before his retirement he had served on an Educational Commission to the United States, and had had opportunity of studying in the New Continent the solution of educational problems, for which previous unofficial travel in that country had partially prepared him. In 1909, one year before his resignation, his appointment to the Presidency of the Educational Science section of the British Association led him to Canada for the third time. Having passed through Winnipeg, the meeting-place of the Association, he was struck everywhere at the want of touch between some phases of life in the Mother Country and in the Dominion. With the aim, therefore, of making a humble contribution to the Cause of Empire, he purchased and founded, on his own responsibility, a Ranch near Calgary, where public-school boys, already properly equipped with a scientific knowledge of the connection between mind and hand, might create a bond between themselves and the Western Canadian, and at the same time enjoy the fellowship of their old comrades and of other English public-school men.

He was inspired thereto by a belief that thus there might come about a gradual assimilation of environment, while Old Country prejudices against the dignity of manual labour would be abruptly wiped out.

It may be added that, since 1910, the experience of the writer has been widened by service under a Western Canadian Provincial Government, in whose service he has been responsible for handling industrial and economic problems of considerable import.

These varied avocations may not be regarded by the English reader as constituting any particular title to be heard. On the contrary, perhaps; though overseas an adaptability for new environments is not regarded as a shortcoming. They have, at any rate, afforded the writer an opportunity of cultivating a certain mental detachment and perspective in his endeavour to trace the connection between English educational problems and the future well-being of the Empire.

To revert for a moment to the writer's own educational work. If it be urged that he has not in his own sphere of duty carried out to their logical issue every one of the principles which are advocated in this book, the justice of the criticism may be at once conceded, with a not unimportant reservation. So inveterate is the disposition of the English mind to acquiesce in the *status quo*, to abhor general principles and their practical application, especially in matters educational; so little disposed are Englishmen to give solid sympathy or support to new enterprises or new methods, even when the arguments in favour of such enterprises and methods are irresistible, that no educational or other would-be reformer can go far towards the attainment of ideals as long as those who are in positions of responsibility are unwilling to touch the burden with one of their fingers. Thus, then, to my theme.

Notes

1 Lord Rosebery, when opening a Drill Hall at Linlithgow on 2nd December 1912, said: "I believe that history, when it comes to sum up this time, will regard it as one of the most astonishing facts in our record and generation that we should have turned a heedless and unattentive ear to the warnings, full of weight and full of experience, of the greatest soldier we have the privilege to possess."
2 Lord Curzon, at the beginning of his stimulating book on *Problems of the Far East*, lends the weight of his personality and eloquence to this doctrine in connection with our Indian Empire, where, if anywhere, the map has been extensively incarnadined with paint and blood. He says: "To those who believe that the British Empire is under Providence the greatest instrument for good that the world has ever seen, and who hold with the writer that its work in the Far East is not yet accomplished, this book is dedicated." Even here, however, carping criticism might interpolate a doubt whether, after all, that part of our Empire (as elsewhere) was not largely won by a few "eccentric" men who would not run in the groove marked out for them by schoolmasters and governments, and who were failures in the eyes of both. They flouted their superiors: they ran away from school and from law: they were "immoral." But these were the men who won the Empire for Downing Street. Heaven was propitiated by the indictment of the culprits, and posterity has built their sepulchres. Thus, in spite of *their* shortcomings, *we* have become "instruments for good."
3 It is true that a philosophising Thales may fall into a well, if he keeps his gaze fixed entirely on the stars. But the man who watches only his feet, and, like Muckrake in *Pilgrim's Progress,* "can look no way but downwards among the mud-heaps," tempts the expert highwayman to break his unguarded head for the sake of the spoil. Moreover, the Teuton has, for the last forty years, been utilising his scientific knowledge for industrial development. His feet and eyes have alike been set towards a clearly defined goal. It will be shown in the following pages that in England there has been, on the contrary, no systematised connection between the academic and the industrial spheres.
4 *Latifundia perdidere Italiam.*
5 See the Report of the Royal Commission on Physical Deterioration, 1904.
6 A decline of 6·3 per cent. in twenty years. The corrected birth-rate was 34·7 per 1000 of population in 1881; 28·4 in 1901.
7 Palmistry, Crystal-gazing, Agapemone, *et hoc genus omne.*
8 *Panem ac Circenses!*
9 The author, who has been a persistent athlete of respectable proficiency throughout the course of a long and arduous life, yields to none in his belief in the physical, mental, and moral benefits of a sane development of bodily activities. It is not, of course, sport as such, but the abnormal craze for vicarious sport, in which he sees a serious sign of national decrepitude. But – a pinch of fact is worth a peck of assertion. Here is an instance. In the dark days of December 1899, when defeat had attended the British arms in South Africa three times in one week, and when at the same time an international cricket match was going on in Australia, his attention was attracted to posters in the evening journals, which proclaimed in letters four inches high that a certain English Cricketer had been "No-Balled," while in insignificant capitals was recorded the announcement "Disaster at Colenso." This advertisement seemed a correct estimate of the interest which the Press expected would be taken by the British public in the two items of news respectively.
10 οὐδὲν κάκιόν ἐστιν ἀθλητῶν γένους. – Euripides.
11 Mr Price Collier, an acute observer from the other side of the Atlantic, gives to Englishmen the following warning: "No successful imperialism is possible to a nation of men who are without charity, without toleration, and without recognition of their own

ignorance and limitations. They must strive for an intellectual magnanimity which enables them to detect the good in manners, morals, governments, and beliefs built upon foundations worlds apart from their own."

12 I make a present of this sentence in advance to my kindly reviewers as "a hit – a very palpable hit."

11

'PUBLIC SCHOOL BOYS EMPIRE TOUR', IN *THE TIMES EDUCATIONAL SUPPLEMENT*, 18TH AUGUST 1931, P. 321.

This document, relating to the connection between the public schools and Empire, records the tour of public school boys to Australia in the early 1930s. Between 1926 and 1939 the School Empire Tour Committee, an offshoot of the Church of England Council of Settlement, organised a series of Empire tours for British public-school boys. The first tour travelled to Australia; the last went to Canada. In between, the tours went to South Africa, New Zealand, East Africa and the West Indies. The purpose of the tours was to encourage Empire settlement, with the boys possibly becoming district officers in India or imperial governors of the Dominions. A significant figure in the organisation of the tours was Lord Hyde, the son of the 6th Earl of Clarendon, who was Under-Secretary of State for the Dominion Affairs and Governor-General of South Africa from 1931 to 1937. Most of the leading public schools had boys aboard the R.M.S. Corinthic *when it departed from Britain.*

Public school boys' empire tour

Start for Australia

The public school boys' tour to Australia which has been arranged by the School Empire Tour Committee has begun this week. The outward trip is being made in the R.M.S. Carinthic, of the Shaw, Savill, and Albion Line, *via* the Panama Canal and New Zealand. The Corinthic is due at Wellington on September 21, and there the party will trans-ship for Sydney, where they will arrive about September 28.

The boys will remain in Australia until December 5, when they will leave Fremantle in the Moreton Bay of the Aberdeen and Commonwealth Line, which is due at Southampton on January 4. The homeward voyage will be made *via* Colombo, Port Said, and Malta. Twenty-two boys are joining in the tour, and they are from the following schools: Marlborough, Harrow, Repton, Eton, Glenalmond, Bradfield, Winchester, Ampleforth, Onndle, Charterhouse, Chillon, Radley, Sedbergh, and Stowe. The director in charge of the tour will be Mr. J. W. Parr, a master at Winchester, who will have as assistants Lieutenant M. E. D. Cunning, an Etonian, now in The King's Royal Rifle Corps, and Mr. D. G. White, of Christ

Church, Oxford, who left England for Australia in June to make the necessary preparations for the party.

In arranging the tour the committee has had the assistance of a representative of the office of the Australian High Commissioner in London, and a message has been received from Australia showing that the arrangements are proceeding satisfactorily, and that the boys will have a warm welcome in the Commonwealth. The itinerary for the tour will bring the members of the party into close association with the life and industry of the country. The principal cities and towns will be visited, and the programme includes excursions to sheep and cattle stations, wheat and fruit farms, and vineyards. Trips have also been arranged to districts noted for their beautiful scenery, and besides meeting men of ripe experience in Australia the boys will be introduced to the youth of the country, and will probably join in their sports and games.

A collection of books has been placed on board the Corinthic at Southampton for the use of the party, and these include volumes having special reference to Australia. On the homeward voyage it is hoped that the boys will be able to leave the Moreton Bay at Suez, visit the Pyramids, and rejoin the ship at Port Said.

12

A VISIT TO THE BOER CAMP – DIYATALAWA, CEYLON

By Annie Jones

From: 'A Visit to a Boer Camp', in *The Cheltenham Ladies' College Magazine* (Autumn 1902), pp. 197–199. Reproduced with kind permission of Cheltenham Ladies' College Archive.

Cheltenham Ladies' College (CLC) was founded in 1853. Leading suffragist Dorothea Beale (1831–1906) was the principal of this college from 1858 to the end of her career as an educator. In the first issue of the magazine, Beale had asked the question as to why a magazine was needed. Her answer was, 'We lose sight of so many old pupils and they lose sight of us, in their distant homes in India, Africa, Australia and New Zealand'. In the years 1880–1914, the magazine contained a significant amount of imperially themed news and features. During the South African War, Annie Jones visited the Boer prison camp that had been established by the British in Ceylon (the first camps, on St. Helena, having been filled). Some 5,000 Boers were interned there during the conflict. Pupils of the college subsequently explored the notion of what is was to be an imperial citizen in the years of peace that followed. In the 1920s, the magazine changed somewhat, to become more internationally themed, reflecting changes in the political climate in the aftermath of war. The documents demonstrate that imperial awareness was not confined to boys' schools in the years between 1880 and 1914 as schools such as CLC also gave their pupils news of the Empire.

WE were staying in Newera Eliya – a plain up among the mountains in the highest part of Ceylon (over 6000 feet above Colombo). Newera Eliya is a lovely place, so unique and diversified – the gorse in parts is quite home-like, the lake and mists remind one of Scotland, and the mimosa trees all over are like the South of France. Then there are the mysterious jungle hills all round – there is nothing like them in Europe. When we decided to go to the Boer Camp we were prepared for a long tiring day, as it is a three hours' train and one hour coach journey each way from Newera Eliya – but it turned out to be the most delightfully easy, comfortable day of sight-seeing I ever remember. We got up at 5.30 and descended in a mist to the station 1000 feet lower. Fortunately the mist soon cleared off after we got into the train, and we passed through most glorious scenery – masses of greenery on either side, brightened here and there by red rhododendrons – then more jungle hills, all shades of lovely greens. Among the trees we noticed wild ginger, which has a sweet spicy smell, blue gum, a few coffee bushes with their dark green leaves and red berries, and occasional creamy orchids and gentians. The little stations go in for flowers. At one – Ohiya – there was a beautiful row of sweet peas (they only grow at a certain height in Ceylon). After much cajolery we managed to get a few pieces from the native porter. Then we passed through a series of tunnels – between each, wonderful panoramic views through a blue haze into the far distance – and on into sight of the Camp an hour before reaching it. It lies in a hollow surrounded by great bare green hills (*not* jungle) round which the train slowly winds to Diyatalawa, the small station about a mile from the Camp. Here we were met by a sergeant with a permit. He seemed rather bored – I don't wonder; he has had so many visitors to meet, and they probably all ask him the same questions. He took us to the Commandant's office to write our names, and then we were put in charge of another "Tommy" to escort us round. He was *most* amiable, and kept on saying "Oh there's no doubt about that," to most of our remarks, such as "What a lot of feeding they must take," and, "They seem to have a very good time," etc., etc.

There are between four and five thousand Boers at the Camp, which is surrounded by a wire fence, guarded of course by our men. The place is lighted by electric light, and there is a wire shoot from the railway station to the Camp for sending down wood and stores. There is a big storage house and a place like a butcher's shop with enormous quantities of beef, etc., hanging up. The kitchens are in different parts of the Camp – they are just open sheds roofed with corrugated iron, as all Camp houses are – with low stone walls to put pans and things on, and built so as fire can be lighted underneath. The Boers do all their own work inside, but coolies are employed to clean up outside. The prisoners amuse themselves in all kinds of ways – they play games, and have a large place for football, hockey, etc., and a large recreation room for concerts (they have a regular band) and acting, boxing, etc. Then there is a school-room, in which we saw one man teaching some language to quite a large class. On the whole, I thought the prisoners a fine lot of men – far nicer than I expected – and for the most part cheerful and happy, and well-behaved. Many of them saluted and said good morning as we passed. Visitors are not allowed to speak to anyone but the shopkeepers. The shops are truly unique – some of the men make such wonderful things out of different kinds of wood – chiefly ebony – and out of cows' horns! (the cows they eat) and shin bones! I cannot remember half the things they make – there are wooden candlesticks, carved boxes, whips, sticks, egg-cups, pen-holders, tumblers (horn), and table-napkin rings, brooches and charms (shin bones), etc., etc. One man, such a nice German, carves most beautiful things in ebony – another takes photographs and sells post-cards with them on – another man paints pictures, etc. Their ingenuity is perfectly wonderful, considering the materials they have at hand.

It was all *so* interesting. The time we spent at the Camp just flew – but it *was* hot, there is no shade there – although of course it is not *real* heat, as the sergeant said, nothing to parts of India. We had a most delicious and welcome tea, before starting back, sent up to the station for us by one of the officers. Going home everything looked even more beautiful in the lovely sunset light than it did in the morning, and when the train stopped at Namioya, although it was dark, we were quite sorry to get out.

13

THE DUTIES AND PRIVILEGES OF IMPERIAL CITIZENSHIP

By Phyllis D. Hemingway, I. 2b.

From: 'The Duties and Privileges of Imperial Citizenship', in *The Cheltenham Ladies College Magazine* (Autumn 1907), pp. 241–246. Reproduced with kind permission of Cheltenham Ladies' College Archive.

Cheltenham Ladies' College (CLC) was founded in 1853. Leading suffragist Dorothea Beale (1831–1906) was the principal of this college from 1858 to the end of her career as an educator. In the first issue of the magazine, Beale had asked the question as to why a magazine was needed. Her answer was, 'We lose sight of so many old pupils and they lose sight of us, in their distant homes in India, Africa, Australia and New Zealand'. In the years 1880–1914, the magazine contained a significant amount of imperially themed news and features. During the South African War, Annie Jones (see document 12) visited the Boer prison camp that had been established by the British in Ceylon (the first camps, on St. Helena, having been filled). Some 5,000 Boers were interned there during the conflict. Pupils of the college subsequently explored the notion of what is was to be an imperial citizen in the years of peace that followed. In the 1920s, the magazine changed somewhat, to become more internationally themed, reflecting changes in the political climate in the aftermath of war. The documents demonstrate that imperial awareness was not confined to boys' schools in the years between 1880 and 1914 as schools such as CLC also gave their pupils news of the Empire.

Introduction.

THAT the British Empire extends over a greater area than do the possessions of any other power, is a fact which bears with it sufficient proof of the responsible position of each individual citizen. It would be surprising to one totally ignorant of history to hear that the origin of this great empire lies in an insignificant island, itself thrice conquered – by Roman, by Saxon, and by Norman; nevertheless, it was through these very conquests that England first entertained the idea of gaining power and influence.

It was only when firmly established as a first-class European power, feared in France and second only to Spain in commercial and naval importance, that England began to realize that in order to maintain her position she must grow, and to grow she must have room. The New World was, as yet, free to all – there it was a case of "catch as catch can," and England, though hampered by Spain, was not behindhand with expeditions, many of which were successful.

The main object of these early settlers was to further trade, and the colonies established at that time may be regarded as the foundation of the Empire. Various other reasons may be given for Britain's later attempts to increase her territory, though generally trade was the governing motive. On one or two occasions colonies were founded in America when bad rule led to the oppression of certain classes at home; and at different times isolated islands have become ours and now serve as naval and military outposts or coaling stations. When the power of France was a menace to Britain, it was through her colonies that we were able to cripple her. Thus Canada and much of what is now the United States changed hands; and at the same time French influence in India was limited to a few parts, while Britain established a firm rule over that country. Australia, one of our more recent acquisitions, was at first chiefly used for convict settlements after the American War of Independence; but in after years it was much resorted to on account of the gold to be found there, and also for its agricultural possibilities.

The more recent additions to the Empire were generally made with aims less selfish than those which prompted our "land-grabbing" ancestors. It has been said that one of the most sacred duties of a Christian nation is to withstand all injustice and oppression in dealing with races under its influence and protection, and this has, for the most part, characterised the attitude of the British to a conquered people.

The foregoing outline of the growth of the Empire will serve to show the unique position occupied by its citizens.

The privilleges of the citizen.

The most striking advantage enjoyed by the Imperial citizen is freedom – freedom to live, work, and speak as he will, freedom which is extended to all those under British protection, freedom which is world famed: it is every citizen's birthright, won by the struggles and sacrifices of his forefathers.

The extent of the Empire ensures power; the Britisher, if not always loved, is certainly respected abroad, and this respect is felt for all inhabitants of the daughter colonies. The growth of the Empire has been the means of removing much of the insular prejudice so typical of the "tight little island." The great lands which Britain now possesses are in themselves the means of an education, serving to broaden her views and sympathies.

Though the Empire cannot be said to be self-supporting, that ideal state of affairs will no doubt be attained in due time. She at least is quite able to defend herself – "independent" seems an inadequate word to apply to her position – no other power is so secure. This is perhaps due to the feeling of unity between the colonies and the mother-country, the mutual sense of obligation, the sympathies of the one with the other. Britain has not attempted to gather round her smaller, weaker, and therefore more dependent states. Her aim is to build up the daughter colonies, so that they may be able to meet the mother country on equal terms. Her ideal has altered since her first attempts at colonization, when a colony was supported merely for the benefit of the Homeland, and its dependent position was considered a necessity.

> "Taught by time, our hearts have learned to glow
> For others' good and melt for others' woe."

The duties of the citizen. True patriotism.

The most important duty of the imperial citizen is to uphold the honour of the Empire. He should not let any action soil its reputation and should be ready to make any sacrifice for its good. To brag of a country's power, and to attempt to justify its mistakes, is false patriotism. A true lover of his country is able to realize when a mistake has been made, and in history there are many instances of the noblest men meeting disgrace and even death because they had bravely denounced some popular movement which they considered injurious to their country's best interests. It is the duty of every citizen, when there is occasion, to make whatever sacrifice is in his power for the sake of the Empire.

The present position of the Empire.

The Empire occupies a very different position now from what it did a century ago. *Then* Britain was the only colonizing power and the greatest military and commercial power in Europe; but other countries have been seized with the desire to colonize and Britain's success is looked upon with envious eyes; not only with regard to colonization, but with regard to trade, Britain has serious rivals. The Empire is no longer so far ahead of the other powers as it used to be, therefore an increase of vigilance and energy is needed to hold it together. The time is past when it lived chiefly by the sword, and it is by other means than by mere warfare that we may fear to be attacked.

A need of men.

The Empire is in need of men, and it is the duty of every man to prepare himself for its service. In order that the Empire may continue in its present position it is necessary to train up men who will in years to come control its affairs. We owe it to our descendants to transmit to them this great Empire strong and united, and because of this the training of every child is of the greatest importance, for how can an Imperial race exist without health and education? All those who in our great cities endeavour to lessen distress and disease among the poor do no small service for the Empire.

It is thought by some to be a drawback that the British possessions are so scattered; this may at times be a source of difficulty, but it might, at least, be partially obviated by an increase of intercourse and a greater display of mutual interest and sympathy. On the whole, those in the mother country do not know nearly enough about the colonies; this state of affairs might be improved by means of early education. After learning the geography and history of their native land, children should next be taught the geography and history of the colonies, and thus should learn to develop an interest in them. The granting of privileges in regard to trade on both sides and interchange of visits are ways of increasing interest and sympathy which might well be extended. Instead of "going abroad" to Europe or Asia, why should we not visit those places with which we are more closely connected? A sure proof of the unity between Great and Greater Britain is the help which the one has so readily rendered to the other when need has arisen during past years. The Empire is bound together by a sense of mutual obligation. England has taught the colonies all she knows, and in return they are able and willing to teach her much.

The duty of the citizen towards inferior races.

The aim of the Empire is to extend to all more ignorant races under its protection the benefits of Christianity, civilization, and education, and to withstand injustice and oppression. A citizen should allow no selfish feeling for his own country to eclipse his concern for the welfare of the Empire. It is left to the individual conscience to see that the privilege of freedom is not abused. Our liberty has been won for us gradually and with difficulty – the foundation stone of our present position being laid by Magna Carta: "to none will we sell, deny, or delay right and justice" – and each advance has brought with it added power and added responsibility.

Conclusions.

In speaking of the relationship between Great Britain and the Colonies, it would be well to compare their present attitude with that of earlier days.

It must not be thought that England was behaving in an unusual manner in her treatment of her American colonies. To use all settlements for the good of the Homeland and to hamper and restrict them in order that they should not become too powerful was the short-sighted aim of all the great colonizing powers of that time. It was because the colonists *were* Englishmen that they resented this unfair treatment, and the wisest men in England realised that they were right. The war which followed could only have terminated in the way it did. The colonists, supported by a sense of justice, received first secret, and later open help from England's enemies. Much might be said on both sides, and it would be well to remember that it was only after England had saved the colonies from their French and Spanish enemies that they raised any objection to British rule; but yet the war was one of England's most lamentable mistakes. It was war for a principle; one of the wisest statesmen of the time, Edmund Burke, said:

"The blood of man should never be shed but to redeem the blood of man. It is well shed for our God, for our kind, for our country. The rest is vanity, the rest is crime."

But good arose from this seeming evil, for England never repeated her mistake. She realized that in future she must grant to her colonies those privileges which experience had taught her were so necessary.

It can now be truthfully said that Britain is the greatest colonising power in the world; the Empire is based on two principles – the spirit of freedom and the desire for unity, and what could be a firmer foundation? Since the founding of the Empire great changes have been wrought for its welfare. It is a mistake to think that because old ways have been successful they are necessarily the ways for the future as well as for the past. We need to realize –

"New times demand new measures and new men:
The world advances and in time outgrows
The laws that in our fathers' days were best."

14

THE LAST DAY OF KHARTOUM

From: J. Grant, *Cassell's History of the War in the Soudan Vol. II* (London: Cassell, 1885–1886), pp. 148–158.

The British Empire and colonial warfare evidently generated a healthy appetite for accounts of the engagements of British troops in the Empire and British rule overseas more generally. The appetite was catered for by publishing houses such as Cassell, founded in 1848. It issued illustrated accounts of the wars in the Soudan (Sudan) and in South Africa, in addition to a history of India. James Grant (1822–1887) was a prolific writer, authoring both fiction and non-fiction works. Born in Scotland, he was a distant relative of Sir Walter Scott. Grant authored the Illustrated History of India *(1876) and the* History of the War in the Soudan *(1885–86). Richard Danes authored the South African volume (see document 15). One review noted of Danes' volume, 'War provides great scope for picturesque and descriptive writing, and in this instance the author has made the most of it'. Indeed, at times the writing in the Boer volume borders on the kind of prose found in the* Boys' Own Paper. *Danes adopts the perspective of the British, describing them as hardy people who had been obliged to assert their dominion over the natives at the muzzle of a rifle. The black population in Africa are not seen in Danes' account as the equals of white settlers. It is likely these books were held by public libraries for the perusal of both youths and adults alike.*

> The Surprise – The Slaughter – The Story of Said and Jacoob – The Greek's Narrative – Gordon Slain and Beheaded – Females sold into Slavery – Horrors of the Scene – Fate of the Arch-Traitor – The Treachery of Farag denied – The Escape of Father Bonomi – The Memorial of the Clan Gordon.

FARAG PASHA is said to have opened the gate in the southern wall early on the morning of the 26th of January, and a vast force of the Mahdi's men, who were close by, flowed like a living stream into the town. On hearing the alarm, General Gordon rushed from the palace, armed with a sword and axe, according to one account; with a revolver only, according to another. He was accompanied by Ibrahim Bey Ruchdi, and about twenty armed men.

On his way to the house of the Austrian consul he was met by a party of the enemy, who fired a volley, and shot him dead. The Arabs, with their spears, then dispatched Ibrahim and nine men, the rest achieving their escape. Abdul Kerim further stated that he had seen General Gordon's body lying outside the palace, without any mutilation except that inflicted by spears, which, according to their custom, they thrust through and through it. Herr Hansal, the Austrian consul, was killed in his own house; but Nicola, the Greek, was made prisoner.

All the Greeks and other Europeans employed in the arsenal had been exterminated, together with most of the notables. Abdul Kerim affirmed that the great majority of the inhabitants fraternised with the Arabs, and that no women or children were slain; also, that all who surrendered their valuables were permitted to go unharmed. But, on the other hand, other accounts, particularly a letter written by one of the captive missionaries to Padre Vincentini at Dongola, and brought there by a messenger, stated that the city had been utterly sacked, and its people put to death, the number of victims being over 2,000. Major Kitchener says 4,000, with 3,327 Regulars and Bashi-Bazouks, and 2,330 of the Shagiyeh tribe, were all slain in cold blood, after laying down their arms. The fact that the massacre had taken place was further confirmed by Wilson and his returning party, who saw dead bodies – many of them tied back to back, evidently before slaughter – floating down the Nile.

It was now believed that there had been in Khartoum a greater number of Europeans than was at first supposed.

One of the latest accounts of the fall of Khartoum was that supplied on the 11th of April to the military correspondent of the *Daily News* at Dongola by two soldiers of Gordon's army, Said Abdullah and Jacoob Mahomet, who were taken prisoners, and sold as slaves to some Kabbabish merchants, from whom they effected their escape at a place called Abandon.

"Khartoum was delivered into the hands of the rebels," they stated; "it fell through the treachery of the accursed Farag Pasha, who opened the gate. May he never reach Paradise! May Shaytun take possession of his soul! But it was *Kismet* (Fate). It was the gate called Buri, on the Blue Nile. We were on guard, but did not see what was going on. We were attacked, and fought desperately, at the gate. Twelve of us were killed and twenty retreated into a high room, where we were taken prisoners. And now came the ending!

"The red flag with the crescent was destined to wave no more over the palace; nor would the strains of the hymn of his Highness the Effendina be heard at evening within Khartoum. Blood was to flow in her streets, in her dwellings, in her very mosque, and on the Kennish of the Narsira. A cry arose: –

"'To the palace! to the palace!' A wild and furious band rushed towards it, but they were resisted by the black troops, who fought desperately. They knew there was no mercy for them, and that even were their lives spared, they would be enslaved, and the state of the slave, the perpetual bondage with hard taskmasters, is worse than death. Slaves are not treated well, as you think; heavy chains are round their ankles and middle. They are lashed for the least offence, till the blood flows."

So these black troops fought desperately, knowing they would receive no mercy. The party the narrators were with could not help being taken prisoners. The house they defended was set on fire; the fight raged, and the slaughter went

THE LAST DAY OF KHARTOUM

on, till the streets were slippery with blood. They saw the hordes rushing towards the palace, but did not see Gordon slain.

They understood that he met his doom as he was leaving it, near a large tree which stands on the esplanade, not a gunshot from the house of the Austrian consul. They did not hear – so they stated – what became of his body, or that his head was cut off. They added that they did not hear that the black troops had given way, nor that the Egyptians fought well; the latter were craven, and had it not been for them, the two soldiers asserted, that in spite of the treachery of many within the city, the Arabs would not have got it.

"I was not at my house," said Penago in his narrative. "I was with some Greeks – eight in all – near the mosque, when we heard a hideous uproar as of men shouting and yelling and women wailing, on all sides. Nearer and nearer did this long-continued roar approach. Men with frightful gashes on their faces and limbs came flying by, and women, with torn garments and dishevelled hair, shrieking and screaming. I shall not forget that horrible din to the day of my death. 'We are lost! we are lost!' we cried; 'the place is taken!' But no one could tell us exactly what the matter was. We ran to the top of the mosque and saw that the town was given up to massacre and bloodshed. We rushed to a house, barricaded the doors and windows, went up-stairs, shut ourselves into a room, and determined never to surrender, but to die like Greeks, and, mindful of our ancestors, fight to the last. I did not see Gordon slain, but everybody in Khartoum knows when the event happened."

Penago then goes on to say, that "an Arab shot him with a gun as he was reading his Bible." This latter detail is most improbable. After that another cut off his head, and put it on a spear, and went forth with it through the city, brandishing it on high. Men shut themselves up in their houses, but the doors were burst in, and the shooting, spearing, and slashing went on in the streets, the market-place, and the bazaars. "It was a horrible scene, this bazaar," said Penago. "Gay curtains, crimson-coloured and orange-striped, golden-edged satins, silks and muslins, lay smeared and splashed with blood; everything was upset, strewed about, and trampled on. Everywhere was the wildest disorder. One corner was so full of corpses and dying that we could not get by."

The havoc went on till 8 a.m., or six hours, according to Major Kitchener. Penago was taken, and had his hands tied behind him, when the Mahdi, he stated, sent word from Omdurman, that Allah had revealed to him that the slaughter was to cease; but it did not. Those who were in hiding were bidden to come forth; but of forty-two Greeks he says only eight escaped, and sixteen Jews were killed. He again adds, "Gordon's head I saw on a spear. It was taken over to Omdurman and shown to Mahomet Achmet."

When it was laid before the Mahdi, a grim smile passed over his face. He gazed long on the countenance. "God be praised!" he exclaimed, "Can this be his?" He made merry at the death. The head was then borne away, and men plucked the hairs out of it and the chin, and spat in his face. "His body was then cut into little pieces. This was his end."

In the *Daily Chronicle* for April 22nd, 1885, is the following news from Dongola: – "We have just got a most authentic account that Gordon's head was cut off, and put on one of the chief buildings at Khartoum. This was kept secret from the newspapers, for fear of exasperating the British public."

But in the account of all that followed, we cannot do better than give the graphic narrative of the two soldiers, Said Abdullah and Jacoob Mahomet, already partly quoted: –

"And now fearful scenes took place in house and building, in the large market-place and the small bazaars. There were the same terrible scenes in the dwellings where the window-sills and the door-lintels were painted *azrek* (blue), where there had been many feasts and fantasias, and where *merissa* had flowed in plenty; and where walls were built of *wahál*, and the roofs formed of dhurra stalk. Men were slain shrieking for mercy, when mercy was not in the hearts of our savage enemies. Women and children were robbed of their jewels of gold and silver, of their bracelets, necklaces of precious stones, and carried off to be sold to the Bishareen merchants as slaves. Yes – and white women, too – Egyptians and Circassians, who wore the *burko* (veil) over their faces; the *rabtah* and the *turbah* (head-dresses) – ladies clad in silk and satin. Mother and daughter were alike dragged from their homes of comfort.

"These were the widows, wives, and daughters of Egyptian officers, some of whom had been killed with Hicks Pasha: wives and children of Egyptian merchants, formerly rich, owning ships and mills, gardens and shops. They were sold afterwards – some for 340 *thaleries* or more; some for 250, according to age and good looks; while the poor black women, already slaves, and their children, were taken off too. These were sold for 100, 80, or 70 *thaleries*. Their husbands and masters were slain before their eyes, and yet we hear it said there was no massacre at the taking of Khartoum!

"This fighting and spilling of blood continued till *dohr* (noon), till the sun rose high in the sky – red, yet darkened by the smoke and dust. There were riot and clamour, hubbub and wrangling over spoil; cursing was heard till the hour of evening prayer; but the muezzin was not called, neither were any prayers offered up on the evening of that dark day . . . Yet the howling herd, possessed by evil spirits and devils, and bespattered with gore, swarming about in bands, found not the plunder they had been promised. Then they were exasperated; their fury knew no bounds, and they sought out Farag Pasha, but he was with the dervishes. 'Where is the hidden treasure of the Greek merchants and Bachalees, of Leontides and Giorgio Themetrio? Yes, and of the Franchesi Marquet, of the Italian Michaelo? Where are all the thaleries of Marcopolo, and of the German tailor, Kleine? We know that those who left Khartoum were unable to carry away their silver, and you know where it is hid.'

"Farag was now questioned, but he swore by Allah, and by the souls of his fathers, back to three generations, that Gordon had no money or treasure. 'You lie!' cried the dervishes; 'you wish, after a while, to come here, dig, and get it all for yourself. If the Inglezzi had no money or silver how did he make all those silver medals we have seen?'

"'Most of them are lead,' replied Farag, 'and he paid every one with paper.' 'It is false,' they replied. 'We are sure you know where the money lies concealed. We are not careful of your life, for you have betrayed the men whose salt you have eaten; you have been the servant of the infidel, and you have betrayed even him! Unless you unfold the secret of the buried treasure, you shall surely die.'

"But Farag, it is said – for we were not there, – seeing that his end was approaching, and that his words were not believed, assumed a proud and haughty bearing, and an attitude of defiance.

"'I care not,' he said 'for your threats; I have told the truth, as Allah knows. There is no money, neither is there treasure. You are *magnoons* (fools) to suppose there is; but if there were, you would not divide it fairly among your followers; you would keep it among yourselves. I have done a good deed. I have delivered to your master the city, which you could never have taken without my help. You would have been beaten back from the trenches by the Inglezzi, who, even now, await their time to punish you; and I have no secrets regarding these, which, if I die, will die with me. I tell you, there is no treasure; but you will rue the day if you kill me.'

"One of the dervishes then stepped forward and struck him, bound as he was, on the mouth, telling him to cease his fool's prophecies; while another rushed at him with a two-edged sword, so that with one blow his head fell from his shoulders. So perished the arch-traitor – may his soul be afflicted! But, as for Gordon Pasha, may his soul be enjoying the fuller knowledge! . . . All the Egyptian men were slain, in spite of their casting themselves down and praying for mercy. Farag Pasha's head was then carried to Mahomet Achmet. We heard this when the Kordofan soldiers, who guarded us at the Dormas Gate, talked of it among themselves. We were there for some days; we saw nothing, but only heard what these soldiers told us. They said two steamers with British had come up, and gone back. We have nothing more to tell you."

"The story of these men, so far as it goes," wrote the correspondent of the *Daily News*, who took it carefully down, "seems perfectly trustworthy."

The correspondent of the *Daily Chronicle* recorded that many little children were spitted on Arab spears in pure wantonness, and that all the relatives of the faithful five hundred under Nusri Pasha, who met and assisted us at Gubat, shared the same fate. It was a scene unparalleled in horror since the days of Tamerlane. When the officers and men of Nusri Pasha's force heard of the massacre of their families, they gave way to the wildest paroxysms of grief, and for a time were quite demoralised by the blow that had fallen upon them.

The bulk of the people willingly joined the Mahdi, who, with his chiefs, speedily organised a complete system of defence for the city, throwing up outlying redoubts, arranged on a tolerably sound military principle, to command the approaches from every point.

He sent out a proclamation demanding fresh levies, stating that the British were few, and that the gates of Paradise were now open to all the Faithful; but he did not enter the town until the third day after its capture. The consul Nicola was spared, and kept as a medical man.

Rosti Penago, the Greek refugee, stated that when he left Khartoum no one lived in the palace, as the bodies of the dead had not been cleared away, and a fearful stench of corpses pervaded the entire city.

The correspondent of the *Daily News*, at a subsequent period, records a curious statement made to Major Turner by one Abdullah Bey Ismail, commander of a battalion of irregular troops, who made his escape after the capture. He denied the treachery of Farag Pasha, who was his brother officer. He stated that twenty days before the fall of the city, Gordon had urged all civilians capable of bearing arms to leave, in order to avoid the threatened famine, and sent a letter to the Mahdi, saying, "Behold these people, now that I have had them six months. Feed and support them. Then as I have done up to the present date, do you in the future."

Abdullah stated that the number of persons left in Khartoum at the time of its capture was only 14,000, including the troops, which is very unlikely; and that Farag was killed because he had served the Infidels. He also thought that the number of slain amounted to about 5,000; but Major Kitchener puts it at 9,657. Several grappled with their murderers, and strangled them in the fury of their despair.

"Gordon," said Abdullah, "with a European doctor, and two other men, killed 200 Arabs from the Palace, and when their ammunition was exhausted, the eastern door was thrown open, and Gordon, calm and serene, smoking a cigarette, and with a sword in his right hand, appeared. There was a pause for a moment, but one near him raised a rifle and shot the General dead. I speak the truth and lie not, Allah knows! The Mahdi, every day after reading his prayers, rises to his full height, and turning to the north, draws his long two-edged sword and cries, 'Woe to you, Stamboul, for this sword is against you!'"

Pitted with spear thrusts, Gordon's body was, no doubt, flung into the Nile, a prey to the crocodiles, so that not even the palm of martyrdom could be laid upon his tomb.

The Roman Catholic missionaries, taken prisoners at El Obeid and Gebel Nuba, seven men and five women, were some of them at this time in Omdurman, clad as dervishes, to save them from insult.

One of the former, Father Bonomi, a captive at El Obeid, afterwards achieved his escape. The first instrument of his deliverance was a letter from the Superioress of the Sisters of Nigritia, addressed to Mgr. Sogaro, Vicar Apostolic of Central Africa. A proposal was made at Dongola to send four camels to El Obeid, for the escape of Father Bonomi and his companions in misfortune. But only one driver, with two camels, could be got. He was to be paid 100 thalers down, and 500 more if he brought back Bonomi safe. The latter had with him in captivity Father Ohrwalder, a Tyrolese priest, and each besought the other to depart on the solitary camel; and ultimately, Father Bonomi, eluding the vigilance of the Arabs, quitted the city, and on the camel began the long and perilous journey, without other food than a few grains of dhurra daily, and generally not daring to approach the wells;

after travelling for thirteen days and nights, he reached Wady Halfa in safety, and thence to Cairo.

Tidings of the fall of Khartoum reached Great Britain early in February. The hard-won victories of our troops had filled every heart with hope that the end of the horrible war was near, and on learning that the advance of the long-delayed expedition had reached the Nile and been joined by Gordon's steamers, every one anticipated that Khartoum would be relieved at last.

Then came the mournful news that all was over; that not only had the long-defended city been captured by treachery, but that its gallant upholder was slain.

A relic of Gordon was given by his sister as a marriage present to the Princess Beatrice – a jade ornament, brought by him from China in 1865, called "The Gem of Bright Gems," and which had belonged to the Emperor Hein Fung.

Among the many public meetings summoned to do honour to his memory was one held in April, 1885, by the clan and surname of Gordon, convened at Aberdeen by the Marquis of Huntly, as chief, and by the Duke of Richmond and Gordon. There were present the Earl of Aberdeen, the Gordons of Essilmont, Banchory, Monar, Craig, Ellon, and other gentlemen of the surname, when it was universally carried that there should be a fitting memorial erected in Aberdeen "to the memory of the late General Gordon, C.B., killed at Khartoum, one of the most distinguished members of the clan."

15

RICHARD DANES, *CASSELL'S ILLUSTRATED HISTORY OF THE BOER WAR* (LONDON: CASSELL, 1902), PP. 1–24.

The British Empire and colonial warfare evidently generated a healthy appetite for accounts of the engagements of British troops in the Empire and British rule overseas more generally. The appetite was catered for by publishing houses such as Cassell, founded in 1848. It issued illustrated accounts of the wars in the Soudan (Sudan) and in South Africa, in addition to a history of India. James Grant (1822–1887) was a prolific writer, authoring both fiction and non-fiction works. Born in Scotland, he was a distant relative of Sir Walter Scott. Grant authored the Illustrated History of India *(1876) and the* History of the War in the Soudan *(1885–86). Richard Danes authored the South African volume. One review noted of Danes' volume, 'War provides great scope for picturesque and descriptive writing, and in this instance the author has made the most of it'. Indeed, at times the writing in the Boer volume borders on the kind of prose found in the* Boys' Own Paper. *Danes adopts the perspective of the British, describing them as hardy people who had been obliged to assert their dominion over the natives at the muzzle of a rifle. The black population in Africa are not seen in Danes' account as the equals of white settlers. It is likely these books were held by public libraries for the perusal of both youths and adults alike.*

Chapter I

The first fight – Talana Hill

IT was a bright October morning. The sun rose over the hill and veldt of a rocky mountainous country in the northern corner of Natal, shedding its rays upon a scene at once awful and inspiring. For there eight thousand men were gathered to strike the first blows of that contest which should decide whether or not the British race should rule in Africa from the Cape of Good Hope to the Zambesi's bank.

This was not the first time that men in arms had met in conflict in those regions. Full many a time had the hardy white settlers who first colonised the country been obliged to assert their dominion at the muzzle of a rifle. But these were unequal conflicts. The Zulus, the original black population, were not the equals of the white men either in arms or in policy; and their savage bravery, supported only by the assegai, had failed before the disciplined valour, the steady conduct, and the gunpowder of the Europeans. But on this day the combatants were more equally matched, and the issue was far more serious than in those days when black aboriginal and white settler met.

Imagine a hill, rocky and precipitous – a hill such as one sees in the Western Highlands of Scotland – with boulders scattered about it as though some giants of old had been playing at "chuckie-stane." Unlike our British hills, however, this hill is not green nearly to the top. It was brown – of a peculiar loam-coloured brown such as the British home-staying person never sees in nature. In a week or so it will be clad with verdure, for soon the summer begins, and with it the rains. But now it is brown, bare and wild. Such was Talana Hill on the morning of Friday, October the 20th, in the year of our Lord 1899.

At the foot of the hill were gathered a brigade of British soldiers, of a quality, perhaps, such as our Army has never seen. Not raw ploughboys, straight from the ploughtail, such as Wellington commanded that day when he stopped the way to Brussels, and, with a sunken road as his only entrenchment, defied for fourteen hours the finest troops in the world and the best artillery, led by the greatest commander since Oliver Cromwell. No! These were not raw lads. They were men who had been "salted" for a tropical clime in Egypt, in India, and in South Africa itself. The Dublins had been in Natal for two years. And they were all burning to wipe out the memory of the disaster at Majuba Hill in 1881. They had heard that the Boers had boasted plentifully of how the red-coated "rooinek" was a poor sort of fellow, who could not shoot, and was a good and easy mark; and they desired to show these hunters and farmers how foolish and unfounded was this contempt.

But where was the thin red line? Where was that red coat of the British soldier which has seen every climate and latitude? The Boers searched for it in vain. For the British War Office had, since the day of Majuba, abandoned the policy of making the British soldier the best living target in the world and had even been brought to believe that a soldier under the scorching suns of India and Africa may march and fight a little better if he be not clad in a garb originally built for London in December. Wherefore the 4,000 men at the foot of the hill were arrayed in a kind of fine canvas, called "khâki," a stuff devised for our troops in India and thus named because of its colour. In the Hindustani tongue, or some dialects thereof, *khâki* signifies "mud." Lord Roberts was responsible for its general use in India.

These 4,000 men, or thereabouts, now assembled at the foot of Talana Hill, comprised a splendid infantry brigade of four battalions,[1] a squadron[2] of mounted infantry, some cavalry, and some irregular Natalian troops, mounted. The footmen were – the 1st Battalion of the Leicester Regiment (the 17th), the 1st Battalion of the King's Royal Rifles (the old 60th), the 1st Battalion of the Royal Irish Fusiliers (the 87th), and the 2nd Battalion of the Royal Dublin Fusiliers (the 102nd). The only cavalry – and even at this stage the want of mounted men was to make itself felt – was the 18th Hussars, under Colonel Möller, in addition to the Natalian volunteers and mounted infantry before mentioned. There were, likewise, three Field Batteries[3] of Artillery – the 13th, 67th, and 69th.

At the top of the hill, another 4,000 were gathered. Brown-faced men these, young and old; farmers, most of them, and farmers' sons, from beyond the Buffalo River. And mixed with them were a few foreigners – Irish and Russian, French and Scandinavian, with here and there a German with stolid face. Soldiers of fortune these: fighting, some for love of the Boers, some for love of money, some for hatred of the English. But the farmers and the farmers' sons fought from necessity, and because Paul Kruger had said that if they did not fight hard and shoot straight the Dutch republics would vanish in the capacious maw of the British Empire.

The composition of the force was two-fold – artillery and mounted riflemen. There were no infantry, in the proper sense of the term. Each man carried a gun, but no sword or bayonet. Nor would swords and bayonets have been of much use to them; for they had not tried these weapons. Their rifles they knew and trusted, and could use them as only hunters born and bred can – with confidence born of usage, and aim steady and true, bred of a clear eye and muscles of iron. Bearded men, most of these, with rough, shaggy heads of hair. Uniform they had none, being dressed in the ordinary every-day dress of a colonial farmer, with hats of all sorts, from a tall and ancient beaver to a slouch felt.

Each man carried a bandolier of cartridges. They had proceeded to the field of battle mounted on hardy, shaggy ponies, of nondescript breed – animals of great endurance, able to live on next to nothing: fast, surefooted, docile. But as the armies faced each other that morning the ponies were in groups in the rear, being loosely tethered and guarded by boys and old men, about one attendant to ten animals. These ponies were, of course, of no use as chargers; but as a means of locomotion, of rendering their riders a mobile force, they were invaluable.

Of guns there were on the crest of the hill of Talana six field-pieces. On the 19th (Thursday) the Dutchmen had thrown up entrenchments – ditches in which the riflemen could lie and take shelter, besides cover for the guns.

And so the sun rose on 8,000 men stern and resolute, armed with weapons of destruction such as no two white nations had ever used against each other before and each resolved to play the man.

Commandant Lucas Meyer, a well-known Transvaal patriot, president of the First Volksraad, held command on the top of the hill. General Symons led the 4,000 men in mud-coloured garments at the foot. It is easy to see that Meyer had the best of the position. He, to begin with held the top of the mountain; he was in an entrenched position; and he was on the defensive.

Scarcely had the sun risen when a gun boomed out, and a shell sailed through the air and dropped near the British camp at Dundee. But either the range was too long – it was about 3,400 yards – or the marksmanship was bad, for the first shell fell far short of its mark; but the third or fourth shot found its range. It was not very deadly, however, for the shells were of the "plugged" variety – *i.e.* not intended or expected to explode, but rather to act like the old-fashioned solid cannon-ball. The first shot was fired at about 5.30; and it caused surprise almost amounting to consternation amongst the British. Let us go back a few hours and see why that should be.

General Symons had been sitting with his advanced camp at Dundee for over a week – ever since the war broke out. His scouts and pickets had, indeed, since the 18th of the month been coming in contact with small detached parties of Boers; but these were not in anything like sufficient numbers to attack the advanced column, and were regarded as scouting and sniping parties. Even thus early in the war, however, we were to feel the difficulty of dealing with an enemy so mobile as this. It was here to-day and gone to-morrow. To-day your scouts, having scoured the country for miles round, bring word that there is not an enemy to be seen within thirty miles of you. And probably your scouts are right

Yet the very next morning, when your camp wakes with the reveille, you find within a few thousand yards of you a whole army, with guns already mounted and rifle-pits dug. That is exactly what had happened in this case. On Thursday our scouts had scouted some twelve or fifteen miles to the bank of the Buffalo River, which formed the boundary between the Transvaal and Natal, and had seen nothing. They reported, quite correctly, "No enemy to be found this side of the Buffalo." And let it be remembered that General Symons had the services of a number of the Natal Mounted Police and Carbineers, men who knew the country by heart, to do scouting work. Yet on Thursday night, Lucas Meyer, gathering together his 4,000 Vryheid farmers, forded the Buffalo River, dragging with him his six field-pieces; and, marching with all the stealthy rapidity of a moss-trooping band of Scottish border raiders, this force swept straight on Dundee.

They might have surprised Symons had not his pickets been particularly alive; but at 2.30 in the morning of Friday a mounted infantry picket of the Dubliners saw something: challenged it: a shot was fired: a private wounded: and the picket was driven in. It was known, therefore, that Boers were near the camp; and immediately on the picket's report, the General sent a party of the Dublin Fusiliers to take possession of a dry river-bed (there called a donga) on the east of the town. This donga was at the foot of Talana Hill, about 1,700 to 1,900 yards from the top, and formed a valuable starting point for the footmen in the battle. It afforded cover from rifle fire, and here troops could be formed for the attack.

At first it was thought in the British camp that the burgher force was only a party of riflemen; but the boom of that first cannon quickly undeceived our men. And General Symons found himself confronted, not by a mere reconnoitring or raiding detachment, but by a force equal in number to his own and armed with long-range field artillery. How those guns were carried to the top of the hill, over rocky ground, in dead of night and silently, was, and remains, a mystery.

For some little time the Dutchmen had all the artillery firing to themselves; but soon our batteries joined in. The 67th, which remained in the camp along with the Leicester regiment as a reserve, opened the ball on our side. The enemy used some smokeless explosive, probably melinite, and the positions of their guns had to be found by watching the flash as each cannon was fired. This is one of the difficulties of modern warfare. In former times the smoke of the powder soon told where the enemy's pieces were; but science has abolished this guide.

Meantime the other two batteries rattled off. The 13th went forward to the right, and the 69th forward to the left. General Symons formed his plan of battle pretty quickly. He was determined to give the Boers a lesson: to show them that the rooinek whom they despised was a good soldier and brave man, and that, to put it in the words of an officer, "Majuba Hill was not a fair sample." So he ordered the battle thus: – The batteries were to shell the burghers' artillery and put it out of action – a thing that ought to be fairly easy with twelve guns against six, with greater skill and with better ammunition.

When their batteries were silenced, ours were to shell the enemy's infantry position and try to demoralise them; or, at all events, to give them something to divert their attention from our infantry. These last were to be formed in the riverbed, and then to climb the hill in loose or open order – that is with plenty of space between the men – so as not to afford too good a target for the marksmen on the hill. They were to take all the cover they could get, and, creeping and rushing alternately, go from cover to cover until the charge was sounded. Then it was to be "Up and at 'em" with the bayonet. Meantime the Hussars were to make a detour round the hill, ready to cut up the retreating foe.

Symons must have had supreme confidence in his infantry to attempt a thing of this kind. To begin with, he was sending 2,000 men to attack nearly double their number, for only the battalions of the King's Royal Rifles and the Dublin and Royal Irish Fusiliers could be spared. The Leicesters must be kept in reserve for contingencies of the fighting, as well as to hold in check any flank attack.

So the men formed up in companies and battalions behind the village of Dundee, eager, expectant, ready; and by half-past five they marched out, the Dublins leading, by half-companies. That first startling shell had dropped just after the "before daylight parade," and the men had had no breakfast. And thus it came to pass that British soldiers went into battle hungry.

I know it is a common superstition that the same British soldier can neither fight nor march unless he has plenty of beef – a superstition encouraged by the author of "Waverley," who makes Charles the Bold speak of "the beef-consuming knaves." If you want to know how the "knaves" can fight on empty stomachs, make the acquaintance of some Boer who was at Talana. If you want to know how they can march, read hereafter the story of the retreat to Ladysmith.

At 5.45 (a.m.) o'clock our batteries had galloped into position, and they and the Boer artillery thundered at each other for nearly two hours. The plugged shells of the burghers did little or no damage; while our men, after they had got the range – and that was in less than twenty minutes – dropped shell after shell into the Boer position with merciless rapidity and precision. Our gunners were using shrapnel, which, when it bursts, sends out a shower of bullets; and as the shells were bursting well, there must have been blood running round the Boer guns. Still, the Dutch gunners, with the stubbornness of their breed, stuck to their work, and for two hours sent down with beautiful accuracy their ineffective missiles amongst our men. As shell after shell dropped about our guns, every time without exploding, our Mr. Atkins began to be merry, and more than one of them was heard to express the opinion that these were made in Germany, and that the manufacturer had sold not only the ammunition, but "Mr. Kroojer" as well. For when soldiers go into battle they do not talk heroic sentiments. They chaff one another and the enemy, and talk about everything except their heroic determination to do or die.

By 7.30 superior armament and ammunition had told their tale, and the artillery on the top of the hill ceased from troubling. One by one the pieces ceased to speak. Whether they were disabled or not, no man can tell to this day; but for the purpose of the moment, it was sufficient that they were silenced. And the men of the 69th and 13th Batteries cheered as they moved their guns forward, and began to shell the riflemen who lined Talana's crest.

From 6 o'clock the three infantry battalions had been lying down in the donga, and their position was trying enough. The rain was beginning to fall in a soaking drizzle, and it continued to fall all day. But the men were cheerful enough, for all that.

By 9 o'clock, the men having then been lying down for three hours or more – the original company of Dublins for double that time – the word was passed, "Unbuckle greatcoats from your waistbelts, and place them on the ground."

It is needless to say that since the battle began the men in the donga had not remained entirely unmolested. They had received a shell or two, and some rifle fire; but the damage done was trifling. Now the work was likely to be hotter, and the men braced themselves to do what had never been attempted before – namely, to carry by a frontal attack an entrenched position held by riflemen armed with the best modern weapons of precision.

It may be remarked that in theory this is impossible – all the best military authorities said so and had been saying so for a dozen years or more. Valour and the bayonet were to be at a discount. Every entrenched position must be turned, and these theories never applied more than on this day, when the men entrenched were the finest shots in the world. But these brave lads, the dashing Dublins, the gallant old 60th Rifles – who does not remember how a handful of them held back an army of Zulus at Rorke's Drift? – the fiery Irish Fusiliers, set out to perform the impossible. Well they knew the cost, but they held life cheap as the price of victory.

To be exact, the work to be accomplished was to march up the hill, first of all up to Peter Smith's Farm, a quiet homestead about half-way up, and surrounded by a not very thick wood. This part of the advance was very easy climbing, but it had the disadvantage of affording no cover until the men should reach a wall running partly up and partly round the hill. The next cover was the wood. From the wood they had to proceed steeply over bouldery, rough ground to a sort of terrace, which formed a kind of break in the hill. Round this terrace ran a second wall, a thick stone one. From beyond this wall the ground was just about as rough as ground could be, and from the end of the terrace to the top of the hill there was an almost perpendicular climb. There is no need to enlarge on the difficulties which such a position presented to an attacking force. It was a perfect Gibraltar.

Quietly and in order, the Dublins leading, the infantry advanced across the first gentle slope, making for the shelter of the first wall. The whole of this slope was open, and well within rifle range, so the order went that the advance was to be by half-companies. So the first half-company,[4] spreading itself out wide as for skirmishing, marched boldly across nearly half a mile of grass veldt, affording them no protection at all. And now blazed out the rifles from the plateau of Talana Hill. From some cause or other the farmers' shooting was not so deadly as it might have been. The Mausers emptied their magazines time and time and again, but of the leading company not a man fell. The infantry shook themselves together.

"Are these the beggars who call themselves marksmen?"

"Oi shud be ashamed av miself av Oi cuddn't hit a whole man at this distance!"

"'Tis a wickud waste av good ammynition, Oi cahl ut!"

"We shall have to send the serrgeant-major to tache thim muskittrry!" Now the sergeant-major's shooting is always the joke of the regiment.

"Sure, bhoys! They think 'tis the band we are, bekase we're marrchin' forrst, an' they don't mane to horrt us."

So the first half-company reached the shelter of the wall; and, lying down behind it, began to fire at the enemy – rather, at the top of the hill; for not a Boer showed himself. At the same time the second half of the same company marched over from the donga; and, as they arrived, they joined in the firing. At last, all were under the shelter of the wall; and then began a move to the wood, and in this stage of the attack a few men were hit.

At last the wood was reached. Welcome shelter! And here the men halted for the word to advance. Their next objective was the second wall above mentioned. It was now about 9.30, and here a terrible blow fell upon the British. General Symons had been galloping about the field, exposing his person with a fine disregard of danger. Bullets fell round him like hail, and his staff suffered heavily. The general was a mark the more conspicuous because he was attended by a mounted orderly who carried a lance bearing a red pennon, this being intended to serve as a landmark for all who came with messages for the general. Unfortunately, it also served to draw the attention of the Boer sharpshooters.

At about 9.30, then, Symons galloped across the open ground to the wood where the men had taken cover to speak a word of encouragement, and to give his final orders for the attack. It seemed as if every rifle on the plateau were aimed at him, and it was matter for marvel that he and his horse were not riddled. But neither was touched. While in the wood, being within fairly easy rifle range, he became the object of further marked attentions from the marksmen. His officers besought him to take cover, to retire, to dismiss the flag-carrying orderly. In vain! It was another case of Nelson and the stars and medals on his coat. "Do you think I'm going to let them imagine that I am afraid?" A bearded Boer looks over the entrenchment. His rifle goes to his shoulder. A careful sight, a long aim, a touch of the trigger, a sharp crack like the crack of a whip, and ere the Boer has emptied out the spent cartridge from his rifle General Symons reels in his saddle mortally wounded. A bullet had struck him in the stomach.

Carried into the village, his one thought is of the field he has left. "Are they – at – the top – yet?" And the doctor soothes him and brings a proud smile to his face by telling him, "Nearly at the top." And then the man of healing science injects morphia, for the pain of the wound is agonising.

The charge of the operations now devolved upon Yule, the colonel of the Devonshire Regiment, who held the local rank of Brigadier-General.

As for the men, nothing could now hold them back; for Symons was a man much beloved. Forward they crept, taking advantage of every boulder and every rock, for the range was shorter now; and any man who was seen was instantly made the target of a hundred rifles. Here the casualties grew more numerous. All the regiments advanced practically together, and in half an hour (at about 10.5) had won as far as the second stone wall. Under cover of this the Rifles and Irish Fusiliers halted for two hours.

The distance from the plateau was, perhaps, 600 yards – rather less if anything – and any man who showed himself dropped at once, lucky if he had only one bullet in him. The artillery on the right and left front were working round for a good position, and continued to shell the entrenchments. Rarely has there been more accurate artillery fire. For two long hours the battle held thus, the Boers showering Mauser bullets on our infantry; our artillery showering shrapnel on the Boer riflemen.

It is not to be imagined that our Lee Metfords did not speak at all. It was not likely that a crack shooting corps like the 60th would lie within 600 yards of the enemy and not burn a cartridge or two. Now there was a Boer, a wily man, and a sharpshooter. A sharpshooter is one who can shoot with the utmost accuracy without appearing to take aim. Up goes the rifle to the shoulder, and almost simultaneously the trigger is pulled. This particular Boer sharpshooter made himself an unmitigated nuisance to a company of the Rifles. Did one show out of cover so much as an inch, the Boer hit him. The captain of the company put his helmet on a rifle and raised it a little above the wall. Two bullets were through it before he could lower it. "Good job a head wasn't in it."

Now in this company of the 60th there was another sharpshooter. And the rest wanted to know, with many expletives, what was the good of him. And they became so vigorous in their remarks that the object thereof was constrained to ask them, "Wot there was to bloomin' well shoot at?"

At last, however, the British sharpshooter found a place whence he could watch the stone behind which his rival was ensconced; and he waited. Now! The least little bit of the Dutchman's head is visible above his boulder. Crack! The Lee-Metford speaks. Cruel fate! Just as Tommy pulls the trigger, another Boer, impelled by curiosity, puts his face above the stone, right in front of the sharpshooter. He drops! And as he drops, derisive laughter shakes the sides of the 60th.

It was no laughing matter for "the other old beggar," who lay with a bullet through his brain; but it furnished matter of merriment for a good hour to that company of the Rifles. To all except one.

The Fusiliers, on the left of the attack, had a curious method of progression. This is how they mounted. There was, running up from the wood nearly to the top of the hill a gully, or cleft in the ground, with precipitous, grey boulder-strewn banks. The Irishmen crawled along, a few at a time, and dropped into this gully, where they could be seen by, but could not see, the enemy. They made their way along it, dodging from boulder to boulder, until they reached the other end. Then, singly, every man making himself as small as he could, they crept out. Every man, as he emerged, crawled for cover to the left; and as soon as a whole section was out and under cover, another started. Of course, those who were out fired as often as they could see anything to fire at.

In this way the line of infantry crept slowly up the hill; and now the men began to drop. "Who's that?" "F Company! Man down." A bullet is through his head. A man crawls ahead to take cover. A groan! "He's hit!" And an officer springs out to bear him to a place of safety. Plucky of you, Captain Weldon. But fatal. For a score of rifles direct their fire at the gallant officer, and he drops, more sorely stricken than the man he went to help.

At noon, for the space of a few minutes, the Dutchmen slackened slightly, and in a minute the word was "Forward!" The "advance" sounded, and in a trice Rifles and Fusiliers were over the wall, bolting across the terrace and scaling the almost perpendicular height at the top of the hill. Here there was no cover, and men fell fast. The King's Royal Rifles were, if anything, leading, headed by Colonel Gunning, as fine an officer as ever wore a sword. He was at the head of his regiment, and nearly at the top of the hill, when he was shot through the brain.

The Rifles went in with a wild yell and a rush that nothing could stop. On top of them came the Dublins and the Royal Irish; and at last the climb was over, the impossible had been accomplished, and those three battalions of British infantry stood victorious on the crest of that blood-stained hill. There was some hot work with the bayonet for those Boers who still remained in the trenches. But few waited the onset. When they found the despised rooinek so close at hand, looking so fierce and determined, and carrying that terrible steel, the Dutchmen, true to those tactics of guerilla warfare which they use so well, ran for all they were worth, mounted the little razor-backed ponies, and were off like the wind. A few, wounded and unwounded, surrendered.

For the infantry, the battle was now over. They had been victorious. They had carried an almost inaccessible position in the face of such rifle fire as the rest of the world could nowhere show. They had proved themselves the true sons of that invincible infantry which drove Napoleon's marshals from the Guadalquivir to the Pyrenees. They had shown that valour may still win battles, that in military matters the personal equation is still something.

But at what cost was the victory won! Symons was down; and it was certain that he would never more lead his old comrades. The King's Royal Rifles had lost, in addition to their colonel, four other officers in killed and seven wounded – in all, twelve officers out of the seventeen who went into action. The Dublins and the Royal Irish Fusiliers had also suffered, but less heavily. They had lost respectively two officers killed and three and five wounded. Of non-commissioned officers and men, the Rifles lost eleven killed and seventy-five wounded, the Dublins four and forty-four, and the Royal Irish Fusiliers fourteen and thirty-one. The proportion of casualties amongst officers was, it will be seen, enormous, and it arose from this fact: in carrying a position by this kind of attack, it is imperative that the men should take cover; and it is the duty of officers commanding companies to select the cover. Now, when bullets are falling like hail it might be that it would be better for officers wishing to survey the ground ahead of them to raise themselves no more than is necessary, so as not to expose themselves. But this has not been the way of the British officer. For good or evil he would never take the least care of himself. If you asked him why, he would tell you: "Must set good example to the men, y' know. Never do to let 'em think we funked." Or perhaps he would tell you, with a stare of surprise, that his business was, in the main, not to take care of himself. And so on the slope of Talana the officers exposed themselves with the cool and careless recklessness of their race and their class, walking when they might have crawled and when crawling would have been quite dangerous enough. In the front the whole time; the whole time as conspicuous as they could well be made by the glitter of their uniform and the carrying of sword instead of rifle. How a single man of them escaped is nothing less than a miracle, for every one of them was, for several hours, a target – a special target – for some of the finest marksmen in the world.

Among others fell Colonel Sherston – "lucky John," they called him – one of the fine fellows who had helped to earn Lord Roberts his famous title of Baron of Candahar. He was serving on the brigade staff here, and by his death the Empire lost a brilliant servant. Colonel Beckett, Major Hammersley, and Captain Lock Adams, staff officers all, were seriously wounded. The King's mourned Colonel Gunning, Captain Mark Pechell – a stalwart man who towered head and shoulders above his fellows, and who led his company up the slope until he was picked off – and Lieutenants Taylor, Barnett and Hambro.

Connor, the adjutant of the Irish Fusiliers, received a mortal wound, and Lieutenant Hill was shot dead. This was not the first time Connor had been under fire; the North-West Frontier of India well knew his fearless form. Best of Irishmen, most dashing of soldiers. His men wept when he breathed his last. The Dublins lost Captain Weldon, who was shot dead instantaneously, and Lieutenant Genge, mortally wounded. And, greatest loss and grief of all, the general, too, proved to be mortally wounded, though he lingered on for several days.

So much for the losses; now for the gains of the victory. To begin with, the Boers undoubtedly suffered heavily from our shell fire. It was known that they had buried or carried away most of their dead and wounded; but about thirty were lying on the plateau, and there was captured a field hospital with seventy more wounded.

As a matter of fact, the whole force ought to have been destroyed, but that they were not was due to two stupid blunders. The 69th Battery was well placed for shelling the retreating enemy, the guns having been dragged forward to Smith's Nek (*Nek* = pass between two hills), whence the defeated commando could be distinctly seen retreating, with guns and all equipment. By all the rules of the art of war, the 69th Battery ought to have plumped shell after shell into this retreating mass of men, galloping after them when they got out of range, and have smashed, pulverised, and destroyed them utterly, and compelled them to abandon their artillery. This chance was, however, thrown away. Why? Nobody knows. The explanation given was that someone had informed the officer commanding the battery that an armistice had been concluded!

Now there is another way of driving defeat home – of turning a defeat into a disaster, a disaster into a rout – and that is by the use of cavalry. As stated before, General Symons had despatched Colonel Moller with 200 or so of Hussars and mounted infantry round the hill, to fall on the enemy's flank. Night fell, and nothing had been seen of Colonel Moller. Firing was heard, late in the day, in the direction of the enemy's line of retreat; and our men hoped and thought that Moller and his men were cutting up the enemy. But Meyer, though defeated, was not routed. When Moller's force put in an appearance on his flank, the wily Dutchman ran away until he had lured the Hussars into a trap, out of which it was impossible to get in the face of 2,500 men with rifles.

When the unfortunate Hussars found themselves entrapped they seized a Kaffir cattle station, and defended themselves bravely enough as long as they could. Then they surrendered.

And that is how the defeated army of Lucas Meyer was able to send 170 British prisoners to Pretoria – the whole cavalry of the force that defeated them. No! Not quite the whole. For a certain Sergeant Baldrey, who was with a troop of thirty separated from the rest, cut his way out, and by the exercise of skill and discretion, as well as bravery, contrived to steer his troop safe back to camp with the loss of three horses only.

It was a great feat, and Baldrey proved once more that there are men who do not hold commissions but who are quite able to lead. Finding that his colonel had blundered into two fresh commandoes of General Joubert's force, Baldrey ordered his men, who were away on the left scouting, to face about. Off they went, but not unperceived. The Boers thought that Baldrey's contingent would ride straight back to Dundee. Not a bit of it. The sergeant was a tactician. So while a Boer party went to cut him off, he headed for the open country. Another Boer party pursued him for half a day, and fired on him; but not a man was hit. It was not until several days afterward that the little band rode into camp. They were obliged to make a great detour to avoid the cutting-off party between themselves and Dundee. And they had to scout every yard of the way, for fear of blundering into a party of the enemy.

Of Boer ponies, Mauser rifles, ammunition, and so forth, there was a good deal left behind in the retreat; and the King's Rifles captured two Transvaal flags – a bit of honour and glory that gallant regiment well deserved.

The material gains of the victory of Talana Hill were not very marked, but the moral gain was enormous. It indeed showed the Boers that "Majuba was not a fair sample"; and it taught our men that even these vaunted marksmen could be overcome, and that, too, when they had the advantage in numbers and the best position. Still, the patriotic Briton could not but lament that the material gain had been so slight.

Chapter II

The causes of the war

IT is impossible to understand the cause of this quarrel without going a long way back – back, in fact, to the beginning of the century. After the Great Prisoner had been immured in St. Helena, when boundaries were being settled, Britain was allowed by the Great Powers to retain Cape Colony, which was then a purely Dutch settlement. Cape Town, and the district round it, had been colonised originally by the Dutch East India Company and many farmers had emigrated thither. Thither also went large numbers of French Protestants, two centuries ago, when their own fair land was made an impossible abode for men who dared to believe according to their conscience. But after the Cape became a British possession, a few English and Scots went there too, and became farmers and traders.

The farms were largely worked by the labour of slaves, the original black inhabitants of the country. In 1811 slavery was abolished wherever the British flag floated, and Parliament voted an enormous sum of money by way of compensation to slave-owners. It was alleged, and it may be true, that the Boers of Cape Colony did not receive their fair share of compensation. At all events, in a few years' time they found themselves with ruin staring them in the face. And so in 1833, and right on to 1837, a large number, many hundreds, packed up their household chattels in waggons, drove their flocks and herds before them, shouldered their muskets, and trekked forth into the wilderness.

They settled to the north of the Orange River, and some even crossed the Vaal River, a stream which runs westward and southward, and eventually pours its intermittent waters into the Orange River. They subdued the country, fought and defeated the Zulus, Basutos, Bechuanas, and other native tribes; and there they lived for nearly twenty years, farming and hunting. As for government, they thought little of it. Each isolated householder kept order in his own domain. The British Government laid claim to their allegiance, but it was given grudgingly, or not at all, until at last, by the agreement of 1852, known as the Sand River Convention, the "Dutch African Republic," or Transvaal, was recognised as independent. British emigrants had been pouring in on the North-East, and had largely colonised the country now known as Natal, of which possession was formally taken by Great Britain in 1843.

The Sand River Convention carved out as independent Boer territory an enormous tract of country north of the Vaal and south of the Limpopo or Crocodile

River, extending east to Delagoa Bay, and west from the Marico River to Fourteen Streams, a country of 110,000 square miles, or 20,000 square miles greater than Great Britain. In 1854 the British Government further conferred independence on those Boers who had trekked north of the Orange but south of the Vaal, under the style of the Orange Free State. The Free Staters, from that day to the year 1899, lived at peace, and apparently in amity, with the subjects of the Queen, who formed their southern, eastern, and western neighbours; and, their country being a fertile one and well enough watered, they speedily became a solid, sober nation of pastoral and agricultural farmers. Their national history, happily, was uneventful.

But with the Dutch African Republic – afterwards called "The South African Republic" – matters were very different. These men seemed to comprise the whole of the more fanatical part of the trekkers – stern Calvinists: more like the Westland Whigs whom Claverhouse hated than like any other men of whom we know. They were the Chosen People. The blacks were the race of Ham – the Hivites and the Hittites, who must either be exterminated or made to labour for the superior race. They passed the *Grond Wet*, or Fundamental Law, declaring that they would "admit of no equality of persons of colour with the white inhabitants either in Church or State." This spirit brought about troubles with the natives; and there were massacres; and vengeances; and more massacres. They even quarrelled with and invaded the Orange Free State in 1857, and tried to impose a union upon the Free Staters. In 1868 Delagoa Bay was annexed – on paper – by Pretorius, the President; but on Britain and Portugal putting in rival claims, the matter was referred to arbitration, and Marshal MacMahon awarded the Bay and the territory a few miles inland to Portugal, which was a blessing in disguise to the Transvaal, as she has discovered in this war.

In 1875 the burghers entered upon a war with Sikokuni, a native chief, and had by no means the best of it. Then Great Britain tried to prevail upon the two Boer States to agree to a federation of themselves, Natal, and Cape Colony; and this might have been accomplished but for the action of the Cape Ministry of the day. The reason assigned for this was the danger from the natives, who were everywhere restive. The Zulus were, in fact, having very much the best of a war that was raging between the Boers and themselves. Then, in 1877 Britain intervened and annexed the Transvaal, it being alleged that the burghers as a whole were agreeable to this course. As a matter of fact, many objected, including one Paul Kruger, who headed a deputation of protest to England.

After the Zulu War, in 1879, in which many Boers fought with us against the natives, some taxation was imposed on the Transvaal to help to meet the expenses. Now the Boers, under their own government, had hardly known the meaning of taxation, and they prepared to resist. They accumulated in every farmhouse stores of ammunition. They bought the best rifles; they formed a secret combination. And at last, just before Christmas of 1880, a large party of farmers, met to celebrate the defeat of Dingaan by Pretorius,[5] rose in open revolt to resist the seizure of a farmer's waggon, which had been distrained upon for taxes. Over a thousand burghers there assembled took an oath not to lay down their arms until independence had been achieved. As each man's turn came, he picked up a stone, and, when he had finished taking the oath, he cast it from him, until gradually a cairn was made. This was at Paardekraal.

The burghers acted with great promptitude, and, to cut a long story short, eventually met and defeated a small force of British soldiers, under Sir George Colley, at Majuba Hill, near the place where Natal, the Free State, and the Transvaal meet. The shooting of the Boers was so deadly that almost every man who showed himself was shot. Sir Evelyn Wood was ordered to quell the rising, and Lord Roberts was also despatched from India. But nothing further was done. The British Government had previously made up its mind to grant independence to the enemy, and a Convention was signed for that purpose on March 21st, 1881.

As the preamble of this Convention gave rise to much dispute, it will be well to summarise it. It declared that the British Government accorded "complete self-government, *subject to the suzerainty* of Her Majesty, her Heirs and Successors." In 1884 a further agitation was begun in the Transvaal for a revision of the 1881 Convention, and in 1884 the British Government consented to a revision. The Convention of London (1884), as it was called, declared that "the following articles of a new Convention should be substituted for those of" the 1881 Convention. It is somewhat important to notice this, because, since the Convention of London did not mention suzerainty, it was contended that suzerainty had been tacitly abolished or purposely dropped.

The words last quoted hardly seem to bear that construction, on the face of them; but it is impossible for any person to speak with real impartiality on the subject, and it probably will be so for many years to come, because the matter has been made one of party politics. And where party politics begin, farewell to impartial judgment. The Macaulay of 1950 will, perhaps, be able to solve the problem. It is certain, however, that "suzerainty" was an unfortunate word to use. "Suzerain" is a feudal term, adopted by us from the French; and it describes this state of things: Suppose, for example, the King of France granted a province to a nobleman, as he did to the first Duke of Normandy. The nobleman, being a vassal of the king, was bound to render him the services contracted for when the grant was made – generally, services in war. The great vassal let out the land in smaller parcels to counts and knights, who became bound to serve him, and these to farmers and husbandmen, who became bound to serve them. Now, the King of France was the suzerain or over-lord of that province. But his powers regarding it were of the slightest – as witness the relations of the Dukes of Normandy and Burgundy with their suzerains, the French kings. Technically, the great vassal owed the suzerain assistance in time of war and certain irregular occasional payments in money or in kind; and he was bound not to make war upon his over-lord.

This state of things, which is really suzerainty, could not possibly be supposed to describe the relations intended to be established between her Majesty and the South African Republic. And, therefore, the term was one of those loose, misleading words, sure at some time to lead to dispute; because its plain, grammatical, legal meaning not being the true interpretation, each side tried to put on it a gloss to suit its own purposes.

This also seems certain: that the Boer view of "suzerainty" was not the British view. The Convention of 1884 contained two other provisions which led to dispute. One was Article 7, which guaranteed to British subjects and loyalists resident in the Transvaal on August 8th, 1881, full civil rights and protection for their persons and property. Article 14 guaranteed to all persons (other than natives) full liberty to enter, reside, or travel, possess landed property of all kinds, carry on trade and commerce in the republic, without being subject to any taxes, general or local, other than those imposed upon burghers.

Not very long after the Convention of London the Transvaalers showed some disposition to extend their boundaries; and, largely to prevent trouble with the natives, who have always hated the Transvaal Dutch, but partly, also, to protect them from oppression, the British Government hoisted the Union Jack in Bechuanaland and proclaimed a protectorate there. This was in March, 1885, and it had the effect of confining the new republic to the Limpopo as its western as well as its northern boundary, and of preventing any possible expansion of territory. The subsequent seizure and colonisation of the country of the Matabele by the Chartered Company of South Africa also shut them in to the north, and left the two Boer republics absolutely surrounded by British territory, except for a strip of the eastern frontier of the Transvaal, marching with Portuguese East Africa (Delagoa Bay).

Here they might have remained peaceful enough, attending to their flocks and herds, their sowing and reaping, had it not been for one fact, which altered the whole aspect of South Africa, and created again a South African question.

In 1886 gold was discovered in the Middleburg district of the Transvaal. More was found in the Witwatersrand. And immediately the little township of Johannesburg, about twenty-five miles away from Pretoria, began to receive the inrush of the hordes who came to hunt for the precious metal. Soon Johannesburg became the largest and most prosperous town in South Africa, and the population was a population of all nations, but chiefly British subjects.

It was the discovery of the gold that made war possible; for it produced the Outlander question, and it led to the Jameson Raid. Finally, it made the Transvaal rich, and thus enabled the burghers to accumulate warlike stores, to construct fortifications, to hire officers from Europe, to employ mercenaries, to convert Pretoria into one of the most formidable arsenals in the world, and to make the South African Republic the best-armed State in Africa. In 1885 the revenue was £177,876. In 1898 it was £3,983,560, and of this £321,651 was from mining prospectors' licences, £668,951 from railway receipts – principally connected with the Rand – and £1,066,994 from Customs, due to the large increase of population on the Rand.

In course of time the Outlanders, as the new population was called, outnumbered the Boer farmers, who regarded the immigrants from the first with mistrust and dislike. For although, as a mining city, Johannesburg was never a centre of lawlessness, vice and debauchery such as were found in the early Californian and Australian goldfields – since the Rand mining was conducted by machinery, and was necessarily an organised industry – yet the pious Calvinistic farmers regarded a town where night was turned into day, where the Sabbath was not strictly observed, where theatres and music-halls existed, as practically a centre of infection. Imagine, if you can, what would have been thought of such a place by the Scottish Whig farmers of Wigton and Galloway in 1600, or even in 1800, and you may have some idea of the Boer feeling.

Ere long the Rand population began to agitate. They found themselves governed, policed, judged by a set of men whom they regarded as ignorant bigots; lazy, unprogressive. They found themselves paying nearly all the taxes, and having no voice in the spending of them. The Volksraad, or republican parliament, was elected by Boers only. Taxation was adjusted, so they said, in order that they, the men who were "making the country" by their capital and their brains, might be practically the only taxpayers. Their children were obliged to be taught in a hybrid Dutch *patois*, or else not go to school at all. Dynamite, an essential in Rand mining, was only obtainable from a concessionnaire, who had bought the monopoly of it from the Government. They were taxed far more heavily than the needs of government required. They had not even the municipal franchise. They complained that there was no justice – in the inferior courts, at all events – between Boer and stranger. They even complained of the corruption of the Government. This was the Outlander question. The time has not yet come when a historian can decide on the rights of this quarrel. Here it is merely intended to state both sides as fairly as may be.

The Boers replied: – We will not give you the franchise in any way on an equality with ourselves, because you outnumber us, and to do this would be national suicide. In President Kruger's words, "How can strangers govern my State?" As to taxation, you came here to get rich; you take your riches literally out of our soil. It is only fair that you should pay more heavily than others. Lastly, we know that you Englanders wish to make this a British State. We will not submit to lose our independence.

After a time, the British Outlanders appealed to their parent Government to interfere; and some remonstrance was addressed to President Kruger. While pourparlers were being exchanged, an association called the Reform Committee appealed to Mr. Cecil Rhodes, the controlling head of the Chartered Company, a man of vast wealth, and influence only surpassed by his ambition, to aid them. And eventually it was agreed that a rising should take place in Johannesburg; and that, if need be, a force of the Chartered Company's men should march from Rhodesia through Bechuanaland and assist the Johannesburgers by policing the town and protecting the women and children.

Dr. Jameson was then administrator of Rhodesia; and he, in December, 1895, got together about 600 men, all mounted, with some Maxim guns, and marched from Mafeking over the Transvaal border. But the movement failed for want of concert. The Johannesburgers, who had been obliged to arm secretly, were not yet ready to rise when, on Monday, the 30th of December, 1895, they heard that "Dr. Jim" and his men were at Krugersdorp, a point about twenty miles west of the golden city. The Boer Executive had been better informed – in time, in fact, to gather together a force of burghers, who blocked the way to the Rand. The republican force met the raiders after these had been marching for ninety hours almost continuously.

Men and horses were tired out when, on the 1st of January, a rifle-fire from the adjacent hills and kopjes brought them to a halt. Cover was sought; but the burghers had selected their position. And although the Englanders fought bravely enough for a time, they finally surrendered. The commandant of the Boer commando at first decided to shoot the prisoners, but eventually thought better of it, and the ringleaders were ultimately handed over to the British Government, were tried in London, convicted of an offence against the Foreign Enlistments Act, and sentenced to varied terms of imprisonment.

The Johannesburgers at once surrendered such arms as they had, on the advice of the British Commissioner at the Cape. And from that time to the outbreak of war, negotiations went on from time to time between the Governments for a removal of the Outlanders' grievances. But the Boers' suspicions were aroused. "You want," they said, "not equal rights, but our country"; and from that time they regarded Mr. Rhodes as a kind of Mephistopheles. And when in the House of Commons Mr. Chamberlain publicly exonerated Mr. Rhodes from blame, "as a man of honour," the Colonial Secretary was regarded as hand-in-glove with their worst enemy. And so, when negotiations reached any stage beyond mere politenesses President Kruger distrusted Mr. Chamberlain and the British Government. He adopted a procrastinating policy. And very soon the British Government distrusted him, too.

Meanwhile the Transvaal Government was arming. Every sixpence it could raise was spent upon munitions of war of the latest and best type. Mauser rifles, Maxim guns, Hotchkiss guns, field artillery and guns of position from the Creusot works in France, shells and cartridges in millions. And as the Boers were no cannoneers, having, for the most part, a pious horror of great machines, German gunners were imported. And French, Russian, and German officers came in and surveyed the country, and prepared to place their knowledge of the art of war at the service of the Boers.

The Free Staters also armed, and concluded a treaty with their cousins mutually to defend the independence of the two republics. Negotiations for the friendly settlement of a dispute are not likely to be successful when neither party trusts the other. And in this case neither party did. Sir Alfred Milner had been sent out to the Cape as High Commissioner after the Raid, to see if he could not restore harmony between the white races there; and ultimately, in 1899, when the Colonial Office persisted in its demands for redress of Outlander grievances, but without inducing the Transvaal to do anything, Sir Alfred Milner suggested a conference between himself and President Kruger. This was held on the neutral ground of Bloemfontein, the capital of the Orange Free State. But again each party thought the other had something "at the back of his mind," as the Americans say, and the conference ended in precisely nothing. This was in May and June of 1899.

War was now in sight. The negotiations still went on; and once or twice it appeared possible that a settlement would be arrived at by peaceful means. But the old distrust prevented the realisation of this hope. The letters between the parties became more bitter and more recriminatory, each not failing to accuse the other of bad faith. The British Government accused the Transvaal Executive of breaking Article 14 of the 1884 Convention (see p. 19) by unfair incidence of taxation, and by rendering life in the republic practically impossible for a self-respecting Briton – in fact, of doing indirectly what would have been a clear breach of agreement had it been done directly.

In August, 1899, the British troops in Natal amounted to about 6,000. In September they were increased by a whole infantry battalion, and several more battalions of infantry and batteries of artillery were sent from England, India, and Egypt, and Sir George White went out as general in command. The Boers were also arming rapidly, and arms and ammunition were arriving daily at Delagoa Bay and the Cape, and being forwarded to Pretoria. The Boers talked of British desire for annexation. The British element feared a Dutch conspiracy – with the republics as a nucleus, but aided by Cape Dutch – to oust our rule from South Africa.

No doubt many Boers had, since Majuba and the Convention of Pretoria, been in the habit of thinking and speaking contemptuously about Britain and the British. They treated the British Outlanders with contempt, often actively and offensively manifested. They regarded the British army as a collection of weaklings, led by idiots: the men being unable to ride, shoot, or take cover – men who would surrender after the first few shots. In fact, of military prestige in South Africa the British had none. The common Boers regarded the Convention of Pretoria not as a magnanimous and generous act, but as a treaty extorted at the muzzle of their rifles. And, no doubt, they expected to be able to defy the British power with success, if not with ease, in view of their increased armaments. Whether Presidents Kruger and Steyn, Mr. Reitz, and General Joubert, who had travelled and seen something of Britain's resources, shared the sentiments of their ignorant countrymen, cannot be told.

Matters were brought to a crisis in the month of September. The British Government became insistent. Sir W. Penn Symons, at that time in command of the forces in Natal, moved his troops up the country to Ladysmith – now a place of historical military interest – and formed a base camp there. This, no doubt, was by way of precaution against a raid; for, as may be seen from the map (p. 5), this part of Natal runs up between the Free State and the Transvaal, and is open to an attack from both sides at once. Moreover, in this neighbourhood are the coalfields of the colony. In September Colonel Moller was sent nearer to the border, to Dundee, with an advanced column; and so quietly was the march made that the townsfolk's first intimation of the presence of troops was the roll of the drums playing them into camp. On October 11th General Symons took over this column.

There is no doubt that these military movements, and especially the increase in garrison, caused much searching of heart amongst the Boers, and afforded them a ground of complaint. "Here," they said, "we are negotiating, and at the same time you increase the number of your troops"; and Cronje, one of their generals, rode into Dundee to ask the meaning of it, and they, too, massed commando after commando on the border. Eventually, on the 9th of October, 1899, Sir Alfred Milner received from Secretary Reitz, of the Transvaal Executive, an Ultimatum. This extraordinary document demanded an assurance that no more British troops should be sent into South Africa; and gave Her Majesty's Government forty-eight hours within which to make up their minds. The Colonial Secretary replied that such terms could not even be discussed.

Then came a proclamation by Mr. Steyn, President of the Orange Free State, denouncing Great Britain and officially casting in his lot and the lot of his people with that of the kindred republic. Blood, as we know on the authority of Sir Walter Scott, is thicker than water; but yet the British people were surprised at this defiance from a country with which we had never had a quarrel. But the die was cast. It was the whole Boer race against the British Empire.

In forty-eight hours from the ultimatum, the burghers were on the move.

Notes

1. Most regiments of British infantry are divided into battalions – two or more of regulars, one or more of militia, and one or more of volunteers, each consisting, when at full strength, of 1,010 men of all ranks.
2. "Squadron' is, perhaps, an improper term to use of mounted infantry. A squadron is a fourth part of a regiment of cavalry on peace footing.
3. A Battery is a party of artillery. Our artillery is not divided into regiments as cavalry and infantry are, but into batteries. A Field Battery consists of six guns, worked by five commissioned officers (major, captain, and three lieutenants), and 176 non-commissioned officers and men of various grades, nine being artificers (collar-makers, etc.) and fifty-nine drivers. The guns used are 15-pounders, sighted to 5,000 yards.
4. A battalion of infantry is divided into companies. A company is composed, when at war strength of 101 privates, five sergeants, five corporals, two lieutenants, and a captain; the last-mentioned is the company commander.
5. Dingaan was a Zulu chief, who almost exterminated the Transvaalers. After defeating them several times and overrunning the country, he was met near the Buffalo River in 1840 by the last force possible for the Boers to collect, and defeated with such slaughter that his power was broken. The Boer general, Pretorius, was ever afterwards regarded as the saviour of his country; and the capital of the young republic was named after him – Pretoria. The anniversary of Dingaan's Day is the great Transvaal festival of the year.

16

S. R. GARDINER, *A STUDENT'S HISTORY OF ENGLAND FROM THE EARLIEST TIMES TO 1885* (LONDON: LONGMANS AND CO., 1892), PP. 952–955.

Samuel Rawson Gardiner (1829–1902) was an Oxford-educated English historian, whose reputation lay in his histories of the 17th century. In addition to these books, he also published school textbooks such as An Outline of English History *(1902) and* A School Atlas of English History *(1892). His assessment of the Indian Mutiny reflects a minor shift in earlier views that had seen British actions as guiltless. Instead, Gardiner perceives Indian culture as in need of reform but believes it best that the Indians are left untouched by the British.*

28. **The Sepoy Army. 1856–1857**. – In **1856,** Lord Canning, a son of the Prime Minister George Canning, became governor-general. By that time some of the dispossessed princes and most of the offended native gentlemen had formed a conspiracy against the British Government, which they held to have been unjust towards them and which in some cases had really been so. The conspirators aimed at securing the support of the Bengal Sepoy army, which had also been alarmed by certain acts in which the Government had not shown itself sufficiently careful of their feelings and prejudices. Most of the Sepoys were Hindoos, and all Hindoos are divided into castes, and believe that the man who loses his caste is not only disgraced in the present life but suffers misery after death. This loss of caste is not the penalty for moral faults, but for purely bodily actions, such as eating out of the same vessel as one of a lower caste. Caste, too, is lost by eating any part of the sacred animal the cow, and, as a new rifle had been lately served out, the conspirators easily frightened the mass of the Sepoys into the belief that the cartridges for this rifle were greased with cow's fat. When, therefore, they bit the new cartridges, as soldiers then had to do, before loading, their lips would touch the cow's grease and they would at once lose caste. It was said that the object of the Government was to render the men miserable by depriving them of the shelter of their own religion in order to drive them to the adoption of Christianity in despair.

29. **The Outbreak of the Mutiny. 1857**. – In the spring of **1857** there were attempts to mutiny near Calcutta, but the actual outbreak occurred at Meerut near

Delhi. There the native regiments first massacred their English officers and such other Englishmen as they met with, and then marched to Delhi, where they proclaimed the descendant of the Great Mogul (see p. 801), who was living there as a British pensioner, Emperor of India. Canning did what he could by sending for British troops from other parts of India, and also for a considerable force which happened to be at sea on its way to take part in a war which had broken out with China. His position was, however, exceedingly precarious till further reinforcements could be brought from England. His best helper was Sir John Lawrence, who had governed the recently annexed Punjab with such ability and justice that the Sikh warriors, so lately the fierce enemies of the British, were ready to fight in their behalf. As the Sikhs did not profess the Hindoo religion, there was, in their case, no difficulty about caste. With their aid Lawrence disarmed the Sepoys in the Punjab, and sent all the troops he could spare to besiege Delhi. Delhi, however, was a strong place and, as the besiegers were few, months elapsed before it could be taken.

30. **Cawnpore. 1857**. – The mutiny spread to Lucknow, the capital of Oude, where the few Englishmen in the place were driven into the Residency with Sir Henry Lawrence, Sir John's brother, at their head, to hold out, if they could, till help arrived. At Cawnpore, not far off, were about five hundred British women and children, and less than five hundred British men were besieged by Nana Sahib, who hated the English on account of the wrongs which he conceived himself to have suffered at their hands. After they had suffered terrible hardships, Nana Sahib offered to allow the garrison to depart in safety. The offer was accepted and the weary defenders made their way to the boats waiting for them on the river, where they were shot down from the bank. Some of the women and children were kept alive for a few days, but in the end all were massacred, and their bodies flung into a well. Only four of the defenders of Cawnpore escaped to tell the miserable tale.

31. **The Recovery of Delhi and the Relief of Lucknow. 1857**. The mutiny, widely spread as it was, was confined to the Bengal Presidency. In Lucknow, though Sir Henry Lawrence had been slain, the garrison held out in the Residency. At last Havelock, a brave, pious officer, who prayed and taught his men to pray as the Puritan soldiers had prayed in Cromwell's time, brought a small band through every obstacle to its relief. Before he reached the place Sir James Outram joined him, authorised by the Government to take the command out of his hands. Outram, however, honourably refused to take from Havelock the credit of the achievement. 'To you,' wrote Outram to Havelock, 'shall be left the glory of relieving Lucknow, for which you have already struggled so much. I shall accompany you, placing my military service at your disposal, should you please, and serving under you as a volunteer.' Thus supported, Havelock relieved Lucknow on September 25, but he had not men enough to drive off the besiegers permanently, and Outram, who, after the city had been entered, took the command, had to wait for relief in turn. Delhi had already been taken by storm on September 10.

32. **The End of the Mutiny. 1857–1858**. – Soon after the relief of Lucknow Sir Colin Campbell, who afterwards became Lord Clyde, arrived with reinforcements

from England, and finally suppressed the mutiny. In **1858** Parliament put an end to the authority of the East India Company (see p. 808). Thenceforth the Governor-General was brought directly under the Queen, acting through a British Secretary of State for India responsible to Parliament. There was also to be an Indian Council in England composed of persons familiar with Indian affairs, in order that the Secretary of State might have the advice of experienced persons. On assuming full authority, the Queen issued a proclamation to the peoples and princes of India. To the people she promised complete toleration in religion, and admission to office of qualified persons. To the princes she promised scrupulous respect for their rights and dignities. To all she declared her intention of respecting their rights and customs. It is in this last respect especially that the proclamation laid down the lines on which administration of India will always have to move if it is to be successful. Englishmen cannot but perceive that many things are done by the natives of India which are in their nature hurtful, unjust, or even cruel, and they are naturally impatient to remove evils that are very evident to them. The lesson necessary for them to learn is the one which Walpole taught their own ancestors, that it is better to leave evils untouched for a while than to risk the overthrow of a system of government which, on the whole, works beneficently. It is one thing to endeavour to lead the people of India forward to a better life, another thing to drag them forward and thereby to provoke a general exasperation which would lessen the chances of improvement in the future, and might possibly sweep the reforming government itself away.

17

E. SALMON, *THE STORY OF THE EMPIRE* (LONDON: GEORGE NEWNES, 1902), PP. 154–163.

Edward Salmon was the editor of United Empire, *the journal of the Royal Colonial Institute. In* The Story of the Empire, *Salmon saw the Empire as a success story, having withstood downturns such as the loss of the American colonies, and discontent in Canada in Australia and at the Cape at the beginning of Queen Victoria's reign. Had she been in full command of the facts, Salmon argued, Queen Victoria would have concluded that the Empire was 'doomed to dissolution'. Cobden and Bright of the Manchester School had argued that colonies were too costly to acquire and yielded few trade benefits. This pessimism had also been circulated in the work of Adam Smith and John Stuart Mill. Conditions in New South Wales were chaotic, as settlers were pitched against convicts, and in New Zealand 10 per cent of the white settlers were escaped convicts. Empire had then gradually been reconstituted during the rest of Victoria's reign. The chapter included here is the penultimate chapter, titled 'Progress All Round'.*

Progress all round – colonial federation – the Boer War – Indian advancement and grievances – the scramble for Africa

GRADUALLY the mists generated by political economy and misapprehension of the trend of events began to disperse. Canada had grown more prosperous, more contented and more loyal under the constitution given to her at the instigation of Lord Durham; Australia was growing rich and increasing rapidly in population under the magnetic influence of the gold discoveries; in New Zealand the aboriginal and the settler had fought out their differences and arrived at an understanding which satisfied both sides; in South Africa the way seemed to be opening to happier relations between the Boer and the Briton, and in India the Crown was sparing no effort to make good the principles of the royal proclamation. A new conception of Empire took possession of the British people if not of British politicians in the sixties, and it is perhaps not unreasonable to give credit in large measure to Canada. Lord Durham's constitution had done its work, and the united provinces were now anxious to be separated again and joined in a federal bond only. Of their loyalty there remained not a shadow of doubt. French Canadian ill-will had so completely disappeared that Sir Etienne Taché declared "The last gun that would be fired for British supremacy in America would be fired by a French Canadian."

In 1864 Nova Scotia, New Brunswick and Prince Edward's Island met to discuss the possibility of federation, and Canada at once saw a way out of its rather unwieldy and uncongenial legislative union. She took part in the movement, and the outcome of the conference was a scheme of federation by which Upper and Lower Canada were given separate provincial legislatures, and both joined with Nova Scotia and New Brunswick in 1867, in a federal union under the name of the Dominion of Canada. Federated Canada lost no time in securing control of the whole of North America unappropriated by the United States: the other colonies, with the exception of Newfoundland which has, unwisely as its best friends believe, rejected the idea, joined the Dominion as occasion offered; in 1885, under the auspices of Sir John Macdonald, her greatest statesman, Canada started the railway which five years later linked her Atlantic sea-board with the Pacific Coast; and the consummation of her progress and her loyalty is that a French Canadian has been her Prime Minister during the past six or seven years. Sir Wilfrid Laurier in the opinion of a good many people, will rank with Sir John Macdonald in Canadian annals as one who aimed at achieving Canada's highest destiny under the British flag.

The success of the Canadian union, combined with the knowledge of German intrigue north of Cape Colony inspired Lord Carnarvon to attempt to remove the discords of South Africa by similar means. Responsible government was granted to Cape Colony in 1872, and he hoped by showing the Boer Republics the advantages of a federal system to repair the blunders of the fifties. The discovery of the Kimberley diamond mines in 1867 had caused new disputes between Boers and British, and the man sent out by Lord Carnarvon in 1876, Mr J. A. Froude, had unfortunately a genius for controversy rather than for diplomacy. Instead of bringing oil to bear on the troubled waters, he lashed them into fresh fury. That the disunion of South Africa was a misfortune was made clear in 1877, when the Zulu impis swept down on the bankrupt and helpless Transvaal. Sir Theophilus Shepstone annexed the Boer State in its own defence, and Sir Garnet Wolseley then Governor of Natal, disposed finally of the native chief Sekukuni, who was the terror of the Transvaal.

Relieved of their fears of the Zulus, the Boers protested against annexation; on Dingaan's Day they rose in arms; Sir George Colley moved against them, took up what should have been an impregnable position on Majuba Hill, was boldly attacked by the Boers and defeated. Sir Bartle Frere was High Commissioner at the time and if he had been supported from home might have saved the situation. But Mr Gladstone, recently restored to office, deemed "magnanimity" the better part of valour and decided to give back the Transvaal without striking a blow for the honour of the flag. If Majuba had been avenged – and the necessary forces were at hand – there would probably have been a very different spirit throughout South Africa during the next twenty years.

As it was the Boer became more than usually insolent, believed himself capable of holding his own against the British power, and embarked on an Afrikander policy which if it succeeded would make South Africa Dutch and not British.

For this propaganda the necessary funds were forthcoming from the proceeds of taxes on the Rand mines opened up by British subjects in ever-increasing numbers since 1884. Boer attempts to expand beyond the frontier allotted to the state were nipped in the bud, and in 1889, Mr Cecil Rhodes then the leading statesman in Cape Colony took steps to secure for the British Empire the country known to-day as Rhodesia. The British South Africa Company has made mistakes – the greatest being the countenance lent by its officers to the Jameson raid – but it has rendered huge service to the British cause in South Africa. The Jameson raid, wrong as it was, had its origin in the over-bearing attitude towards British subjects, of the Boer oligarchy which had grown fat on British industry. The Boers, fearful of being swamped by the British, denied all semblance of citizen rights to the Outlanders, and repudiated the suzerainty of Queen Victoria.

After long negotiations it became apparent that the issue would be war, and as the Imperial Government keep no troops in self-governing colonies, ten thousand men were despatched to Natal as a measure of precaution. The Boer Republics – the Orange Free State, with whom we had no quarrel, not less than the Transvaal – saw in that step a menace, and with a temerity which would have been wholly admirable if it had not been a little insane, sent forth an ultimatum demanding the withdrawal of the British troops within forty-eight hours. There could be but one answer to such a demand. That answer was a war which found us unprepared – to our eternal honour as Sir Wilfrid Laurier has suggested – but the Empire had only to put forth its strength and the fate of the petty Republics was sealed. South Africa's destiny is British, and when the Boers have settled down to self-government under the Union Jack the federation of this group of colonies will be more practicable than it proved to be whilst Dutch pretensions were given free play under a pseudo-Republican régime.

The failure of the federal movement in South Africa owing to racial prejudice, was not more conspicuous than its failure in Australia during a third of a century owing mainly to provincial jealousies – an equally potent force. In the fifties when federation might have been inaugurated simultaneously with the concession of self-government; when Earl Grey at home and Governor Fitzroy, William Wentworth and Edward Deas Thomson in the colonies, urged its adoption in however tentative a form, Lord John Russell declared that it was premature. It would have been easy to unite the Australian, even the Australasian, colonies for general purposes in 1852; every year of delay strengthened the provincial sentiments of the colonists, permitted frontier customs houses to appear and brought local men to the front who being someone in their own colony were not anxious to assist the creation of a big state which would swamp their personality.

The necessity of federation was shown by the repeated conferences held by the various colonies for the settlement of common questions. New Zealand in any case has never shown much desire to be associated more closely with Australia, and as her own federal system, slender as it was, gave way to a central government in 1875 she was not an encouraging example to set before the Australians. In 1881 Sir Henry Parkes, who had risen from a toy-maker-and-seller to be the chief of Australian statesmen, made an effort to bring the colonies into line, but his efforts were defeated by Victoria. Two years later when the whole of Australia was scared by the activity of Germany in New Guinea, into consciousness of the dangers latent in separation, a new scheme was advanced and resulted in the creation of a body, without power and invertebrate to the last degree, known as the Federal Council. It was treated with scornful contempt by Sir Henry Parkes, who could not forget the rebuff of 1881.

Had Sir Henry Parkes taken a broad patriotic view of things he would have accepted the Federal Council, poor affair though it was, as a beginning and have built up from it. Four or five years more went by and again Australia was brought face to face with facts by the report of an Imperial officer on the shortcomings of Australian defence arrangements. Once more Sir Henry Parkes moved; a great convention met in Sydney and drafted the Commonwealth Bill of 1891; but the bickerings and pretensions of provincial politicians whose loyalty to the federal movement did not go beyond the lips, occasioned more delay and it really seemed that the new scheme would be as hopeless as its predecessors. Fortunately it was decided to take the matter out of the hands of the politicians and refer it to the people themselves. The referendum left no doubt as to what the people desired; they were cordially in favour of union; the federal bill was safe; the measure was sent to London, passed through the Imperial Legislature in 1900, and on the first day of the new century, Australia entered formally on her new life of nationhood achieved under the auspices of the British flag. She has surmounted her earliest difficulties under the joint control of Lord Hopetoun, the first federal Governor, and Mr Edmund Barton, the first federal Premier. New Zealand remains outside the federation as Newfoundland remains outside the Canadian; but New Zealand has more reason. Twelve hundred miles separate her from Australia, and she prefers to continue to be, what she has for the past decade been, an isolated forcing-house of great social experiments. But socialistic as she is, New Zealand has shown that she is second to none in her loyalty to the Empire, and she is affording the most interesting proof of the compatibility of extreme democracy and thorough Imperialism.

The conditions of progress in India are naturally very different from those which obtain in the great colonies: India is governed despotically but the despotism is one of benevolence. Her viceroys have spared no pains to govern in the interests of India not less than in the interests of Great Britain, and to compass at once the ends of freedom and of security. Essentially unlike the colonies of Australia or Canada as India is however, the movement within her borders has been in the same direction. The wave of Imperialism which swept over the British dominions during the seventies did not leave India high and dry. In 1877 Queen Victoria was proclaimed Empress by Lord Lytton at a great durbar on the ridge above Delhi. India, the empire of the Moguls, became an empire once again, but an empire within an empire. Lord Lytton's successor Lord Ripon took India a step along the other road which is characteristic of the time. He made some almost revolutionary changes in freeing the native press from all trammels and calling into existence the elements of local self-government. Leading natives have a larger share in the control of their own affairs to-day than ever before. An informal deliberative assembly whose proceedings are not always wisely directed but which serves the purpose of ventilating grievances legitimate or illegitimate meets every year. Side by side with the development of local self-government, a new source of Imperial strength has appeared in the forces voluntarily held in readiness by the native princes to assist the Central Government whenever occasion demands. The difficulty under which the British Raj has always laboured has been to find sufficient employment in responsible positions for those members of leading families who in other days would have been called upon to govern and to fight. Idle hands must be ever ready for mischief in India as elsewhere. Lord Curzon, the present viceroy, had made a material advance by providing military employment for a number of cadets of princely and aristocratic families, a step which received the cordial approval of the King Emperor in the first year of his reign.

In India as in other directions the interval between the Mutiny and the death of Queen Victoria was one of consolidation and progress. It was also a period of expansion. Under the Crown the frontiers of India have been considerably extended; the rest of Burmah has been annexed owing to the intrigues of the King with the French, and the north-west frontier has been pushed further back into mountain recesses in response to the movements of Russia in Central Asia. In 1878 India was involved in a second costly and disastrous but not inglorious war in Afghanistan, ending in the placing of the British nominee Abdurrahman on the throne at Kabul, where he remained in reasonable security till his death. Nor is it only in India that expansion has been witnessed. A quarter of a century ago, Africa was the dark continent. To-day it is parcelled out among the European powers into spheres of influence. The scramble for Africa on the East and the West, on the North and the South was maintained during the eighties and part of the nineties unremittingly. British possessions in Nigeria, in Central Africa, in Uganda are flanked by French, German, Portuguese and Belgian, and the responsibilities they involve would in themselves be no mean charge if they were the whole instead of a tithe of British Colonial cares. In 1882 Great Britain was left single-handed to rescue Egypt from rebel clutches, and fifteen years later she disposed of Mahdism in the Soudan. She has regenerated Egypt, and her control extends along the whole length of the Nile. Some day it is the ambition of statesmanship to place Cairo in the North in direct telegraphic and railway communication with Cape Town in the South!

18

VICTORIA AND HER COLONIES

From: J.M.D. Meiklejohn and M.J.C. Meiklejohn, *A School History of England* (London: Alfred Holden, 1902), pp. 449–463.

John Miller Dow Meiklejohn (1836–1902) was an Edinburgh schoolmaster. A Scottish academic who graduated from the University of Edinburgh and a journalist who was noted for his authoring of school textbooks, he also published the textbook The British Empire: Its Geography, Resources, Land-ways and Waterways *(1891). In the chapter included in this volume, 'Victoria and Her Colonies', Meiklejohn argues that the British had improved conditions in India and prevented famine. This positive viewpoint has been challenged by recent historical accounts which castigate the British for simply leaving the famine to market forces. Parallels have been drawn between British responses to the Indian famines and the mid-19th-century Irish famine. Meiklejohn's assertion that railways had benefited India is also now contradicted, with argument made that they were not used to alleviate famine. Lord Lytton, Viceroy of India (1876–1880), is seen by his critics as contributing to the devastating Indian famine of 1876–1878 by allowing 6.4 million hundredweight of wheat to be exported to England. What is evident is that Meiklejohn's account gave schoolchildren the impression that Britain's was by 1901 a benevolent empire which had stabilised itself after mid-century turbulence.*

1. **Our Colonies before the Queen's Reign**. – During, and up to the end of, the great wars with France in the eighteenth and the beginning of the nineteenth centuries, the history of our colonies had been more or less intimately bound up with the history of England itself, and especially with the history of its wars. The war with France gave us Canada in the year 1763; thus, too, most of the West Indian Islands fell into British hands. A belief that Napoleon would attempt to occupy the Cape of Good Hope induced the Stadtholder of Holland to 'lend' Great Britain that colony in 1795, and the loan was turned into a permanent possession in 1814. So, too, both Gibraltar and Malta were occupied as naval outposts to keep watch and guard over threatened danger either from France or Spain. In India we find a small trading company planting weak mercantile settlements on the coast, and gradually growing in wealth and territory till British influence overshadowed the whole Peninsula. But the directors of the East India Company never looked on India as anything but a huge trading-mart. They developed the country, it is true, but they developed it not for the sake of the country itself, but for the sake of the increased dividends which that development would enable them to pay to their shareholders at home. Always and for everything the colonies depended on 'home,' and were governed

from home; but the reign of Victoria brings us to a time when the colonies began to develop by themselves and for themselves, gradually winning the privilege of self-government and working out their own history in their own way. No longer either (with one notable exception in South Africa) was war with any European people to bring us fresh territory. Most of the colonial expansion which took place during the reign of Victoria was due to the researches of intrepid explorers, and to quiet, steady work on the part of individual traders, or great trading companies; or, if war with a savage tribe or nation did occur, then that war was waged because an uncivilised and warlike native people is always a grave danger to the civilisation near it.

2. **Greater Britain**. – War then had gained for us a very large part of our Empire; but peace was to develop those acquisitions, and the profound quiet that followed the year of Waterloo was to witness the growing up of a Greater Britain beyond the seas. Wars there were with various savage tribes who resented the coming of the white man into their territory, but for the most part no very strong resistance was made, except in India, to the progress of British civilisation and settlement. That work proceeded steadily. Our colonies gradually enlarged their borders, and from a state of infancy grew into the condition of political manhood. Yet when they had attained to man's estate, they never forgot that they were the children of the mother-country, and always looked to, and spoke of, her as home. Though widely sundered by sea and land, the British Empire is one united whole, and two main causes serve to keep that whole together. These are – sentiment – a loving attachment to the mother-land – and, in the second place, a strong feeling of loyalty to the person of the reigning sovereign. Therefore it is that, in all the wars Great Britain has recently been involved in, colonial men of British blood have been instantly eager to lend aid to the old country. Canadian boatmen helped Wolseley up the Nile in his gallant, though fruitless, attempt to rescue General Gordon in 1885; Australian horsemen served both in the Mahdist wars and in the 1900–1 expedition against Pekin; and when the South African war of 1899–1901 burst out there was not a corner of the British Empire, where white men dwelt, that did not send its sons to stand by England in the hour when its authority in South Africa was in danger of disappearing altogether. The history of England in the latter half of the nineteenth century comprises far more than the history of England itself. As Kipling puts it –

'What do they know of England,
Who only England know?'

Therefore it behoves us to know something about the history and development of some at least of our more important dependencies – of India, of Australasia, of Canada, and South Africa.

3. **India**. – About the year 1815 the East India Company could call itself master of hardly a quarter of the present Indian dominions. Bengal was British, and a broad strip on the east coast; Ceylon we had taken from the Dutch, in 1795, being confirmed in the possession of that island by the Peace of Amiens (1802).

On the West we had little more than the island of Bombay, and one or two trading settlements near it. On the other hand, many princes, such as the Nawab of Oudh and the Nizam in the Deccan, had bound themselves to the Company by treaty, to put the control of their foreign policy in British hands, and to assist the Company with men and money in time of war. There were, however, two groups of warlike native peoples who held themselves resolutely aloof from British influence – the **Mahrattas** in the West and the **Sikhs** of the **Punjab**. The Mahrattas were little more than freebooters, and could not, and did not, offer any organised resistance, so that by the year 1818 their independence came to an end. They were disturbers of the peace of India, and had therefore to be put down. Far otherwise was it with the Sikhs. Their great chief, Runjit Singh (who died in 1839), had made of the whole nation a powerful fighting machine, which was a standing menace to British supremacy in India. In 1845 these warlike fanatics, with a mad notion that they might overrun the whole of India, invaded the British North-West Provinces. Checked by Sir Hugh Gough at the bloody battles of Ferozeshah and Sobraon (1846), they renewed the war with desperate valour two years later, and finally surrendered after the British victories of Chillianwallah and Guzerat (1849). Lord Dalhousie, then Governor-General of India, annexed their country, the Punjab, and by an able and just administration transformed the Sikhs into the most faithful of our Indian subjects in the short space of eight years. Great Britain very soon reaped the advantage of treating the conquered Sikhs well, for in the Great Mutiny of 1857 they not only remained quiet, but lent valuable aid to the British arms.

(i) The names of the principal Mahratta chiefs were Scindiah, Holkar, and the Gaikwar of Baroda.
(ii) The **Sikhs** were originally a religious sect believing in the existence of one Spiritual God, and rejecting all worship of images. They now, along with the **Gurkhas** of Nepaul (whom we conquered in 1814), furnish the finest native regiments in the British service.

4. **Afghanistan**. – Afghanistan is a country of high tablelands, lofty mountains, and rich narrow valleys, which lies between the British Empire in India and the Russian Empire in Asia. The present ruler, or Ameer, likens it to a mountain-goat lying between a lion and a bear. England and Russia have in that part of the world been constantly intriguing against each other; and it is of very great importance that Afghanistan, which is a 'buffer' state, should be friendly to the English Government. In 1838 Lord Auckland determined to put on the throne of Afghanistan, Shah Sujah, a nominee of his own, and expel Dost Mohammed, the then Ameer, who had been intriguing with the Russians. With this object British troops entered the country and garrisoned the fortified cities of Kábul and Kandahar (1839). For two years the garrisons held their own, but with great difficulty, being constantly harassed by risings of the Afghans, who hated the foreign nominee. In course of time the whole country

rose, and the British garrison of Kábul was forced to surrender on terms to Akbar Khan, the son of Dost Mohammed. The terms were that the British should give up all their money and all their guns, in return for which they were to have a safe-conduct to the frontier. The column started – four thousand fighting men and 12,500 camp followers (January 1842), but the treacherous Afghans had not the faintest intention of keeping to their side of the bargain. The hills swarmed with bloodthirsty barbarians, who hung upon the march of the British troops, and attacked them incessantly. By the time that the British army had got through the Khoord Kábul Pass, three thousand corpses lay upon the blood-stained snow. Here and there the Afghans put up strong barriers to impede the march of the retreating army, then rushed in among the pent-up crowd, and slaughtered them right and left by scores. Of the whole army, only one man – Dr. Brydone, a surgeon – reached the fort of Jellalabad alive. In Jellalabad alone, and in Kandahar, did the British manage to hold their own. To take revenge for this disaster General Pollock with a new army entered Afghanistan again, and re-occupied Kábul (1842), and an inglorious end was made to the whole affair by permitting Dost Mohammed to return to the throne from which we had injudiciously expelled him.

(i) **Afghanistan** means the *stan* (or country) of the Afghans; as Hindustan is the country of the Hindus, Kurdistan, of the Kurds, etc.
(ii) At a conference held outside Kábul, the British Resident was shot dead by Akbar Khan (the son of Dost Mohammed) with the very pistol that he had the day before presented to the Afghan leader. This was in the end of 1841.
(iii) **Jellalabad** is a town about seventy-seven miles east of Kábul.

5. **Roberts's March**. – Once again were we destined to interfere in the internal affairs of Afghanistan, and once again, but for a brilliant feat of arms, with doubtful success. In 1878 the Ameer, Shere Ali, was invited to receive a British Resident. He refused. War followed, and a Resident, Sir Louis Cavagnari, was forced on the recalcitrant ruler. Then, as in 1842, the Resident was murdered – chopped to pieces by the long Afghan knives in the streets of Kábul (1879). General Sir Frederick Roberts thereupon fought his way into the country through the gloomy mountain passes, and was occupying Kábul, when he heard that a British force had been severely defeated at the Battle of Maiwand, and forced to fly for refuge behind the walls of Kandahar (1880). Then followed one of the greatest marches in history. Over roads that were nothing but the boulder-strewn beds of dried-up torrents, through a country swarming with savage tribesmen, Roberts covered the 300 miles that lay between Kábul and Kandahar in 23 days. Kandahar was relieved on the 31st of August 1880, and the very next day, recking nothing of his long and toilsome dash, Roberts fell upon the Afghan army and inflicted on it a crushing defeat. Soon after that Afghanistan was evacuated, and Abdurrahman Khan was placed upon the throne, which he still (1901) continues to occupy.

6. **The Progress of India**. – Since the second Afghan War (1878–80) no war of any great moment has disturbed the peace of India or its borders. In 1885 Thebaw, the King of Burma, proclaimed his intention of driving the English into the sea, but his proclamation only resulted in his dethronement, and in the placing of the whole of Upper Burma under the British rule (1886). The annexation of Burma was the final rounding off of the British Indian Dominions, over which Queen Victoria was proclaimed[1] Empress in 1877. But war and territorial expansion has not been all the history of India throughout the Queen's reign. Even more important has been the protection afforded by the British rule to life and property. Thuggism – an organised system or brotherhood for murdering travellers – was finally repressed in 1848. Slavery, too, was put an end to in the year 1843, previous to which time natives had been in the habit of selling themselves for debt – enslaving themselves for a few shillings. In 1834, just after some disastrous floods in Calcutta, children were openly hawked for sale about the streets. Even famine has been robbed of its most hideous terrors by the energy of British officials, and famine has been combated in two ways – by providing abundant supplies of water, and also by providing quick means of communication – by irrigation and by railways. The Ganges Canal alone supplies water to hundreds of thousands of peasant-cultivators; the Madras Presidency is covered with thousands of tanks for conserving the precious water; and in Northern India there is the largest artificial reservoir in the world, which covers an area larger than that of London. Water makes the crops grow, but railways must carry them. After the Queen had been on the throne sixteen years, there were only 21½ miles of railway in India. A great plague and famine smote the country in 1860, and by 1868 there were 4000 miles of line. To-day there are over 22,000. 'Wasted lands, blight and famine, plague and earthquake, roaring deeps and fiery sands' were once the scourges of India. Some of these are so still, but what the hand of man can do to make them lighter has been done by the thoughtful, beneficent British Raj.

7. **China**. – One of the chief crops in India is opium, and an attempt to force Indian opium on the Chinese brought us into collision with that people in 1839. At the end of the war in 1841, the Chinese were compelled to cede to us the island of **Hong-Kong,** at the mouth of the Canton River, which occupies one of the most important positions for trade in the country. A second war with China (1857–60), in which Pekin was entered by British troops, resulted in the opening of several ports to English commerce. Not until the year 1898 was Great Britain to acquire any further possessions in China. In that year the town of **Wei-hai-wei** was handed over to this country as an offset to the Russian possession of Port Arthur, on the north shore of the Gulf of Pe-chi-li; but Great Britain has done all she could to hinder any European occupation of Chinese territory on a large scale. She has attempted to maintain the principle of the 'open door' – that is, the right of every nation to trade with China, but not to encroach on Chinese territory. However, after 1895 (when the war between China and Japan ended victoriously for the latter country) a 'scramble' for China set in, and both Russia, France, and

Germany succeeded in obtaining for themselves some very valuable possessions. These encroachments led to the Boxer outbreak of 1900. A sect of fanatics, who called themselves by the name of Boxers, goaded to fury by the presence of the European intruders, rose in arms. They murdered the white missionaries, wherever they could find them, and in the summer of 1900 laid siege to the European legations in Pekin. The lives of the Europeans in Pekin were despaired of, till at length an international relief-force fought its way to the Chinese capital, and found the little European garrison still gallantly holding its own. The Chinese Question still remains to settle.

8. **Australasia**. – Australia, alone of all our colonies, has been able to develop itself entirely undisturbed by war. Not so, however, the sister-colony New Zealand. In that island, the Maoris – a fierce and able race of man-eaters – offered a strenuous resistance to the progress of British civilisation, and were only subdued, after much hard fighting, in 1869. Yet the early history of the Australian colonies – peaceful though it was – is not a very bright one. Year by year from 1788 (when New South Wales was founded) ship-loads of convicts were landed on the shores of the island-continent, and transportation to Western Australia only finally ceased in 1868. This steady influx of ruffianism checked all real attempts at colonisation, and up to 1851 Australia was mainly known as a struggling pastoral country which could produce only a little wool, tallow, and hides. But in 1851 gold was discovered in New South Wales, and also at Ballarat in Victoria. The news spread all over the world, and, before three years had passed, over a quarter of a million settlers had arrived. From that time the advance of Australia was assured. Some of those who came to find gold found none, but settled down as industrious and hard-working settlers on the land. Great cities sprang up – Sydney, Melbourne, and Adelaide; the pastoral industry, which fed the gold-diggers, took a new lease of life; railways and telegraphs (notably the great Overland Line which crosses the Continent from Adelaide to Port Darwin) were constructed; and each colony grew into a prosperous and self-governing community, but each keeping to itself. That separation ceased in 1900, and all the five colonies of Australia, together with Tasmania, formed themselves into a united **Commonwealth**. The infant Commonwealth, assured of a happy and glorious future, celebrated its first birthday on New Year's Day, 1901.

(i) The **Maoris** of New Zealand, for all their intelligence and cleverness, are a dying race. They number now only 40,000, less than half as many as there were a hundred years ago. Alone of all natives under British rule, they are privileged to send members to the Colonial Parliament which sits at Wellington.
(ii) New South Wales was the mother-colony of Australia, and Victoria, Queensland, and Tasmania were offshoots from it.
(iii) The **Duke** of **Cornwall** and **York** (King Edward VII.'s eldest surviving son and heir) formally opened the first Parliament of the Australian Commonwealth at Sydney in the early summer of 1901.

9. Canada. – Australia found herself a united nation in 1901, but the example of Federation had been set by another great colony thirty-four years before. In 1867 some of the most important colonies in British North America formed themselves into a self-governing Union called the Dominion of Canada. Quebec and Ontario, New Brunswick and Nova Scotia, were the first colonies to join in the Dominion; and gradually the other colonies, as they have successively been carved out of the lands of the Great West, have come into the Dominion. Only Newfoundland has chosen to stand aloof. – The history of Canada throughout the Queen's reign has been on the whole an eminently peaceful one. There was in 1837 a trifling rebellion in the provinces of Ontario and Quebec (or, as they were then called, Upper and Lower Canada) due to a demand of the inhabitants for increased political rights; and in 1870, and again in 1885, one Louis Riel, a French half-breed, raised the Indian and half-white hunters of the West, with the cry that the Dominion Government was attempting to deprive them of their hunting-grounds. Both of Riel's rebellions were very easily crushed. The disturbances arose from the fact that in 1869 the Dominion Government had bought out the territorial rights of the Hudson Bay Company west of the Red River, and had sent officers to survey and register the lands with a view to future settlement. Riel persuaded his ignorant following of Indians and half-breeds that the lands they hunted over were going to be taken from them. Since Riel's last rebellion nothing has occurred to disturb the peaceful development of the Dominion – a development to which a powerful aid was lent by the completion of the Canadian Pacific Railway from Montreal to Vancouver. This railway, more than anything else, has made the Dominion one country.

(i) The constitutions of the Dominion and of the Australian Commonwealth very much resemble each other. In each case a combined Federal Parliament controls affairs that affect the whole country; while each province or state has its local Parliament to manage its own local affairs.

(ii) The **Hudson Bay Company** was founded in 1670. Charles II. gave to his cousin, Prince Rupert and a few others, two and a half million square miles round and behind Hudson Bay, for which he stipulated to receive a yearly rent of two elks and two black beavers. The Company had the right of fur-trading over the whole of Canada, except in the settled East, from Hudson Bay to the Pacific. It exercised no government over this vast extent of country, except what little control it could exert over the half-breeds and Indians from its scattered trading-posts.

10. The Scramble for Africa. – Long before the Queen ascended the throne, Great Britain had established herself at various points on the Guinea coast, and she was also permanently settled in Cape Colony on the South. In 1884–85 a sudden zeal for colonisation seized some of the countries of Europe, whose vast industries and perpetual production required new markets for their wares. The French began to push inland from Senegambia to the valley of the Niger, and the Germans established themselves both on the East and West coasts of the Continent. It was impossible for Great

Britain not to become a competitor in the race. The result has been the annexation of vast blocks of territory. In 1886 the Royal Niger Company established, through the medium of trade, an influence over the whole of the lower valley of the Niger, and this enormous territory was taken over by the Imperial Government in 1900 and renamed Nigeria. On the East a narrow strip of coast between Mombasa and Witu, granted (1888) by the Sultan of Zanzibar to the Imperial British East Africa Company, gradually grew into the huge British East Africa Protectorate – a million square miles in extent – which stretches back to the head-waters of the Nile. More important than any is the occupation of Rhodesia, which began in the year 1890. Thanks to the energy and foresight of the South African statesman, Cecil Rhodes, the whole of the region north of Bechuanaland up to Lake Tanganyika is in British hands. Thus, with this vast extension and the annexation of the Transvaal and the Orange River Colony (1900), the whole of temperate South Africa flies the British flag.

(i) Mashonaland was the first country of Rhodesia to be settled by the British. A little to the west lies Matabeleland, till lately an independent kingdom of ferocious and warlike natives. The Matabeles' chief occupation was raiding and murder, and in 1893 they attacked the British settlers in Mashonaland. The Matabele warriors were defeated with great slaughter; their King, Lobengula, died a fugitive; and Matabeleland became part of Rhodesia.

(ii) The possession of Rhodesia is additionally important because through it is building the Capetown to Cairo Railway, which will run, with but one short break, entirely through British territory.

11. **South Africa** (i). – The Cape Colony, the most important colony in South Africa, was captured, for the second time, by Great Britain out of the hands of the Dutch, in 1806, and the British possession of the country was finally confirmed in 1814. The white inhabitants of the Colony were mainly Boers or pastoral farmers, many of whom were holders of slaves. In the year 1833 the House of Commons gave freedom to all slaves throughout the British colonies, and this Act gave great offence to the Boers, who were by no means friendly to the British Government, and who, besides, were very insufficiently compensated for the slaves they were compelled to release. For this and other reasons thousands of the Cape Colony Boers moved off, at the beginning of the Queen's reign, into the unknown North. This movement is known as the Great Trek,[2] and the emigrant Boers were called Voortrekkers.[1] Their wives and children went with them; their tented waggon was their home; and, though they took also considerable numbers of cattle and sheep, it was upon their guns that they depended both for food and for protection against the savage tribes by which they were surrounded. After desperate struggles with the ferocious Zulu and Matabele warriors, the Boers succeeded in establishing three republics – Natal (1839), the Transvaal (1852), and the Orange Free State (1854). Her Majesty's Government were, however, of opinion that the Boers, even though they had left the Cape Colony, still remained British subjects, and, in pursuance of that opinion, Natal was declared British territory in 1843. As for the other two states,

they were too far off, it was thought, and their country was too poor to make it worth while to bring them under British control, and they were therefore left alone.

(i) The special history of Cape Colony itself consists principally of wars with the Kafirs of the Eastern Border. There were eight of such wars between the years of 1811 and 1880, and most of them resulted in fresh annexations of territory.
(ii) Not only did the Boers complain of insufficient compensation for their slaves – their property (for a slave worth £500, in some cases only £48 was received) – but they, in common with the English settlers, also blamed the British Government for their weak and vacillating policy in dealing with the Kafir cattle-raiders of the Eastern Border.
(iii) The Orange Free State was a British colony for a short time (1848–54), under the title of the Orange River Sovereignty.

12. **South Africa** (ii). – The Orange Free State remained quietly within its borders, and not until 1867 did anything of moment happen to disturb its tranquil career. In that year diamonds were discovered on the Vaal River, and in 1871 Great Britain annexed the neighbouring district of Griqualand West, which included the now immensely valuable diamond-mines of Kimberley. The Free State Boers complained bitterly, for they alleged that this territory belonged to them. However, they were satisfied by a payment of £90,000, and, though there lingered a feeling of soreness at what they considered to be an unwarrantable encroachment on their dominions, no further unpleasantness ensued, and they continued to develop their country quietly and prosperously. Far otherwise was it with their brethren across the Vaal. They had lost (1877) and regained (1881) their independence,[3] and, having regained it, were disposed to look down on Englishmen, whom, after the defeat of Majuba, they regarded as a beaten and contemptible nation. They were not in the least grateful to Great Britain for having saved them from the formidable power of the Zulus (1879); much less were they grateful for the restoration of their independence, which they conceived they had won, and could keep, by their own straight shooting. Suddenly in 1886 it was announced to the world that immensely rich gold-mines had been discovered on the bleak and barren Witwatersrandt,[4] where the large and wealthy town of Johannesburg now stands. The Transvaal Boers, from being a poor and struggling nation of cattle-farmers, became rich and prosperous, and at the same time swollen with the pride of riches. Though the authority of Great Britain over them was of the slightest, they determined to throw that authority off; and further they conceived, in an indistinct sort of way, the mad idea of expelling British authority from all South Africa, and of turning the country into one vast Boer confederation. On the 11th of October 1899 the Transvaal, with the Orange Free State for an ally, embarked on war with Great Britain, with the result that the names of both these states have disappeared from the list of independent, or semi-independent, nations.

(i) The first South African diamond was found among the playthings of a Boer child, who had been playing with it along with other bright-coloured stones.

VICTORIA AND HER COLONIES

(ii) The **Zulus** had been organised into a formidable military power by their great King, T'saka, and this warlike people, under T'saka's grandson, **Cetewayo,** constituted a grave danger to the neighbouring countries of the Transvaal and Natal. Great Britain declared war against the Zulu King in 1878. Cetewayo's warriors wiped out a whole British regiment at **Isandula,** and, after some mismanagement and great difficulty, were finally defeated by Lord Chelmsford at the Battle of **Ulundi** in 1879.

(iii) The slender authority which Great Britain exerted over the Transvaal was (chiefly) that conferred by a treaty known as the **London Convention** (1884). This Convention gave to Great Britain the right (among other things) to veto, if it chose, any treaty which the Transvaal might conclude with a foreign power.

Landmarks in colonial development

Canada.	**1763.** Canada ceded by France to Great Britain.
	1783. The **independence** of the **United States** recognised.
	1791. The Quebec Act.
	UPPER and LOWER CANADA divided, and each given a government of its own.
	1867. The **Dominion** of **Canada** founded.
	1886. Canadian Pacific Railway completed.
India.	**1757. Clive's** victory of Plassey.
	Foundation of British supremacy in India.
	1774–85. Warren Hastings Governor-General.
	1842. Destruction of a British army by the Afghans.
	1849. Annexation of the **Punjab.**
	SIKHS finally subdued.
	1857. The **Indian Mutiny.**
	1858. Government of **India** assumed by the **British Government.**
	Rule of the East India Company ended.
	1877. Queen Victoria proclaimed **Empress of India.**
Australasia.	**1788.** First **Convict Settlement** at **Sydney,** N.S.W.
	1834. First Settlement in **Victoria.**
	1835. First hut built on the site of Melbourne, now a city of half a million people.
	1840. New Zealand declared a British possession.
	1851. Discovery of **Gold** in New South Wales and Victoria.
	1856. Responsible government granted to New Zealand.
	1900. Australia and Tasmania form themselves into the Australian **Commonwealth.**
	The First Parliament of the Commonwealth opened by the Duke of Cornwall and York at Sydney in 1901.

South Africa.	**1835–37. Great Boer Trek** into the **Free State** and **Natal**.
	1843. Natal annexed to the British Crown.
	1852. Independence of the **Transvaal** recognised.
	1854. Independence of the **Orange Free State** recognised.
	1867. Diamonds discovered in **Griqualand West**.
	1877. The **Transvaal annexed** by Great Britain.
	1881. The Transvaal restored to independence.
	1886. The **Witwatersrandt Gold-fields** declared open.
	1890. Mashonaland settled.
	1895. Dr. Jameson's Raid into the Transvaal.
	1899. War with the Transvaal and Orange Free State.
	1900. The **Transvaal** and **Orange River Colony** become **British possessions** again.

Notes

1 At DELHI, the ancient capital of the Great Moguls.
2 *Trek* is the same word as 'drag' or 'draw.' Oxen dragged the waggons of the Emigrant Boers, and hence 'a trek' means 'a journey.' Voor-trekker – pioneer – one who treks voor (in front of) every one else.
3 See p. 439.
4 *White-water's-ridge*.

19

C.R.L. FLETCHER AND R. KIPLING, *A SCHOOL HISTORY OF ENGLAND* (OXFORD: CLARENDON, 1911), PP. 240–241.

Charles Fletcher (1857–1934) was a fellow of All Souls and a strong Conservative. His racist views created suspicion at the Clarendon Press. Rudyard Kipling (1865–1936) is also a figure who now divides opinion due to his views on the native peoples of the Empire. In contrast with the work of Gardiner, Fletcher and Kipling's 1911 text was more rabid in its treatment of colonial peoples. The book was written in praise for the National Service League. Much like Salmon's work in document 17, this school text warns of the threat to the British Empire. It critcised figures from English history such as Oliver Cromwell (whose Protectorate had led to a distrust of the army) and prime ministers such as Pitt the Younger who had not supported investment in the armed forces. A racist description of the West Indian is followed by the assertion that the British rule of India has been 'to the good of all' and the mutiny the result of British 'carelessness and mismanagement of its vast Empire'.

The West Indies, &c.

There are other countries, like Ceylon, the West Indies, the several stations on the North-west African coast, Singapore on the Straits of Malacca, Guiana on the north coast of South America, and islands too numerous to mention, both in the Pacific and Atlantic Oceans, which belong to Great Britain. But most of these are called 'Crown Colonies' and do not enjoy any form of Parliamentary government nor need it. The prosperity of the West Indies, once our richest possession, has very largely declined since slavery was abolished in 1833. There is little market for their chief products, and yet a large population, mainly black, descended from slaves imported in previous centuries, or of mixed black and white race; lazy, vicious and incapable of any serious improvement, or of work except under compulsion. In such a climate a few bananas will sustain the life of a negro quite sufficiently; why should he work to get more than this? He is quite happy and quite useless, and spends any extra wages which he may earn upon finery.

Future of the Empire

What the future of our self-governing and really great Colonies may be, it is hard to say. Perhaps the best thing that could happen would be a 'Federation' of the whole British Empire, with a central Parliament in which all the Colonies should get representatives, with perfect free trade between the whole, and with an Imperial Army and Navy to which all should contribute payments. But where and when shall we find the statesman great and bold enough to propose it?

Our Indian Empire

Our Indian Empire must be treated to a few lines by itself. It is not a Colony but a 'Dependency of the Crown'. The extension of our rule over the whole Indian peninsula was made possible, first by the exclusion of any other European power (when we had once beaten off the French there), and secondly by the fact that the weaker states and princes continually called in our help against the stronger. From our three starting-points of Calcutta, Madras and Bombay, we have gradually swallowed the whole country; though some states keep their native princes, these are all sworn dependants of King George as 'Emperor of India', just as in feudal times a great feudal earl was a sworn subject of his king. Our rule has been infinitely to the good of all the three hundred millions of the different races who inhabit that richly peopled land.

Its growth till 1911

Until 1858 the old 'East India Company', founded at the end of Elizabeth's reign, was the nominal sovereign. Its early conquests had been made over the unwarlike races of Bengal and of the South; next, in the reign of George III, over the gallant robbers who swarmed over the central plains and were called Mahrattas. Early in Victoria's time we had to meet those magnificent fighters the Sikhs of the Punjaub, and the fierce Afghans of the north-western mountains. Both gave us from time to time terrible lessons; but British patience and courage triumphed over all. As we conquered them, so we enrolled in our Indian army all the best fighting men of these various races; of that army the Sikhs are now the backbone; but the Afghans have still to be kept at bay beyond the northern mountains. They are the 'tigers from the North'; and, if our rule were for a moment taken away, they would sweep down and slay and enslave all the defenceless dwellers on the plains.

The Indian Mutiny, 1857

In 1857 our carelessness and mismanagement of this vast Empire, together with the religious fear inspired among the Indians by the introduction of European inventions such as steam and railways, brought about the most serious danger that ever threatened British India, a mutiny in our Indian army. The instigator of the revolt was a man who claimed to be the representative of the old Mahratta rulers; the rebels took Delhi, the oldest capital city of India, and set up a shadow of an Emperor. They perpetrated terrible cruelties upon defenceless English women and children. But Southern India remained perfectly loyal and quiet; so did several of the old native princes; while the gallant Sikhs and the Ghoorkas of Nepaul came to our help in crowds. British troops were poured in as fast as possible, though in those days that was not very fast. The siege of Delhi and the relief of Lucknow were the greatest feats that were performed; and the names of John Lawrence, John Nicholson, Colin Campbell and Henry Havelock became for ever immortal. When the Mutiny was finally put down in 1858 the Crown took over the sovereignty from the East India Company, which ceased to exist; and, twenty years later, Queen Victoria was proclaimed 'Empress of India'.

20

TWENTY-SECOND STORY. – THE GROWTH OF THE EMPIRE

Lesson 43. – In the East

From: *The Patriotic Historical Reader Book V: Thirty Stories and Biographies from 1688–1897* (London: William Collins, 1898), pp. 208–216.

These documents are taken from school 'readers' issued by several leading publishing houses at the end of the 19th and the very early 20th centuries. They were used to provide exercises in reading and comprehension and also moral instruction in elementary schools. From 1883, the educational code suggested that one reader used in reading classes be in the field of history. They were not used primarily for the teaching of history, but rather historical understanding as a by-product of providing a sense of national citizenship. The readers use an essentially Whig approach to the past and they attempt to draw into the imperial fold children of the working class. The depiction of the English people as 'adventurous' and 'sea faring' across the centuries is a recurring theme. What was then recent imperial history was presented to the child as a logical growth of older trends established at or before the time of Elizabeth I. Emphasis was on imperial figures as role models in character. Historians note the absence of Scottish or Welsh figures, excluded in favour of English. Document 23 is taken from a senior reader aimed at an older child, compared to those for which documents 20–22 were intended.

1. It was not till the latter half of the eighteenth century, that Britain began to surpass other European nations in colonising in the East. Let us first take note of our island possessions far over the sea, to the east of Australia or New Zealand. In another part of this book, we have read how Captain Cook explored the east coast of that great island in the year 1770, and took possession of it in the name of the mother country.

2. Some years passed away before we made any attempt to settle people there, and when we did begin, what a start it was! We sent over to Botany Bay some ships containing nearly eight hundred convicts with their guards. Such was the strange colonisation of what is now, without doubt, one of the most prosperous colonies in the whole of the Empire.

3. The only idea the Government at home had of that glorious southern land was, that it would suit very well for felons to spend their years of exile in, especially as it was fifteen thousand miles away. This was the strange beginning of the colony of New South Wales.

4. For years after the settlement of the colony, voyages of discovery were chiefly confined to the coast. The names of Bass and Flinders will ever be remembered in connection with this pioneer work. Bass was a surgeon and Flinders a midshipman in the Royal Navy, and at first, their journeys were made in a little boat eight feet long, called the *Tom Thumb*.

5. Later on, more ambitious voyages were made. In a small schooner they sailed round Van Diemen's Land (now Tasmania), proving it was an island, and at the same time explored its rivers and harbours. Flinders, whose name should ever be remembered as the bold pioneer in Australian discovery, was raised to the rank of Captain. In his ship, the *Investigator*, which was expressly fitted out for the service, he minutely explored the shores of New Holland, as it was then called, and was the first to give the island its name of Australia, that is, the Southern Land.

6. It was, however, a quarter of a century after the founding of the colony of New South Wales, before much was known of the interior of the island continent. The Blue Mountains seemed an impassable barrier, but at length Mr. Bass, by means of iron hooks fastened to his arms, succeeded in scaling their precipitous sides, and was let down by ropes. After about fifteen days' exertion he gave up the task as hopeless.

7. At length, in 1813, a passage was found, leading to the pastoral lands now known as the Bathurst Goldfields, and this is now the Great Western road of the colony. Next follows the story of the many attempts to penetrate into the interior, and to cross the mighty island. With these journeys are linked the names of Mitchell, Eyre, Kennedy, Stuart, Burke, Wills, and others. The story of the trials and hardships they endured forms a bright spot in the history of Australia.

8. Today the scene is changed. Where, in the early days of this century, roamed races of savage men of the lowest type, little better, indeed, than wild beasts, stand vast cities, such as Melbourne, Sydney, and Adelaide. The ground, which was then covered with the rude huts of the aborigines, is now the scene of some of the busiest life in the world.

9. Sixty years ago, for example, Collins' Street, Melbourne, now one of the finest thoroughfares in the world, was only covered with the rude dwellings of the early settlers. The discovery of gold, which caused a wild rush of settlers from Europe, did much to largely increase the population of the island, and gave a great impetus, which the country much needed. But beside its mineral wealth, the land depends largely on its production of corn, and the rearing of sheep.

10. New Zealand, discovered by Tasman in 1642, was visited by the renowned Captain Cook in 1770. In the early years of the century, missionaries established stations in North Island, but it was not till 1839 that a society was formed inland for the purpose of colonising the island, and in 1841 New Zealand was proclaimed a British Colony. The aborigines or Maoris, as they call themselves, were fierce savages, in the early days of our colonisation. They are gradually dying out. The colony is very flourishing, doing a great and increasing trade in frozen meat, wool, gold, and corn.

11. Turning our faces home again, we shall have to pass India, but the story of our conquest of that great peninsula has been told in previous lessons. The English started their connection with this land in 1600, when Queen Elizabeth granted a charter to the East India Company for exclusive trade with that country, and the story for the next century and a half is one concerning trade only.

12. We have described the rivalry which sprang up between the English, French, and Portuguese, which resulted in the supremacy of the English being declared. The story of the next hundred years is taken up with the attempts of the English to establish themselves as masters all over the country. In connection with which you have read the stories of Clive, Hastings, and others, and of the proclamation of the Queen as Sovereign of the whole land in 1858.

13. Sailing west from India, we come to Africa, in which several valuable parts of our Empire are situated. We have in previous lessons read of the explorations of men like Livingstone, into the interior of the dark continent, until now we are able to write:

"The mystery of old Nile is solved: brave men
Have through the lion-haunted island passed,
Found the source at last."

14. The news brought home by travellers as to the great wealth of the continent, especially as to gold and diamonds, caused, just as it did in Australia, a rush of men hungry for wealth. We were not, by any means, the first European nation to colonise Africa. The Dutch preceded us there, and it was that nation that occupied what is now known as Cape Colony, and cleared the land of its wild animals, made roads, and planted the country. We have established ourselves there, by force of arms, and the greater part of South Africa is now under British influence and protection, and we are today the masters of a territory large enough to receive our colonists for generations to come.

15. Such, then, is the story of our expansion of our Empire towards the West. History teaches us that the enlarging of a country's territories brings with it great responsibilities on the home country. The stability of our rule over these important and far distant colonies, depends entirely on the way in which the mother country treats the colonists. Good government will bind them, and has bound them, to us, in bonds of love and unity, and in times of danger they will be to us, and we to them, as friends and brothers, whose cause is one.

Lesson 44. – In the West

1. In the early years of the seventeenth century, European travellers began to lift the veil which hid the interior parts of the North American continent. Both English and French settlers were busy in the same parts of the world. Jamestown was started fifty miles up the river of the same name, while Champlain, a Frenchman, founded Quebec in 1608. In the year 1620, the second English settlement was planted by the Pilgrim Fathers at New Plymouth.

THE GROWTH OF THE EMPIRE

2. Passing on to the beginning of the reign of Charles the Second, we find the king assigning an immense tract of North America to Ashley Cooper and others. The land was looked upon as a region capable of producing all sorts of tropical vegetation, and was called Carolina in honour of the English King. It stretched from the Atlantic to the Pacific, and included the southern states of America.

3. The first batch of emigrants sailed from our shores in 1670, and from that period dates the opening up of the North American continent. In the north, too, hardy travellers began to penetrate into the interior.

4. It is to a famous French traveller, Jacques Cartier, that we owe our earliest knowledge of this territory. In 1535 he discovered the St. Lawrence, and gave the name of Canada to the country. The origin of the name is interesting. Cartier, who mixed much with the native Indians, often heard them use the word "Kanata," and this he thought must be the name of the whole country, hence the name Canada. The Indian word simply means village.

5. The French explored and developed the greater part of Canada, and towards the end of the seventeenth century, La Salle explored Western Canada and the basin of the Mississippi, to which the French naturally laid claim.

6. The historical events in connection with our possessions in the West, have been told in previous lessons. In the year 1759, the immortal Wolfe gained the mastery over the French at Quebec, though he himself fell in the hour of victory, while in the next year Montreal was surrendered to us, and Canada was completely conquered. As a result of this, by the Treaty of Paris in 1763, Great Britain obtained nearly the whole of the French possessions in the New World.

7. Just twenty years after this, however, we had to sign another treaty in which we lost what were called the United States. Still Canada remains with us to this day, the most extensive of our colonial possessions, comprising, as it does, nearly the whole of America north of the United States.

8. The story of our possessions in America after the War of Independence has, on the whole, been peaceful. Our Government of the country was at first marked by distrust of that portion peopled chiefly by the French. On the conclusion of the American War, and the acknowledgment of the United States as free and independent, many thousands of the people moved across the northern borders into the British territory, as they did not wish for separation from the mother country.

9. Many of them settled in that part of Canada along the upper reaches of the St. Lawrence. Thus, while the majority of the people in the lower part, towards the north of the river, were of French nationality, the others were of British descent.

10. The island of Newfoundland was visited by early colonists from Iceland and Greenland, and being rediscovered by John Cabot in the reign of Henry the Seventh, was called the New Found Land, and claimed as a British possession.

11. Out in the far west, on the shores of the Pacific, lies British Columbia, the development of which dates from the discovery of gold there, over thirty years ago. The nature of the country prevents its being used for agriculture to any great

extent, though as settlements are springing up in the eastern portions along the great Canadian Pacific Railway, there may yet be a development of the trade of the colony in this direction.

12. There are many other places out west whose history and development are of great interest, but we have said enough in the last two lessons to show that the British Empire is a great one, the greatest, indeed, that the world has ever seen.

21

INSTRUCTIVE STORIES FROM ENGLISH HISTORY, HOLBORN SERIES HISTORICAL READER

(London: Educational Supply Association, 1900), pp. 135–144.

These documents are taken from school 'readers' issued by several leading publishing houses at the end of the 19th and the very early 20th centuries. They were used to provide exercises in reading and comprehension and also moral instruction in elementary schools. From 1883, the educational code suggested that one reader used in reading classes be in the field of history. They were not used primarily for the teaching of history, but rather historical understanding as a by-product of providing a sense of national citizenship. The readers use an essentially Whig approach to the past and they attempt to draw into the imperial fold children of the working class. The depiction of the English people as 'adventurous' and 'sea faring' across the centuries is a recurring theme. What was then recent imperial history was presented to the child as a logical growth of older trends established at or before the time of Elizabeth I. Emphasis was on imperial figures as role models in character. Historians note the absence of Scottish or Welsh figures, excluded in favour of English. Document 23 is taken from a senior reader aimed at an older child, compared to those for which documents 20–23 were intended.

LVII. A terrible siege

re-bel-led	cru-el-ty	butch-er-ed	mu-ti-ny
Luck-now	go-ver-nor	pro-vi-sions	bul-lets
mi-se-ry	stud-ded	Have-lock	High-land-ers

THE year after peace was made with Russia new troubles came upon England. The native soldiers in India rose against their English officers and rebelled against our rule. One day you will read a full account of this mutiny and how it was put down. I will only attempt at present to tell you what passed at one great city called Lucknow.

Before the rebels came there we had time to prepare for their coming. The governor brought all the English and their friends into a strong place with a wall and a ditch all round it. And here he stored up provisions and mounted his guns.

At last the rebels entered the city and attacked the place. They planted their guns on the top of the houses, and day after day shot and shell came thick and fast. Many of our people were killed. No place was safe. A shell would sometimes come through the roof and burst in the room. The governor himself was killed in this way whilst writing at a table.

But most of the deaths were caused by bullets. One who was present says, "A man could not show his nose without hearing the whiz of bullets close to his head. To walk slowly was in some places very, very dangerous; and many a poor fellow was shot who was too proud to run past places where bullets danced on the walls like a handful of peas in a frying-pan."

The siege began on the 1st of July, 1857, and no help came until the 25th of September. What misery our countrymen had to bear during these three months no one can tell! Sickness from want, work, and worry, brought more to an untimely end than the bullets of the enemy. Men could not be found for all the work to be done. Some of the horses went mad from want of water and proper food. Others were shot, and no one could be spared to bury them.

Meanwhile the siege went on. Though thousands of the enemy were trying to get inside, they could not succeed. At all hours of the day and night our men had to keep watch. No one could count on an hour's sleep. "At any moment you might hear the cry of 'turn out,' and you had to seize your musket and rush to your post."

Still our brave countrymen would not give up. They trusted in God and waited in hope, and they waited not in vain. Help was brought to them by the famous General Havelock and his brave Highlanders.

LVIII. The Victoria Cross

| me-dals | res-cue | he-ro-ic | sur-round-ed |
| ex-plod-ed | ser-geant | ar-rang-ed | lu-ci-fers |

You have often seen soldiers with medals on their breasts showing that they have been in war and have done their duty. There is one medal, called the *Victoria Cross*, which is more highly prized than any other; for it shows that the soldier who wears it has done some famous deed in battle, or has risked almost certain death to rescue a comrade in great peril.

In putting down the Indian Mutiny many noble fellows won this medal by their heroic conduct. I will give you one example. The head-quarters of the rebels was the city of Delhi, which was taken by our troops after a siege lasting some months. My story relates to the way in which our soldiers got an entrance into the city.

Delhi was surrounded by walls, and it was the object of our troops to get in through one of the gates. So it was decided to blow up one, called the Cashmere Gate, with gunpowder. Powder-bags had to be placed under the gate, and then exploded, in the face of the enemy. But who would undertake such a task?

Six brave men stood forward, ready "to do or die." Let us hear what Sergeant Smith, one of these men, has to tell us: –

"At the word of command we six rushed toward the gate. Salkeld and Burgess reached it first. One of the others was killed in front of me, and the remaining two fell into the ditch. I placed my bag and that of the poor fellow, lying dead beside me, under the gate, and then arranged the fuse.

"Salkeld, while lighting the fuse, was shot in the thigh, and rolled over into the ditch. Burgess then took the match. I told him to fire the charge and keep cool. He turned round and said, 'It won't go off, sir; it has gone out, sir.' I gave him a box of lucifers, and, as he took them, he let them fall into my hand, he being shot through the body.

"I was then left alone; and keeping close to the charge, seeing from where the others were shot, I struck a light, when the fuse went off in my face, the light not having gone out, as we thought. I took up my gun, and jumped into the ditch. I stuck close to the wall, and by that I escaped being smashed to pieces."

Four of this brave band lived long enough to receive the Victoria Cross, but Salkeld died of his wounds a few days after.

As soon as the gate was blown up our soldiers poured in, and after hard fighting the city was won The rebels, not killed or taken, escaped by the opposite gate. The neck of the mutiny was now broken, and before the close of the year (1857) India was again almost at peace.

LIX. The Princess Alice

| A-lice | me-mo-ry | Vic-to-ri-a | ar-ran-ged |
| re-quest | cof-fin | vir-tues | lus-tre |

WHAT the rose is among the flowers of the garden that the Princess Alice was among the children of the Queen. Her memory is dear to every English heart from the sweetness of her temper and the tenderness of her heart.

When her father, the good Prince Albert, was dying, it was she that stood at his bedside and watched him from hour to hour. When her brother, the Prince of Wales, was at the point of death, it was she that helped him to recover by her careful and skilful nursing.

In 1862 she became the wife of Prince Louis of Hesse. She had therefore to leave her beloved England, and to live in Germany. There she soon gained the love of the German people, and many are the stories they tell of her kindness to those in distress. Here is a copy of a letter she once wrote to her mother, Queen Victoria: –

> "Some days ago I went with Christa to a poor sick woman in the old town, and what a trouble we had to find the house! At last we went through a little dirty court, up a dark ladder, into a small room, where the poor woman and her baby were lying in bed. There were four other

children in the small room, the husband, two other beds, and a stove. There was no bad smell in the room, and it was not dirty.

"I sent Christa downstairs with the children. Then I cooked something for the woman with her husband's help, arranged her bed a little, took the baby from her, bathed its eyes, which were very sore – poor little thing – and put everything in order. They did not know at all who I was."

But she who had brought comfort to so many sorrowing hearts was not spared from the deepest grief herself. In 1873 one of her children, a boy little more than two years old, fell from an open window in the palace. The child had climbed to the window, and before a hand could be stretched out to save, he had lost his balance and fallen upon the cruel stones of the courtyard below. The Princess, who was in the next room, heard the fall, and rushed in terror down the stairs to find her child lifeless.

Five years later, in 1878, the Princess nursed her husband and children, who were all attacked by the same disease. One of the children died, but all the rest recovered. Then the mother had to tell them of the death of their sister. This threw her little son into such grief, that she could not help clasping him in her arms and kissing his lips. That kiss was death to the Princess. She caught the disease and died, and great was the grief of us all.

"'Clever and kind and good,'
Her virtues lent a lustre to a throne;
A pattern to the greater world she stood,
A blessing to her own."

LX. Defence of Rorke's Drift

| main-body | re-treat | hos-pit-al | breast-work |
| bis-cuit | cir-cle | re-tir-ed | he-roes |

WHO has not heard of those brave black men, called Zulus, with whom we were at war a few years ago? In the end they were defeated, but early in the war they cut to pieces a body of troops left in charge of our camp, while the general with the main-body was absent.

The victors then pushed on to Rorke's Drift in the hope of destroying the stores left there in charge of a mere handful of soldiers. The brave defence made by these men not only saved themselves from destruction, but kept open a safe passage for our troops, who were now in full retreat.

An hour and a half before the Zulus reached Rorke's Drift two of our horsemen rode up with the news of their advance. At once every man set to work to prepare for the defence. They were but eighty in all, and ten of them were sick. They had two buildings to defend – one was used as a hospital, and the other as a store-house.

Loop-holes were knocked in the walls, waggons were drawn up in front, and bags of maize and anything that came to hand were placed as a breast-work all round. In case the enemy should force their way inside this fence, an inner ring was made of large biscuit boxes.

At half-past four in the afternoon the attack began, and it lasted until four the next morning. Three thousand of the enemy raged around our small band of eighty, and more than once on that fearful night seemed on the point of breaking through the ring of our defences and dealing death on all sides.

The hospital caught fire, and the Zulus broke into it before all the sick could be removed. Some Welsh soldiers here fought like heroes to save their comrades from death. The outer ring had to be given up, but nothing the enemy could do, though they fought like lions, could drive our men from the inner circle.

Through all the hours of that dreadful night the English soldiers "never wasted a shot." When the enemy retired at four in the morning, it was found that thirteen of our small band lay dead and nine wounded. The Zulu loss amounted to five hundred.

LXI. Great improvements

| im-prov-ed | com-par-ed | an-swer | tele-graph |
| in-stru-ment | twink-ling | lu-ci-fer | po-lice-men |

QUEEN VICTORIA began her reign in 1837. What wonderful changes have taken place since then! How much better off we are than people used to be! Every little boy and girl now learns to read, and when they have learnt they can always buy or borrow a good book. Printing is now so cheap that a penny, or even a halfpenny, will buy a paper for boys and girls full of stories and pictures.

It is wonderful what we can do with a penny. For a penny we can send a letter to a friend from one end of the country to the other. And for a penny a mile we can be carried ourselves from one town in England to any other.

Our fathers and grandfathers could not do such things with a penny when they were young. It was Rowland Hill that first thought of the plan of the penny postage. He said, if only a penny was charged, so many people would write letters that it would pay well to send them. His plan was tried, and found to answer even better than he expected.

When Queen Victoria came to the throne railways had already begun to be made, but most of them have been laid down since. Before her reign few people went more than ten or twelve miles from their homes. In the place they were born, there most of them stayed to the end of their days. But now nearly every one goes about the country, and sees all he can for himself. If wages are low in one part of the country, a working man can now pack up his tools and go to another part.

And, then, what a wonderful messenger is the telegraph! We can now send a message hundreds of miles off in the twinkling of an eye. The train can go fast, but he is a creeping snail compared with the telegraph. Many a thief has been caught by the help of the telegraph. The rogue has got into a train, and thinks himself a lucky fellow to have escaped. The train takes him hundreds of miles away in a few hours; but on stepping out of the carriage at the end of his journey a policeman's hand is laid on his shoulder, and he is a prisoner. A message has been sent by telegraph since he entered the train.

Among the many wonders which have ceased to be wonderful, because they are so common, is that of the lucifer match. We have now only to rub a match against the side of the box, and in a moment light springs out of darkness. Fifty years ago it was a hard task to strike a light. Sparks had to be got from a bar of steel by striking it with a flint-stone; then the sparks had to drop on some tinder, made of burnt rags, before a light could be got. Five or ten minutes passed away, sometimes, before this could be done. Fancy a poor father or mother having to do all this in the middle of the night, with the baby screaming all the time!

These are only a few of the great improvements that have taken place since our good Queen began to reign. But they ought to be enough to make all little boys and girls very thankful for the great blessings they enjoy under her rule.

God save the Queen.

22

THE YOUNG BRITON'S HISTORY READER (GLASGOW: COLLINS, 1904), PP. 88–93.

These documents are taken from school 'readers' issued by several leading publishing houses at the end of the 19th and the very early 20th centuries. They were used to provide exercises in reading and comprehension and also moral instruction in elementary schools. From 1883, the educational code suggested that one reader used in reading classes be in the field of history. They were not used primarily for the teaching of history, but rather historical understanding as a by-product of providing a sense of national citizenship. The readers use an essentially Whig approach to the past and they attempt to draw into the imperial fold children of the working class. The depiction of the English people as 'adventurous' and 'sea faring' across the centuries is a recurring theme. What was then recent imperial history was presented to the child as a logical growth of older trends established at or before the time of Elizabeth I. Emphasis was on imperial figures as role models in character. Historians note the absence of Scottish or Welsh figures, excluded in favour of English. Document 23 is taken from a senior reader aimed at an older child, compared to those for which documents 20–23 were intended.

24. Setting Free the Slaves.

1. In some parts of America, and in the islands near, it is very hot. The heat is good for the growing of sugar, cotton, and coffee, but white people cannot work in the fields.

2. Our forefathers had not the same feeling for their fellow-men as we have. They looked down on the black men, or negroes, and thought little more of them than they did of animals.

3. It was the custom to buy and sell them, and to make them toil in the fields like cattle. These poor slaves had no rights, but were forced to obey their masters in all things. Life for them, unless they had kind masters, was very hard.

4. They were brought chiefly from Africa, where they were stolen from their homes. Then they were placed on board ship and carried to America, or to the West Indies.

5. The sea passage was full of misery. The ships were crowded, and the negroes could come on deck, only for a short time each day, in fine weather. On almost every trip a number died, and their bodies were thrown into the sea.

6. When the ships reached land, the negroes were put up for sale. Sometimes a boy was sold to one man, while his sister was sold to another living miles away. Thus they were parted, and never saw each other again.

7. The slaves had to toil very hard. They did not get any money, but their masters gave them food and clothes, and huts in which to live. Some of the masters were kind, and tried to make life as cheerful for the poor negroes as they could.

8. Other owners treated their slaves badly, and flogged them if they did not work hard enough. This slave-trade went on for a long time, and even good men did not see what wrong they were doing.

9. A man named Granville Sharp began to stir people up, by telling them about the cruel things that were done. He said it was a shame that there should be a single slave in the British Empire.

10. Very soon many good men came to his help. They wrote letters in the papers, and held great meetings all over the country. But many years passed before the freedom of the slaves was brought about.

11. Then a large sum of money was given to the owners of the negroes in the West Indies. This was to make up for their loss, and, on a certain day, all the slaves there were set free. It is our proud boast that no one can be a slave under the British flag.

12. This law was passed shortly before Queen Victoria came to the throne, and now there are few countries where men can keep slaves.

23

THE FIRST ENGLISH COLONIES, OR THE WORK OF RALEIGH AND HIS FRIENDS

From: *Macmillan's New History Readers: Senior* (London: Macmillan and Co., 1902), pp. 158–165.

These documents are taken from school 'readers' issued by several leading publishing houses at the end of the 19th and the very early 20th centuries. They were used to provide exercises in reading and comprehension and also moral instruction in elementary schools. From 1883, the educational code suggested that one reader used in reading classes be in the field of history. They were not used primarily for the teaching of history, but rather historical understanding as a by-product of providing a sense of national citizenship. The readers use an essentially Whig approach to the past and they attempt to draw into the imperial fold children of the working class. The depiction of the English people as 'adventurous' and 'sea faring' across the centuries is a recurring theme. What was then recent imperial history was presented to the child as a logical growth of older trends established at or before the time of Elizabeth I. Emphasis was on imperial figures as role models in character. Historians note the absence of Scottish or Welsh figures, excluded in favour of English. Document 23 is taken from a senior reader aimed at an older child, compared to those for which documents 20–23 were intended.

WHILE men like Drake were plundering the Spaniards upon the seas, there were other Englishmen, equally brave and daring, who were striving to plant colonies, which should make the New World English instead of Spanish territory. Of these founders of colonies in the reign of Elizabeth, the chief were Sir Walter Raleigh and Sir Humphrey Gilbert. Although they did not altogether succeed, yet it was through their efforts that the first settlements were founded, which have since grown into the United States of America. So if we regard Drake as the forerunner of England's naval greatness, we must also consider Raleigh as the pioneer of her colonial empire.

Like Drake and many other Elizabethan sailors, Raleigh was born in Devonshire, probably in 1552. The house in which he was born was in sight of the sea, and this may have influenced him in loving seafaring pursuits. We do not know much of his early years, but at the age of seventeen he went over to France to fight for the Protestants, who were being oppressed by the Catholics. There he stayed for six years, and on his return he made his appearance at Elizabeth's Court, where he soon gained the queen's favour owing to his good looks, his energy, and fine abilities.

Raleigh, however, longed for something better than the life of a courtier, and in 1578 he set sail with his kinsman, Sir Humphrey Gilbert, on an expedition to attack the Spaniards and to discover the North-West Passage. This enterprise proved unsuccessful, and in 1580 Raleigh accepted a command in Ireland. There was then a rebellion in that country, and Raleigh had to take his share in suppressing the revolt. This he did with some severity, and was rewarded for his efforts by a grant of 18,000 acres of land in Munster, which he colonised by introducing Englishmen to populate the estates.

When Raleigh returned to England, he was again admitted to the royal favour of his mistress, who admired his ready speech and charming manners. By Elizabeth he was promoted to high offices; and, when he became Captain of the Queen's Guard, he was brought into constant communication with his royal mistress.

In the meantime, Sir Humphrey Gilbert had procured a commission which gave him liberty to go in search of heathen lands and to take them in the name of the queen. As a first step towards this project, Gilbert formed a company, and received much assistance. On August 5th, 1583, three ships with some intending colonists landed in the harbour of St. John's, Newfoundland. Gilbert summoned all the inhabitants and traders of that port, read the queen's commission, and in her name took possession of the town and district within a radius of 200 leagues.

Thus the first English colony was proclaimed, and England took the first step towards founding her great empire. The experiment of colonising Newfoundland failed, for discontent and sickness compelled Gilbert to return. Gilbert reluctantly took to his little ship, having with him his friends with whom he had encountered so many storms and perils. The weather was very rough, so rough that the oldest mariner aboard had never seen more outrageous seas. The little frigate was wrecked in the night, and neither the vessel nor any of its crew was ever seen again.

Gilbert's work, however, was not allowed to lapse. For many years Raleigh had been pondering over the best way to colonise countries on the other side of the Atlantic. The King of Spain claimed nearly the whole of America as his own, but the Spaniards had not settled in any of the districts on the Atlantic coast of what we now call the United States. Raleigh received a patent allowing him to acquire any heathen lands which he might discover, and so he determined to try his fortune in that district of North America.

Raleigh accordingly fitted out an expedition, and his ships touched the American coast off the shore of the present State of North Carolina. They returned to England with a glowing account of the fertility of the soil, the charm of the climate, and with rumours of the abundance of gold and pearls. So pleased was the queen, that she suggested the name Virginia for the new colony.

In 1585 an expedition of 108 settlers sailed for Virginia under the command of Sir Richard Grenville, a cousin of Raleigh, and a fighting sea-captain like Drake.

THE FIRST ENGLISH COLONIES

Owing to various causes, however, the colony did not prosper, and the colonists were glad to be brought home by Drake in 1586.

For a time, then, the founding of colonies did not seem a success. But still a beginning had been made, and we shall find that after a while Englishmen profited by these early efforts of the Elizabethan navigators and adventurers. The year 1588 brought Raleigh more exacting work, for when the Armada sailed up the Channel in the month of July, he was in his proper place on board the fleet, which was chasing the Spanish ships up the Channel and through the North Sea to their destruction.

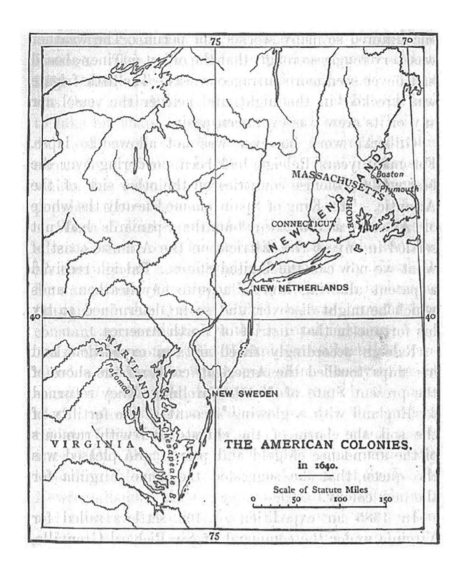

THE AMERICAN COLONIES, in 1640.

THE FIRST ENGLISH COLONIES

The next year we find Raleigh joining an expedition under Drake to take vengeance on the Spaniards. This, however, accomplished little, and then Raleigh betook himself to his Irish estates, living pleasantly at his house at Youghal. It is during this sojourn in Ireland that he tried the experiments of planting tobacco and potatoes, both of which had been brought over from America.

In 1591 he was back in England, urging the queen to take part in an expedition against Spain. It was in that year that his cousin, Sir Richard Grenville, sailed with Lord Thomas Howard to take the Spanish fleet of treasure ships on their return from South America. But the Spaniards heard of this design, and sent fifty-three ships of war to act as a convoy. The story of Sir Richard Grenville and his little ship, the "Revenge," has been told in a noble ballad by Tennyson. Suffice it to say that this grand hero fought to the last with one ship against fifty-three; and, when he was carried dying to the stately Spanish flag-ship, he rose upon their decks, and he cried:

> "'I have fought for Queen and Faith like a valiant man and true;
> I have only done my duty, as a man is bound to do:
> With a joyful spirit I, Sir Richard Grenville, die!'
> And he fell upon their decks and he died."

Returning to Raleigh, we find he offended Elizabeth in 1592, and by her he was thrown into the Tower. He soon regained his liberty, and again determined to seek new lands beyond the seas. This time he made for Guiana, a region between the Amazon and the Orinoco. He received much encouragement, and took command of the expedition in person. The Orinoco was explored for several hundred miles, and Raleigh brought home glowing reports of the fertility of the soil and of a region of untold wealth, which was called El Dorado, or the Golden Land.

Raleigh intended to return to Guiana the next year, but in 1596 Elizabeth needed him to accompany an expedition she was sending against the shores of Spain. It sailed under the command of the Earl of Essex and Lord Howard, and not only destroyed Cadiz, but worked immense harm to Spain. It is pleasing to note that Raleigh was so successful in his share of the work that, on his return, Elizabeth again received him into her favour.

The long and glorious reign of Elizabeth was drawing to a close, and when she died in 1603 Raleigh had to deal with James I., who deprived the brilliant courtier of most of his offices. Raleigh, too, was charged with being concerned in a plot to deprive James of the throne; and although there was no truth in the charges brought against him, he was found guilty of treason, and imprisoned in the Tower for twelve years. While there Raleigh could not be idle. He was still haunted with dreams of the finding of rich lands, and he contrived to write the *History of the World*.

At length, in 1607, after his liberation, Raleigh conducted his last expedition to Guiana in search of gold. On his arrival in South America he was attacked by the Spaniards, whom he defeated; but the gold mine of which he dreamt was not discovered, and he returned to England a disappointed man.

He was received with marked displeasure on his return by James I., who declared his intention of punishing all those who had committed acts of violence against the Spaniards. Raleigh was finally condemned to death on a false charge of treason. It was October 29th, 1618, that Raleigh mounted the scaffold and addressed the people in a touching speech, which he thus concluded: "So I take leave of you all, making my peace with God."

As soon as everything was ready, Raleigh turned to the executioner and asked to see the axe. He ran his finger down the edge, saying to himself, "This is a sharp medicine, but it is a sound cure for all diseases." He then knelt down and placed his head upon the block. Some one suggested that he should lay his face towards the east. "What matter," said he, "how the head lie, so the heart be right?" After he had prayed awhile, the headsman gave two blows, and the head was severed from the body. So died this brave and gallant Englishman, whose remains were buried by his faithful wife in St. Margaret's, Westminster.

24

CHAMBERS NEW GEOGRAPHICAL READERS, BOOK VI, BRITISH COLONIES AND DEPENDENCIES (LONDON: W. & R. CHAMBERS, 1898), PP. 31–40; 76–77; 100–103.

These extracts are taken from geographical readers and textbooks used in the classroom during the period 1900–1939. They demonstrate that geography teaching and texts could either use a rather dry, 'almanac' approach to presenting the Empire, with the emphasis on facts, or conversely, take the form of fairy stories which might capture the attention of younger children. Like the history readers presented earlier in this volume, the geography readers could include a largely positive account of the British Empire (as is the case in document 24). A frequently appearing word in these readers was 'strange', used to describe non-Anglo cultures, with the implication that British – or as it was invariably used, 'English' – culture was the 'norm' (a particular feature of document 26). The Collins reader opened by calling the growth of the British Empire 'a most marvellous story' and asserting that children should do their best to maintain what had been won. The Empire, it stated, stood for 'freedom and justice', and children should 'live good and useful lives' to maintain the Empire.

9. The peoples of India – I

1. We must now learn something of the races who inhabit our Indian Empire. The first thing that strikes us is the immense number of the people, no other country in the world, except China, containing nearly so many. Altogether, the population is about 287,000,000, of which the province of Bengal alone has some 67,000,000, or as many as England, Scotland, and France put together.

2. We are accustomed to speak of the people of India as Hindus; but only three-fourths of the people of the country really belong to this religion. Besides these, there are some 57,000,000 Mohammedans. They are descended from those conquerors who in ancient times poured through the northwestern passes and established themselves in the country. In the mountainous parts, again, there are other races, not so numerous, who are supposed to be older than any of the others. Doubtless they are the descendants of the first inhabitants of the country, who were gradually driven away from the plains by invaders, just as in this country the ancient Britons were driven westward by the Anglo-Saxons.

3. The Hindus of the northern plain differ greatly from those of Southern India. The former are olive-coloured in complexion, something like Italians, and are generally tall and good-looking; while the latter are nearly black, and much shorter in stature. The Mahrattas, in the north-west of the Deccan, are a bold and hardy people. In former days they were not conquered by the British without great trouble; but now that the country is settled, they are peaceful and industrious. The same may be said of the Sikhs of the Punjab region, who make the finest cavalry soldiers in Asia, and were not overcome by the British until after many battles had been fought.

4. A totally distinct race are the Parsees, who came from Persia, and are now settled in the neighbourhood of Bombay. They make excellent traders, and readily adapt themselves to British customs. A team of Parsee cricketers visited this country quite recently, and played several matches. The Parsees still retain their ancient faith, which is known as fire-worship.

5. With respect to the religious beliefs of these races, the Mohammedan 'has but one God, and Mohammed is his prophet.' His Bible is the *Koran*, and his weekly day of rest is Friday. Frequent prayers and fastings are required from all true believers, and they must not drink wine or eat swine's flesh. They are also required to make pilgrimages to Mecca, the birthplace of their prophet. The Mohammedan temples are called *mosques*. They have gilded domes, and are adorned with towers, from which the priests summon the people to prayer at certain hours every day.

6. The religion of the Hindus is Brahminism. The sacred books of the Brahmins, which are much older than our Bible, contain some very excellent teaching. At the present day, however, Brahminism is really a gross form of idolatry. Temples abound everywhere; nearly every village has one. Every day, crowds of worshippers pay their devotions to their god, bringing him little offerings of rice, fruit, or flowers. Bulls, and even monkeys, are looked upon as holy, and must on no account be killed. The Brahmins, indeed, eat no animal food, considering it wrong to kill any creature; and even eggs are forbidden, because they contain the germs of life.

grad'-u-al-ly, step by step.	a-dapt', suit.
com-plex'·ion, the colour of the skin.	pil'-grim-age, a journey made to a sacred place.
stat'-ure, height of any animal.	sum'-mon, call.

10. The peoples of India – II

1. The most curious custom of Hindu society is that the people do not mix freely together as in this country. They are divided into a great number of classes, or castes; and persons belonging to one of these divisions must not meet with those of another grade. The Brahmins, or priests, form the highest class, and a Brahmin would consider himself degraded by sitting down at the same table or drinking out of the same vessel with any one not belonging to his order. When the Prince of Wales visited India in 1875, one of the great native princes could not, for fear of losing caste, sit down to a banquet with him.

2. The poorer classes of Hindus – and the majority of them are poor – lead very homely lives. Their cottages are generally nothing more than mud walls roofed with bamboo, and the furniture is most scanty. Indeed, their simple wants are easily satisfied. They eat no flesh; and a few of the commonest utensils, to prepare their meal of rice or bake their cakes, are all that they need for cooking purposes. They never use chairs. When they wish to rest, they squat upon the ground; and one cannot pass a village without seeing numbers of them resting in this their favourite attitude. A mat serves them for a bed, and upon this they coil themselves when they want to sleep.

3. By far the greater number of the people of India are engaged in agriculture. Their methods of cultivation, however, are of the most unskilful kind, and have probably lasted for centuries without change. A Scotch or an English farmer would smile to see the clumsy ploughs drawn by oxen, and the crops roughly cut down with the sickle. But such is the fertility of the soil, that it produces abundant harvests, which not only supply the native population, but also leave a good deal over for export. It has been estimated that if the soil of India were skilfully cultivated, it would provide food for more than 400,000,000 people.

4. In the cities of India the people are, of course, engaged in other work. The higher classes make good merchants and traders. Some of the better educated are in the service of the government, or on the staffs of newspapers. Others, again, are skilful workers in metals, and produce many tasteful articles of jewellery. In the manufacture of gold brocade, shawls, muslins, and articles requiring beauty of design and fine work, the Hindus are very clever.

5. Besides the peoples we have already mentioned, there are the Singhalese in Ceylon, and the Burmans in Burma. The former are an idle, cheating people; but the latter are industrious and honest. In both places, Buddhism is the chief form of worship. It is very like Brahminism with its numerous temples and idols, but the foolish custom of caste is unknown.

de-grad'-ed, lowered in character.
ban'-quet, feast.
ma-jor'-i-ty, greater number.
at'-ti-tude, position.
ag'-ri-cul-ture, tilling the ground and raising crops.

sic'-kle, a large hooked knife for cutting down grain.
a-bun'-dant, very plentiful.
gold bro-cade', a silk stuff on which figures are wrought in gold.
de-sign', form; plan.

11. What Britain has done for India

1. Never before, in all history, has it been the lot of so small a country as Britain to rule over so large and populous a dependency as that of our Indian Empire. Of the total population of 287,000,000 which that empire contains, about 200,000,000 are under the direct government of Britain. The remaining 80,000,000, though in name ruled by native princes, are for the most part subject to Britain, and own our Queen as Empress.

2. For the purposes of government, India is divided into eight provinces. Supreme over all these is the Viceroy or Governor-general, while at the head of each division is placed a Lieutenant-governor or Chief Commissioner. The Viceroy lives at Calcutta in a splendid building called Government House. Here, with the aid of his council, he directs the affairs of the empire. He is, of course, subject to the government at home, and is in constant communication with the Secretary of State for India. Ceylon is a separate crown colony, and the governor is therefore not under the Viceroy of India.

3. For defence, India has an army of 219,000 men. Of these, 73,000 are British, and the remainder native troops, drilled and commanded by British officers. Besides this regular army, the native princes can together muster a very large force, which would make common cause with our army against an invader.

4. Great Britain has nobly performed her duty to her great dependency. Foremost among the advantages that India has derived from our occupation is the blessing of a just and settled form of government. Before Britain stepped in, the country had for long been the prey either of invaders from without, or of cruel, greedy princes from within. Under such a state of things industry could not flourish, and the people could not be contented or happy. Now, all this is changed. The country is secured by the strong arm of Britain from danger of every kind, and it is making rapid improvement in every way.

5. Besides the protection thus afforded, Britain has done much for India in various ways. Formerly, dreadful famines were frequent in certain districts, owing to the failure of the rains. But the making of canals, for the purpose of irrigation, has done much to remedy these evils. Excellent roads have been made in different parts, harbours have been improved, machinery has been introduced; and thus manufactures and trade have been encouraged.

6. But perhaps the greatest boon of all has been the laying down of railways in every part of the country. Over 18,000 miles have already been completed; and a traveller can now land at Bombay, and by this means be conveyed north-eastward to Calcutta, south-eastward to Madras and Southern India, northward to Peshawar at the mouth of the Khaibar Pass, and in fact to nearly all parts of India. We have also introduced the telegraph and an excellent postal system.

7. A scheme of elementary education has been established for the lower classes, as well as universities in five of the chief cities for higher education. Christian missionaries, too, labour among the people with untiring zeal, teaching them to 'turn from their dumb idols.' Thus, the natives are no longer oppressed as their forefathers were by former conquerors, but are now treated as equals; and it may fairly be hoped that a brighter future is in store for them.

pop'-u-lous, having a large number of people.	rem'-e-dy, cure.
su-preme', highest in rank or power.	boon, gift or favour.
mus'-ter, raise; gather.	con-veyed', carried.
op-pressed', treated harshly.	pass, a narrow passage through a mountain-range.

24. Races of British South Africa

1. British South Africa is very thinly populated, the total number of people of all races being only about 2½ millions, of which Natal contains nearly one-fifth. At present, Europeans are but a small proportion of the whole, and are mostly settled in the older parts of Cape Colony, where they form the majority of the inhabitants.

2. Of the white races, the *British* are most numerous in the eastern half of Cape Colony, while the *Dutch* are found chiefly in the western districts. The former are the more enterprising, and carry on nearly all the trade of the country. The railways, telegraphs, and other undertakings of the last thirty years, are mostly due to the British. The Dutch are chiefly farmers, and are slow to join in any new movement. They still speak their own tongue, but English is, of course, the official language of the country.

3. Of the coloured races, the *Kafirs* are much the most numerous. They are of a very dark brown colour, and are tall, strong, and handsome. They are a warlike people, and do not take willingly to labour, cattle-rearing being the only occupation for which they have any liking. Some of them are now giving up the savage ways of their forefathers, and adapting themselves to European customs, wearing clothes, and endeavouring to speak the English language.

4. The *Hottentots*, the old inhabitants of the country, are of a yellow-brown colour, short in stature, and of a mirthful disposition. They have now dwindled down to a very small number; but *half-castes*, or people of mixed Dutch and Hottentot blood, such as the *Griquas*, are numerous. They make good herdsmen, wagon-drivers, and labourers generally, and are very honest and trustworthy. In the towns are numbers of *Malays*, whose ancestors were brought from the East Indies by the Dutch. They are good fishermen, and many of them also make skilful artisans. They still keep their old Mohammedan faith.

5. With the exception of Natal, which is a separate crown colony, the whole of British South Africa, and the various races inhabiting it, are under the control, more or less direct, of the Cape Parliament, which is formed on the British model. At the head of all is a Governor, or High Commissioner, appointed by the crown.

en'-ter-pris-ing, bold and clever.
of-fi'-cial lan'-guage, the language used by all those connected with the government of the country.
oc-cu-pa'-tion, kind of work.

mirth'-ful, happy.
dis-pos-i'-tion, nature.
an'-ces-tors, forefathers.
art'-i-san, one skilled in any art or trade.

33. Productions of Australia – II

1. Australia has a splendid share of birds, but they are more noted for their gay plumage than their song. Though not musical, however, their cries are often very diverting. A sort of kingfisher, nicknamed the 'laughing-jackass,' is the most peculiar in this respect. It gives out its laughter-like notes at intervals during the day, and hence it has obtained the name of the 'bushman's clock.' There is also

the crow, which has a cry like a baby; the magpie, with its droll warble and sly tricks; the mocker, which imitates the barking of dogs or the whistling of men; and the beautiful lyre-bird, so called because its tail is formed like that instrument. The bower-bird, too, is well deserving of mention. Its nest, or rather its house, is formed like a gallery, and is decked with showy feathers and other gay coverings.

2. The Australian bush is also the great home of the parrot family, which are to be seen of all sizes and all colours; while on the seashore is found the large crane, wading about tall and stately. The largest bird of the continent, however, is the emu, or Australian ostrich, but it is much smaller than the African ostrich. It is often hunted with horses and dogs, and affords excellent sport. Its feathers are of little or no value; its eggs are made into drinking-vessels. The bustard, or wild turkey, is found on the plains, and its flesh is considered a luxury. This bird and some others do not sit upon their eggs, but cover them up with leaves and grass, and leave them to be hatched by the heat of the sun.

3. Australia is very rich in minerals, gold and copper being especially abundant in several parts. The gold mines of Victoria and New South Wales rival those of California; and, as we shall see, it has been owing to the plentiful supply of the 'yellow metal' that these colonies have grown so rapidly.

4. The copper mines of South Australia are among the richest in the world, and so abundant was the yield of this mineral at the time of first discovery, that it was obtained in large quantities both on and near the surface. Some of the older mines have now been worked out; but as the 'finds' extend over a very large area, the supply is not likely to fail for a long time to come.

5. The aborigines of Australia are generally called Austral negroes, to distinguish them from the African negroes, to whom they are much inferior. They are perhaps the lowest of all savage races, wearing scarcely any clothes unless compelled, building no houses, and cultivating no land. Efforts have been made to improve them, but they are very unwilling to engage in steady labour, though 'black boys' are sometimes employed on cattle stations, where they are very useful in the sheep-washing season.

6. Away from the haunts of the white man, the Australian 'blacks' give themselves up to hunting and fishing. They show great skill in tracking and running down game, and in capturing emus and kangaroos. They are, however, fast dwindling in numbers, it being estimated that there are now only some forty or fifty thousand of them, and the great majority of these are found in Queensland and the remote northern districts.

plum'-age, feathers.
di-vert'-ing, amusing.
ab-or-ig'-in-es, the first inhabitants of a country.

lux'-u-ry, a delightful thing.
haunts, places to which they often go.
re-mote', far distant.

25

R. FINCH, FRGS, *THE KINGSWAY BOOK OF GEOGRAPHY STORIES* (LONDON: EVANS BROTHERS LTD, 1919), PP. 76–82; 152–157;195–199.

These extracts are taken from geographical readers and textbooks used in the classroom during the period 1900–1939. They demonstrate that geography teaching and texts could either use a rather dry, 'almanac' approach to presenting the Empire, with the emphasis on facts, or conversely, take the form of fairy stories which might capture the attention of younger children. Like the history readers presented earlier in this volume, the geography readers could include a largely positive account of the British Empire (as is the case in document 24). A frequently appearing word in these readers was 'strange', used to describe non-Anglo cultures, with the implication that British – or as it was invariably used, 'English' – culture was the 'norm' (a particular feature of document 26). The Collins reader opened by calling the growth of the British Empire 'a most marvellous story' and asserting that children should do their best to maintain what had been won. The Empire, it stated, stood for 'freedom and justice', and children should 'live good and useful lives' to maintain the Empire.

IX. Peter goes hunting

PETER and Jack had had a very happy day. There was always great fun when cousin Jack came to stay with Peter. They had played at hunting all the morning in the woods – hunting elephants, lions, rhinoceroses, and other fierce beasts. Of course, really, there was not a creature in the woods fiercer than a rabbit, but all boys and girls know what fun it is to make-believe. Now they sat in their little white beds talking things over. For when Jack was staying with his cousin the two boys always slept in the same room – that was part of the fun.

"What a pity it came on to rain this afternoon!" said Peter. "It quite spoiled our game."

"Yes," answered Jack; "but, after all, we had quite a jolly time in grandfather's room. You know it was not at all bad to go there and see real elephant tusks, rhino' heads, antelope heads, and all that sort of thing, after playing at hunting. It made me wonder what it must be like to go on a real hunt with real guns, real blacks, real forests, and real wild animals."

Peter agreed. He and Jack had been surprised to find how quickly the time flew by in the Wonderful Room. There was so much to see there, and almost everything seemed to have a story to tell if it could only speak.

Then Jack noticed the blue stone. It was hanging on its queer necklace round Peter's neck.

"Hullo!" he said, "you still wear your funny stone! Doesn't it make you feel like a girl?"

"Rot!" replied Peter. "It's a lucky stone, Jack – like yours, only much better. You carry yours in your pocket; I prefer to carry mine round my neck. It's a magic stone, you see."

Jack laughed. Peter flushed, and felt a little annoyed. Presently he said, "How would you like to go on a real hunt, Jack?"

"Oh!" Jack answered, with a yawn, for he was getting rather sleepy, "I suppose it wouldn't be bad fun. How would you like to go yourself?"

"I?" said Peter, as he turned the magic stone over and over in his fingers, "I only wish I really could." . . .

He had hardly got the words out before Jack and the bedroom and everything else passed away into a blackness. The strange magic of the stone had begun to work.

For Peter had wished. And when people carry wishing-stones strange things happen, even if they only wish by accident.

* * * * *

The next thing Peter remembered was that he was crouching down behind a big thorn-bush with several other black boys. Somehow or other Peter did not think it strange to be a black boy; he understood all the others were saying, and felt quite at home in this great, wild land. The hot sun did not trouble him a bit, although his head was bare. The only clothing he wore was a fine *kaross*, or apron of leopard-skin. He held a knob-stick in his hand like the other boys, and in the loop of the raw-hide thong which bound his waist he carried three or four light throwing spears.

His necklace with the queer blue stone was the envy of all the others, for they knew it was magic.

The boys were watching the top of a low, rounded hill not far away. There, up on the sky-line, stalked seven giraffes, which as yet had not found out they were being watched. This was because the wind blew from them towards the boys, who knew quite well that the only way to get near such shy creatures was to creep up towards them against the wind. If the wind had been blowing in the opposite direction the keen scent of the giraffes would have warned the animals long ago that man-enemies were near.

Soon a large number of men crept up to where the boys were hidden. Two were white men and carried fine guns; close behind them were blacks, who held spare guns and cartridges ready for their masters to use. All formed part of a big hunting party. There must have been at least two hundred of them. For when one goes hunting in Africa in the "Land of Big Game" one cannot go alone. All food and other things likely to be wanted on the journey must be carried on the heads of native porters, for there are no roads – only tracks through the bush. It is necessary, too, to take a large number of blacks to act as "beaters" in rounding up the game, and to help to skin the animals killed, and so forth. Peter, then, was one of a large hunting party; he was "on *safari*," as they say in Africa.

The giraffes still browsed on the tender shoots of the low, flat, umbrella-like trees that were scattered thinly over the hill. The party crept a little nearer, making use of every bush for shelter. Soon they were close enough for the white men to take a fair shot. At the very moment when the bigger of the two hunters was about to pull the trigger the old male giraffe, which was leader of the herd, turned his head towards the danger. But he was too late. Crack! Crack!! went the heavy sporting rifles, and the big giraffe dropped with hardly a struggle. The rest of the herd made off in long, loping strides at great speed, and the hunters, with their swarm of blacks, scrambled up the hill to their prize.

There was big talk round the camp fires that night. A native had come in from a village a few miles away with the news that five big elephants had raided the fields of maize, millet, and cassava, and had even pulled off the roofs of the native huts to look inside for grain. For the blacks in this country store their grain in huts built almost exactly like the ones they live in. The only difference is that the store-huts are built on raised platforms to protect the grain from rats, white ants, and other creatures. The poor people were in terror lest the elephants should eat up all their food, or even kill their wives and children. They begged "the great white hunters" to bring up their guns to put an end to the danger. It was about six o'clock in the morning when the elephants came, the native said; and he believed that they would come again at the same time on the morrow.

The hunters were glad to hear the news. So far they had not shot a single elephant. They had followed their *spoor* – the great round footprints which showed plainly on soft, barren ground, and they had crept along the elephant-tracks through the bush without getting near enough to get a shot. They had begun to fear lest they should have to go back without even a pair of tusks, for it was now early in January, and soon the time of the "big rains" would come, when hunting is difficult and uncomfortable. Here was a grand chance. They made up their minds to start at dawn.

Very early next morning, while the red glow still lay on the eastern rim of the sky, the party made ready for the start. Peter and the other boys were very excited. Not that an elephant hunt was anything new, but they felt angry at what the elephants had done and wanted to see them killed.

Soon the native beaters came across the *spoor* – big, black, round footprints where the elephants had crossed a large patch of burnt grass. Every one went cautiously now, for the footprints were fresh that morning. By and by they heard a crashing in the thick bush, and the best trackers went on ahead to see how many elephants there were. Presently they came back. "Five," they said, "and one is an old male elephant, the biggest and the fiercest we have seen since we were born."

The hunters looked to their guns. The native beaters spread out in two big "wings," so as to get behind the herd and drive it towards the white men. Peter and another boy stayed behind to carry some of the little clips of cartridges for the hunters. Half an hour passed and nothing happened. Then suddenly there was a trumpeting roar in the distance and the thud of heavy feet upon the ground, and a crashing and rending among the thornbush and trees in front of the waiting guns, as the herd charged down upon them, led by the old elephant, trunk uplifted and red mouth open.

"Crack!" went the heavy rifle. But the old bull elephant still charged on. Crack! Crack!! – two more shots. One of the bullets had found him, for he staggered and fell on his knees. The hunters dashed from their hiding-place to put an end to him. But directly he caught sight of them he rose to his feet again, and with a squeal of pain and rage rushed madly at his foes. Peter bounded off to the nearest tree, and in a twinkle had clambered up into its thick umbrella top. It was not a big tree. But it was not very easy for even a big elephant to uproot it, even if it pressed the whole weight of its great body against it.

The hunter was a brave man and stood his ground. He took steady aim at the charging mountain of flesh and fired again – this time at the angry little red eye of the monster. The shot missed its mark, however, and sunk into the tender part of the trunk where it joins the head. The heavy shock of the bullet was enough to bring up the raging beast, which stood for a moment swaying as if it must fall. The hunter seized his chance and ran for the bush. What became of him Peter did not know. He heard crashings and heavy tramplings as the other four elephants plunged through the trees, and he heard, too, the shrill cries of the spearmen and beaters as they pursued the animals. He was much more interested in the big wounded elephant, which still stood swaying from side to side and feeling gently with his long trunk at the terrible wounds he had received. "What if he catches sight of me?" thought Peter. He knew only too well what would happen. Once within reach of that squirming trunk he would be pulled to the ground, flung high in air by those terrible tusks, and then trampled into a red pulp by those enormous feet. He held his breath in fear. He drew himself as near the bushy top of the tree as he dared.

At that moment the wounded monster caught sight of him. With a scream of rage he charged up to the tree and bore with his whole weight at the trunk. The tree swayed dizzily, and Peter had all he could do to keep his perch. Again and again the angry creature pushed heavily at the tree. He even twined his trunk around it and tried to uproot it. But the tree still stood. Then he stood quiet for a moment, as if he were thinking. Peter wondered what would happen next. Would he be kept prisoner until he fell down through exhaustion?

Peter had not long to wait. The huge elephant rearing itself upon its hind legs and pressing its great forefeet in the lowest fork of the tree, pushed its trunk up towards the boy, who cried out in terror as it nearly reached his bare foot. Up and up it squirmed, just like a big snake. Peter watched the curling, grasping end of it as it stretched nearer and nearer. He shrieked in terror and, bending down, pulled his foot up to his body. Then he remembered the magic stone. Just as the squirming tip of the elephant's trunk had seized his toes he clutched the blue stone and wished for safety.

* * * * *

"Come along, Peter! It's time to get up, old man!" cousin Jack was shouting in his ear. "I've been pulling your toe for nearly five minutes. Wake up!"

And Peter sat up in bed, rubbing his eyes sleepily.

"What on earth have you been dreaming about?" went on Jack. "You've been yelling at the top of your voice and talking all sorts of rubbish."

Peter was silent. Perhaps if he told Jack, his cousin would only laugh.

The boy who went to British Columbia

JACK BROWN had been plucking peaches all day long – lovely ripe peaches kissed by a hot summer sun until they had turned golden and rosy – and yet he had not eaten a single one. It was not because they belonged to his master, for Jack had been told that he could eat as many as he liked. It was because there were so many of them, and because Jack had been amongst them every day now for more than a week and had got tired of tasting them. In the great orchard where he stood he could see hundreds of peach trees standing in long, straight rows which stretched ever so far down to the lake. Every one of these trees had borne its golden burden of ripe fruit; many were now plucked bare, but there were still a great many whose branches bent to earth under their heavy load.

It was very hot, although it was late afternoon. Jack's broad, shady hat had not been able to keep the sun from tanning his face a rich deep brown. He wore light clothes, and his shirt-sleeves were tucked up above a pair of strong brown arms. He stood watching the men at work packing the ripe fruit into the big white square boxes that were to take it many miles to the great factory where it would be sorted, washed, and packed in cans by machinery. Tall waggons drawn by big brown horses came down between the rows of peach trees and went back piled high with boxes of fruit. It was all very wonderful, he thought.

Only a few years ago Jack had stood hungry, ragged, and barefooted outside a shop window in a mean London street, peering in at the good things to eat. What he liked to look at best were the tins with pictures on them telling of the lovely fruit hidden inside. He never dreamt in those days that by and by he would be in the land where that golden fruit grew; still less did he dream that the time would come when it would be no treat for him to eat ripe peaches, and when he could handle thousands of them without longing to taste a single one.

Yet here he was in British Columbia – six thousand miles from the wretched slum in which he played as a little boy – with plenty to eat and drink, a good home, kind friends, and ever so many interesting things to do every day. There were times when it seemed too good to be true. Then he remembered how, when father died and he was left alone, kind people had taken him to a big house where were lots of other poor, lonely little boys like himself; had fed him, clothed him, and taught him to read and write and make himself useful. Then had come the great day when he left the home to go to Canada with several other boys. They went in a fast train to Liverpool, and there were placed on board a big steamer, which took them many hundreds of miles across the Atlantic Ocean to Montreal. Jack still remembered what a wonderful voyage it was. It was summer-time, and the sea was never very rough. Once they passed two huge icebergs towering high and white above the blue sea; they had floated down all the way from the polar seas and the frozen land of the seal and white bear. They saw a school of whales, too; Jack watched their black humps rolling over in the sea and the thin fountains of spray that they kept sending up into the clear air through their blow-holes.

After the sea voyage there was the long, long journey by train across Canada to British Columbia. It was a Monday, he remembered, when they left Montreal, and the great engines roared on and on, and the train rumbled along behind them for nearly a whole week, day and night, without stopping except at big towns. There were lots of people on the train. All had brought food for the week. Some had even little oil cooking stoves with them for boiling water for tea, though plenty was to be had from the men on the train. At night they pulled out boards from under the seats or drew them down on hinges from the sides of the train to form beds. Most of the people were new to Canada and were going out to the Far West to make new homes on the wide prairies or to seek their fortunes in the goldfields and forests of the new land. It was a long and tiring journey, especially where nothing was to be seen for three days by the broad grass lands of the plains. But when the plains were left behind and the great engines began to labour as they puffed their way up among the hills towards the Rocky Mountains, Jack saw the most wonderful sights he had ever seen. From the window he could see high mountains with the white snows glistening upon their lofty peaks. They looked very near, although they were still miles away. And when at last the train was amongst them, rushing along the bottoms of deep valleys, or crawling along narrow ledges above frowning precipices, or tearing across high trestle bridges over torrents that foamed and roared thousands of feet below, Jack could hardly tear himself away from the window. It was all so wonderful and strange. Climbing up the steep slopes were thick forests of straight larches and spruces – just like regiments of soldiers, Jack thought. And above them were the white snows – snows that had been there for ages. Jack never forgot this journey.

It was in this land of snow-capped mountains, dark forests, rushing rivers, and fertile valleys that Jack was to find his new home. He was met at a little station by the lake-side by the farmer who was to be his master for some years. They went on board the lake steamer, and after nearly a day's journey on the lake stepped off at the little landing of the fruit farm. The farmer called it a "ranch" – not a farm. Here there was a wide, flat plain, shut in, it seemed, by mountains thickly clad with spruce and larch and hemlock – but not high enough to have snow upon them. Sometimes, however, you could see, far off and high up, the white gleam of the distant snow ranges.

Jack found plenty to do. The fruit had nearly all been picked, and the farmer was getting ready for the winter, laying in stores of wood for the fires which would have to be kept burning night and day for many weeks. For though summers are hot in this part of British Columbia, winters are cold; the lakes freeze over, and the snow lies deep. Jack was surprised, though, when winter came, to find that he did not feel the cold nearly so much as he expected. Perhaps it was because the air there is so dry.

There was not much farm work to be done when the snows came. The horses and cattle had to be fed, of course; and there was wood to fetch in, and there were odd jobs to do about the house. It was a wooden house, very strongly built. Jack could see that the wood had come from the forests that grew not far away across the plain on the first slopes of the mountains. The farmer and his sons often went hunting there, especially in winter; and Jack went with them. They shot birds, squirrels, deer, and other creatures. There were, too, great flights of wild geese and duck upon the frozen lake. In summer, too, they hunted deer, and sometimes came across the lynx – a great cat with tufted upright ears and fierce yellow eyes that looked you through and through.

The farmer was fond of telling the story of his great adventure with a grizzly bear – a monster who stood eight feet high upon his hind legs and nearly crushed him to death in his strong paws. "There are still plenty of them up in the bush, boys," he would say, "so watch out for them." Jack had long ceased to be afraid of rattlesnakes. At first he was scared almost to death when the boys told him how common they were. Now he knows that he must be alert when he hears the warning rattle, and that one sharp cut with a stick will settle most rattlers if you catch them in time.

When the snows melted every one was very busy. Fields had to be ploughed, for the farmer grew corn as well as fruit; and trees had to be examined and cared for, so that the fruit harvest might be a good one. Then came the time of blossom, when the plum and pear orchards were white with snowy bloom and when peach trees and nectarines were heavy with flowers. The hardest work of all came when the ripe fruit was ready to be gathered, and when every one had to toil and toil to get it all in before the first early-morning frosts came.

What interested Jack most was the Indian village at the foot of the hills, where a little river ran down to the lake. He had read a lot about Indians, and was just a little disappointed with the first ones he saw at the lake-side station. They were rather wretched-looking objects, and not at all like the grand fellows of the storybooks. They earned their living on the station doing all sorts of odd jobs. But in the Indian village there were Indians quite like the real ones, especially when on certain days there was a great pow-wow and feast. Some of them were quite rich men, owning land, horses, and cattle, and ranging through their own forests in search of game. One or two had been great travellers, and, luckily for Jack, could speak English fairly well. They were great story-tellers, too, and told him of the wonderful things to be seen far away in the north – how men braved the Arctic snows to seek for gold, and how the lumbermen cut down the great forest trees and floated them down the rivers. Some had lived near the shores of the Pacific, and had seen the rivers there so full of salmon that men could catch them with their hands. They told him of the huge nets and the queer salmon-wheels used to net the fish, and of the thousands of men who worked hard day and night in big factories canning the salmon. But perhaps the most interesting of all their stories were those which told of the old days before the white men ever set foot in the Indian country, of the great fights between rival tribes, of the magic of the medicine men and of the struggles with the pale-faces.

* * * * *

Some day Jack hopes to go with his master down to Vancouver, the great city which has grown up on the Pacific coast, where the steamers start on their five thousand-mile voyage to China and the East of Asia. There he will once more see crowds of busy people, brightly-lit streets, rushing street-cars, and big buildings, which will remind him of the London he left several years ago.

Jack is doing well, too. He has saved a good deal of money, and is looking forward to the time when he can buy a small fruit ranch of his own.

The story of Hassan

HASSAN lives in a small village near the great river of Egypt, which here is nearly a mile wide, although it is a long, long distance to the sea.

Hassan is dressed in a loose white cotton coat which reaches nearly to his ankles. Over it he often wears another of bright blue. On his head is a white cap folded in many folds, something like the turbans that the Hindus wear. His feet are bare, but when he has to walk a long distance he puts on straw sandals, which he keeps on his feet by gripping between his big toe and the rest a little thong. His father is quite a poor man, and although Hassan is not very old he has to work hard in the fields to help keep so large a family, for Hassan has three brothers and two sisters.

The house they live in is poor too; it is built of sundried bricks made from mud and straw, and whitewashed to keep out the heat of the burning Egyptian sun. But they are quite content, for they are much better off than some of their neighbours, who have to live in dirty hovels of mud-plastered branches. Let us peep into the house: how cool it is inside! But there is not much furniture – only a few mats and a number of pots of earthenware. In the corner of the room is a carved box, into which Hassan has never been allowed to peep. It contains his father's treasures, and will become his when his father dies, for Hassan is the eldest son. By its side is a little low stool, on which stands the queer little stove and coffee ladles and cups which his father uses when he has his great treat – a cup of good coffee.

Around the little white house is a small patch of garden, where they grow beans and other vegetables, as well as maize or millet, which is ground at home in a stone mill to make coarse flour for bread. Hassan's mother does this; she puts the grain upon the lower stone and then turns the upper one round and round, crushing the grain between them. When Hassan's sisters are big enough they will learn to grind the corn, too; it is very tiring work.

From the low doorway of the house you can see the cotton fields and sugar plantations where Hassan and his father work every day. Here and there are groves of tall palm trees with long, slender stems crowned with a cluster of broad, fan-like leaves of a most wonderful green. Looking towards the river you can see beyond it the high cliffs of fiery red and golden yellow sand which mark the beginning of the great desert. Hassan has never been there, but he has talked much with Arab children who have come in with their fathers from the desert, and he knows, too, that in spring the strong winds drive before them high whirling clouds of desert sand that blot out the light of the sun. It is terrible then; for the fine, sharp sand finds its way into everything; it clog's one's eyes, ears, and nose, and almost suffocates those boys and girls who are unlucky enough to be outdoors when the desert wind is blowing.

Hassan and his father work very hard in the cotton, maize, sugar-cane, and bean fields. For in Egypt there are at least three harvests in the year – one of grain and two of vegetables. By February the fruit trees are all in full bloom and the corn is standing high. For winters are very mild in Egypt; really the Egyptians have no winter such as we have in Britain, although the nights are sometimes very cold. In March the crops begin to ripen, and harvest is finished by the end of April. Egypt has always been famous for its grain. When the children of Israel were starving they went down into Egypt for corn; many other Eastern peoples did the same. To-day Egypt is most famous for her fine cotton, which is sent in large steamers to Britain to feed the looms of Manchester and other big "cotton towns." It is strange to think that a cotton frock worn by a little English girl may have been made from cotton that grew in far-off Egypt.

Where Hassan lives it very rarely rains, and if it were not for the great river nothing would grow in the fields. Both Hassan and his father have worked hard at keeping clear the long water-channels and little canals along which the precious water is taken to the fields from the river when it rises, as it always does in early summer. For then the Nile is fed by heavy rains near its sources in the heart of Africa, and it rises higher and higher until it overflows its banks. All the fields near the river are flooded. When the river begins to go down in August it leaves behind a rich mud, which will help to grow next year's crops. Once upon a time all the water was allowed to drain off the land, and at low Nile farmers were often in sad straits for water. Nowadays a great deal of the Nile flood is held back by huge dams which British engineers have built across the river. The Nile boats go up and down through locks at the end of the dam.

Hassan loves to see the grumbling camels ploughing in the rich Nile mud, or to watch them walking round and round driving the big *sakieh*, or water-wheel, whose buckets lift the water out of the canals and pour it into the channels to water the fields. Sometimes the work is done by patient oxen, and often by men or boys. But the latter work what are called *shadup* – leathern buckets slung from one end of a long pole hung across another, something like a see-saw. At the other end is a heavy weight. When the weight is lifted, down goes the bucket into the water to be filled; when the weight is let go it fetches up the bucket of water, and men seize it and pour it into the channel higher up. Both plans are just clever ways of raising water from one level to another.

Besides helping to plough and sow, Hassan breaks up the clods of earth with his mattock, scares away the clouds of birds that come to feed on the growing crops, and takes his share in gathering the wheat, barley, lentils, beans, and clover, or the cotton, sugar-cane, rice, and tobacco.

Best of all, Hassan likes to wander down to the banks of the great river, where he and other brown boys throw off their blue and white gowns and bathe in its warm waters, or sit on a high yellow rock to watch the big-sailed boats and swift steamers going up and down. Many of the steamers carry tourists who have come from all parts of the world to see the wonders of Old Egypt. Some of them come ashore near by to visit the ruins of a great temple which Hassan knows well. He has often looked at the strange carvings on the huge broken pillars, and has wondered what they mean. There are beautiful little pictures in stone of birds and animals, men and women, kings and queens, all arranged in long lines with lots of curious marks that he cannot understand.

He asked his father about it all one night when the work was done for the day. His father told him a wonderful story of the days when the Egyptians were a great people and the masters of the world; when they built great cities and marvellous temples, and built them so well that even to-day many of them are still to be seen. Hassan is proud to think that he belongs to the same race, although his people to-day are ruled by another nation from the western seas. He often begs to hear more of the wonders of Old Egypt, of the great tombs built by the kings and queens, of the huge figures carved in the rocks by the river.

As Hassan sits by the water he sees long white rows of pelicans fishing in the shallows among the reeds. Not far off is a string of flamingoes, dazzlingly white in the hot sunlight. Hassan gives a shout and claps his hands. At once the flamingoes take to flight; and as they spread their wide wings their under feathers show delicate pink and red as they wheel across the water. Away they fly, stretching their long necks straight in front of them and their long legs straight behind. Hassan has often found their nests – queer little towers of mud with a little grass tucked in on the top. On them squat mother flamingoes with their long legs sprawling and their funny necks twisted and turned so that their heads lie on their backs looking towards their tails!

The sun is low over the western desert – a ball of fiery red in a sky full of gorgeous colour, such as we never see in our grey island home. It is time for him to go home. Women clad in black, with their faces covered to the eyes, and carrying, balanced on their heads, jars of water, go up from the river to the village, their anklets clattering musically as they walk. Past the creeper-covered stones and hanging bells of yellow and scarlet blossom, past long lines of graceful palms, and through the green clover fields runs the well-worn path to the village. The white houses look beautiful beneath the shady grove of palms – until one gets near enough to see the ugly bundles of firewood on the roofs and the crumbling mud of the walls.

Hassan goes in, taking no notice of the swarm of hungry dogs that prowl about the streets. His supper of lentils and coarse bread is ready for him. There is a little talk about the doings of the day. Then Hassan and his brothers and sisters roll themselves up on their reed mats to sleep. Far away from the outskirts of the village comes the steady beat of a "tom-tom": an Arab camp is pitched there. The last thing Hassan remembers is the great white Egyptian moon which stares in at him through the opening high up in the wall.

26

E.C.T. HORNIBLOW, *LANDS AND LIFE: HUMAN GEOGRAPHIES, PEOPLE AND CHILDREN OF WONDERFUL LANDS* (LONDON: GRANT EDUCATIONAL CO., 1930–1935). EXTRACT TAKEN FROM THE 1944 EDITION. PP. 7–19; 103–108.

These extracts are taken from geographical readers and textbooks used in the classroom during the period 1900–1939. They demonstrate that geography teaching and texts could either use a rather dry, 'almanac' approach to presenting the Empire, with the emphasis on facts, or conversely, take the form of fairy stories which might capture the attention of younger children. Like the history readers presented earlier in this volume, the geography readers could include a largely positive account of the British Empire (as is the case in document 24). A frequently appearing word in these readers was 'strange', used to describe non-Anglo cultures, with the implication that British – or as it was invariably used, 'English' – culture was the 'norm' (a particular feature of document 26). The Collins reader opened by calling the growth of the British Empire 'a most marvellous story' and asserting that children should do their best to maintain what had been won. The Empire, it stated, stood for 'freedom and justice', and children should 'live good and useful lives' to maintain the Empire.

The Negro of the burning sun

As you will see later, I am a black man. My home is in Africa, where the sun is always very hot. That is why I do not wear many clothes.

My little sons and daughters wear none at all, when they are tiny. They would not be happy if they did.

I am very proud of all my family, with their shiny, smiling faces, and their nice, black, woolly hair.

Their teeth are white and strong, because they clean them every day. This is how they do it. A piece of twig is split at one end many times, and with this *brush* they rub their teeth very clean.

My children, their *mummie*, and myself are very happy. We have many friends, who live near us.

We do not buy our goods in shops, like you. Oh, no! My wife grows maize, and grinds it into flour. Out of this she makes a nice porridge in our large iron pot; of course, she puts in other things as well – especially plenty of *salt*. Sometimes we have meat.

My work is to look after my cattle.

I live in the *Hot Grasslands*, where there is plenty of long grass, taller than I am. My cattle feed on the shorter and juicier grass.

At night I drive them home, so that the wild animals will not kill and eat them. Many wild animals live near my home.

I have seen wild *elephants*. Once an elephant nearly killed me when I was hunting, but I shot him just in time. with my bow and arrow.

That is why I am now a rich man and have many cattle. I sold the ivory from his tusks for ever so much money. I got one hundred pounds for each tusk.

I wish I could shoot another, but elephant hunting is very dangerous and very difficult. To kill him, one has to shoot very hard in one of his small eyes. It is no good shooting at any other place, because his skin is inches thick – so thick that even a bullet from a gun bounces off it.

What a lovely smooth coat the *zebra* has! I have often seen a herd of these feeding on the grass, or drinking at a lonely pool.

I do not like the *rhinoceros*, which is very fierce. If you annoyed him, he would tear you to pieces with his one sharp, curved horn. I keep away from him. I do not like him at all!

But I love to see the tall, long-legged *giraffe*, reaching up with his long neck to nibble at the young, juicy leaves of a tree.

Herds of *antelope* also roam near my home, and I often hunt them.

Antelope meat is very nice to eat. When I am lucky enough to shoot one of these timid animals, I invite all my friends to a feast. We stay up all night, eating, drinking, and dancing. We negroes like dancing very much. The banging of a monkey-skin drum always makes me want to dance.

The *lion* and the *leopard* are no friends of mine, because they would kill my cattle if I was not very careful.

You would like to see my house. I made it myself, with the help of my wife and children.

First, I fixed long, thin poles into the ground to make a ring. These I joined together at the top to form a dome. Over this round shape I laced thin sticks and pieces of the long, thick grass. Last of all, I thatched the top with another layer of thick grass.

I think my home looks very nice. It is very comfortable inside, for *Mummie* and the girls have made many grass mats. They also find plenty of work to do in the fields, for they grow all our food. But they always find time to play with the new-born baby, who rolls in the sun.

But I am proudest of my three sons. They love to help me look after my fine cows and bullocks. Yesterday, my youngest one took them down to the *water hole* for the first time. He is only five years old. But he *can* shout!

The best treat for my two elder sons is to go hunting with me and my friends. For their last birthdays, I made each of them a real bow and some arrows. Already they have brought home something for dinner!

But my other little son is only five. He also would like to go hunting with me. But I have told him he must first grow older, bigger, and stronger.

Yesterday he took his elder brother's bow and some arrows, and tried to shoot with them. *He almost poked out my dog's eye with one of the arrows!*

Some time ago, my brother, who is not as rich as I, came to live with me. He brought his wife and all his belongings.

The picture shows you how he arrived at my home.

He rode on an ox with a humped back and two great horns. On either side of the saddle hung all his goods in two sacks. His wife led the ox.

I have heard that in your country the woman would have had the ride, while the man would have walked! I think that would be very strange.

The boys and girls of this country love to play in the shallow river for hours and hours. That is where we get our drinking water.

Every morning, when the women and girls fill the water-pots, all the children have great fun splashing each other in the cool water.

But if they see an *alligator* – don't they run! It is very sensible of them to keep out of such danger. One of my friends has now only one leg. When he was a boy, he once trod on an alligator that was hiding in the muddy river. He tried to run away, but not before the beast had snapped off his right leg with one bite.

We negroes do not have many worries. We have plenty to eat, plenty of sport, and plenty of play.

We laugh and dance and sing, and are very happy.

My little son is ever so happy. He is always smiling, and I have never seen him cry.

(1) Why are the Negro children happier with no clothes on?
(2) Describe the Negro's face and head.
(3) Give the names of some wild animals that live in the land of the Negro.
(4) Why does the Negro dislike the lion?
(5) Draw a picture of the Negro's home.
(6) Say how this house was made.
(7) What games are played by the boys and girls of this land?
(8) How is the grass in this land different from that in our own land?
(9) Draw a bow and some arrows.
(10) *Make models in clay or plasticene* of the Negro's hut, his bow and arrows, or of any other things mentioned in this chapter.

The frizzy-haired cannibals of New Guinea

The people of this land are very proud of their huge mops of frizzy hair. The larger and thicker they grow, the prouder they are. These mops are often propped up with bamboo sticks on which large feathers are tied.

How would you like to wear a long bone or shell through the middle of your nose? Many of these people always wear one of these things. The longer it is the prouder they are! Yet it never seems to get in the way of the wearer.

The home of these people is in one of the biggest islands in the world.

What a strange house they live in! It is very large – larger than the biggest school that was ever built.

The whole of one tribe lives in this large house. That means that there are more than one hundred men and women, and perhaps more than two hundred children – all living in the same house!

It reminds us of Saba's home, that we read of in Chapter 4.

This huge building is made of wood, and has a thick, thatched roof.

It is built on posts driven into the ground. To get into it, the natives have to climb up steep steps. In one part of this large house the tribe keeps many ugly images, which they think are mighty *gods*. Other rooms hold many spears, arrows, and thick wooden clubs, for these people are very fond of fighting other tribes.

Once they were *cannibals*. This means that they *ate* the flesh of men and women. But they always kept the heads of those who were their enemies. These heads they hung up, to show how brave they were, and the man who had the largest number was the most important man.

That is why these men are sometimes called the *Head-hunters* of New Guinea.

Now, perhaps, you can see why they all live together, and why their houses are built *on piles*, and are often built in the water.

They do these things so that they can easily defend themselves against their enemies.

But all the houses of this land are not large like this.

Some are stranger still. They are built on the top of a tall tree – just like the nest of a bird. Most of these houses are very well made, and have thatched roofs. To get into their house, the father, mother, and children have to climb up a very shaky ladder. The sides of this ladder are made of rope, with pieces of cane, tied to the rope, to act as steps.

At night this ladder is always pulled up, so that no one can get in.

I should not like to live in a house like this. Would you?

(1) What is a cannibal?
(2) Make a drawing of one of their very large houses – built on piles.
(3) Why do so many people live in the one large house?
(4) Draw a picture of one of the *tree-houses*. (Don't forget the ladder.)
(5) Why do these people wear bones or shells in their noses?
(6) Say why you would not like to live with these people.
(7) Make a model of a tall tree. Then build a *tree-house* on the top of it. Don't forget the ladder.
(8) Why do these people build their houses in the trees?

27

COLLINS' WIDE WORLD GEOGRAPHY READER: THE BRITISH EMPIRE (LONDON: WILLIAM COLLINS, 1901–23), PP. 83–87.

These extracts are taken from geographical readers and textbooks used in the classroom during the period 1900–1939. They demonstrate that geography teaching and texts could either use a rather dry, 'almanac' approach to presenting the Empire, with the emphasis on facts, or conversely, take the form of fairy stories which might capture the attention of younger children. Like the history readers presented earlier in this volume, the geography readers could include a largely positive account of the British Empire (as is the case in document 24). A frequently appearing word in these readers was 'strange', used to describe non-Anglo cultures, with the implication that British – or as it was invariably used, 'English' – culture was the 'norm' (a particular feature of document 26). The Collins reader opened by calling the growth of the British Empire 'a most marvellous story' and asserting that children should do their best to maintain what had been won. The Empire, it stated, stood for 'freedom and justice', and children should 'live good and useful lives' to maintain the Empire.

37. Like and unlike

1. In some respects South Africa is like one or more of the other great divisions of the British Empire, and in others it is quite different. For instance, South Africa resembles Australia in having western and central deserts, and in having its mountains and more fertile tracts along the east and south coasts. In both lands droughts are common, and the soil needs to be irrigated; in both, agricultural and pastoral pursuits occupy most of the inhabitants; but South Africa is mainly peopled by native races, while the inhabitants of Australia are nearly all of Anglo-Saxon descent.

2. Great mountain ranges, that form terraces, run along the coasts of South Africa. Extending inland from the terraces are lofty plateaus, the general level of which is about as high as Snowdon, but there are parts which have a much greater elevation.

3. South Africa resembles Canada in having its white population consisting of two different families. In Canada about two-fifths of the whites had French ancestors, and the rest are mainly of British origin; so in South Africa the British are greatly outnumbered by the Dutch.

4. In the physical features of Canada and South Africa, however, there is great difference. Canada is well supplied with navigable rivers and inlets of the sea; South Africa lacks these. The presence of the mountains on or near the edge of the plateaus in South Africa prevents the formation of useful rivers, and increases the difficulty of constructing railways between the coast and the interior.

5. West winds from the sea are rain-bearers to the British Isles, but not to South Africa. There the west winds are not very strong, and as they blow from a cooler to a warmer district, they retain most of their moisture. The wet winds in South Africa blow from the south and the east, but their passage is checked by mountains from ten to twelve thousand feet high, and consequently the interior has a small rainfall.

6. Owing to the rapid fall of the land from the mountains to the coast, the rivers on the south and east of South Africa are practically useless for navigation; nor are they of much service for irrigation.

7. The Orange River[1] is the longest in South Africa. It rises in the mountains on the east coast, where there is an abundant rainfall, and it enters the Atlantic Ocean after a course of twelve hundred miles; but it has a bar at its mouth, and great rapids in its course; and its volume is so much diminished by evaporation in the Kalahari Desert that this alone would prevent it being used as a waterway.

8. South Africa is also unlike both Canada and Australia in that its States are neither united nor equally advanced in civilisation. Some of the States of South Africa are self-governing, others are under imperial or colonial officers, and in certain territories the regulations of the South African Company have the force of law.

9. Comparing South Africa with India, we find that while the former grows barely enough food for the comparatively small number of its inhabitants, the latter supports a teeming population; but the two countries are alike in that the population is mainly native.

10. "In certain districts of South Africa there is an overwhelming majority of dark-skinned people, and in these districts the social and political conditions are those of India. That is to say, the coloured races are controlled and governed by the handful of Europeans resident among them."

11. The unproductiveness of the soil of South Africa is partly the result of the insufficient and uncertain rainfall in the interior; it is also in a great measure due to the unprogressiveness of the Dutch farmers.

12. This is what was said of them a hundred years ago, and it might be said of them, though to a less extent, even now: – "The Dutch farmers never assist the soil by flooding. Their only labour is sowing the seed, and leaving the rest to chance and the excellent climate. Their ploughs, harrows, and utensils of husbandry are clumsy and ill-formed; but they cannot be prevailed upon to make any alteration in their method of farming."

38. The settler in South Africa. – I

1. Those who do not know South Africa often think of it as another Canada or another Australia, but that is a mistake which cannot be made by anyone who has intelligently read the last chapter. "South Africa is a black man's country, ruled by the white man. It is India, with the climate of Australia."

2. Another mistake that is sometimes made is to regard the diamond and gold-bearing regions of South Africa as representative of the whole country; but, "remarkable as has been the mineral development, it is the veld and not Kimberley or Johannesburg which characterises South Africa.

3. "Once beyond the barrier ranges, undulating plains spread on every side. The surface of the earth is broken only by rounded and flat-topped masses. There is neither tree nor shrub, homestead nor boundary, to arrest the eye. At most, a line of mimosa bushes marks the track of the periodic water-course, and the brown earth at our feet is studded here and there by stunted bushes. Such is the veld, and such is the characteristic landscape of two-thirds of settled South Africa."

4. Is South Africa, then, a land to be avoided by the British and other white races? Certainly not. To think that would be as great a mistake as those which have just been pointed out. Over the greater part of the country the climate is an excellent one for the white man, and the many opportunities of meeting with success, through the abundant sources of wealth awaiting him, have given rise to the saying that "Fortune knocks at a man's door once in every other country; in South Africa she knocks thrice."

5. The Rand, the chief gold-field of the Transvaal, alone produces more of the most precious metal than the whole of Australasia and America. Kimberley has almost a monopoly of the world's diamond industry; and there are stores of silver, iron, coal, copper, and tin waiting only for capital and skill to unlock them. There is hardly any valuable mineral of which South Africa has not a good share.

6. The low-lying coast lands produce the spices and fruits, sugar and coffee, tea and indigo, of the tropics. The highlands and karroos are excellent grazing country. The fertile areas from Cape Town to the Zambesi grow to perfection every product of the warm and temperate regions. "Nature has withheld no good thing from South Africa, except plenty of wood and plenty of water."

7. The development of the land, however, has not kept pace with the production of gold. Agriculture, except in a few spots, is carried on in a very primitive way, consequently enormous quantities of provisions have to be imported, and upon these heavy taxes are levied.

8. Knowing these facts, it is not surprising to find that living is "dearer and poorer in South African towns than anywhere else in the British Empire." Before the great war, which began in 1899, the price of eggs in Johannesburg was from five to six shillings a dozen, milk was one shilling and sixpence per quart, butter five shillings a pound, and cauliflowers five shillings each. In Rhodesia even higher prices had to be paid.

9. Agricultural settlers are the great need of South Africa, but the man who desires to succeed must be prepared to toil early and late, and before settling down he should become acquainted with the country and with colonial ways. All parts are not alike suitable for the same kind of farming, and methods which are successful in the British Isles and other countries are not always the best that can be employed in South Africa.

10. If the new colonist can afford to travel about the country, he can in that way obtain the knowledge which will help him to make a wise choice of a farm. Many new-comers acquire invaluable practical experience by taking service with a farmer in a fertile district.

11. A very popular way of gaining colonial knowledge and experience, while earning a good living, is by joining one of the forces of mounted police, as the members of these bodies travel over large areas, and have excellent opportunities for observation.

39. The settler in South Africa. – II

1. The principal labour employed upon South African farms, whether agricultural or pastoral, is that of natives and other coloured races. Very few farmers are willing to offer such wages or furnish such accommodation as would satisfy Europeans. White men, therefore, who wish to undertake farm work in South Africa, have little chance of doing so, except upon their own land.

2. In order that the farm may prove remunerative, it must be near a railway, it must consist of good soil, and it must have water. The scarcity of water on the surface is, as you know, a general difficulty in South Africa; and, except in Natal, artificial irrigation is everywhere necessary. By the drought of 1897–98 more than half the wheat and maize, or "mealie," crop was lost, together with half the rye, a third of the barley, and a fifth of the oats.

3. On many farms there is a stream of water for a part of the year, and across this dams are constructed, so that reservoirs are formed. In some places use is made of natural subterranean reservoirs, the water being obtained by means of artesian wells, or raised by pumps worked by windmills. The settler must be prepared for a long, dry winter, as well as for great summer heat.

4. South Africa is a great grazing country. Flocks and herds are the chief wealth of the natives and of the white farmers, but, of course, all parts are not equally suitable for cattle, horses, or sheep, and it is only in a few specially favoured spots that all three will thrive, and where grain can also be successfully grown.

5. "Where sheep will thrive, horses may die of the dreaded horse sickness; where cattle grow fat and sleek, sheep may starve; and where sheep can hardly find a living, the cultivation of the soil yields splendid returns."

6. The area suitable for sheep is much more extensive than that on which grain can be grown. In some parts the sheep are pastured on grass, but on the high plains of Cape Colony, and on the country north of the Nieuwveld Mountains, they feed

on succulent plants – that is, plants with leaves, stems, and roots, thickened by nature to contain stores of moisture, that they may withstand long droughts.

7. Goats flourish in South Africa, and ostrich farming is more profitable than sheep farming, although the former is a very speculative industry. Besides large numbers of the common goat, there are great herds of the Angora variety, which furnishes mohair. This animal is a native of the central plateau of Asia Minor, and of the highlands of Persia and Kashmir. It was introduced into South Africa from Asia Minor about the middle of the nineteenth century.

8. The Angora goat is rather smaller than the common domestic kind. It has a small and pretty head, surmounted by horns from eighteen to twenty-four inches in length. The fleece is white and shiny, and falls in natural ringlets almost to the ground. Each goat yields five or six pounds of hair, which is usually worth about twenty shillings. The mohair is exported chiefly to England, and is there made into braid, covering for buttons, shawls, &c. Bradford and Norwich are seats of this manufacture.

9. The ostrich is a native of South Africa. At first the feathers were obtained by hunting and killing the wild birds. The next step in the industry was the rearing of birds which had been caught when young; but as the birds, when full-grown, were fierce and unmanageable, only a few were kept. At length there was invented an incubator, by which the eggs could be hatched, and by this means many generations have been brought up entirely by hand; and, through being accustomed to man from birth, the birds have become increasingly tame.

10. Ostriches are kept on farms[2] throughout Cape Colony, but not beyond its bounds. The chief districts are Oudtshoorn, on the south coast, and Albany, in the eastern province. The price of the feathers varies very much, as the demand depends on the caprices of fashion.

11. The oldest of the Cape industries, however, is the cultivation of the vine. This is mainly followed on the mountain slopes, and in the valleys in the south-western corner of the colony. Soil and climate are so suitable, that the vineyards are six times as productive as those of Europe, and eight times as prolific as those of Australia; but the wine has not found favour, and consequently the amount exported is small.

12. The vineyards are very picturesque. The houses are usually quaintly-built, old Dutch dwellings, with coal-black thatched roofs and whitewashed walls. The vines are grown without any support, and, seen from a distance, they have the appearance of currant bushes.

Notes

1 See coloured illustration opposite page 90.
2 See coloured illustration opposite page 90.

28

B. G. HARDINGHAM, *ROUND THE GLOBE: THE FOUNDATIONS OF GEOGRAPHY* 1 (LONDON: THOMAS NELSON AND SONS, 1934), PP. 5–13; 73–86; 113–129.

These extracts are taken from geographical readers and textbooks used in the classroom during the period 1900–1939. They demonstrate that geography teaching and texts could either use a rather dry, 'almanac' approach to presenting the Empire, with the emphasis on facts, or conversely, take the form of fairy stories which might capture the attention of younger children. Like the history readers presented earlier in this volume, the geography readers could include a largely positive account of the British Empire (as is the case in document 24). A frequently appearing word in these readers was 'strange', used to describe non-Anglo cultures, with the implication that British – or as it was invariably used, 'English' – culture was the 'norm' (a particular feature of document 26). The Collins reader opened by calling the growth of the British Empire 'a most marvellous story' and asserting that children should do their best to maintain what had been won. The Empire, it stated, stood for 'freedom and justice', and children should 'live good and useful lives' to maintain the Empire.

The veld

1 Far, far away to the south, across the sea, the sun shines down upon a very strange country. It is a wide, open land covered with grass and bushes.

There are very few trees, and the light brown soil is covered with stones; among these stones the grass grows in spiky tufts.

This land is called the "veld." All kinds of animals find a home there. Great lions make their dens in the caves, while the jackals live not far away.

Long ago the animals had this land all to themselves, and Tsuro, the hare, was the cleverest of them all. Many were the tricks which he played upon his companions.

You may have heard of some of them in the stories of Brer Rabbit. For it was the men who came to live on the veld who first told the stories about Brer Rabbit.

2 The men of the veld are black. They carry spears for hunting.

The rivers and pools give them water and fish. There are plenty of animals for food, and there is plenty of room to grow corn for porridge.

There are millions of these black people living on the veld. But many of the large animals went away long ago.

The black men, who are called Kaffirs, do not make their houses of bricks, like ours. They make them of grass, and each house is shaped like a round beehive.

Not far away from the houses the women make the gardens. Instead of using a spade or a fork to dig, they use a pointed stick, or a heavy piece of iron fixed in the end of a handle to make a kind of hoe.

It is very hard work to dig with a tool like that.

Sometimes the rain is scarce, and then the people starve, for the animals move away to the places where there is water.

3 When night has fallen, and the baboons who rob the fields in the daytime are asleep, young and old gather around the fire beside the round grass huts to listen to the tales of the days of long ago.

The firelight dances upon the black faces of the boys and girls, and men and women; and the old man who tells the story moves his hands and shakes his spear as he tells of the doings of the old days.

Many of his stories are about animals, and very good they are; but some of them are real fairy stories, and as the old story-teller goes on the hearers draw in their breath and say "Ah! Ah!" Here is one of his stories.

Why the lion roars

In former times the lion did not roar; he had a thin piping voice like that of a goat which says, "Meh, meh, meh."

One day while walking about, the lion met the hare, who was busy felling a tree to get some honey from a bees' nest.

When the hare saw the lion, he said to himself, "I will teach you something."

So he called to the lion, and said, "Grandfather, how is it that a big animal like you has such a little voice? You go about like a goat saying, 'Meh, meh, meh.'

"I will show you how you can get a big voice, so that all the other animals will be afraid of you."

"Will you, indeed?" replied the lion. "Very well."

Then the hare took a piece of honeycomb, covered with bees, and said to him, "You must eat this. Whatever happens, do not spit it out, but close your mouth and swallow it."

So the lion put the honeycomb in his mouth, and the bees began to sting his tongue, causing him great pain. However the lion kept his mouth closed, as he had been told, but the pain made him say "M-r-r-r."

"That's it, grandfather," cried the hare, dancing about like a mad thing. "Don't you see how much bigger your voice is?"

"M-r-r-r," roared the lion, unable to stand the pain of the bee stings any longer. "M-r-r-r."

"Eh, behold, grandfather, that is indeed a voice that suits you," said the hare.

Ever since then the lion has always roared – "M-r-r-r, M-r-r-r."

The blackfellows

1 Far, far away on the other side of the world lies the Never-Never Land. It is one of the strangest countries in this wonderful round world of ours.

For thousands of years no one ever heard anything at all about it. Even when people did find it, and came back to tell others about it, no one would believe them.

This land is strange, and different from anywhere else upon earth. It is part of the great big island of Australia.

Think of a land where the swans are coal-black. There are animals with wings which lay eggs as hens do. The dogs do not bark and the birds do not sing. It all sounds too strange to be true.

Let us pretend to pay a visit to this strange country with its queer birds and beasts.

2 It is early morning and still quite dark. Presently it begins to get light. We begin to see queer shapes around. They are just like ghosts in the grey light. There are tall, strange-looking trees, and bushes all around us.

As we watch we see a grey shape slink between the bushes, and then we hear a fearful howl. It is Old Man Dingo, the wild dog. He has been watching us, but he will not come near us.

He is about as big as a wolf, and is brownish-yellow in colour. He does not like men, and no one has ever tamed him or made a friend of him.

He is the same as the wild dog that lived long, long ago in our own country when the world was young.

3 By this time it is quite light. All around us we see hundreds of strange-looking plants.

There are bushes that look just like clumps of feathers. Everything is grey, while even the grass, where there is any, is white.

The trees are even more strange. They grow up quite straight, and are very tall. They have no branches, except right at the very top.

One thing that we shall not be able to find very often in this strange land is water. We could walk for miles and miles and miles, and we should not see a river, or a stream, or water of any kind.

If we looked up we should only see the clear blue sky above us, with no clouds, and the sun blazing down. That is why everything is so grey.

It does not rain very often in this part of the world, and so the plants have had to learn how to live without water.

4 The animals are as strange as the plants. There is one big animal. He is really the cousin of the rat, only he is about four feet high when he sits up.

This is Old Man Kangaroo.

He does not walk about, but takes big jumps. His hind legs are very big and strong, while his front legs are only just two little paws.

Mother Kangaroo is very careful of her babies. When they are tiny she carries them about in a kind of pocket in front of her.

It looks very strange to see a little furry head popping slyly out of this pocket as Mother Kangaroo goes hopping along.

Then there is the squirrel which lives in the trees. It has skin between its legs on each side, just like a pair of wings, to help it as it leaps from tree to tree.

Even the birds are different in this strange country. Many of them cannot fly, but stalk along on their tall thin legs. One bird called an "emu" is something like an ostrich. It has a long neck and long legs, as you can see in the picture.

Some of the other birds are like parrots, with wonderful colours, but they never sing. They only make a squawking kind of noise.

5 There are not many people in the Never-Never Land. They are called blackfellows, but they are not really black. Their skin is just the colour of a piece of chocolate.

They do not need to wear clothes, for the weather is very hot and dry.

They have to keep moving from one place to another to find food, so they do not need a house. They do not know how to make tents like the Red Indians or the Lapps.

In fact they are very, very poor. They do not know how to use bows and arrows. They have no cups or pots or pans.

Their house, when they have one, is just a big piece of bark. It is curved over to make a shelter from the sun and the wind. Often they do not use even this covering, but sleep on the ground.

6 The little blackfellow cannot read or write. He knows nothing about history or geography, for he never goes to school.

Yet he knows many things that you or I could not understand. He soon learns which things are good for food. He can even tell where water can be found.

He is very clever at noticing the marks left by different animals. He can tell if a frog or a snail has passed along. He knows where to look for the honey bees that live under the ground.

Then, too, he can make a fire without matches. He does this by rubbing two pieces of wood together. (See next page.)

He can make sharp knives out of pieces of stone and is a clever hunter. To kill a squirrel or a bird he throws a piece of wood at it.

This piece of wood is curved like a man's elbow, and is called a boomerang. It spins in the air as it is thrown. If it does not hit the thing at which it is thrown the boomerang spins back to the person who threw it.

7 The blackfellows live on all sorts of strange things. Sometimes the blackfellow is lucky enough to kill a kangaroo or a wallaby. A wallaby is like a little kangaroo.

When this happens the family have plenty to eat for a few days. At other times the women go out looking for frogs and snails. They also eat snakes and caterpillars.

At certain times of the year they pick berries and wild fruits. They also dig up different kinds of roots.

When the blackfellows travel the man takes his boomerang and his spear. The woman picks up the baby and off they walk.

They have no furniture to move and no clothes to pack. When they come to a place where there is food they stop.

The old men among the blackfellows know many stories. One of them is a very pretty story about the Rainbow.

The rainbow

Once there was a widow who was very lonely. She lived with her four children in a little camp by herself. Her name was Dee-ree-ree.

After a time a man called Bibbee came near her camp.

This made Dee-ree-ree much afraid. That night she could not sleep. She kept crying out, "Dee-ree-ree, wyah, wyah."

Now Bibbee heard her crying and wondered what was the matter. The next morning he went to the little camp and asked what had happened.

"I was afraid," said the widow. "I thought I heard some one walking about."

"You need not be afraid," said Bibbee. "There is no one near but myself, and I do not want to hurt you."

The next night Bibbee heard the widow crying again, "Dee-ree-ree, wyah, wyah, Dee-ree-ree." This went on all night.

Next day Bibbee went to the widow and said, "Why are you still afraid? Marry me and I will take care of you."

But she did not want to do that.

Then Bibbee set to work and built a beautiful arch of many colours. It curved across the sky. It was a roadway from the earth to the stars.

When the lonely widow saw this she was more afraid than ever. She did not know what this arch could be.

So she called "Wyah, wyah," for a long time.

Then she looked to see if she could see Bibbee, but she could not.

At last the widow went to look for Bibbee. She took her four children and went over to his camp. When she had found him, she asked what the strange thing was.

"I made it," said Bibbee, "to show you how strong I am. You will be quite safe if you marry me."

So the widow said she would marry Bibbee, and they lived very happily together.

Years afterwards, when they died, they became birds. Now Dee-ree-ree is the wagtail. All through the summer nights she cries "Dee-ree-ree, wyah, wyah, Dee-ree-ree."

Bibbee is the woodpecker, and he is always climbing trees. He is trying to get up to the sky again.

And that is how the first rainbow was made, say the blackfellows of Australia.

Anula of sunny Ceylon

1 Anula is a little brown girl. Her skin is not chocolate-brown like that of the golliwog people. It is a beautiful golden brown colour.

Anula is seven years old. She is a very happy little girl although she lives in a very poor home, far away in the island of Ceylon.

You would be surprised if you could see the house in which Anula lives. It is just a tiny mud hut about as big as a small stable.

There are no windows. The walls are built of mud and stones, and are very low. The roof seems almost too big for the hut. It is made of palm leaves. It hangs down so low that the walls are almost hidden behind it.

If the roof were not made like this the walls would soon be washed away by the rain.

This tiny hut is the home of nine people. There are Anula's four brothers and her little sister. Then there are her father and mother as well as her grandmother.

How crowded they all must be. It must be very stuffy, too, for the weather in Ceylon is very hot.

However, Anula and her family only sleep in the hut. They spend most of the day out of doors.

2 The hut stands in a pretty garden. It is not a garden like those we see in England. There are all kinds of strange plants in it.

In one corner there is a group of tall coco-nut palms. Not far away is a clump of what looks like tall grass. The leaves are very long, and the stems are higher than a man.

This is sugar cane. Inside the thick knobby stems is a very sweet juice from which sugar can be made. The children are very fond of a piece of this sweet green cane. They suck it like a stick of barley sugar.

Then there are tall plants with very wide leaves, called banana plants. The fruit grows in a big clump hanging from the stem of the plant. Bananas grow pointing upwards, as shown in the picture.

The bunches of bananas which we see in greengrocers' shops are taken from this big clump.

The rest of the garden is covered with bushes of different kinds. Most of these bushes bear berries or fruit.

Between the bushes we see clumps of spiky green leaves growing. These leaves grow from what look like big turnips. The turnips are covered with golden yellow scales.

These are pineapples.

Perhaps you thought that pineapples grew on trees? They do not. They grow in the ground. They have a root like a carrot. When the pineapple is cut this root is left in the ground.

Pineapples are very cheap in Ceylon. We could buy five of them for a penny.

3 There is no fence or hedge round Anula's garden. On the other side of the bushes are the fields. In these fields rice is grown.

Every morning, as soon as it is light, Anula's father and two of her big brothers get up and get ready for work.

They have not many clothes to put on. Each wears a piece of cloth wrapped round his waist and reaching almost to his feet On their heads the men wear broad-brimmed straw hats.

Each man takes his breakfast with him wrapped up in a piece of cloth.

At midday Anula and her mother set out for the fields. They take with them the food for the men's dinner.

The men eat their dinner together. After they have finished, Anula and her mother gather up the scraps that are left over and return home.

In the afternoon they make ready for the evening meal, and cook the breakfast for the next day.

4 On some days the boys and men gather coco-nuts. The coco-nut palms always grow near the sea. The tall palms are never straight, but lean over to one side.

The people of Ceylon have a saying, "Whoever has seen a dead monkey, a white crow, and a straight coco-nut tree will live for ever."

Anula likes to go down to the coco-nut groves, for then she can watch the fishermen at work. These fishermen use some of the strangest boats in the world. Each boat is made from a log of wood with two or three planks on top. (See page 115.)

The boat is so narrow that it would roll over and over in the water. So to stop this the fishermen fasten a float on one side at the end of some big poles.

The boat is driven along by a big square sail. This is fastened to two tall masts made from bamboo poles.

Sometimes, when the wind is strong, one of the fishermen has to climb out along the poles and sit on the float. This stops the wind from turning the boat over.

Anula likes to watch the boats as they glide along.

5 Sometimes Anula's father goes into the town. When he does this Anula loves to go with him.

The two big white bullocks are harnessed to a cart. It is a very big heavy cart with two large wheels. Over the top of the cart is a big curved roof of woven leaves.

Anula likes riding in the cart. It is rather bumpy but it is great fun.

At these times Anula wears her best clothes. She has a bright blue cloth wrapped round her, and wears a pretty red jacket with yellow braid. In her ears she wears little silver ear-rings, and on her arms are several bangles.

The road winds along between tall shady trees. Bright-eyed monkeys chatter from the branches, and there are many beautiful birds.

Along the road there are all kinds of people to be seen. They all wear clothes of very bright colours.

A porter strides along with a big box on the top of his turban. There are several women carrying baskets of fruit. One old gentleman has a long white beard and a big turban.

At one place the road crosses a stream, and here, one day. Anula saw some elephants. They were having a bath.

It was such fun to see the big creatures squirting water over themselves from their trunks. The elephants of Ceylon do not have tusks.

6 The town itself was crowded with people. Anula loved to watch the monkeys and the crows.

The monkeys would sit on the roof of a house watching the shops. They would wait until the shopman's back was turned; then they would steal down and snatch perhaps a bunch of fruit.

Over the roofs they would go one after the other. Then they would stop and pull the fruit to pieces, chattering all the time.

There were many crows. They, too, sat on the roofs and played tricks on people. They were very fond of rolling stones down the roof.

An old crow would fly up to the roof of a house with a stone in his claw. Then he would let it go. Down the stone would roll "Bumpety – bump – bump" over the tiles.

Then the old crow would put his head on one side as much as to say, "That was a good one," and away he would fly for another stone.

7 Sometimes when Anula's father went to the market they saw a conjurer. The conjurer would do very many strange and wonderful tricks. He could make a plant grow from a seed under a cloth. Sometimes he had some snakes which crawled all over him.

The trick which Anula liked best was what the conjurer called his little pet duck.

First he took the half of an empty coco-nut shell. This he placed on the ground between two stones. Then he filled it with water.

Next he took a piece of wood about as big as a man's thumb. He took this out of his ear. At one end of the piece of wood he put a bent match, and a straight match at the other end.

The conjurer then told every one that this was his little pet duck. It would do whatever he told it. He put it on the water in the coco-nut and walked a little distance away.

Then he said, "Swim," and the duck moved to the side of the shell. When the conjurer said, "Turn round," the duck turned round. If he said, "Dive," it would sink to the bottom of the shell.

Anula thought this was very clever.

Adam's footprint

Anula's home is near a tall mountain called Adam's Peak. Her mother told her how it was given its name.

Long ago, she said, the first man and woman were driven out of the lovely Garden of Eden. At first they did not know where to go.

They stood looking about them until at last Adam said, "We will go towards the sunrise." So they set off towards the East.

Now Adam and Eve were very tall. We should call them giants, for Adam was twelve times as high as a man is today. He walked with great strides across the earth, and Eve followed him weeping.

They travelled over tall hills and through deep valleys. Even the deepest rivers only reached to their knees. At last they came to the wide plains of India.

Here Adam and Eve stopped to rest. On their left was a great wall of mountains whose tops seemed to touch the sky.

So when they went on they turned away from the mountains. They went towards the south for a long time.

At last they reached the sea. The land came to a point, and then to an end. In front of them and on all sides was deep blue water.

"Let us go back," said Eve.

"No, I am going on," said Adam. "See, there is the land again."

As he spoke he pointed over the sea. When he tried to wade through the sea he found that it was too deep for him.

So he picked up some large pieces of rock and threw them into the sea to make stepping-stones. Then he and his wife walked across safely.

This bridge of rocks is still there. It is called "Adam's Bridge," and it reaches from India to Ceylon.

After Adam and Eve had reached Ceylon they saw two tall mountains before them. Adam said he would climb to the top of the one that was nearest to them.

When he had reached the top Adam looked round. He could see nothing but sea all around, while behind him was the bridge of rocks which he had made. He could go no farther, for he was on an island.

When he saw this he was much vexed. He thought of the lovely garden he had left, and he stamped his foot in anger.

He stamped so hard that he made a deep footprint in the mountain top. This footprint is still there.

Thousands of people go to see it every year. It is called Adam's Footprint, and the mountain is called Adam's Peak.

29

SCHOOL DRILL

From: 'School Drill', in *The Globe*, 15th July 1889, p. 1.

These documents show the ways that Lord Meath's influence was felt in the popular realm. Meath (1841–1929) was educated at Eton College, later becoming a diplomat and a prominent Conservative member of the House of Lords. By means of the Empire Day Movement (EDM) and the Duty and Discipline Movement (DDM), the attempt was made to shape children as imperial citizens. Earlier in his life, in publications such as Social Arrows *(1887), he had shown an interest in the provision of outdoor play space for children that had the aim of making fitter citizens. He then turned his attention to imperial concerns, although there was of course some connection between physical fitness and preparedness for imperial defence as the 20th century arrived. Empire Day was marked through the Edwardian era into the 1920s and 1930s, before finally disappearing in 1958 when Harold Macmillan renamed it Commonwealth Day. The overall success of these initiatives is subject to debate. Some children simply enjoyed Empire Day but did not pay much attention to the message. The DDM had a membership of 4,200 in 1917. It is reasonable to suggest that these movements and their value systems were at their peak in the period between 1900 and 1914, although they continued well into the 20th century. During the 1920s, the BBC and its radio broadcasting had some impact of the marking of Empire Day, moving it into the home, where once it had been a largely public celebration. The article by Cyril Norwood, headmaster of Marlborough College at the time of writing, notes the ways in which by the mid-1920s the imperial outlook was now combined with an internationalist outlook. The more militaristic and jingoistic aspects of Empire celebrations that were sometimes visible before 1914 had dissipated in the aftermath of the grim carnage of the First World War.*

The School Board for London has undoubtedly done a good work in organising a system of drill for the pupils in its schools. The voluntary schools are not indeed excluded from its benefits, and the proceedings at the Royal Albert Hall yesterday afforded proof that many have been glad to avail themselves of the advantages offered. Both boys and girls attended in considerable numbers, and the Commander-in-Chief, who was present on the occasion, observed that it made his heart glad to see the efficiency which had been reached. No reasonable person can doubt the desirableness of physical education for the children in our public elementary schools. The benefit of teaching "extra-subjects" to boys and girls whose lot in life most needs be manual labour, often of the severest kind, is problematical, but a boy will at least be none the worse a workman for having had his muscles properly developed. Judicious drilling is allowed on all hands to be promotive of health, and to improve the *physique* of our town-bred children is at least as important as to cram their memories. From this point of view there is no reason why girls should not be drilled as well at their brothers, and we are glad to read that the female contingent at the Albert Hall, under the generalship of Miss Ely, made a creditable display. On other grounds the drilling of our boys is, of course, much more necessary. No nation can afford to despise the physical development of its youth. It is of pressing urgency alike for the enterprises of peace and of war. London kids have, it is true, found favour with the recruiting officer, even in comparison with the best from the country and the provincial towns. They are to a remarkable degree, the equals of those brought up under healthier surroundings. And, this being so, there is all the more reason why natural aptitude should be supplemented by skilful training. It is hardly worth while to notice the absurd objection to school-boy drilling that it tends to foster the spirit of militarism. Men are not more likely to wish for war because they have learned how to make proper use of their arms and legs.

30

'LADS' DRILL ASSOCIATION', IN *VOLUNTEER SERVICE GAZETTE*, 19TH JUNE 1903, P. 530.

These documents show the ways that Lord Meath's influence was felt in the popular realm. Meath (1841–1929) was educated at Eton College, later becoming a diplomat and a prominent Conservative member of the House of Lords. By means of the Empire Day Movement (EDM) and the Duty and Discipline Movement (DDM), the attempt was made to shape children as imperial citizens. Earlier in his life, in publications such as Social Arrows *(1887), he had shown an interest in the provision of outdoor play space for children that had the aim of making fitter citizens. He then turned his attention to imperial concerns, although there was of course some connection between physical fitness and preparedness for imperial defence as the 20th century arrived. Empire Day was marked through the Edwardian era into the 1920s and 1930s, before finally disappearing in 1958 when Harold Macmillan renamed it Commonwealth Day. The overall success of these initiatives is subject to debate. Some children simply enjoyed Empire Day but did not pay much attention to the message. The DDM had a membership of 4,200 in 1917. It is reasonable to suggest that these movements and their value systems were at their peak in the period between 1900 and 1914, although they continued well into the 20th century. During the 1920s, the BBC and its radio broadcasting had some impact of the marking of Empire Day, moving it into the home, where once it had been a largely public celebration. The article by Cyril Norwood, headmaster of Marlborough College at the time of writing, notes the ways in which by the mid-1920s the imperial outlook was now combined with an internationalist outlook. The more militaristic and jingoistic aspects of Empire celebrations that were sometimes visible before 1914 had dissipated in the aftermath of the grim carnage of the First World War.*

THE Annual Report of the Lads' Drill Association for 1902 has been received, and it is with the greatest pleasure that we call attention to the excellent work performed by the Association, the objects of which are to encourage systematic physical training in schools and the formation of Cadet Battalions and Corps throughout the country. As regards the latter, the Lads' Drill Association has already achieved a good deal in obtaining the following concessions for cadets from the War Office: (I.) A grant of Substantive in place of Honorary Commissions for Cadet Officers, thereby enabling them to attend Schools of Instruction. (II.) Full recognition of the right of all ranks in Cadet Corps and Battalions over 17 years of age to count their service as qualifying for the Volunteer Officer's Decorations and the Long Service Medal respectively. (III.) Sanction for a simpler uniform. (IV.) Grant of free ammunition. (V.) A definite place and recognition in the Table of Contents of the Army List, for Cadet Corps, Companies and Battalions – a very great convenience to all interested in them. (VI.) The approval by the Secretary of State for War of the placing of non-uniform School Cadet Corps on the same footing as those already existing. The Association also announces its intention to work on until the rudiments of Military training are brought within the reach of every able-bodied subject of His Majesty in the British Isles, and until it has obtained the full recognition by Government of the Cadet System as the basis of Home Defence. The Earl of Meath, President and Chairman of the Association, in an Introduction to the Report, says: The Lads' Drill Association by its proposals – (1) That physical training should be systematically given in schools; and (2) That as far as possible every lad between the ages of 13 and 18 should be made capable by adequate training to defend his country – believes that it is urging two very important steps towards the improvement of the physique of the population, and the rendering of the men of these islands fit not only, if necessary, to take part in the defence of their country, but also to maintain our position amongst the nations in the labours of commercial and industrial life which in these days of keen competition require the highest physical and intellectual qualities. Sir J. Whitworth, forty years ago, said that the labour of a man who had gone through a course of military drill was worth 1s. 6d. a week more than that of one untrained, as, through the training received in military drill, men learned ready obedience, attention and combined action, all of which were so necessary in work where men had to act promptly and together. "In Germany manufacturers consider the service of a man who has undergone the methodical physical and military training of the German army as worth *twice* as much as that of a man who has been exempted from it; indeed all competent observers agree that one of the chief factors in the extraordinary commercial and industrial success of Germany is the education and discipline thus received. The German methods are, however, enforced by conscription. In Great Britain we desire the benefits above-mentioned, but we are not prepared to submit to that form of coercion. The Lads' Drill Association believes that the plans it recommends affords the only means by which the physical evils universally admitted to exist can be dealt with, and yet conscription be avoided."

THE Report of the Lads' Drill Association for 1902 states that the demonstration given in the Albert Hall on June 7, 1902, in the presence of T.R.H. the Prince and Princess of Wales, produced very valuable results, and was speedily followed by the appointment of Col. Malcolm Fox as Inspector of Physical Training to the Board of Education. It is stated that "the Cadet movement is advancing all along the line." From Lord Salisbury downwards the opinion has steadily gained ground in the minds of all classes that every male capable of bearing arms should be taught how to use them in the defence of his country. In addition to the military advantages of Cadet training, the Report of the Lads' Drill Association refers also to its physical, moral and social advantages. The suppression of hooliganism amongst the rough lads of our towns is acknowledged to be one of the most pressing social questions of the day. Undoubtedly the most efficient method of checking this evil is to bring these lads under some form of military discipline.

The Boys' Brigade and the Church Lads' Brigade have proved that drill is a most efficacious means of getting hold of boys. But, admirable and deserving of all support as these organisations are, many, if not most, of those who have been brought into closest and most direct relations with hooliganism in its acute phases, would agree that there are two reasons why these brigades cannot be expected to cope alone with this particular evil. Very justly it is pointed out that they attract the better intentioned rather than the rougher and more lawless set of boys, who, unhappily, are not prepared to submit themselves to anything in the way of religious obligation; whilst they lack just that force of actuality which has such a magnetic attraction for the young, and the boys have an uneasy feeling that they are, after all, only playing at soldiers. The actuality, however, is not absent from the Cadet organisations, and it is greatly to be hoped that the public generally will not fail to add to its support, and that financial assistance which is necessary to place such battalions on a sound working basis.

31

'THE DUTY AND DISCIPLINE MOVEMENT', IN *THE TIMES,* 5TH NOVEMBER 1913, P. 6.

These documents show the ways that Lord Meath's influence was felt in the popular realm. Meath (1841–1929) was educated at Eton College, later becoming a diplomat and a prominent Conservative member of the House of Lords. By means of the Empire Day Movement (EDM) and the Duty and Discipline Movement (DDM), the attempt was made to shape children as imperial citizens. Earlier in his life, in publications such as Social Arrows *(1887), he had shown an interest in the provision of outdoor play space for children that had the aim of making fitter citizens. He then turned his attention to imperial concerns, although there was of course some connection between physical fitness and preparedness for imperial defence as the 20th century arrived. Empire Day was marked through the Edwardian era into the 1920s and 1930s, before finally disappearing in 1958 when Harold Macmillan renamed it Commonwealth Day. The overall success of these initiatives is subject to debate. Some children simply enjoyed Empire Day but did not pay much attention to the message. The DDM had a membership of 4,200 in 1917. It is reasonable to suggest that these movements and their value systems were at their peak in the period between 1900 and 1914, although they continued well into the 20th century. During the 1920s, the BBC and its radio broadcasting had some impact of the marking of Empire Day, moving it into the home, where once it had been a largely public celebration. The article by Cyril Norwood, headmaster of Marlborough College at the time of writing, notes the ways in which by the mid-1920s the imperial outlook was now combined with an internationalist outlook. The more militaristic and jingoistic aspects of Empire celebrations that were sometimes visible before 1914 had dissipated in the aftermath of the grim carnage of the First World War.*

THE DUTY AND DISCIPLINE MOVEMENT. – Lord Meath appeals for public support of the "Duty and Discipline Movement," founded by him on June 16 last. The objects of the movement as declared at the inaugural meeting are: – (1) To combat indiscipline in the national life, especially in the home and in the school; (2) to give reasonable support to all legitimate authority. The movement deals with principles only, not with methods. The cooperation of all who feel that the prevalent slackness and indiscipline amongst all classes constitute a real and serious danger to society and the State is invited by the promoters of the movement, of which Lady Barrington and Lord Meath are joint presidents. Its office is at 117, Victoria-street, S.W., and full particulars of the movement, as well as a list and prices of the literature issued by it and a form of adherence for signature, will be furnished to any who apply to the hon. secretary, Miss Isabel Marris. Funds are urgently needed, and may be sent to Lord Meath or to the hon. treasurer at 117, Victoria-street, S.W., or to Messrs. Coutts and Co., 440, Strand, marked for the "Duty and Discipline Movement Fund."

32
'PATRIOTISM PLEA: CELEBRATION OF EMPIRE DAY IN SCHOOLS', IN *THE SCOTSMAN*, 28TH JUNE 1938, P. 7.

These documents show the ways that Lord Meath's influence was felt in the popular realm. Meath (1841–1929) was educated at Eton College, later becoming a diplomat and a prominent Conservative member of the House of Lords. By means of the Empire Day Movement (EDM) and the Duty and Discipline Movement (DDM), the attempt was made to shape children as imperial citizens. Earlier in his life, in publications such as Social Arrows *(1887), he had shown an interest in the provision of outdoor play space for children that had the aim of making fitter citizens. He then turned his attention to imperial concerns, although there was of course some connection between physical fitness and preparedness for imperial defence as the 20th century arrived. Empire Day was marked through the Edwardian era into the 1920s and 1930s, before finally disappearing in 1958 when Harold Macmillan renamed it Commonwealth Day. The overall success of these initiatives is subject to debate. Some children simply enjoyed Empire Day but did not pay much attention to the message. The DDM had a membership of 4,200 in 1917. It is reasonable to suggest that these movements and their value systems were at their peak in the period between 1900 and 1914, although they continued well into the 20th century. During the 1920s, the BBC and its radio broadcasting had some impact of the marking of Empire Day, moving it into the home, when once it had been a largely public celebration. The article by Cyril Norwood, headmaster of Marlborough College at the time of writing, notes the ways in which by the mid-1920s the imperial outlook was now combined with an internationalist outlook. The more militaristic and jingoistic aspects of Empire celebrations that were sometimes visible before 1914 had dissipated in the aftermath of the grim carnage of the First World War.*

"It is of the utmost importance that the spirit of patriotism should be fostered among our children," said Mr J. Graham Downes, president of Edinburgh Chamber of Commerce, at a meeting of the Education Committee of Edinburgh Town Council yesterday.

The Committee were considering a list of school regulations, including a proposal that, as at present, Empire Day might be celebrated in the schools at the discretion of head teachers.

Mr Downes, who is a co-opted member of the Committee, moved that Empire Day "shall" be celebrated in the schools. "There should be a periodical reminder of the wonderful heritage we have," he said, "not from the point of view of music-hall jingoism, but to arouse in the children a sense of responsibility for the privileges which they enjoy. We are far too diffident about impressing upon our children the wonderful heritage to which they have fallen heir, and for which they will be responsible in the years to come. We know that the ideals for which we stand are definitely in danger."

Councillor Clark Hutchison, seconding, remarked that in the present unsettled state of affairs a great deal depended on the British Empire.

"An extraordinary thing"

Councillor Stewart Lamb said it had always seemed to him an extraordinary thing that Empire Day was celebrated with the greatest enthusiasm in every part of the Empire overseas from Montreal to Sydney, and with least enthusiasm at the centre of the Empire.

Councillor Mrs Woodburn moved that the regulation should not be altered. In most schools, she thought, Empire Day was celebrated. If a mandatory regulation was adopted, the tendency might be to over-exaggeration. If the celebration of Empire Day were made obligatory, a similar course should be taken with regard to lectures by accredited representatives of the League of Nations Union. It was very important at the present time that we should have an international outlook rather than one restricted to our own Empire.

Dr Peter Comrie, seconding, said that the regulation leaving the celebration of Empire Day to the discretion of head teachers had been in operation until now, and had worked very successfully. In practically all schools there was an instruction that notice be taken of Empire Day in some form. All their schools did not possess halls to which the children could be taken in order to celebrate Empire Day.

Supporting the celebration of Empire Day in all schools, the Rev. Canon R. J. Mackay said it was responsibility that they were trying to bring home, not the waving of flags.

It was decided by 15 votes to 8 that the celebration of Empire Day be compulsory in the schools, as suggested by Mr Downes.

33

'EMPIRE DAY IN CHELTENHAM', IN *THE CHELTENHAM LADIES' COLLEGE MAGAZINE* (AUTUMN 1907), PP. 260–264. REPRODUCED WITH KIND PERMISSION OF CHELTENHAM LADIES' COLLEGE ARCHIVE.

These documents show the ways that Lord Meath's influence was felt in the popular realm. Meath (1841–1929) was educated at Eton College, later becoming a diplomat and a prominent Conservative member of the House of Lords. By means of the Empire Day Movement (EDM) and the Duty and Discipline Movement (DDM), the attempt was made to shape children as imperial citizens. Earlier in his life, in publications such as Social Arrows *(1887), he had shown an interest in the provision of outdoor play space for children that had the aim of making fitter citizens. He then turned his attention to imperial concerns, although there was of course some connection between physical fitness and preparedness for imperial defence as the 20th century arrived. Empire Day was marked through the Edwardian era into the 1920s and 1930s, before finally disappearing in 1958 when Harold Macmillan renamed it Commonwealth Day. The overall success of these initiatives is subject to debate. Some children simply enjoyed Empire Day but did not pay much attention to the message. The DDM had a membership of 4,200 in 1917. It is reasonable to suggest that these movements and their value systems were at their peak in the period between 1900 and 1914, although they continued well into the 20th century. During the 1920s, the BBC and its radio broadcasting had some impact of the marking of Empire Day, moving it into the home, where once it had been a largely public celebration. The article by Cyril Norwood, headmaster of Marlborough College at the time of writing, notes the ways in which by the mid-1920s the imperial outlook was now combined with an internationalist outlook. The more militaristic and jingoistic aspects of Empire celebrations that were sometimes visible before 1914 had dissipated in the aftermath of the grim carnage of the First World War.*

Empire Day

Empire Day was celebrated in Cheltenham (which Miss Beale once called an "Imperial town") with much enthusiasm. The local branch of the Victoria League carried out well an excellent idea. Miss Ethel Smith, aided by many good workers, and seconded by Miss McLea, the hon. secretary of the Cheltenham branch of the League, undertook to present scenes from the native life of our Eastern and

Western Colonies. The Winter Garden, which was used for the representation, was decorated with flags, streamers, etc. The Mayor of Cheltenham opened the proceedings at the afternoon meeting, and then Mr. Vincent Smith, President of the Cheltenham branch, read the results of the competition for prizes and certificates offered by the League to the children of the elementary schools for essays on subjects connected with the Empire. After this came the entertainment proper, – a series of animated pictures, the intervals of time between the scenes being filled up with national and patriotic songs given by an immense choir of children under the conductorship of Mr. Teague. In the evening the same programme was gone through again with even greater enthusiasm. From the *Cheltenham Examiner* we quote a passage describing the principal items: –

> "Friday witnessed in the Winter Garden two great gatherings which will long live in the memory, for their human interest, their artistic charm, and their patriotic import. As spectacles they are not likely to be eclipsed; as celebrations, intended primarily to impress and interest the young, they were susceptible of some improvement, by a reduction of the speech-making. The children can sing themselves into patriotism, and that is enough. . . . Songs and pictures: they satisfy the primal instincts. . . . The heart must have grown sadly old and cold that did not beat with quickened pulse in the presence of all that wonderful young life, so joyous and expectant, so rich in possibility. And when the eye turned away from the serried ranks of children (symbols of the future) to the flag-draped stage, tender reverence for the past was (or should have been) summoned up by the vision of the great White Queen, daughter of Alfred's House, and, like him, gravely sweet and nobly wise; the good Queen whose gracious face and memory are linked, by the truest instinct, with the thoughts of Homeland and of Empire which it is the function of this blithe May festival to awaken. The afternoon of Friday was the ceremonial occasion; in the evening, when there was less to say, the programme of songs and tableaux was carried through with perhaps still greater effect – at all events as regards the tableaux, or 'animated scenes,' to term two of the three accurately.
>
> "First, for a few personal references. The moving power behind these celebrations is the local branch of the Victoria League, an organisation which is doing much, by educational methods, to promote Imperial sentiment. The combination of Miss McLea, the hon. secretary of the League in Cheltenham, and Miss Ethel Smith, of the Ladies' College, supplied the idea and the execution. Miss Ethel Smith, as all who have seen a Guild performance at the Ladies' College know, has a genius for stage management, in union with an educationist's enthusiasm for making a stage picture as instructive as thorough study of detail can ensure. The aim being to instruct as well as entertain the children, the work could not

have been in better hands. Much skilful help was forthcoming. Mr. Sidney Herbert, of the Ladies' College Art staff, painted the scenery; Mrs. McLellan, of the same College, trained the dancers; Colonel Ashburner turned his ingenious hand to supplying the 'properties'; Miss Kernahan painted the Arms of the Colonies; and for costumes, some (in the Indian scene) were lent by Mrs. Golding, but most of the dresses were specially made by Mrs. Waterfield and other ladies in working parties. It is to the credit of the workmanship that is survived the ordeal to which it was subjected by the two hundred exuberant youngsters taking part. These were selected from among the elder scholars in the different schools; they threw themselves into the performances with natural delight and proved responsive and intelligent.

"The beginning of what may prove a long series of graphic lessons gave two illustrations of East and West, to which was added, as a fitting finale, an allegorical representation of the United Empire. When the curtain was first drawn, a beautiful picture was disclosed of the holy city of Benares, its turrets silhouetted against an evening sky. To the banks of the Ganges had thronged pious Hindus from many parts, wearing the distinctive dresses of their province or calling, and many bearing floral offerings for the temple. The careful study of costume satisfied not a few critical eyes in the audience. The ensemble reproduced the variety and brightness of Oriental colour, touched by the solemnity of the shadows. A little more action among the crowd of pilgrims would, perhaps, have added to the realism, but individual groups largely supplied the sense of movement. All the more characteristic types were introduced. A white robed Brahman was seen distributing Ganges water to pilgrims round him: a learned Pundit was reading and expounding to a group of listeners: rosary and garland sellers, fruit and pottery vendors were offering their wares. Red turbans from Western India gave vivid splashes of colour to the miscellaneous throng of sight-seers, soldiers, and pilgrims, intent on watching, at one time a snake charmer, and at another a wedding procession, headed by the bridegroom (the bride has been left at home). His approach was announced by the vigorous beating of drums: and a dance by Nautch girls, the dance undeniably Eastern in character, though too energetic, we were told, to be an absolutely faithful representation, closed the scene.

"From the land of sunshine the picture changed to Our Lady of the Snows: to the primitive Canada of the Indians and the early traders. The Indians of Miss Ethel Smith were of the true Fenimore Cooper pattern, not those that wear top hats wildly out of fashion, smoke short clays, and carry gamps. The picturesque Indian of romance, unspoiled by firewater, was seen in all his barbaric splendour, with crest of eagle feathers, and ornaments of porcupine quills, wampum, and beads, and (presumably) the scalp girdle, though an anxious scrutiny was unrewarded by the sight of scalps. This was the boys' scene, albeit the squaws, some with 'papooses' (if that is the word – Fenimore Cooper is a distant memory!) played no unimportant part. It was a Bull Dance that day: the Good Spirit was to be invoked for a plentiful supply of buffalo, and invoked he was accordingly. The ritual was concisely described in the programme thus: 'The dance is directed by a master of the ceremonies, with a drum and rattle accompaniment. The characters are eight persons representing the buffaloes, which may be expected from any of the four quarters: and, facing the eight, four other persons, of whom two, dressed in black with white spots, symbolise the starry night, and two, dressed in red with white streaks, represent the ghosts driven away by the light of day. The performers hope to secure the arrival of the buffaloes in a lucky moment whether by night or day. After the dance enter two grizzly bears, growling ferociously. The food given to them by the squaws is snatched away by "bald eagles" (with white heads) who, in turn, are chased away by "antelopes" (with yellow heads), who seize and eat the food, but are disturbed by the Evil Spirit (in black, with white stripes). His attack is met successfully by the "medicine man," who drives him away.' All this was gone through, needless to say, with keen enjoyment by the young performers: but the dramatic climax was reached with the entrance of a party of white traders, who, after securing respectful attention by a harmless pistol shot, proceeded to barter with the noble savage, the pipe of peace then circulating and the 'pipe dance,' accompanied by a fearsome flourish of tomahawks, bringing matters to a highly animated finish.

"While the educational side of this may be regarded as ethnological rather than anything else, the third item emphasized the spirit and teaching of Empire Day very strikingly. It was, strictly, a tableau, representing Britannia and her Colonies and Dominions. The details had been most carefully arranged, so as to convey facts to the youthful mind. Second to the interest of the living picture, and greatly accentuating it, was Mr. Herbert's finely conceived coast scene, with a sea suggestive of the colour of Henry Moore, and far stretched headlands. Britannia, who was personified with charm and dignity by Miss Counsell, was enthroned overlooking the wild waves she rules. Supporting her were England, Scotland, Ireland, and Wales, attended on the right by the Channel Islands and the Isle of Man: and in the order of their foundation or annexation her 73 children, racial or political, entered to do her reverence. The Continents around which the Colonies were grouped were personified by ladies almost as queenly as Britannia herself: they carried emblems, and wore distinctive dresses, America being arrayed in yellow, Europe in dark blue, Asia in white, Africa in red, and Australasia in green. The arms of many of the Colonies were displayed, and to make the whole thing at once more effective artistically and more instructive geographically, islands forming part of Colonies were personified by little girls dressed in light blue, varied by collars of the colour of the Continent to which they belong. Naturally the eye alone could not satisfy the sentiment of the situation, and appropriately it was at this point in the programme that all present on either side of the footlights joined in singing 'The Empire Flag,' and then 'Rule Britannia' – that lady rising from her shield-flanked seat in acknowledgment of the delicacy, and justice, of the compliment."

In this final tableau several members of the C. L. C. staff and old pupils took part. Many pupils were present at the rehearsal of the entertainment on the previous day.

At College prayers on Empire Day a short address was given by the Vice-Principal on the responsibilities of empire. The lesson and collects were appropriate to the occasion, and the hymns sung were the National Anthem and Mr. Rudyard Kipling's *Recessional*.

34

EMPIRE DAY PAGEANT AT PERTH

From: 'Empire Day Pageant', in *Dundee Evening Telegraph and Post*, 24th May 1921, p. 1.

These documents show the ways that Lord Meath's influence was felt in the popular realm. Meath (1841–1929) was educated at Eton College, later becoming a diplomat and a prominent Conservative member of the House of Lords. By means of the Empire Day Movement (EDM) and the Duty and Discipline Movement (DDM), the attempt was made to shape children as imperial citizens. Earlier in his life, in publications such as Social Arrows *(1887), he had shown an interest in the provision of outdoor play space for children that had the aim of making fitter citizens. He then turned his attention to imperial concerns, although there was of course some connection between physical fitness and preparedness for imperial defence as the 20th century arrived. Empire Day was marked through the Edwardian era into the 1920s and 1930s, before finally disappearing in 1958 when Harold Macmillan renamed it Commonwealth Day. The overall success of these initiatives is subject to debate. Some children simply enjoyed Empire Day but did not pay much attention to the message. The DDM had a membership of 4,200 in 1917. It is reasonable to suggest that these movements and their value systems were at their peak in the period between 1900 and 1914, although they continued well into the 20th century. During the 1920s, the BBC and its radio broadcasting had some impact of the marking of Empire Day, moving it into the home, where once it had been a largely public celebration. The article by Cyril Norwood, headmaster of Marlborough College at the time of writing, notes the ways in which by the mid-1920s the imperial outlook was now combined with an internationalist outlook. The more militaristic and jingoistic aspects of Empire celebrations that were sometimes visible before 1914 had dissipated in the aftermath of the grim carnage of the First World War.*

2500 school children take part

Empire Day was celebrated by Perth school children in the City Hall this afternoon, when a pageant depicting in symbolic fashion the bonds of friendship existing between the Mother Country and the Dominions was given

Senior school children to the number of about 2500 took part. The central figure, that of Britannia (Mrs A. E. Cox, Dungarthill) in tableau, with figures representing England, Scotland, Ireland, and Wales in national costume in attendance, symbolised the Empire in unity. To the feet of Britannia were brought produce of Canada, West Indies, Africa, India, East Indies, and Australasia by pupils dressed in the national costumes

In song and recitation the freedom and might of the Empire found expression in Rudyard Kipling's "Big Steamers," recited by Miss Rumgay, and the children's songs by the same author saluted the flag of the Red, White, and Blue.

Sir Samuel Chapman in an address spoke of individual duty to the Empire, and said it was a magnificent thing to find children playing their parts so well in song and acting, as it spoke to the spirit of unity and a keen appreciation of the duty which would be theirs in the future.

The tableau, which was in every way a success, was arranged by Mr William Paterson, Central School, and Mr Dougald Walker, Northern District School, at behest of the Education Authority.

35

'CHILDREN'S EMPIRE DAY BROADCAST', IN *THE DAILY INDEPENDENT*, 25TH MAY 1936, P. 11.

These documents show the ways that Lord Meath's influence was felt in the popular realm. Meath (1841–1929) was educated at Eton College, later becoming a diplomat and a prominent Conservative member of the House of Lords. By means of the Empire Day Movement (EDM) and the Duty and Discipline Movement (DDM), the attempt was made to shape children as imperial citizens. Earlier in his life, in publications such as Social Arrows *(1887), he had shown an interest in the provision of outdoor play space for children that had the aim of making fitter citizens. He then turned his attention to imperial concerns, although there was of course some connection between physical fitness and preparedness for imperial defence as the 20th century arrived. Empire Day was marked through the Edwardian era into the 1920s and 1930s, before finally disappearing in 1958 when Harold Macmillan renamed it Commonwealth Day. The overall success of these initiatives is subject to debate. Some children simply enjoyed Empire Day but did not pay much attention to the message. The DDM had a membership of 4,200 in 1917. It is reasonable to suggest that these movements and their value systems were at their peak in the period between 1900 and 1914, although they continued well into the 20th century. During the 1920s, the BBC and its radio broadcasting had some impact of the marking of Empire Day, moving it into the home, where once it had been a largely public celebration. The article by Cyril Norwood, headmaster of Marlborough College at the time of writing, notes the ways in which by the mid-1920s the imperial outlook was now combined with an internationalist outlook. The more militaristic and jingoistic aspects of Empire celebrations that were sometimes visible before 1914 had dissipated in the aftermath of the grim carnage of the First World War.*

THE stage is set for the Derby, and to-night Phillip Allingham, a breezy talker on the life of a cheapjack (a calling which he has followed for many years) is coming to the microphone to give some of his experiences while working as a huckster on Epsom Downs.

It is from the humorous angle that he will look at the Epsom crowds in his talk to-night in the Northern programme.

Prior to this, the Preston Cecilian Choir broadcast to Northern listeners in a programme with the B.B.C. Northern Orchestra.

Their programme to-night will include "The Watches Carnival," by Percy Fletcher.

'CHILDREN'S EMPIRE DAY BROADCAST' P. 11.

Outstanding for National listeners is Arthur Schnitzler's "Liebelei," translated from the German and adapted for the microphone by Marianne Helweg, prior to which listeners have half an hour with Louis Levy and his orchestra in more music from the movies.

This, the eleventh broadcast in the series will include "Melody from the Sky," and two other film selections, "Limelight" and "Follow the Fleet," from the new Fred Astaire and Ginger Rogers picture now playing in the West End.

Broadcasters from five continents within the Empire are taking part in a special Empire Day transmission for children to-day. Sir William A. Wayland, chairman of the Empire Day Movement, opens the programme with a talk on the meaning of Empire Day.

36

'THE KING'S EMPIRE DAY BROADCAST', IN *THE EVENING NEWS*, 25TH MAY 1940, P. 2.

These documents show the ways that Lord Meath's influence was felt in the popular realm. Meath (1841–1929) was educated at Eton College, later becoming a diplomat and a prominent Conservative member of the House of Lords. By means of the Empire Day Movement (EDM) and the Duty and Discipline Movement (DDM), the attempt was made to shape children as imperial citizens. Earlier in his life, in publications such as Social Arrows *(1887), he had shown an interest in the provision of outdoor play space for children that had the aim of making fitter citizens. He then turned his attention to imperial concerns, although there was of course some connection between physical fitness and preparedness for imperial defence as the 20th century arrived. Empire Day was marked through the Edwardian era into the 1920s and 1930s, before finally disappearing in 1958 when Harold Macmillan renamed it Commonwealth Day. The overall success of these initiatives is subject to debate. Some children simply enjoyed Empire Day but did not pay much attention to the message. The DDM had a membership of 4,200 in 1917. It is reasonable to suggest that these movements and their value systems were at their peak in the period between 1900 and 1914, although they continued well into the 20th century. During the 1920s, the BBC and its radio broadcasting had some impact of the marking of Empire Day, moving it into the home, where once it had been a largely public celebration. The article by Cyril Norwood, headmaster of Marlborough College at the time of writing, notes the ways in which by the mid-1920s the imperial outlook was now combined with an internationalist outlook. The more militaristic and jingoistic aspects of Empire celebrations that were sometimes visible before 1914 had dissipated in the aftermath of the grim carnage of the First World War.*

The first factor is speed

IN the words of the King's eloquent Empire Day broadcast, all who love the ideals of freedom, justice and peace have to be armed afresh with 'endurance and self sacrifice'.

It is fortunate that the King could send this rallying call to the ends of the earth, certain of response, because the British Commonwealth would have never been created or held together without the cement of these three ideals. The splendid help in men and supplies coming from every quarter of the Commonwealth has behind it faith and confidence in the spirit of the Mother Country to withstand all the shocks that may fall upon the civil population during the next few weeks or months. The Prime Minister has warned us that civilians must before long suffer battle-front casualties like the men in arms or in the air. As long as they are shared and accepted in the same front-line spirit the enemy will not shake the nation by either invasion, death or panic.

But practical as well as spiritual readiness is essential, and it requires a day-by-day and night-by-night vigilance in every home; watchfulness and cheerful trust has to be shown. It is in this key that Mr Bevin today exhorts the men and women who can win the war in the workshops to redouble effort and output. The Germans have thrust so far by sheer weight of mechanised munitions. This is why they broke through the Ardennes, hitherto supposed to be an impregnable bottle-neck of forest, rock and river. The strength of the defensive, so much of which was derived from the experience of the last war, may partly have failed through faulty military dispositions. But the crashing force of Hitler's "mechanised Atilla" is the supreme surprise. The enemy has simply to be out-mechanised, and it is possible to do it. Speed is now the first factor.

37

THE EMPIRE AND THE LEAGUE OF NATIONS: THEIR REAL MEANING AND IDEALS

[Address by Dr. Cyril Norwood of Marlborough College, May 30th, 1925.]

From: C. Norwood, 'The Empire and the League of Nations: Their Real Meaning and Ideals', in *The Cheltenham Ladies' College Magazine* (Autumn 1925), pp. 74–79.

These documents show the ways that Lord Meath's influence was felt in the popular realm. Meath (1841–1929) was educated at Eton College, later becoming a diplomat and a prominent Conservative member of the House of Lords. By means of the Empire Day Movement (EDM) and the Duty and Discipline Movement (DDM), the attempt was made to shape children as imperial citizens. Earlier in his life, in publications such as Social Arrows *(1887), he had shown an interest in the provision of outdoor play space for children that had the aim of making fitter citizens. He then turned his attention to imperial concerns, although there was of course some connection between physical fitness and preparedness for imperial defence as the 20th century arrived. Empire Day was marked through the Edwardian era into the 1920s and 1930s, before finally disappearing in 1958 when Harold Macmillan renamed it Commonwealth Day. The overall success of these initiatives is subject to debate. Some children simply enjoyed Empire Day but did not pay much attention to the message. The DDM had a membership of 4,200 in 1917. It is reasonable to suggest that these movements and their value systems were at their peak in the period between 1900 and 1914, although they continued well into the 20th century. During the 1920s, the BBC and its radio broadcasting had some impact of the marking of Empire Day, moving it into the home, where once it had been a largely public celebration. The article by Cyril Norwood, headmaster of Marlborough College at the time of writing, notes the ways in which by the mid-1920s the imperial outlook was now combined with an internationalist outlook. The more militaristic and jingoistic aspects of Empire celebrations that were sometimes visible before 1914 had dissipated in the aftermath of the grim carnage of the First World War.*

JUST a week ago at Marlborough the Duke of Connaught visited us and did us the honour of declaring open a Memorial Hall which we have built to commemorate those of our school who fell in the War. Round the walls of that hall there are carved in stone the names of 733 boys and 8 masters who gave their lives, and over the entrance doors on either side we have carved the one word "Remember." In speaking this morning that memory is naturally uppermost in my mind. For what did these men die? For what were the million lives which our country sacrificed given? Those men died for an ideal, and because this country and the allies followed a true ideal in the end they won. It is of that ideal that I want to speak.

Perhaps there is another scene which is fresh in your memories, or at any rate in your reading. Last Sunday was Empire Sunday, and the King and Queen went to Wembley and joined in a great national service of thanksgiving and prayer. All the wealth of the many countries and races which own our flag was gathered there. For what does all that stand? The leadership in the development of the world which has been granted to this race of ours – how are we going to use it? For ourselves or as trustees? Are we going to think of the glory and the greatness of the British Empire as ends in themselves, or are we going to take pride in the British Empire rather as an instrument of the Kingdom of God?

You will see straight away that I regard this subject as at bottom religious, for you cannot without disaster separate politics from religion. They have been too often separated in the past, and it is my hope that the coming of women into politics will mean that more weight will in future be given to principle. Therefore I am not going to apologise for starting with the plain elementary rules of our religion. The religion of Christ teaches us that there are two kinds of values, spiritual and material. The material are the sort that the more you have of them the less there is for other people, and Christ said of these that they do not matter, they are not the things for which we ought to strive. We ought to strive for the other values, the spiritual, of which the more we have the more there is for other people; those eternal values are truth, beauty and goodness. These are the things that matter – truth, beauty, goodness – and he that hath these has Christ, has eternal life.

Christianity shows us, in the light of modern knowledge, a most wonderful process beginning before the dawn of all history. It shows us the beginning of life in the very humblest forms and gradually developing until men come upon the earth; it shows us men again developing until they found families and tribes and peoples and kingdoms and can till the earth, and build, and lay the foundations of science and art. Then after ages of that developmen Christ came, God taking upon himself man's nature in order to show us the way of further development; and the future progress of mankind depends upon how far as individuals and as nations we can follow the way which He showed us. That Way is Love; love seeking to make the eternal values – truth, beauty, goodness – the possession of all men. That is why all politics depends at bottom on religion, for politics is nothing else than the process by which in the life of our own nation, as one among other nations, we seek to give effect to the ideal which Christ has set before us. I want you, with the religious ideal in your hearts, to think of your country and of the British Empire as something which may be used as a great instrument for the building of the Kingdom of God. I remind you that everyday when you say the Lord's Prayer you pray that that Kingdom may come on earth as it is in Heaven, and we ought to mean something when we say that. We ought to mean that religion will enter into our politics.

Now we know that one of the very hardest things which our religion tells us to do is to love our neighbours as ourselves, and one of the first difficulties which you find in politics is how to love your own country without regarding other countries with hostility. We feel that it is right to be patriotic and we feel that it is easy to imagine circumstances in which our patriotism might conflict with the ideal of peace between all nations, in which it might be easy and natural for many to say that the followers of the League of Nations are unpatriotic. Let us try to be clear about patriotism. Enthusiasts are in such haste for the brotherhood of man and the Kingdom of God on earth that they are apt to abuse patriotism and the patriot, and their sneers offend honest men and women. We are descended from countless generations who have survived because they knew how to hold together and be loyal to one another; this instinct has possessed the tribe, the city, and the nation. No man can live by himself or entirely for himself. He must be shaped by the local circumstances which gave him birth and environ his life. When the Psalmist in exile cries "If I forget thee, O Jerusalem, may my right hand forget her cunning" does it not stir a pulse in our hearts too? Jesus, when He beheld the city, wept over it. Why? Because it was His city. And do we not feel with Him, and feel that He was right? When the dying John of Gaunt in *Richard II* bursts out into his magnificent panegyric "This blessed plot, this earth, this realm, this England," does he not carry us with him all the way, and have we anything but contempt for the denationalised person, the superior person, the person who is the friend of every country but his own? No, the instinct as an instinct is profoundly right; it only needs to be used in the right way.

The teaching of Our Lord gives another and a deeper emphasis and lifts the whole subject on to a higher plane. He does not think of His nation first and foremost, but of mankind as a whole. He came into the world as human and divine to show the kinship of all men with Divinity, to set a new value on human personality, and to break down the barriers of rigid, exclusive, neighbour-hating nationalism. St. Paul in the Epistle to the Colossians shows how the higher ideal is superimposed on the life of the law. He tells them that they have put on a new man "where there is neither Greek nor Jew, Barbarian, Scythian, bond nor free: but Christ is all, and in all." And again, "And above all things these put on charity, which is the bond of perfectness. And let the peace of God rule in your hearts, to the which also ye are called in one body."

There we have the ideal, the Christian ideal, and if we can get it into our hearts we shall have no difficulty in being at once patriots and members of the League of Nations; and members of the League of Nations just because we are patriots. The League of Nations does not mean that all nations are equal and alike, but that they have all their rightful place in the great family of God and all of them have their work to do in His service. The true Christian will love his country intensely just because it has this special service to render, and at the same time will recognise that other countries have their contribution to bring. That is the ideal and meaning of the League of Nations.

We have to face the fact that there are people in the world who say that they stand for their country whether it be right or wrong, even those who, if they would not say it aloud with Machiavelli, certainly seem to think it, that they prefer their country to the salvation of their soul. There have been all sorts of influences which have gone to make popular theories that it is right for nations to be utterly selfish and to seek to pile up riches and power for themselves at the expense of their neighbours. The first and most powerful is just natural human greed; then there is Darwinism, the belief that the survival of the fittest is the law of nature which we cannot avoid. Again there are developments and perversions of the doctrines recently universal in Germany, that the State is an end in itself, above the ordinary moral law, and the object of the State is to cause the noblest race and the highest culture (that is, of course, always another name for ourselves) to survive and to possess the world. Such are the people who say that you cannot alter human nature, that war has gone on always in the past and always will go on in the future, that you may trust in God if you like but you should never forget the real safeguard, which is always to keep your powder dry, and if possible get your blow in first.

You hear people call that common-sense; I would rather call it common delusion. The fact remains, and history shows it, that the man who is blind to and despises moral issues does his country more harm than good, and if there are enough of these short-sighted patriots it is only a question of time before they ruin their country. Thereof the supreme example in our own times is the great empire of the Hohenzollerns which lost the war ultimately because it was utterly and entirely in the wrong.

You are all familiar with the political maxims which Europe has been content to put prior to the maxims of the Gospel. They are simply that if you wish for peace you should prepare for war, and that you should strive to arrange Europe in so delicate a balance of opposing powers that neither side will be willing to attack the other. But if, at any time, it is quite safe to grab something owing to the weakness of your neighbours then in the interests of national expansion and out of love for your own country you should grab it.

A short survey will make my point clear. It was the Reformation that first broke Europe into two hostile camps, and through the end of the 16th century and into the 17th they fought continuous wars of Catholic and Protestant ending in a system of mutual toleration, not because they thought it was the right thing but because they had fought themselves to a standstill. As soon as those wars ceased there began the long career of Louis XIV devoted to the end of making himself and France supreme in their mastery over the Continent. He failed, and in the end the Treaty of Utrecht was made, a world settlement according to the ideas of the time, based on the Balance of Power. A short period of peace followed, and then in 1740 there came to the throne of Prussia an unscrupulous rascal called Frederick the Great, and his ambitions to make his country a leader by the process of war inspired war in three continents. He did not go to his grave before there arose one greater than he, Napoleon, who carried the eagles of France over all Europe in pursuit of the same vision of empire. Again there was ultimate failure and another world settlement at the Congress of Vienna, again based on the Balance of Power, and meant to last for all time. Once more there was a short and uneasy period of peace, no man trusting his neighbour very much, and then came the ambitions of Napoleon III and the rise of Prussia. France was struck to the ground, and there followed the period during which the German Empire organised its strength for the great adventure in its turn: result the World War of our own times. There has followed the peace, so called, made at Paris after the latest failure of the enterprise, out of which was born the hope of the League of Nations and of a new way of international life. But the danger is that while we talk of the League as the hope of the future we are steadily drifting as a matter of practical politics towards the reintroduction of the old system of the Balance of Power and counterbalancing armaments. Need I remind you that the adventures of Louis XIV cost Europe lives that may be counted by the ten thousand, the adventures of Napoleon cost lives by the hundred thousand, the adventure of Germany cost lives by the million. The next adventure which, unless a change comes over the heart of the world, we may obviously expect within the next hundred years, will destroy European civilisation. So I put it to you that it is a very practical question whether the ideal of the League of Nations is to succeed or not, because it involves with it whether we and our civilisation are to survive or not.

I want you to think on which side you are going to stand in your citizenship, because if you regard your country as a supreme end in itself you are bound to fall into the old error of armaments and the Balance of Power which has ruined Europe three times running. But if you take firm hold of the Christian idea that all humanity constitute the children of God, and that every nation and race has some special contribution to make to the well-being of the whole, then you cannot fall into crude courses of selfishness. The wealth of a country consists in the character, health, fitness, goodness and true happiness of its men and women. Therefore the Christian patriot will take the keenest of interests in municipal and national politics, and in international politics it will be his object that his country shall so play its part as to lead humanity forward.

The highest English patriotism, the truest Imperialism to-day is to support that cause and those ideals for which the League of Nations stands, for we can do more than any other country on its behalf. We stand geographically between the Old World and the New. Our ships, our trade, our ideas and our language reach to every continent and to every sea. The truest service of patriotism, as I see it, is to try to lead the world on to that state where mankind shall seek to be governed by justice and by law. Such a patriotism fulfils the law of God, and at its noblest, that is when it is Christian, it is an effective destroyer of rancour and jealousy, a stimulus to all honourable conduct and noble effort, a part of the poetry of life. But like all great and noble things, like all Christian things, it is very hard. Yet it may be that we shall be able to do something to bring nearer the day which Isaiah saw long ago, imperfectly and far off, the day of God's promise, "It shall come that I will gather all nations and tongues, and they shall come and see my glory."

38

THE REPORT OF THE INTER-DEPARTMENTAL COMMITTEE ON PHYSICAL DETERIORATION (LONDON: HMSO, 1905), PP. 13–17.

Whilst the working classes' poor physical condition had been noted by several commentators before 1900, the early 20th century saw a new anxiety as to the implication of this condition for the future of the Empire. The 1904 report was conducted in the wake of the South African War (1899–1902) by the Balfour Conservative government (1902–1905), and in many ways attempted to make sense of why the British had struggled to overcome their Boer opponents. The report focused on the apparent deterioration of working-class youth who had volunteered for service. It noted that 37 per cent of the recruits were unfit for service. This undermined the idea of British racial superiority that had supported the imperial mission. The committee, appointed by the Duke of Devonshire, Lord President of the Council, on 2 September 1903, was chaired by Almeric W. Fitzroy (1851–1935), a civil servant who had been Clerk of the Privy Council since 1898. Evidence was provided by 68 witnesses and it made 53 recommendations, leading to better nourishment in schools and a greater emphasis on physical education in the curriculum, with medical inspections to be undertaken to a greater extent. The 46th and 47th recommendations argued for the value of clubs and the cadet corps and urged that grants should be made available for them to exist; so, too, should lads be made to attend continuation classes at which drill and physical exercise should be permanent. Further reforms were suggested in relation to working-class housing, and the report also addressed the problem of overcrowding. However, one commentator suggests that the report did little to identify the exact causes of deterioration.

PART II.

I. Introductory

67. It has now been seen that there are no sufficient *data* at present obtainable for a comparative estimate of the health and physique of the people, and the Committee have indicated the measures that, in their opinion, should be adopted in order to supply the want, but before concluding their task they deemed it their duty, under the fuller explanation of their commission, by which their Order of Reference was supplemented, to consider the causes and conditions of such physical degeneration as is no doubt present in considerable classes of the community, and to point out the means by which, in their opinion, it can be most effectually diminished,

and more especially to discuss this aspect of the question as it affects the young during the three periods of infancy, school age, and adolescence.

68. It may be as well to state at once that the impressions gathered from the great majority of the witnesses examined do not support the belief that there is any general progressive physical deterioration.

69. The evidence of Dr. Eichholz contains a summary of his conclusions on this point, so admirably epitomising the results of a comprehensive survey of the whole subject, that the Committee cannot do better than reproduce it in full at this stage of their report: –

"(1) I draw a clear distinction between physical degeneracy on the one hand and inherited retrogressive deterioration on the other. (2) With regard to physical degeneracy, the children frequenting the poorer schools of London and the large towns betray a most serious condition of affairs, calling for ameliorative and arrestive measures, the most impressive features being the apathy of parents as regards the school, the lack of parental care of children, the poor physique, powers of endurance, and educational attainments of the children attending school. (3) Nevertheless, even in the poorer districts there exist schools of a type above the lowest, which show a marked upward and improving tendency, physically and educationally – though the rate of improvement would be capable of considerable acceleration under suitable measures. (4) *In the better districts of the towns there exist public elementary schools frequented by children not merely equal but often superior in physique and attainments to rural children.* And these schools seem to be at least as numerous as schools of the lowest type. (5) While there are unfortunately, very abundant signs of physical defect traceable to neglect, poverty, and ignorance, it is not possible to obtain any satisfactory or conclusive evidence of hereditary physical deterioration – that is to say, deterioration of a gradual retrogressive permanent nature, affecting one generation more acutely than the previous. There is little, if anything, in fact, to justify the conclusion that neglect, poverty, and parental ignorance, serious as their results are possess any marked hereditary effect, or that heredity plays any significant part in establishing the physical degeneracy of the poorer population. (6) In every case of alleged progressive hereditary deterioration among the children frequenting an elementary school, it is found that the neighbourhood has suffered by the migration of the better artisan class, or by the influx of worse population from elsewhere. (7) Other than the well-known specifically hereditary diseases which *affect poor and well-to-do alike*, there appears to be very little real evidence on the prenatal side to account for the widespread physical degeneracy among the poorer population. There is, accordingly every reason to anticipate RAPID amelioration of physique so soon as improvement occurs in external conditions, particularly as regards food, clothing, overcrowding, cleanliness, drunkenness, and the spread of common practical knowledge of home management. (8) In fact, all evidence points to *active, rapid improvement, bodily and mental, in the worst districts*, so soon as they are exposed to better circumstances, even the weaker children recovering at a later age from the evil effects of infant life. (9) Compulsory school attendance, the more rigorous scheduling of children of school age, and the abolition of school fees in elementary schools, have swept into the schools an annually increasing proportion of children during the last thirty years. These circumstances are largely responsible for focussing public notice on the severer cases of physical impairment – just as, at a previous stage in educational development, they established the need for special training of the more defined types of physical deficiency – the blind, the deaf, the feeble-minded, and the crippled. (10) The apparent deterioration in army recruiting material seems to be associated with the demand for youthful labour in unskilled occupations, which pay well, and absorb adolescent population more and more completely year by year. Moreover, owing to the peculiar circumstances of apprenticeship which are coming to prevail in this country, clever boys are often unable to take up skilled work on leaving school. This circumstance puts additional pressure on the field of unskilled labour, and coupled with the high rates of wages for unskilled labour, tends to force out of competition the aimless wastrel population at the bottom of the intellectual scale, and this, unfortunately, becomes more and more the material available for army recruiting purposes. (11) Close attention seems to be needed in respect of the physical condition of young girls who take up industrial employment between the ages of fourteen and eighteen. The conditions under which they work, rest, and feed doubtless account for the rapid falling off in physique which so frequently accompanies the transition from school to work."

70. Testimony is almost unanimous as to the improving conditions under which the denizens of large towns are called upon to exist. Rookeries are being dispersed, enclosed yards opened out, cellar-dwellings and back-to-back houses are disappearing. One-roomed, two-roomed, and three-roomed tenements, with more than two, four, and six occupants respectively are diminishing; the figures for the years 1891 and 1901 under each class in the Administrative County of London and in Lancashire are as follows: – from which it appears that the rate of improvement has been more marked in London in regard to the overcrowding of one-room tenements, and in Lancashire in respect of the other two classes. With an increase of wages a fall in the prices of food, coal, and clothing has taken place, more than counterbalancing the rise in rent, which, in itself, is largely due to the higher wages paid in the building trade.

	One-roomed tenements with more than two occupants.		Two-roomed tenements with more than four occupants.		Three-roomed tenements with more than six occupants.	
	1891	1901	1891	1901	1891	1901
London	56,727	40,762	55,020	50,304	24,586	23,979
Lancashire (Administrative County, together with 15 County Boroughs).	5,007	4,256	16,001	10,277	8,704	6,437

71. Mr. C. S. Loch, in his interesting evidence, furnished the Committee with reasons for believing that improved resources have been accompanied by an upward movement in social ability or competence, with the result that a certain amount of advantageous expenditure has gone in better houses, and in the purchase of more food, and of food particularly good for children, and he also thought the same conclusion might be drawn from the large decrease in child pauperism.

72. Further, the water supply has been enormously improved, both in purity and quantity; legislation has greatly extended the liabilities of owners and occupiers under the Public Health Acts and the Housing Acts, and under the said series of Acts wide powers have been placed in the hands of local authorities for cleansing unhealthy areas, closing insanitary houses, preventing overcrowding, abating nuisances and enforcing generally a higher standard of sanitation; machinery exists for the inspection and purification of cowsheds and dairies, pauperism has diminished, better and more complete accommodation is provided for the sick poor, the conditions of labour touching young persons and women, in factories and workshops, have been greatly ameliorated, and all the children of the State in workhouse schools, reformatories and industrial institutions, are started in life under far better auspices than formerly.

73. On the other hand, in large classes of the community there has not been developed a desire for improvement commensurate with the opportunities offered to them. Laziness, want of thrift, ignorance of household management, and particularly of the choice and preparation of food, filth, indifference to parental obligations, drunkenness, largely infect adults of both sexes, and press with terrible severity upon their children. The very growth of the family resources, upon which statisticians congratulate themselves, accompanied as it frequently is by great unwisdom in their application to raising the standard of comfort, is often productive of the most disastrous consequences. "The people perish for lack of knowledge," or, as it is elsewhere put, "lunacy increases with the rise of wages and the greater spending power of the operative class; while a falling wage-rate is associated with a decrease of drunkenness, crime, and lunacy." Local authorities, moreover, especially in the rural districts, are often reluctant to use their powers, and in these circumstances progress, unless stimulated by a healthy public conscience in matters of hygiene, is slower than might be wished.

74. An apt illustration of the widely different views held by competent observers is afforded by the interesting evidence of Mr. J. B. Atkins, London Editor of the *Manchester Guardian*, who, with a view to investigations of his own on the subject, has collected a large body of testimony, some of which he was good enough to lay before the Committee, showing in immediate juxtaposition what may be perhaps best described as the empirical and statistical methods of arriving at a conclusion.

75. The operation in different directions of the aforesaid ameliorative tendencies, and of the influences that incline towards the arrest of progress, combined with the spread of education, has, as Dr. Eichholz pointed out, had the effect of stratifying the population and concentrating the classes that require special treatment:

> "There is an upper class, well-to-do and well cared for, to whom our methods afford every chance of mental and physical improvement. They come out well, and furnish a population probably not excelled by any in this country or in any other. At the other end of the scale we find the aggregation of slum population, ill-nourished, poor, ignorant, badly housed, to a small extent only benefited by our methods of training. They are the degenerates for whom this enquiry is presumably instituted. Between these two is the third and largest stratum consisting of the average industrial artisan population in which the breadwinners are in regular employment. It is the aggregation of the slum population which is largely responsible for the prominent public notice called to their physical condition."

76. In a similar vein, Dr. R. J. Collie, one of the medical staff of the late London School Board, says –

> "Physical infirmity is practically confined to the poorest and lowest strata of the population, whose children are improperly and insufficiently fed and inadequately housed, and where parents are improvident, idle, and intemperate."

77. If this be so, as the Committee are inclined to think, the task of dealing with a concentrated rather than a scattered evil manifestly presents fewer physical difficulties.

78. The Committee have advisedly abstained from framing an estimate of the number of persons living under depressed conditions on the basis of the calculations made by Messrs. Booth and Rowntree. First, they have not the means of doing so; and, secondly, the different estimates of the number of underfed children, which they have had to consider, seem to show that there must be some very variable element which interferes with the acceptance of such conclusions as resting on generally accepted *data*. It may be stated also that

Mr. Loch, in the course of his evidence, questioned the method on which the calculations leading to these conclusions had proceeded, and he subsequently put in a Memorandum explaining the grounds of his dissent. This Memorandum, which confirms the Committee in the belief that the matter is attended with great difficulty, will be found in the Appendix, and is a valuable contribution to the literature on the subject.

II. – Urbanization of the people

79. Turning to the general causes in operation that are calculated to arrest and depress development, the collection of the majority of the population in the large towns is the most evident and most considerable; but even here the evil is not so great as the form in which it is commonly stated might suggest.

80. According to the classification adopted in the Census returns for England and Wales the urban population is 77 per cent. of the whole, whereas fifty years ago it was only just over 50 per cent. It is the fact that for every person who in 1851 lived in a town, about three are so situated at the present time, but it must be remembered that the term "urban" merely means those districts that for the purposes of local administration have an urban organization, and that a large portion of the urban population is living under conditions as healthy as any that obtain in rural districts, and indeed enjoys superior advantages, owing to the greater completeness of sanitary legislation for such areas, and the higher conception of duty that governs their administration. Further, it is the case that towns have now a death-rate which is lower than was that of rural districts fifty years ago.

81. If a comparison could be made between the numbers living in slum quarters now and in the middle of the last century there might be some nearer approach to an effective conclusion as regards the results of urbanization, making due allowance for the improvement of life, even under the most degraded conditions, that has undoubtedly taken place. To this fact both Drs. Chalmers and Niven, Medical Officers of Health for Glasgow and Manchester respectively, testify on the strength of the evidence supplied by the vital statistics touching such quarters. In opposition to such testimony it is not sufficient to say, as one witness did, that he attaches little importance to an improvement of vital statistics, because it is simply raising an inferior limit. The theory that the processes by which life is preserved are themselves a cause of degeneration, by prolonging the lives of the unfit, is open to the criticism that of all the discriminating agencies to produce the survival of the fittest disease is the worst, for the injury to those that survive is so serious that all measures which combat disease tend to improve the race. But be the circumstances what they may on this point, there is reason to fear that the "urbanization" of the population cannot have been unattended by consequences prejudicial to the health of the people, and these have been considered under the three heads of (i.) *Overcrowding*, (ii.) *Pollution of the atmosphere*, and (iii.) *The conditions of employment*.

i. Overcrowding

82. Overcrowding still stands out most prominent with its attendant evils of uncleanliness, foul air, and bad sanitation.

83. The problem is by no means a new one, however its conditions may have become aggravated in recent times. So long ago as the year 1598 the Privy Council addressed a letter to the Justices of Middlesex, inveighing against the owners of tenement houses for the abuses they encouraged; "the remedie whereof cannot be sufficientlie provided in havinge an eye to these persons that take those howses, beinge so great a nomber, and they cannot be justlic corrected untill they be taken with some offence, but in severe punyshinge those landlords that lett out those small tenements (parcells of howses and chambers) unto unknowne and base people and from weeke to weeke, not regardinge what the persones are that take the same, but to rayse a vile and unconscionable lucre."

84. This is not quite the official language of the present day, but among the opinions collected by the most modern investigator occur the following:

"Overcrowding is the great cause of degeneracy"; "Drink is fostered by bad houses"; "Crowded homes send men to the public house"; "Crowding the main cause of drink and vice."

85. The permanent difficulties that attach to the problem reside, as the same witness has shown, in the character of the people themselves (their feebleness and indifference, their reluctance to move, and their incapability of moving), and in the obstacle this presents to the best directed efforts on the part of the local authority to employ their powers.

86. It has been suggested that interference "by administrative action and penalties at each point at which life falls below a minimum accepted standard" is the way by which the problem must be approached, and the occupation of overcrowded tenements seems to afford the best opportunity for the application of the doctrine. The evil is, of course, greatest in one-roomed tenements, the overcrowding there being among persons usually of the lowest type, steeped in every kind of degradation and cynically indifferent to the vile surroundings engendered by their filthy habits, and to the pollution of the young brought up in such an atmosphere. The general death-rate in these tenements in Glasgow is nearly twice that of the whole city, and the death-rate from pulmonary tuberculosis is 2·4 per thousand in one-roomed tenements, 1·8 in two-roomed tenements, and ·7 in all the other houses. In Finsbury, again, where the population of one-roomed tenements is 14,516, the death-rate per thousand in 1903 was 38·9, yet the rate among occupants of four or more rooms was only 5·6, and for the whole borough 19·6. Similarly a comparison between the population of Hampstead and Southwark, in respect of their ability to withstand disease and death, shows an expectation of life very largely in favour of Hampstead, at birth the relative figures being 50·8 and 36·5 years, at five, 57·4 and 48·7, illustrating the waste of material during the first

years of life. From another table, furnished by Mr. Shirley Murphy, the Medical Officer of Health for the administrative County of London, it appears that in seven groups of districts with an increasing amount of population living in overcrowded tenements the infant death-rate has followed the increase; that is to say, in districts with under 10 per cent. of the population living under these conditions the death-rate was 142 per thousand, and then, as the proportion of people living in overcrowded tenements increases, so does the infant death-rate, going from 180 to 196, and then to 193, and then going on to 210, 222 and 223.

87. Facts like these show where the root of the mischief lies, and surely the time is ripe for dealing drastically with a class that, whether by wilfulness or necessity, is powerless to extricate itself from conditions that constitute a grave menace to the community, by virtue of the permanent taint that is communicated to those that suffer under them, and of the depressing effect that the competition of these people exercises on the class immediately above. The Committee think that with a view to setting a term to these evils the Local Authority should, in the exercise of their power to treat "any house or part of a house so overcrowded as to be dangerous or injurious to the health of the inmates" as a nuisance, and for the abatement of the same, notify that after a given date no one-roomed, two-roomed, or three-roomed tenements would be permitted to contain more than two, four or six persons respectively. The change might be brought into operation gradually, so as to treat the worst cases first, and render it easier to provide for the displaced families, but in every case handled it must be made plain that in the event of non-compliance recourse would be had to the compulsory closing of the tenement in question.

39

MORRIS DANCES

Mr Cecil Sharp's lecture at Queen's Hall

From: 'Morris Dances: Mr Cecil Sharp Lecture at Queen's Hall', in *Westminster Gazette*, 1st June 1910, p. 8.

These documents show the ways in which amateur dramatics (masques) and dance could be utilised in the context of popular culture and Empire. Dances and plays could contain a strong imperial message, and dance was also seen as a form of physical exercise. Cecil Sharp (1859–1924) founded the English Folk Dance Society in 1911. It built on the work of the Folk Song Society that had been established in 1898. Members of this society included Ralph Vaughan Williams, Percy Grainger and George Butterworth. Sharp made endless bicycle trips through the English countryside, gathering songs and dances in his notebooks, and also travelled overseas to the USA, to gather folk dances that had been taken to the New World by English settlers. Grace Kimmins (1871–1954) was known for her work in London settlements and her work with children who had disabilities. The Bermonsdsey settlement was particularly interested in the question of children's play. Kimmins established the Guild of Play in 1895 to provide 'vigorous happy dances for recreative purposes on educational lines'. Enid Blyton (1897–1968), a qualified teacher, authored the play for children titled The Union Jack *and it appeared in one of her early works, the three-volume* Teacher's Treasury, *published in the mid-1920s. The* Union Jack *introduces figures such as James Wolfe, Lord Clive of India, David Livingstone and Cecil Rhodes, who are depicted as 'men who made the Empire great'.*

Morris and Country dances formed the subject of an interesting lecture delivered by Mr. Cecil J. Sharp in the small Queen's Hall yesterday afternoon. No one knows more about the subject than Mr. Sharp, whose efforts as a collector and investigator in this field are so well known, and as he has the knack of imparting his knowledge in the most interesting manner, his remarks were as entertaining as they were instructive. In view of a recent newspaper controversy, some polemical observations were perhaps anticipated by some, but the lecturer contented himself with laying down two general principles which can hardly fail to gain the assent of most. The first was that it behoved all students and collectors to play fair with the public by reproducing both folk dances and folk tunes with the strictest accuracy, since this was a duty which they owed alike to the past, the present, and the future. Secondly, he suggested that this was not only the more honest course but also the one likely to conduce to the most satisfactory results aesthetically. In other words, the more closely we could get to the dances as they were originally danced, the more artistic, characteristic, and generally pleasing were they likely to be. Unfortunately, as Mr. Sharp went on to say, the tendency was quite natural, although reprehensible, in the case of some folks to reproduce not the songs and dances which actually were sung and danced, but those which it was supposed ought to have been sung and danced; and the two things were not necessarily the same at all. Mr. Sharp then went on to explain the difference between the Morris and the Country dance, and told his hearers much which was probably news to them. As to the supposed Moorish origin of the Morris, he put forward tentatively a more recent theory, which certainly had the merit of ingenuity. This was to the effect that the Morris was originally a dance in honour of Mars, who, he recalled, was originally the god, not of War but of Spring, and that it took its name from this fact. He went on to explain that it was never, as some people supposed, an every-day dance, indulged in by the peasantry at large, but one strictly reserved for special and ceremonial occasions, and danced solely by specially trained exponents. It was, indeed, regarded as the greatest possible honour to get into the village team or side of Morrismen – as an instance of which Mr. Sharp mentioned that an old worthy who died in Herefordshire not long ago requested actually to be buried in his Morris shirt. Many other interesting facts and anecdotes figured in Mr. Sharp's remarks, which were charmingly illustrated in addition by practical examples of the various dances described, performed by the students of the South-West Polytechnic, Chelsea, S.W.

40

THE MASQUE OF THE CHILDREN OF THE EMPIRE

From: G. T. Kimmins, *The Masque of the Children of the Empire* (London: J. Curwen & Sons, 1909).

These documents show the ways in which amateur dramatics (masques) and dance could be utilised in the context of popular culture and Empire. Dances and plays could contain a strong imperial message, and dance was also seen as a form of physical exercise. Cecil Sharp (1859–1924) founded the English Folk Dance Society in 1911. It built on the work of the Folk Song Society that had been established in 1898. Members of this society included Ralph Vaughan Williams, Percy Grainger and George Butterworth. Sharp made endless bicycle trips through the English countryside, gathering songs and dances in his notebooks, and also travelled overseas to the USA, to gather folk dances that had been taken to the New World by English settlers. Grace Kimmins (1871–1954) was known for her work in London settlements and her work with children who had disabilities. The Bermonsdsey settlement was particularly interested in the question of children's play. Kimmins established the Guild of Play in 1895 to provide 'vigorous happy dances for recreative purposes on educational lines'. Enid Blyton (1897–1968), a qualified teacher, authored the play for children titled The Union Jack and it appeared in one of her early works, the three-volume Teacher's Treasury, published in the mid-1920s. The Union Jack introduces figures such as James Wolfe, Lord Clive of India, David Livingstone and Cecil Rhodes, who are depicted as 'men who made the Empire great'.

The Prolocutor –

Here in this scroll I hold is writ a story, the story of the Life of England, how the great centuries came and passed, and of the lessons they taught and held. Of this story many of ye know full well the tale already, yet ye shall now have a rendering of a fuller telling, and as the Centuries of England pass, with pomp and pageant, before you, ye shall see the best and the noblest of their time in their coming and going, and the part that each plays in the building up of our mighty Empire.

Here shall ye see, symbolled in music and movement, those inner things in human history to which the present is ever a child, but which the time to come knows and sees with the great eye of discernment.

Great Beauty has been in the past, but the great abundance of the beauty of our nation has yet to be. In this Masque of the Children of Bermondsey behold, then, a little of the beauty that IS, and behold, in presentation, some of the beauty that WAS. Watch, then, to my calling, like some wizard who unlocks strange things and wonderful, the Centuries of England, each with her symbol, her offering to the life of the nation.

Thus shall those of the seeing eye, and of the hearing ear, and of the understanding heart learn and grasp the meaning of the great message of Unity, which we celebrate throughout the length and breadth of our mighty Empire.

The glory of the Coronation Pageant may be centred at Westminster, but the glint of the beauty reaches to Bermondsey and Chailey, and no children in the mighty Empire rejoice with fuller rejoicings, nor offer with greater loyalty their gifts of affection at the feet of their Sovereigns than do these children of to-day.

Enter BRITANNIA *to music.*
Takes up position in centre of hall.

Father Time –
    Behold, the Spirit of Youth!
    With them all things are possible.
To audience –
    You, too, were young – *your* pulses thrilled
    As theirs in merry jibe and jest,
    Your veins with warm young blood were filled,
    And Youth gave to you of its best.
    Listen, as now my tale unfolds,
    Of History, and the great, grand Past,
    And watch the brave of old appear
    As o'er them all the spell is cast.
    Listen, and learn! . . . Musicians, speak!
    And summon hence –
                     Alfred the Great.

Alfred the Great

England of the Saxons

Enter –
    STANDARD BEARER.
    ALFRED THE GREAT.
    SAXON, carrying ship, to represent the founding of the Navy.
    SAXON, carrying books, to represent the learning of the period.
    SAXON, carrying candles, invented by Alfred the Great, to mark the time of day.
    NEATHERD, carrying crook.
    WIFE, carrying cakes.

FATHER TIME *speaks* –

Ye shades of the Past Centuries, come hither, and lay your offerings at the Nation's feet. Alfred the Great!

ALFRED, *laying a boat, emblem of the founding of the Navy, at the feet of* BRITANNIA, *speaks* –

> Now may God bless this England's isle,
> And grant it fail not in the times to be.
> Teach well the people – bid them read and learn;
> Mark well the hours, and build great ships
> For England's honour both by land and sea.

> "Comfort the poor, protect and shelter the weak, and with all thy might right that which is wrong. Then shall the Lord love thee, and God Himself shall be thy great reward."
>
> – *Alfred the Great's last words.*

William the Norman

England of the Normans

Enter –
> STANDARD BEARER.
> WILLIAM THE CONQUEROR.
> EARL DE WARRENNE.
> NORMAN SOLDIER.
> NORMAN, carrying Domesday Book.
> NORMAN, carrying Curfew Bell
> NORMAN, carrying Forest Laws.
> LANFRANC, Archbishop of Canterbury, carrying model of Harrow Church.

FATHER TIME *speaks* –
> William the Norman, what hast *thou* to say?
> The Norman Line hast made a mark,
> It stretches o'er this land from north to south.
> Come hither at my bidding, and do homage.

WILLIAM THE NORMAN *speaks* –
> William the Norman bids you hear
> How England by his help was greater made than ere before,
> Greater in buildings, first in warfare, both on land and sea.
> I fortified your castles, like the grey pile in Sussex by the Ouse, in Lewes,
> Where in the holy church lie bones of Gundrad, daughter of mine, and of her husband, William de Warrenne.
> I loved this England, and I wished it well, right through the centuries to be.

Richard Cœur de Lion

England of the Crusaders

Enter –
>STANDARD BEARER.
>RICHARD CŒUR DE LION.
>CRUSADER.
>SAINT HUGH OF LINCOLN, carrying model of Lincoln Cathedral.
>BLONDEL, the Minstrel Troubadour.
>ROBIN HOOD.
>A KNIGHT TEMPLAR.
>FATHER TIME *speaks –*

>Behold, Richard Cœur de Lion!
>Richard of the Lion Heart,
>Whose tales of fighting in the Holy Land inspire us yet.
>Step forth, and play thy part.

RICHARD CŒUR DE LION *speaks –*
>For this great land I battled oft in distant climes,
>Saw countries new – new forms of speech – new merchandise,
>Opened up pathways to the East by travel,
>Even as we fought for those opprest.
>Never will England hear of weakness unprotected,
>Of unjust war, or tyranny,
>O England! ever fight for home and freedom,
>Enlarge thy boundaries and thy trades,
>Till East and West come under thy great rule.

Edward III

England and her Church

Enter –
>STANDARD BEARER.
>EDWARD III.
>BLACK PRINCE.
>WILLIAM OF WYKEHAM, Bishop of Winchester.
>WYCLIFFE, carrying Bible.
>JOHN GOWER, Poet.
>CHAUCER, carrying "Canterbury Tales."

FATHER TIME *speaks* –
   Thou mighty Edward! last of a long line, step forth.

EDWARD III *speaks* –
   Each in his part wideneth the bounds of this great land.
   Mother Church enlighteneth vision, and teaches us the knowledge of all time.
   The Church doth teach us ever best that gentleness,
   And love of neighbours, and of justice
   Must ever be the link that binds lands each to each.

Henry V

England of the preaching friars

Enter –
   STANDARD BEARER.
   HENRY V.
   DUKE OF BEDFORD.
   ARCHER.
   SIR JOHN FASTOLF.
   SIR JOHN OLDCASTLE (Lollard).
   RICHARD WHITTINGTON, Mayor of London, carrying his ship "The Cat."

FATHER TIME *speaks* –
   Thou kingly warrior, great in life and death,
   Give us thy message from the shadowy past.

HENRY V *speaks* –
   We of this 14th century bring our offerings due,
   And lay them at the Nation's feet.
   Offerings of learning – of liberty of thought and action, and of travel.
   Great is this England, and still greater year by year.
   Yet live we in the promise of mightier days and fuller powers.
   God grant it.

Edward V

England of the Middle Ages

Enter –
   STANDARD BEARER.
   EDWARD V.
   LITTLE DUKE OF YORK.
   QUEEN MOTHER (ELIZABETH WOODVILLE).
   RICHARD CROOKBACK.

BRACKENBURY, Governor of the Tower, with keys.
CAXTON, the Master Printer.

FATHER TIME *speaks* –
   Thou child of troubled face and wrinkled brow,
   Full short the part that thou dost play.
   Yet what the future held no man can tell.
   Step forth, and let us hear thy message.

EDWARD V (*the child King, and his brother, clad, as in the famous picture, in black velvet with garter, steps forth, and speaking sadly, says*) –

   Naught but my youth have I to offer.
   A boy king, loving my people, with my life to live.
   I would fain give my tale of years to service for my country,
   And to the past have added yet a mighty gift.
   But strong walls do entomb me, and prisoners are we in this free land.

Queen Elizabeth

England of the new learning

Enter –
   STANDARD BEARER.
   QUEEN ELIZABETH.
   WILLIAM SHAKESPEARE.
   SIR WALTER RALEIGH.
   SIR FRANCIS DRAKE.
   SIR PHILIP SIDNEY.
   SIR THOMAS POPE.

FATHER TIME *speaks* –
   There stands Queen Bess, the mightiest of monarchs.
   Come, lady, forth.

QUEEN ELIZABETH *speaks* –
   Forsooth, make way,
   No candles for our guidance, thank ye, but plain words.
   Sail East, sail West, take compass, book, and charter,
   And plant our flag in other lands.
   At home make wide the path of knowledge till all walk therein.
   Dance, laugh, and sing, be merry and rejoice;
   Peace, and let England merry be in deed and truth,
   The spacious land where all are free.

Charles I

England under the Puritans

Enter –
>STANDARD BEARER.
>CHARLES I.
>LORD STRAFFORD.
>PURITAN FATHERS, with model of "Mayflower."
>CROMWELL.
>JOHN MILTON, carrying "Paradise Lost."
>JOHN BUNYAN, carrying "Pilgrim's Progress."

FATHER TIME *speaks* –
>And yonder cometh Charles the Stuart.
>Yet pause, that he may speak and make his link
>In this great tale we now unfold.

CHARLES I *speaks* –
>Fair is my country; yet the stir of discord and of fighting fills the land.
>I fear me, 'tis my crown, my life they seek.
>So be it. I lay my life, myself, as offering at my country's feet.

George III

England militant

Enter –
>STANDARD BEARER.
>GEORGE III.
>NELSON.
>GEORGE WASHINGTON and Cherry Tree.
>SIR RICHARD ARKWRIGHT (Spinning Frame).
>SAMUEL JOHNSON (Literature).
>SIR JOSHUA REYNOLDS (Art).

FATHER TIME *speaks* –
>The time speeds on, the present draweth nigh.
>I see before me visions of brave deeds of mighty progress.
>King George III, step forward bravely, and thy tale unfold.

GEORGE III *speaks* –
>And now the picture widens.
>Nelson, and truth, and bravery, and courage

March hand in hand to certain victory.
Old England changes, adding glory to past glories,
And long years bring we as of offerings meet.

Queen Victoria

England of commerce and science

Enter –
  STANDARD BEARER.
  QUEEN VICTORIA.
  STEPHENSON, carrying Steam Engine.
  DARWIN and an Ape.
  LIVINGSTONE, the Explorer.
  ROWLAND HILL (Penny Postage).
  JOHN RENNIE, carrying model of London Bridge.

FATHER TIME *speaks –*
  No words of mine are wanted.
  O maiden Queen, come forth, that all may do thee honour.
  Victoria the Good!

QUEEN VICTORIA *speaks –*
  Peace to my people,
  Life to the arts, the sciences, the wealth of England.
  Forward the learning and the arts,
  And ever may the flag protect us far and near.

The daughter nations

Enter –
  INDIA –
  STANDARD BEARER, bearing Flag with Elephant, and INDIAN, carrying spices, tea, and coffee.
  CANADA –
  STANDARD BEARER (Beaver on Flag) and CANADIAN carrying corn.
  AUSTRALIA –
  STANDARD BEARER (Kangaroo on Flag) and AUSTRALIAN carrying fruit.
  NEW ZEALAND –
  STANDARD BEARER (Sheep on Flag) and COLONIST carrying wool.
  SOUTH AFRICA –
  STANDARD BEARER (Ostrich on Flag) and KAFFIR carrying gold, diamonds, etc.

THE DAUGHTER NATIONS, in unison, uplifting their standards –
   Recitative – Distant lands salute thee, great Britannia;
   Bring their tributes – bow the knee.
   Rule us wisely, and for ever
   Loyal subjects will we be.

The Twentieth Century Child –
   The gifts I bring thee are but small,
   And I come hindermost of all.
   Child of the Empire, grant to me
   All my life through to work for thee.
               (*Offers a ball.*)

BRITANNIA –
   Hear ye, good people, links with all the ages!
   Take ye my thanks, across the whirl of time.
   Rich the inheritance – great the varied stages
   By which ye brought this nation to its prime.
   Prize ye the history linking Past and Present;
   Value the bond which binds us each to each;
   Grant that the chain between us ne'er be lessened,
   Nor dimmed the glory which the Past doth teach.
   Rather let one and all link hands in token,
   In pledge that History's tale be understood.
   Past, Present, Future, all in thee unshaken,
   Linked in one vast, great, living brotherhood.

The Prolocutor *speaks, linking Parts I and II.*
   Farewell! the centuries so closely woven
   With all the rich great history to be –
   Remember now the ages long forgotten,
   And in this Masque the truth of History see.
   Learn that in Unity lies perfect progress,
   Above the Past, above the Present, too,
   Aye – and above the Future of our Empire
   The Flag of Unity flies high and true.
   Till o'er the great wide world the message thrilling
   May through the centuries its burden ring –
   From hearts of women, men, and little children
   The heartfelt, earnest prayer – GOD SAVE THE KING.

At the words "God Save the King" the whole of the Centuries salute Britannia, who then passes slowly to end of hall or stage, followed by the kings, standard bearers, and representatives of the centuries, the procession beginning with Victoria and ending with Albert the Great. Slow, impressive music will be found very effective for this part of the Masque, or, if preferred, the children could take up their positions to the music of a march.

41

'THE UNION JACK', IN *THE TEACHER'S TREASURY* (LONDON: HOME LIBRARY BOOK CO., VOL. 2, 1926), PP. 49–62.

These documents show the ways in which amateur dramatics (masques) and dance could be utilised in the context of popular culture and Empire. Dances and plays could contain a strong imperial message, and dance was also seen as a form of physical exercise. Cecil Sharp (1859–1924) founded the English Folk Dance Society in 1911. It built on the work of the Folk Song Society that had been established in 1898. Members of this society included Ralph Vaughan Williams, Percy Grainger and George Butterworth. Sharp made endless bicycle trips through the English countryside, gathering songs and dances in his notebooks, and also travelled overseas to the USA, to gather folk dances that had been taken to the New World by English settlers. Grace Kimmins (1871–1954) was known for her work in London settlements and her work with children who had disabilities. The Bermonsdsey settlement was particularly interested in the question of children's play. Kimmins established the Guild of Play in 1895 to provide 'vigorous happy dances for recreative purposes on educational lines'. Enid Blyton (1897–1968), a qualified teacher, authored the play for children titled The Union Jack *and it appeared in one of her early works, the three-volume* Teacher's Treasury, *published in the mid-1920s. The* Union Jack *introduces figures such as James Wolfe, Lord Clive of India, David Livingstone and Cecil Rhodes, who are depicted as 'men who made the Empire great'.*

Scene. – Two children are sitting at desks or a small table in centre of stage. At back is a curtain or screen, behind which is a big chair raised and draped to represent a throne. School books are on the table, and the children are learning their lessons.

JACK. Australia, India, Canada, New Zealand, my goodness, what a lot of land belongs to our Empire!

MOLLIE. It says in my book that the sun never sets on the British Flag. Just fancy millions of Union Jacks waving in different winds all over the world!

JACK. It's a jolly fine flag, and a pretty one too. Look, here's one I bought yesterday to wave to-day. (*Pulls a Union Jack from his pocket.*)

MOLLIE. Jack, isn't it a funny flag. Three different crosses all put together. I'd like to know exactly how it came to be put together, and why it's called the Union *Jack*, and when it all happened and everything!

JACK. Oh, Mollie! Read your history and you'll know.
MOLLIE. Yes, but reading about it is different from really *knowing* about it. I'd like someone who's seen it all to tell me about it.
JACK. There isn't anyone who can do that. People don't live for hundreds of years, you silly!

> (*The curtain at the back is suddenly pulled, revealing Father Time sitting in the raised chair, holding a sickle. Mollie and Jack stare in amazement.*)

MOLLIE. Who are you?
FATHER TIME. I am someone who *has* lived for hundreds of years. I am Father Time! I have reaped with my sickle more years than anyone can guess! I have seen all the Kings and Queens of the world, the Emperors and the Saints, the Priests and the Peoples.
JACK. Then perhaps you know how the Union Jack was made and everything about it.
FATHER TIME. I do.
MOLLIE. Oh tell us, do tell us!
FATHER TIME. I will bring others here who will tell you better than I. They come from down the centuries, men and women of far-away days. Each had a share in the making of your flag. (*Claps once loudly.*)

> (*Steps heard outside. Enter St. George carrying a pole with his flag flying from the top. Salutes Father Time.*)

FATHER TIME. Show these children your flag and tell them who you are.
ST. GEORGE (*turning to children*). I am Saint George of England.
MOLLIE (*excited*). I knew you were. You killed a dragon, didn't you?
ST. GEORGE. I killed a far greater dragon than the stories say. I was a Christian soldier who tried to overcome the dragon of evil by the sword of good. This is my flag, the plain red cross on a white ground. I carried it into many a hard battle, and brought it through many conflicts unstained and honourable.
JACK. I wish I'd been with you, Saint George. I'd have helped you.
MOLLIE. So would I. We thought of you a lot yesterday, because it was Saint George's day. We flew your flag in the garden.
ST. GEORGE. I am proud to hear you say so. I am the Saint of Merry England, and my red cross is on her flag.
FATHER TIME. Stand back, Saint George, and make room for another.

> (*St. George stands back. Steps heard. Enter St. Andrew, bearing a pole with his flag, a white diagonal cross on a blue ground. He bows to Father Time, then faces children.*)

FATHER TIME. Do you know who this is, Jack?
JACK. Yes. Saint Andrew!

St. Andrew.   Saint Andrew for Scotland! And here on my flag is the cross I brought her.
Mollie.   Are you the Saint Andrew in the New Testament? Did you know Simon Peter?
St. Andrew.   He was my brother. Together we served the greatest Master in the world, Jesus Christ. When I was crucified for him, the white cross became my symbol, and is on my flag.
Jack.   It's on our flag too. Look!

>   (*Holds up his Union Jack, and points to white pieces on it.*)

St. Andrew.   I am proud to see it there.
Father Time.   Here is the third Saint. Make room, Saint Andrew.

>   (*St. Andrew stands on other side of Father Time, opposite St. George. Enter St. Patrick, bearing flag with a red diagonal cross on a white ground. He bows to Father Time.*)

Jack.   By your flag I can tell who you are!
Mollie.   So can I! You're Saint Patrick!
St. Patrick (*smiling*).   Yes, I am Patrick, the Patron Saint of Ireland.
Jack.   I've read all sorts of stories about you. How you were born in Scotland and went to Ireland –
Mollie.   And destroyed all the snakes there, and were loved by all the people.
St. Patrick.   My work was the same as Saint Andrew's. I lived to preach the good and the right.
Mollie.   You must have done it well, because there are scores of places in Ireland called after your name.
St. Patrick.   I loved the Irish and I was proud to give them my flag. Here it is, a diagonal red cross on a white ground. (*Shows it.*)
Jack.   It's on *our* flag too (*points to it on Union Jack*), and so is Saint George's and Saint Andrew's!
Father Time.   And now you know who gave you the crosses on your flag – Saint George, Saint Andrew, and Saint Patrick. Are you satisfied now?
Jack.   Not quite, Father Time.
Mollie.   We'd like to know how the three crosses became *one* flag, if you don't mind, and *how* it was decided.
Jack.   And *who* decided it and everything!
Father Time.   That can be told you. But this time you will not see Saints, but Kings and Queens and soldiers, in whose lives the flags were chosen and altered.
Mollie.   How lovely to see Kings and Queens!

>   (*Steps heard outside. Enter two soldiers wearing Crusader-uniforms of white surcoats embroidered with red cross of St. George. They salute Father Time and Saint George, then turn to face children.*)

JACK. What soldiers are you?
MOLLIE. And why do you wear the cross of Saint George?
1ST SOLDIER. We are Crusaders, who fought against the Turks centuries ago, to free the Christians from their cruelty.
2ND SOLDIER. We wear Saint George's cross because he came to us in a vision one night and urged us on to victory. He is the patron saint of soldiers!

(*Steps heard outside.*)

FATHER TIME. Stand back, Crusaders.

(*Crusaders stand aside. Enter two more soldiers and salute Father Time and St. George. They wear shorter coats than the Crusaders and have the red cross embroidered on them.*)

FATHER TIME. Well, soldiers, I have called you for a purpose! Tell these children the meaning of the cross on your uniforms.
1ST SOLDIER (*turning to children*). We are soldiers of the sixteenth century, and we wear these red crosses because in our time our Kings shouted "Saint George for England" when they rushed into battle!
2ND SOLDIER. And because the people of England so often saw the cross of Saint George on our uniforms, they began to take it as a symbol for their country.
1ST SOLDIER. They began to want the cross on their flag, so that other countries might know that good Saint George's cross stood for England!
JACK. Wasn't it on the English flag then?
2ND SOLDIER. No, only on our uniforms, until the year 1645, when soldiers wore red coats – look!

(*Enter two soldiers in red coats and salute.*)

JACK. Oh, the red cross has gone! What a pity.
1ST RED-COATED SOLDIER. *Not gone altogether, my boy.*
2ND SOLDIER. England was too fond of the red cross to let it go. She put it in her flag.
1ST SOLDIER. And there it is to this day!
MOLLIE. But who said it was to be put there?
FATHER TIME. We will see. I hear someone coming who will tell you that.

(*Soldiers stand back. Enter King James I. Bows to Father Time.*)

FATHER TIME. I have called you here to tell these children the part you took in founding the national flag of England.
KING JAMES (*turning to children*). I am pleased to tell you. What exactly would you like to know?
MOLLIE. Was it you who said the Saint George's cross was to be put in our flag?
KING JAMES. *I* first authorised its use, little girl, and I well remember the day. It was April 12th in the year 1606. I sent out a proclamation to say that the English flag from that day was to be the flag of Saint George.

'THE UNION JACK'

MOLLIE. But how did it get the name of *Jack*? It seems so funny for a flag to have a man's name!

KING JAMES (*proudly*). It was I who gave it that name too. I always used to sign my name as Jacques, and so the flag was called Jack too!

JACK. We still call it the Union *Jack*, all these years afterwards.

KING JAMES (*displaying St. George's flag*). But my flag is very different from yours.

JACK. Weren't you King of Scotland as well as of England?

KING JAMES. Yes. I was the first King to be ruler of both countries – but in my time they still had separate flags.

MOLLIE (*to Father Time*). Who began to put the flags together, Father Time?

FATHER TIME. Our next visitor will tell you.

(*King James stands back, and Queen Anne enters and curtseys to Father Time. She carries the flag of 1707, i.e. a flag comprising St. George's cross and St. Andrew's, with a ground of blue.*)

MOLLIE. Oh, are you a Queen? I've never seen one before!

QUEEN ANNE. I am Queen Anne. What do you want of me?

JACK. What is that flag you hold in your hand?

QUEEN ANNE. The flag showing the Union between two great countries, England and Scotland. For many, many years they had been enemies, but ever since the Scottish King James had come to the English throne, wise men hoped that the two countries would be joined.

MOLLIE. And when you came to the throne, did you join up the two flags?

QUEEN ANNE. No, not until the year 1707, the middle of my reign. Then, on a royal proclamation, the English flag of St. George was changed to the flag I am holding. Here it is, with the cross of St. Andrew behind the cross of St. George! (*Points to each on her flag.*)

JACK. What a funny flag! It looks sort of unfinished!

FATHER TIME. Well, now you shall see it finished!

(*Enter King George III, bearing with him the Union Jack proper. Bows to Father Time and turns to children.*)

MOLLIE. Oh, there's the proper Union Jack!

JACK (*to Father Time*). Who is this who is carrying it, Father Time?

GEORGE III. I am King George III of England. In my reign Ireland became joined to England, and so her cross of St. Patrick was put into the English flag too. (*Points to it in Union Jack.*)

MOLLIE. Was that very long ago?

KING GEORGE. It was in the year 1801, and ever since then your flag has remained the same.

JACK. There's not room for any more crosses on it, so perhaps it always will remain the same!

FATHER TIME. Now you have seen all you asked me to show you. Is there anything more you want to know about the flag of your country?

JACK. I suppose we couldn't talk to the men who made it the flag of other countries too? It says in my history book that the sun never sets on the Union Jack, so it must have been taken all over the world!

FATHER TIME. You shall see those who took it and planted it in far-away lands.

(*Enter James Wolfe, salutes Father Time and salutes the flag held by Queen Anne.*)

JACK. Who are you, and why do you salute that flag instead of this one? (*Points to Union Jack.*)

J. WOLFE. I am James Wolfe, young sir, and I salute this flag because it is *my* flag. That is the flag I fought under in Quebec, when I won Canada for England.

MOLLIE. Oh, are you really James Wolfe? I've read all about how you fought the French and won Canada from them.

(*Footsteps heard. Wolfe stands back.*)

JACK. Who's this, I wonder?

(*Enter Clive and salutes same flag as Wolfe. Salutes Father Time also.*)

MOLLIE. Oh, are you Lord Clive, who won the battle of Plassy?

CLIVE. I am, and that (*pointing*) is the flag I fought for.

JACK. Did you plant it in India for us?

CLIVE. Yes, with the help of my men, I saved India for the British Empire, so that now her flag waves proudly over it.

(*Stands back. Enter Captain Cook, salutes same flag, and Father Time.*)

JACK. What country did *he* get for us, Father Time?

C. COOK. A great country, my boy. I am Captain Cook, and I took that flag to Australia and to New Zealand, and there it flies to this day! It was a glorious day when I first flew it there!

JACK. All these explorers seem to have used the unfinished Union Jack, Father Time! Aren't there any that planted the Union Jack that *we* know in the countries they discovered?

FATHER TIME. We shall see.

(*Enter Livingstone and Rhodes. Salute the Union Jack proper, and also Father Time.*)

FATHER TIME. Here are two men who know *your* flag, Jack!

MOLLIE. Who are they?

CECIL RHODES. I am Cecil Rhodes, and I put the Union Jack in Rhodesia, a great tract of Africa.

LIVINGSTONE. And I am David Livingstone, who worked for God and England in Africa, and now our flag flies where I worked!

'THE UNION JACK'

JACK.   What a glorious story our Union Jack has behind it!

FATHER TIME.   And it will make even more glorious stories for itself, if you boys and girls grow up to love it and guard it! Make it stand for justice and liberty all the world over, and the Union Jack will never be lowered!

MOLLIE AND JACK (*together*).   Father Time, we will!

> (*Queen Anne gives her flag to Father Time and he holds it. Explorers, Saints, Kings, and Soldiers are grouped round him. Jack and Mollie stand one at each side of him.*)

FATHER TIME.   Now let us sing the song of the Union Jack, and then we must say good-bye!

SONG

(*Either sung or recited by all*)

> Now let us all salute the flag
> On which are countries three,
> The flag of Britons, great and small
> That waves on land and sea.
> And let us bring to mind the men
> Who helped our flag to make,
> The saints and soldiers and the Kings
> Who fought for England's sake.

Chorus.
> May the flag for ever fly,
> In honour far and wide.
> And be for ever down the years,
> Our nation's love and pride.

> On this our Empire Day we'll sing
> Of deeds of long ago,
> And praise the men who helped to make
> The flag we're proud to know.
> The men who left their homes behind
> And far from England sailed,
> The men who bravely fought and won,
> The men who fought and failed.

Chorus.
> May the flag for ever fly, *etc*.
> May Britain always proudly keep
> Her good and mighty name,

And loyal may her Empire be
And one with her in fame.
For loyal daughters, sturdy sons
May Britain never lack,
And proudly down the future, fly
The glorious Union Jack.

Chorus.
    May the flag for ever fly, *etc.*

CURTAIN

Note. – This song can be sung, with a little adaptation, to the tune of "The British Grenadiers."

42

THE BRITISH EMPIRE LEAGUE
Meeting in Leamington

From: 'The British Empire League', in *Leamington Spa Courier*, 6th June 1896, p. 6.

These reports, taken from the contemporary newspapers, show the imperial loyalty leagues 'in action'. The British Empire League was founded in 1895 and was, in effect, a replacement for the Imperial Federation League, which had dissolved in 1893. It took a role in organising the imperial conferences of 1897, 1902, 1907 and 1911, and lobbied for the introduction of an imperial 'penny post'. Another aspect of its work was to organise imperial exhibitions. Imperial statues were unveiled as a result of its work and the British Empire Club opened in St. James Square in 1910. The League of Empire (LOE) focused on education and staged ten imperial education conferences in 1907 in London. Out of these conferences emerged the Imperial Union of Teachers in 1913. A number of textbooks were overseen by the LOE. A. F. Pollard's book The British Empire: Its Past, Its Present, and Its Future *was one of the first to be published. The LOE also had its own publication, called the* Federal. *Lord Meath was one of the LOE's vice presidents. The Victoria League, founded in 1901, was an organisation which included more women. Its emphasis was on producing hospitality, friendship and education through and about the Empire. It established branches across the Dominions and set itself the task of providing information about them. Libraires were established in New Zealand, Australia, South Africa and Canada. Correspondence schemes were established, and it also opened the Ladies Empire Club in Grosvenor Street. After the South African War, it tended war graves, and in the 1920s it began to host overseas students.*

Under the auspices of the British Empire League a meeting was held in the Mayor's Parlour of the Town Hall, Leamington, on Thursday afternoon, for the purpose of hearing an address from Mr F. Faithfull Begg, M.P., a member of the executive of the League, on the importance of securing the permanent unity of the Empire. The League is the outcome of a conference held on July 20, 1894, when it was unanimously resolved to establish an association with the object of maintaining and strengthening the connection between the United Kingdom and the outlying portions of the Empire, by the discussion and promotion of questions of common interest, more particularly those relating to trade arrangements and mutual defence. – The Mayor (Alderman Dr. T. W. Thursfield) presided, and among those present were Mr Freeman Murray (secretary), Councillor Heath Stubbs, Misses

Stubbs, Dr. Otho Wyer, Mr R. P. Yates, C.C., Mr F. Glover, Councillor Overell, Dr. Douglas, and Councillor Richards.

The MAYOR, in opening the proceedings, said they were met there that day – in very small numbers, it was true, because that was merely a preliminary meeting – to consider the claims of the British Empire League, and they had the great advantage of Mr Faithfull Begg, who had come down to explain the matter more particularly to them. He took it that the League had for its purpose – irrespective of politics of any degree – the desire to bring under the notice of all patriotic Englishmen the necessity of drawing closer together, not only for the purposes of defence, but also for the purpose of developing and holding that which the bravery and wisdom of our forefathers had bequeathed into our hands. One of our very greatest poets had said

> Who knows ought of England
> Who only England knows?

and there was no more pregnant sentence than this. The British Empire did not consist of the forty millions of people who lived within the two or three islands which constituted the British islands, but it consisted of hundreds of millions of people, amounting, he believed, to something like four hundred millions of people scattered over the vantage spots of the earth. Over the temperate regions of the globe whereever we found them we should find British colonies and British stations; and there the industry, the patriotism, and the energy which had carried our country to those regions and had sufficed to develop one of the noblest empires the world had ever seen, not bound together by a miserable system of universal military service, but by the silken cords of commerce, consanguinity, and community of language. All thinking men had observed this was not quite sufficiently strong a bond to hold it together in the face of our numerous enemies, and quite recently we had had loudly expressed threats towards us. When this was the case all Englishmen might join together and unite, irrespective of what their politics were. What we wanted to do was to bind together this noble inheritance, and he was sure Mr Begg would give them an interesting account of how it was best to be done, and how the present leaders of the League believed it could be done. He only hoped this might be the commencement of a condition of things which would spread all through the British Islands, and that we might find in the future our inheritance would be more firmly held and more closely nipped together, and foreign nations, who were jealous of our progress, would then think twice before they dared to attack us. He commended the League to all patriotic Englishmen from the bottom of his heart. (Applause.)

Mr FAITHFULL BEGG, M.P., said the Mayor, in his opening remarks, had correctly explained the object of the present meeting. It was a preliminary meeting with the view to interesting the people of Leamington in the work of the British Empire League. That League, although in one sense a new organisation, was really the outcome and the following up of a movement which had been going on in this country now for a great many years. The British Empire League was the lineal descendant of the old Imperial Federation League, and hoped to carry on and extend the work which the latter carried on so successfully in this country for so many years. It might be asked why it was necessary to make any alteration in the constitution of the body which preceded the British Empire League? Well, from his own point of view, he could answer that in a sentence. The old League did an immense amount of good work, but, with all deference, he would say that it took rather a narrow view of the great subject it had been constituted to discuss and promote. It practically decided, in its later stages, to confine its operations, almost entirely, to the consideration of the question of Imperial defence. It was undoubtedly a question of enormous importance, but everything which had happened recently had gone unquestionably to show that they could not separate from the question of Imperial defence that of Imperial trade, the latter being the subject for which the former existed. He thought, therefore, the present was the most comprehensive view of the subject, and that the British Empire League was in a position to more fully realise the hopes and wishes of those who believed in the permanent unity of the British Empire than its predecessor, holding the views it did, could possible be. Although at the time he regretted the dissolution of the old League, he thought he had already come to see that the advantage which had followed had not been little, but, on the contrary, be believed in the new boby which had now been formed, they had an institution capable of carrying out, in the fullest possible manner, all that was necessary to be done in order to bring constantly and persistently before the minds of the British people what was involved in that great question. Passing on to speak of the interdependence of the various parts of the Empire and their common interests, he said that unless the people were willing to come down from the position of a first-rate power to that of a second, third, or even fourth-rate State, it was impossible for the United Kingdom to contemplate a severance between itself and its dependencies. Although they must preserve a united front agains, foreign aggression, there was absolutely no necessity for their going further than the question of defence. In other words, he was perfectly satisfied that no member of the League would propose that anything like foreign aggression should be part of its policy or anything in the nature of defiance of foreign nations. The old motto of "Defence not Defiance" might be taken as the basis of any question in this country in regard to the augmentation of our fleet or the strengthening of our communications. In regard to this question of Imperial Federation, the Canada Club was a sufficient reflex of the general tendency and tone of the Canadian nation as existing among Canadians residing in London. At a recent meeting Mr Chamberlain made a most remarkable speech, in which he devoted himself to the consideration of the very problem they were discussing that afternoon. The right hon. gentleman laid it down as a first principle that the question of trade, the establishment of a zollverein, must precede any question of wider, and in one sense more important, question of how we were to provide from a mutual source for mutual defence. There was also present, no doubt, in Mr Chamberlain's mind that we had had a rude shock lately, a species of awakening in connection with Imperial policy, in which we had found that this country stood open to attack in so many parts of the worid, that we had at the moment almost no allies, but, on the contrary, that there were many who would be ready to pull us down from the position we had attained. Although we were now in quieter waters, he (Mr Faithfull Begg) was not aware that any one of these problems had been solved, although it was satisfactory to hope they were on the way to a solution. He thought, that during the recent threatenings, the country did consider the position of affairs, and rose to the occasion and showed that under no consideration would they allow their interests to be tampered with in any part of the world whatever. (Applause.) The policy of the League were to abstain, in the first place, from embarking upon political controversy in any shape or form; in the second place they also abstained from adopting extreme views of fiscal or financial policy. The object was to promote discussion throughout the country. In conclusion, he hoped they would not only join the League, but do all they could to further the object of it by getting a large membership for it in the important town of Leamington. (Applause.)

The MAYOR proposed "That this meeting approves of the object of the League, and hereby decides to establish a local committee, to be called the Leamington Committee."

Dr. DOUGLAS seconded, remarking that as an old Federation League member, he felt it was incumbent upon him to join the new League. He hoped the members of the institution would see their way to impress upon Government the necessity of teaching to the children attending our schools something of the great duties and liabilities of citizenship.

The motion was carried.

Mr FRANK GLOVER moved that the following should form the local committee: – The Mayor, Dr. Douglas (hon. sec. *pro. tem.*), Councillors Heath-Stubbs, Molesworth, Richards, and Overell, Mr H. Field, Mr M. P. Lucas, the Rev. Dr. Nicholson, Mr Gordon Bland, Mr F. Glover, Dr. Otho Wyer, and Mr R. P. Yates. In regard to the subject of schools, a small book by Mr H. Arnold Foster – "The Citizen Reader" – had come to his hands, written with the special object of teaching these Imperial matters, and if copies of this could be placed in the hands of teachers in Board Schools and other educational centres, very much good might be done.

Mr YATES seconded, and observed that, as far as his experience went, all our colonies were anxious to join in some system of Federation.

The motion was carried.

The MAYOR, in moving a vote of thanks to Mr Faithfull Begg, said that in every national school in France the ensign was displayed, and in the United States the same custom was in vogue, the children being drilled and made to salute the national flag. He did not see why that should not be carried out in this country, and he suggested that the Leamington School Board should adopt some such custom.

Councillor HEATH STUBBS seconded, and it was carried, Mr FAITHFULL BEGG responding.

A vote of thanks to the Mayor, proposed by Mr BEGG, and seconded by Mr FREEMAN MURRAY, closed the proceedings.

43

'THE LEAGUE OF EMPIRE', IN *THE GAZETTE*, 2ND DECEMBER 1905, P. 5.

These reports, taken from the contemporary newspapers, show the imperial loyalty leagues 'in action'. The British Empire League was founded in 1895 and was, in effect, a replacement for the Imperial Federation League, which had dissolved in 1893. It took a role in organising the imperial conferences of 1897, 1902, 1907 and 1911, and lobbied for the introduction of an imperial 'penny post'. Another aspect of its work was to organise imperial exhibitions. Imperial statues were unveiled as a result of its work and the British Empire Club opened in St. James Square in 1910. The League of Empire (LOE) focused on education and staged ten imperial education conferences in 1907 in London. Out of these conferences emerged the Imperial Union of Teachers in 1913. A number of textbooks were overseen by the LOE. A. F. Pollard's' book The British Empire: Its Past, Its Present, and Its Future *was one of the first to be published. The LOE also had its own publication, called the Federal. Lord Meath was one of the LOE's vice presidents. The Victoria League, founded in 1901, was an organisation which included more women. Its emphasis was on producing hospitality, friendship and education through and about the Empire. It established branches across the Dominions and set itself the task of providing information about them. Libraires were established in New Zealand, Australia, South Africa and Canada. Correspondence schemes were established, and it also opened the Ladies Empire Club in Grosvenor Street. After the South African War, it tended war graves, and in the 1920s it began to host overseas students.*

The League of Empire

The subjoined letter is one a number received by the head master of St. Ann's School, Hanwell, from Bengal through the instrumentality of the League of Empire. We understand the St. Ann's School children are also in correspondence with schools in the West Indies and Canada. The children manifest great interest in this new departure. The work can be done at home or in school as a lesson in composition. The schoolmaster does not suggest the topic for the letter, but, of course, takes advantage of the errors, if any, to offer useful hints. The letters are sent off as originally drafted by the scholars themselves.

Farm House, Kalimpong, Bengal, Oct. 20th, 1905.

Dear Friend, – I am very pleased to tell you that we have joined the League of Empire. I think it will be a great help in our correspondence, and hope to receive nice interesting letters from you. I am living in the St. Andrew's Colonial Homes in Kalimpong, a small district in British Bhutan. It is 26 miles east of the town of Darjeeling, and 36 miles north of the nearest railway station, – its name is

Silliguri. The climate of Kalimpong is mild and very healthy; we are away up in the country 4,500 ft. above sea level, and about two days' journey from Calcutta. We have no railway nearer than Silliguri, except the little toy railway as it is named because it is so small, which leads a little to the west. The scenery and surroundings are very picturesque, and very pleasant to the eye. There is a big bill towering above us, then smaller hills and fertile valleys with miniature rivers flowing through them. I will now tell you a little about our Homes. The land is about 400 acres. We have a farm where six boys are learning to be farmers. They have enough cattle to supply our cottages with milk and also beef; then there are horses, pigs, goats, sheep and poultry. There are carpentering works in which I am a full-timer; we make a lot of furniture, but are learning other useful things. There are seven cottages, three for girls, and four for boys (twenty-six in each). I belong to I Company, Bengal Cadets, and am a Corporal of No. 4 Section, which is composed of the Farm House Boys. We have drill in full uniform every other Saturday, and physical drill once a month. Our recreation consists of football and cricket, and the girls play hockey. We saw the British and Goorka troops returning from the Thibetan expedition. The poor men must have endured great hardships, as they looked rather worn out. They had with them a wild ass which they had captured, also some Yak cows with their calves; these animals have very long hair which protects them from the cold. The troops had two Maxim guns with them, which they used with acme effect amongst the poor Thibetans. There is a huge market or Indian bazaar in Kalimpong, it is generally crowded on Wednesdays and Saturdays, which are market days. There are many different tribes, and I will mention some. There are Bhutias, Nepaulese, Sepchees, Chinamen and some of the natives of the plains, such as merchants, who supply the stores for our homes. There are very few European people, and these are missionaries of the Church of Scotland. There is also s District Judge and an engineer. An Indian fair is held in Kalimpong, which is called a Mela; it is very interesting to watch all the different grades of cattle and ponies. The natives here are very fond of European games and delight in football. We have no wild animals except leopards – which now and then carry away a goat, sheep. or pig, but are very timid of man. Before I close I will tell you a little of myself. I was born in Bangalore in the South of India in the year 1899. I have been almost through the whole of India. I stayed in Allahabad for five years, where I spent some of my happiest days. I was also in Madras for five years. Madras is a very nice place, but it is too hot in the hot season. The sea is about two miles from the town. I used to love to have a moonlight party on the sands and to go for a good swim. At Madras they had a small menagerie which contained six Royal Bengal tigers, a lion and a lioness, a rhinoceros, and many different kinds of animals and birds. In Calcutta, where I lived a few months, is a much larger Zoo. I have exhausted my news, and close now, but hope to receive a long letter from you in a few weeks. – I am, yours sincerely,

PERCY DAVIS.

44

LORD BALFOUR AND THE VICTORIA LEAGUE

Closer union of British subjects

From: 'The Victoria League', in *The Scotsman*, 1st July 1922, p. 9.

These reports, taken from the contemporary newspapers, show the imperial loyalty leagues 'in action'. The British Empire League was founded in 1895 and was, in effect, a replacement for the Imperial Federation League, which had dissolved in 1893. It took a role in organising the imperial conferences of 1897, 1902, 1907 and 1911, and lobbied for the introduction of an imperial 'penny post'. Another aspect of its work was to organise imperial exhibitions. Imperial statues were unveiled as a result of its work and the British Empire Club opened in St. James Square in 1910. The League of Empire (LOE) focused on education and staged ten imperial education conferences in 1907 in London. Out of these conferences emerged the Imperial Union of Teachers in 1913. A number of textbooks were overseen by the LOE. A. F. Pollard's book The British Empire: Its Past, Its Present, and Its Future *was one of the first to be published. The LOE also had its own publication, called the Federal. Lord Meath was one of the LOE's vice presidents. The Victoria League, founded in 1901, was an organisation which included more women. Its emphasis was on producing hospitality, friendship and education through and about the Empire. It established branches across the Dominions and set itself the task of providing information about them. Libraires were established in New Zealand, Australia, South Africa and Canada. Correspondence schemes were established, and it also opened the Ladies Empire Club in Grosvenor Street. After the South African War, it tended war graves, and in the 1920s it began to host overseas students.*

A LARGE and distinguished gathering assembled under the auspices of the Victoria League at the London Guildhall yesterday afternoon. The Lord Mayor was chairman, and among those supporting him were the Dowager Countess of Jersey (president of the Victoria League), the Earl of Balfour, Sir Joseph Cook (High Commissioner for Australia), and Mr W. Ormsby-Gore, M.P.

The Lord Mayor recalled that it was just twenty-one years since the Victoria League was formed. It was founded on the death of Queen Victoria – in her memory and in her name. Its object was the promotion of closer union between British subjects living in different parts of the world.

The Earl of Balfour proposed a resolution – "That in the opinion of this meeting, the practical and non-party work of the Victoria League for the Empire deserves the heartiest support of all British people." He said the Victoria League was totally free from that tinge of controversy which followed all work in countries where freedom of discussion was the rule. What was the inherent difficulty or problem of the British Empire? The problem which had assailed many countries they did not suffer from. There was no difference of opinion between them and the great self-governing Dominions which were the backbone, the essential element in "this brotherhood of co-operating States." That was not our difficulty. Our difficulty was neither moral nor legal; it arose from no collision of interests from no differences of language or laws. It arose largely – almost entirely he ventured to say – from physical conditions. Compare our special problem with that of the United States. The United States began with the thirteen colonies along the eastern seaboard of the great Continent of North America, and gradually they spread westward, and in that process of colonisation the same kind of hardships assailed the emigrants from the East. In fact, they were much greater than the difficulties which in these modern days assailed the emigrants sailing from these shores.

America's advantage over Britain

"But they had one great advantage over us," the Earl of Balfour proceeded, "due to geographical situation. Those who gradually settled the land were bound to each other by means of communication – by a train of settlers, so that when the furthest and remotest parts of the Continent were settled there was one nation of which all the members were in direct physical, as it were, and material connection by land with all the others.

"How different and how much harder is the destiny that we have to accomplish, the problem we have to solve. We are separated from the nearest of the great Dominions by the whole width of the stormy Atlantic; and as for Australia and New Zealand they are, as we all know, at the very Antipodes, the parts of the earth most distant from the Motherland, that central community from which they issue, whose laws and institutions they have carried to the uttermost parts of the world. In these circumstances it is quite inevitable that, human nature being what it is, the communities that we have planted or that they have planted themselves, put it as you like, those remote regions should have as their main preoccupation the immediate pressure of the necessity of concentrating their attention upon their local problems, upon their local difficulties, upon the development of uninhabited or, at all events, uncivilised land of a community as free, as cultured as that from which they sprang. That is a preoccupation which may well absorb all the attention of these fellow-citizens of ours. And yet if either they or we allow ourselves, under pressure of our own local difficulties and problems, to forget our common origin, allow ourselves to be cold or even lukewarm in our Imperial patriotism, then this great experiment of the British Empire, new as it is in the whole history of the world, is doomed either to failure or to the most qualified of successes. It can only be what providence intended it to be. In addition to all these local patriotisms, however warm they be, we always add as the background of our political and national thought the notion that we are common members of a common family.

Problem can be solved

"I do not suppose that the problem is easy of solution," the Earl of Balfour went on. "It is not easy, but it can be solved, and I boldly maintain that the kind of work this League has done and is doing is this kind of work which is eminently calculated to further the great object which I have described."

Outlining the work of the League, the Earl of Balfour said that it was a great aid to preserving that community of spirit which was the essential background of any true Imperial patriotism. It was not merely the outgoing emigrant whose path they desired to smooth, whose passage from the old country to the new they desired to make easy, whose introduction to a new life they aimed at facilitating; they also had to think of those who came from distant countries and visited again the Motherland. (Cheers.)

The Earl of Balfour pointed out that as the result of the exertions and labours of the League the whole life of the Empire was affected. He wished, as a result of their labours, that no man henceforth coming to these shores from the Dominions in the right spirit should feel himself a stranger in his father's house, and that all those who left these shores to carry on civilisation in the remote regions should feel that in those remote regions they had friends.

The work of the Victoria League was summarised by the Dowager-Countess of Jersey, who mentioned that 10,000 English wives of Australian soldiers had gone to Australia, and a great many of those were welcomed by members of the League. She also said she was told 36,000 English women went to Canada (Applause.) Children in England were put into communication with children overseas, and since the war there had been 15,000 fresh links created in this way. (Applause.)

Sir Joseph Cook, in seconding the resolution proposed by the Earl of Balfour, humourously suggested that the reason so many Englishwomen had become the wives of Australians was because the "diggers" knew a good thing when they saw it. (Laughter and applause.)

The resolution was carried unanimously.

45

THE TEACHING OF GEOGRAPHY FROM AN IMPERIAL POINT OF VIEW, AND THE USE WHICH COULD AND SHOULD BE MADE OF VISUAL INSTRUCTION.[1]

From: H. J. Mackinder, 'The Teaching of Geography from an Imperial Point of View and the Use Which Could and Should be Made of Visual Instruction', in *The Geographical Teacher*, Vol. 6, No. 2 (1911), pp. 79–86.

The Colonial Office also engaged in an imperial education project. At the time of the accession to the throne of Edward VII, it established the Visual Instruction Committee at the suggestion of Michael Sadler, Director of Special Enquiries at the Board of Education. Lectures and lantern slides were to be provided for use in schools. One of the individuals who was co-opted in this project was Sir Halford Mackinder, who was, at the time of writing, director of the London School of Economics (1903–1908) and MP for Glasgow Camlachie. He was a founder of geopolitics and a pro-imperialist who became a staunch anti-communist during the First World War. As a member of the Visual instruction Committee of the Colonial Office, he wrote the paper included here. It is noted by imperial historians that the Committee for Visual Instruction was one of the only government-sponsored Empire propaganda initiatives, and it was not a huge success, as it garnered no financial support and its methods soon became outdated. Mackinder was also chairman of the Imperial Shipping Committee and Imperial Economic Committee. Another of his articles was published in the National and English Review *in 1905, titled 'Man-Power as a Measure of National and Imperial Strength'.*

I VENTURE to hope that the subject which I have been asked to present to you this afternoon may have a double interest. I desire to approach you in the first place as educational experts, and to ask your attention for a special mode of teaching, and in the second place as Imperial representatives, and to suggest to you that the mode in question may have peculiar value in regard to the maintenance and progress of our Empire.

The phase of Imperial history upon which we have entered is concerned with the consolidation rather than the extension of the Empire, and I think it will be agreed that in this work of consolidation the part of the teacher must be as great as that of the statesman. New conditions prevail to-day in every part of the King's Dominions. In the Mother Country and in the Self-Governing Dominions beyond the seas we have to do with a league of democracies, which are becoming equal in status, although various in power. Under such conditions a certain unity of policy, without which the Empire will exist merely in name, is to be obtained only by the free consent of the several peoples. This consent, if it is to be relied upon, must be based on a reasonable agreement in regard to aims, and sympathy in regard to difficulties. The chief enemies of such agreement and sympathy are ignorance and local prejudice. These are the devils which it is the part of the teacher to exorcise.

Nor is it only in the Self-Governing Dominions that the Empire is to-day based on consent. Are we not entitled to say, in view of the small military force which we maintain, that our position in India is now due rather to the service which we render than to the fact of conquest? Moreover, with the progress of education is it not clear that the longer the British Raj lasts the stronger will become the new sense of Indian unity? For the peace and progress of India it is therefore necessary that there should be great classes among the Indian peoples who freely consent to the endurance of our rule, because they appreciate what India has gained from British justice, what to-day she obtains from the Empire in the way of peace, and how difficult and gradual must be her advance to fitness for self-government. So it happens that here in Britain in the way of democracy, and in India in the way of education, we have now advanced so far that safety is only to be found in stepping still further forward on to the sure ground of a widespread understanding and discretion. Need I add in this connection that in using the word 'Imperial' in the title of my address, I have had no thought of treating it as the equivalent of 'Imperialist.' My wish has been to indicate opposition on the one hand to a merely scientific, and on the other hand to a merely insular point of view. If education is to build up the Empire it must aim at supplying not merely knowledge but a motive, and that motive must spring from a wide, not a narrow, outlook.

It is necessary to my argument that, with your permission, I should devote a few moments to the significance of another of the words in my title. By geography I do not intend a knowledge of place names. I do not even mean a knowledge chiefly of facts. I refer rather to a special mode and habit of thought, to a special form of visualisation which I cannot otherwise describe than as 'thinking geographically.' The mind has an eye as well as an ear, and it is possible to train this eye by appropriate methods to as much accuracy and readiness of thought as may be imparted by the ordinary literary methods to the mind's ear. It is, of course, true that many people visualise literature, and *see* the printed page rather than *hear* the voice of the author. Such visualisation is, I venture to say, a perversion of literature, and a waste of the visualising power. The music of language was meant to be heard. The power of visualisation was meant for real things, rich in shape and colour, not for the combinations and permutations of the letters of the alphabet. Let our literary teaching appeal to the mind's ear, and our geographical and historical teaching to the mind's eye. As Thring of Uppingham had it, 'the true geographer thinks in shapes.' May I add, 'and the true historian in movements'?

Will you forgive me if for a moment more I dwell on this point, for it is essential to the object which I have in view. We have geographical thinking in its rudimentary form in the eye for the country which characterises the fox hunter and the soldier. But many a countryman and officer has the eye for a bit of solid country under his feet and within the circle of his horizon, without having the power of roaming at ease imaginatively over the vast surface of the globe. This is true even of many travelled men. How much more of the untravelled majority!

The real geographer prefers a map without names. He broods over it by the hour together, for it is rich in suggestion. He *sees* the world-drama as he reads his morning paper. He gesticulates unconsciously as he thinks. Within limits his wordless language has great resource, for whereas in ordinary talk we can make only one statement at a time, many thousand statements are made simultaneously in a map. The trained geographer, when he considers a fact, sees it on a background of kindred facts. In other words, he sees it in perspective of space, just as it is characteristic of the historian that he sees each occurrence in perspective of time.

These trained powers of outlook are close kin, are they not, to what we know as judgment in the ordinary affairs of the world? The sense of geographical and historical perspective goes far to make the statesman, whether in politics, or strategy, or commerce. I submit that the man who has once acquired the habit of geographical thinking approaches every problem of great affairs with the more surety and resourcefulness. His mind's eye sees beyond the horizon with the same accuracy and vividness with which the parochial eye sees within the horizon. He finds the same joy in the contoured map *without names* that a born and trained musician finds in the silent reading of a musical score. The index to his mental stores is geographical. He looks over his mind's map to recover a lost fact, for his habit of association is of ideas with places. To teach geography and history aright we must train the artistic eye to appreciate topographical forms, and the dramatic eye to people them afresh with past humanity. In a word, I plead for the cultivation in geography and history of that visualising power which in rudiment is natural to the child and the savage, but which tends to wither rather than to expand in the presence of the printed page and of the ribbons of landscape seen through the windows of a railway carriage.

Now, how do these ideas bear on the teaching of children? Everyone will remember the surprise with which a few years ago we realised the possibilities of what is known as brushwork for the artistic training of children. I believe that there lie similar possibilities for their general mental development in the realm of geography. The appeal to what I may describe as a concrete rather than an abstract philosophy is, in my experience, of absorbing interest to boys and girls of twelve years old. I have urged lately the possibilities of such teaching in some little books for children, and perhaps I can best and most quickly convey my idea by sketching the scheme which I have there drawn for a four years' course appropriate to children between the ages of nine and thirteen. The pupil is first incited to read, with mastery, the nameless map of the land-relief of Britain, building up mental pictures from it, and associating history with it. Then the lands immediately beyond the Channel are described in similar fashion, the essentials of European and Mediterranean history being revealed in the national contrasts of to-day. Then the outlook is broadened so as to include the world-wide stage of modern life, the climatic contrasts being pictured in the order of their discovery. Finally, with powers prepared and strengthened in the previous stages, the pupil is asked to visualise with a single grasp our whole world of varied scene and incessant change. Almost every problem of to-day is a whole-world problem, and the power of comprehensive outlook is of the first importance for the citizens of an empire. I believe that it is possible by right geographical teaching to send forth pupils, even from the primary school, with something of what used to be known as 'humane' culture in them. By training the power of visualisation I believe that we can at a relatively early age impart a sense of mental perspective which does not come by less concrete methods until later years – too late for the schooling of the majority. With the habit of distinguishing the significant from the insignificant, and with a chart in the mind upon which to enter new facts in due position, even the halfpenny newspaper may contribute to further education in after life.

At this stage I would ask you to consider two incidental points. In the first place you will have noticed that I have not hesitated to build history into my geography. If historical action is to be properly visualised it must obviously be upon a geographical stage. We frequently speak of a joint subject which we call History and Geography. I believe that we should rather teach Geography and History, and this not merely because the 'stage directions' must necessarily precede the successive acts of a drama, but also because for the vast majority of people the present must ever be more important than the past, and should therefore stand in the foreground. Unless, perhaps, in the case of the national epic, where the burnt cakes of Alfred and the disobedient waves of Canute have what I may describe as a saga value for the maintenance of the race, I believe that history should be taught to children incidentally to the existing facts of political geography. So shall we impart the historical sense in regard to the affairs of to-day, rather than a merely romantic interest in the past. Moreover, there is a practical reason in favour of this course. In these days, when international affairs have become worldwide, it is necessary that the great human contrasts which are the outcome of universal history should be generally known, and that – to take only a single category, by way of illustration – the distinction of Christian, Mohammedan, Hindu, and Buddhist should be generally realised in some degree of historical perspective. But within the limits of the Elementary School there is not time for another subject, especially for one so vast as World-history. Even the national epic of England begins to lose its simplicity and its dramatic force in the later stages, when the stories of Ireland, Scotland, Canada, India, and France must to some extent be grafted upon it. I speak after experiment when I express my conviction that it is possible to convey the essentials not only of geography, but also of universal history, by beginning our geographical teaching with the Homeland, there learning to read the geographical alphabet, and thence proceeding through the lands of the world in such order that the incidental history falls roughly into its chronological sequence. Thus I would describe the geography of Egypt first, and then in succession, let us say, Palestine, Greece, Rome, Constantinople, Mecca, Italy, the Oceanic Lands of Europe, the East Indies, the West Indies – as it were, a world-long Odyssey. In each case would be clearly visualised first the land-relief and the play of air and water upon it, then the living contrasts and the historical movements from which they have ensued. Even the national epic of Britain itself will be the more clearly and the more fruitfully realised if it is built up on a vivid mental picture of the British Isles. Let us mentally see rather than hear of the fertile lowland near the Continent, successively conquered by Roman, Saxon, and Norman, and then the hill countries of the oceanic border still peopled by the Gael and the Briton. Within the plain of England itself let us realise the contrast of town and country, London and the Shires, for English history down to the time of the Industrial Revolution was essentially the story of a single city and a single countryside.

My other incidental point regards the futility, as I think it, of prescribing for a subject of teaching or examination the geography of the British Empire. 'Little they know of England who only England know.' Still more truly may it be said, little they know of the British Empire who only the Empire know. England is surrounded by external powers of nature and man, but the British Empire is, as it were, threaded through the other powers as the weft through the woof of a cloth. In the poet's phrase the shuttles of the Empire's loom are driven through the neutral spaces of the ocean. The postal route from Calais to Brindisi, essential to the efficiency of the British Empire in modern peace time, is threaded through the Alpine tunnels. The significance of such a station as Hong Kong lies wholly in its relation to neighbouring China and to the eastern seaways. British trading communities and His Britannic Majesty's Consuls are in every land. For the practical purposes of the British citizen the Empire is an influence which pervades all lands and all the sea, though its radiating centres are in the regions coloured red on the map. The question is one of perspective. Let us first teach children to read the map and to think geographically, then let us regulate and broaden their imagination through wider and wider fields until at last they can grasp the globe in the background of a thought, and place a given detail in its world setting. The idea of a world-price for wheat may, for instance, call up a picture of the globe bearing its grain harvests in all their due positions and seasons. It is there in the mind, available for reference if necessary, and giving surety and richness of thought. But through all, let our teaching be from the British standpoint, so that finally we see the world as a theatre for British activity. This, no doubt, is to deviate from the cold and impartial ways of science. When we teach the millions, however, we are not training scientific investigators, but the practical striving citizens of an empire which has to hold its place according to the universal law of survival through efficiency and effort. The special virtue of thought by visualisation is that it prompts doing rather than merely knowing.

The Imperial attitude enters when we come to consider the point of view from which our young citizens thus reconnoitre the world which is to be the scene of their life's action. Our task as teachers of the twentieth century, responsible for the next generation, is to secure that our pupils shall view the world not merely from the standpoints of England, Scotland, Ireland, Canada, Australia, New Zealand, South Africa, or India, but that they shall identify themselves with the British Empire, which is far more complex than its component parts, and therefore demands higher powers of visualisation. This very difficulty of imagination is, however, the measure of the importance and urgency of the task. The conquest of space by speed has in our time reduced the relative significance of near and easily apprehended things. Must we not readjust our educational methods to the new situation?

For reasons such as these it was that a Departmental Committee was in the autumn of 1902 appointed by the Secretary of State for the Colonies to consider on what system teaching in regard to the Empire might best be developed. I will conclude what I have to say by a few words descriptive of the work of this Committee, although that work by no means covers the whole field which I have traversed this afternoon.

The Visual Instruction Committee of the Colonial Office began by reporting that children in any part of the Empire would never understand what the other parts were like unless by some adequate means of visual instruction, and further, that as far as possible the teaching should be on the same lines in all parts of the Empire. The Committee were then empowered to take practical steps with a view to the realisation of their ideas. It was decided to make a beginning by an experiment on a small scale, and for this purpose to invite the three Eastern Colonies of Ceylon, the Straits Settlements, and Hong Kong to bear the expense of a small book of lantern lectures on the United Kingdom for use in the schools of those colonies. Further editions of these lectures have since been issued to suit the special requirements of other parts of the Empire, and at the present time the lectures on the United Kingdom are in use in Ceylon, the Straits Settlements, Hong Kong, Mauritius, Sierra Leone, the Gold Coast, Southern Nigeria, Trinidad, British Guiana, Jamaica, and in the following Provinces of India: – Madras, Bombay, Bengal, the United Provinces, the Punjab, Burma, Eastern Bengal and Assam, the Central Provinces, the North-West Frontier Province, and British Baluchistan. In short, system has been introduced throughout the tropical zone of the Empire.

Having thus completed an instalment of their task, the Committee turned to a fresh aspect of their work, the preparation of illustrated lectures on the Overseas Dominions and India as well as on the United Kingdom. At this point, however, they were met by a difficulty. There are no doubt in the open market many excellent photographs and lantern slides available for illustrating the chief lands of the Empire, but they have usually been collected either without system by passing visitors whose main object was other than educational, or by residents who, from the very fact of their familiarity with the scenes, are apt to omit pictures of the contrasts which for the stranger are most salient. Such considerable collections as are available have usually been made for special purposes, as for the promotion of religious missions, or of emigration. Moreover, there are frequent difficulties of copyright. The experience of the Committee therefore convinced them that if this part of the work were to be done as well as it could be done, it was advisable to have the illustrations prepared on a uniform system by an artist specially commissioned and instructed for the purpose. They were so fortunate as to interest in their work at this stage Her Majesty the Queen, and through her powerful and gracious support, and that of Lady Dudley and a Committee of Ladies who were good enough to collect a considerable sum of money for the purpose, they have been able to make a beginning of a work which it will take some time to complete. The Committee's artist, Mr. A. Hugh Fisher, has travelled through India, Canada, Australia, New Zealand, the Fiji Islands, Singapore, North Borneo, Hong Kong, Wei-hai-wei, Somaliland, Cyprus, Malta, and Gibraltar, everywhere collecting material according to the directions of the Committee for the purpose of constructing illustrative lantern slides. Eight lectures on India were issued last December, and to illustrate them a set of 480 slides. These may be obtained, a considerable proportion of them coloured, for the sum of £50, or uncoloured, except in the case of the maps, for the sum of £26.

In one respect the slides illustrative of the Indian lectures represent an important advance on those of the United Kingdom. They include more numerous maps of the land-relief to which the pictures are related, so that the ideals which I have endeavoured here to sketch are more nearly attained. For the sake of accuracy in dealing with so vast a region the text of the lectures has been minutely revised by a number of our chief authorities on Indian subjects, but this has not been allowed to interfere with vividness in the interchaining of the maps and pictures, so that the challenge to visualisation might not be lost. At the present time three other similar courses of illustrated lectures are being prepared, respectively on Australasia, Canada, and the ring of Imperial stations round Europe and Asia from Gibraltar to Wei-hai-wei. It is intended that these shall be issued in the course of the present year. The hope of the Committee is that educational authorities may take the scheme up, and supply schools with the illustrative material by a system of loan. Already the Scottish Provincial Committee, and the Army Council in respect of the Army Schools, have adopted this course.

One last point should perhaps be dealt with. There are now many methods of depicting scenes to the eye, among them, of course, the ubiquitous cinematograph. At present, at any rate, for the purposes of school teaching, unless under exceptional circumstances, the cinematograph appears too cumbrous and too expensive; but apart from these practical difficulties, I venture to plead for the simplicity of the lantern slide. Our object in Visual Instruction is not to render thought unnecessary, but rather to call forth the effort of imagination. Personally, I disbelieve in complex apparatus for teaching, wherever it can be avoided. The young child loves the battered doll, which amply serves to focus the imagination. Similarly, I believe that the good teacher can make the blackboard and the lantern slide speak to better educative purpose than he could the cinematograph. The picture palaces of the present moment debauch the imagination by relieving the spectator of all effort. The picture painted by the artist is more stimulating than the photograph for the very reason that it suggests rather than reproduces. Visual Instruction, it must be remembered, aims at increasing the mental powers in a particular direction, and for this purpose we must not render unnecessary effort of the mind. When the child gesticulates in reply to a question we may know that the mind's eye is at work. Does not the distant look in the more mature eye betoken a similar fact?

May I summarise the four points which I have endeavoured to make. They are –

(1) That with the exception of the national epic, our teaching of history, essential for the citizens of a modern democracy, should for children be incidental to geography;
(2) that geography thus lifted to be the chief outlook subject in our school curriculum should be taught by methods which demand visualisation;
(3) that we should aim at educating the citizens of the many parts of the British Empire to sympathise with one another and to understand Imperial problems by teaching geography visually, not only from the point of view of the Homeland, but also of the Empire; and
(4) that among many other excellent aids to such teaching, there is now becoming available an apparatus of illustrated lectures prepared under the authority of the Visual Instruction Committee of the Colonial Office.

Note

1 A paper read at the Imperial Education Conference arranged by the Board of Education.

46

BOARD OF EDUCATION, *HANDBOOK OF SUGGESTIONS* (LONDON: HMSO, 1937), PP. 416–419.

The extracts shown here reveal the changing intellectual outlook in teaching after the First World War. Document 46 advocates internationalism and the teaching of the work of the League of Nations rather than celebration in the classroom of imperial battles and militaristic figures in British history. In document 47 we can see a change in the approach that authors of history texts adopted in the 1920s and 1930s.

B. British history as a part of world history

17. Some ways of dealing with ancient history. – No course of History can be satisfactory that leaves the pupil with the impression that the story of the world began with Julius Cæsar's visits to Britain. To give an adequate picture of the history of the Ancient World is of course impossible, but since we all enjoy the fruits of ancient wisdom and civilisation, many teachers may think that we ought to know something of how these things came to be. Some teachers, accordingly, commence the course by making the Bible their main source for ancient history, adding such references to the ancient empires of Egypt, Assyria and Persia as are necessary. Other teachers make a practice of giving at a suitable stage in the school course, a very simple sketch of world history by means of biographical studies of outstanding figures, leading the pupil to see, not merely disconnected lives, but something of the character of the civilisations which they represent. The important thing in such teaching is to concentrate on those parts of the world's story from which modern civilisation can trace a direct descent, i.e. Palestine, Greece and Rome; it is easy to waste time on stories of primitive man or to devote too much attention to stories of the Asiatic Empires and Egypt. But, through Ancient History rightly taught in biography and story and picture, the pupil may learn to recognise what we owe to Greece and Rome: the feeling for beauty and the beginnings of scientific thought and method, on the one hand, the spread of law and order, on the other; and how the fusion of the two made western civilisation, as we know it, possible. Again, he may be shown how, as the Middle Ages drew to their close, renewed interest in the ancient Greeks and Romans altered the outlook of all western peoples, and how the university and the printing press passed on the inheritance.

In Ancient History, some of the more important stories of the ancient world which the pupils have learnt at the Junior School stage might be reviewed, and where possible a few lessons might be given on some of the main features of the early civilisations which those biographies and stories illustrate, especially where they bear on our own history.

18. Linking up British history with world history. – Where a series of lessons on the Ancient World is given, it is usually followed by the topics chosen from British history with allusion to the concurrent stream of general history, and experience shows that this is a practicable plan of attacking the wider relations of History. Though time is seldom found for the systematic teaching of foreign or world history, the course should make it possible for children to see such parts of our own history as are parts of world movements in due proportion. For example, if such topics as the following are dealt with boldly and simply the children may be expected to have a better understanding of our own history: Britain as a province of the Roman Empire; the raids and settlements of the Northmen; the Crusades, the Renaissance and the Reformation; the expansion of Europe overseas; the position of Spain under Philip II, of France under Louis XIV and Napoleon; the unification of Germany and Italy; the development of the United States of America; and the international growth of modern industry and commerce.

19. The League of Nations. – If the teacher brings to his work a broad conception of the treatment of the history of Great Britain and the British Commonwealth of Nations, dwelling not less upon the points of contact between nations than upon the differences which have separated them, he will naturally wish that the children should learn something of the League of Nations and of the ideals for which it stands. In most cases, opportunity will offer, not only in the History lessons, but at other times, for drawing attention to that form of international co-operation which the League represents. It may be pointed out that in the modern industrial world the increased communication between nations, owing to improved methods of transport, the economic interdependence of nations upon one another, and above all the vast scale and terrible machinery of modern warfare, have made it necessary that the peoples of the world should combine with their natural sense of local patriotism a conception of their common interests and duties.

This subject is dealt with more fully in the Appendix at the end of this volume.

C. Some examples of the way in which the school course may be dealt with

20. The teacher should make his own selection of periods and topics. – The teacher will naturally himself determine what period of History he will deal with at any particular stage and what topics he will include in his treatment of that period. Something has already been said as to the kind of selection that may be made from the field of Ancient History; but it may be found useful to give some examples of the way in which a typical course in History may be handled in accordance with some of the principles mentioned in the opening sections of this chapter. These examples, however, are only intended to suggest a method of approach; they are not offered as the basis of a school syllabus, nor is it to be expected that any one school could deal satisfactorily with all of them.

47

H. MARTENS AND E. H. CARTER, *HISTORIES. BOOK IV. THE MODERN AGE* (OXFORD: BASIL BLACKWELL, 11TH EDITION, 1952). FIRST PUBLISHED 1931. PP. 183–189; 320–322.

The extracts shown here reveal the changing intellectual outlook in teaching after the First World War. Document 46 advocates internationalism and the teaching of the work of the League of Nations rather than celebration in the classroom of imperial battles and militaristic figures in British history. In document 47 we can see a change in the approach that authors of history texts adopted in the 1920s and 1930s.

36. Rhodesia: Livingstone and Rhodes

"For those who deserve well of their country."

I

South Africa is the name of that part of the British Commonwealth of Nations which lies south of the great River Zambesi. One of the men who did most to spread British influence in the lands *north and west of the Boer provinces* (the Transvaal and Orange Free State) travelled without weapons among entirely uncivilized natives for many years, won their love and trust, and left a name that they still remember with affection. How he achieved all this can be read in the wonderful book of his "Travels." His name was *David Livingstone* (1813–1873). He was brought up as a very poor boy in Scotland, near Glasgow, but he determined to become a Christian missionary, and struggled hard to educate himself. At the age of ten he went to a cotton-mill. But he learnt Latin at odd minutes whilst he was at work and by studying late at night, though he had to be in his mill by six o'clock in the morning. Years afterwards, when he was alone in parts of Africa which no other white man had ever seen, he used to cheer himself by repeating the old Latin hymns of the mediæval Church.

Dr. Livingstone went to Africa (1840) early in Victoria's reign, when very few Englishmen except the *missionaries* had crossed the Orange River into

Bechuanaland. Livingstone was not only a missionary but an explorer. He was not content to settle and to teach in one place, but went on farther to the north until he reached (1851) the *Zambesi* river high up in its course. This great river, the second largest in Africa, the Portuguese had only known at its mouth; but Livingstone traced the whole of it, and in doing so (as you will see by a look at the map) he journeyed right across the African continent.

Later in his life he went even farther north, discovering the great lake Nyassa, and the *Victoria Falls*, which he named after his Queen and which are more wonderful than those at Niagara, and the river called Lualaba, which is really a part of the River Congo though no one guessed it. He and his wife were very practical

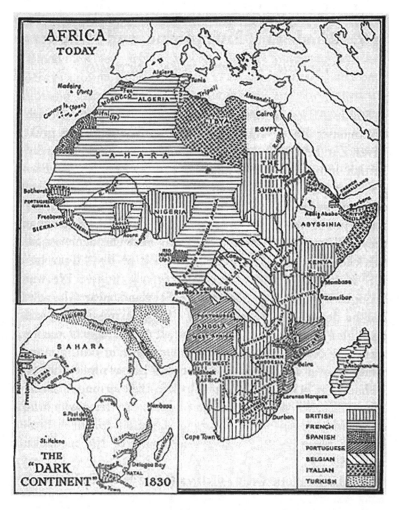

Figure 47.1 In the larger map, the areas left unshaded, or partly shaded, represent territories which have some form of native government.

people. He built with his own hands three houses, besides schools, in different parts of South Africa, as he was a good carpenter and worker in iron; whilst his wife made the candles, soap, and clothes. One of the places in which he settled was infested with lions, which killed his cattle. Livingstone organized lion-hunts, and in one of these was nearly killed, for he wounded a lion thirty yards away, which then sprang on him and crushed his left shoulder.

Livingstone came home in the middle of these journeys, and aroused great interest in Africa by what he told people. Then he returned to Africa and for a long time no news of him reached Great Britain, and people wondered what had happened. An American newspaper arranged for a search to be made, and sent out H. M. Stanley, a Welshman. *Stanley* started from Zanzibar, and two years later (1871) he found Livingstone at Ujiji, more keen than ever on the people and problems of Africa. He would not go back to the coast with Stanley, though he went with him half-way to Zanzibar.

Then Livingstone turned towards the interior again, and two years later, without any white man as his companion, he died in the middle of the "Dark Continent," to which he had devoted his life. The British Government had given a good deal of help to Livingstone when he was exploring, but it did not wish to undertake the task of governing the great Zambesi country which he had found. Private people, however, were more adventurous; missionaries and traders followed Livingstone, and at last there came the second of the great men who have joined the fortunes of South Africa with those of the British race.

II

This second man was quite unlike Dr. Livingstone. His name was *Cecil Rhodes* (1853–1902), and he was born and bred in an English parsonage. He was not a missionary and explorer as Livingstone had been, but a politician and a business man, who had gone originally to Natal for the sake of his health. When he was an undergraduate at Oxford, whilst rowing he caught a chill which affected his lungs, and the doctor gave him six months to live; but he grew up a strong man over six feet high, and looked like a Viking with his blue eyes and light hair. Livingstone had tried to interest the British in Africa chiefly because he wanted to help the natives and to teach them to live better. Rhodes was thinking chiefly about getting white people to live and work in Africa, and tried to make the best arrangements he could to persuade them to go.

Diamonds were found in Bechuanaland, and all sorts of companies set about to get them. Cecil Rhodes thought that this was a mistake, and gradually he made one great company, which had control of many of the diamond mines in South Africa. He did this by persuading the other people to join his company or by buying their rights from them. Later he became the head of one of the largest of the *gold-mine* companies. When he had had so much success he became more ambitious, and he began to plan for a great British colony in the country farther north – *Matabeleland and Mashonaland* – where Livingstone had lived. Since Livingstone's death little had been done there, but now (1889) Rhodes had a new Charter given to a company that he formed. As he was a man of great wealth and became Prime Minister of Cape Colony, he was able to use his company to bring the Zambesi country into the British Empire.

The *British South Africa Company* which Rhodes founded reminds us of the East India Company and the other old companies of Tudor and Stuart times, which went out to trade in new countries. Rhodes was quite sure that it was a good thing to spread British influence wherever he could. He was most active in pressing our claims in Central Africa, and the great colony now called after him, *Rhodesia*, his company ruled for many years, though it has now been replaced by a regular government (1921), just as the East India Company was replaced in India.

Rhodes valued money as a means to power, and gave it as a means to spread British influence and ideals. His policy aimed at co-operation on equal terms between the Dutch and the British, and the federation of the two Dutch republics and the two colonies in the British Empire (the Cape and Natal) in a United South Africa. His idea came to pass at last after his death, when the *Union of South Africa* (1909) was made by the free act of all the colonies. Rhodes was "ever the most practical of visionaries and the most visionary of men of business." His idea of a United South Africa was but a step in a larger plan; he hoped that some day the British Empire would stretch right through Africa from Cape Colony in the south to Egypt in the north. "That is my dream," he once said to a friend showing him a map of Africa, "all British."

To bring this about he worked hard to have a *railway* and a *telegraph* line from the Cape to Cairo. When he died (1902) only a small strip of German territory broke the long British line. Then, since the peace (1919) following the First World War, this strip which used to belong to German East Africa, has been administered under a British Mandate.

Cecil Rhodes lies buried on the summit of one of the Matopo Hills in Matabeleland, a resting-place intended by him for "those who deserve well of their country." The whole of his vast fortune, some six millions, he left to found scholarships and to help Universities.

58. The League and a Twenty Years Crisis (1919–1939)

The creation of the League of Nations was, it was then hoped, the most significant result of the Versailles Treaty (1919) that ended the First World War. Due mainly to the suggestion of Woodrow Wilson, the President of the United States – though his country refused to join it – the League was intended to be a kind of World Parliament of the nations. Its main object was to settle disputes between nations by *arbitration*[1] instead of by war, to improve labour and health conditions throughout the world, to secure just treatment for natives – in fact, to provide for the security, peace, and welfare of mankind.

The League did much useful work. Its *Health Organization*, for example, established at Singapore a Centre of Intelligence for all the countries of the Far East as regards the spread and prevention of diseases such as cholera and plague; and it helped to organize and combine the campaigns of various countries against malaria and cancer, leprosy and sleeping sickness.

The *Mandates Commission* of the League looked after the more backward countries for which various nations had been given mandates as trustees, and it had tried to see that those nations carried out their duties.

Closely connected with the League was the *International Labour Office* – a great clearing-house of information for the world in matters to do with trade and industry and conditions of employment.

But the League of Nations failed in its main task. It did not succeed in enforcing its will and preventing war. In spite of the failure of a *Disarmament Conference*, Britain remained disarmed – even when Hitler reoccupied the Rhineland contrary to the Treaty of Versailles.

The League did not prevent Poland seizing Vilna, nor later on did it prevent Japan (1931) marching into Manchuria and Italy into Abyssinia (1936) and Germany (1935) re-arming.

Figure 47.2 A Russian caricature, depicting a European tour of the Angel of Peace, and some of the danger spots shown as bombs – such as Austria, Danzig, Memel (on the boundary between Germany and Lithuania, which the latter seized in 1924), and the Saar (returned to Germany after a critical election in 1935).

There were Great Powers who were satisfied with their position in the world, such as Great Britain, the U.S.A. and France; there were other Powers which were dissatisfied, such as Germany and Italy and now also Japan. But the problem of ensuring *peace* is no new one – it has been rarely absent in human affairs; and it is not surprising that the League failed to find a solution in twenty years to a problem which had baffled statesmen for centuries.

During the great World Crisis (1930–1934)[2] in Trade and Industry – with its worldwide unemployment and unrest – Hitler and the Nazis in Germany, following the previous example of Mussolini and the Fascists in Italy, seized power (1933), while Soviet Russia continued with great energy and foresight to industrialize and modernize itself. Spain was torn by civil war (1936–1939) during Franco's rise to power. In due course Germany and Italy and (later) Japan[3] formed the "Berlin-Rome-Tokio Axis" for defence, so they pretended, against Bolshevism and against what they called the "plutocratic [wealthy] democracies." The rest of the world craved for peace, which the League had failed to maintain.

In 1939 we were again at war, and in this terrible Second World War the U.S.A. and the U.S.S.R. in due course became Allies of the British Commonwealth, of France, and of China. Forty "United Nations" fought for what President Roosevelt defined as the *Four Freedoms* – "freedom from want, freedom of religion, freedom of speech, freedom from fear, everywhere in the world." And, as we all know, this grim universal war became a *total* war, in which not only the sailor, the soldier and the airman, but also every man, woman and child, every village, town, factory and farm, had a part to play.

In 1940 – the most critical of all years in our long history – Britain, by saving itself in the *Battle of Britain*, in due course saved the world, thanks to its courage and endurance in the German "blitz" when the R.A.F. earned from our great Prime Minister, Mr. Winston Churchill, the immortal tribute: "Never in the field of human conflict was so much owed by so many to so few."

Notes

1 *I.e.,* by an arbiter – by a judge or judges.
2 See end of chapter 48 on America.
3 See end of chapter 47 on Japan and China.

48

A WONDERFUL ESCAPE

By H. W. Boyler

From: 'A Wonderful Escape', in A. R. Buckland (ed.), *Boys' Own Book of Heroism and Adventure* (London: RTS Society, 1914), pp. 311–331.

These extracts are taken from boys and girls' magazines and annuals in the years 1880–1939. They were a response to the publications known as 'penny dreadfuls' (serialized, sensationalistic stories of crime and horror). Amongst the earliest of these new kind of magazines was the Boys' Own Paper (BOP), *published by the Religious Tract Society (RTS) in 1879.*

The founding values of this publication, and others that followed, was the belief that the youth would read and have instilled in them Christian moral values. In its early phase the BOP *stressed the missionary aspect of Empire, perhaps not surprising, given that the clergymen who had founded the RTS in 1799 had, four years earlier, founded the London Missionary Society. The paper and its companion the* Boys' Own Annual, *promoted the British Empire, particularly in their first decade. Among those who wrote for the paper were Arthur Conan Doyle, R. M. Ballantyne, Jules Verne and G. M. Henty. Alfred Harmsworth noted that his stable of publications aimed to eradicate 'the miserable literary rubbish, in which murders, thieves and other criminals are raised to the position of heroes'. The* BOP *reflected Britain's position as a leading imperial power and its description of the races of Empire invariably include pejorative language. By 1900 the* BOP *was being challenged by other titles, such as those published by Edward Brett. Other titles included* The Boys of the Empire, *published by Andrew Melrose and edited by Howard Spicer; G. A. Henty's* The Union Jack; *and* Young England: An Illustrated Magazine for Boys Throughout the English Speaking World *(first appeared in 1880 and published by the London Sunday School Union). By the later 19th and early 20th centuries, another crop of youth publications had appeared, among which were* Chums *(1892);* Union Jack *(1894), founded by Alfred Harmsworth;* Pluck *(the full title of this publication was* Stories of Pluck: a high class weekly library of adventure at home and abroad, on land and sea, *1894);* Gem *(1907); and* The Magnet *(1908), for which Charles Hamilton (known as Frank Richards) wrote the Greyfriars stories. The* Girl's Own Paper *was edited first by Charles Peters (1880–1907), whose aim was to 'foster and develop that which was highest and noblest in the girlhood and womanhood of England . . . putting the best things first and banishing the worthless from his pages', and second by Flora Klickmann (1908–1931), who made the magazine a monthly publication. It was aimed at the middle-class English gentlewoman and in that respect tended to reflect the shift between an ideology of domesticated feminism transforming into an appreciation of the 'modern woman' who played sport, rode a bicycle and*

DOI: 10.4324/9781351024822-50

would perhaps eventually migrate to the Empire. Most of the features were educational and improving in their nature. Contemporary concern for physical fitness can be seen in magazines for both boys and girls. E. C. Dawson, author of document 50, was rector of St. Peter's, Edinburgh, and also authored Lion-Hearted *(1909) and* Missionary Heroines in India: true stories of the Wonderful bravery of patient endurance of missionaries in India, *published in the 1920s.*

Being the story of the career and imprisonment of Slatin Pasha among the Dervishes, and his miraculous escape after twelve years.

AT the invitation of General Gordon, Lieutenant Slatin left Vienna at the end of 1878. He was then an officer in the Austrian army, and had had some experience of the Sudan and the Arab tribes there. Although quite young, being only twenty-two years of age, Slatin had made a favourable impression on Gordon. The latter, on his taking over the care of the Equatorial provinces of Egypt, remembered the clever young Austrian officer and wrote offering him an appointment as Governor of the distant province of Durfur. Little did Slatin dream that seventeen years would elapse before he should see his home again.

In Slatin's account of this part of his life[1] he writes –

"As I stepped over the side (of the boat) he (Gordon) said –

"'Good-bye, my dear Slatin, and God bless you; I am sure you will do your best under any circumstances. Perhaps I am going back to England, and, if so, I hope we may meet there.'

"These were the last words I ever heard him utter; but who could have imagined the fate in store for both of us? I thanked him heartily for his great kindness and help, and on reaching the river-bank I stopped there for an hour, waiting for the steamer to start. Then I heard a shrill whistle and the anchor being weighed, and in a few minutes Gordon was out of sight – gone for ever!"

Unfortunately, Slatin was handicapped at the start because General Gordon was considered by the natives to be the cause of many ills that then troubled them, and he, Slatin, had the same blue eyes and shaven chin. He was, indeed, throughout the whole of his career in the Sudan, considered to be Gordon's own son.

Slatin journeyed to Dara, which was his headquarters, with the newly appointed Sanitary Inspector, a much older man than himself, and who was mistaken for the Governor. Indeed, Slatin lent himself to the deception by riding in advance and giving himself out as one of the new Governor's escort. It was the month of Ramadan, the great Mohammedan fast, and Slatin and his companion, Dr. Zurbuchen, were glad of the chance for a rest this gave them before the welcoming festivities began. During Ramadan, which the Arabs keep strictly, the people fast during the day until sunset, when they make up for the hungry hours. Rudolf Slatin thus describes the scene on the evening of his official arrival at his post:

"At sunset the gun boomed out the signal that one day more of Ramadan had gone; and now the hungry and thirsty inhabitants, their daily fast over, hurried to their evening meal. The chief men of the place now came to see us, and asked us to dine with them. They were followed by a host of servants bearing roast mutton, fowls, milk, and rice – which is usually eaten with hot melted butter and honey – and dishes of asida (meat spread over with a very fine layer of dukhu flour, over which sauce is poured, and on top of all is a thin layer of paste, sprinkled with sugar); this completed the menu. In a few minutes the ground just outside the house, which had been sprinkled with fine sand, was spread with carpets and palm mats, and on these the dishes were laid. Zogal Bey began distributing the viands amongst those who had come to welcome me, including the servants, but keeping, of course, the best dishes for the more select company. We now sat down, and the tearing and the rending of the roast sheep began with a vengeance; of course knives and forks were out of the question."

They were interrupted during this primitive feasting by the news of a disturbance at an outlying post, and by midnight of this his first day of office Slatin was on his way to put down Sultan Harun, who had been giving a lot of trouble, and whom Slatin had secret orders from General Gordon to quell. Slatin was very young, and eager. He says, "I was delighted at the thought of a brush with Sultan Harun. The idea of difficulties and fatigue never crossed my mind; all I longed for was a chance of showing my men that I could lead them."

On the march, owing to want of rest, Slatin became ill and complained of a bad headache. An Arab companion produced a man who he said was a better doctor than the one at Dara.

"All right," said Slatin, "but how is he going to cure me?"

"Oh, it is very simple. He places both his hands on your head and repeats something; then you get perfectly well."

"Then let him come at once," cried Slatin.

In a few minutes Ahmed ushered in a tall dark man with a white beard. Without hesitation the "doctor" placed his hands on Slatin's head, pressing his temples, muttered a few words, and spat in his face! Slatin jumped up and knocked the man down. The latter then explained that "Headache is the work of the devil, and I must drive it out; several passages from the Koran and sayings of holy men direct that it should be chased away by spitting, and thus his evil work in your head will cease!" Slatin laughed, gave the man a dollar, and sent him away; but the headache remained.

During this expedition each day brought its own more or less exciting incident. On one occasion they came across a number of trees laden with beehives. For fear of the venomous insects they were compelled to camp about two miles off, and even then they had to start an hour before dawn, such was the dread inspired by these little dealers in sweetness and death. But one man, when he saw the hives, had fallen out of the ranks and had attempted to procure some honey. He was brought in afterwards, a terrible sight. "His face was swollen beyond all recognition, and his tongue protruded to an enormous size from his widely distended mouth." He was unconscious and soon died.

On another occasion Slatin found two pretty little black babies deserted on the top of a rock. The mother was not far away; she had been unable to escape with them in time. We like Slatin's account of his treatment of these mites. "Dismounting, I went up to them, and they began to cry and cling to each other; so, taking them in my arms, I told my servant to bring me some sugar from my travelling-bag. This pacified them at once, and, smiling through their tears, they munched what to them was probably the nicest thing they had ever tasted. Then taking two of the red handkerchiefs (a supply of which I generally carried about to offer as presents), I wrapped the babies up in them, laid them down on the rock again, and moved on some distance. Looking back, I saw a human being, evidently the mother, creeping down the rocks. Then, joyfully seizing her little ones, she fondled them most lovingly. She had got back her naked treasures clothed in lovely garments, and licking lips all sticky with their feast of sugar."

A little later Slatin assembled all the women, whom he had commandeered to carry corn. He then set them free, and told them that next time he hoped to find their husbands more submissive, as in that case husbands, wives, and children need never be separated. "A wild shriek of joy, a mutter of gratitude, and they were off like gazelles released from a cage."

Doubtless you all know the story of "Taffy and the Welshman." Well, Slatin's case was something like that of Taffy. He had set out to catch and punish the disloyal Sultan Harun. He did not succeed in this; but when he was nearing home (Dara) again, he learned to his consternation that the wily Harun had got round him (Slatin) and had attacked Dara, looting and burning some small villages near by! Incidentally he learned that his enemy had been influenced by his example in liberating the captured women. However, this did not save the wily Arab, for a little later on Slatin overtook him and scattered his force, Harun being killed in the conflict.

About this time, Dr. Felkin, who was journeying from the interior bound for Europe, arrived at Dara. Our only excuse for mentioning him here is because of a most amusing incident connected with a camel – an animal unknown to the doctor's black companions, who had come from Mtesa's dominions. Dr. Felkin was doubtful if his people would stand the sight of a camel, let alone mount one; but Slatin sent for a beast belonging to a merchant, which was very big and fat. "By this time the envoys and others had arrived, and the camel appearing suddenly round the corner caused almost a stampede. Dr. Felkin explained to them that the camel was a most patient and docile animal, on which they would have to make the remainder of their journey to Egypt, and that there was no cause for fear. Still, they kept a respectful distance from the alarming beast; and when I told my kavass to mount and make it get up and sit down, their astonishment was boundless. At length, one more courageous than the rest, volunteered to mount. Timorously approaching the animal, he was assisted into the saddle, and having safely got through the operation of rising, with a beaming countenance he surveyed his friends from his lofty seat, and proceeded to make a speech to them on the pleasures of camel-riding. Apparently he had invited them to share these pleasures with him, for suddenly, without a moment's warning, they rushed at the poor animal in a body, and began swarming up it. Some tried to mount by the neck, others by the tail, and half a dozen or so clung to the saddle trappings. For a moment the camel seemed stupefied by this sudden attack, but recovering its presence of mind, it now lashed out in all directions, and in a moment it had freed itself completely from every unfortunate Waganda who had been bold enough to approach it. I do not think I ever laughed so much in my life."

But, unhappily, from this time on there was not much laughter for Slatin. He was kept busy with administrative duties, with his would-be extortionate tax-gatherers, with the petty chieftains and office-holders about him, and especially with the discontented slave-dealers whose dreadful business had been so ruthlessly interfered with by General Gordon while Governor-General of the Equatorial provinces. One great source of trouble were the gellebas, or traders, whose complaints to headquarters of stolen caravans and rifled harems, gave the Governor much trouble. Once he had these claims added up, and found they totalled more than the entire wealth of the Arabs against whom their claim lay.

As the result of a visit to Khartum, Slatin was made Governor-General of Darfur, instead of Governor, or Mudir, of merely the department of Dara. He received also the title of Bey at the same time, and proceeded to take up his quarters at El Fasher, then the seat of the local government.

It was while making a sort of progress through his dominions that the Governor-General observed the strange form that an oath of fealty took. Four sheikhs, who had been troublesome, tendered their submission and brought tribute to the new ruler. They became entirely friendly, and wished to take an oath of allegiance. "The ceremony was performed as follows. A horse's saddle was brought and placed in the midst of the assembly, and on this was laid a large earthenware dish filled with burning charcoal. A lance was then fixed to the saddle, and the head sheikhs, with their attendants, now came forward, and, stretching out their hands over the lance and burning charcoal, they recited the following words with great solemnity: 'May my leg never touch the saddle, may my body be smitten with the lance that kills, and may I be consumed by the burning fire, if I ever break the solemn oath of fidelity which I now make to you.'"

But now the Arabs, inflamed by the Mahdi, were everywhere rising over the Sudan. Massacres, burnings, and pillage, accompanied by horrible cruelties, were practised on those who would not submit to this religious fanatic and recognize his divine mission, which was to drive out every foreigner, European or Egyptian, from the Equatorial provinces.

Slatin in his own province strove valiantly against the rising forces of the Mahdi in vain. He was eventually taken prisoner, and carried to Omdurman, which had already fallen into the cruel hands of the Mahdi. Here he was a witness of the final scenes which resulted in the fall of Khartum and the death of General Gordon. What must have been Slatin's feelings as the head of his friend and chief was exultingly shown him by the brutal soldiers of the Mahdi! Previously Slatin had said that "there was no small advantage in being a fatalist." But in spite of the patience which had become part of his nature during the trials and sufferings of the early part of his imprisonment, he could not repress a strong shudder as the gruesome burden was uncovered before him. But let me quote his own words –

"The blood rushed to my head, and my heart seemed to stop beating; but with a tremendous effort of self-control I gazed silently at this ghastly spectacle. His blue eyes were half opened; the mouth was perfectly natural; the hair of his head, and his short whiskers, were almost quite white.

"'Is not this the head of your uncle, the unbeliever?' said Shatta, holding the head up before me.

"'What of it?' I said quietly. 'A brave soldier who fell at his post; happy is he to have fallen; his sufferings are over.'

"'Ha, ha!' said Shatta, 'so you still praise the unbeliever; but you will soon see the result;' and leaving me, he went off to the Mahdi, bearing his terrible token of victory.

"I re-entered my tent. I was now utterly broken-hearted: Khartum fallen, and Gordon dead!"

A few days after the fall of Khartum, Slatin was still more rigorously treated than before. This was in consequence of some letters of his to Gordon that had fallen into the Mahdi's hands. He was taken from his ragged tent where he had been confined and carried to the general prison. Here his chains were increased in number and weight, a heavy iron bar being added. At night time he was bound with other prisoners by a long chain. Forbidden to speak, under penalty of a severe flogging, and nearly starved, he soon found that, bad as his treatment had been before, it was now infinitely worse. He was compelled to sleep on the bare ground, with a stone for a pillow, and had not a poor black woman taken compassion on him and cooked his small allowance of grain, he would have been compelled to eat it uncooked. For many months he lay like this, forbidden to speak, and his distress further increased by witnessing the sufferings of poor Lupton Bey, who was confined in another corner of the prison enclosure.

Slatin's submissive spirit, however, during a visit to the prison of the Khalifa, procured a slight amelioration of his treatment. He was allowed to receive a little food from outside, and to pay short visits to some of his fellow-prisoners. At this time he notes a curious fact. Small-pox had broken out at Omdurman (where was the prison), and great numbers of the people were carried off by the disease. Even the prison officials were attacked, while many of them died. But none of the prisoners took the disease during the whole time of Slatin's imprisonment here.

Lupton Bey (one of Gordon's officers) was by this time very ill. But he and Slatin used to accompany the other prisoners, who were engaged in building a new prison-house, to the place where they got the stones. Slatin did not carry stones himself, but acted as architect, his heavy chains precluding him from the former task. About this time they had a gleam of hope that their sufferings would be lightened, the Khalifa (the second man in rank to the Mahdi) being announced as about to visit the captives.

Slatin had been advised by an Arab friend to humble himself. And here I should like to say that this is the thing I most dislike in our hero's narrative. He was (and is) physically brave, but he did not scruple to lick the dust off his captor's boots, and, worse still, to appear to abjure the religion of his countrymen and to conform outwardly to that of Mohammed. During all the twelve years of his captivity he appeared to be a devout Mohammedan, though in his heart he declared himself a Christian. Nay, he even went so far as to call the crowds of worshipping Arabs, as they knelt in the mosque, "hypocrites." And he was kneeling with them handling the Mohammedan rosary, but repeating the Lord's Prayer in his mind while his lips were uttering the Mohammedan formula!

On the present occasion, in reply to the Khalifa's inquiry as to his condition, Slatin replied –

"Master, I belong to a foreign tribe; I came to you seeking protection, and you gave it to me. It is natural for man to err, and to sin against God and against each other. I have sinned; but I now repent, and regret all my misdeeds. I repent before God and His Prophet."

The immediate result of this appeal was that both Slatin and Lupton had their irons removed, and they were bade to accompany the Khalifa to his house. Here they were exhorted to become Mohammedans and to renounce Christianity. "Lupton and I assured him that we should never leave him of our own free-will; that all the pleasures of the world would never tear us from his side; and that it was only by being constantly in his presence that we learnt to act in such a way as would lead to our salvation." The Khalifa, according to Slatin, "was thoroughly taken in by our mendacity."

Well, that sort of thing must be condemned. Life is valuable, and should not lightly be thrown away; but truth, principles and beliefs are worth more than life, and should be upheld at all costs.

Taking, for a second time, the oath of allegiance to the Mahdi, Slatin was now a comparatively free man; that is to say, he was not in irons or in prison. But he was no less a prisoner, being compelled to serve his masters in any capacity they chose. His movements were restricted also, so that he found it impossible to stray more than a short distance from the Khalifa's door, of whose household he had become a member. In other words, from a prisoner he had become a slave, to walk beside his master when the latter went out on horseback, to keep watch at the door, and also at times to act as the Khalifa's secretary. As a last act of degradation Slatin was compelled to sign a document declaring that he had become a Mohammedan of his own free will, and that he now had no desire to return to his own country. Shortly after, however, he got into greater favour with the Khalifa, who granted him a piece of ground close to his own residence, to build a house upon, and offered him "some wives," really slaves who should work for Slatin, himself a slave. This offer he was able to decline without offending his master. He then proceeded to erect his house – three huts within an enclosure. He had with him an old Darfurian servant and a few effects, a share of the loot of Khartum. His own money, about £40, was also returned to him, and, for a captive, Slatin might consider himself comparatively well off. But none knew better than he on how unstable a basis he stood. At any moment he might come under the displeasure of his patron, the consequences of which would be dreadful. He had been the Khalifa's superior in the Darfur days, and now this man was at all times anxious to show how he could lord it over his former white master. Slatin felt that the Khalifa was continually on the look-out for occasions of humiliation and degradation. Thus he was made to walk barefoot beside his master's horse, was sent to prison for trifling causes, and made to keep guard with the other slaves.

His anxiety to escape increased, but the distance to the Egyptian frontier was so great, and the desert was so difficult to traverse, that he knew his case was hopeless without outside help and organization. His many efforts failed, one after the other. Once or twice, after several years' captivity, he managed to get word, through travelling merchants whom he bribed, to his far-off relatives.

In the mean time, the Mahdi died, and Khalifa Abdullahi, Slatin's master, was appointed the new ruler of the Sudan. Slatin now began seriously to plan an escape. He never felt safe for a moment, for he knew that, however friendly the Khalifa might appear outwardly, he did not in the least trust his captive, but kept a continual and harassing watch on his movements. Father Ohrwalder, a fellow-countryman, who was also a captive in the Khalifa's hands, but was allowed a small measure of freedom, used secretly to visit Slatin about this time. They comforted each other by hopes of release or escape, but could do nothing but wait with patience for that happy and far-off time. Then a letter arrived from Slatin's brothers and sisters, giving him the sad news of the death of his mother. The broken-hearted captive was compelled by the Khalifa to read out the contents of the letter.

"Ah," said the latter, "your mother was not aware that I honour you more than any one else, otherwise she certainly would not have been in such trouble about you."

He was, however, allowed to write home, practically at the Khalifa's dictation, and to ask for money to be sent him and also a few articles for presents. By means of inverted commas and exclamation marks he managed to convey to his relatives how "happy" and contented (!) he was, and to urge again that some measures might be taken for his release. Poor Lupton had been dead a month now, and Slatin was allowed to settle his poor friend's family affairs.

A truly terrible affair, and one typical of the Khalifa's rule, occurred about this time. An expedition had been sent against the Batahin tribe, north of the Blue Nile. Sixty-seven of the men, together with their women and children, were captured and brought in. The women and children were separated, and the men condemned to death. The Khalifa had three large scaffolds erected in the market-place, to which the prisoners were taken. It is an awful picture that Slatin depicts in his book, "Fire and Sword in the Sudan" –

"After a quarter of an hour the Khalifa got up, and we all walked on behind him. Arrived at the market-place, a terrible scene awaited us. The unfortunate Batahin had been divided into three parties, one of which had been hanged, a second had been decapitated, and a third had lost their right hands and left feet. The Khalifa himself stopped in front of the three scaffolds, which were almost broken by the weight of the bodies, whilst close at hand lay a heap of mutilated people, their hands and feet lying scattered on the ground; it was a shocking spectacle. They did not utter a sound, but gazed in front of them, and tried to hide from the eyes of the crowd the terrible sufferings they were enduring. The Khalifa now summoned Osman Wad Ahmed, . . . a member of the Batahin tribe, and pointing to the mutilated bodies, he said, 'You may now take what remains of your tribe home with you!' The poor man was too horrified and shocked to answer. . . . Each one of these sixty-seven men had met his death heroically. The Khalifa's work was done; he was satisfied with it, and rode home."

Slatin's outraged feelings were in time soothed by the receipt of letters from his far-off home. There was also in the box a fitted bag for the Khalifa, and other presents, also £200 in money, which, to his surprise, he was allowed to keep. Also, for the first time for six years, he heard news of the outside world – the box contained some old newspapers. The Khalifa was in an unusually good temper because of a recent success of his troops, and invited Slatin's brothers and sisters to come to Omdurman. It is needless to say that the captive brother did not second the invitation.

The condition of the Sudan, never very comfortable, became at this time one of acute distress. Owing to the continued warfare, and to the storing up of grain by the Khalifa and his lieutenants, gaunt famine faced the wretched inhabitants. Slatin tells how one day he saw three wild-eyed starving women seated round a young donkey, tearing out its entrails with their teeth! Mothers sold their children to save their lives, and it was more than feared that cases of cannibalism occurred. Hundreds of dead bodies were daily floating down the Nile past Omdurman, while the streets were littered with the bodies of poor wretches who had died where they lay, too weak to hold out longer. The Khalifa favoured his own tribe, and collected what corn was left for their benefit. This tribe, the Taaisha, was gradually brought to Omdurman, where a large section was forcibly cleared of its inhabitants to make room for them. That by these actions he was estranging the rest of his followers did not trouble him. He had his kinsmen and his own tribe about him now, and could ignore the rest. Indeed, so secure did he feel his position to be that he actually sent letters to Queen Victoria, to the Sultan of Turkey, and to the Khedive of Egypt, summoning them to submit to his rule and adopt Mahdism.

Slatin had now (1889) been about ten years a captive when General Grenfell and the Egyptian army utterly defeated a Mahdist force, under Nejumi, which had started to subjugate Egypt itself. It was the beginning of the end of Mahdism; but weary years were yet to elapse before Slatin could effect his escape. Indeed, the misfortunes which began to overtake the Khalifa rendered his position more and more precarious. Yet he continued to embarrass Slatin by sending him more wives, which was a source of expense and much anxiety and worry. Many he refused to take, but fear of offending the Khalifa obliged him to do what he could for the poor creatures given him, and to make some arrangements for their comfort. Yet he had scarcely enough allowed him for his own subsistence.

Sometimes the situation became especially painful; as, for instance, when he returned home one day and found his house full of women, all relatives of the Khalifa's latest gift, headed by a loquacious old lady, who introduced herself as his mother-in-law! Poor Slatin, the slave of a tyrant, what could he do? What he did was to order them a meal, and then turn them all out, ordering his servants not to readmit them. Then he sent this newest "wife" after them, with a few presents and a message that she was free. But this action was followed by renewed suspicion on the part of his master, who made him shift his household to a place nearer his own, where all his movements could be more closely watched.

After the news of the fall of Kassala arrived at Omdurman, the Khalifa made a further attempt to tie Slatin to his side, or to render him harmless. This was by offering him yet another wife (!), this time a cousin of his own. But the nimble wit of Slatin enabled him to escape the dreaded gift by pointing out that the lady in question, being a descendant of the Prophet, should not be exposed to the danger of disgrace through the quick temper of a foreigner. But all the same this refusal of a bride related to the Khalifa himself offended the latter greatly, and now Slatin became very, very anxious to escape. He had frequently made attempts to induce the Austrian Consul-General at Cairo to assist him, but hitherto unsuccessfully. That the Khalifa had not already taken his life appears to have been due chiefly to the man's vanity at having as his slave one who had been governor of his own country and tribe.

A stricter watch was set on Slatin's every movement. He was seldom allowed in the town, and never to make visits to acquaintance. He had, however, the care of the Khalifa's numerous watches and clocks, and thus was compelled to visit from time to time the shop of an Armenian watchmaker. But he never confided in the shopkeeper, and those whom he wished to meet there generally made some short purchase in excuse. These brief meetings enabled a few words only to pass between the customers. Most of his time was spent at the Khalifa's gate reading the Koran, and in attending prayers five times daily.

But Slatin had two friends who were not easily discouraged by repeated failures to reach his ear. The Austrian Consul-General, who held a large sum of money for the purpose, and Major Wingate, succeeded in getting through various small sums of money, very considerably diminished ere they reached his hands. Again and again what seemed perfect plans were made, only to be frustrated. The Arab friends Slatin had made would have assisted him, but one was executed and the others feared the vengeance of the Khalifa after the escape became known.

It was a Dongola camel-postman who at last got into direct communication and arranged a meeting in the mosque, after prayers, where he handed Slatin a message from Colonel Schæffer, saying that the bearer was a trustworthy man. He may have been trustworthy, but he was dilatory and timid, and when notice began to be taken of his presence in Omdurman he fled.

The Austrian Consul and Major Wingate now made an offer of £1000 to an Arab merchant if he succeeded in effecting Slatin's escape. This was in the winter of 1893, but it was not until the middle of next summer, 1894, that he received word that full preparation had been made for his flight, with every prospect of success. On July 1 he was warned that the start would be made the next night, and that he should plan to leave as much time as possible between his starting and before his escape would be noticed. A relative of the contracting merchant, named Ahmed, accompanied him as he quitted the mosque the next night – "with bare feet and armed only with a sword, we hurried along the road. . . . and turned off in a north-easterly direction."

The night was dark and cool, as the rainy season had begun. All was favourable, but their camels and attendants were not at the appointed place, and, bitterly disappointed, they had to return, thankful to get back without observation. Two days later he learnt that the Arabs had considered the risk of capture too great.

Then followed several months of further plotting and planning, until in the middle of January of 1895 a man jostled him in the street and whispered, "I am the man with the needles." Slatin had been previously warned that such a message would introduce a new agent and a new scheme of escape. But this man also failed, and begged for a letter to Major Wingate asking for more money. This was the more disappointing, as the man had brought a letter from Father Ohrwalder, who had already escaped to Egypt, recommending him as a trustworthy agent.

Dejected, Slatin was returning to his house, when he met Mohammed Ahmed, the first agent, who whispered to him in passing, "We are ready. The camels are bought; the guides are engaged; the time arranged for your escape is during the moon's last quarter next month. Be ready!"

Then, about the end of January, another agent, employed by the Austrian Consul and Major Wingate, arrived in Omdurman and told Slatin to be ready to escape.

Which to choose? It was an embarrassment of offers, occurring as they did simultaneously. In the end he wisely decided to escape by the first assistance that offered.

On February 17th Mohammed whispered to Slatin that the "camels would arrive the next day, that they would rest two days, and the attempt would be made on the night of the twentieth."

The night arrived. At ten o'clock the Khalifa had retired. "I arose," says Slatin, "took the farwa (the rug on which we pray) and the farda (a light woollen cloth) on my shoulders, and went across the mosque to the road that leads north. I heard a low cough, the signal of Mohammed, the intermediary in my escape, and I stood still. He had brought a donkey. I mounted, and was off. The night was dark. The cold northerly wind had driven the people into their huts and houses."

They reached the outskirt of the town, and there a man met them with a saddled camel.

"This is your guide," said Mohammed; "his name is Zeki Belal. He will guide you to the riding camels that are waiting concealed in the desert. Make haste. A happy journey, and God protect you."

An hour's ride brought them to the travelling camels, and at sunrise they reached Wadi Bishara, when Slatin was able to get a good look at his two guides. Zeki was a young fellow, with a downy beard, while the other man, Hamed Ibn Hussein, was middle-aged. All three travelled at their swiftest, the start of only twelve hours, as estimated by Slatin, not being much when they were mounted only on inferior beasts.

During the first day's hurried rush they were alarmed by a party of Arabs whom they saw in the distance, and who recognized the presence of a white man. A bribe of twenty dollars secured a promise of silence from the leader. This was a truly hard day. They pushed on for twenty-one hours without stopping, eating nothing, and only once having a drink of water. Even now they proposed but to rest an hour for the sake of the camels. But the poor beasts were done up, and refused food. The fugitives could not wait, as every hour lost increased their danger. So the tired animals were urged on, though they could go no faster than a walk, and the sun had risen the second day before they found themselves on the high ground north of Metemmeh. They had still a day's journey to reach the spot, near Berber, where a change of camels awaited them. They struggled on until afternoon, and then were compelled to conceal themselves in the rugged ground of the Gilif range of hills while their beasts rested and recovered strength, or until the guides could procure other mounts.

Once within shelter of the rocky Gilif hills, Slatin was left hidden, while the guides took the camels to a spring of water at some distance. For a week Slatin and Hamed lay hidden in the rocks, while Zeki went on a two days' journey to procure help from some relatives of his. Slatin's thoughts were of his home and companions at Omdurman, and of that other and dearer home in far-off Austria, that had begun to loom on the horizon of his mental vision. But his musings were cut short by the sight of an Arab who had approached and caught sight of them, endeavouring to steal off without being observed. Hamed started after the man, and brought him to Slatin with the information that all was well, as the stranger proved to be a relative and might be useful. Fortunately this proved to be so, yet the Arab confessed with a grin that his first intention on seeing the slenderly guarded white man was to come back at night and rob him. The newcomer recognized in Hamed a former benefactor, and in gratitude led the fugitives to a more secure hiding-place about a mile away. This was a tiny cave in the rocks, where they lay securely hidden until the return of Zeki.

This time of waiting was a severe trial, especially as both water and provisions began to fail. Slatin remained in the cave during the daytime, but went off some distance to sleep at night, his companion keeping watch from a neighbouring height. This continued for several days, when Zeki returned with two fresh camels. That night the party rode cautiously without stopping, covering half the remaining distance to the relief party. They now reached the most critical stage of their flight, the approach to the Nile, which they had to cross at all hazards, and which would have many people about its banks.

The way was fearful travelling, a sandy waste thickly covered with stones, small and large. In sight of the Nile Slatin was again left alone while his companions went off into the night to reconnoitre and see if they could get tidings of the relief party. About dawn Hamed returned alone, with disappointment on his face. He informed Slatin that they must return to the desert and remain hidden until the next night, as there were too many people about. Building a screen of loose stones, the fugitive remained all day on his back, his spirits at a low ebb, and courage nearly gone. "God have mercy on me!" he cried, at the bitter disappointment. "Let me see my friends and dear ones, my fatherland again!"

Then Hamed returned and informed Slatin that all was well, and that that night he would be safely across the river, the most dangerous part of his journey over. At nightfall he arrived in sight of the Nile once more, at a spot near the fifth cataract, about fifty miles north of Berber. Here his faithful guides, who had done so much to ensure his safety and comfort since leaving Khartum, left him. Two new guides led the way to the river-bank after two hours of watchful riding. The passage across the river was made in a small boat, which was sunk after they had crossed. The camels were made to swim across, with the help of inflated skins, at different points in order, though it was quite dark, not to attract too much attention, for orders had come down the river to have all ferries and roads watched.

Once across the Nile, another day had to be spent in hiding, as it was not yet safe to travel by day. The march over the rough stones into the hills completely exhausted Slatin, so that he could only stumble on, staggering like a drunken man. Night brought his guides, and also the news of a providential escape from a body of Dervishes who passed that way. Fortunately the camels had been hidden, and so escaped seizure. Starting at midnight, the party pressed on with all speed for two days, almost without a halt, urging the camels to their utmost. The way was largely desert, inhabited chiefly by wild asses.

Arrived at the Nuranai hills, Slatin had trouble with his new guides, very different men from the first two. These were continually grumbling, and were careless besides, for they managed to drop their charge's sandals on the way, a loss that caused him much trouble afterwards. They were also afraid of the consequences to themselves should their participation in Slatin's escape ever be known. So Slatin was easily persuaded to accept a substituted guide who lived in the district whom they brought to their employer, and to bid these timid guides farewell.

In one respect the change of guide was disastrous. The man was faithful enough, but the extreme roughness of the way, and bad food combined with his considerable age, broke him down after a couple of days' further travelling, and Slatin had to mount him on their only camel, and walk the last four days himself. As his sandals had been lost by the second set of guides, this was a terrible business, and soon he was limping painfully along, leaving tracks of blood on the stones. Then the camel hurt its foot, and also began to limp. However, Slatin succeeded in making a sort of shoe for the poor beast from a piece of cloth, and slowly the crippled trio proceeded north.

But the end of his troubles was now near. On the 16th of March the town of Assuan came in sight. He was received with great delight by the English and Egyptian officers of the garrison, though they would not let him change his tattered garments for more civilized clothing until they had taken a photograph!

Everywhere the news of Slatin's miraculous escape was received with gladness, and telegrams of congratulation and offers of help were numerous. When he reached Cairo he met his friend Wingate Bey, "to whom I can never sufficiently show my gratitude in word or deed." Here he also met his old friend and companion in captivity, Father Ohrwalder. The changes that had taken place in the civilized world during his twelve years of captivity almost stunned him – he said it made his "head feel heavy, as though he had just woke up from an evil dream."

Thus, after seventeen years in the Sudan, twelve of them in durance, Slatin returned once more to his home and his kindred. But not for long, for presently he was back again in Egypt, helping the Government with his unique knowledge of the languages and the country known as the Equatorial provinces or Sudan, and what is really remarkable, he is at the present time Inspector-General of the Sudan.

Note

1 *Fire and Sword in the Sudan,* by Rudolf C. Slatin Pasha, C.B.

49

BOUND IN BENIN

A story of the massacre

By Lieut. A Manson

From: 'Bound in Benin', in *The Union Jack*, 18th March 1897, pp. 1–4.

These extracts are taken from boys and girls' magazines and annuals in the years 1880–1939. They were a response to the publications known as 'penny dreadfuls' (serialized, sensationalistic stories of crime and horror). Amongst the earliest of these new kind of magazines was the Boys' Own Paper (BOP), *published by the Religious Tract Society (RTS) in 1879.*

The founding values of this publication, and others that followed, was the belief that the youth would read and have instilled in them Christian moral values. In its early phase the BOP *stressed the missionary aspect of Empire, perhaps not surprising, given that the clergymen who had founded the RTS in 1799 had, four years earlier, founded the London Missionary Society. The paper and its companion, the* Boys' Own Annual, *promoted the British Empire, particularly in their first decade. Among those who wrote for the paper were Arthur Conan Doyle, R. M. Ballantyne, Jules Verne and G. M. Henty. Alfred Harmsworth noted that his stable of publications aimed to eradicate 'the miserable literary rubbish, in which murders, thieves and other criminals are raised to the position of heroes'. The* BOP *reflected Britain's position as a leading imperial power and its description of the races of Empire invariably include pejorative language. By 1900 the* BOP *was being challenged by other titles, such as those published by Edward Brett. These titles included* The Boys of the Empire, *published by Andrew Melrose and edited by Howard Spicer; G. A. Henty's* The Union Jack; *and* Young England: An Illustrated Magazine for Boys Throughout the English Speaking World *(1880), published by the London Sunday School Union. By the later 19th and early 20th centuries, another crop of youth publications had appeared, among which were* Chums *(1892);* Union Jack *(1894), founded by Alfred Harmsworth;* Pluck *(the full title of this publication was* Stories of Pluck: a high class weekly library of adventure at home and abroad, on land and sea, *1894);* Gem *(1907); and* The Magnet *(1908), for which Charles Hamilton (known as Frank Richards) wrote the Greyfriars stories. The* Girl's Own Paper *was edited first by Charles Peters (1880–1907), whose aim was to 'foster and develop that which was highest and noblest in the girlhood and womanhood of England . . . putting the best things first and banishing the worthless from his pages', and second by Flora Klickmann (1908–1931), who made the magazine a monthly publication. It was aimed at the middle-class English gentlewoman and in that respect tended to reflect the shift between an ideology of domesticated*

DOI: 10.4324/9781351024822-51

feminism transforming into an appreciation of the 'modern woman' who played sport, rode a bicycle and would perhaps eventually migrate to the Empire. Most of the features were educational and improving in their nature. Contemporary concern for physical fitness can be seen in magazines for both boys and girls. E. C. Dawson, author of document 50, was rector of St. Peter's, Edinburgh, and also authored Lion-Hearted *(1909) and* Missionary Heroines in India: true stories of the Wonderful bravery of patient endurance of missionaries in India, *published in the 1920s.*

Chapter I

FAREWELL TO HOME – IN THE TROPIC OF CANCER – A PERSISTENT BORE – WHERE ARE WE BOUND FOR? – THE SECRET SIGNALS – A DRUNKEN SKIPPER – OPEN MUTINY.

It was a beautiful evening in the early summer, and the setting sun was darting red beams athwart a lovely valley in the West of England.

On a rocky ledge of an eminence, forming one of a range of hills that bounded the valley on one side, a solitary man was standing looking down with sad eyes on a lonely farmhouse, embosomed among the trees at the foot of the hill.

He was young, and strongly-built, dressed in the style of a well-to-do farmer's son, and he stood with one hand in the pocket of his buckskin breeches, and the other grasping a stout blackthorn, handsomely mounted in silver.

His face was still bare of beard, and the soft felt hat pushed off his brow showed a wide and capacious forehead, that matched well with the set of his wilful-looking mouth.

He had been standing in this pensive attitude for some time, when appearing to be actuated by a sudden impulse, he raised the hand which held the stick, and, shaking it gently at the lonely farmhouse below, murmured:

"Good-bye, father and mother. Good-bye, George. Goodbye, little Lizzie. You'll none of you see me any more!"

He then turned swiftly, and, with a firm, determined step completed his ascent of the hill.

On reaching the top, he saw in the distance the long, white line of road, winding away for miles, till it was lost in the mystery of the horizon, and far away to the right a confusion of red roofs, and one solitary tower, standing calm and majestic, looking down on the wide stretch of open country.

He descended the hill, and, in the course of an hour's sharp walking, set his feet on the high road, and left the hills behind him.

Exactly four weeks after that an advertisement appeared in all the London papers to the following effect:

"John, – Come back. We have found out our mistake. Come back and forgive us. Your father is very ill. – LIZZIE."

The person to whom this was addressed never saw it, for he was at that time on the wide Atlantic, rapidly approaching the Tropic of Cancer.

He was pacing the deck in a pensive mood, looking at the dancing waves, or watching the flight of a sea-bird from the neighbouring islands; but there was an expression on his face as if the present scene was veiled to his eyes, and he was recalling the bygone years.

Figure 49.1 The carriers started off at a quick trot, the bodies of their prisoners dangling and swaying from the poles.

"Enjoying the beauties of the ocean, my friend?" said a slightly nasal voice behind him, and, at the same time, a somewhat rude and heavy hand was laid on his shoulder.

He turned with an expression of annoyance on his face, which was not lost on the intruder, and replied:

"No. I was thinking of something far different."

"Surly cub!" muttered the gentleman, with the nasal voice. "No getting alongside of him. I'll wake him up presently, I doubt. Hallo! There's that son-of-a-gun up to his tricks again!"

As he spoke, a small, thin man, with a deep scar down one side of his face, peeped up the hatchway, and made signs to the man at the wheel, who watched him attentively, and nodded as if in assent.

"There's some etarnal villainy brewing. Of that I'm sartin sure. But what it is I can't at present fathom."

These words were not spoken aloud. They were merely thought in the recesses of the gentleman's brain.

"I wish that lad was not so perky. We might together find out something that would be valuable to us. Hallo! there, mister," said he, walking close up to the young man, whose name, as we learned from the advertisement, was John – John Gower. "Can a body have a few minutes' confidential chat with you, without crowding you too much?"

John looked up with the same shade of annoyance in his face as before; but something in the expression of the man's keen, grey eye, caused him to relax, and he replied:

"Certainly, if you wish."

"Thanks," said the man, in so peculiar a tone that John glanced at him suspiciously, and felt inclined to take huff again.

The next words that fell from the stranger's lips made John Gower open his eyes.

"Are you aware where this old tub is going to?"

"Why, to Rio. You knew that before you took your passage in her, surely?" replied John, regarding the man with eyes that seemed to say: "You've been having a glass too much, my good friend."

"She is not going there!"

"Where is she going, then?"

"That I cannot say, though I can make a very good guess."

"You are a strange man."

"You are a stranger man, not to be able to trust the evidence of your senses."

"My senses give me no evidence that the vessel is going anywhere but on her rightful course."

"Have you seen the skipper lately?"

"Not for some little time."

"You will be astonished to learn that he is in his cabin as drunk as a lord, and the ship's course has been altered without his knowledge."

"Why, man, you must be crazy!" said John; but at the same time a vague uneasiness took possession of him, as he looked in the man's earnest face.

"Look! look!" he whispered in John's ear. And he pointed to a curious scene that was taking place a little distance from them.

The same diminutive man, who had given the signal before, was now telegraphing to the man at the wheel, who, with the same rapt attention on his face, was endeavouring to read the signs.

At last, with a nod and a smile of satisfaction, that had a grim significance for the two watchers, the man at the wheel gave the other to understand all was clear, and the latter descended to the regions below.

"What had better be done?' asked John, now convinced there was something going as it ought not to go."

"What say, if we pop down and try and see the skipper?"

"I am ready. Shall we go at once?" "Yes."

They walked across the deck, and descended to the captain's cabin. They were the only passengers, with the exception of the person they had seen signalling to the man at the wheel. The mate was ill – had been taken seriously and mysteriously ill soon after they had entered the Channel, and had been in bed ever since.

They knocked at the door, and a hoarse voice bade them enter.

The room reeked with odours of stale tobacco and of old rum.

For some few minutes they could discern nothing clearly; but, as their eyes got used to the murk, they saw the skipper sitting in an armchair at the other end of the table, a pitiable spectacle of helpless intoxication.

A half-emptied glass and a wholly-emptied rum-flask stood on the table near him, and the table was stained and ugly with the spilled liquor.

The drunken skipper took no notice of the entry of the two men. He was too far gone in insensibility.

They tried to rouse him; but he only snorted in an imbecile manner, and they regarded each other in dismay.

The American said in a low tone:

"I fear he is in the hand of an astute villain who keeps him plied with drink."

"Oh, you do – do you?" cried a mocking voice from the door behind them. And, turning, they saw the wizened face of the man they had watched on the deck grinning at them malevolently.

"Perhaps," he said, in the same mocking tone, "you would like to run this vessel yourselves. I have noticed you very busy of late prying into what you have no business with."

"No business, do you say?" demanded Cyrus Fadden, as we may now call the American without further mystery. "No business? When we book our passage for Rio, and find we are being taken to goodness knows where?"

"What authority have you on board this ship?" asked John.

"Authority enough to have you pitched overboard, if you are not civil!" snarled the man, with a sudden change from his crafty manner to a fierce, aggressive ferocity.

"Indeed?" said John.

"Yes, indeed. Get out of this cabin at once! It is a private place, where neither you nor your Yankee friend have any business. Clear out, or I'll have you chucked out!"

John strode forward with some idea of chastising his insolence, when the small man stepped back, uttered a loud cry of rage, and, the door flying open, half a dozen of the crew rushed in, their faces aflame from drink, uttering loud yells.

"Ah! this is a mutiny!" cried Cyrus. "Old man, wake up. They are robbing you of your vesse.

Before he could utter another word, he was felled to the floor, and John, attempting to assist him, found himself involved in the same plight.

One of the armed ruffians had struck him a heavy blow on the temple, from which a thin stream of blood was now flowing, and he lay dazed and wondering on the ground.

Before he could make an effort to rouse himself, he found himself seized by a group of men, and hurried from the cabin.

Chapter II

THE LEADER EXPLAINS HIS PLAN – ADRIFT ON THE OCEAN – CYRUS SHOWS HIS SKILL – FREE ONCE MORE – THE CAPTAIN DISAPPEARS – BORNE ON BY THE CURRENT.

The two men, finding themselves thus violently assaulted, struggled desperately with their assailants; but numbers prevailed, and, with a heavy groan of despair, John fell to the ground.

There was a chorus of mocking laughter, as the victory was thus declared in favour of the mutineers, and the two prisoners were quickly deprived of the power of making any further resistance.

"What is your purpose? What do you mean by such conduct as this?" asked Cyrus.

"What are you going to do with us?" said John.

"Well, we don't want your blood on our hands; we know it's useless to attempt to come to terms with you; so all we can do is to turn you adrift, and give you a chance for your lives. If you lose them it won't be our fault."

"Do you really intend to do what you have said?" asked John, looking at the man with horror, as he stood before him grinning with all his might.

"We do that, my boy, as you will very soon find out. Lift them up, men, and bring them on deck. They won't have another chance of interfering in the management of this vessel."

"Interfering with the management?" said John indignantly. "You mean, interposing to save the vessel from the hands of a rascal like you?"

"Do I? Well, very likely we mean the same thing. You are talking very big just now. In a short time, maybe, you will not make so open a mouth."

"What do you intend to do with us?"

"Haven't I told you? Why, we're going to put you in a snug little boat – you and your friend, and the drunken skipper – and send you on a cruise round the Gold Coast. We are bound there, too, and we shall load the ship with gold, and you will tear your hair with envy to think you were such fools as to interfere where you had no business."

Then, seeing John was about to retort with one of his hot remarks, the leader of the mutineers went on:

"Bring them up to the deck. No more palaver. We'll settle their business in a brace of shakes."

"Bring them along, men, and fetch up the skipper, too. We'll send them all adrift together."

"Nay, man, you will never be so reckless!" pleaded John Gower, overcome with the horror of the situation.

"Bring them along!" was the only reply. And the crew, grinning with ferocious glee, set about their task with every appearance of supreme enjoyment.

John was the first to be carried to the deck, and there he was thrown down with brutal violence.

In a few minutes Cyrus was brought up also, and, last of all, the skipper, still insensibly drunk.

The boat was quickly got ready, and lowered to the water, and, when this was done, the leader came over to where the prisoners were lying, and, touching them by turns with his foot, said contemptuously:

"Now then, carrion! Come along. Your gig is ready, and you are going for a sail on the sea – the salt, salt sea!"

He looked demoniacal as he uttered these words, and the crew around laughed aloud.

"But, surely," said John, "you will unbind us? You will not turn us adrift in this fashion?"

"Surely," he replied, mimicking John's manner of saying the word – "surely, but we are. It's more merciful, you know. If you had the use of your limbs, you'd be trying to save yourselves, and so prolonging your misery. No, no. We are too humane for that. You go just as you are, and the quicker will be the end of you. That's genuine humanity – isn't it, men?"

"Ay, ay, sir!" was the fierce response. And the leader winked and chuckled at his villainous crew.

"Age before honour!" cried the mutineer leader, in a mocking voice; "the old gent first."

Immediately there was a rush made upon Cyrus, who was, of course, incapable of defence, and he was lifted and carried to the side of the vessel. Some tackle was fastened to his body, and he was dropped over the side, where a man stood upright in the boat, to receive and unfasten the body.

"Next one!" cried the leader. And John was lifted, and in a few moments thrown down on top of his companion.

The drunken skipper, still insensible, came down last.

Then the man loosened the rope that held the boat to the vessel's side, seized it in his hands, and was hoisted up.

"Good-morning to you!" cried a mocking voice from above. "Good-morning, and good luck!"

In a few minutes the vessel had spread her sails, and was flying over the face of the waters.

Cyrus at once began a persistent course of wriggling and writhing, which lasted for some time, and then, to the astonishment and delight of John, he bent over him with arms free, and with a gleaming knife in his slender right hand.

"They are not quite so clever as they thought themselves. We will not die with our arms fettered, at all events. We will have a struggle for life. Cheer up, lad. While there's life there's hope. There are ships on the ocean, there are islands in the sea, and there are currents which may bear us to the land. What, man, we are not dead yet. Look on the sunny side."

All the time he was speaking, he was busy at John's bonds, and, in a surprisingly short time, had them lying in pieces in the bottom of the boat.

"There, lad. Now you are a free man again. Look up – pluck up spirit, and battle for your life."

John looked at him with surprise, and wondered for a moment or two if this was the same man who had caused him such annoyance on the deck of the vessel but a few short hours before?

So soon as his arms were unbound, he sat up in the boat, and looked around him o'er the wide waste of waters on which they were floating.

"What do you think will become of us?" he asked of his companion presently, as the latter appeared absorbed in deep thought.

"In a few hours – a very few hours, we shall be in sight of land."

"What?" said John incredulously. "In sight of land?"

"Yes. Look, the boat is moving, without any help from us. We are in a gentle current, which I have no doubt will presently increase in force, and drift us at last to land."

As Cyrus predicted, so it came to pass, and towards evening they became aware the boat was moving rapidly in a straight line.

Towards morning they saw there was a gradual change, both in the scene and in the skipper. His eyes stared wildly, and he began to rave.

They watched him closely; but he took no notice of anything they said or did to him.

When the sun had risen high in the heavens, he started to his feet.

They tried to persuade him to lie down, for he was imperilling the safety of the boat; but he appeared endowed with extraordinary strength, and they were obliged to quit their hold on him to avoid being pitched into the sea.

Directly they released him he drew himself up to his full height, and before they could guess his intention, sprang with a wild cry into the waves.

They could render the poor wretch no assistance, for the boat drifted rapidly on, and they had no means of staying her course.

He came to the surface once with a white, bewildered, terrified face, and then sank for ever.

"It is the best thing that could happen to him," said Cyrus Fadden. "He has escaped much misery."

John Gower answered with a deep sigh.

Chapter III

IN BENIN BIGHT – A CROWD OF BLACKS – THE BLACK CHIEF – WE WILL NOT KNEEL – TIT FOR TAT – AN UNPLEASANT JOURNEY – ARRIVAL AT THE TOWN.

On went the boat. No sign of land was seen all that day, and the night fell at last, and their eyes closed in broken and uneasy slumbers.

When they again awoke, it was with a confused feeling that they were again on board the ship, and surrounded by the angry mutineers.

A few seconds sufficed to dispel the illusion.

They were surrounded, it was true; but by a dreadful-looking mob of ferocious blacks, who were chattering and gesticulating in the most alarming manner.

"Hallo!" said Cyrus, regarding the ugly crew, "we have got into unpleasant company. I trust they are not cannibals, though I fear the taste is somewhat prevalent in these parts."

"Where are we?" asked John, in a tone of wonder and apprehension combined.

"I cannot precisely say. But I have been once before in the Bight of Benin, and if I am not mistaken it is somewhere in that neighbourhood we are at this present moment. This is either an island, or part of the mainland of the Gold Coast, on the west coast of Africa – in fact, of that much I am sure."

"The Gold Coast. That rascal mentioned the place, you remember?"

"I do. And it was to that part of the world they themselves were bound in my opinion."

John was about to make some answer, but before they could say another word, the black mob made a rush on them, and they were dragged unceremoniously out of the boat, and some yards inwards towards a giant tree, whose leaves and branches made a pleasant shade in the fierce sunlight which was now beginning to stream down from the cloudless sky.

Beneath this tree was seated a fierce-looking and immensely corpulent black man, who regarded the prisoners with a ferociously-gleaming eye, as they were dragged and pushed into his presence.

The men who accompanied them went down on their knees, and grovelled before this black fellow, and they made signs to the prisoners to do the same.

"They want us to kneel," said John, looking at his companion.

"So I see," was the quiet rejoinder. "What is your opinion? Had we better do it?"

"Certainly not!" cried John Gower, with a look of scorn in his eye. "Kneel to a black rascal like that? I'd rather be shot at once!"

"Oh, as for that, shooting on the spot is not much in their line. They like something more protracted."

"Do you mean torture?" asked John, blanching a little.

The other nodded his head, and smiled grimly.

"I don't care!" said John. "Let them do as they will, they shall not make me go down on my knees to any black rascal in the world."

"Bravo, lad! My sentiments exactly!"

This little dialogue had taken but a few seconds in delivery: but it was too long for the blacks, whose impatience displayed itself in loud cries.

John had opened his mouth to say something in reply to his comrade, when a fellow who had stolen up behind them with a heavy club dealt him a terrific blow on the back of the head, and he went down like a log of wood. The next instant Cyrus lay beside him from the same cause.

John, though stunned for the instant, was up again in a remarkably short space of time, and, seeing the man with the club standing near him, he launched his left with terrific force straight into the face of the negro, who, with a shrill cry, occupied the spot from which John had just risen, and lay there as if he had been smitten with his own club.

"Well done, lad!" cried Cyrus, who had lifted his head from the ground just in time to see the punishment of the aggressor. "A true British blow, straight from the shoulder. The black fellow seems to have taken it to heart."

There was a sudden and ominous silence of the black mob, as they witnessed this daring deed on the part of one whom they had supposed would be overcome with fear at the mighty presence in which he stood.

Presently the chief spoke. He seemed to give an order, and the next moment a crowd of blacks, armed with spears, rushed forward and the two prisoners were thrown to the ground in spite of their desperate struggles to throw off the enemy.

They were soon bound securely with withes, in a manner which would have taught the mutineers a wrinkle could they have seen the process.

A few minutes after there came a tremendous yell from the back of the crowd surrounding them, and four men drew near bearing long poles in their hands. Two of these they thrust brutally under the thongs which bound the hands and feet of the two Englishmen, and lifted them by this means from the ground.

The agony was exquisite as they hung with all their weight by their wrists and ankles, and, in a few seconds, the withes that bound them began, as it were, to eat into the flesh, from which the blood soon streamed.

This agony was increased when, at an order from the chief under the tree, the carriers started off at a quick trot, and the bodies of the prisoners dangled and swayed from the poles.

They rested once or twice, for the bearers' sake – not for theirs – on the terrible journey, and towards evening they were startled for an instant out of the consciousness of their sufferings by a deafening din of drums and trumpets which arose in the distance before them.

"We are approaching a town of some sort," said Cyrus hopefully. "Then we shall be released."

John only answered with a groan.

Cyrus was right. On looking around them with pained and swollen eyes, they saw they were entering a long lane of huts, and that crowds of blacks were thronging round to catch a glimpse of the white prisoners.

Presently they were borne in another direction out of the straight line, and were at length thrown down unceremoniously in a dark and ill-smelling hut.

As his bruised limbs touched the ground, John fainted away.

Chapter IV

ALONE IN THE HUT – A MYSTERIOUS VISITOR – A NOVEL EXPERIENCE – A FRIGHTFUL JOURNEY – THE COVERED STREAM – THE HUT.

When John again recovered his consciousness, he found himself in a dismal, ill-smelling place, with a half-open door through which there was a glimpse of sunlight, and of waving branches.

It was some time before he could recall all the incidents that had led up to his present predicament, and then, looking about him, he missed his companion.

"Fadden!" he cried – "Fadden! Where are you?"

There was no answer, and a great terror took possession of his soul. Was it possible that anything had happened to his friend?

He raised himself with difficulty on his elbow, and strove to pierce the gloom of the further corners of the hut. There was neither movement nor sound.

He called aloud once more, and then thought he detected a faint rustling in the further corner, where he could dimly perceive a heap of rushes, or some similar material.

His fixed his eyes on this, and called out again.

There was no answer, but there was a decided movement in the heap.

While he was racking his brain to find out what this might portend, and wondering whether some drunken black, or mayhap some venomous beast, had taken refuge there, he was startled by seeing the mass of material moved aside at the bottom, and a pair of gleaming eyes fixed intently upon him.

"A wild beast," he said to himself. "But of what kind?"

What beast did he know of that had eyes like that?

A still more decisive movement took place, and he saw the head and shoulders of a man protrude from the mass.

The shoulders were those of a man of immense size, and the head and face were also of giant proportions. What was his astonishment, then, when the figure, having entirely withdrawn itself and stood upright, he saw it was the figure of a man scarce four feet high, whose arms, hanging by his side, allowed his fingers to rest on the floor, exactly as in the case of the larger monkeys.

The black, cavernous eyes gazed at him with great intensity; but he saw, to his surprise, they were not fixed on him with a ferocious look, but rather with a mild and gentle expression, which did not tally with the wild and uncouth appearance of the rest of the frightful figure.

"Who are you?" asked John, almost unconsciously; for he had no idea the figure would understand his question.

"Ju-Ju man – Mahlki. Come help white man."

The young Englishman looked at the strange being, and was inclined to think he was the victim of some illusion of the senses.

The voice of his strange visitor was wonderfully deep, and made the air vibrate like the pedal of an organ, or the boom of a big bell.

"Where is my friend? Where is the other white man? Do you know?"

"Ju-Ju man – medicine man – know all things," was the solemn reply.

"Does he, by George!" exclaimed John, beside himself with surprise at the fact of the strangeness of the visitor, and his being able to speak English.

"Can he tell me where my friend is?"

"Yes."

"Where is he?" said John, a prey to the most poignant emotion, caused by the strange solemnity of the dwarf's manner and the sudden disappearance of his comrade.

"He go to King's palace. He there now. He sacrifice to Marimbo, the great King's god."

"What!" cried John, in a voice that quivered with horror. "When did they take him? Why did they not take me, too?"

"You go to-night."

"Ha, ha, ha!" shrieked the excited man, in a burst of hysterical laughter. "Are they going to sacrifice me, too?"

"Yes. All white men come on shore go to be sacrifice to Marimbo."

"Excellent! And what is the precise nature of the ceremony? Do they take long about it?"

"Yes, long, long time."

"Ah, just so! They spin it out a bit. Didn't I understand you to say just now that you had come to help the white man?"

"Yes."

"How do you propose to do it?"

For answer the black drew a gleaming blade from under his dark woollen garment, which entirely concealed his short legs, and advanced on the captive.

For one moment John had the wild hope that the dwarf was intent on slaughtering him, and he welcomed the merciful death that would save him from the lingering tortures he knew by repute.

To his increased astonishment, the black, instead of sticking the knife into the white man's breast, slipped it beneath the withes that bound his ankles, and set his legs free. The next instant he had done the same to his arms.

"Come with me. I put you hide."

"My good friend – for such in intention I see you are – I couldn't move to save my life; my limbs are dead. All the blood has been forced out of the arteries, and the doors closed against any return."

"Your legs, your arms, stiff?" said the dwarf, looking at the captive, and a little puzzled by the speech he had just used.

"Stiff, my good fellow, conveys no idea of the case. They are dead, as far as fitness for active service is concerned."

"Then Mahlki carry white man on his shoulder."

"My excellent Ju-Ju man, you could not do such a thing. I have not been feeding very well of late, but I am too heavy."

With a curious look in his face, the dwarf stepped forward, and before John could guess his intention had put his arms around him and hoisted him to his monstrous shoulder as easily, it seemed, as he would have lifted a cat.

"I carry you little way; then I give you something make walk, run, jump."

He approached the door, when a renewed feeling of distrust coming into John's mind, he said loudly:

"Where are you going to take me?"

"Hush! Not talk, not cough, not sneeze. Marimbo hear. Kill both. Go fast. Not long."

Resigning himself to his fate, in which, in spite of the grimness of his surroundings, John could not help detecting a tiny grain of humour, he allowed the dwarf to carry him from the hut.

The burst of blinding sunshine, as they came out into the open air, destroyed his visual organs for the time, and all was blank.

He was conscious, though, of an awful stillness in the air, and not a sound of bird or beast was to be heard.

"Where are all the people?" he asked in wonder.

"Hush! Not talk. Marimbo hear. Kill both at once."

John could feel a tremor pass through the dwarf's limbs as he spoke, as though he were fully convinced of the presence of some great danger, from which they could be saved only by the greatest precautions.

With rapid strides, despite the by no means insignificant weight he carried across his shoulder, the dwarf proceeded along a narrow lane, bordered on each side by thickly growing shrubs and a kind of latticework.

A few minutes after they had entered a patch of long, thick grass, amid which the dwarf deposited his burden, motioning the white man to follow him on hands and knees through the jungle.

The way was comparatively easy for John, as the wide shoulders of the dwarf cleared his passage for him, and by . . .

50

FROTH

By the Rev. E. C. Dawson

From: Rev. E. C. Dawson, 'Froth', in *Boys of the Empire*, 1st December 1900, p. 111.

These extracts are taken from boys and girls' magazines and annuals in the years 1880–1939. They were a response to the publications known as 'penny dreadfuls' (serialized, sensationalistic stories of crime and horror). Amongst the earliest of these new kind of magazines was the Boys' Own Paper (BOP), *published by the Religious Tract Society (RTS) in 1879.*

The founding values of this publication, and others that followed, was the belief that the youth would read and have instilled in them Christian moral values. In its early phase the BOP *stressed the missionary aspect of Empire, perhaps not surprising, given that the clergymen who had founded the RTS in 1799 had, four years earlier, founded the London Missionary Society. The paper and its companion, the* Boys' Own Annual, *promoted the British Empire, particularly in their first decade. Among those who wrote for the paper were Arthur Conan Doyle, R. M. Ballantyne, Jules Verne and G. M. Henty. Alfred Harmsworth noted that his stable of publications aimed to eradicate 'the miserable literary rubbish, in which murders, thieves and other criminals are raised to the position of heroes'. The* BOP *reflected Britain's position as a leading imperial power and its description of the races of Empire invariably include pejorative language. By 1900 the* BOP *was being challenged by other titles, such as those published by Edward Brett. These titles included* The Boys of the Empire, *published by Andrew Melrose and edited by Howard Spicer; G. A. Henty's* The Union Jack; *and* Young England: An Illustrated Magazine for Boys Throughout the English Speaking World *(1880), published by the London Sunday School Union. By the later 19th and early 20th centuries, another crop of youth publications had appeared, among which were* Chums *(1892);* Union Jack *(1894), founded by Alfred Harmsworth;* Pluck *(the full title of this publication was* Stories of Pluck: a high class weekly library of adventure at home and abroad, on land and sea, *1894);* Gem *(1907); and* The Magnet *(1908), for which Charles Hamilton (known as Frank Richards) wrote the Greyfriars stories. The* Girl's Own Paper *was edited first by Charles Peters (1880–1907), whose aim was to 'foster and develop that which was highest and noblest in the girlhood and womanhood of England... putting the best things first and banishing the worthless from his pages', and second by Flora Klickmann (1908–1931), who made the magazine a monthly publication. It was aimed at the middle-class English gentlewoman and in that respect tended to reflect the shift between an ideology of domesticated feminism transforming into an appreciation of the 'modern woman' who played sport, rode a bicycle and would perhaps eventually migrate to the Empire. Most of the features were educational and improving in their nature. Contemporary concern for physical fitness can be seen in magazines for both boys and girls. E. C. Dawson, author of document 50, was rector of St. Peter's, Edinburgh, and also authored* Lion-Hearted *(1909) and* Missionary Heroines in India: true stories of the Wonderful bravery of patient endurance of missionaries in India, *published in the 1920s.*

THOUGH some things are bound to be, we are not bound to be them. That, I take it, needs no demonstration. But it may be all the better for a little demonstration. Let me use as an illustration that very common thing, froth.

In the first place, what is froth? The dictionary definition is that it is the bubbles caused in liquors by agitation. But, of course, that depends upon the liquors which are agitated. If the liquor holds all kinds of solids in solution it is easy to shake it into froth. Soapy water, for example, or beer, or porter, froth up at once. Sea-water, which is full of salty matter, works up into dense flakes of white, spumy foam when it is lashed into waves. The muddy water of most of our lowland rivers swirls into foam at every weir. Even the highland waters do the same, because they are charged with the peaty deposit which stains them their beautiful amber. But absolutely pure water will not make froth. There is never any foam on the tumbled surface of the fresh spring which wells up straight from the clean heart of the rock. That is just where it is. You are bound to get froth in a world of mixed motives. There is no frothy talk among the angels. We may be sure of that. Their service is pure and simple and with no dregs of selfishness in it. When they rest not day and night crying Holy, holy, holy, and when they gather in their thousands of thousands and make their united voices heard, as it were the voice of a great multitude, and as the voice of many waters, and as the voice of mighty thunderings, shouting Alleluia, it is because they are expressing exactly what they feel, and what they mean to carry into action whenever the occasion arrives.

But the world is not like that – yet. And we must take the world as we find it. And so long as men are what they are, we are bound to have froth. One must expect froth whenever men's minds are stirred. One even welcomes a certain amount of froth, as a sure sign that things are not stagnant. If there is no froth you may be sure there is no movement.

Jingoism is froth, if by jingoism you mean music-hall shouting, and bellowing of patriotic songs. But when the nation is moved to its depths, all sorts of queer stuff comes to the top. One would rather the rotten stuff was not there, but, since it is there, its very appearance is one of the signs of the general stir.

Things are stirring just now, thank goodness. No one can lie a-bed comfortably unless he has got a doctor's certificate. He has got to show why he does not take his proper part in all that is going on. The school does not want him unless he will do something for its honour somehow, at his games, or, if he is only capable of swotting, at least, with his brains. College does not want him unless he means to buckle to. The captain of the boats calls on him first thing, if he is a likely chap, and the captain of the eleven looks him up, if he hears a good report of him; and if he is no use to either, he is expected, at all events, to subscribe to all that is going on. Besides which, he is required to pass his examinations within a given period, or quit.

And life everywhere is just as hard upon a fellow after he goes out into the world. It really is counted bad form to do nothing for anybody. That old American story seems likely to come out true. "How do you define a gentleman?" "One who does nothing." "Oh! we call that sort a tramp." *Punch* has lately set a smart quip circulating. "What are you going to do this mornin', eh?" asks one young gilded loafer of another. "Oh, I dunno. Rot about, I 'spose, as usual." "Oh, but I say, that's so rotten." "Well," replies his friend, "what else is there to do, you rotter?" That's an amiable way of laughing out of court what we all cordially despise. The moneyed and titled idler has made a long stride towards the ranks of the workers when he has discovered that he is a "rotter." As much a rotter as the worst of them who goes to rot at the lazy corners of the dirty East-end alleys. No fellow now has a chance of being respected unless he does *something*. His very valet will make a grimace at him.

Of course this general stir-about whips up a great deal of froth and fume. It is sickening to hear some people talk. They work themselves out in talk. And it grows upon them. They begin to think that they have a mission to tell other people what they ought to do. They do not stop to ask whether they have yet made any start of doing anything themselves. They just put on full steam, like a ship at anchor in a muddy harbour, churning up froth in grand style, but not making an inch of way.

And the provoking thing is that they often get the credit for what the silent busy workers are achieving. Oh! it is a paying thing in this poor, silly world, is frothy talk, and it makes one properly mad to see it.

But we really need not concern ourselves with such things. It is the weakest and most foolish of mistakes to allow oneself to be disgusted and turned aside from the right way because one does not like all the companions he must meet there. The question, of course, is, Does the Way go in the right direction? and not What sort of people get into the Way? *We*, at all events, may go at some pace without fuss. What if the others waste their breath in shouting, we need not stop to listen, but just ride on. Gaily coasting down hill, steadily pedalling all along the levels, grinding doggedly in the face of the adverse wind, and sticking to our work on the long weary rises, we can keep on our way, and let those follow who will.

In his essay on Robespierre, Mr. John Morley compares the flashy French orator with such men as Jefferson and Washington, who also had to take their part in forming a new nation. While Robespierre poured out speech after speech, which threw his hearers into ecstacies of delight, it was said of Jefferson by one who knew him intimately that he seldom uttered three sentences together, and of Washington that he was not heard to speak ten minutes at a time.

Unhappy Robespierre! Did he ever think of the uselessness of it all, as he lay that miserable last day of his life, with his once fluent mouth shattered by a pistol ball, and waiting to hear the curses of the people as he too was dragged, all shattered and dishonoured, to the guillotine?

Well, we must not run away with the idea that all words are froth. Only let us take care that ours are not. And since froth there must be, let us not be disheartened or too much troubled about it, but go on our way to serve God and our country, as though we heard it not.

51

THROUGH PERIL TO FORTUNE

The strange adventures of two young Britons in the heart of Africa

By W. Shaw Rae

From: 'Through Peril to Fortune: The Strange Adventure of Two Young Britons in the Heart of Africa', Chapter 1. *The Union Jack*, 15th October 1898, pp. 1–4.

These extracts are taken from boys and girls' magazines and annuals in the years 1880–1939. They were a response to the publications known as 'penny dreadfuls' (serialized, sensationalistic stories of crime and horror). Amongst the earliest of these new kind of magazines was the Boys' Own Paper (BOP), *published by the Religious Tract Society (RTS) in 1879.*

The founding values of this publication, and others that followed, was the belief that the youth would read and have instilled in them Christian moral values. In its early phase the BOP *stressed the missionary aspect of Empire, perhaps not surprising, given that the clergymen who had founded the RTS in 1799 had, four years earlier, founded the London Missionary Society. The paper and its companion, the* Boys' Own Annual, *promoted the British Empire, particularly in their first decade. Among those who wrote for the paper were Arthur Conan Doyle, R. M. Ballantyne, Jules Verne and G. M. Henty. Alfred Harmsworth noted that his stable of publications aimed to eradicate 'the miserable literary rubbish, in which murders, thieves and other criminals are raised to the position of heroes'. The* BOP *reflected Britain's position as a leading imperial power and its description of the races of Empire invariably include pejorative language. By 1900 the* BOP *was being challenged by other titles, such as those published by Edward Brett. These titles included* The Boys of the Empire, *published by Andrew Melrose and edited by Howard Spicer; G. A. Henty's* The Union Jack; Young England: An Illustrated Magazine for Boys Throughout the English Speaking World *(1880), published by the London Sunday School Union. By the later 19th and early 20th centuries, another crop of youth publications had appeared, among which were* Chums *(1892);* Union Jack *(1894), founded by Alfred Harmsworth;* Pluck *(the full title of this publication was* Stories of Pluck: a high class weekly library of adventure at home and abroad, on land and sea, *1894);* Gem *(1907); and* The Magnet *(1908), for which Charles Hamilton (known as Frank Richards) wrote the Greyfriars stories. The* Girl's Own Paper *was edited first by Charles Peters (1880–1907), whose aim was to 'foster and develop that which was highest and noblest in the girlhood and womanhood of England . . . putting the best things first and banishing the worthless from his pages'*, and second by Flora Klickmann (1908–1931), who made the magazine a monthly publication. It was aimed at the middle-class English gentlewoman and in that respect tended to reflect the shift between an ideology of domesticated feminism transforming into an appreciation of the 'modern woman' who played sport, rode a bicycle and would perhaps eventually migrate to the Empire. Most of the features were educational and improving in their nature. Contemporary concern for physical fitness can be seen in magazines for both boys and girls. E. C. Dawson, author of document 50, was rector of St. Peter's, Edinburgh, and also authored Lion-Hearted *(1909) and* Missionary Heroines in India: true stories of the Wonderful bravery of patient endurance of missionaries in India, published in the 1920s.

Chapter 1

CAMPED ON THE NIGER – FIGHT WITH A WHISTLE-SNAKE – "THE CHILD OF THE MOON" – AN ALARM.

By a camp-fire in the woods, on the banks of the Upper Niger, lay two young Englishmen – Sidney Palmer and Clement Chiffney.

The taller and stouter of the two was Chiffney – a fine, athletic youth, of two-and-twenty, whose clear, fresh features indicated that he was not long from home.

He looked now a picture of sturdy health; yet only three months before he had been stricken down by wasting fever.

Sent out to a commercial situation at Bruss, Chiffney had been attacked by the almost inevitable malarial disease, and had been warned to leave the coast at once, if he would not lay his body in the "white man's grave!"

Clement's first intention had been to return home, although such would mean the ruin of his business prospects; but he had gladly changed his plans, on the invitation of his old friend Sidney Palmer, now a trader on the Benin River, who was about to make a journey into the interior, and cordially invited his former chum to accompany him.

The proposal to seek renewed health in the interior of Africa seemed startling at first; but the idea was sound. The unhealthy zones of that Continent lie usually round its coast, and on the low-lying deltas and lagoons fringing the shore-line. Beyond these fœtid belts, inland, on the higher, drier, breezy levels, a perfect sanatorium is generally found.

So it was, at least, in Chiffney's case.

The erstwhile fever-stricken invalid was now as strong and robust, as hale and hearty, as ever he had been. Now he lay on his side, sound asleep, his curly head pillowed on his stalwart arm, breathing with the freedom and regularity of a child.

Sidney Palmer, as already indicated, was of slighter build than his friend; but perhaps more lithe and active. His well-tanned skin bore the signs of long residence under a burning sun.

Possessed of a small capital, Sidney had been, for the past few years, a merchant-trader on the Benin River; one of those sturdy pioneers of British commerce – one of the shrewd, yet daring, adventurers who have carried Britain's trading-flag all over the world, opening fresh markets for the benefit of all concerned.

Ever with a keen eye to the main chance, Palmer was on a business journey now, his object being partly to extend his sphere of operation, partly of a more private nature, as will soon transpire.

Night was passing. Palmer, like his chum, was reposing; but, instinctively alert and vigilant, his watchfulness quickened by his recent training, Sidney permitted himself but a "dog's doze." Every now and again one of the quivering eyelids would partially open, and a scintillating glance be shot around. Occasionally he would stir himself to replenish the fire; for wild beasts abounded in the forest, and flame is the best bulwark against such night prowlers.

Suddenly he started, both eyes opened wide and bright, as a soft whistle fell upon his ear – the sound low and melodious, as though it issued from human lips.

Instantly he sprang to a sitting position. His hand was instinctively outstretched to the wood-pile; and, grasping a faggot, the youth gazed eagerly in the direction of the sound.

Into the circle of light a sinuous body was advancing – a snake, of about four feet in length, slender in body, with flat, venomous head. Dark-brown in colour, it was mottled with black marks. The reptile was crawling towards the slumbering man, creeping leisurely, and its procedure was most singular. With each revolution of its coils, it raised its head and neck, passing them forward with something like a peacock's gait; while at every strut it gave vent to its low, seductive whistle.

Scant time spent Palmer in watching. He knew the crawling figure too well. The faggot was firmer clutched, waved in the air, then hurled full at the interloper, striking the reptile fair on the swelling neck, instantly interrupting its chuckling whistle.

At once a wild commotion sprang up, the stricken snake wriggling and struggling, curling and whirling like a live firework; then, leaping to his feet, the young man further joined in the fray, delivering several more smashing blows with a fresh faggot, quickly beating the life out of the reptile. Then, with one foot placed firmly on the venomous head, with its protruding fungs, Palmer slashed through the neck with his hunting-knife, kicked aside the severed body, and, picking up the head and poison-bags on the point of his blade, dropped them into the fire, remarking:

"That makes sure. Now there is one demon less in this world!"

"Eh! Ah! What's the row? Had a visit from a fiend?" queried Chiffney, sitting up, and rubbing his bewildered eyes.

"Yes," replied Palmer, throwing himself on the ground again, beside his friend, "a veritable demon, in truth – a whistle-snake. These reptiles are as deadly as the American rattlesnakes, to which they bear some resemblance, as they cannot move upon their prey without a warning. That whistle has saved the life of many a man. If ever you hear it again, Clem, look out; act promptly. Their sting is always fatal; generally, death follows almost instantly. In other cases, a few hours of madness intervene; but the end is always the same. Nothing can save from the venom of the whistle-snake. You saw me cut off the head and throw it into the fire? Cases have been known of men treading barefoot upon, or even handling, the head of such a reptile, dead for hours, when the poison somehow infecting the victim, the unfortunate man dies shortly afterwards, just as though he had been stung by the live reptile. Oh, they are fiendish creatures!"

"Not very pleasant neighbours; hope there are no more about," commented Chiffney.

"Say, Sid," he added, "how much further have we to go are you reach the spot for which we are making? This river seems interminable, and we have to work our own passages now. It seems months since I left Brass, feeling weak as water – luckily, at that time, having black fellows to row me. Then up we went, I improving daily, portering past falls, towing up rapids, past Rabba, Bussa, through Gompa, Say, and all sorts of unpronounceable places, till we reached Gao. Then we gave up our big boat, discharged our crew, purchased that small craft there (pointing to a canoe drawn up on the bank), and have been 'paddling our own canoe' ever since. How long is it to last, old man?"

"Tired of the life?" queried Palmer. "Never mind, Clem, the trip has done you a world of good. You are a very different man from the corpse-like creature that was borne away from Brass. You feel well, don't you?"

"Fit as a fiddle, and right as ninepence!" cried Chiffney gaily. "I'll show you that by my appetite at breakfast, by and by. By George! I could do with a bit of deer-meat now!"

And the youth cast a hungry glance at a koodoo, which, ahot the previous evening, had been hung up on the tree under which the voyagers had fixed their camp.

"Of course, I like this living," continued Clem. "By George! it's a real pleasure to work when one's thews and sinews are strung to concert-pitch; but one likes to see the end. Where is this wonderful valley of yours, with its marvellous diamond. You might run over the story again, Sid, as I was scarcely alive when you first told it me."

"It is not much of a story, Clem, and it may not have any definite end," laughed Palmer.

"Of course, the ostensible reason for my journey was to extend my up-river connection, which I have done, most satisfactorily; but, privately, I mean to look for 'The child of the moon.'"

Throughout the lower delta there is a legend of a wonderful point of fire, that glitters at full-moon, on a mountain-top. It can only be seen from a valley, and all attempts to locate the luminosity have proved fruitless. The natives hold it as sacred, calling the fire-point "child of the moon," and the vale "the valley of moonlight."

"I have heard the yarn repeatedly, and did not pay much attention to it at first; but latterly it has occurred to me that this 'child of the moon' may be a great diamond, or other precious stone, on which the moon, striking at a certain angle, reflects a stream of light into the centre of the valley. If so, the jewel must be an immense one – probably worth a fabulous sum. It's only a notion, of course – very likely I'm wrong; but I want to look into the thing."

"And whereabouts is this 'valley of moonlight'?" queried Chiffney.

"It cannot be far distant now," replied Palmer. "It is said to lie close by the river, on this side of the mysterious old city of Timbuctoo. Now, Timbuctoo is the next town of any importance above us. But I have a more authentic guide. I can locate the valley exactly. See here."

Then Palmer drew a small piece of paper from his pocket, on which were the characters:

18 deg. 8 N.
0 deg. 25 W.

"I'm no good at cryptograms," said Chiffney, shaking his head.

"Why, man, it's clear enough," laughed Palmer. "It reads: 18 deg. 8 min. north latitude, 0 deg. 25 min. west longitude. These are the bearings of the 'valley of moonlight.' It's merely a memorandum. With this, and with my sextantette, and chronometer, I can always work my reckonings."

"We are now nearing the spot. Soon we shall be able to test the merits of the legend. Should there be anything in it, we may become possessors of fabulous wealth (for, of course, we shall go share and share alike, Clem). If not, we shall be none the poorer; and when we return, you will have gained that which is better than wealth – health; while I shall have developed my business.

"Hi! Look out! Get you 'barker' ready!" cried Palmer, suddenly interrupting himself.

52

'DAVID LIVINGSTONE: MISSIONARY AND EXPLORER', IN *YOUNG ENGLAND*, VOL. 34 (1912–13), PP. 219–223; 263–296.

These extracts are taken from boys and girls' magazines and annuals in the years 1880–1939. They were a response to the publications known as 'penny dreadfuls' (serialized, sensationalistic stories of crime and horror). Amongst the earliest of these new kind of magazines was the Boys' Own Paper (BOP), *published by the Religious Tract Society (RTS) in 1879.*

The founding values of this publication, and others that followed, was the belief that the youth would read and have instilled in them Christian moral values. In its early phase the BOP *stressed the missionary aspect of Empire, perhaps not surprising, given that the clergymen who had founded the RTS in 1799 had, four years earlier, founded the London Missionary Society. The paper and its companion, the* Boys' Own Annual, *promoted the British Empire, particularly in their first decade. Among those who wrote for the paper were Arthur Conan Doyle, R. M. Ballantyne, Jules Verne and G. M. Henty. Alfred Harmsworth noted that his stable of publications aimed to eradicate 'the miserable literary rubbish, in which murders, thieves and other criminals are raised to the position of heroes'. The* BOP *reflected Britain's position as a leading imperial power and its description of the races of Empire invariably include pejorative language. By 1900 the* BOP *was being challenged by other titles, such as those published by Edward Brett. These titles included* The Boys of the Empire, *published by Andrew Melrose and edited by Howard Spicer; G. A. Henty's* The Union Jack; Young England: An Illustrated Magazine for Boys Throughout the English Speaking World *(1880), published by the London Sunday School Union. By the later 19th and early 20th centuries, another crop of youth publications had appeared, among which were* Chums *(1892);* Union Jack *(1894), founded by Alfred Harmsworth;* Pluck *(the full title of this publication was* Stories of Pluck: a high class weekly library of adventure at home and abroad, on land and sea, *1894);* Gem *(1907); and* The Magnet *(1908), for which Charles Hamilton (known as Frank Richards) wrote the Greyfriars stories. The* Girl's Own Paper *was edited first by Charles Peters (1880–1907), whose aim was to 'foster and develop that which was highest and noblest in the girlhood and womanhood of England . . . putting the best things first and banishing the worthless from his pages', and second by Flora Klickmann (1908–1931), who made the magazine a monthly publication. It was aimed at the middle-class English gentlewoman and in that respect tended to reflect the shift between an ideology of domesticated feminism transforming into an appreciation of the 'modern woman' who played sport, rode a bicycle and would perhaps eventually migrate to the Empire. Most of the features were educational and improving in their nature. Contemporary concern for physical fitness can be seen in magazines for both boys and girls. E. C. Dawson, author of document 50, was rector of St. Peter's, Edinburgh, and also authored* Lion-Hearted *(1909) and* Missionary Heroines in India: true stories of the Wonderful bravery of patient endurance of missionaries in India, *published in the 1920s.*

David Livingstone: missionary and explorer

A centenary worth celebrating

IT is immensely interesting to walk through the grey old Abbey of Westminster, and, passing from one honoured tomb to another, to think of the strangely different places that gave birth to the men whose dust lies there.

From all parts of our island they have come – from feudal castle and rose-covered cottage, from lonely farm and crowded street, from factory town and village green. Every class has contributed at least someone to represent it – wealth and poverty, spacious opportunity and cruel straits, the favourites of fortune and the children of the workhouse, all have helped to make that ancient building the most sacred spot in the whole of the British Empire.

There are tombs there which have become places of pilgrimage for English-speaking visitors from all parts of the world. One of the chief of these is the grave of David Livingstone. This year, this month, there will be a notable increase of such "pilgrims," for the centenary of his birth, which is to be so widely celebrated, has concentrated attention afresh on the pathetic story of his death and the stirring story of his life.

Even those people who "take no stock" of religion, and have no belief in the labours of our missionaries, extol the pluck and enterprise of Livingstone the explorer, and testify to the value of what he accomplished. But how much more fully can *we* appreciate him and his work, who revere him as the Great-heart of African travel, whose lofty character and unshakable integrity were as notable as his geographical discoveries?

It is good to think that so much of the Southern and Central regions of Africa were opened up by one who was a great missionary as well as a great explorer, and who never for a moment in pursuing any scheme of travel forgot that he was a Christian. The man who did more than anyone else to fill in the great blanks in the map of the Dark Continent was a man who knew his Bible from end to end, guided himself by its counsels, and relied on its promises.

Heredity and early training – both of these can be cited as having made Livingstone the man he was. The dogged, never-say-die determination which he showed to the very last may have had its springs in that fighting ancestry of his. (His great-grandfather fell at Culloden, striking for Bonnie Prince Charlie, and his grandfather sent several of his sons into the King's Service during the long duel between Britain and France, which closed with Trafalgar and Waterloo.)

But probably he owed more, very much more, to his early training in the little house at Blantyre, in Clydesdale. For both his parents were deeply religious, and the atmosphere of devotion and implicit trust in God which pervaded the home was one which permeated his whole life. Most of you boys who read this magazine would have called it a strict home, but it made for strength and "grit" and endurance. The religion that was taught there was *lived* by both parents; it was a daily reality, and not an occasional exercise. Their children were not likely to "pass through it" as a phase. It was, and it remained, a part of their very being.

One cannot say to which of his parents David owed most. They were very diverse. The father was kind of heart, but undoubtedly grave and austere, shaking his head mistrustfully at the thought of the children of godly parents needing or wishing for any books beyond the Bible and certain theological works.

Mrs. Livingstone, the mother, on the other hand, seems to have been a sweeter, brighter, and more liberal nature, winning her boys' love by her sympathy and delighting them, of a winter's night, by her fireside recital of old legends and traditions. From her David inherited the buoyancy which in later days carried him past many a crushing disappointment, and the sense of humour which relieved many an exasperating situation. An African pioneer missionary has need of both those qualities in a large degree.

The little household was one in which every penny had to be looked at; there was but little to spend, little time to spare, little respite from hard toil. Consequently, David grew up without false notions of self-pity. A man so trained could bear much, put up with much, and go far without complaining.

School was much akin, and David went to it very early. At the age of ten he was a wage-earner in the local cotton mill (think of that, in view of our factory laws of to-day!). The hours were outrageously long – from 6 a.m. to 8 p.m. – and the occupation was tiresome, not to say tiring; the child's small, deft fingers being kept busy "piecing or joining such of the threads of cotton as might break while they were being spun and wound on the bobbins of the loom."

Yet the craving for knowledge, the Scotch eagerness for education, was not extinguished by this long and close day's work. Livingstone has told us himself how he spent his evenings. "With a part of my first week's wages I purchased Ruddiman's 'Rudiments of Latin,' and pursued the study of that language for many years afterwards with unabated ardour at an evening school, which met between the hours of eight and ten. The dictionary part of my labours was followed till twelve o'clock, or later, if my mother did not interfere by jumping up and snatching the books out of my hands. . . . I read in this way many of the classical authors, and knew Virgil and Horace better at sixteen than I do now" (*i.e.*, in 1857).

With the same spirit and the same willingness to grind at the difficult parts, he read other books on widely different subjects, among which travel and missionary adventure figured, as we know. His trick of propping up some book on a convenient ledge while his hands were busy with the threads is an old and oft-told story.

That he had also outdoor and open-air tastes we know, and he himself attributed much of his keenness for the green fields and the quiet woods, and for the living creatures of all sorts that ran, or flew, or swam, to the contrast of those long hours of work with the free roamings through the pleasant countryside.

One delightful anecdote of these days is thus related in Mr. Edward Hume's "Life of Livingstone." "David and his brother had been after trout, and they had hooked and landed a salmon. Difficulties of transport at once arose. The law against the taking of salmon was strict, but the prospects of a dainty meal were irresistible. Youthful ingenuity triumphed, and the big fish was conveyed home in brother Charles's trousers. Charles, needless to say, was a younger brother."

Boyhood's happy irresponsible years passed all too quickly. At the age of eighteen David became a spinner in the mill; it meant harder work, but it also meant bigger pay. A proportion of his new earnings went to buy books, and he not only read, but thought:

"And the thoughts of youth are long, long thoughts."

His fancy was beginning to travel into the future and to wonder what his life-work would be.

He seems to have had some good counsellors in addition to his parents. He owed much, for instance, to one of these, David Hogg by name. The latter said to the young factory hand, as he stood by his deathbed, "Now, lad, make religion the everyday business of your life – not a thing of fits and starts; for if you don't, temptation and other things will get the better of you." That was good counsel well put, and Livingstone was true to it throughout his career. His religion assuredly could never be called spasmodic – "a thing of fits and starts."

Great, also, was his debt to Dr. Thomas Dick, of Broughty Ferry, a self-taught philosopher, whose books saved young Livingstone from the distressing doubts which arose from the widely prevalent fear that the teachings of religion and science were not reconcilable.

But the man who, more than any other, was responsible for making Livingstone a missionary was a German, Dr. Karl Gützlaff, the apostle of China, whose great life-work was well known in the last century, and who had many English acquaintances. His fervid appeals to young men to take up service in the field of medical missions drew many responsive hearts in Britain and America.

In Livingstone's case the seed fell on prepared soil, for in his home there had always been the missionary spirit. His father had formed a little missionary society in the village. Moreover, throughout the country a general spread of interest in foreign missions was taking place. David conceived the idea of preparing himself for work in China.

To this end he went to Glasgow to study, settling himself in cheap lodgings, contenting himself with the plainest fare, and using to the full his new opportunities both in the lecture-room and at his studies. Two winter sessions he spent in preparation, and during the second he offered himself to the London Missionary Society.

The usual time of probation and training followed a tentative acceptance, and his ability in preaching and public prayer seemed so poor that he was on the point of being rejected. But after some further preparation he was passed, and he entered on the completion of his studies, taking his much-coveted medical degree at Glasgow University in November, 1840.

To China, however, he could not go. Britain was at war with that country. Conversations with Robert Moffat, who had just returned from South Africa, induced him to think of going thither. Livingstone had been "profoundly impressed by his story of work among the Bechuanas and bushmen. 'By and by,' says Moffat, 'he asked me whether I thought he would do for Africa. I said I believed he would if he would not go to an old station, but would advance to unoccupied ground, specifying the vast plain to the north, where I had sometimes seen, in the morning sun, the smoke of a thousand villages, where no missionary had ever been.'"

Livingstone made the proposal to the Society, and the latter endorsed it. Accordingly, in that same month of November, he turned his back on home and friends, on Glasgow and London, and set sail for the continent which was to be for ever coupled with his name.

A three months' voyage (*viâ* Rio Janeiro) to the Cape, and then six or seven hundred miles of travel in his slow, jogging oxwagon to Moffat's missionary station of Kuruman, cut deep into the year. But he remembered Moffat's hint, and, after a few weeks' rest, he pushed on northward for some three hundred miles, reaching at last the country of Sechelé, Chief of the Bakwain.

Here his strong personality and, still more, his medical knowledge won him almost instantly a welcome, and, like his Lord and Master in Galilee, the young missionary found himself besieged by the sick and suffering. This popularity gained him permission to open a school, and the Chief not only had the children assembled, but provided them with food as well.

We get a characteristic picture of Livingstone at this time. Drought was playing havoc with the lands of the Bechuana tribe, and, although there was a river, the natives had no notion of irrigation.

Livingstone therefore began to teach them, as Moffat had taught the men of Kuruman, to dig little canals and so carry the water right and left from the broad waterway. Everyone caught at the idea. "Even the professional rain-maker to the tribe, laying aside a very natural jealousy, joined in the work. And then might have been seen, for the first time on record, the spectacle of these dusky Bakwains labouring without wages, picking out the earth with sharpened sticks, and carrying it away in their cloaks, in tortoise-shells, and in wooden bowls to the rapidly rising dam."

Returning to Kuruman in June, 1842, he made sundry long excursions, building on the hope that the London Missionary Society would grant him permission to push outward and found a new station. One of these reconnoitring journeys was on ox-back to the land of the warlike Matabele.

The following summer brought the desired permission, and he decided on the hill-country of the Bakhatla for his new sphere of work.

Thither he went, and, building a strong, roomy hut, there he dwelt for three long years. The place was well watered and very beautiful (the valley lies about a hundred miles due west of what is now Pretoria), but it was haunted, nay, infested by lions. The natives were none too courageous, and Livingstone and Mebalwe, one of his teachers, went out one day to "stiffen" a hunting party.

An attempt to hem in a group of lions failed, the latter breaking through the circle, and as they returned Livingstone and his assistant came suddenly on one of the lions. He fired both barrels, and was reloading, ramming down the bullets in his old muzzle-loader, when a warning shout made him turn quickly. "Looking half round," says Livingstone, relating the now well-known story in one of his books,

> "I saw the lion just in the act of springing upon me. He caught my shoulder as he sprang, and we both came to the ground together. Growling horribly close to my ear, he shook me as a terrier dog does a rat. The shock produced a stupor similar to that which seems to be felt by a mouse after the first shake of the cat. It caused a sort of dreaminess, in which there was no sense of pain or feeling of terror, though quite conscious of what was happening.
>
> "Turning round to relieve myself of the weight, as he had one paw on the back of my head, I saw his eyes directed to Mebalwe, who was trying to shoot him at a distance of ten or fifteen yards. His gun, a flint one, missed fire in both barrels; the lion immediately left me, and, attacking Mebalwe, bit his thigh. Another man, whose life I had saved before, after he had been tossed by a buffalo, attempted to spear the lion while he was biting Mebalwe. He left Mebalwe and caught this man by the shoulder, but at that moment the bullets he had received took effect, and he fell down dead."

It was a narrow escape, and to the end of his life Livingstone suffered from the effects of that encounter. His left arm was smashed and the flesh badly lacerated. A false joint formed in due time, and never again could he raise a gun to his right shoulder.[1]

At the close of 1843 Livingstone learned that Moffat was returning to Kuruman after a visit to England, and went to meet him. The meeting was fraught with consequences, for Moffat had brought his family, and the eldest daughter, Mary, a lively, laughing girl, pleased David greatly, and the following summer saw the two engaged. She made him a splendid wife, for she brought to him not only true affection, but hearty sympathy with all his aims and labours.

The early years of Livingstone's married life were years of great discomfort, not to say hardship.

Twice he had to move his home, and the move meant housebuilding under a burning sun, with all the ordinary work of a mission to be carried on as well. Two little children took up much of his wife's time, tireless though she was in her teaching and her tendance of the sick. A drought, long and pitiless, was laid to the charge of the "new religion," and few converts were made, so strong was the prejudice aroused.

About this time, Livingstone came into contact with the Boers, and was forced to recognise that they were hostile, or, at least, suspicious. Their treatment of the more docile native tribes was too harsh, often too brutal, to commend itself to "the black man's friend," and at a later date their enmity to the newcomer took a dastardly shape.

Once more he determined to break new ground. In June, 1849, he set out, and because the risks were very great he left wife and children at Kolobeng.

The route was northward. With him were two notable hunters, Mr. Oswell and Mr. Murray, and the former, a great admirer of Livingstone, was actually financing the whole "trek." What a noble fellow William Cotton Oswell was, and what an intrepid sportsman, was told, some years ago, in the pages of this magazine.

The journey was a terribly trying one. Fearful thirst, tormenting insects, deep sandy tracks, in which the waggon wheels sank, pitfalls dug for wild beasts and lightly covered over, the jealous opposition of a powerful Chief – all these were "against them for evil." But at last they struck a great sheet of water. It was Lake Ngami, and they were the first white men to set eyes upon it.

It was in Oswell's company, a little later, that Livingstone, pushing onward, came upon the magnificent Zambesi River – a discovery of first-class importance. He questioned the natives as to what lay to the northward, and it was then that there came to him the idea of penetrating into those unknown regions and finding an outlet route to the coast, along which civilised commerce might come and go (thus helping to break up the slave trade).

Reluctantly he forced himself to see that it would be better to send his loved ones to England and face this pioneer task singly, and Oswell's splendid generosity enabled him to do so. After some delay, his ox-waggon journey from Cape Town began – first to Kuruman, thence through the country of the Bakwains to Linyanti, where the Chief of the Makololo gave him the heartiest of welcomes.

From here Livingstone obtained the loan of twenty-seven tribesmen, and in the Chief's own canoe he set out on his long journey to the coast. At first easy and pleasant and full of interest, it gradually resolved itself into a battle of one fever-weakened white man's will against scarcity of food, reeking forests, matted jungle, floods and accidents, and opposition of extortionate tribal chiefs. But at long last the sea came in sight, and Livingstone, "spent and emaciated, tottered down the hillside" into the Portuguese town of St. Paul de Loanda.

"Never shall I forget the luxurious pleasure I enjoyed," he writes, "in feeling myself on a good English couch after six months' sleeping on the ground." Everyone vied with each other in ministering to his comfort, and honours came to him from England. It had been a truly heroic feat.

But an even finer one was the return. Resisting the urgent entreaties of his friends and the tempting offer of a passage home on a British man-of-war, Livingstone, after a needful rest, set his face again towards the swamps of Linyanti. He had promised the Chief that he would restore him the twenty-seven men, and he knew they would never find their way back alone. Through innumerable perils he led them back, and redeemed his promise. Little wonder that the respect and love of the native African for this indomitable "Ingerasa" (Englishman) was deep and enduring!

And, let it be said, such actions of Livingstone were not the outcome merely of a sense of honour. His love for the native, his pitiful compassion for their needs, were as sincere as his indignation at their unjust treatment by Boer or Briton. He knew their good qualities, and he championed their rights with a fearlessness which brought him many enemies.

David Livingstone: missionary and explorer

A centenary worth celebrating

Part II

LIVINGSTONE had found that his western route to the sea was one that would be useless to the trader. He therefore prepared to try one to the east.

Using the Zambesi river for a certain distance, he was brought by his native boatmen to within sight of the stupendous cataract which he loyally named the Victoria Falls. He gazed at the spectacle with almost breathless wonder – the greatest waterfall in the world.

It was the year 1855, and not until May, 1856, did he reach Quilimane, on the shores of the Indian Ocean. The journey had been a very trying one, and the dangers from wild beasts, drowning, sunstroke, and pugnacious tribes had been very great. Yet he had accomplished it, and, to his infinite credit, without taking the life of a single opponent, even in self-defence.

Then at last Livingstone felt free to pay the long-looked-for visit to England. He had been in Africa sixteen years, and wife and children awaited him. His return was the signal for an outburst of universal praise and appreciation. Learned societies *fêted* him, and wherever he went he was an object of admiring interest.

It was all very distasteful to such a man, and equally tiresome was the need of completing his book on African exploration. He lectured up and down the country to audiences of all kinds – religious bodies, business men, university undergraduates, factory hands. And everywhere the note he struck was the same – Britain's duty to Africa.

Believing that he could do better service if he were not pledged to missionary work only, he resigned his official connection with the L.M.S., though he continued on friendly terms with its supporters. The thing he had closest at heart was the opening up of Africa to Christianity and commerce, and the suppression thereby of the iniquitous slave trade, which could not otherwise be got at.

As a potent aid, in this direction, he rejoiced when Lord Palmerston's Government appointed him H.M. Consul in East Africa, and gave him the command of an exploring expedition. They also put at his disposal a small steamer for river work. Then, amid a chorus of friendly speeches and well-wishes, Livingstone, with his wife and youngest son, went back to the continent which he had learned to love.

In the exploration that followed his return to Tete the immense expanse of a new lake – Lake Nyassa – was reached. In 1861 Livingstone had the satisfaction of conducting the first party of men representing the new Universities Mission to their sphere of work. They were under the leadership of Bishop Mackenzie.

Lake Nyassa was a favourite hunting ground of the slavetrader in those days, and Livingstone's heart burned at the unspeakable cruelties and almost incredible extent of the awful traffic. He implored the home Government to interfere by placing even one armed steamer on the lake (none were sent until long after – in the year 1892).

On the 27th April, 1861, a great blow fell upon Livingstone in the death of his wife, stricken by fever. She was laid to rest "under a baobab tree in beautiful Shupanga." Sick at heart, he braced himself to take up anew his work, and found in it his best relief from the sense of loss and sorrow.

There was distraction enough. On revisiting Tete he found famine, and in the villages bordering the lovely Shiré River the slave trade had left a desolation. Livingstone writes:

> "Dead bodies floated past us daily, and in the mornings the paddles had to be cleared of corpses, caught by the floats during the night. For scores of miles the entire population of the valley was swept away. . . . Ghastly living forms of boys and girls, with dull dead eyes, were crouching beside some of the huts. A few more miserable days of their terrible hunger and they would be with the dead."

The year 1863 saw the recall of the expedition, and, handing over the Government steamer to the British naval authorities at Mozambique, Livingstone proceeded to navigate his own little boat, the *Lady Nyassa*, across the Indian Ocean to Bombay – a really wonderful feat for a landsman – in the hope of finding a purchaser for her. He had spent £6,000 on her, and though he eventually sold her for £2,300, the whole proceeds were lost by the failure of an Indian bank.

Back once more in England, he was appointed by the Government to conduct another exploring expedition in the heart of Africa. The money voted him was contemptibly small, but he got together his caravan – Sepoys, native Africans, camels, mules, donkeys, etc. – and started off from Zanzibar, westward and then south-westward. The human part of his company proved a bad lot, and the animals grew sick and died off with rather alarming rapidity. One of these rascally natives went back to Zanzibar and there circulated a report that Livingstone had been murdered. The rumour reached England, and a search expedition was actually sent out; of course it was found that the story was baseless.

But the man who was being inquired about so anxiously was facing death in other forms than the assassin's spear – sheer hunger, trackless wastes, soaking tropical rains, recurring fever, and, direst of all, a lost medicine chest. He had "fits of insensibility and of temporary paralysis." When, therefore, he struggled out on to the shores of Lake Tanganyika – wooded gloriously and of bewitching beauty – there was nothing for it but to rest and recruit his strength.

When he resumed his journeyings, one of his discoveries was the great lake Bangweolo, which he was the first white man to set eyes upon. Again he was laid low by fever. Then it was that, by the almost tender consideration of an Arab slave trader, he was conveyed to Ujiji, his destination.

What a strange situation it must have seemed to Livingstone! – to be helped by a representative of the very power he was heart and soul intent on destroying.

But it was an unhappy waiting-time, to lie weak and ill at Ujiji. It was a den of thieves, a nest of raiders and murderous ruffians, who fed with human spoils the caravans bound for Zanzibar.

Up again at last, he pushed on to Manyuema, where he believed he should find the headwaters of one of the great African rivers. There again he was stricken down. His followers deserted him – all but the faithful Chuma, Susi, and Gardner – and for three months he lay in his poor hut, tortured by depression and by bodily sores and ulcers.

When at last he was able to proceed he came into frequent contact with the slave-hunters. One sudden murderous attack on a laughing, chattering crowd in a riverside village, which he witnessed one July morning, and which resulted in the death by gunshot wounds and drowning of some 350 innocent victims, left him maddened with indignation that such things should be. The entry in his journal is eloquent of his feelings.

These and similar horrors which he witnessed made him physically ill, but he felt he must get back to Ujiji. The journey was terrible – between five and six hundred weary, difficult miles. On the way he was more than once nearly transfixed by spears of natives lurking in the belief that he was one of their enemies. And when he arrived at his goal it was to find that his goods had been looted and sold by an Arab scoundrel to whom they had been despatched.

It was while he was still reeling under this staggering blow that he was found by H. M. Stanley – sent out by the *New York Herald*, because the world wanted to know what had become of the veteran explorer, lost to sight for two long years.

The scene has been described too often to need re-telling here. Stanley's coming was incalculably cheering to Livingstone. Hunger, anxiety, solitariness were at an end – for the time being. He could ask countless questions and receive news of the great world from which he had been so long shut out.

But it meant much – very much to Stanley also. It was not merely that his search was ended, his mission accomplished. It was that in Livingstone he found a unique personality – someone the like of whom he had never met elsewhere. As a war correspondent Stanley was familiar with courage and endurance, but these virtues were blended in this travel-worn, solitary Briton with other qualities of a rarer kind.

From that memorable night when the two men sat together on the verandah of the little hut, and talked – and talked – while the great stars burned overhead and the hours flew by with winged feet, till the day on which they parted, and each went his own way, the bond of friendship grew ever stronger. Here is Stanley's tribute: –

"For four months and four days, he and I occupied the same house, or the same that . . . and the longer I lived with him the more did my admiration and reverence for him increase." And again: "His gentleness never forsakes him; his hopefulness never deserts him." "His religion is constant, earnest, sincere *practice;* it governs his conduct, not only towards his servants but all who come in contact with him."

One likes, too, these other things which Stanley noticed and which his biographer, Mr. Hume, thus summarises: –

"His guilelessness, his animal spirits, his whole-hearted laugh that was infectious, his prodigious memory, the tenacity of his beliefs, his huge diary crammed with notes and observations, his eyesight keen as a hawk's, the stoop of his shoulders, and his clothes, patched but scrupulously clean."

Each of the two parted from the other with pain of heart. But Stanley was going back to Europe and congratulations and eager audiences, and it is on the grey-haired veteran turning back to "finish his task" while yet longing for home, that the eye rests most tenderly and reverently.

Stanley had promised to send him fifty carriers as soon as he reached the coast. He kept his word – they were picked men, and they proved loyal and staunch, it is good to know. But the weather was awful, rain fell incessantly, roads disappeared, food grew scarce, and at last even the iron will of Livingstone could not combat the distressing weakness and agonising pain of the illness that again had seized him.

On April 27th, 1873, he makes the last entry in his journal: "Knocked up quite . . . We are on the banks of the Molilamo." The party had halted, a hut was erected, and the dying leader was sheltered as comfortably as was possible. He grew weaker, but the end found him kneeling in prayer by his rude couch, with his face buried in his hands.

Between midnight and dawn his watchful followers found him – dead. Then, in awe and dismay, they took counsel together, and they came to a great resolve. It was to carry him whom they had loved and revered so long step by step over hill and plain, through marsh and forest to the coast, so that he might lie amongst his own people in the land far across the seas. And that heroic feat they fulfilled in the face of every fear and difficulty. No tribute that has ever been paid to Livingstone surpasses that act of supreme devotion.

One of that heroic band of natives accompanied the embalmed body which the liner brought home to England, but two others – the faithful Susi and Chuma – were brought over in time to be present on April 18th, 1874, at the stately and impressive service in Westminster Abbey, when the honoured remains which they had shielded so well were laid to rest.

Of David Livingstone it may indeed most truly be said,

"He being dead yet speaketh." In the splendid courage, the dogged persistence, the single-minded purpose, the untarnished honour of the great missionary-explorer, there is inspiration of the finest sort for every boy of the English-speaking race.

Note

1 Long years after, indeed, that false joint served a sad but useful purpose. For by means of it the embalmed body of Livingstone, when brought to England, was identified beyond doubt by Sir William Fergusson and other medical men.

53

THE FOUR ADVENTURERS
No. 1. – The Initiation

By Robert Harding

From: 'The Four Adventurers', in *Chums*, Annual for 1927–1928, pp. 396–398.

These extracts are taken from boys and girls' magazines and annuals in the years 1880–1939. They were a response to the publications known as 'penny dreadfuls' (serialized, sensationalistic stories of crime and horror). Amongst the earliest of these new kind of magazines was the Boys' Own Paper (BOP), *published by the Religious Tract Society (RTS) in 1879.*

The founding values of this publication, and others that followed, was the belief that the youth would read and have instilled in them Christian moral values. In its early phase the BOP stressed the missionary aspect of Empire, perhaps not surprising, given that the clergymen who had founded the RTS in 1799 had, four years earlier, founded the London Missionary Society. The paper and its companion, the Boys' Own Annual, *promoted the British Empire, particularly in their first decade. Among those who wrote for the paper were Arthur Conan Doyle, R. M. Ballantyne, Jules Verne and G. M. Henty. Alfred Harmsworth noted that his stable of publications aimed to eradicate 'the miserable literary rubbish, in which murders, thieves and other criminals are raised to the position of heroes'. The* BOP *reflected Britain's position as a leading imperial power and its description of the races of Empire invariably include pejorative language. By 1900 the* BOP *was being challenged by other titles, such as those published by Edward Brett. These titles included* The Boys of the Empire, *published by Andrew Melrose and edited by Howard Spicer; G. A. Henty's* The Union Jack; *and* Young England: An Illustrated Magazine for Boys Throughout the English Speaking World *(1880), published by the London Sunday School Union. By the later 19th and early 20th centuries, another crop of youth publications had appeared, among which were* Chums *(1892);* Union Jack *(1894), founded by Alfred Harmsworth;* Pluck *(the full title of this publication was* Stories of Pluck: a high class weekly library of adventure at home and abroad, on land and sea, *1894);* Gem *(1907); and* The Magnet *(1908), for which Charles Hamilton (known as Frank Richards) wrote the Greyfriars stories. The* Girl's Own Paper *was edited first by Charles Peters (1880–1907), whose aim was to 'foster and develop that which was highest and noblest in the girlhood and womanhood of England . . . putting the best things first and banishing the worthless from his pages', and second by Flora Klickmann (1908–1931), who made the magazine a monthly publication. It was aimed at the middle-class English gentlewoman and in that respect tended to reflect the shift between an ideology of domesticated*

DOI: 10.4324/9781351024822-55

feminism transforming into an appreciation of the 'modern woman' who played sport, rode a bicycle and would perhaps eventually migrate to the Empire. Most of the features were educational and improving in their nature. Contemporary concern for physical fitness can be seen in magazines for both boys and girls. E. C. Dawson, author of document 50, was rector of St. Peter's, Edinburgh, and also authored Lion-Hearted *(1909) and* Missionary Heroines in India: true stories of the Wonderful bravery of patient endurance of missionaries in India*, published in the 1920s.*

Chapter 1

A strange meeting-place

DICK HASTINGS jumped from his compartment on to the weedy platform of Matapore railway station with a large smile and a thrilled heart. He had no luggage but a stout walking-stick, which he twirled in the air and, because the station boasted but a solitary oil lantern secured by a bracket over the carved arch of the exit porch, missed the head of the native ticket-collector standing in the shadow by inches.

Yesterday Dick, in fluent Hindustani, would have told this official of the Great Indian Peninsula Railway to "get out of it!" But to-day, this night, the white man not only gave up his ticket with a good-natured "salaam," but pressed a glittering rupee into the grimy black palm. The old fellow had grinned at the stick incident. At the sight of the coin he croaked like a happy frog, and bowed till his turbaned head touched the donor's feet.

Yesterday Dick was a shipping clerk who toiled eight hours per diem in a small wooden hut dumped between two gigantic cranes at Bombay Docks; a big, boyish, out-of-place sort of chap, who strolled about amongst the piles of discharged fruit cargoes with a pencil sticking out from under the rim of his white topee, for ever bemoaning the day when he had attached himself to the Oriental Steam Navigation Company, Limited, in order to see India.

"See India!" he had often grumbled, making a club of *The Bombay Times* and swiping at flies and wasps that couldn't tell the difference between his head and the water-melons in baskets on the quay. "I've been here for two years an' haven't been outside o' Bombay yet! Bombay's all right – granted; but one gets fed up with seein' it for – let's see – twice three-six-five days. Hi, Framji" – this to a fat, jolly-faced Parsee who wheezed on a high stool in front of a dog-eared pay ledger – "Hi, babuji! Are there any elephants besides you in this continent?"

The babu, who liked Dick hugely, in spite of his chaff, and saw under the boy's fretfulness the humour of a roving spirit, assured him that there were. "Plentee in the jungles, sahib," he declared with an oily chuckle, "and other monkeys, too!" And as the *pukka* jungles were a good half-way between Victoria Terminus, Bombay's railway palace, and Agra, where the Taj is, Dick fumed all the more and studied the "Employments Vacant" columns of *The Pioneer*.

This admirable paper and Dick's restless nature were the means of transforming him from a *dufta wallah* (office clerk) into a daring adventurer in a single week. Of course, physiologically it had been a gradual process – a battle between the inner Dick, who fretted for the jungles, bazaars, temples, black-magic, and the mysterious India he had never seen, and the outer Dick, who pushed a shipping pen for sixty rupees a month in order to "buy a new topee occasionally," as he termed it.

But it was *The Pioneer* that brought matters to a head – at least, indirectly. Directly, it was "The Gentlemen Adventurers" its special representative so often reported upon; that gallant band of men who, purely for the love of adventure, cleared up crimes the mysteriousness of which had long baffled the police and even (although this was only hinted at) the impregnable Secret Service.

The job Dick applied for was not printed in the "Situations Vacant" columns, however, but in the news paragraphs. A man named Drake Weston, with two of his trusty compeers, had – after completely hoodwinking and outwitting a gang of the cleverest criminals the Punjab unfortunately possessed – unearthed in the vaults of a solitary temple a box containing bright new rupees that for an anxious month had been missing from the Delhi bank.

"What you do, mister?" Framji expostulated loudly; and declared on the second day of the barbaric exhibition: "You no fit for an offeece, man! You too much of a strong fellow, mister; a man with a fist for a gun, not for a pen."

"You're talking absolute sense," Dick grinned. "Don't know of a way out for me, I s'pose?"

"Why not you join Mister Drake Weston and his party?" the babu replied; which suggestion caused Dick to grab him roughly by the arm.

"How? When? Where?" he bellowed, almost rocking his office companion off his seat.

"My aunt's brother – that is, my uncle – was once a *syce* (native groom) in the employ of the gentleman in question, mister, and –"

"Y'mean – y'know – where Drake Weston is?" queried Dick eagerly.

"Where he is *sometimes* to be found."

And so it was that Dick spent a brain-fagging evening poring over a sheet of foolscap, which same sheet, covered with clumsy scrawl, reached Drake Weston at the Excelsior Hotel, Agra, the following day; a scrawl that so interested the addressee that he replied to it immediately.

Upon receipt of Weston's reply Dick put in for his week's leave, and, after two days and nights in a second-class compartment of the Punjab mail, alighted at Matapore jungle station in the liveliest of spirits.

Truly had that particular train been the means of conveying him to an atmosphere of romantic adventure. The things he had imagined in his adventurous mind, although presented differently, stood before him in actual fact. A crackling wood fire glowed in the small compound behind the station, round which darkclothed natives were warming themselves – for the night air was keen – and talked like a lot of rooks as they handed round the silver-mouthed hookah and dented brass coffee bowl. Their ruddy faces regarded him with friendly nods as he passed with his stick tucked under his armpit gun fashion.

A narrow path twisted towards an horizon of tall trees, above which a round moon shone in a clear starry sky. A jungle moon that flooded the forest with the gossamer light of mystery. The path lost its firmness in small scattered earth lumps, and eventually disappeared in a mass of dense undergrowth where sun-bleached scrub, thorn and cactus bushes thrust up ugly and grotesque heads.

Knee-deep Dick paused and glanced back. The fires in the compound were tiny pricks of light now. The station resembled a small, solid fort standing out blackly against the velvety sky.

It was marvellous in how short a time one could escape from civilization, he thought; wonderful to find himself in the real moonlit wilds!

Close in front of him lay the fringe of the jungle: the entrance to a kingdom that had a law of its own and a population of its own. He could hear some of its denizens; see others. The weird whispering chorus of thousands of insects incessantly filled his ears. The hiss-hiss of snakes brushing through creeper-leaves and tall grasses made him wish that leggings or putties encased his trousered legs and that his shoes were good stout boots. A disturbed parakeet flew screaming from a tree into the shadowy gloom of the forest. A sleep-disturbed monkey grimaced down upon him wrathfully, and then, untwisting its tail, climbed to a higher branch. Between the trees, which he had now almost reached, deer glided in twos and threes, stopping occasionally to listen, and at the sound of his footfalls disappeared like shadows.

Dick thrilled and marvelled as he stood watching it all, and was glad that the mysterious Drake Weston had not fixed upon the inside of the jungle for their meeting-place. The letter in his pocket implicitly stated that he must carry no arms. Why, Dick could not fathom. But as long as one wasn't expected to venture any farther inland it didn't matter much, for a few friendly monkeys, insects, parrots and deer meant no harm to anybody. His stick was good enough for a snake or two. But, he decided, as he peered into the moon-speckled three-columned distance, a chap would be a first-class ass to potter about in there without a quick-firing repeater.

"At the outskirts of the jungle just outside Matapore station," the leader of the gallant band had said in his letter.

"Well, here I am!" said Dick, sticking his topee on his cane so that the cool breeze could fan his brow. "And at the day and hour appointed; I hope I'm not in for a leg-pull!"

He had never once queried the sincerity of the appointment. He could not connect the gallant leader of adventure's band with leg-pulling. And yet – He gazed around and realized that he was tremendously alone.

Suddenly his ears tingled and twitched at the sound of a voice calling from somewhere:

"Hullo-a! Is that a man or a two-legged tiger?"

With quick-beating heart and darting eyes Dick hastily replaced his topee and, cupping his hands, thankfully shouted back: "Hullo!"

Came the scrunching of feet in the undergrowth, followed by a cheery: "Oh, there you are, are you? Evening, Mr. Hastings!"

Chapter 2

A queer interview

DICK blinked as in a dream when a black figure came out of the shadow of the trees, a figure the moonlight quickly introduced as a small man clad in shorts, shirt, and putties; a man who with hands in pockets came towards him as if the jungle were the most natural meeting-place in the world.

His topee was tilted at the back of his head, and there was such a comical grin on his lean face that Dick – towering above him with a face that did not disguise his disappointment at beholding in the most daring adventurer in India a man so small of stature – was compelled to put on a grin of his own.

A hand shot out from one of the pockets and gripped Dick's fingers so heartily that he gave forth an involuntary howl.

"Jolly pleased to meet you, old son!" greeted the man with the iron grip jovially. "You're the fellow-me-lad who wrote me that letter about wanting to be put in the way of real-stuff adventure, aren't you?"

"That's me," confirmed Dick, rubbing his still smarting fingers. "And you are – ?" he added, looking down upon his new acquaintance curiously.

"Oh, I'm Drake Weston all right," the other assured him, his comical grin spreading wider across his angular face. The hand with the iron grip rose to Dick's shoulder, gave it a good-natured jerk, and then flattened itself on the boy's back so chummily that he grunted like a pig.

"I've got a bit of a fire round here," the owner of that hand declared as Dick pushed up the peak of his topee away from his eyes. "Let's do our bit of chin-wagging round it, shall we?"

Without waiting for Dick's answer, he turned and began wading through the undergrowth with such rapidity that the boy – who was now fully convinced that Weston's grip, at least, was a thing to fear and avoid – tripped over thick roots that wound round his trousers like the tentacles of an octopus in his endeavour to keep pace.

At length they came to a small clearing where the stumps of recently felled trees shone like huge mushrooms in the moonlight. An enchanting spot that could very well be the playground of jungle fairies had not a small brushwood fire crackled away in the middle of it, thrusting out dragon-tongued flames that licked thirstily into the air and caused long yellow fingers of light to flicker grotesquely on the trunks of the surrounding trees.

"Must keep up a good blaze," said Dick's companion, "'cause o' wolves."

"Wolves?" repeated the boy queryingly, hopping on one leg in order to extricate a sharp thorn that had got into his shoe. "Why, I didn't know that wolves abounded in Indian jungle forests, Mr. Weston."

"They don't, Mr. Naturalist. I meant wild dogs, really. I know those silent, never barking beasts that prowl about in packs. Quite as cowardly as wolves when alone, but when they're together and hungry, it's hard cheese on the tiger or anything else on four or two legs they happen to take a fancy to!"

He suddenly darted forward a few paces and kicked a loose branch into the fire.

"Take a pew, old sport," he invited, indicating the stump of a hundred-year-old toon tree.

"You want to join us?" he questioned.

"I do very much, Mr. Weston."

"Why? By the way, chuck that mister o' yours overboard. It makes me feel like a bank clerk," declared the other, grinning like a Cheshire cat. "Why?" he repeated.

"Because I'm fed up with being a clerk myself, sir – Ow!"

The hand with the iron grip had encircled Dick's ankle and jerked upward, so that the boy felt himself shot from his seat, and landed on his back with such force that he squeaked like a cat.

"And your 'sir' makes me feel like a young subaltern," this extraordinary man confessed, raking the fire with Dick's cane and then sticking it in the centre and watching it catch alight while the boy gamely collected himself together again.

54

'HINDU WOMEN', IN *THE GIRL'S OWN PAPER* (1881), PP. 118–119.

These extracts are taken from boys and girls' magazines and annuals in the years 1880–1939. They were a response to the publications known as 'penny dreadfuls' (serialized, sensationalistic stories of crime and horror). Amongst the earliest of these new kind of magazines was the Boys' Own Paper (BOP), *published by the Religious Tract Society (RTS) in 1879.*

The founding values of this publication, and others that followed, was the belief that the youth would read and have instilled in them Christian moral values. In its early phase the BOP *stressed the missionary aspect of Empire, perhaps not surprising, given that the clergymen who had founded the RTS in 1799 had, four years earlier, founded the London Missionary Society. The paper and its companion, the* Boys' Own Annual, *promoted the British Empire, particularly in their first decade. Among those who wrote for the paper were Arthur Conan Doyle, R. M. Ballantyne, Jules Verne and G. M. Henty. Alfred Harmsworth noted that his stable of publications aimed to eradicate 'the miserable literary rubbish, in which murders, thieves and other criminals are raised to the position of heroes'. The* BOP *reflected Britain's position as a leading imperial power and its description of the races of Empire invariably include pejorative language. By 1900 the* BOP *was being challenged by other titles, such as those published by Edward Brett. These titles included* The Boys of the Empire, *published by Andrew Melrose and edited by Howard Spicer; G. A. Henty's* The Union Jack; *and* Young England: An Illustrated Magazine for Boys Throughout the English Speaking World *(1880), published by the London Sunday School Union. By the later 19th and early 20th centuries, another crop of youth publications had appeared, among which were* Chums *(1892);* Union Jack *(1894), founded by Alfred Harmsworth;* Pluck *(the full title of this publication was* Stories of Pluck: a high class weekly library of adventure at home and abroad, on land and sea, *1894);* Gem *(1907); and* The Magnet *(1908), for which Charles Hamilton (known as Frank Richards) wrote the Greyfriars stories. The* Girl's Own Paper *was edited first by Charles Peters (1880–1907), whose aim was to 'foster and develop that which was highest and noblest in the girlhood and womanhood of England . . . putting the best things first and banishing the worthless from his pages', and second by Flora Klickmann (1908–1931), who made the magazine a monthly publication. It was aimed at the middle-class English gentlewoman and in that respect tended to reflect the shift between an ideology of domesticated feminism transforming into an appreciation of the 'modern woman' who played sport, rode a bicycle and would perhaps eventually migrate to the Empire. Most of the features were educational and improving in their nature. Contemporary concern for physical fitness can be seen in magazines for both boys and girls. E. C. Dawson, author of document 50, was rector of St. Peter's, Edinburgh, and also authored* Lion-Hearted *(1909) and* Missionary Heroines in India: true stories of the Wonderful bravery of patient endurance of missionaries in India, *published in the 1920s.*

Hindu women

IN no part of the world, says Dr. William Knighton, are nobler specimens of female humanity to be found than in India. The history of the country abounds with instances of the noblest devotion, unswerving fidelity, high principle, and sublime self-renunciation on the part of its women. Nor can anyone have been long resident in India without witnessing such. I have lived in Ceylon, in Bengal and in Oudh, and I have seen something of many districts and provinces lying between these distant regions, and everywhere I have witnessed the noblest instances of devotion and self-denial on the part of the women.

And yet the lot of the Hindu woman is unspeakably sad. She is married at so early an age that choice on her part is impossible. She accepts her destiny. She looks up to her husband as a sort of deity – she has been so taught from her earliest years – and a very debased, earthly, selfish, and altogether contemptible sort of deity he too often proves himself to be. But for her there is no hope, however vile and contemptible he may prove. In life and death she is his. And if death takes him and she is left to widowhood, sad indeed is her lot. She may not immolate herself on the funeral pyre of her husband, a stern English Government forbids that, and she is doomed in consequence to gloom and sadness, and if childless, to one meal a day, one garment, a total deprivation of all ornament, and all that in her eyes makes life worth living. Her existence is bound up in his, and her affections are called forth powerfully, first for her husband and secondly for her children. And for the childless widow a far more miserable life remains.

The principal duties of the Hindu woman of the middle class at home are grinding the corn with a little hand-mill, similar to that so often referred to in the Bible, washing the floor where they cook and eat, drawing water, scouring the metal vessels, the cooking utensils, the jugs and plates; of course many of the more wealthy are exempt from these duties, but the vast majority perform them. The kitchen must be washed every day; when I say the kitchen, I mean that part of the house in which cooking and eating are carried on, for a large part of the religion of the Hindus consists in cooking and eating in a proper and in a religious manner. The shadow of a low-caste man falling on the food of a high-caste Brahmin, whilst that food is in preparation, will be sufficient to defile it, and the whole will be thrown out in consequence.

The well at which water is drawn is a frequent resort for gossip. It is usually early in the morning and in the afternoon, from four to six, that water is drawn. Friends meet there, and interesting little details of household management and village life are exchanged. Some of the women will carry as many as three water-pots on their heads, one over the other, and sometimes one or two on the head and one under the arm. Women of different castes must not touch each other's vessels. This is a matter of great importance. Deadly feuds may be the result of thoughtless imprudence in this respect. Families of the higher classes who are wealthy often engage men or women of the fisherman's caste to carry water for them. But the young women usually like the duty, if the well be not too distant, and, in towns, the wells are usually in the gardens or yards of their own houses, rendering any journeys to a distance for the purpose unnecessary.

Few people in the world are more religious than the women of India, but theirs is a zeal for religion without knowledge. They perform their service to the gods and goddesses of their faith unremittingly, particularly to the goddesses, and fail not to bathe in the sacred Ganges, or any other accessible river, on days of festivals, at the changes of the moon, and such like. From this service they expect good in this life rather than happiness in another. They are full of superstitious terrors; in fact they are amongst the most timid and fearful people on the face of the earth. The evils against which they contend by their religious services are their own, or their husband's or their children's illness. Being full of affection and concern for their children, they will go to any inconvenience or expense possible for *their* welfare. If sickness visits them it is attributed to some angry god or goddess, who must be propitiated by religious offerings, by prayers, by devotion, or human mortification. They will use medicines, but too often, alas! the physicians whom they are able to consult are little able to help them, and not unfrequently but experimentalise in their endeavours to do good. If the sickness be long continued or dangerous, they will promise a young kid as an offering to some goddess in expiation, hoping thereby that the sick loved one may be restored to health. Should the child recover they believe their prayers have been heard, and the vow is performed. Priests often work upon their credulity, and the credulous women will believe any story they may tell them. In this matter they will often act in opposition to their husband's wishes, although in other respects attentive and dutiful.

A Hindu wife never mentions the name of her husband. It would be esteemed an indelicacy or an insult if she were to do so. If he have a son then he is spoken of as that son's father. *Gopal's father*, the wife will say, ordered it, not *my husband* ordered it – *our man*, or some equivalent expression, if he have no son, is the nearest approach to indicating him distinctively. Nor does the husband mention his wife's name – he will call to her, *O mother of Gopal*, or if there be no child, *O housewife*, but never by her name.

Although distinctly regarded as an inferior by the husband, with whom she does not even take her meals, always waiting till he has finished, yet the treatment she experiences is not usually bad. There are of course tyrants and cruel husbands in all countries, but so far as my experience went in India, I do not believe that the average treatment of women by their husbands in that country is worse than that in England, rather better I think amongst the lower orders; but in the upper ranks of life the husband has a power and an authority which are quite unknown in Europe, and which of course will often be abused by unfeeling and tyrannical men, particularly amongst the uneducated, and it is unfortunately too often the case that, in remote districts especially, even the wealthy are uneducated. I have heard it remarked that those who have had the advantages of European culture amongst the upper classes make better husbands and better sons than others.

The chief education of a girl in India has for centuries consisted in learning how to dress the dishes most prized, to do rough needlework, to behave seemly in company, and sometimes a little singing and instrumental music. Mental nurture and training is the great want. Reading and writing have been for centuries denied to her, and considered unnecessary. Young men have been laughed at over and over again, both in Calcutta and in the Upper Provinces, for having had the boldness to teach their wives to read and write. And this they have been obliged to do stealthily – not openly in the light of day, but, in a clandestine manner, after dinner, at night. Nor is it uncommon still to hear such exclamations as these: "What nonsense! for a woman to read and write! What's the use of it? A foolish proceeding! something new and senseless!" and such like. But a better day is dawning for women in India.

restrained him. I kept it back from him lest there should be disappointment, and I thought the surprise would be so delightful if there was not."

"And the happiness was dashed just as it ought to have been realised! But I am thankful, thankful on your account, Katie, that you can feel about it as you do. Your heart cherishes no bitterness though the grief has been so bitter."

"Oh, Mr. Walmer, don't speak to me like that, don't! If you knew all, you would chide rather than comfort. You would bind me down in the valley of humiliation, out of which I have vainly endeavoured to find a way, and you would help me to take part against myself. I must tell you that I never thought it possible that I could feel towards my bitterest enemy as I have felt towards Frank; and when the dear fellow came and asked me to forgive him, I said, 'Don't come near me. You've disappointed me – oh, bitterly;' as if myself, you know, and my disappointment were all that mattered."

The very recollection, and it was an ineffaceable one, so overcame her that she burst into a flood of tears; but he spoke to her firmly, reminding her of the necessity she was under to keep quiet.

"Tell me anything that will be a relief to you," he said, "but do not get excited. You felt sorry, I am sure, that you had spoken harshly, when he was penitent."

"Yes, more especially when I heard him crying in his room, as I think only Frank ever does cry. I went to him and made it up; but all night through the words seemed to be turned against me and spoken to myself. 'You have disappointed me, oh, bitterly!'"

"You felt then that more than Frank had ever disappointed you, your conscience telling you so, was that it?"

"Yes, and I thought, what if He were to forbid me to come near?"

"Ah, what indeed? What for any of us! But then Frank's tears would never make you, tender-hearted as you are, relent to him as sweetly as God relents to you. Did you think of that also?"

She shook her head slowly, while her eyes were full of a new-born confidence.

"I think, Katie, where the Spirit has been so certainly chiding and upbraiding, all that is left to my humble instrumentality is to apply the consolation. This is very evident, you have been chastened as a child and not beaten like an enemy; in all the trial God has been with you. Now you made one little remark with respect to Frank which I should like you, as you have been reasoning from him to yourself, to apply in another way. You said you believed if he had known your plans for him he would have been good, though he ought to have been independent of incentives. I should like to see him here."

Thanking the kind clergyman for the words he had spoken to her, Katie went in quest of her brother, glad to know that the spiritual skill and insight that could adapt itself to her case would meet the recreant schoolboy's also.

Nor was she mistaken, for Frank's face, after he had been in conversation with his minister, was happier than it had been since his return home; he said to her also, in a very shy whisper, "Katie, Mr. Walmer says that since you have forgiven me, I may feel sure that God will forgive, and do you know I almost believe that He does."

It was only two evenings after this that Mr. Walmer called again. His kind face was rippling into so many smiles that Katie, a little intolerant of such manifest exultation where so dark a shadow had fallen, wondered what was the cause of it. Something more than the well-spring in himself, she felt sure. "I have just come from the train," he said to Mrs. Oxley, "and I think I have some good news for you. I have been to see Dr. March about Frank, and he has consented to take him back again, fully persuaded that it is the right thing to do. I told him that I would be surety for his good behaviour. He owned to me that he was very sorry for the lad; he said his abilities were of a high order, and he had never been guilty of anything criminal, but he was too much carried away by his great flow of animal spirits, and – . However, we won't talk about his faults. We'll give him time to mend them. Now Katie, will you be the bearer of the good news to Frank, or shall I?"

But Katie couldn't speak. She thought the joy was going to make her as ill as the grief had done, and only by a strong effort did she regain composure.

Mr. Walmer hastened home to escape the thanks which followed him next morning in a beautiful little note, still preserved among his most fragrant epistolary treasures. So there was "clear shining after rain," and at the expiration of the holidays Frank, with a chastened gladness, took up his cross and returned manfully to the field where he had been worsted.

Before leaving he did not say anything about a possible Senior Wranglership *in futuro*, nor even about Scholarship, and B.A.'s, but he went, promising by God's grace to be a more diligent, steadfast, and obedient scholar than he had been, and by God's grace he kept his word. Nor were a sister's fond hopes concerning the immediate result of this extra year at school doomed to disappointment.

55

ON THE PURCHASE OF OUTFITS FOR INDIA AND THE COLONIES

By Dora De Blaquiere

From: 'On the Purchase of Outfits for India and the Colonies', in *The Girl's Own Paper* (1889), pp, 68–69.

These extracts are taken from boys and girls' magazines and annuals in the years 1880–1939. They were a response to the publications known as 'penny dreadfuls' (serialized, sensationalistic stories of crime and horror). Amongst the earliest of these new kind of magazines was the Boys' Own Paper (BOP), *published by the Religious Tract Society (RTS) in 1879.*

The founding values of this publication, and others that followed, was the belief that the youth would read and have instilled in them Christian moral values. In its early phase the BOP *stressed the missionary aspect of Empire, perhaps not surprising, given that the clergymen who had founded the RTS in 1799 had, four years earlier, founded the London Missionary Society. The paper and its companion, the* Boys' Own Annual, *promoted the British Empire, particularly in their first decade. Among those who wrote for the paper were Arthur Conan Doyle, R. M. Ballantyne, Jules Verne and G. M. Henty. Alfred Harmsworth noted that his stable of publications aimed to eradicate 'the miserable literary rubbish, in which murders, thieves and other criminals are raised to the position of heroes'. The* BOP *reflected Britain's position as a leading imperial power and its description of the races of Empire invariably include pejorative language. By 1900 the* BOP *was being challenged by other titles, such as those published by Edward Brett. These titles included* The Boys of the Empire, *published by Andrew Melrose and edited by Howard Spicer; G. A. Henty's* The Union Jack; *and* Young England: An Illustrated Magazine for Boys Throughout the English Speaking World *(1880), published by the London Sunday School Union. By the later 19th and early 20th centuries, another crop of youth publications had appeared, among which were* Chums *(1892);* Union Jack *(1894), founded by Alfred Harmsworth;* Pluck *(the full title of this publication was* Stories of Pluck: a high class weekly library of adventure at home and abroad, on land and sea, *1894);* Gem *(1907); and* The Magnet *(1908), for which Charles Hamilton (known as Frank Richards) wrote the Greyfriars stories. The* Girl's Own Paper *was edited first by Charles Peters (1880–1907), whose aim was to 'foster and develop that which was highest and noblest in the girlhood and womanhood of England . . . putting the best things first and banishing the worthless from his pages', and second by Flora Klickmann (1908–1931), who made the magazine a monthly publication. It was aimed at the middle-class English gentlewoman and in that respect tended to reflect*

390 DOI: 10.4324/9781351024822-57

the shift between an ideology of domesticated feminism transforming into an appreciation of the 'modern woman' who played sport, rode a bicycle and would perhaps eventually migrate to the Empire. Most of the features were educational and improving in their nature. Contemporary concern for physical fitness can be seen in magazines for both boys and girls. E. C. Dawson, author of document 50, was rector of St. Peter's, Edinburgh, and also authored Lion-Hearted *(1909) and* Missionary Heroines in India: true stories of the Wonderful bravery of patient endurance of missionaries in India, *published in the 1920s.*

WHETHER our journeys be to the far East, or to the East Coast of England only, the subject of wearing apparel is the first to be considered, for the whole family, beginning even with the master of the house, will certainly require the needful changes of raiment to make their stay enjoyable, and the body comfortable under all the circumstances which may befall them. Whether the journey be long or short, suitable clothes for each member, little or big, must be thought of, and this is, perhaps, one of the really difficult things which fall on the shoulders of the much-tried mother and wife. Of course, if she be well off, she has only to take the money, and order so many of everything and anything, and she runs through her long list of wants with a light heart. The shopkeepers will generally assist her – if she be not a woman of practical knowledge and determination – to a great number of things she does not need, and she will perhaps leave out many things she really cannot manage without, and which have to be supplied in the near future at great expense, and in that hurry of departure which makes even the most careful reckless and extravagant.

But be the outfit Indian, Eastern, Colonial, or only for the English seaside, or a Continental journey, it is well to begin the campaign with a chat with some friend who knows the locality, if possible; then with your father or husband, or whoever manages the financial family matters, so as to find out whether the family wants can be fully supplied, or only partially so, and how much money can be allowed to provide for everything.

It is not easy for men to realise the wants of women and children, so it is well if the wife, mother, or daughter have a dress allowance, and in that case she can go to the fountain-head with quiet confidence, and say, "I can manage with £30, £40, or £100," as the case may be. But this can only be done after a careful inspection of the family wardrobe, and much thought and careful management, so that she can make every shilling go as far as possible. The only practical way to arrive at the real state of things, is to make a list of the existing wardrobe, and another of what is needed to bring the stock for everyone up to the mark of efficiency. A separate list should be made for each member of the family, and a careful account given of the condition of the articles in hand, and of what she thinks will be needed to add to that stock. In case of very long voyages, such as that to New Zealand or to Queensland, the Cape or India, all the old and half-worn things will have to be used for the voyage; and, in most instances, this provision will pretty well exhaust the ordinary clothes in stock, for we no longer have the amount of clothes which our grandmothers thought needful. Many ladies content themselves with half a dozen of everything, and prefer to purchase underclothing as it is needed; never thinking of laying in garments which must be stored up unused in drawers and cupboards, until the very patterns in which they are made become old-fashioned, and the calico yellow and musty, before it comes into daily wear. I have often seen people with underlinen twenty years old, made up at the time of their marriage, and stored up to be carried about as useless lumber ever after. Perhaps if they be methodical people they make a struggle to wear things in turn, which mends matters a little.

The good old days of Indian outfits, of dozens and dozens of underlinen, and hundreds of dresses, seem to have passed away, to return no more. Locomotion and the parcel post, and also improved methods of manufacturing materials, combined with new ways of looking at the sanitary and hygienic questions of dress, are amongst the reasons for this change. The adoption of woollen underclothing for hot as well as cold climates, the use of spun silk for underclothing for men as well as women, and the introduction of the different forms of combination underlinen, have all of them done wonders towards increasing our comfort, and decreasing our thousand cares and worries.

The new rule as regards underwear, which we endeavour to follow to-day, is that of wearing the least amount of clothing possible, combined with the greatest degree of warmth; and where this rule is understood and adopted, and successfully applied to daily life, it will be found the greatest help in all matters connected with outfits. The use of the "combination garment" does away with one garment completely – the chemise – and thus our outfit is simplified at once. So what we have to consider are combinations, corsets, stockings, and petticoats, which would constitute the smallest amount of underclothing we could have. The addition of other articles would be a question of individual preference. For very hot climates, woollen underwear seems to be the safest in every way, and nothing can exceed the beauty of our English manufactures of thin woollen, thin merino, and Indian gauze, which range in price from eight shillings and sixpence to twelve shillings and sixpence each, and which, with care in the mending and in the washing, will wear extremely well.

They should be selected to fit well, but not tightly; as if tight, no allowance is left for shrinking, and consequently they will not wear well, but will fall into holes wherever there is a strain upon them. Fine wool or silk is supplied at most shops for darning them, and also printed directions for washing them. I have found that the ironing is about the most important part to attend to, for they must be ironed while damp, with a cool iron, so as to preserve their elasticity. There are several ways of washing them – the paraffin method answers well; also with borax, or with a little lump of ammonia in the water. A simple method is to make a lather first, by dissolving the soap in hot water, and boiling till quite dissolved and in a lather, using a pound of soap to four gallons of water, or in that proportion at least. (Add two teaspoonfuls of borax if the articles be coloured.) Do not rub the things at all, but simply draw them through the hands, over and over again.

Soap should never be rubbed upon them, as it makes all woollen or knitted things hard. Wring lightly at first, then rinse through two, or even three waters, which should be warm; in fact, quite as warm as the original lather, about 90° to 96° Fahrenheit. There seem to be only two or three rules for observance in washing flannels or woollen woven undergarments: Never to wash nor rinse in either hot or cold water, as both of them cause the flannel or woollen to shrink very suddenly, whereby it retains the soap in its texture, and is discoloured, drying like a piece of parchment. Neither should woollens be submitted to great heat when drying, and when possible should be dried in a shady place in the open air. No soap should ever be rubbed on anything woollen, but a hot lather should be employed, and when just warm throw in your woollens, drawing them through the water with your hands, but not rubbing them. The best heat will be what is called "tepid" or "loo-warm."

I have been thus particular in describing the washing of flannels and all other woollens, as it is equally important to a gentleman's clothing as to a lady's; for this is emphatically the day of woollens in every part of dress, and nothing is so annoying as to have a nice suit of tennis flannels spoilt, or some possibly expensive underclothing.

Amongst the valuable suggestions recently made, is the use of fine "Nun's veiling" for either ladies' or gentlemen's underwear. Either in white or cream, it makes beautiful combinations and nightgowns. It is both light and warm, and less heavy than flannel. There is another material called "woollen gauze," also elastic woollen fabrics in various qualities.

All of these make useful garments for the outfit, and good paper patterns for combinations are now very easily procured. In India, needlework is done in each household by the tailor attached to it; but he will always require a pattern to work by, and in most Eastern countries cotton muslins may be found, which have been too little thought of hitherto by Europeans. Some of these, notably those made in Syria and Arabia, and in Turkey, make very pretty and well-wearing frocks. In fact, we are manufacturing the same muslins in England, and many people are wearing them under various names, generally claiming the East as their origin.

It seems best to be guided by common sense in all matters relating to your outfit. In the present day, too large and varied a one is a source of worry only, for there are now few countries where shopping for necessaries cannot be performed quite as cheaply as at home. Illustrated fashion magazines give an idea of what other people look like, so far as the outer woman is concerned; and good paper patterns, as I have said before, are not difficult to obtain.

Some practical suggestions on the outfits now thought needful by the principal firms of tradesmen in the metropolis, may be obtained by writing for their price lists, which may be consulted with profit as to the best things to take, and all the new improvements. As a rule the quantities are far too large, and this may always be provided against. The woman who has habituated herself to wear combination under-garments is, of course, better off than her sister who wears the old-fashioned chemise and drawers, for she has only one garment to think about, and for travel and residence in foreign countries that means not a little additional rest and comfort. There is also a very good nightgown combination, which is most comfortable for hot countries; and, indeed, some ladies in the East have followed the example of their husbands, and adopted a night garment not unlike a bathing-gown, with loose drawers and a jacket, so as to have the advantages of a pyjama. These may be made in some pretty-coloured material, such as batiste, or printed and coloured linens or cottons; and if the trousers be made on the model of the divided skirt – even though in your nightgown – you may be decently visible when passing from room to room in your needful journeys to the children and their apartments.

With regard to the amount of clothing to be taken, it is naturally difficult to advise where personal circumstances respectively must differ so widely, where climate demands consideration, and where habits of life are quite altered. The social aspects of life also demand consideration, for if you intend to enter into society, you must provide yourself with suitable dress. Tennis also demands a suit of flannels, and so does boating. In this respect a gentleman is much better off than a lady, for his suit of dress clothes is unchangeable, and if made by a good tailor, in a modern fashion, he will be presentable anywhere; and on no journey should he be without it, for it is impossible to foresee the treats he may miss, or the discomforts he may be put to, for lack of it. And it seems to me that an Englishman never looks so thoroughly a well-bred gentleman as in that dress suit which has been so much abused. But for travelling, the English-woman is also fortunate, for since the introduction of black lace dresses for both day and evening wear, she can supply herself with a well-arranged skirt, and have two bodiced made to it; one for the daytime, and one for evening, and this will take the place of two dresses. This gown, with a well-made black silk, a tailor-made travelling gown, and two or three blouses of foulard and sateen, will, I think, supply all the dress you need, even for a prolonged journey, either on the Continent or elsewhere. For a sea voyage, you would have to add something looser in the way of a dress; perhaps one that will put on and off easily, and yet look pretty and suitable. In my next article I shall enter into the question of "travelling outfits," which usually present a very mountain of difficulties to everybody.

56

A GIRL IN THE BUSH

By H. C. Storer

From: A. R. Buckland, 'A Girl in the Bush', *Empire Annual for Girls* (London: RTS, 1910), pp. 283–291.

These extracts are taken from boys and girls' magazines and annuals in the years 1880–1939. They were a response to the publications known as 'penny dreadfuls' (serialized, sensationalistic stories of crime and horror). Amongst the earliest of these new kind of magazines was the Boys' Own Paper (BOP), *published by the Religious Tract Society (RTS) in 1879.*

The founding values of this publication, and others that followed, was the belief that the youth would read and have instilled in them Christian moral values. In its early phase the BOP *stressed the missionary aspect of Empire, perhaps not surprising, given that the clergymen who had founded the RTS in 1799 had, four years earlier, founded the London Missionary Society. The paper and its companion, the* Boys' Own Annual, *promoted the British Empire, particularly in their first decade. Among those who wrote for the paper were Arthur Conan Doyle, R. M. Ballantyne, Jules Verne and G. M. Henty. Alfred Harmsworth noted that his stable of publications aimed to eradicate 'the miserable literary rubbish, in which murders, thieves and other criminals are raised to the position of heroes'. The* BOP *reflected Britain's position as a leading imperial power and its description of the races of Empire invariably include pejorative language. By 1900 the* BOP *was being challenged by other titles, such as those published by Edward Brett. These titles included* The Boys of the Empire, *published by Andrew Melrose and edited by Howard Spicer; G. A. Henty's* The Union Jack; *and* Young England: An Illustrated Magazine for Boys Throughout the English Speaking World *(1880), published by the London Sunday School Union. By the later 19th and early 20th centuries, another crop of youth publications had appeared, among which were* Chums *(1892);* Union Jack *(1894), founded by Alfred Harmsworth;* Pluck *(the full title of this publication was* Stories of Pluck: a high class weekly library of adventure at home and abroad, on land and sea, *1894);* Gem *(1907); and* The Magnet *(1908), for which Charles Hamilton (known as Frank Richards) wrote the Greyfriars stories. The* Girl's Own Paper *was edited first by Charles Peters (1880–1907), whose aim was to 'foster and develop that which was highest and noblest in the girlhood and womanhood of England . . . putting the best things first and banishing the worthless from his pages', and second by Flora Klickmann (1908–1931), who made the magazine a monthly publication. It was aimed at the middle-class English gentlewoman and in that respect tended to reflect the shift between an ideology of domesticated feminism transforming into an appreciation of the 'modern woman' who played sport, rode a bicycle and would perhaps eventually migrate to the Empire. Most of the features were educational and improving in their*

DOI: 10.4324/9781351024822-58

nature. Contemporary concern for physical fitness can be seen in magazines for both boys and girls. E. C. Dawson, author of document 50, was rector of St. Peter's, Edinburgh, and also authored Lion-Hearted *(1909) and* Missionary Heroines in India: true stories of the Wonderful bravery of patient endurance of missionaries in India, *published in the 1920s.*

"THERE you are, Phœbe; you've broken the handle of mother's best sugar-basin! I never saw the like of you!"

"Can't help it; 'specks I was made that way. It's better to break things than to have dirt."

"Don't wrangle, girls," interposed the delicate, gentle mother. "You've both got your faults, you know. One of you might bring me in some wood; I've got a pie to make before the bread is ready to put into the oven."

Phœbe, thrusting her feet into a pair of her father's watertight boots – for it was winter, and everything was very muddy – went out of doors and started to split firewood.

The Morrison homestead was a substantial, square, one-story wooden building, with a veranda in front and a lean-to kitchen at the back. Within, everything was as bright and clean as soap and elbow-grease could make it. A cheerful atmosphere of industry pervaded the home. The girls worked hard, with a good deal of clatter and occasional bickerings, but on the whole they were good-natured, and brimming over with animal spirits. There was always something to be accomplished, something done to earn a night's repose. Cows had to be milked, butter churned, bread to be baked, and clothing to be made and repaired. There was no want, but no superfluity.

The father, a hard-working man, had taken up a Crown section of land on easy terms. But stock was dear, and there were many losses, and it took him all his time to meet his rent and taxes and to keep his family of growing boys and girls, who were always tearing their clothes and wearing out their boots and shoes.

The situation was a very beautiful one. The farm lay on the slopes of a range of hills close to the west coast of the North Island of New Zealand. From the windows magnificent views were obtainable of plain, river, lake, and mountains to where the eastern sky was fretted by the conical peaks of the Coromandel peninsula and Te Aroha Mountain.

When Phœbe re-entered the house, carrying an armful of firewood, Mary was busily employed counting out the weekly wash preparatory to bundling it up and taking it down to the spring which served as their laundry.

"I say, mum, how much soap have we got?" she asked, stopping her work.

"I never thought of that till now. You'll have to go over to the store for some, and there are a lot of other things wanted."

"All right," she readily answered, nothing loath to exchange the variety of a ride and a chat with the storekeeper's daughters for the routine of house-work.

A white mist was driving up from the coast, obliterating the landscape and soaking everything out of doors; but Mary was too well accustomed to these atmospheric conditions to take any notice, so, fetching a bridle from the storeroom, she went off to catch her horse.

He was in a paddock which was fenced off from the Bush, but cumbered with fallen timber, round which Dick, her horse, dodged and doubled, in company with three foals, who greatly enjoyed the fun. After chasing round for nearly half an hour, Mary succeeded in running them into the stockyard. His mates crowded about Dick's heels, so she could not approach him from that quarter. Nothing daunted, Mary climbed on to the top rail of the yard, from which coign of vantage she managed to slip the bit into his mouth and get the bridle over his head. Wielding a switch right and left on to the heads and withers of the foals, she quickly dispersed them, jumped on to Dick's back, and trotted to the house for her saddle.

The condition of the roads would have filled a town-bred girl with dismay, but Mary Morrison was too well accustomed to the mud and slush to take any notice of them. She trotted through deep pools and along the edge of steep cuttings without any sense of fear.

The storekeeper carried on his business in a small, one-roomed building with two windows and a door. As he ran a farm as well, his daughters attended to the requirements of customers. The dwelling-house was within a few feet, so, finding the door locked, Mary passed on and knocked. Her summons was quickly answered.

"How d'ye do, Mary? So glad to see you. It's a treat to have company on a wet day. Mrs. Smith is here too, and we're having a cup of tea; you're just in time."

"But look at my boots and skirt! They are a mass of mud."

"That's all right! Here's an empty sugar-bag for you to place your feet on. Hurry up before the tea gets cold."

The talk grew general, and drifted from one topic to another, until, the winter afternoon beginning to close in, the two visitors rose to go. But first they had to make their purchases in the store, and, as is usually the case when one is doing household shopping, it was a curious, heterogeneous collection, comprising jam, calico, biscuits, and ointment.

"As I am riding your way I'll carry that box of ointment for you," remarked Mrs. Smith, slipping it into her pocket.

When the purchases had been stowed away into sugar-bags and satchels for safe transit by horseback, Mrs. Smith and Mary set off in pouring rain, heralded by the loud barking of five dogs. The riders were good friends, but the same could not be said of their dogs. They yapped and barked and snarled at each other regardless of the commands of their respective owners. It was not easy travelling, riding down a steep track rendered greasy by the rains, cumbered as they were with "cargo." It called for careful management to prevent the horses from slipping. But the journey was safely accomplished, with no greater incident than a fight between two of the dogs.

A little later, a sunny February day, with a gentle breeze to counteract the heat of the sun, found all the little world of Wenley in holiday trim. From every point of the compass they came, in buggies, in drays, on horseback – but chiefly on horseback: the bachelor from the lonely Bush wharé, the small farmer and the station owner, the school teacher and the parson and the Maoris – all got up in their best, and for one day at least in the year all grievances and differences were forgotten. For it was the children's annual picnic, and every one was determined to give the "kiddies" a good time.

The place of meeting was an ideal one – an almost level paddock sloping gently towards the virgin bush, where tree ferns waved their plumes to the summer breeze and nikau palms stood in stately order, lances in rest, guarding the portals of the forest king.

> The wind in the tree-tops was scarcely heard,
> The streamlet repeated its one silver word,
> And far away, o'er the depths of the woodland,
> Floated the bell of the parson bird.

As the Morrison family rode down the Bush track it was a gay and animated scene that presented itself to their view. Several tents had been patched to afford shelter from the sun and to serve as dressing-rooms and nursery where the babies could be put to sleep. The provision wagons had been drawn to one side, and on one of these a gramophone poured out popular melodies and reproduced the notes of famous singers. Boys ran hither and thither; girls moved about in twos and threes, looking, in their bright prints and muslins, like moving flowers; while their elders stood round or sat on empty boxes exchanging news, the mothers keeping a watchful eye on the toddlers, who trotted about or sat on the grass like daisies.

"Take me down! Take me down!" shouted wee Bobbie Morrison, who had ridden in front of his father. The sight of so many people had worked his excitement, which had been gathering momentum since daybreak, to an uncontrollable pitch.

"What do you want to get down for?" inquired Phœbe, in a tone of gentle teasing.

"Me want to wun a wace; me want to win a saddle!"

While the mother exchanged greetings with those close at hand the father tethered the horses, and the girls slipped to the dressing-tent to change their heavy riding-skirts for dainty white frocks.

"Ain't you girls ready yet?" exclaimed Harry Falconer, a young farmer who seemed to find pleasure in Mary's company. He had been watching for their arrival, and had placed himself at hand ready to act as cavalier. "Hurry up; there's rare fun going on here!"

"All right, I'm coming," said Mary. Then in a whisper to Phœbe: "I say, is my belt straight at the back – and how does my back-hair look?"

"Don't blush, Mary; you'll do. Harry will not see anything to criticize."

Mary bobbed out of the tent, and was quickly annexed by Harry, who bustled them along to where the company were drawn up in a double line with a clear course between.

A three-legged race for girls was in progress, and every one was convulsed with amusement.

In front were two slight girls, a white girl and a Maori. These two adapted their movements to each, and got over the ground with surprising agility; but the real interest was centred on the next pair, two fat, good-natured lassies of ten or thereabouts, with no more suppleness in them than two bags of flour. They rolled and they lurched along, until finally they collapsed in a laughing heap.

The banging of tin cans and cries of "Tucker's ready! tucker's ready!" proved a welcome diversion, for the fresh air and exercise had put an edge on even the most jaded appetites. Tea was carried up from the camp-fire in kerosene tins, and ladled out by a jolly, fat Maori woman; while sandwiches, cakes, and pastry were quickly unpacked and transferred to trays, from which they disappeared with an amazing rapidity.

When the elders and the little ones had been served, Harry Falconer and the two girls joined a group of old schoolfellows, and there was much banter and harmless persiflage as they heartily enjoyed their alfresco meal.

"What race are you going in for, Harry?" asked Mary.

"I'm going in for the surprise race."

Just then the starter came along calling for all those who had entered for this event. Harry jumped up, threw off his coat, and ran for the starting-point.

This had some excitement about it, for many of the contestants were in good training. To the delight of Mary and Phœbe, Harry came in first. He ran freely and gracefully, and was followed home by a Maori.

"But where's the surprise?" asked Phœbe.

"The surprise lies in the fact that there is no prize," answered Harry, laughing.

The day was brought to a close by an exhibition of dancing by men. The prize was carried off by a fat Maori, dressed in black-and-white check riding-pants and white silk shirt. He went through the antics of the cake-walk with the ponderousness of an elephant waltzing, and with a seriousness of demeanour which threatened to upset the gravity of the onlookers.

As Mary and Phœbe rode home in the clear evening light under a sky dappled with crimson cloudlets, Phœbe exclaimed, with a deep sigh, "Hasn't it been a perfect day!" Simple joys, these!

Some weeks later Mary propounded a bold and surprising plan. "I wonder how dad will manage about the mail-carrying contract?" she said to Phœbe, as she pressed out a linen blouse.

Phœbe, who was cleaning the forks and spoons with a great clatter, ceased working.

"Why, what's the trouble? Can't Jack go on carrying it?"

"No, he's been offered a billet as chain-man with the surveyors who have been at work near here, and he wants to accept it. Mother thinks he ought to, as it might lead to something permanent, but dad says he can't manage without the money."

She started to iron a pile of children's pinafores; then suddenly laid down her iron with a clatter that made Phœbe jump.

"I'll tell you what; I'll do it, and you can take turns with me!"

"You'd never manage it! Just look how early you'd have to start! And it would be dark in the winter before you'd get home. It would be horribly cold, too, and the roads swimming in mud. You'd soon get sick of it! It's ten miles each way to Glen Thompson, and you'd have to go twice a week. And it's a big load to carry too!"

"I know all that," replied Mary placidly, "but I'm going to do it, all the same. It will help dad, and I know he's pushed."

The plan announced, Mary met with a good deal of opposition, especially from her mother; but she was determined, and finally she got her way.

The mail-carrying was quite pleasant work in the summer and autumn, but when the dark, short, winter days came it proved very trying. But the "mailman" was grit all through, and held bravely and cheerily on, always willing to oblige any one by making little purchases or by taking parcels.

Yet she had at least one fright.

On a cold, dark evening in the middle of June the mail was very late in reaching Glen Thompson. The launch which brought it up the creek from the railway had run on to a sandbank, and so had delayed it for hours.

It was close on five o'clock before Mary rode out into the gloom on her ten miles' journey over the hills. There had been a good deal of carting done, and the road was very heavy. It was too dark to pick out the track. All she could do was to stick to her saddle and trust to her horse to carry her through.

Not a sound was to be heard. Even the night-birds had retired to their nests. The chill darkness wrapped her round like a winding-sheet. Beneath her was the reflection of the stars in the liquid mud, as the horse sank up to his knees, drawing out his feet again with a noise like a pistol-shot.

When Mary felt as though she had been travelling thus for weeks and years, she began to feel that the junction in the road where she would have to turn off to the Wenley post-office ought to be near. The question in her mind was, "Will Dick be able to pick it out in the dark?"

She stopped, and peered into the darkness.

That gate looming like a blotch – it ought to be on her right hand. She pulled the rein, and presently found herself jammed against a fence.

"This won't do, Dick!" she exclaimed aloud, her courage rapidly oozing away.

"Hullo! Is that you, Mary?"

The cheery tones of Harry Falconer's voice rang through the night, shattering the miserable loneliness and bringing tears to Mary's eyes for joy.

"I'm here, stuck up against a fence!"

"Hold on, I'll be there in a minute."

Was any one ever more welcome? In a trice Harry had seized her bridle and half-led, half-dragged her horse back on to the track. Then, taking her mail-bag, he mounted his own horse and rode on at her side.

What a relief it was to feel at ease in the saddle! At first Mary was too overcome to say a word, but when she regained her composure natural curiosity asserted itself, and she asked –

"However did you happen to be here?"

"When I went for my letters, the postmistress told me of the delay, so I came out to meet you – in case you might get lost, you know," he concluded rather lamely.

"How good of you!" she exclaimed fervently.

His heart gave a bound of delight and then thumped against his ribs like a flail against a barn floor.

As for the poor little "mailman," the coldness, the awful loneliness, the utter weariness had all vanished before the delightful consciousness of being cared for.

> Love took up the harp of life, and smote on all the chords with might,
> Smote the chord of self that, trembling, passed in music out of sight.

They did not talk much as they plodded side by side through the mud, but an infinite content filled their hearts and minds.

A year later Harry took his bride home.

57

THE BOYS' BRIGADE GAZETTE

From: *The Boys' Brigade Gazette*, 1st December 1892, pp. 149–170.

The final documents in this volume demonstrate the ways in which youth organisations of the period were underpinned and indeed inspired by the Empire. The Boys' Brigade (BB) and the Boy Scout and Girl Guides movements encouraged the youth to demonstrate patriotism and self-discipline, and to acquire skills that could be used in the colonial context. The BB was founded in 1883 as a Christian youth movement by William Alexander Smith (1854–1914). Smith had been a Sunday School teacher and a member of the rifle volunteers. The aim of the BB was 'The advancement of Christ's kingdom among Boys and the promotion of habits of Obedience, Reverence, Discipline, Self-respect and all that tends towards a true Christian manliness'. It introduced boys to semi-military discipline, gymnastics, summer camps and religious services. Robert Baden-Powell (1857–1941) became a vice president of the BB in 1903 and there were close links between the BB and the scout movement before 1914. Robert Baden-Powell was also on the committee of the Duty and Discipline Movement which Meath founded just before the outbreak of the First World War. Baden-Powell was very much an imperial figure, serving in the British army, travelling to India, Afghanistan, and East Africa, and participating in the South African War, taking great credit during the siege of Mafeking. During the war he had utilised boy messengers and this proved to be the origins of the scout movement. As was noted in Baden-Powell's obituary, scouting was seen as a system of education which combined 'chivalry and patriotism'. His book Scouting for Boys, *which appeared in the Edwardian era, can be seen as a founding document of this youth movement, a movement which then also encompassed girls as the Girl Guides were founded in 1910 by Powell's sister Agnes. Both movements were subsequently established across the British Empire.*

Head-quarters notes

MR. J. CARFRAE ALSTON, Brigade President, and Mrs. Alston, sailed from Liverpool on Friday, 25th November, for a tour in Egypt and the Holy Land.

WE have the pleasure of publishing this month an unusually full report of the highly successful series of Meetings held at Sheffield on Friday, 28th October, in connection with the Annual Meeting of the Brigade Council.

QUITE a number of Public Meetings fall to be chronicled in this number of the *Gazette*, in the reports of which some very interesting addresses will be found. It is clear that Battalions and Companies throughout the country are realizing more and more the benefits that flow from such Meetings, in stimulating interest in the movement.

WE are sure that the decision of the Executive Committee to hold another great Exeter Hall Meeting on Friday, 2nd June, 1893, will be hailed with satisfaction throughout the whole Brigade. Further particulars will be found on page 157.

WE would draw special attention to the *Annual Appeal of the Finance Committee,* on behalf of the Head-Quarters' Fund, which will be found on page 163; and would express the hope that there will be a very generous response from the friends of the Brigade in all parts of the country. The amount asked from the general public is *Six Hundred Pounds,* and, considering the magnitude of the work now undertaken by the Brigade, this cannot be considered a large sum.

ALONG with this number of the *Gazette,* the Executive Committee have the pleasure to publish their *Eighth Annual Report,* which is in all respects the most satisfactory Report that has ever been issued from Head-Quarters.

THE Executive Committee are extremely fortunate in being able to follow up Professor Drummond's great success of last year, *Baxter's Second Innings,* with so worthy a successor as the Rev. Professor Marcus Dods' *Union Jack,* a Christmas Gift-Book that we are sure will go straight to the heart of every Boy in the Brigade, as we hope Officers will see that it goes into the *hands* of every Boy.

MAY we express the hope that a copy of *The Boys' Brigade Scripture Union Card,* with its Daily Bible Readings for the year, will also be put into the hands of every Boy in the Brigade, unless in cases where another form of Card may be already in use.

THE issue by the Executive Committee of the very admirably compiled *Manual and Firing Exercises for The Boys' Brigade* will remove a long-felt difficulty; and once the new *Infantry Drill* has ceased to be "Provisional," it is hoped that the Committee will complete their work in this direction by compiling a Drill Manual for The Boys' Brigade on the same simple, clear, and satisfactory lines.

THE Brigade Secretary has received numerous letters asking questions on various points of drill, nearly every one of which could be satisfactorily answered by a reference to the article on the "New Drill" on page 131 of the *Gazette* of 1st October, 1892.

ALL effective Companies ought to be in full working order by this season of the year, and Captains who have not already done so should send to Head-Quarters without delay for their supply of necessary Forms and New Session's Membership Cards.

WE have received the Annual Reports of the Belfast, Bristol, Glasgow, Liverpool, London, and Sheffield Battalions. As we shall have something to say about the Battalion Reports in an early number, we shall be glad to have 12 copies of the Report of each of the other Battalions as soon as published.

MANY very admirable *Company Cards* are also coming to hand, and we would ask every Captain to send a copy of his Company Card to Head-Quarters.

Mr. W. Irving Smith, well and favourably known throughout the country for his lectures on Sunday School Work and Methods, writes as follows to the Brigade Secretary: –

> "I keep an eager and sympathetic eye on your sanctified ingenuity to catch and keep the dear lads of 12 to 17. Your movement touches and utilizes many springs of Boy nature. The wooden gate-post does not grow; the healthy young tree does. The young tree is rooted in the soil; the post is a branch broken off. There is a good deal of 'wooden-post' work in attempts to hold the big Boys."

The Boys' Brigade has lost one of its truest Officers and best friends, in the death, at the early age of 37, of Mr. Reginald A. Bewes, Captain, 5th Plymouth Company, and until recently President of the Plymouth Battalion of The Boys' Brigade. Mr. Bewes was one of the prime movers and chief supporters of The Boys' Brigade in the West of England, where he was widely known and universally esteemed. He has all along taken a very warm and active interest in the work of the Brigade, and indeed in all work having for its object the social or religious welfare of Plymouth. In The Boys' Brigade he will be sorely missed; and we are sure that the loving sympathy of all his brother Officers will be extended in their hour of trial to Mrs. Bewes and her three children, and to the large circle of friends who now mourn his loss.

Officers wanted

MOST of us will find, stored somewhere among our childhood's memories, the recollection of having a binocular put into our hands. We put the small end to our eyes, and, perhaps not being properly focussed, we saw nothing clearly. Then the wrong end was tried: "Oh! Wonderful! How large our garden was! How small every body looked! What a long way off everything seemed to be!"

Faith has been likened to a telescope, for it brings the future near, and makes it real to us; so much so, that faithful men live less for the present life, and more for the life to come. But the Devil is cunning, and somehow he manages to trick us, and gets us to put the wrong end to our eye; so that instead of the telescope bringing the future life right into our everyday life, it looks a long way off – a very unreal thing, and we live for the moment.

Does this not give us a peep into the reason why there should be a call for such a heading as "Officers Wanted" in *The Boys' Brigade Gazette*? Young fellows get so much engrossed in the present, and the future seems so far off, that business becomes magnified as the most important thing with some; intellectual culture with others; some think all the world of athletics; and to some a dance or other social engagement must not be missed on any consideration, although the following morning it leaves little more satisfaction behind it than does a burst soap bubble – damped spirits and no result.

The earnest Brigade Officer has trumped the Devil's trick, and to his eye of faith, a line of brave stalwart men are seen plodding manfully through life; one is in the forefront of missionary enterprise away in the heart of Africa; another is a skilled doctor combating disease on the plains of India; a third gathers his family and neighbours around him on the quiet Sundays, away in the Far West of Canada, and tells them the story of the Cross; while one and all, in humble or high positions, at home or abroad, have a warm shrine in their hearts for the Captain and Officers of their Company of The Boys' Brigade, who gave up so many evenings for them, and laid themselves out to do them good, and to make of them true and happy men.

But we Officers know *more* than this. Where is the man who will not say that The Boys' Brigade has done more for him than he has for The Boys' Brigade? Who of us did not at one time feel afraid of Boys, fancying they were laughing at us in their sleeves when we tried to teach them, and knew that the tell-tale colour was mantling our cheeks as we meekly said, "Please be quiet, Boys!"? And do you not remember how this was all changed when we exchanged the pleading tone for the command, "Attention!"? Or how trait upon trait, hitherto latent in your character, have been developed, and unknown resourcefulness called forth to meet the hundred-and-one emergencies of a single season's drill?

Now, to know this and to keep it to ourselves is *wrong*. Boys can be got by the hundreds, but where are the Officers to come from? Trace the history of every lapsed Company, and in nine cases out of ten, no Officers could be found to take the places of those compelled to resign, by reason of removal or some other cause.

Let every one of us – and there are 1618 of us – try to induce at least one friend or acquaintance to become an Officer of the Brigade. Try to put the right end of the telescope to his eye. Tell him it is astonishing how readily he can with the confidence of the Boys by taking an interest in them, and laying himself out to make them happy. Once gained, that influence may be used in drawing them to *Our Friend and Master*. Boys are wonderfully responsive to anything which young fellows may do for them. We are more or less their heroes, and they watch us with uncommonly sharp eyes.

Tell him this all means self-denial, but it carries its own reward with it. We have to make such engagements *first engagements*, and the social functions consequently suffer. But cannot we well afford to let them suffer? While they amuse for the time, they give no real satisfaction if sought after for our own pleasure.

Tell him this the first time you see him, and use all your influence to get him to start in, right away. Then you will have done him a life-long kindness, and through him, his fellow Officers, and perhaps five hundred Boys may pass through his hands, and *you* will be at the beginning of it all.

Is it worth doing? Do it well and wisely. Ask your Great Captain how, and to whom, you are to speak, and so soon as you have your marching orders, go. Then by Christmas time the staff of Officers in The Boys' Brigade may be swelled by hundreds, and perhaps the Company Enrolment Forms at Head-Quarters will be run out.

"Is it a vision, or is it a dream?
I know not, for 'things are not what they seem.'

"'Tis a cold grey morn, and I think I stand
Alone, in the midst of a desert land.

"I can see no tree – no flower will grow:
Ah, me! I remember I would not sow.
                2 Cor. ix. 6.

"Others were busy, their gardens are bright;
Alas! for me, only mildew and blight.
                Gal. vi. 7.

"The Master called, but I would not go;
Oh! how can I reap? I refused to sow!

"He bade me some precious seeds to set:
I answered, 'I go,' *but not yet! not yet!*

"Many were patiently kneeling around,
Putting dull brown seeds into dull brown ground.

"Their ground is now full, the harvest they wait,
                John iv. 36.

"While I stand and mournfully cry, 'Too Late!'
                Hos. viii. 7.

Brigade Council meeting at Sheffield

The EIGHTH ANNUAL MEETING of the BRIGADE COUNCIL was held in the Y.M.C.A. Buildings, Sheffield, on Friday, 28th October, 1892, on the invitation of the Sheffield Battalion Council.

The plan of moving the Council Meeting from one large centre to another has been more than justified by the experience of the last few years, and certainly the Meetings just held at Sheffield have proved no exception to this rule.

The arrangements made by the local Battalion Council were characterised by great forethought and thoroughness, and the impression produced upon the Officers who visited Sheffield for the purpose of attending the Meetings, was one that will not soon pass away.

The proceedings of the day began with a Devotional Meeting held at 1 o'clock, to ask God's blessing on the work of the Brigade. No one who was present at this meeting could have failed to realize where the motive of the work and the secret of its success lay, as one after another of the Captains led in prayer, asking God's blessing on the Boys, the Officers, and the future of the movement. The meeting was in every way most helpful and stimulating, and formed a fitting prelude to the important business of the day.

The Council Meeting proper took place at 4 p.m. Officers representing Companies were present from London, Liverpool, Manchester, Plymouth, Derby, Nottingham, Hartlepool, Hull, Newport (Mon.), Edinburgh, Glasgow, Belfast, and other towns, besides a large representation of the Sheffield Battalion.

Mr. J. CARFRAE ALSTON, Brigade President, occupied the chair, and was supported by members of the Executive Committee from various parts of the Kingdom.

The meeting having been opened with prayer by the Rev. J. R. HILL, M.A., Captain 1st Brighouse Company, the Brigade Secretary read the minutes of last Annual Meeting, which were approved.

The CHAIRMAN, in moving the adoption of the Annual Report of the Executive Committee, which was in the hands of the members of Council, spoke as follows: –

The Brigade President's address

GENTLEMEN, – The Annual Report of the Executive Committee, which I have the honour of submitting for the acceptance of the Brigade Council, is the fullest and, I think, the most interesting of the eight which have now chronicled the history and operations of this organization.

In reading it you feel what a strong hold the movement is taking and how widespreading are the influences brought to bear on the Boyhood of the country. You recognize what a powerful mechanism you have in your hands and how great the responsibility in using it aright.

Let us examine for a few minutes some of the details presented in this Report, which is really the narrative of your own year's work sifted and arranged by Head-Quarters. Let us see what there is to warrant our congratulations and, more profitably, to note what demands improvement.

The nett increase of 72 Companies on last year's strength is undoubtedly satisfactory, and when we find that 143 new Companies were enrolled against 89 in the preceding year, we have proof of the vitality of the movement in many localities and through many channels. But, unfortunately, we have not secured the gross increase, for no less than 17¼ per cent. of the Companies we saw on the roll at 31st May, 1891, have been lost to us from causes which have already been suggested, discussed, and lamented. Our loss from these causes is much too heavy; but I do hope that through forethought and good guidance it may become gradually less and less. I can assure you the Executive Committee exercises as much care and supervision as possible in the initial stages of Company formation. Were the future prosperity of new Companies to depend solely on the completeness of scheduled information, the Executive would no longer have to grieve over such lapses as have hitherto occurred.

But, gentlemen, you have after all a substantial increase, and we have warrant for believing that the quality of our Companies is steadily improving, both for work and for what the actuaries call "expectation of life."

In any conjectural figures upon which we have ventured from time to time, we have generally stated our rank and file, with Non-Commissioned Officers, at 20,000 Boys. I am glad to say that the ascertained number is 1000 over that estimate – nay, more, the Secretary, by some happy process, shows one file better, as an earnest, no doubt, of this season's successful recruiting. Head-Quarters are nothing if not exact, and 21,000 *and two* is therefore the total strength. This gives an increase of over 21 per cent. on last year.

What have the Companies to say about these Boys is a point on which the statistical columns of the Report throw a tell-tale light, and here we are at once met with a slight disappointment. The increased numbers have not shown the same regular attendance at Drill as compared with last year. Officers should see wherein this falling-off originates, and guard against themselves being found at fault. Let them make their Drill precise, interesting, even brilliant, plenty of go in it, full steam on; Officers and Boys at the pitch of excited attention, with the desire to make each movement a finished performance, so that when "stand easy" comes there is a pant of satisfaction all round. Let them encourage emulation among Non-Commissioned Officers to get the best out of their squads, and among the Boys in each squad to rival the others in attendance and attention.

Drill and discipline, on which we set such store, must not be allowed to fall flat or to become slovenly or stale. If so neglected we shall lose immensely in the efficacy of that great lever through whose power the Brigade works out its ends.

You will observe an increase of five Battalions on the year, viz., Aberdeen, Bristol, Liverpool, Newport (Mon.), and Nottingham. By the sub-division sanctioned in the exceptional case of London that Battalion now becomes three, which brings up the actual number to 16 in all.

Very nearly one half of the Companies, and of the Boys of the Brigade, are now grouped under the control of Battalion Councils, and we are entitled to look for many advantages in such consolidation. The statistical columns before us do not, however, deal with many phases of Battalion work which yield good results in most of these centres. But we gather this fact from these figures that, in attendance at drill the Battalion Companies are 2½ per cent. better than the average of all the outlying Companies. And another feature presents itself unexpected where claims on Company funds are numerous – this, that Battalion Companies contribute a higher average rate to Head-Quarters than do the others – or 15s as against 12s. 7½d. per Company. Our Treasurer will fully appreciate the necessity of immediately creating more Battalions. Like all good treasurers he longs for revenue.

The Report takes note, with approval, of the increasing number of Companies which have established Bible-Classes in connection with their work. More than

52½ per cent. of the Boys of the Brigade have now the opportunity of attending such classes. But let us always attach more weight to the manner in which these classes are appealing to the Boys, and to their proper management, than to the mere numbers of them.

The average attendance of the 11,050 Boys who had this privilege afforded them was somewhat under 50 per cent. Making allowance for other duties and similar classes claiming their presence, apart from the Company Bible-Class, this average is too low, and if you glance at the details of this attendance you will see how startling is the divergence of the figures which produce the average.

Just compare an average attendance of one-tenth of a Company's roll with the splendid and possible achievement of the 1st Belfast and 1st Glasgow with over 94 per cent.; the 73rd Glasgow and 1st Bannockburn with over 93 per cent.; and the 2nd Hastings with more than 92½ per cent. – not to mention other instances in which the Bible-Class is evidently an attraction and a profit to the Boys, and must be a pleasure and a strength to the Officers.

I feel justified in saying that the attendance for the whole Brigade under this head is lower than it should be.

Now, we have surely a right to expect that the Address at the Drill Meeting should be found holding a prominent place in the 254 Companies which have no Bible-Classes. It would appear, however, that of these, only 31 report "Regular" Addresses, and [Illegible text] have them more or less frequently.

The best state of things would be that all of the 490 Companies in the Brigade should have both Bible-Class and Drill Address; there are 221 in this ideal position. The next best would be that all had one or the other; 234 fulfil this condition. On the other hand, it is to be hoped that some error in the returns, or very exceptional causes, make it appear that eight Companies have neither Class nor Address.

Consider that the Brigade is a two-sided organization – the one disciplinary by military methods, the other religious. These two should be well balanced, so that we may always be able to honestly assert that the one side is used only to secure the attainment of those higher ends aimed at in the other. A Company with drill alone, and no religious guidance by its Officers, would certainly be an anomaly in The Boys' Brigade, and one in which there is provided a maximum of drill and a minimum of religious supervision cannot be said to be on the strongest lines for the main purpose of our existence.

Again, let us admit that there are other opportunities and means by which the Boy is influenced, still, I think that our Officers should gather up and bring into the Company environment all the religious instruction, by word and example, which their close sympathetic relationship to their Boys enables them to apply with such advantage.

I have ventured to dwell on some of these results obtained from the statistical columns, to get below the surface a little, and to speak more strongly than the Executive require to do in a general report of the year's work. When we are here in Council assembled it is better to search for any weak place in the wall of our fortress than to crow on the perfect parapet.

The one thing that seems always to bulk most largely as our mainstay and prime requirement – the one that comes to the front at all points, at drill and in recreation – is the personal fitness of our Officers. The Executive have always this subject before them, and they can but press upon those who are engaged in this stimulating and remunerative work how much their example in word, in tone, in conduct, can influence our 21,000 Boys, and through them thousands more in this land. A true sense of unfitness and of responsibility will work wonders on us all.

A prominent paragraph in the Report refers to the value of the Public Meetings which have been held. There is no doubt that when the work of the Brigade is presented as an object-lesson by the presence of the Boys, much public interest is at once excited. In many places where the Brigade is unknown or misunderstood the appearance of the Brigade Secretary or of a Company would at once furnish information and arguments in favour of the movement. There is one thing very much needed at the present juncture, and that is a Travelling Secretary in addition to a resident one. Did funds permit he might open new ground which now lies fallow for lack of knowledge of what the Brigade is and what it can do; he could visit existing Companies, shake them up and set them right where needful, or stimulate and encourage where they are doing well. From what I know of the demands made on Mr. Smith to give addresses and to inspect Companies and Battalions here, there, and everywhere, and of the success which has attended the meetings convened for him, it is evident how much value is attached to personal contact. Were he to accept all the invitations offered, the work of the Head-Quarters' Office would soon fall sadly into arrears.

The paragraph on Instrumental Bands may well break into poetry when dealing with that branch of the work. Boy life goes in for thumping and blowing as well as for drilling and marching. The Brigade is all the better for the Companies whose good friends have enabled them to add Bands to their other attractions. Musical training is a great privilege for the Boys, and one is astonished to find that 11 per cent. of the strength is engaged in adding the exhilaration of music to the evolutions of Drill.

There are, indeed, Bands and Bands, and we must not look for the same effects from the little squad tootling bravely on the modest flute as from the full Band with sonorous brass. Speaking in a musical county like Yorkshire, and before the Battalion Officers whose splendid Band – that of the 1st Sheffield – added so much to the success of the Exeter Hall Meeting, I can only point to what can be done towards perfection in this department.

The organization of the Brigade still moves forward in other countries and friendly intercourse is maintained with our Head-Quarters. We receive many pleasant communications on Brigade work, and have been favoured with interesting calls from strangers, who, while on tour in this country, do not lose the opportunity of making acquaintance with the Secretary and the Brigade Office.

In the "Baxter" correspondence we had several excellent papers from Boys in American and Canadian Companies. In The United States the numbers now stand at our figure of six years ago, and since they have organized Divisions with suitable centres we shall soon hear of rapid progress in that energetic country.

With these remarks, I beg to move the adoption of the Report.

The Rev. ALFRED L. BICKERSTAFF, M.A., St. Nicholas' Church, Nottingham, and Captain of the 12th Nottingham Company, in seconding the adoption of the Report, expressed his belief that the Brigade was being increasingly recognised as a powerful means for advancing Christ's Kingdom, and for training the future men of England in righteousness, soberness, and godliness. Personally, the work appealed to him most strongly. From the time he first grasped the idea of the Brigade, he had looked upon it as a splendid instrument for influencing Boys, and his subsequent experience had only confirmed this impression – made him believe in it with all his heart. He considered the Brigade was an institution which was thoroughly "up to date." Special weapons were needed against special sins in particular states of society. No one could doubt that lawlessness and disregard for authority were among the marked characteristics of the age, and the Brigade seemed exactly to meet this present-day need. He rejoiced that the spiritual side of the work had been so strongly emphasised that day. We must keep ever before us the thought that it was a work for Christ, and that we sought to lead the Boys to Him.

Mr. GEORGE P. REYNOLDS, Newport (Mon.) Battalion President, in supporting the adoption of the Report, congratulated the Executive on the high standard which they kept up in the publications issued from Head-Quarters. He referred specially to the *Gazette*, which in matter and style, he thought, reflected great credit on the Executive of the Brigade. He believed that the Brigade owed no small part of its success to the uniformly high "tone" which was maintained in everything that emanated from the Head-Quarters' Office, and he trusted that the Executive would maintain in the future the policy which had yielded such good results in the past. He had much pleasure in supporting the adoption of this most gratifying Report.

The Report was unanimously adopted, and, on the motion of Mr. Samuel Osborn, Sheffield Battalion Treasurer, a hearty vote of thanks was awarded to the Office-Bearers and Executive Committee, a similar compliment being paid to Major Adam Elliot Black, C.A., and Major Arthur Hart, C.A., Glasgow, for their kindness in auditing the Brigade Treasurer's Accounts.

The Office-Bearers and Executive Committee for the ensuing Session were then elected as follows: –

Brigade President – Mr. J. CARFRAE ALSTON.
Brigade Secretary – Mr. WM. A. SMITH.
Brigade Treasurer – Mr. JOHN LAMMIE.

Members of Executive Committee.

Mr. EDWIN ADAM, *Edinburgh Battalion Secretary*.
Mr. LEONARD E. STONEMAN, *Plymouth Battalion Secretary*.

Mr. WILLIAM M'VICKER, *Captain, 1st Belfast Company.*
Dr. HERBERT LANKESTER, *Captain, 13th London Company.*
Mr. SAMUEL OSBORN, *Sheffield Battalion Treasurer.*

Interesting statements were then made by Officers from different parts of the country.

A battalion head-quarters

Mr. LEONARD E. STONEMAN, Plymouth Battalion Secretary, said that one of the chief reasons for Companies lapsing in Plymouth was the difficulty of obtaining the use of rooms to drill in. Church Officers could always accommodate a Bible-Class or Boys' Service, but not a Drill Meeting. To obviate this, the Battalion Council had rented the first floor of a large warehouse, and, in addition to a Drill-Room, had furnished a comfortable Reading-Room and a Gymnasium. The Battalion Head-Quarters was managed by a staff of four Officers, who reported to the Battalion Council. On Sunday evenings at 8.15 a Lantern Service was held, with an average attendance of over 200 Boys. The rooms were open every evening from 8 to 9.30. The street in which the premises were situated had a poor reputation, but the Officers had determined to alter this, and, although the rooms had only been open a short time, a great improvement was manifest in the neighbourhood. They were carrying the war right into the Camp of the enemy, and thus seeking to advance Christ's Kingdom.

The work in Ireland

Mr. WM. M'VICKER, Captain, 1st Belfast Company, in reporting on the work in Ireland, said: –

The 1st Belfast Company, with which I have the honour and pleasure of being connected, continues to retain the interest of its members. The past Session has in every way been most encouraging. The attendance at both Drill and Bible-Class has been wonderfully regular. The attendance at Sunday School has also been good. The Drill of the Company was at the close of the Session better than at any previous time, and the *esprit de corps* very strong. A pleasantly successful Inspection brought to a close a Session that for the most part gave much satisfaction to those interested, and since then the First Summer Camp has done much to increase the feeling of brotherliness and to draw Officers and Boys nearer to each other. It is not therefore to be wondered at that when, a week ago, the Officers once more stood opposite that long line of bright faces, all eager and ready for the commencement of another Session, it was with emotion that our Father in Heaven was thanked for having been pleased to lead to the formation of The Boys' Brigade. Nor is the experience of the Officers of this Company unique; that of others in Belfast has equalled and in some ways even surpassed it, that helping to show that when loyally worked in accordance with the spirit of its

Constitution, there are few, if any, organizations working specially among Boys so well calculated to benefit them as the one which brings us together this afternoon. I need not say anything of the work of the Belfast Battalion Council more than that it is moving along quietly and in a fairly satisfactory manner. There are now in the Battalion 17 Companies and, judging from last Session's work, much good is likely to be done in that just entered upon. The Dublin Battalion Secretary reports steady progress and fair prospects there, and some at least of the country Companies are beginning the work of the Session enthusiastically and with much hopefulness.

The new London battalions

Dr. HERBERT LANKESTER referred to the recent division of the London Battalion into three distinct Battalions. He reminded the Council that towards the close of Session 1890–91 six "District Battalions" were formed, but these were really Sub-Committees without any power to act in many ways. They were, however, felt to be a step in the right direction, but only a step, and in the course of last Session it gradually became evident that the London Battalion as then existing was hindering rather than helping on the work in these "District Battalions." With some difficulty a scheme was devised which met with the approval of very nearly all the members of the Council, and was in due time sanctioned by the Executive of the Brigade. The scheme, which took effect from 1st September, divides the London Postal District into three parts, viz., "South London," "West London," and "North London," the river separating the first from the last two, while these are divided from one another by the main roads that run nearly due North from the West end of Westminster Bridge. A "Central Committee" has been formed to which matters affecting the whole of London can be referred; but the South London Battalion is as distinct from the West as Sheffield is from Plymouth. The size of London is so enormous that even this division is felt to be only a temporary plan, and that in course of time there must be still further cutting up, so it was decided to number all the London Companies consecutively, irrespective of the Battalion which they had joined. To carry out this a new Brigade Official was created in the shape of a "Registrar," whose sole duty it is to see to the designation of the Companies. Dr. Lankester mentioned that during last Session (with the partial division) much more had been done than in previous years in the shape of combined Church Parades, Gymnastic and other inter-Company Competitions, and that already there were signs of still greater advance in this direction during this Session. He mentioned also that, as the Honorary Secretary of the Church Missionary Society's Medical Mission Fund, he was going to try and form a branch of that Fund among the Church of England Companies of the Brigade in the hope of raising sufficient to support one or more beds in one of the Mission Hospitals abroad. He hoped that those connected with other Denominations might see their way to do something in the way of interesting the Boys in Missionary work.

The Manchester district

Mr. R. R. SHAW, Captain, 1st Ladybarn (Manchester) Company, in reporting on the work in the Manchester District, said: –

The Brigade Movement appears to be only in its infancy in Manchester and District. Three Companies are doing well, and others are being formed. In reference to the Ladybarn Company, of which I have the honour to be Captain, the interest of the Boys is well sustained. A short time ago a Brass Band was started, and is a great attraction. The Local Board kindly provided a room in the village for practice, and if the Company had been unknown before, the strains of music soon wakened the neighbours to a knowledge of its existence. A photograph of the Company recently appeared in a local magazine, and, as a result, efforts are now being made to establish other Companies in the district. The influence of the Company is very marked amongst the Boys; their attendance at the Bible-Class almost equals their attendance at Drill, and the majority of the members second the efforts of the Officers to maintain the dignity and efficiency of the Company.

How to conduct an ambulance class

Mr. J. DOUGLAS HAY, Convener, Ambulance Committee, Glasgow Battalion, gave a short sketch of the Ambulance work being carried on in the Glasgow Battalion, where over 300 Boys are at present undergoing a course of Ambulance Instruction. Referring to the work of Boys' Brigade Ambulance Classes in general, he said: –

In the first place, it is necessary to secure the requisite number of Boys who are 14 years of age, a medical man, and a nice, quiet hall. It is a good plan to ask other Companies to join your Boys, but do not let the class exceed 26 or 30 Boys. The Doctor should be a young man, because as a rule he has more time than a large practitioner, he is not called away so often, and can generally always be present. Having secured the Boys, the Doctor, and the hall, the next move is to become connected with the St. John's or St. Andrew's Ambulance Association, and this is done by writing to the Secretary of the Association, stating that a class has been formed made up of members of various Companies of the Brigade, it will meet on such and such a day, at a certain hour, and will be instructed by Dr. So-and-so. Make arrangements for a supply of diagrams and stretchers. The St. Andrew's make no charge whatever, but I do not know how the St. John's Association do. An Officer should be selected to act as Class Secretary, and he will act as Captain of the class, and should not allow the other Officers to interfere with the work. He will keep the roll and score off the name of any Boy absent twice, because if the Boy loses a lecture or two he throws the whole class back. Some Officers are afraid to start classes, as they think the Boys are unable to pick up the big names. Now there should be no big names. If the instructor knows his work he will use as simple words as possible; and yet, though simple, the lectures should be none the less thorough. At the close of the tenth or twelfth lecture the Examination takes place, and those Boys who pass are entitled to wear The Boys' Brigade Badge. In the St. Andrew's Association the names of the Boys who pass are all entered on the roll. Stretcher Drill should be taught to all the Boys, because as much depends in some cases on how a patient is lifted as on the dressings. Doctors as a rule are not practically acquainted with the commands for Stretcher Drill, and it is preferable to have a competent Instructor for that part of the work. We teach our Boys Friendship, but what does Friendship avail in cases of accident? I think Oliver Wendell Holmes sums that up beautifully thus: –

"Friendship's blind service, in the hour of need,
Wipes the pale face and lets the victim bleed;
Science must stop to reason and explain;
Art claps his finger on the streaming vein."

In The Boys' Brigade we want to combine Art with Friendship, and so put it in the power of our Boys to be a means of practical help and blessing to those around them.

Had time permitted, many equally interesting statements might have followed, but "time and tide wait for no man," so after a hearty and well-deserved vote of thanks had been awarded to the Chairman, the Eighth Annual Meeting of the Brigade Council was closed with the Benediction.

Brigade council dinner and conference at Sheffield

ON the invitation of the Sheffield Battalion Council, the Officers attending the Brigade Council were entertained to Dinner on the day of the Council Meeting in the Albany Hotel, where they were met by a large number of the Officers of the Sheffield Battalion.

Mr. ARTHUR U. COLE, Sheffield Battalion President, occupied the chair, and among the guests present, other than Brigade Officers, were Mr. E. J. KENNEDY, of the Y.M.C.A., Exeter Hall, London; the Rev. V. W. PEARSON, B.A., Head-Master of Wesley College, Sheffield; Mr. WM. JERVIS, Secretary of the Y.M.C.A., Sheffield; and Mr. EDWARD P. BLAKENEY, representing his father, the Venerable ARCHDEACON BLAKENEY, D.D., who deeply regretted his unavoidable absence owing to a previous engagement, and who had shown his warm interest in the movement by holding a Drawing-Room Meeting at his residence in the earlier part of the week, at which from 70 to 80 gentlemen were present to hear about the work of the Brigade, with a view to securing the interest of additional men as Officers in the Sheffield Battalion.

Mr E. J. KENNEDY spoke a few words of warm commendation of the work of the Brigade, which, he said, was in some respects more important, and was certainly more full of promise than the work in which he himself was engaged. The Y.M.C.A. got the young men too often when their characters were seared and the usefulness of their lives ruined by sinful courses. The Brigade, on the other hand, got the Boys when their lives were fresh and young, and their characters at that formative period when there was some hope of moulding them for goodness and for God. He rejoiced in the success of the Brigade, and hoped that some definite steps might be taken to secure for the Church and the Y.M.C.A. the harvest of young men who, in increasing numbers, must pass out each year from the ranks of The Boys' Brigade. He counselled the Officers to stick to the wildest Boys, for excess in mischief generally indicated excessive force of character, and if these Boys were won over they would prove our greatest strength in the future.

While the tables were being cleared an interval was allowed for conversation, after which the Rev. Herbert Reid, Captain 2nd Dundee Company, was called upon to open the discussion on the question raised in his article in last *Gazette*,

What shall our boys read?

The discussion which followed, if it did not elucidate the matter much, was at least lively enough, and helped to call attention to the question as to how far we should seek to regulate our Boys' reading. The side eddies into which the discussion flowed at times were numerous. Jules Verne found a most enthusiastic champion in the Edinburgh Battalion Secretary, who saw in him the pioneer of modern scientific invention. Another Officer objected to the discussion being confined to story-books, as he found that his Boys enjoyed such books as Green's "Short History of the English People," and Farrar's "Early Days of Christianity;" and with regard to Boys' papers, the preponderance of opinion was clearly in favour of the new periodical *Boys* rather than its rival *Chums*, while our old friend, *The Boys' Own Paper*, seemed still to hold the field. A well-known London Officer said that his difficulty was to know whether, supposing he were to start a lending library among his Boys, there was any chance of more than the covers being returned; but the unvarying testimony of those who had tried it was that when due care was taken to put the right books in the library, and when a proper register was kept, the books were not only read but returned. In the system adopted by one Captain, each Boy handed in a list of the numbers of the books he wished. When one of these was given out to him, a diagonal line was drawn through the number on the list from left to right, and when it was returned, another from right to left, forming a cross. At the conclusion, the opinion of the meeting seemed to be divided on the proposal contained in the paper, and after some further discussion, the matter was finally left in the hands of the newly appointed Executive. *(See Note in "Our Bookcase" on page 170).*

The next subject, viz.: –

How to get the boys to attend church

was introduced by Mr. GEORGE P. REYNOLDS, Newport (Mon.) Battalion President. Some of his Boys used to attend in the gallery, but he had once had occasion to call them to order, and since then they had been conspicuous by their absence. He wished to know if any brother Officer could help him out of his difficulty. Captain the Rev. J. R. Hill (one of the "original" Officers of the 1st Glasgow), after venting his indignation at seat rents, told how the young people in his Church had been formerly relegated to the back seats of the gallery, where they could neither see nor hear, but that in spite of the protests of a few old ladies, the front seats were now reserved for the children, who were marched there straight from the Sunday School. But the best solution was that of the Captain who told how, when his Chapel was being enlarged, the Boys of his Company had subscribed several pounds towards the Building Fund. In return for this, they had allocated to them two of the best seats, to which they had the exclusive right, where they could go whenever they pleased, and take a "chum" with them; and so the Boys had come to feel that they had a "proprietary interest in the Chapel."

The discussion was brought to a close by a few remarks from the BRIGADE SECRETARY. The Conference, he said, if it had done nothing else, had at least shown what an amount of life and reserve power was lying dormant in the Brigade, and if Captains, instead of sending in as "Company Items" the usual paragraph telling how Lieutenant-Colonel So-and-so had inspected the Company, how pleased he had been with the drill, which he had never seen better performed, how it quite put the Volunteers in the shade, and almost rivalled the Regulars – if instead of the stereotyped paragraph which no one read but those immediately interested they would tell something of the real living work in which they were engaged, with their difficulties, and how they were overcome, the *Gazette* would become a much more living influence among the Officers of the Brigade.

Regret was the feeling indexed on all faces when the Chairman announced that it was time to close the Conference. Doubtless there were many other matters regarding which some would have liked to unburden themselves had time permitted, but as the Secretary reminded us, the Conference is still open – in the pages of the *Gazette*.

Proposed public meeting and demonstration in Exeter Hall

FROM all quarters representations have reached the Executive Committee, pointing to the desirability of following up the brilliant success of May last, by holding another Meeting and Demonstration in Exeter Hall in the course of the coming year.

At the recent meeting of Executive Committee, held at Sheffield on the occasion of the Annual Meeting of Brigade Council, the matter received very careful consideration, with the result that the Committee are now in a position to announce that the second PUBLIC MEETING and DEMONSTRATION of THE BOYS' BRIGADE will be held in EXETER HALL, LONDON, on FRIDAY, 2ND JUNE, 1893.

In its main features the Meeting will follow the lines laid down with such satisfactory results in May last, while at the same time the Committee hope that the interest taken in the coming Meeting throughout the Brigade will be even more widespread than before. There is no reason why such a Gathering as this should not assume the character of a GREAT NATIONAL DEMONSTRATION OF BOYS' BRIGADE LIFE AND WORK. Why should we not have representations of Officers and Detachments of Boys from all parts of the country? We believe that the expense incurred would be justified many times over by the interest and enthusiasm which would be aroused.

The Sheffield Battalion set a noble example to the whole Brigade by the enterprise displayed last May, when the splendid Band of the 1st Sheffield Company was sent up to London at great expense, in order to furnish the music at Exeter Hall. And not less was the Brigade indebted to the unwearied efforts of the Officers of the London Battalion for the success which attended the Meeting. Is it too much to hope that the other Battalions throughout the country may aspire to the honour of having a share in the success which we are sure will attend the coming Meeting, by taking a hearty interest in the arrangements and endeavouring to have some representation of their Officers and Boys present at the Meeting?

Battalion Councils and Officers of Companies are therefore invited to give the matter their early and earnest consideration, and, if willing to co-operate in any way, are requested to communicate with The Brigade Secretary, Head Quarters' Office, 68 Bath Street, Glasgow, stating clearly and fully (1) What they are prepared to do; (2) the number of Boys who would take part; and (3) the time (in minutes) which they would occupy.

The Committee will also welcome suggestions from Officers as to any way in which the arrangements could be improved, or the interest in the Meeting increased. All communications to be addressed to The Brigade Secretary.

District battalions

AT the Meeting of the Brigade Executive Committee, held at Sheffield on Saturday, 29th October, the following important resolution was passed: –

> "The Executive Committee, having carefully considered the desirability of allowing as many Companies as possible to obtain the advantages of being grouped in Battalions, is now prepared to consider applications from Companies in any District for sanction to form themselves into a Battalion, in accordance with Article 7 of the Constitution, under a local designation which shall define the limits of such Battalion."

Battalion jottings

Battalion Secretaries are invited to send, for this Column, Notes on all matters of general interest in connection with the work of their Battalions. Contributions should not exceed 400 words.

Aberdeen

THE Ambulance Classes so successfully conducted last winter have been resumed this year. Dr. Kelly, a distinguished graduate of Aberdeen University, is the teacher.

IT is proposed to hold a Public Meeting on Tuesday, 20th December, to stir up interest in The Boys' Brigade. Several distinguished gentlemen are expected to take part.

UNUSUAL interest is being manifested in our work at this time, and several new Companies are about to be started.

Dublin

THE Ambulance Committee has been at work, and Classes will begin in a week or two.

THERE is a Drill Class for Officers every Saturday evening, with Mr. Woodhead, the Battalion Adjutant, as Instructor. The attendance of Officers is not as satisfactory as the Drill Committee would desire.

THE Executive Committee have enrolled two Companies since the opening of the Session, and there are several others in process of formation.

Edinburgh

THE Sixth Annual Report of the Edinburgh Battalion again records a decrease in the number of Companies. Against this, however, is set off the fact that the number of Boys enrolled has not similarly decreased, and the Report shows advance in Bible-Class work, and even more notably in Ambulance.

FOR the present season the Battalion programme has been fixed tentatively as follows: – Swimming Gala, Thursday, 23rd February; Church Parade, Sabbath, 2nd April; Inspection, Thursday, 13th April; while a Camp will be held in the Trades' Holiday week in July.

THE formation of a Battalion Military Band has been sanctioned by Council, and steps will at once be taken to have it started so that it may take part in the Battalion events in spring.

THE Meeting of Council on Monday, 12th December, is to take the form of a Social Gathering and informal Conference. Any Officers of the Brigade who may be in the neighbourhood will be made very welcome on sending their names to the Battalion Secretary.

Glasgow

AT a recent meeting of the Battalion Council, Mr. David Laidlaw, Battalion President, was, on the occasion of his marriage, presented by his fellow Officers with a Silver Salver, suitably inscribed, as a mark of their esteem for him, and their appreciation of his services to the Battalion. The presentation was made by Mr.

William Kidston, Captain 9th Glasgow Company, whose remarks were enthusiastically applauded by the Officers.

THE Bible-Class Committee have again issued a complete schedule of the work to be undertaken by them among the thirty-two Classes, including names of visitors, dates of Official visits, and dates of Missionary and other addresses.

THE Drill Committee are making arrangements for holding several Classes for instruction in Physical Exercises, Infantry Drill, etc., for Officers, which are to meet in Volunteer Drill Halls in different parts of the city. The Committee hope to hold in January Joint Drills to enable Companies to practise Battalion Drill, and trust that they will be largely taken advantage of.

TWELVE Ambulance Classes have been started throughout the Battalion with about 300 names on the roll. The Committee are now much better able to supply the necessary diagrams, etc., which ought greatly to assist the medical gentlemen who have so earnestly taken up the work.

THE Recreation Committee have decided to hold the next Swimming Gala in October, 1893, as that time of year has been found by experience to be the best. They have been reluctantly compelled to abandon their desire of starting District Gymnastic Classes owing to the impossibility of securing suitable halls. There is a falling off in the number of Companies which have entered for the Football Challenge Cup, but there is every prospect of the contests proving as keen as in former Sessions.

THE number of Boys who had entered their names by 31st October for the first Battalion Summer Camp is more than enough to ensure its success, and the Committee have been enabled to commence some of the numerous arrangements which are required. They have extended the time for receiving names until the 31st December, as there were several Companies which owing to various causes could not spread the information among their Boys by the date first given.

Liverpool

THE First Annual Report of the Liverpool Battalion has just been issued. It shows that at 31st May the strength of the Battalion was 8 Companies, 26 Officers, and 302 Boys. A copy of the Report is being sent to every Clergyman and Sunday School Superintendent in the city.

THE Council are arranging to have definite subjects brought up for discussion at each meeting. The first subject considered was the conduct of Bible-Classes, and many useful hints were received by all.

IT is proposed to have a Public Drill Competition and Demonstration some time early in the year.

North London

IT is very gratifying to note the deep interest which is now being shown by Superintendents of Missions and Sunday Schools in the work of The Boys' Brigade in this district. This is assuredly due to the publicity given to the grand aim and object of our Organization at the Exeter Hall Meeting of May last, coupled with the high moral tone that characterized that Meeting. It is only now, as the winter's work is commencing, that one can say what a grand success attended our first public gathering. It is needless to say that a large number of new Companies is expected to be enrolled in this Battalion before the end of the present Session.

South London

THE First Council Meeting of the new South London Battalion was held on Monday evening, 12th September, in the Parochial Hall, attached to St. Paul's, Westminster Road.

MAJOR JONES being Convener of the Meeting and Acting Secretary, the next Senior Captain, the Rev. Mr. Latham, occupied the chair, and opened with a prayer.

MR. F. F. BELSEY (ex-Mayor of Rochester), was unanimously elected Battalion President; Mr. Ernest A. Millar, Brixton (Captain 37th Company), Vice-President; Mr. Frederick Bridges (Brockley), Battalion Treasurer; Major E. Jones, Battalion Secretary; and Messrs. W. J. Booer (Captain 24th Company), and W. H. Shemeld (Lieutenant 52nd Company), were elected delegates to the Central Committee.

IT was then resolved that the South London Battalion join in a combined Inspection on Whit-Monday next, in conjunction with the other new Battalions, *i.e.*, West London and North London, the Secretary to communicate with the other Battalion Secretaries with that object.

IT was also decided to hold a separate Battalion Inspection next year at the Crystal Palace in connection with the Demonstration of the Sunday School Union, provided the matter could be arranged on the same lines as that carried out this year by the late South-East District Battalion.

IT was decided to form groups of Companies in several districts with a view to holding Battalion Drills, Church Parades, etc. A combined Church Parade, Summer Camp at Hayling Island, and other business were deferred until next Council Meeting in October.

THE October Council Meeting was held in St. Thomas's Church Hall, Waterloo Road, on Monday evening, 10th October, when three new Companies were enrolled.

ARRANGEMENTS with the North and West London Battalions were gone into relative to the combined Inspection at Pinner on Whit-Monday, and the independent Inspection at the Crystal Palace in June next.

THE Camp at Hayling Island in July was discussed, and the Secretary was requested to institute enquiries as to cost of transper head.

West London

IT has been decided to hold the Meetings of Battalion Council, in rotation, at the Head-Quarters of the different Companies. A Battalion Card has been printed, giving particulars of place and date of these Meetings, a note of forthcoming Battalion events, the Battalion Rules and Regulations, and information with regard to the different Companies comprising the Battalion.

AT last Meeting of Council the following resolution was passed: "That considering the conflicting interpretations of the New Drill Book, and the fact that it is only 'Provisional,' it be decided to continue the use of 'Infantry Drill, 1889,' in this Battalion until the end of the present Session."

(A few copies of "Infantry Drill, 1889," may still be had at 1s. 2d., carriage paid, from Head-Quarters' Office, 68 Bath Street, Glasgow. Officers requiring these should apply at once, as the book is out of print, and cannot be replaced).

Newport (Mon.)

ON Sunday, 9th October, four Companies, numbering about 100 strong, attended the Morning Service of the Havelock Street Presbyterian Church, with which the 1st Company is connected. The Rev. J. Glyn Davies preached a very able sermon, and as it was the Anniversary Sermon, the Church was crowded.

A GRAND SOCIAL MEETING was held at the G. W. Restaurant on Thursday, 20th October. After ample justice had been done to a capital tea, a very good programme was gone through, consisting of Songs and Recitations by Officers and Boys, Musical Drill by Squad from 4th Company, Selections by 6th Band, cornet duet by Bandmaster Gabb and Lieutenant H. Williams. A new feature was a Lantern Exhibition by Captain and Lieutenant Lawrence, 1st Cardiff. The views were items of interest connected with the Brigade and our Summer Camp. In the interval Captain Reynolds, Battalion President, presented the Battalion with a magnificent Cup as a Football Trophy. The Cup is quite unique in design, being supported by three rifles and bayonets, and has several Brigade engravings on it. The evening was brought to a close by the presenting of Prizes to the successful competitors in an essay competition, entitled, "Five Days with the Newport Battalion in Camp at Bridgend."

A BATTALION AMBULANCE CLASS has been formed, and the Boys show great interest in this work. Dr. A. Garrod Thomas. J.P., has kindly undertaken the duties of lecturer, and is ably assisted by Mr. T. R. Fifoot, Army Medical Staff.

ARRANGEMENTS have been made for holding the First Battalion March-Out. Everything augurs well for the most successful Session the Battalion has yet seen.

Nottingham

A VERY successful meeting – particulars of which will be found in another column – was held on 31st October in the Mechanics Institute, and called forth an amount of enthusiasm which was entirely unexpected from an audience most representative, and composed of gentlemen of nearly all shades of religious opinion, who were unanimous on the subject of The Boys' Brigade, and declared that it was doing a grand work in Nottingham, and must spread very rapidly in the town.

A PROMINENT Christian worker (Mr. Thornton, J.P.) took the Chair, and addresses were given by Mr. William A. Smith, the Brigade Secretary; the Rev. L. H. Gwynne; the Rev. Frank Woods; the Rev. J. F. Makepeace; the Rev. E. E. Coleman; and Mr. J. A. Dixon, the Battalion President. The meeting was a thorough success, and will no doubt add largely to the number of Companies in the town. Our thanks are due to the Brigade Secretary and all who helped to make the meeting such a success.

THE Battalion Executive has decided to commence an Inter-Company Football Competition during the present winter, and a Sub-Committee has been appointed to draw up the rules and make all arrangements.

To supply a long felt want an Officers' Drill Class will shortly be commenced, under the able guidance of Captain Brewill, Robin Hood Rifles, who has most generously given his services and placed his office at the disposal of the Officers for the purposes of the class. This move is sure to add largely to the efficiency of "non-military" Officers, and so make the Brigade more popular for young men who have had hitherto no knowledge of the intricacies of a "Red Book."

Plymouth

Opening of Battalion Head-Quarters

ON September 23rd the Mayor of Plymouth presided at a meeting, held in the Drill Room, to inaugurate this new departure in the work of The Boys' Brigade. He was supported by Revs. Dr. Chapman, M.A.; D. F. O. Poulter, M.A. (Captain, 1st Stonehouse (Devon) Company); J. T. Maxwell, R. Waters, and the Officers of the Plymouth Battalion. After singing and prayer, Captain Wright (Secretary of the Head-Quarters Staff) having explained the purposes for which the rooms would be used, the Mayor said that it gave him great pleasure to declare the building open. Other addresses followed, all the speakers expressing their hearty approval of the work. The Brass Band of the 1st Plymouth and the Drum and Fife Band of the 3rd Plymouth played selections during the evening. There was a large attendance of the public as well as of the Boys.

THE new Battalion Head-Quarters is situated in Kinterbury Street, and consists of a Reading and Games Room, open every evening from 8 to 9.30 to all Boys who have had their cards of admission stamped at the previous weekly Drill; a Gymnasium, open on Tuesdays and Thursdays with a paid Instructor, and on Fridays, when the Adjutant is in charge; and a Drill Hall, capable of holding 300 people, which is available, at a small charge, for all Companies who cannot get accommodation at their own quarters. In this hall a Lantern Service is held every Sunday evening from 8.15 to 9.15, to which all Boys are invited. The average attendance is about 240. There is also a small Officers' Room. A Shorthand Class is held on Saturday evenings, and Dr. Willoughby (Lieutenant, 2nd Plymouth) is giving a series of Ambulance Lectures on Mondays. A Lending Library will be started in January. Two Officers and two Non-Commissioned Officers are on duty every evening. At 9.20 the Scripture portion for the day is read and prayer offered.

Sheffield

A HIGHLY interesting Drawing-Room Meeting in connection with the Boys' Brigade movement in Sheffield was held on the evening of Tuesday, the 25th October, when some 70 or 80 gentlemen, most of them unconnected in any way with The Boys' Brigade, accepted the very kind invitation of the Venerable Archdeacon Blakeney, D.D., Vicar of Sheffield, and Chaplain-in-Ordinary to Her Majesty, to meet Mr. W. A. Smith, founder of The Boys' Brigade; Mr. D. A. Hunter, Liverpool Battalion President; and Mr. J. A. Dixon, Nottingham Battalion President and Captain of the Notts County Cricket Team.

THE earlier part of the evening was occupied with conversation and light refreshments, and afterwards short addresses were given, questions and discussion following. A brief outline of the history of the movement was given, its methods and mode of working explained, the beneficial effect the Brigade exerted not only on the Boys but also on the Officers, and its grand aims, physical, moral, and spiritual, were all dealt with. The Archdeacon expressed his entire sympathy with the objects of the Brigade, and his hope that that meeting would be the means of strengthening and developing the movement in Sheffield. It is encouraging to see that this hope is being realised. Already several offers of help, both personal and pecuniary, have been received, and the Officers of the Sheffield Battalion are deeply indebted to the Archdeacon for his kindness, and to those gentlemen who helped to make the meeting so great a success.

FRIDAY, the 28th October, was another red-letter day in the annals of the Sheffield Battalion, this being the occasion of the Annual Brigade Council Meeting, which was this year held in Sheffield. After the Council Meeting, Officers dined together at the Albany Hotel, rather more than 60 gentlemen sitting down to dinner. A report of the Dinner and the Conference which followed will be found on another page.

HAD it been possible to take advantage of this special opportunity a Public Meeting would have been held in the town; and although this could not be arranged, it is hoped that at an early date it may be possible to hold a meeting of this character in Sheffield.

THE third Annual Report (1891–92) of the Sheffield Battalion has now been issued, and shows a very satisfactory state of affairs, except as regards the Treasurer's Balance Sheet, which shows a considerable deficit.

The work abroad

WE have such a mass of home intelligence for this number of the *Gazette*, that we must confine our notice of the work abroad to a very few extracts from the latest *Bulletin* and the letters received in the course of the past two months.

The Boys' Brigade in the United States of America

The third number of *The Boys' Brigade Bulletin*, the official organ of The Boys' Brigade in The United States of America, is largely taken up with an account of an intensely interesting meeting held under the auspices of The Boys' Brigade, by the noted evangelist Mr. Mills, in the Mechanics' Pavilion, San Francisco, at which no fewer than 4,000 Boys and 1000 adults were present.

Mr. Mills preached a striking discourse from the text "As my beloved sons, I warn you" (1 Cor. iv. 14). We only wish it were possible to reprint *verbatim* this remarkable address, which appears to have been listened to with rapt attention by the vast audience. We give the closing passage.

(Several Ministers had spoken after the conclusion of Mr. Mills' address, and in doing so had referred to the time when, as young men and even as Boys, they had joined the American Army to take their part in the War.)

Mr. MILLS then said: –

"We have heard about joining the Army from two or three, and what one Minister said reminded me of a young man who wanted to join the Army, and his mother would not let him. She didn't want him to go, but he went up to his room and wrote down something on a paper, and brought it down to her and he said: 'Mother, here are some things I can say, and some things I want to say. First, my country needs me; second, my country calls me; in the third place, I am willing to go. Now, mother,' he said, 'are you going to prevent me from writing down there, 'I will go?' And she said: 'I don't feel that I could do that. My boy, you may write down, 'I will go;' but I want to ask you this: Will you not go away again, and just sit and think over God's claim on you, as you have been thinking over the claims of your country? I want you to go and spend some time – half an hour or more – just thinking about God's claims the way you have been thinking about your country. And he went off and sat down, and thought about it, and finally he wrote down: 'God's work needs me;' and then he wrote down: 'God calls me;' and then he had quite a struggle before he could write down and say: 'I am willing,' and finally he wrote down and said: 'I will go.' Now, Boys, if there was a war to-day, I suppose you love your country enough to want to enlist in the Army; but I tell you there is a terrible war, the war against sin, and God wants His people to stand out squarely for Him. Before we separate this afternoon, I want every Boy here who means to be a loyal soldier for Jesus Christ – and I will tell you what that means – it means to be always on His side; it means to be always obedient to Him, obeying orders and doing what He tells you – I want every Boy that means to be obedient to Christ, to be a loyal soldier of Jesus Christ, to stand up one after another, and say, 'I will go.' How many are willing to speak it out to-day, and so enlist in Christ's Army? Just stand up and say to Jesus, 'I will go.'"

[A large number of Boys stood up and said, "I will go."]

Mr. Mills. – "How many Boys here are ashamed of their Brigade uniform? Stand up. [No one stood up.] Then don't be ashamed of the uniform of Jesus Christ."

The Rev. J. Q. ADAMS, San Francisco, writes: –

"During the three years of its history the 1st San Francisco Company Boys' Brigade has been such a power along all lines of our Church work as has no other of our Societies. To cite only one result, thirty Boys have come from its ranks into full Church membership."

Mr. T. FRANK FERNALD, Secretary, Eastern Division, writes on 1st November as follows: –

"Companies are being organized in all directions in our Division. The International Christian Workers' Convention, which is to meet in Boston 10th to 16th November, is the great event of the season. The great head centre will be Tremont Temple, with its seating capacity for 3000 persons, while two large Churches have been engaged for the overflow meetings. The Boys' Brigade subject is to be presented on Monday evening, 14th. We are to have the first hour of that evening for an address and opportunity for questions, ending with Exhibition Exercises by one Company on platform. Our Companies, now composing the 1st Massachusetts Battalion, will attend in their new uniforms and sit upon the platform. We expect to have a Boys' Brigade Gathering before the Convention dissolves. Officers from all parts of this country expect to be present, and will be entertained in my District, thereby giving us better opportunities for becoming acquainted with each other. The 1st Boston Company will provide accommodation for the 1st Clinton Company and others who come from a distance. It seems like a great wave that is to roll over the land, just from a small beginning, only six months since when we first made an attempt to inform the people on the subject of The Boys' Brigade. Truly we can say, 'Behold how great a matter a little fire kindleth.'"

Full particulars regarding the formation and enrolment of Companies in The United States may be obtained at any of the following Divisional Offices: –

WESTERN DIVISION. – Mr. A. H. Fish, 58 Nevada Block, San Francisco, Cal.
CENTRAL DIVISION. – Rev. H. H. Russell, 399 Thirty-third Street, Chicago, Ill.
EASTERN DIVISION. – T. F. Fernald, 38 Burrough Street, Jamaica Plains, Mass.

Any friends who desire to subscribe to *The Boys' Brigade Bulletin*, the official paper of The Boys' Brigade in The United States of America, may have it sent regularly for one year from the U.S.A. Head-Quarters, by sending name and full postal address, along with Money Order for 2s. 6d. to Mr. A. H. Fish, Brigade Secretary, 58 Nevada Block, San Francisco, Cal., U.S.A.

The Boys' Brigade in Canada

The Rev. T. F. FOTHERINGHAM, M.A., 107 Hazen Street, St. John, N.B., Canada, writes as follows, under date 31st October: –

"I have just returned from the meeting of our Sunday-School Committee in Toronto. I had the pleasure of attending the meeting of the Presbyterian Ministerial Association and listening to a very lucid account of The Boys' Brigade by Rev. Mr. Young, formerly Captain of the 1st Niagara Falls Company, now of St. Enoch's Church, Toronto. I was asked to speak, and the subject was pretty thoroughly thrashed out in an hour-and-a-half's discussion. Something may follow. I have several orders for packages of literature in consequence."

The Boys' Brigade in South Africa

WE have two letters from Mr. JOHN C. HARRIS, Ivy Villa, Buitenkant Street, Cape Town, Captain 1st Cape Town Company. The following are extracts: –

"We have 29 Boys on the roll. Have had nine drills. The instructor is a Quartermaster-Sergeant in the Royal Artillery, an earnest Christian, and a thoroughly good fellow. Our average at the Drills has been 24. We mean business, and feel very confident that under God's blessing we may reach many of these Boys for Christ. It is found that the coloured 'Boy,' although possessing many of the main characteristics of his white brother, has in addition a few developments of 'original sin' which call for much patience and tact. Our Company is not confined to coloured Boys, and has some white and several of colour. Of course it is a mixture of nations, as is found here, including Kaffirs, Basutos, one or two Malays, Zulus, and several of *all sorts*. We are adhering to the instructions in the 'Manual' as far as possible, but in little minor details have to adapt ourselves to the peculiarities of the people. We hope to get a Gymnasium, Boys' Room, Ambulance, and Night School later on.

"Interest in The Boys' Brigade is being awakened, and the local papers are giving us encouragement and publicity. Tell your home Companies to pray for these new and coloured comrades."

The Boys' Brigade in the West Indies

We have an interesting letter from the Rev. CHARLES RIDGE, Captain of the newly formed 1st Kingstown, St. Vincent, Company, in which he says: –

"To date, I have received 46 Application Forms, and expect at least a dozen more, and should be glad if you will forward me Membership Cards. As soon as the Cards come we shall have a Public Meeting, preceded by a 'March-out.' His Honour, Colonel Sandwith, R.N., at present administering the Government here, has taken kindly to the movement, and has granted us the use of the Court-House grounds for drill. I expect soon to report to you the formation of a Company at Georgetown – 23 miles from here. We are trying to arrange for a Detachment to visit Georgetown early in the coming year. There is also the prospect of a Boys' Brigade Company being formed under the direction of the Anglican Church here. I know they are meeting for drill, and I intend recommending them to apply to Head-Quarters for enrolment. We accept your suggestion as to name – "1st Kingstown, St. Vincent" – and shall be glad to be noticed in your Report and *Gazette*."

List of battalion secretaries

THE following list of Battalion Secretaries is published in order that friends desiring information regarding the work of the Brigade in any town where a Battalion Council exists, may be able to communicate direct with the Battalion Secretary.

Officers desiring to communicate with each other in towns where no Battalion Council is formed, are referred to the list of Captains' Names and Addresses published in the Annual Report.

Particulars of Companies formed during the current Brigade year will be supplied on application to the Head-Quarters Office.

BATTALION SECRETARIES.

ABERDEEN. –	Mr. J. W. JACKSON, 14 Esslemont Avenue.
AYR. –	Mr. JAMES S. HUNTER, 5 Bellevue Crescent.
BELFAST. –	Mr. JOHN M'NEILL, 12 May Street.
BRISTOL. –	Mr. WALTER COOK, 1 The Polygon, Clifton.
DUBLIN. –	Mr. W. CONNOR, 8 Upper Beechwood Avenue, Rathmines.
DUNDEE. –	Mr. EBENEZER HENDERSON, 10 Whitehall Street.
EDINBURGH. –	Mr. EDWIN ADAM, 21 Castle Street.
GLASGOW. –	Mr. Mr. JAS. D. ROBERTON, 68 Bath Street.
HARTLEPOOL. –	Mr. F. H. INGHAM, 10 Olive Street.
LIVERPOOL. –	Mr. WM. NICHOLL, Studley, Blundellsands.
N. LONDON. –	Mr. E. W. LYONS, 4 Scarbro Rd., Stroud Green, N.
S. LONDON. –	Mr. Edward JONES, 73 Brook Street, Kennington Road, S.E.
W. LONDON. –	Mr. J. A. ROBSON, 30 Chepstow Place, Bayswater, W.
NEWPORT. (MON.) –	Mr. DAVID G. GRIEVE, Peterstone Villa, Park Square.
NOTTINGHAM. –	Mr. W. HENRY NEWHAM, 89 Robin Hood's Chase.
PLYMOUTH. –	Mr. LEONARD E. STONEMAN, 7 Huntiscombe Place.
SHEFFIELD. –	Mr. J. A. INGLIS, 96 Harcourt Road.

Boys' Brigade portraits

Professor HENRY DRUMMOND, F.G.S., F.R.S.E., *Honorary Vice-President of The Boys' Brigade.*

IN the Gallery of our Portraits none has a greater right to appear than that of Professor Drummond. He has been one of the warmest friends and advocates of the Brigade from the very first. He has pled for it before the public with force and discrimination – in the meeting in Queen's Rooms, Glasgow, in January, 1889; by his effective article in *Good Words* of February, 1891, of which 35,000 copies were subsequently printed; by his stirring address on "The Brigade as a Field of Work for Young Men" at the great meeting in Exeter Hall in May, 1891; and by addresses in many other public meetings in Great Britain, America, and Australia.

But Professor Drummond is not only an advocate of the Brigade: he is a friend of the Boys. His official title is Vice-President: his real relation to the Boys is something far closer. We may venture to say that there is not a Boy in all the Brigade who does not personally know and love the author of Baxter – Baxter's father, we were going to say, but he is rather Baxter's Big Brother, and the Big Brother of every Boy in the Brigade who knows and loves Baxter. The Boys know that the Professor loves them; that he understands them; that he has been through their temptations; and that he can help them to face and overcome them. That is why we call him their Big Brother.

Professor Drummond is famous as a Writer of Books; but in this portrait he is more like a stone-breaker. Most authors and professors get photographed indoors, with their hats oft and their gowns on – in a chair or at their study tables – reading or contemplative. Now, Professor Drummond is as good a student as any man; but this open-air portrait which we have chosen of him is more characteristic than a portrait in an arm-chair or at a desk. The first time the writer of this sketch was with Professor Drummond was on a frozen loch, skating; and the second was on the top of a mountain, climbing; the third was on a cricket-field; the second last was on a boat in a northern river, whipping it for salmon; and the very last was on a football ground on the day of a great match. Between that skating and this football, lie some sixteen years, and during that time Student Drummond, Traveller Drummond, Professor Drummond, and Drummond bearing the message of his Master, has been, summer and winter, the inhabitant and lover of the open-air, with its freedom and its freshness upon all his work of hand, and heart, and brain.

In this portrait Professor Drummond is far afield. He has been over the larger part of the world; but his most lonely and adventurous journey was that taken through a part of Central Africa, for the purposes of geological exploration. He has told us the story in his "Tropical Africa." This portrait shows us what he looked like when he was "on the tramp," and carried his hammer and his rifle with him.

The heartfelt prayer of every Boy in the Brigade is that his Big Brother may look as healthy and as happy for many, many years to come; and tramp up and down God's earth, and among God's breezes, and while he discovers many secrets of nature, continue to tell Boys and men alike *The* Secret which has made his own life so healthy and happy and helpful.

Head-quarters' fund

Annual appeal by the finance committee

THE following is the full text of the Annual Appeal issued at this date by the Finance Committee of the Executive: –

DEAR SIR OR MADAM, –

We now desire to thank those friends of the Brigade who contributed so generously to the Head-Quarters' Fund for the past year, and at the same time most earnestly to solicit a renewal of their kind support.

It will be seen from the *Annual Report* that the Brigade has *increased very largely* during the past Session, and in its 490 Companies has now an *enrolled strength* of no fewer than 1,618 *Officers* and 21,002 *Boys* in The United Kingdom alone, not counting the very large development of the work in other parts of the world.

The distribution of strength within The United Kingdom is as follows: –

	Companies.	Officers.	Boys.
England,	222	754	9,562
Scotland,	230	720	9,735
Ireland,	38	144	1,705
	490	1,618	21,002

When we point out that the whole of this large and united body comes under the supervision of the Executive it will be apparent that in mere matter of office detail – Secretarial and clerical – not to speak of outlay in promoting and improving the Organization, there must needs be much labour and considerable expense.

The efficiency of the management and the profitableness of these outlays are evidenced by the present position of the Brigade. Its consolidated strength and its expansive force are the results of the work done by Head-Quarters during the past nine years.

But continuous and successful progress must of necessity involve a steadily increasing demand on our resources. We have bid for success and secured it, but this can never mean cessation of effort or curtailment of expenditure. Rather must the Executive keep in the van and leave nothing undone to raise the strength of the Organization, and to increase the value of its work.

Now that the Trust Fund, raised for the payment of the Brigade Secretary's salary for a term of four years, is exhausted, the full burden of this annual charge is added to the other requirements that have to be met by the Head-Quarters' Fund. This renders *an assured and sufficient yearly income absolutely indispensable.*

After deducting the anticipated Contributions from Companies, we estimate that the *requirements of the Executive will amount to not less than £600 for the coming year.*

When we take into account the importance and extent of the work and the beneficial results which have followed the operations of the Brigade throughout the whole country, this sum, which we now ask the public to contribute, cannot be considered a large one.

We beg to urge our Appeal the more earnestly, as the response to the Appeal issued for last year's need – for the same amount and on the same grounds – resulted in only £163 10s. of *Annual Subscriptions.* An inevitable and heavy draft on the amount contributed as *Donations* has considerably diminished the balance which we hoped to have carried to Reserve.

From the above statement of our strength it will be seen that *our field is The United Kingdom,* and, therefore, *The Boys' Brigade is a National Institution.* We therefore ask and expect all friends of the movement – everywhere – to aid us in the efficient maintenance of the Head-Quarters of this National Institution.

Will those who have not yet had their attention directed to our necessities become Annual Subscribers to the Fund; and may we ask those who have given us Donations to repeat, to some extent, their liberality year by year?

We desire to emphasise what has already been said, that *the needs and claims of the Head-Quarters' Executive are quite distinct from those of the Battalion or the Company.* We gratefully recognise that there are many warm friends of the Brigade throughout the country, who are already liberal supporters of the Companies in which they are particularly interested; but we would, nevertheless, ask them, together with the others on whom no call has yet been made, to consider the importance of maintaining in a state of completeness and efficiency that part of the Organization upon which the welfare of the whole movement so very largely depends.

We therefore beg to ask for this Appeal your kind consideration, and trust to receive a favourable response.

Yours faithfully,

J. CARFRAE ALSTON,	. *Brigade President.*
HERBERT LANKESTER, M.D.,	. *Captain, 13th London Company.*
JOHN LAMMIE,	. *Brigade Treasurer.*

The Executive's Finance Committee.

HEAD-QUARTERS' OFFICE,
68 BATH STREET,
GLASGOW, *1st December, 1892.*

The first List of Contributions for the present Session, including some already received, will be published in "THE BOYS' BRIGADE GAZETTE" *of 1st February, 1893.*

Company contributions

THE Brigade Treasurer has the pleasure to acknowledge receipt of the undernoted Company Contributions to Head-Quarters' Fund for Session 1892–93.

The Treasurer would remind Officers Commanding Companies that the time has now come for sending in their Contributions for the current Session, in accordance with Article 12 of the Brigade Constitution.

All Company Contributions should, if possible, be sent in *before the end of December*, or, failing that, at the earliest possible date thereafter.

Company contributions for session 1892–93.

6th	Paisley,	£0	10	6	42nd	London,	3	0	0
1st	Alva,	0	10	0	1st	Cannock (Staffs.),	0	10	0
3rd	Sheffield,	0	10	0	1st	Barnard Castle,	0	5	0
8th	Bristol,	0	5	0	1st	Bath,	0	10	0
1st	St. Le'n'rds on-Sea,	1	0	0	2nd	Guernsey,	0	10	0
1st	Rutherglen,	0	10	0	12th	Belfast,	1	0	0
1st	Burslem,	0	10	0	2nd	Ilfracombe,	0	10	6
51st	London,	0	5	0	7th	Dundee,	0	10	0
2nd	Motherwell,	0	10	0	4th	Aberdeen,	0	10	0
67th	Glasgow,	0	10	0	1st	Marple-Bridge,	0	10	0
1st	Carrickfergus,	£1	0	0	14th	Belfast,	1	0	0
38th	Glasgow,	0	10	0	12th	Sheffield,	0	7	6
6th	Belfast,	1	0	0	1st	Muiravon,	1	0	0
1st	Acton,	0	10	0	19th	London,	0	10	0
1st	Hartlepool,	1	0	0	4th	Bristol,	0	15	0
1st	Chester,	0	10	0	1st	Wokingham,	1	0	0
93rd	Glasgow,	1	0	0	1st	Deal,	0	10	6
1st	Aberdour,	0	10	0	4th	Liverpool,	1	0	0
2nd	Birkenhead,	1	1	0	6th	Bristol,	0	10	0
1st	Darlington,	0	10	0	1st	Cardiff,	1	1	0
3rd	South Shields,	£0	10	0	3rd	Jarrow,	0	10	0
5th	Newport (Mon.),	0	5	0	1st	Maidstone,	0	6	0
10th	Dublin,	0	10	6	9th	London,	0	10	0
2nd	Kirkcaldy,	1	0	0	2nd	Richm'nd (Surrey),	1	0	0
1st	Belfast,	1	1	0	1st	Inverkeithing,	0	14	6
43rd	London,	1	1	0	3rd	Croydon,	0	10	0
2nd	South Shields,	0	7	6	36th	Glasgow,	0	15	0
12th	Nottingham,	0	10	0	5th	London,	1	0	0
7th	Liverpool,	0	10	0	1st	Stowmarket,	0	10	6
6th	London,	1	1	0	1st	Boston,	0	10	0
1st	Plymouth,	1	1	0	28th	Glasgow,	0	10	0
1st	Yeovil,	0	10	0	91st	Glasgow,	1	0	0
35th	London,	0	10	0	82nd	Glasgow,	1	1	0
8th	London,	1	0	0	2nd	Clydebank,	1	0	0
52nd	Glasgow,	1	1	0	2nd	Aberdeen,	0	10	0

1st	{ Ladybarn (Manchester), }	0	10	6	1st	Yalding,	1	0	0
1st	Brislington,	1	0	0	3rd	Birmingham,	0	10	0
3rd	Hanley,	1	0	0	115th	Glasgow,	1	0	0
98th	Glasgow,	0	10	0	105th	Glasgow,	0	10	0
1st	London,	1	0	0	3rd	Hull,	0	10	0
3rd	Perth,	1	1	0	1st	Torquay,	0	10	6
4th	Dublin,	1	0	0	3rd	Carlisle,	1	0	0
114th	Glasgow,	0	10	0	1st	Grangemouth,	1	0	0
1st	Woolwich,	1	0	0	1st	Oughtibridge,	0	10	0
41st	Edinburgh,	1	0	0	6th	Nottingham,	0	5	0
45th	London,	1	0	0	1st	Turvey,	0	5	0
3rd	West Hartlepool,	0	5	0	1st	Elie,	1	0	0
83rd	Glasgow,	0	10	0	1st	Mold,	1	1	0
1st	Kirkinner,	1	0	0	1st	Largs,	1	1	0
5th	Bristol,	£1	0	0	2nd	Lurgan,	0	10	0
1st	Bishop's Stortford,	0	7	6	2nd	Leeds,	1	1	0
2nd	Dumbarton,	0	10	0	7th	Nottingham,	0	10	0
1st	Dundee,	1	0	0	4th	Enfield,	1	0	0
1st	Bonhill,	0	10	6	1st	Greenock,	1	1	0
2nd	Glasgow,	0	10	0	28th	Edinburgh,	0	10	0
25th	Glasgow,	1	0	0	7th	Aberdeen,	0	10	0
59th	Glasgow,	0	15	0	1st	Ayr,	0	10	6
1st	Edinburgh,	0	10	0	3rd	Ayr,	1	0	0
36th	London,	0	5	0	15th	Edinburgh,	1	0	0
2nd	Dunmurry,	0	5	0	1st	Coatbridge,	1	0	0
1st	South Shields,	0	10	6	1st	Sherb'rne (Dorset),	0	10	0
15th	Glasgow,	0	10	6	33rd	Edinburgh,	1	0	0
39th	Edinburgh,	1	0	0	8th	Belfast,	1	0	0
1st	Campbeltown,	0	15	0	52nd	London,	0	6	0
2nd	Grantown,	0	10	0	4th	London,	0	10	0
76th	Glasgow,	0	10	0	1st	Erskine (Gl'sgow),	0	10	0
5th	Glasgow,	0	10	6	38th	London,	0	10	0
5th	Ayr,	0	10	6	11th	Bristol,	0	10	0
1st	Newport (Mon.),	1	1	0	1st	Stanwix,	0	10	0
7th	Sheffield,	0	10	0	10th	Sheffield,	0	5	0
5th	Paisley,	1	0	0	12th	Glasgow,	0	10	6
3rd	London,	0	10	6	1st	Atherton,	0	10	0
1st	N'we'stle-on-Tyne,	0	5	0	9th	Edinburgh,	0	10	0
6th	Glasgow,	1	1	0	1st	Coleraine,	1	0	0
					5th	Darlington,	0	10	0

Parade addresses – a suggestion

To the editor of "the Boys' Brigade Gazette."

DEAR SIR, – The figures given by the Brigade President in his speech at Sheffield brought out one very striking fact, namely, the large proportion of Companies which have no *Regular* Address at their week night Parades. According to the new Report, 22 have none at all, and over 200 report "occasionally." When there is, in addition, no Bible-Class in connection with a Company, the result must be that the Brigade is exercising little *direct* spiritual influence over the members of that Company; and even when a Bible-Class exists there must always be a large number who, on account of Sunday labour (such, *e.g.*, are milk boys), or for other reasons, cannot attend the Class. As a matter of fact, it is common to find, as Major Alston pointed out, that the Company Bible-Class is attended by only 50 per cent. of the members.

But even where there is a flourishing Class, attended by all the members, still the week-night Address holds a unique place by itself. For, do what we like, the Boys *will* get the idea into their heads that because the Class is a Bible-Class, and meets on Sundays, therefore it is the correct thing for the Officers to "talk religion," and for them to listen – in a general way. On the Tuesday night the Boys are in their work-a-day garb, and a short, homely Address carries an air of reality with it.

No doubt it is difficult to get the right sort of speaker, and it is more difficult still, when you have got him, to keep him within the statutory eight minutes; but when care is taken in selecting speakers, and when they are made aware beforehand of what exactly is wanted, the thing can be done. The plan adopted by some Captains of sending out, before the beginning of the Session, a list of the dates – which the speakers fill up as it suits their convenience – is becoming more common, and generally secures a good supply. Could something not be done to foster this branch of the work?

The Sheffield meeting must have set some of the delegates thinking. The direction which the thinking took in one case was this, What a lot of grand Addresses the Boys must be listening to week by week here and there throughout the country! Could some of these not be made available for our guidance and stimulus? A Captain, let us suppose, has just listened to a really striking Address – an experience he will have once a year, or seldomer – and he feels that it would be exceedingly helpful to other Boys as well as his own. Let him be encouraged, then, to send in a report of it to the *Gazette* Committee. Let them select the best sent in and publish it in the next issue. It will be a stimulus to the rest of us, and it will let us see what the Brigade is actually doing in this line.

Then if, at the end of the year, it was found that these Addresses possessed sufficient merit, they might be published in book form. Such a book, containing a dozen earnest, straight talks with the Boys, got up in the neat way for which Brigade publications are now famous, and published, say, at 1s., under some such title as "Sure and Stedfast," would I am sure have a wide circulation. It would, I believe, meet a want often felt. Some of us, I suppose, have sometimes taken one of our Boys along to our rooms on a Sunday evening to have a quiet talk with him about *the* object for which The Boys' Brigade exists, and we have felt what a poor job we have made of it, how cold we have been, how much we might have said but didn't; and as we are shaking hands with him we feel how much we should like to place in his hands a book containing a few plain earnest words on the subject, which he might read and ponder at his leisure.

And when the end of the Session comes round and we have our older Boys along to receive their Discharge Certificates, and we are feeling that they are now passing beyond our reach without perhaps the object of our connection with them being fulfilled, we would like to be able to present, as a parting gift, some memento of the old associations, which by the very aroma of its pages – straight from parade – might recall the quiet talks and the earnest words of the days gone by. – I am, yours sincerely,

HERBERT REID.

DUNDEE. *8th Nov., 1892.*

(The GAZETTE *Committee will be much pleased to carry out Mr. Reid's idea, and with that purpose in view will be glad to receive from Officers the MS. of any* PARADE ADDRESSES *that may seem worthy of a place in the* GAZETTE. *These must be written out in accordance with the Notice to Correspondents on the last page of the* GAZETTE, *and should not exceed 1,500 words.)*

Public meeting at Nottingham

IMPORTANT ADDRESSES.

"THE extension of the work of The Boys' Brigade" is the war-cry of the Nottingham Battalion, and following the example of other centres where Public Meetings have been held with great advantage to the movement, the Battalion convened a Public Meeting on Monday evening, 31st October, in the Mechanics' Institute, with the above most desirable object. Invitations had been sent to Clergymen, Sunday School Superintendents, and others interested in the welfare of Boys, and as a result a very representative audience assembled to hear the story of The Boys' Brigade, its aims and objects, from the lips of its founder, Mr. W. A. Smith of Glasgow, the Brigade Secretary.

The chair was taken by Mr. H. E. THORNTON, J.P., a well-known Christian worker, and amongst others present were: – Mr. J. A. Dixon, Battalion President; Mr. W. H. Newham (Captain 1st Nottingham), Battalion Secretary; Mr. J. H. Farmer (Captain 3rd Nottingham), Battalion Treasurer; Rev. Frank Woods, M.A., Vicar of St. Andrew's Church; Rev. T. H. Fitzpatrick, Old Radford Church; Rev. L. H. Gwynne, Vicar of Emmanuel Church; Rev E. E. Coleman; Rev. J. F. Makepeace; Mr. J. Hall, Captain 7th Nottingham; Rev. S. W. Chorlton, Captain 8th Nottingham; Rev. C. B. Porter, Captain 11th Nottingham; Rev. D. H. Dolman, Lieutenant 5th Nottingham; Rev. N. Heelas, M.A., Lieutenant 10th Nottingham; Mr. County Alderman Robert Mellors, President, Pleasant Sunday Afternoons; and Messrs. E. G. Moore, A. T. Oliver, T. W. Baker, H. W. Caswell, and F. E. Rushworth.

The meeting having opened with the Boys' Brigade hymn, "Soldiers of Christ, Arise," the Rev. F. WOODS offered prayer, and the CHAIRMAN explained the objects of the meeting, and in doing so said the Brigade was doing a good work in Nottingham, and had his entire sympathy. It should be part and parcel of the work of every Christian Church, and he hoped that the sphere of operations would be, as the result of the meeting, considerably extended.

The BRIGADE SECRETARY, who was very heartily received and attentively listened to, gave an interesting statement of the origin, progress, and present position of the Brigade, and sketched in detail the varied methods and many sided developments of the Organization, laying particular stress on the high Christian aims which the promoters of the movement have consistently kept in view from the very commencement, and which are more strongly emphasized to-day than ever they were before.

A powerful appeal for the boys

The Rev. LLEWELLYN H. GWYNNE, Vicar of Emmanuel Church (formerly Lieutenant 1st Nottingham Company), then gave an account of the history of The Boys' Brigade in Nottingham, and in doing so said: –

It was, I believe, nearly six years ago that Mr. J. A. Dixon had the honour of bringing to Nottingham the news of The Boys' Brigade. St. Andrew's Church was the first to have the pluck to start a Company, and Dr. Windly the first Captain of the first Company ever started in this town. From that time up to last year the movement did not make rapid strides. A few isolated Companies were doing their best with varied success, but we knew very little of each other. About a year ago an effort was made to bring the Companies together, and a District Committee was formed from the Officers of the existing Companies to see how we stood and how we could best further the movement. The District Committee did its work well, the number of Companies increased, and, acting under sanction of Head-Quarters, the Nottingham Battalion was formed, with our illustrious Mr. Dixon as President, and hard-working Mr. Newham as Secretary. The position of the Battalion at the present stands thus: Number of Companies, 10; number of Officers and Boys, 478. This is all that is to be said about the Nottingham Battalion. I should, however, like to say something about our own Nottingham lads, for whom I think this movement most helpful. There are in our own town thousands of Boys between the age of 13 and 19, over whom nobody seems to have much control. They are known best, I think, by the name "hobbledehoys." They seem to us to be in that unformed age. Their bodies are unformed, and their minds are unformed. They cannot stand still, they will trip up any other Boy in the street, pick a quarrel, and have it out round the corner – not that they have any hatred or malice, but by way of letting off superfluous steam. I have had the privilege of working among lads in the slums of London for nearly three years, and another three years among the lads of Derby, but for check and independence I have never come across anything like the Nottingham "hobbledehoy." As soon as he leaves the day school he asserts himself; he has no natural respect for anyone. Policemen have a "high old time" with him; Sunday School Teachers and Church dignitaries are all the same to him. He is rough, undisciplined, a great deal of the blackguard about him, and often selfish. But he is a rum mixture of good and bad. There is any amount of uncouthness, and what one naturally dislikes about him, but there is any amount of pluck and endurance about him also. He will half starve himself all the week to save up sixpence to see "Notts County" play "Notts Forest." He will go without his dinner on Saturday, walk three miles and play football all the afternoon without a crumb to eat since breakfast, and come back whistling. Why, there is pluck and energy enough there to be of immense usefulness to the Christian Church, if we could only guide it into the proper channel! What are we doing for the lads? Nothing, or very nearly nothing. We look down our Churches on Sunday, he is not there; we go to our Mission Rooms, he is not there either; we look for him in our Children's Service, we don't see him. Where is he? I saw one of our lads passing my house the other day in his football things, and knowing him very well, asked him to come in to tea. "Doant care if I do," said he, in the polite Nottingham way. He came, and in the course of our talk I asked him what he did on Saturday nights. "Oh," he said, "our gang goes down Market Place, sits on any empty stall, buys 'baccy' in turn, and sings 'Hi-Tidley-Hi-Ti,' or 'What Cher,' or something lively like." 'And on Sunday?" "Oh," he said, "we have a walk on the Forest, and then down the Mansfield Road, and walk about till bedtime." Yes, my friends, that's where they are on Sunday night, loafing about our streets, smoking and swearing and hustling the passers-by; there we should find them sometimes, using foul language, and being ruined wholesale. We look after our children, and we look after our grown-up people; but when our Boys get to a certain age we let them drift away from us altogether, and go to the bad. There is a hole somewhere in the net of our Church work to lose hold of our lads at such an important age as this. And look! look at the difficulties the poor fellows have to contend with. It was not very long ago that our market places on Sunday were lecture halls for Scepticism and Infidelity. The men in the factories have been steeped in it. The coarse rough element, the foul jokes, the cursing and swearing in these workshops make it hard work for a Boy to keep his purity and goodness. There was a lad here who seemed going wrong some time ago. I asked him to come up to my house and have a talk. I asked him what was wrong about him. He was a fine plucky lad, not at all the Boy to cry, but he stood up straight before me and looked me fair in the face, and the tears ran down his cheeks as he said, "You don't know what the temptations of a factory are, Sir. You wouldn't be good if you had to work in our factory." I told him I had to fight just as hard as he did against temptation, perhaps much harder. But there the fact remains, and my heart fairly ached for the lad who found it such hard work to be godly in a Nottingham factory. There is no grander sight on God's earth than to see a lad struggle against his temptations and fight against his passions, and to stand up pure when all around are impure – to stand up a brave, holy lad when all around are cowardly and giving way to their sins. Poor Boys, so much seems against them. With their strong passions and their ignorant weaknesses they do want some one to help them – indeed they do. Shall we stand by idly and wait until their wills are weakened by excesses and their lives fouled with sin before we put out our hands to help them? Of all the times in a man's life it seems to me his Boyhood is the most important. We know how hard it is to work amongst them. We know it rather lowers our dignity to be checked a bit by them. We know how Superintendents of [Illegible Text] Sunday Schools are at their wits' end to know how in the world to keep them. From the speech of Mr. Smith to night we know too what a change The Boys' Brigade made amongst his Boys. Let us try it more among our Nottingham Boys. If we instil a little discipline into them, that will be something; if we teach them respect for somebody, that is something too, if they learn obedience, that is something better still. But even these, though excellent, are not all: our object is to win [Illegible Text] and keep them as true soldiers of Jesus Christ. There is no reason why every Chapel and Church in Nottingham should not have a Company of The Boys' Brigade, for I firmly believe that [Illegible Text] movement is the link (which has almost been lost) in the chain and the mending of the hole in the net, of our Church work.

Mr. J. A. DIXON, Battalion President, said the objects [Illegible Text] the Brigade only wanted to be better known to make it [Illegible Text] greater success. It would bring into active work young [Illegible Text] who would not undertake any other Christian work.

Mr. County Alderman ROBERT MELLORS said the Brigade seemed eminently suitable to become part of the grand [Illegible Text] the Pleasant Sunday Afternoon movement was doing. [Illegible Text] often had applications for membership from youths under [Illegible Text] (the minimum age for joining the Pleasant Sunday Afternoon) they had no alternative but to refuse the applications. Many of the applicants would not attend Sunday Schools, and it [Illegible Text] him great pain to refuse their offers. He asked as to [Illegible Text] approximate cost of starting a Company, as to the supposed warlike effect on existing Companies of the Boys being allowed to use rifles, and said if these questions were answered satisfactorily he would no doubt be able to do something towards forming a Company.

The Rev. FRANK WOODS asked that it should be made perfectly clear to the meeting that each Company acted entirely on its own initiative as regards the religious principles involved, and in doing so bore testimony to the splendid work The Boys' Brigade was doing, as evidenced in the Company in connection with St. Andrew's Church.

The Rev. J. F. MAKEPEACE (Sherbrooke Road) and the Rev. E. E. COLMAN also spoke, and said with what pleasure they had listened to the speeches. There was a great field in Nottingham for Boys' Brigade work, and they hoped to be able in time to help in it. Mr. J. BOWLEY thanked the Battalion for holding out the helping hand, and on behalf of the Bulwell Church authorities had great pleasure in accepting same. He hoped they would be able to form a Company, and so open out an entirely new district. The Rev. NEWTON HEELAS and Mr. F. E. RUSHWORTH also spoke.

Mr. W. H. NEWHAM said the Battalion Executive were forming an Officers' Drill Class under the direction of Captain Brewill (Robin Hood Rifles), who had most generously offered his services and the use of his office for the purpose. The speaker hoped that any gentleman requiring further information would apply to one of the Officers or to himself.

Mr. W. A. SMITH, in reply, gave particulars of the cost of equipping a Company, which might be almost as moderate as the Company chose to make it. He said that the model rifles used in the Brigade were not recommended for a first Session, and gave it as the result of all his observation that the Brigade was developing the very opposite of a warlike spirit among the Boys. He assured the meeting that the Brigade Constitution left every Company entirely under the control of the Church with which it was connected, as to the particular form which the Christian training and religious instruction of the Boys should take.

With another Boys' Brigade Hymn and the Benediction the meeting ended. Already a stir is being made in certain places which must result in further Companies being formed as the Brigade gets better known. No doubt the different Sunday School organizations in the town will sanction the movement, and so help to swell the number of Boys already enrolled under the noble banner, which has for its motto, "The Advancement of Christ's Kingdom," thus helping its members to become true "Soldiers of Christ." For this we are working, and we pray that at no distant date The Boys' Brigade may be a great factor for good, not only in Nottingham, but over the whole earth.

RESTLESS, active, high-spirited, the Boy of our day requires to be handled by men of courage and spirit and energy, dashed with fine tact and vigorous temper.

"YOU have not yet taught me the guards," said a lad who was being taught sword exercise. "You do the cuts, my Boy," was the reply; "let the other fellow do the guards." We must teach our Boys to act on the offensive. – *W. T. Paton.*

Public meeting at Kirkcaldy

A PUBLIC Meeting and Demonstration was held in the Corn Exchange on Thursday evening, 10th November. Mr. MICHAEL B. NAIRN was to have occupied the chair, but an apology for unavoidable absence was read from him, and SHERIFF GILLESPIE was called to the chair. He was accompanied to the platform by Mrs. Nairn and party, Rev. John Campbell, Rev. John Clark, Rev. A. Macmillan, Rev. W. J. Macdonald, Rev. William Fairweather, Rev. J. Balfour, Major Tait, Major Storrar, Mr. William A. Smith, Brigade Secretary; Mr. James Leask, Captain 1st Burntisland Company; Mr. William Balfour, Captain 1st Aberdour Company; Mr. Andrew Morton, Captain 2nd Kirkcaldy Company; Messrs. A. Thomson, J. F. Clark, George Ferguson, James Hogarth, D. Henderson, Alexander Beattie, R. Heggie, R. Herriot, J. G. Lornie, and numerous other gentlemen. After "Onward, Christian Soldiers!" had been sung by the audience, to the accompaniment of the Brigade Flute Band, prayer was engaged in by the Rev. John Campbell.

SHERIFF GILLESPIE, in opening the proceedings, said The Boys' Brigade was indeed one of the most remarkable movements of modern times. The founders of it put in the very forefront as their motto "the advancement of Christ's Kingdom," and the promotion of true Christian manliness among Boys. They did not consider that wisdom and manliness were at all incompatible with Christianity. Their methods were based on an accurate knowledge of the Boy character, and so successful had they been that, though the movement was only nine years old, something like 21,000 members were enrolled. In every place where the Companies had been at work, according to the lines laid down by the founder, there had been a marked improvement in the tone and conduct of the Boys. This success had been brought about by the constant and untiring interest of the Officers in the Boys, and where failures had arisen, it had been by the Officers not keeping in touch with the Boys. And there was also a reflex benefit to the Officers, giving them a field of service which might otherwise have lain idle. One is a Volunteer, and knows his drill well, which is a good thing, but it is better if he takes up with The Boys' Brigade, and puts his knowledge to a beneficent use. Another is a good cricketer, and The Boys' Brigade furnishes an outlet for him in taking an interest in the Boys' games. Again, a man, young or old, may have a taste for music; he can be training a Band for the Brigade, thereby providing an additional attraction. In short, it furnished an outlet for miscellaneous gifts, which might otherwise have been wasted.

After a display of Musical Drill by the Boys of the 2nd Kirkcaldy Company, the Rev. W. J. MACDONALD delivered a bright and interesting address on

Boy life and its needs

These needs, he said, were first to be ascertained, and to do that they required simply to study the animal in its native, wild state. They must watch the Boy when he was left to himself. They wanted to make the Boy a useful member of society, and to run in harness under common yoke, and so they must begin by studying the Boy unyoked. They could not command nature, and so they must obey it. He was afraid many people in treating with Boys went to their inner consciousness, and there evolved some glorified personage whom they would have the Boy to resemble. If they went to the nature of the Boy they found three things – there were a great many others. All Boys they would find wanted to be men. There was an old saw that "Boys will be Boys," but he thought that a great mistake, because Boys would be men if they got their own way. The imitative faculty was strong in all natures, and so they must train the manliness that wanted to be men. They must teach the Boy that manliness was a thing to be got by following Christ; and they must make it Christian manliness. A second thing Boys loved was movement. He thought a Boy was about the nearest approach to perpetual motion that could be got. A Boy might be described as a miscellaneous collection of legs and arms, which were in perpetual motion, served by a steam boiler always at high pressure. Now, if they had the motion they must regulate it, not check it. There were two kinds of motion. There was destructive motion, which must be checked, and constructive motion, which should be fostered – they must turn the love of motion into good movements. They ought not to begin with the Boy on the Sunday School form alone. That was not a natural place for a Boy. They must go to the cricket field and the football field, because these things, if regulated, were good. And then, in the third place, Boys preferred command to advice. Boys did not like Sunday Schools, or lessons, or going to Church. Naturally they didn't, but there was a wonderful love of command amongst them. They did not need to be bribed with sugar or stories. They had simply, as the chairman had already said, to provide them with a cap and belt, and say to them, "You are a soldier," and they would stand to be lectured for a whole hour. Therefore they must cultivate the native animal, and work up from that, for they could not go against it. This, he pointed out in conclusion, was what The Boys' Brigade had done.

MAJOR STORRAR, in the course of an address on the "Moral value of Drill and Discipline," said that the Brigade, beginning with *esprit de corps*, led to true soldierism, which was the cementing together of class to class and rank to rank. The Boys and Officers were united in one large family, with one common centre. It further taught the valuable lessons of reverence, courtesy, obedience, and other virtues, and he hoped the present meeting would be a stimulus to the Brigade in this district, and increase its numbers.

Sheriff Gillespie at this stage had to leave the meeting, and Major Tait was called to the chair.

Mr. WM. A. SMITH, Secretary and founder of the movement, then delivered an address descriptive of the Brigade work generally, and told the story of its origin, progress, and present position.

The Rev. A. MACMILLAN bore personal testimony to the good work done by the Company in connection with his own Congregation. He emphasized the movement as a thoroughly religious one, and hoped soon to see half-a-dozen Companies in Kirkcaldy.

During the evening the Boys went through various manœuvres very creditably, and the Band discoursed with remarkable ability several hymns and other selections. The proceedings closed with the usual votes of thanks and the Benediction.

Public meeting at Thurso

The Boys' Brigade in the Far North

THE Boys' Brigade has of late been creating a good deal of stir in the North, and the visit of Mr. Wm. A. Smith, Brigade Secretary, to Wick and Thurso has given a stimulus to the movement, which ought to result in an increase in the number of Companies in Caithness, and a quickening of life in those already formed.

After travelling from Glasgow on Tuesday, 4th October, Mr. Smith paid a visit on the evening of the same day to the newly-formed 1st Thurso Company, which he found drawn up, awaiting his arrival, in the Artillery Drill Hall. 59 Boys, with their Officers, stood on parade, and received the Brigade Secretary with the General Salute. After a careful inspection of the ranks, the Boys were put through some drill, and were afterwards drawn up for the closing Service, when they were addressed by the Brigade Secretary. Mr. Smith, who is a native of Thurso, said that he never felt more proud of being a Thurso Boy himself than he did on that occasion. He had seen a good many Companies in all parts of the country, but he had never seen a Company that impressed him more with the splendid possibilities of The Boys' Brigade than did the 1st Thurso Company. He was delighted to see such a fine turn-out of Boys. He congratulated them on the progress they had already made in their drill and the perfect silence and steadiness which they observed in the ranks. He hoped that every Boy would strive to make himself a model of attention and good behaviour, and endeavour in every way to be a credit to his Company. He urged the Boys to be just as regular and punctual in their attendance at the Company Bible-Class on Sunday morning as they were at drill on Tuesday night.

Mr. Smith got a hearty cheer for his address, and the meeting was closed with prayer and praise.

On Thursday, 6th October, Mr. Smith travelled to Wick, where he had the pleasure of inspecting the 1st Wick Company in the evening, a note of which will be found among "Company Items."

On Friday evening, 7th October, an important Public Meeting was held in the Artillery Hall, Thurso, Mr. Wm. M'Kay, Chief Magistrate, in the chair. The occasion was used to enlist public sympathy with the movement, and although the night was extremely stormy, there was a good attendance of all interested in work among the young. The Boys of the 1st Thurso Company, to the number of about 70, all wearing the smart cap of the Brigade, were seated in front, and commanded much appreciative attention on account of their smart and cleanly appearance. After singing, and prayer by the Rev. Mr. Connell,

The CHAIRMAN briefly declared the object of the Meeting, and said that he could not forget first of all to say how proud they all were that a Thurso Boy was at the head of this Brigade movement. Mr. Smith, who was present himself, would tell them later on the history of The Boys' Brigade. Nor could he forget that it was Mr. Smith's father, the late Major Smith of Pennyland, whose memory would ever be cherished in Thurso, who had been instrumental many years ago in starting the Volunteer movement in this town. Mr. Mackay then related some amusing reminiscences of his own Boyhood in Thurso, and went on to say that in his young days there were four "armies" among the Boys, and that he was a Sergeant in one of them himself. Amid great laughter he mentioned the distinctive names of the "armies:" the "Fisherbigginers," the "Ellaners," the "Booraktooners," and the "Newtooners." He was afraid, however, that their motives were not so peaceful nor so pure as are the motives of the present-day Boys' Brigade. After remarking on the benefits that Boys would derive from membership in the Brigade, Mr. Mackay concluded by saying that he would with all his heart support this movement, and he hoped its fruit would remain after many years.

The Rev. Mr. KELLY next addressed the meeting, making an exceedingly happy and practical speech. He was so glad that a Company had been formed at last, and he was sure the Boys would be immense gainers by being associated with it. Speaking of "Boy Life and its Needs," Mr. Kelly mentioned companionship, exercise, hobbies, and reading, as indispensable things to the living of a full, happy life. He was glad the Boys of Thurso were now banded together to be trained in ways of orderliness, and to become mutually helpful to each other in so many ways. He, too, would do all that lay in his power for the advancement in every way of The Boys' Brigade in Thurso.

Mr. WM. A. SMITH was warmly applauded as he rose to give an address on the origin, aims, and methods of the movement. Mr. Smith dwelt at length upon the circumstances that led to the formation, by himself and others, of what is now a very powerful organization. The figures to-day are: Companies, 500; Officers, 1600; Boys, 21,000. The movement has spread to The United States and Canada, to South Africa and the West Indies. At the close of his most interesting and inspiring address, Mr. Smith complimented in very high terms the 1st Thurso Company and its Officers. Since coming North he had been delighted to meet in the streets of Thurso a large number of Boys who, instead of the usual aimless grin peculiar to Boys, had met him with the smart, soldier-like salute characteristic of the Brigade. He trusted the Boys would not forget the Bible-Class on Sunday mornings, for the religious part of the work was by far the most important. He would watch with very great interest the career of the "1st Thurso," and he was certain Officers and Boys would give a splendid account of themselves in the days to come.

The Rev. Mr. CONNELL expressed the pleasure he had in being present, and his conviction that the Thurso Company would be a great success.

During intervals in the speech-making, several solos and part-songs were sung, including the well-known Brigade Hymn, "The March of the Boys of Britain," which was rendered with great spirit by Mr. Leslie. A collection was also taken for the funds of the Company.

At the close the Boys were presented with their Membership Cards by the Chairman, each Boy making a smart salute as he came up to receive his Card.

The meeting was throughout a most enthusiastic one, and seemed to show that The Boys' Brigade has already won the hearts of the people of Thurso.

On Sunday morning, 9th October, the Opening Meeting of the Company Bible-Class was held, and was addressed by the Brigade Secretary. The Class will be conducted by the Captain of the Company, Mr. Wm. Campbell, who is also President of the Thurso Y.M.C.A., assisted by the Lieutenants. The Opening Meeting was well attended, and altogether a most successful start has been made.

Public meeting at Falkirk

A SOCIAL and Public Meeting of the Companies in Falkirk and district was held in the West United Presbyterian Church, Falkirk, on Friday evening, 18th November. Tea was served to the Boys of the Companies in the Church Hall at 7 o'clock, after which they marched into the Public Meeting in the Church. Henry Forrester, Esq. of Kinnaird, occupied the chair, and was supported on the platform by Mr. Wm. A. Smith, Brigade Secretary; Rev. Messrs. Taylor, Graham's Road U.P. Church; Kerr, Muiravon; Merrilees, Bainsford; Jaffrey, Camelon; and Messrs. Ralph Stark, Camelon; J. C. Rennie, J. A. Henderson, etc. There was a large turnout of the members of the Brigade from Falkirk, Larbert, and Shieldhill. The meeting opened with the 100th Psalm, followed with prayer.

The CHAIRMAN then delivered a very appropriate address, in the course of which he said he was pleased to see that the Brigade had the sympathy of so many, and that it had obtained so happy results. The Brigade was not started a day too soon, and he was sure that when it had shown so much usefulness in the early stages of its career, it would prove as years rolled on more and more a valuable adjunct to the various agencies at work to train the Boys to a pure and noble manhood.

The BRIGADE SECRETARY then addressed the Meeting. He could not help feeling that the Brigade was in a very sound state in Falkirk. Mr. Smith sketched the rise and progress of the movement, mentioning that there was a band of Zulu Boys in Africa who wore the same uniform as that worn by the Boys of Falkirk and other Companies. The Boys' Brigade was formed because there was a felt want of something to take up the interest of the Boys, to keep them in the Sunday School, and to make Christian men of them. It would be a great pleasure to go back to Head-Quarters at Glasgow and report the high state of efficiency in which the Boys were found that night.

An exhibition of Physical Drill with Arms was given by the Boys of the 1st Larbert Company with precision and ability. Several songs, etc., were also contributed, and after the usual votes of thanks the Meeting was closed with the Benediction.

> "The five cardinal principles of success are order, industry, economy, perseverance and punctuality. Of course, we are speaking now of temporal and human agencies, and not of those which are eternal and divine. Without saving faith in the Lord Jesus Christ, no possible combination of moral or mental traits can prevent utter failure. But, even among the children of light, the lack of the five great principles which we have enumerated will render life comparatively futile and fruitless. Youth is the time to cultivate these great forces of character. A few are endowed with them all, but the vast majority of persons are naturally deficient in one or more of them. Fortunately, however, they can be cultivated, and, if Boys and Girls will make special and continued efforts in this direction, they will surely succeed, and succeed so thoroughly that the principles mentioned will become a second nature."
>
> – *The Boys' Brigade Bulletin.*

The "boys' room"

How it strikes a stranger

HAVING heard that a Room for the Boys of the 1st Glasgow Company has been opened in the Free College Church Mission Buildings, North Woodside Road, I dropped in on a recent evening to see what it was like, and to ascertain if it was likely to fulfil the aims and objects for which it was established. It may be here stated that this development of Brigade work has been made with the view of minimising what is known as "corner standing," by inducing the Boys to spend their evenings pleasantly and usefully, reading healthy literature or playing innocent games, in a comfortable room set apart for the purpose. The objects aimed at being so commendable I was anxious to know how far the efforts of the promoters were being supported, and accordingly the other evening I ascended the well lighted stair, and soon found myself at the door of the "Boys' Room."

Attractive comfort

On opening the door the first thing that struck me was the comfort and attractiveness of the Room. The walls were hung with beautiful pictures and illumined texts, the gifts of friends, as well as several military pictures, while with commendable loyalty a portrait of Her Majesty The Queen was accorded a prominent position. The temperature of the Room was all that could be desired, and the whole scene and surroundings presented a striking contrast to the cold, bleak, and breezy street corner, and any Boy of sense could not for a moment be at a loss to determine which to prefer.

Discipline and respect

I had scarcely time to look about me when I was observed by one of the Boys, who, in accordance with one of the Regulations of the "Boys' Room," called out "Attention!" when all the Boys stood up with military precision, and remained standing till I had returned the compliment by saluting, after which they all sat down quietly and resumed their various recreations. I have had occasion to visit various institutions, and my experience of such is that the visitor is almost invariably received with a stare from all present, while one or two, more forward than the rest, may venture to make a half-audible remark, more personal than polite. Here then was a new experience for me, and the respect shown made me think a good deal of the Boys of the Brigade and their teaching.

Order

The poet has declared that "Order is Heaven's first law," and certainly *order* is the first law of the "Boys' Room." To ensure this an Officer and two Non-Commissioned Officers are present every evening the room is open. On the occasion of our visit we were cordially received by two of the Lieutenants of the Company, and there were some thirty Non-Commissioned Officers and Boys amusing themselves. Some were reading, and the supply of literature was both varied and attractive; others were turning over the pages of the illustrated magazines. Here were two youths engaged in a friendly game of draughts, flanked right and left by sympathetic companions whose interest in the game was second only to that of the players. In the corner were a number of Boys engaged in a new game, called "Bogey Man," the science of which they explained to me with respectful enthusiasm, as if anxious to induce me to take part in it with them. In an adjoining room I found a number of Boys engaged in a game of bagatelle, some of them displaying considerable skill in handling the cue. All were happy, and entirely at their ease. There was no feeling of restraint experienced by the Boys present, yet there was an utter absence of that boisterous noise and "horse play" which have been so long associated with Boys' gatherings, and which we "grin and bear," regarding them as natural concomitants, to be endured because some one, before the days of Boys' Brigades, declared utterly regardless of consequences, that "Boys will be Boys."

Home influence

Some people might be apt to think that the promoters of "Boys' Rooms" were undermining home influences and seeking to break up the family circle. They have no such intention, and I am certain they would abandon the scheme tomorrow did they for a moment suppose that it would have such a tendency. The "Boys' Room" is not meant as a counter-attraction to home, but as a preventative against the formation of the objectionable practice of "corner-standing," with its attendant evils, or as an inducement to abandon such habits [Illegible Text] they have already been acquired. Young lads fresh from school are sent to offices, factories and shops, where they are engaged all day. Being in this way suddenly deprived of the company of their comrades during the day, they long for the evening when they can meet them and discuss their plans and projects. When the weather is cold or wet the difficulty is to know when they can meet to spend their leisure hours. For at least [Illegible Text] evenings in the week the Boys of the 1st Glasgow Company can meet in comfort in the "Boys' Room," and spend a few hours together in a pleasant and profitable manner. That they appreciate this boon is evinced by their presence in such large numbers, as well as by their tidy appearance and exemplary conduct. I hope the time is not far distant when there will be a "Boys' Room" opened in connection with every Company [Illegible Text] the Brigade, believing, as I do, that they are destined to accomplish much good –

"Behold in these what leisure hours demand,
Amusement and true knowledge hand in hand."

58

PATRIOTISM; OR, OUR DUTIES AS CITIZENS

Camp fire yarn. – no. 26. Our empire: how it grew – how it must be held

From: Robert Baden-Powell, *Scouting for Boys: A Handbook for Instruction in Good Citizenship* (London: Pearson, 7th Edition, 1915, reprinted 2004), pp. 273–281.

The final documents in this volume demonstrate the ways in which youth organisations of the period were underpinned and indeed inspired by the Empire. The Boys' Brigade (BB) and the Boy Scout and Girl Guides movements encouraged the youth to demonstrate patriotism and self-discipline, and to acquire skills that could be used in the colonial context. The BB was founded in 1883 as a Christian youth movement by William Alexander Smith (1854–1914). Smith had been a Sunday School teacher and a member of the rifle volunteers. The aim of the BB was 'The advancement of Christ's kingdom among Boys and the promotion of habits of Obedience, Reverence, Discipline, Self-respect and all that tends towards a true Christian manliness'. It introduced boys to semi-military discipline, gymnastics, summer camps and religious services. Robert Baden-Powell (1857–1941) became a vice president of the BB in 1903 and there were close links between the BB and the scout movement before 1914. Robert Baden-Powell was also on the committee of the Duty and Discipline Movement which Meath founded just before the outbreak of the First World War. Baden-Powell was very much an imperial figure, serving in the British army, travelling to India, Afghanistan, and East Africa, and participating in the South African War, taking great credit during the siege of Mafeking. During the war he had utilised boy messengers and this proved to be the origins of the scout movement. As was noted in Baden-Powell's obituary, scouting was seen as a system of education which combined 'chivalry and patriotism'. His book Scouting for Boys, *which appeared in the Edwardian era, can be seen as a founding document of this youth movement, a movement which then also encompassed girls as the Girl Guides were founded in 1910 by Powell's sister Agnes. Both movements were subsequently established across the British Empire.*

Hints to instructors

The use of a large Map of the Empire is very desirable for illustrating this. The Arnold-Forster* or the Navy League or the League of the Empire Map are very good, and we hope to issue one specially designed for the Boy Scouts.

Look up the local history of your neighbourhood, and give your scouts the more interesting and dramatic bits of it, on the actual scene of the events if possible.

Our empire

ANY of you who have travelled much about this country by train, going for your holidays and so on, know how two or three hours will take you a good long distance and six or eight hours will take you to the other end of England.

Well, if instead of hours you travelled for as many days, even six or eight days would take you a very little way over our Empire. It would get you into Canada, but you would want several more days – not hours – to get you across that country. Eighteen days' hard travelling day and night would get you to India or South Africa, but either of these are little more than half way to Australia. And all that distance off, across the seas, on the other side of the world, we have a British country into which you could put nine Great Britains and Irelands.

9	United Kingdoms	=	1 Australia.
10	United Kingdoms	=	1 Canada.
6	United Kingdoms	=	1 India and Burma.
5	United Kingdoms	=	East Africa, Uganda, and Soudan.
5	United Kingdoms	=	South Africa.
1	United Kingdoms	=	New Zealand.
1½	United Kingdoms	=	Nigeria.

Then there are numbers of smaller Colonies or Dependencies, such as Guiana (nearly as big as the United Kingdom), North Borneo, New Guinea, Somaliland, Straits Settlements, Gold Coast, West Indies, Tasmania, etc., and numbers of islands in every sea all over the world.

Our Colonies together are something like forty times the size of the United Kingdom at home.

Our fellow-subjects amount to four hundred millions, and comprise almost every known race. Almost every known species of wild animal occurs in British territory.

It is a magnificient Empire over which the Union Jack flies, but it is still only at the beginning of its development. The territories are there, but the people are only coming. The white population of all these Colonies only amounts to a little over a quarter of the population of our crowded little island. We have nearly forty-four millions here; they have among the Colonies a little over eleven millions.

Many of you scouts, as you grow up, will probably become scouts of the nation, and will find your way to some of the Colonies to help to push them up into big prosperous countries.* Your scout's training will come in very useful to you there. But when you go there you must be prepared to work, and to work hard, and to turn your hand to any kind of job.

How our empire grew

ALL those vast Colonies did not come to England of themselves. They were got for us by the hard work and the hard fighting of our forefathers.

AMERICA. – When we first got to America it took Sir Walter Raleigh, Captain John Smith, and other great pioneers four or five months to get there in their little cockleshells of ships, some of them only 30 tons measurement – no bigger than a Thames barge. Nowadays you can get there in five or six days, instead of months, in steamers of 30,000 tons.

Think of the pluck of those men tackling a voyage like that, with a very limited supply of water and salt food. And, when they got to land with their handful of men, they had to overcome the savages, and in some cases other Europeans, like the Dutch, the Spaniards, and the French; and then they had hard work to till the ground, to build settlements, and to start commerce.

Hard sailoring, hard soldiering, hard colonising by those old British sea-dogs, Sir Francis Drake, Sir Walter Raleigh, Hawkins, Frobisher, and, best of all to my mind, Captain John Smith.*

He left Louth Grammar School in Lincolnshire to become a clerk in an office, but he soon went off to the wars. After two years' fighting he returned home.

He admitted he had gone out as a 'tenderfoot', and had not properly prepared himself as a boy for a life of adventure; so he set to work then and there to learn scouting. He built himself a hut in the woods, and learnt stalking game, and killing and cooking it for himself; he learnt to read maps and to draw them, and also the use of weapons; and then, when he had made himself really good at scoutcraft, he went off to the wars again.

He afterwards became a sailor, fought in some very tough sea-fights, and eventually, in 1607, he went with an expedition to colonise Virginia in America. They sailed from London in three ships, the biggest of which was only 100 tons, the smallest 30 tons. But they got there after five months, and started a settlement on the James River.

Here John Smith was captured by the Red Indians one day when out shooting (as you have seen by the play in Chapter 1), and they were proceeding to kill him when the King's daughter, Pocahontas, asked for him to be spared. After this the Red Indians and the Whites got on good terms with each other. Pocahontas became a Christian, and married Smith's lieutenant, Rolfe, and came to England. After many strange and exciting adventures in America, John Smith got much damaged by an accidental explosion of gunpowder, and came home ill. He eventually died in London.

He was a splendid character – and always did his duty in spite of all temptations to let it slide. He was a tremendous worker, very keen, and very brave. He was never defeated by any difficulty however great, because he was always cheery under the worst of circumstances. His motto was, 'We were born not for ourselves, but to do good to others,' and he acted up to it.

IN SOUTH AFRICA we had to drive out the Dutch and then fight the natives for our foothold, which once gained we never let go – and though it has cost us thousands of lives and millions of money we have got it now.

AUSTRALIA was got by our sailor-adventurers, like Captain Cook, outstripping all other nations in their plucky navigation of immense unknown oceans.

INDIA was practically in possession of the French when Clive and Wellesley drove them out, and then in turn had to fight the hordes of fighting natives of the interior, and gradually, foot by foot, by dint of hard fighting, we have won that country for our Empire.

EAST AFRICA, Uganda, and the Soudan beyond Egypt, and Somaliland have also been fought for and won in quite recent times.

And now in all of these we are spreading the blessings of peace and justice, doing away with slavery and oppression, and developing commerce, and manufactures, and prosperity in those countries.

Other nations could formerly only look on and wonder, but now they too are pressing forward in the race for empire and commerce, so that we cannot afford to sit still or let things slide.

We have had this enormous Empire handed down to us by our forefathers, and we are responsible that it develops and goes ahead, and above all that we make ourselves fit and proper men to help it to go ahead. It won't do so of itself, any more than it would have become ours of itself. If we don't do this some other nation will take it from us.

If our island of England were attacked and taken, down comes our Empire like a house built of cards.

We have had this danger always, even before our Empire was a paying one and worth taking. Nowadays it is much more tempting for other people to take. We defeated determined attacks of the Dutch upon us in the old days. The Spaniards with their Armada attempted to invade us, when, largely thanks to a storm, we defeated them utterly. Then the French, after a long struggle to best us, had their invasion stopped by Nelson's victory at Trafalgar, and their harmfulness ended by Wellington at Waterloo. The French Emperor had been so sure of success that he had had medals got ready to commemorate the capture of England. And since helping in the defeat of the Russians in the Crimea we have been at peace with our Continental neighbours.

Let us hope that this peace will remain permanent.

How the empire must be held

PEACE cannot be certain unless we show that we are always fully prepared to defend ourselves in England, and that an invader would only find himself ramming his head against bayonets and well-aimed bullets if he tried landing on our shores.

The surest way to keep peace is to be prepared for war. Don't be cowards, and content yourselves by merely paying soldiers to do your fighting and dying for you. Do something in your own self-defence.

You know at school how if a swaggering ass comes along and threatens to bully you, he only does so because he thinks you will give in to him; but if you know how to box and square up to him he alters his tone and takes himself off. And it is just the same with nations.

It is much better that we should all be good friends – and we should all try for that – no calling each other names, or jeering; but if one of them comes along with the idea of bullying us, the only way to stop him is to show him that you *can* hit and *will* hit if he drives you to it.

Every boy should prepare himself, by learning how to shoot and to drill, to take his share in defence of the Empire, if it should ever be attacked. If our enemies saw that we were thus prepared as a nation, they would never dare to attack, and peace would be assured.

Remember that the Roman Empire 2,000 years ago was comparatively just as great as the British Empire of to-day. And though it had defeated any number of attempts against it, it fell at last, chiefly because the young Romans gave up soldiering and manliness altogether; they paid men to play their games for them, so that they themselves could look on without the fag of playing, just as we are doing in football now. They paid soldiers to fight their battles for them instead of learning the use of arms themselves; they had no patriotism or love for their grand old country, and they went under with a run when a stronger nation attacked them.

Well, we have got to see that the same fate does not fall upon our Empire. And it will largely depend upon you, the younger generation of Britons that are now growing up to be the men of the Empire. Don't be disgraced like the young Romans, who lost the Empire of their forefathers by being wishy-washy slackers without any go or patriotism in them.

Play up! Each man in his place, and play the game!* Your forefathers worked hard, fought hard, and died hard, to make this Empire for you. Don't let them look down from heaven, and see you loafing about with hands in your pockets, doing nothing to keep it up.

Hints to instructors

Teach the words and choruses of:

> 'The Maple Leaf' (Canada), 'The Song of Australia', and other Colonial songs.*
> 'God Bless the Prince of Wales'.
> 'Rule Britannia'.
> 'Hearts of Oak'.
> 'The Flag of Britain'.
> 'God Save the King'.
>
> (J. S. Maddison, 32 Charing Cross.)

Apply to Secretary, League of the Empire, Caxton Hall, Westminster, S.W.

Explore Westminster Abbey, St Paul's Cathedral, the Temple Church, etc., with following books:

Books to read

'St Paul's Cathedral' and 'Westminster Abbey', both by Mrs Frewen Lord, 1s. (Published by Clowes and Son, Charing Cross.)
(Excellent short histories of our famous men and their deeds.)
'Travels of Captain John Smith', by Dr Rouse. 6d. (Blackie.)
'The Story of Captain Cook', edited by John Lang. 1s. 6d.
'Deeds that Won the Empire', by Fitchett.*
'Heroes of Pioneering' (in America, India, Africa), by Sanderson. (Seeley.) 2s. 6d.

Excellent Lantern Slide Lectures can be got on hire from the League of the Empire, Caxton Hall, Victoria Street, London, on the history of our Colonies and Empire.

Display*

JOHN NICHOLSON was one of the finest among many fine Britons who helped to rule India. On one occasion he had a meeting of a number of chiefs at a time when they were beginning to show some signs of mutiny. The most important one of these chiefs was called Mehtab Singh, and just before the meeting he told the others that he for one was not afraid of the Englishman, and that he meant to swagger into the room with his shoes on. (It is the custom in India for natives to take off their shoes on entering the presence of a superior just as in England you take off your hat on coming in.) And he did so. He walked in before them all with his shoes on.

Nicholson did not appear to take any notice of it and went on with the meeting; but at the end of it, just as they were all leaving, he suddenly stopped Mehtab Singh, and ordered the others to wait. He then reprimanded him for his insolence, and ordered him to take off his shoes then and there and to walk out with them in his hand before all the other chiefs. And so he had to go, hanging his head with shame, disgraced and humbled by the firmness of the British ruler.

This makes a good subject for a display.

Scene in a great tent or hall in India.

Nicholson (with a black beard), in a dark suit, sitting on a throne in the centre, with several British and native officers in red tunics grouped behind him. Native princes, seated in chairs in semi-circle to either side of him, all with white socks or bare feet, except Mehtab Singh, who has black shoes on, put out well before him for all to see.

Nicholson rises, signs to the chiefs that they may go.

All rise and bow to him, with both hands to the forehead.

As they turn to go he stops them.

'Stay, gentlemen, one moment. I have a matter with you, Mehtab Singh! Thou camest here intent to show contempt for me, who represent your Queen. But you forget that you are dealing with a Briton – one of that band who never brooks an insult even from an equal, much less from a native of this land. Were I a common

PATRIOTISM; OR, OUR DUTIES AS CITIZENS

soldier it would be the same; a Briton, even though alone, amongst a thousand of your kind, shall be respected, though it brought about his death. That's how we hold the world. To plot against your master brings but trouble on yourself. Take off those shoes.'

Figure 58.1 Face – dark rouge, not black. Dress – big turban, coloured dressing-gown and girdle, white socks and black shoes.

[Mehtab starts, draws himself up, and glares at Nicholson angrily.]

Nicholson [very quietly and deliberately] – 'Take – off – those – shoes.' [Points at them.]

A pause. Mehtab looks round as if for help, takes a step towards Nicholson, but catches his eye, and stops. He sinks slowly on one knee, head down, and slowly takes off his shoes.

Rises, keeping his head down, slowly turns – Nicholson still pointing – and walks slowly out, shoes in hand.

[If a longer scene is required Nicholson might then address the chiefs on the might of Britain, which, though a small country, is all powerful for good of the world, and so he, as representing her, stands one among them for the good of the whole. And that if they want peace and prosperity they themselves must be loyal and true to the hand that is arranging it. Nicholson's words are splendidly rendered in the poem by Henry Newbolt.]

59

HOW INDIA DEVELOPS CHARACTER

From: R. Baden-Powell, *Indian Memories: Recollections of Soldiering, Sport, Etc.* (London: Herbert Jenkins), pp. 106–122.

The final documents in this volume demonstrate the ways in which youth organisations of the period were underpinned and indeed inspired by the Empire. The Boys' Brigade (BB) and the Boy Scout and Girl Guides movements encouraged the youth to demonstrate patriotism and self-discipline, and to acquire skills that could be used in the colonial context. The BB was founded in 1883 as a Christian youth movement by William Alexander Smith (1854–1914). Smith had been a Sunday School teacher and a member of the rifle volunteers. The aim of the BB was 'The advancement of Christ's kingdom among Boys and the promotion of habits of Obedience, Reverence, Discipline, Self-respect and all that tends towards a true Christian manliness'. It introduced boys to semi-military discipline, gymnastics, summer camps and religious services. Robert Baden-Powell (1857–1941) became a vice president of the BB in 1903 and there were close links between the BB and the scout movement before 1914. Robert Baden-Powell was also on the committee of the Duty and Discipline Movement which Meath founded just before the outbreak of the First World War. Baden-Powell was very much an imperial figure, serving in the British army, travelling to India, Afghanistan, and East Africa, and participating in the South African War, taking great credit during the siege of Mafeking. During the war he had utilised boy messengers and this proved to be the origins of the scout movement. As was noted in Baden-Powell's obituary, scouting was seen as a system of education which combined 'chivalry and patriotism'. His book Scouting for Boys, *which appeared in the Edwardian era, can be seen as a founding document of this youth movement, a movement which then also encompassed girls as the Girl Guides were founded in 1910 by Powell's sister Agnes. Both movements were subsequently established across the British Empire.*

> Killing Ennui – Tommy Atkins as a Sportsman – Spies in Disguise – A Sham Fight – The Perfect Soldier – Learning to Observe – Night Operations – The Man Who Made Grimaces – The Modern Training – Interesting the Men – Sir Bindon Blood's Views on Cavalry – An Irate General – The Woman Abroad – The Scout Mistress – The Rani's Answer – A Fearless Rani – Colonel Alexander Gardiner – His Romance – A Tragedy

THERE is no doubt that the best preventative of disease in India is plenty of work, occupation and exercise. It is the ennui that kills. The difficulty is to make the work interesting so that it does not become a treadmill of drudgery. For the officers shooting, pigsticking, and polo all offer their attractions and make them far more healthy as a rule than are the men. Our Colonel was so fully impressed with the value of keeping up the health of his officers that, instead of keeping the weekly holiday as determined by regulations on Thursday, he moved it to Friday, and thus made the week-end into an outing by removing the mess into the jungle and leaving only the orderly officer to take charge of the regiment during Friday, Saturday, and Sunday. Those of the men who were good shots and capable of looking after themselves were also encouraged, during the hot weather, to go and live out in camp for several days at a time. The Government allowed a certain number of sporting guns for this purpose, and a large number of the men availed themselves of the privilege and made themselves into self-reliant, capable bushmen.

There was too much of a tendency to coddle the men during the hot weather. Native syces, or grooms, were supplied by Government to look after their horses; but we made the men groom and feed their horses regularly, as it gave them exercise and occupation. At least once a week we had all-night field-days. Then also a great deal of our drill and instruction was competitive between squads, sections or troops. Latterly the system of teaching the men to be scouts came in as an additional form of training, which appealed to the men and gave them plenty of outdoor exercise by day and by night.

It was reported to me *sub rosa* that one of the men when in hospital confided to his nurse: "This new Colonel is the devil to work us; but the worst of it is, the more we work the more healthy we are."

The need of a practical training in scouting had often been in my mind even as a young officer, and I had carried out a good deal of it in my early days in India. But its importance was brought home to me more especially in the campaign against the Matabele in 1896, where I found that, although we had plenty of men who were willing and eager to undertake adventurous rides against the enemy, they were seldom able to bring back the sort of information that we wanted and not be led away by chances of little fights and scraps on their own. So when I got to India after Matabeleland I set to work systematically to train the men in the points in which I found them deficient in practical soldiering. People seemed to think, and indeed many outsiders still do, that if a man could march past and look well on parade, he was therefore a perfect soldier; but in reality he was only a part of a machine. This was all very well for show purposes but not the slightest use against a really active fighting enemy in the field. Our men came to us as lads from their Board Schools, well grounded in the three R's of reading, writing, and arithmetic, but without any manliness, self-reliance, or resourcefulness. These were points which we had to put into them and which could not be merely taught in theory; but they came through the practice of the different duties which go to make up effective scouting.

I remember in Ireland, during the early days of my attempts, taking my squadron out of barracks at Dundalk in the late evening. We swam our horses across the tidal river before getting on to our ground among the hills. Here we had plenty of moorland where men could easily lose their way unless they watched their courses by the stars. They were given duties to perform generally in pairs or singly, in order to develop their self-reliance and intelligence. As they were out all night they brought rations with them and learnt how to make their fires in hidden places and to cook their food for themselves. Their ingenuity was exercised in finding fuel, and I complimented one patrol in particular for the excellent fire which they had made, whose embers could have cooked a splendid meal. My admiration was lessened when later a farmer came to the Colonel demanding compensation for a gate which they had pulled down and burnt.

In India night operations of this kind were of course the delight of the men, especially as we generally acted in opposing forces of a few scouts against each other on two sides. On one of these occasions I bivouacked with one party of scouts, and, knowing that the other side were as yet a good many miles distant, I suggested to them to have a little camp fire to themselves with songs and chat. We talked on many subjects of interest, but I could not help noticing that one of the men was continually leaving the circle and going out into the darkness for a few minutes and returning again. At last, noticing his continued restlessness, I feared he might be ill, and I told my sergeant to question him. I overheard his reply. "Oh no, there is nothing the matter with me, but that beggar Fox is on the other side, and I can't help feeling he is creeping around and watching us." There is no doubt the men got to take an intense interest in scouting, which outweighed all other considerations with them.

I did not allow a man to take up scouting unless he was capable both as a horseman, marksman, and swimmer. In this latter particular a man was merely questioned as to his capabilities, but the time arrived when we actually put him to the test. On one occasion in the course of our work we had to swim a big canal, and one of the scouts in swimming over was apparently playing the fool, diving down and bobbing up again, making most fearful grimaces, which drew roars of laughter from his assembled comrades, until it suddenly struck them that he was actually in distress, when some of them promptly went to his rescue and brought him ashore. On inquiry it turned out that he had never learnt to swim, but like the man who volunteered to play the violin, "he had never tried but he supposed that he could!"

One of the points of modern training of soldiers which astonishes an outsider is the amount of tactical instruction which is given to the men themselves. In the course of manœuvres the tactical situation and object of the day's work is carefully explained to the men in the beginning of the day. And then from time to time a halt is called and further explanations are given of the progress and developments that have taken place. In this way every individual man understands what is going on, and therefore plays his part in the general scheme with far greater interest and intelligence.

In cavalry manœuvres we introduced an extra bit of realism which was of additional interest and practical value. We allowed each side to use three spies in disguise, whose duty it was to find out all they could about the enemies' moves. This was good practice for the spies and sharpened their intelligence and, at the same time, was valuable in teaching the men to be cautious when speaking to strangers. It is a common fault with soldiers that, when they understand a field-day and take an interest in it, they are ready to answer questions and to explain the scheme to any onlooker who shows a desire for information. For this reason in South Africa our plans were often given away to specious gentlemen who were in reality Boer spies. But in manœuvres, with the knowledge that spies were about, men became very cautious about giving away information, and in many cases, thinking that they were speaking with such people, they made up wonderful yarns in order to mislead them. Soldiers are rapidly learning that cunning which completes the four C's of soldiering, viz., Courage, Commonsense, Cheerfulness, and Cunning.[1]

In India when we had had a field day it was usual to issue in the evening, for the information of all ranks, a short narrative illustrated by a sketch plan of what had gone on during the day, pointing out the reasons, mistakes, and good points of the actions. I take one from many examples; a non-military reader can easily grasp it. "The Southern division in column of route on the main road learnt that the enemy's division was about two miles distant to its left. Leaving the road our division formed into preparatory formation with one brigade in front and two in the second line. Our scouts soon signalled that the enemy was in sight approaching our left front. Our guns came into action at once against the enemy's main body, and were replied to by his artillery almost immediately due north of them. Our division took ground to the right and thus drew the enemy on to attack it. Then the enemy formed line preparatory to charging, but our division still kept on its course across the front of the enemy in preparatory formation, thus causing him to alter his direction (which it was almost impossible to do in good order when committed to line), and at the same time drew him across the fire of our guns. At the last moment our division, wheeling each brigade into line to its left, charged the enemy in double echelon in good order, and was awarded the victory."

It will be seen that in carrying out this plan the enemy were not only drawn across the front of our guns, but also across that of their own artillery, and were thus prevented from firing into our division. The General Commanding expressed himself highly pleased with the whole manœuvre, and especially with the good scouting of Lieutenant Garrard's patrol, which gave exact information as to the whereabouts and movements of the enemy."

Another method of interesting the men in their regiment and in military history generally was this. At the commencement of each month a calendar was printed and issued to every man for that month, giving all events of interest which had happened to the regiment during its career in that month. Taking haphazard the calendar for October, the following incidents occur.

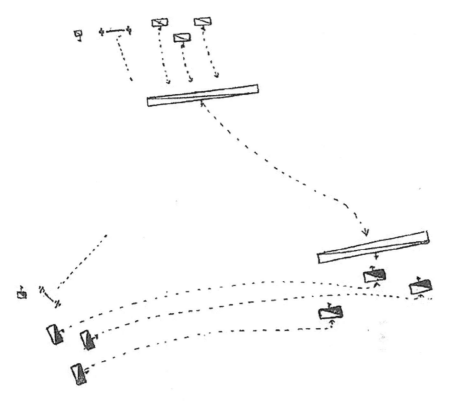

Figure 59.1 Our plan of attack

These I enumerate here without going into detail as given in the copy issued to the regiment:

Oct. 1710. The regiment was employed in covering the siege of Mons till its surrender on the 20th October.

Oct. 1796. The regiment proceeded to Ireland to suppress Rebellion, the French being prepared to assist the Irish.

Oct. 1812. The regiment covered the retreat of General Hill's column from Burgos, etc.

Oct. 1816. The King of the Belgians appointed Colonel.

Oct. 1854. The regiment landed in the Crimea and took part in the charge of the heavy brigade at Balaclava on the 25th.

Oct. 1893. Regiment landed in India.

Before undertaking a long march in India to attend manœuvres, or on change of station, each man was supplied with a leaflet giving an account of the country through which the march would take him, giving its history, especially from the military point of view, with descriptions of any battles and events leading up to them which would be of interest to the reader. The dates and distances of the different marches day by day were also given for their information.

Sir Baker Russell used to say that the duty of cavalry was to look smart in time of peace and to get killed in war. We hear from time to time that modern conditions of war render cavalry obsolete; yet each new campaign proves the contrary. Sir Bindon Blood, although he had not served in the cavalry himself, was broad-minded enough to recognise value in that force, and in forming his columns for fighting over the Malakand Pass he insisted on having a certain proportion of cavalry with him, and, although there was much opposition and criticism of the idea, he showed the wisdom of his prevision. At a critical period of the fighting he was able to deliver an unexpected charge of cavalry upon these mountain warriors, who had never seen any number of horsemen before, and the effects were very far-reaching. It was both refreshing and encouraging to see the General, after having thus used cavalry on active service, coming out in peace time to watch that arm at its drills and training, in order that he might himself improve his knowledge of the details of its work. It is not every infantry general who would take the trouble to do this.

His inspection of a regiment was of a far more practical type than was customary in the old days. Formerly it would have been thought unfair to a regiment to inspect it without first sending a definite programme of all that the General intended to see during his annual inspection of the corps and its barracks. This programme, which I actually remember as a printed one, was handed to the regiment weeks beforehand, so that everybody had ample opportunity for working up and rehearsing his own particular share in the demonstration of the great day. Everything had to be spick and span, horses had a good drink of water the last thing before the General came round, in order to fill up the hollows in their flanks, every subaltern had his card on which the Sergeant-major had noted the different items of information about which the General was likely to ask questions. It was certain always that the General would ask the price of one or other article of the soldier's kit. It was said of one subaltern that in reply to the General's question: "How much does a towel cost?" the poor boy, utterly at sea, suggested four shillings. The General stormed out: "Do you pay four shillings yourself?" and the subaltern, quick to see some error, hurriedly ejaculated: "Yes, sir, four shillings – a dozen."

As a subaltern of experience and observation I very soon realised in the course of a few inspections that a General felt bound to find fault with something or other in each troop, and he would hover about until he could find something unsatisfactory. He would be glad to let off a little steam over that, and then to go off elsewhere. So I made it my business to oblige him, and though I had things as good as could be where it was essential, I took care to have a dirty stable lantern where the General could not miss seeing it. He would jump to this at once. "What's this? Just look at that. I have never seen such a filthy, disgraceful sight in all my life. Aren't you ashamed of it yourself, sir? Your horses are in good condition, your men are smart and clean, your stables are in good order. I'm surprised that you should allow such a thing as this dirty lantern to be here. I am surprised; it just spoils what would otherwise be a very good troop." And with that he would strut off to try and find fault with the next troop, outwardly fuming, but inwardly pleased that he had discovered something wrong, and which when he came to put it on paper appeared too silly for serious notice.

You hear varied opinions about India as a place for women. Most men will tell you it is no place for ladies; many of the ladies themselves will tell you it is a delightful country. One thing is certain – they cannot remain on the Plains in the hot weather. They have, therefore, to leave their husbands at their duty with their regiments, or in their offices, while they flock to the hill-stations and start additional homes in the cooler climate. There they can be extremely useful to their mankind, because, whenever a married man wants a little leave, it needs but a telegram from his wife in the hills to say that she is desperately ill, and his senior officer cannot well refuse to let him go. When some of the unhappy single officers have seen themselves done out of their leave in this way, and have had to do duty for their married comrades, they eventually get driven in self-defence to take a wife themselves, and that is another reason why India is a good country for ladies – from their point of view.

Of course we in England know that the ladies in India, unlike those at home, are entirely given up to frivolity and scandal; we are perfectly sure of that, just as sure of it as was that prelate who, on the voyage out to take over his see in India, wrote an encyclical, or whatever it is called, to his future subjects, telling them that they must at once put a stop to all their former immorality! He was rather surprised to find himself coldly received, and his sermons not well attended. It is possible that he did not stay long enough in the country to realise that society was no worse in India than anywhere else, possibly rather the other way, because troubles come more frequently there, home is further away, and dangers are closer at hand. These facts promote stronger sympathies, more lasting friendships and greater personal pluck and self-sacrifice than elsewhere, among women as among men. I do not say that there are no frivolities, no back-bitings, no tea-table talk, because no doubt these do exist, but to nothing like the extent that some people would make out.

The greatest complaint in the country amongst the women is that there is so little for them to do, their occupations and amusements are necessarily limited by climate and locality, and it seems to an outsider that their main object in life is to get all the pleasure they can out of theatricals, dances, and picnics, without any serious aim in their occupation. Still, if one could look below the surface, there is much good work going on as well. Soldiers' wives and children and the men in hospital are the care of the better class of officers' wives; while devoted women doctors and teachers are doing an enormous amount behind the zenana screens to educate and bring out the native ladies to be more of a power in the land, and there is no doubt that their work is beginning to tell and will tell more widely in the next generation or two.

A new occupation also has lately started, fortunately for me, in a direction in which I have a say personally, and that is in the development of the Boy Scout

Movement. This at first glance would appear to be entirely men's work; but, as we find in England, there are many centres in which there are plenty of boys but no men to take them in hand. The ladies have come forward and proved themselves most able organisers and instructors of scouting work, and their field in this direction is now enlarged by the institution of the Wolf Cubs, or branch of Junior Scouts for small boys of from nine to eleven, who are more particularly amenable to instruction by ladies. Also the Girl Guides have now made a great start in India, and promise to exercise a most valuable influence in the education of girls in that country. The principles on which they are trained are very much the same as those which guide the education of the Boy Scouts, but the details are those which apply to womanhood, in the shape of nursing and housekeeping, and the many details connected therewith.

In these directions there is great scope for active and enterprising women, where their time will be well spent in doing a national work instead of in loafing and frivolity. What is to be the future of the native women, when once they come to the fore after being educated by their Western sisters, is a very big problem. The possibilities before them are very great, for they are naturally adaptable and quick to learn. They have, moreover, pluck and devotion equal to that of any other race, if we can judge by the instances which have made their reputation in history, in spite of the bonds which have been so tightly drawn round them in the past. I will merely quote two out of the many which could be cited.

When the Sikhs were fighting against us in 1846 they were under the rule of a queen, the Rani Jindan. She was a very strong lady politically, and she had a notion that her great rival in power was her own army, which was growing a bit too strong for her. She therefore rather welcomed the chance of its suffering at the hands of the British, so she took care not to equip it too well. Just before the battle of Sobraon the Sikhs, realising that they were becoming inefficient from want of food and ammunition, sent a deputation to Lahore, where the Rani then was, to address her on the subject. She received the deputation in the great hall; she herself remained behind a screen, as was the custom for ladies, while their spokesman represented their difficulties. When he was but half-way through his speech she slipped off her petticoat and, rolling it up in a ball, hurled it amongst the astonished deputation, accompanied by a torrent of abuse, telling them to "get out and take to wearing petticoats themselves, as they were nothing better than a pack of old women, and that if they were afraid to fight she would go and lead the army herself." This so roused them that they gave the equivalent to three cheers and told her they would hammer the English somehow, even without any food or ammunition. And they went back – and got hammered.

The other case was that of the wife of Dhyan Singh, as recorded by Colonel Alexander Gardner. This old warrior, who was at the time an officer in the Sikh Army, describes how Rajah Dhyan Singh was treacherously murdered by Lehna Singh and Ajit Singh. Dhyan's wife was the daughter of the Rajput Chief of Pathankot. When she heard of the death of her husband, she vowed that she would be burnt on a funeral pyre, and, though a very young girl, she showed no hesitation about doing so; but said that before she became sati, that is, a self-immolated widow, she would like to have the heads of Lehna Singh and Ajit Singh, the murderers.

Colonel Gardner says in the simplest way: "I myself laid their heads at the feet of Dhyan Singh's corpse that evening The sati of his widow then took place, and seldom if ever have I been so powerfully affected as at the self-immolation of the gentle and lovely girl, whose love for her husband passed all bounds. During the day, while inciting the army to avenge her husband's murder, she had appeared in public before the soldiers, discarding the seclusion of a lifetime. When his murderers had been slain she gave directions as to the disposition of his property with a stoicism and self-possession to which no one beside her could lay claim. She thanked her brave avengers and declared that she would tell of their good deed to her husband when in heaven. There was nothing left for her, she said, but to join him." There was a little girl of nine or ten present at the scene who was passionately fond of the murdered rajah. She tried to get upon the pyre with the young widow, but was prevented by the onlookers, whereupon she ran away to the battlements of the city and threw herself from them. Colonel Gardner writes: "We picked her up more dead than alive, and the beautiful devotee seated on the pyre consented to take the child in her lap to share her doom. She placed her husband's diamond egret in her turban and she then fastened it with her own hands in the turban of her step-son, Hera Singh; then smiling on those around she lit the pyre, the flames of which glistened on the arms and accoutrements, and even, it seemed to me, on the swimming eyes of the soldiers. So perished the widow of Dhyan Singh, together with thirteen of her female slaves."

I always regret that when I first went to India I did not get the opportunity of seeing Colonel Alexander Gardner, who died shortly afterwards in Srinagar, and was buried in the British cemetery at Sialkote. He was a wonderful character. In his old age, at ninety-three, he was as upright as a ramrod and stood six feet four in his stockings. He spoke English with some difficulty, having spent practically all his life in Afghanistan and Northern India, and when he spoke it was with a strong Scottish accent. He had gone as a boy sailor to the coast of Asia Minor, had sought adventures ashore and had thence drifted into Persia, where he took service as a soldier and gradually established himself as a man of standing and authority. Then he became an Afghan and married under romantic circumstances.

He had been told off with some of his horsemen to capture a great lady of a political rival's family, and was successful only after a desperate fight extending over many miles. He was specially told off to take charge of the lady during the escape from her would-be rescuers, and as he rode alongside her camel he noticed a very beautiful girl who was her companion, and at the end of the enterprise he asked for this girl as his wife in return for his services on the occasion. It turned out a very happy marriage for the time that it lasted.

He was continually employed in forays and border wars and saw an immense amount of fighting. One time when away from his fortified home, engaged in one of these raids, he received a message recalling him to his chief, who was being hard pressed by enemies. He reached his chief just in time to find him surrounded by the enemy, with only twelve survivors left of his bodyguard, with whom he was trying to cut his way through. Gardner succeeded in reaching him and rescuing him. But his chief told him with a stony countenance that his own fort had been taken by the enemy and his wife and baby murdered. Gardner stated that he felt a stern pleasure when, on reaching his home, he saw that the number of dead enemies far exceeded that of the defenders; but these had all been slain to a man, with one exception. An old priest had endeavoured to save the child, but had all his fingers cut off and his arm nearly severed by a scimitar in doing so.

Gardner then migrated to the Punjab and joined the service of the great Sikh leader Ranjit Singh, and was a General in the Sikh army when they were fighting against us at Sobraon, but was not in the field himself, being employed at Lahore in command of the reserves. At that time there were no less than forty-two European officers in the service of Ranjit Singh. Gardner's knowledge of the inner life of the Indians was probably unrivalled by that of any other white man, and equally his experience in actual fighting in the field. He bore the scars of some twenty wounds on his body, and owing to a severe wound in his throat he carried a pair of iron pincers with which he had to hold his neck whenever he wanted to swallow or to drink.

Note

1 If ever a campaign showed the value of these attributes the present war has done so, and has proved that our men are possessed of all, especially the very important one, under the circumstances, viz., Cheerfulness.

60

CAMP FIRE YARN. NO. 33

Our Empire

From: Agnes Baden-Powell, *How Girls Can Help to Build Up the Empire: The Handbook for Girl Guides* (London: Thomas Nelson, 1912), pp. 405–412.

The final documents in this volume demonstrate the ways in which youth organisations of the period were underpinned and indeed inspired by the Empire. The Boys' Brigade (BB) and the Boy Scout and Girl Guides movements encouraged the youth to demonstrate patriotism and self-discipline, and to acquire skills that could be used in the colonial context. The BB was founded in 1883 as a Christian youth movement by William Alexander Smith (1854–1914). Smith had been a Sunday School teacher and a member of the rifle volunteers. The aim of the BB was 'The advancement of Christ's kingdom among Boys and the promotion of habits of Obedience, Reverence, Discipline, Self-respect and all that tends towards a true Christian manliness'. It introduced boys to semi-military discipline, gymnastics, summer camps and religious services. Robert Baden-Powell (1857–1941) became a vice president of the BB in 1903 and there were close links between the BB and the scout movement before 1914. Robert Baden-Powell was also on the committee of the Duty and Discipline Movement which Meath founded just before the outbreak of the First World War. Baden-Powell was very much an imperial figure, serving in the British army, travelling to India, Afghanistan, and East Africa, and participating in the South African War, taking great credit during the siege of Mafeking. During the war he had utilised boy messengers and this proved to be the origins of the scout movement. As was noted in Baden-Powell's obituary, scouting was seen as a system of education which combined 'chivalry and patriotism'. His book Scouting for Boys, *which appeared in the Edwardian era, can be seen as a founding document of this youth movement, a movement which then also encompassed girls as the Girl Guides were founded in 1910 by Powell's sister Agnes. Both movements were subsequently established across the British Empire.*

How it grew – how it must be held

Hints to instructors

The use of a large map of the Empire is very desirable for illustrating this. The Arnold Forster, the Navy League, or the League of the Empire Maps are very good.

Look up the local history of your neighbourhood, and give your Guides the more interesting and dramatic bits of it, on the actual scene of the events if possible.

Any of you who have travelled much about this country by train, going for your holidays and so on, know how two or three hours will take you a good long distance, and six or eight hours will take you to the other end of England.

Well, if instead of hours you travelled for as many days, even six or eight days would take you a very little way over our Empire. It would take you into Canada, but you would want several more days – not hours – to get across that country. Eighteen days' hard travelling day and night would take you to India or South Africa, but both of these are little more than half-way to Australia. And all that distance off, across the seas, on the other side of the world, we have a British country into which you could put nine Great Britains and Irelands.

9	United Kingdoms = 1 Australia.
10	United Kingdoms = 1 Canada.
6	United Kingdoms = 1 India and Burma.
5	United Kingdoms = East Africa, Uganda, and Sudan.
5	United Kingdoms = South Africa.
1	United Kingdoms = New Zealand.
1½	United Kingdoms = Nigeria.

Then there are numbers of smaller colonies or dependencies, such as Guiana (nearly as big as the United Kingdom), North Borneo, New Guinea, Somaliland, Straits Settlements, Gold Coast, West Indies, Tasmania, etc., and numbers of islands in every sea. Our Colonies together are something like forty times the size of the United Kingdom.

Our fellow-subjects amount to four hundred million, and make up *one quarter of the whole human beings in the world*, and comprise almost every known race. Almost every known species of wild animal occurs in British territory. It is a magnificent Empire over which the Union Jack flies, but it is still only at the beginning of its development. The territories are there, but the people are only coming. The white population of all these Dominions only amounts to a little over a quarter of the population of these crowded little islands. We have nearly forty-four million here; and of these people over four and a half million live in London. In Glasgow or Liverpool there are nearly eight hundred thousand people.

Many of you, as you grow up, will probably find your way to some of these splendid and fruitful Colonies, and help to make them into big prosperous countries. Your Guide's training will come in very useful to you there. But when you go there you must be prepared to work, and to work hard, and to turn your hand to any kind of job.

CAMP FIRE YARN. NO. 33

How our empire grew

The British Empire is composed of the British Isles and those overseas Dominions in the table above.

Nothing in history is comparable to this enormous prosperous realm known as the British Empire, with the sea for its streets, and with a sacred duty to carry light into all the dark places over the whole world. The British Empire is three times as big as the whole of Europe, and four times as big as the United States of America.

When we first went to America it took Sir Walter Raleigh, Captain John Smith, and other great pioneers four or five months to get there in their little cockleshells of ships, some of them only 30 tons burden – no bigger than a Thames barge. Nowadays you can go there in five or six days, instead of months, in steamers of 30,000 tons.

Think of the pluck of those men in tackling a voyage like that with a very limited supply of water and salt food. And when they got to land with a handful of men, they had to overcome the savages, and in some cases other Europeans, like the Dutch, the Spaniards, and the French; and then they had hard work to till the ground, to build settlements, and to start commerce. Hard sailoring, hard soldiering, hard colonizing by those old British sea-dogs – that is what made British character with grit in it.

All these immense Colonies did not come to the English of themselves; they were got for us by the hard work and the endurance and bravery of our forefathers.

In CANADA the Army has had famous men who served in the campaigns which placed the Dominion under the Union Jack. They can point to their glorious deeds when they took Fort Ogdensburg, and in the hard fighting at Lundy's Lane. They were in the Red River Expedition, and helped in the suppression of Riel's Rebellion.

In SOUTH AFRICA more than a hundred years ago we established our rule of freedom and fairplay in struggles with the Hottentots and the Dutch, in which the Cape Mounted Rifles fought valiantly. The Natal Carabineers were the finest regiment of that colony, and the regiment of Rhodesian Horse behaved gallantly in helping us against the Matabele and many savage tribes.

AUSTRALIA happily had no wars in her conquest, but was got for us by our sailor men (like Captain Cook), who outstripped all other nations in their plucky navigation of immense, unknown oceans. The Australian soldiers came to the help of Britain in the Sudan and also in the South African War.

The NEW ZEALANDERS had a long ten years' contest with the native Maoris. Their Riflemen and City Guards are the sons of the Englishmen who fought for us at Ranagiri and Gate Pahs.

The vast extent of INDIA has all been conquered bit by bit to form one enormous country loyal to our King, and the natives furnish us with a splendid army, composed of the brave Sikhs and Gurkas, the troops of Gwalior and the Frontier Force, and the "Guides," a crack corps of picked men, always ready for instant service.

East Africa, Uganda, and the Sudan beyond Egypt, and Somaliland have also been fought for and won in quite recent times.

And now in all these countries we are spreading the blessings of peace and justice, doing away with slavery and oppression, and developing commerce and manufactures.

Other nations could formerly only look on and wonder, but now they, too, are pressing forward in the race for empire and commerce, so that we cannot afford to sit still or let things slide.

We have had this enormous Empire handed down to us by our forefathers, and we are responsible that it develops and goes ahead, and, above all, that we make ourselves fit and proper subjects to help it to go ahead. It won't do so of itself, any more than it would have become ours of itself. If we don't do this, some other nation will take it from us.

Patriotism

We all want to help our country, and wish to be of use for the advancement of the Empire.

The Rev. J. Purvis, in addressing some Guides, said: "As you are moulding your minds and your bodies at the present time, so will they act in the future, either as a drag or for the advancement of this glorious nation."

Let every Guide think of her country and help its advancement.

A girl patriot who helped her country at the time of the American War was the Duchess of Sutherland, who, when she was only twelve years old, raised a Sutherland regiment. This brave girl then reviewed her men, 1,000 strong, from the windows of her aunt's house in Edinburgh, only regretting that she could not be in command.

Patriots

In our country we do not lack heroines, and can boast of many who have endured terrible sufferings and have gone through all kinds of dangers for duty and their country.

Read. – So long as tongues can speak, the stories of the valiant deeds of these patriots will be told to eager listeners and proud hearts.

We have a long-ago heroine in our Queen Boadicea, who governed in Norfolk. When she found that the Romans had taken possession of London, she gathered together a very large army of Britons to try and turn out the enemy. She cleverly took the opportunity when the Roman chief had gone away to fight up in the north. She bravely rallied a large force, and urged them to march on London. The queen led her army on, and, inspirited by her, they attacked the Romans suddenly, and massacred the whole garrison.

However brave or great the deed seems, a woman is no heroine if it cost her nothing to do it.

You should read Whittier's account of the brave old American lady, Barbara Fritchie, who, even when over ninety years of age, risked her life in defending the flag of her country. You would all admire the noble self-sacrifice of Lady Catherine Douglas for her king. It was when King James the First of Scotland and his queen had arrived to stay in the abbey at Perth for some great festivities, and were just preparing to retire for the night, that they were alarmed by the tramp of soldiers in the abbey garden. The rebel Graham had come with three hundred armed men to kill the king. The terrified ladies of the Court attempted to close the door, but the lock was found to have been broken, and the great bar which bolted the door had been removed. One of the maids of honour, Lady Catherine Douglas, bravely, and without hesitation, thrust her arm into the staple-rings in the door and the wall so as to bar the door, and for a short time held the door shut. With rough soldiers trying to force the door, what could a girl's tender arm do against them? It was soon broken. The soldiers got in, and finally found the king, who had hidden himself. The queen tried to save him by throwing herself between him and the ruffians; but they were roughly separated and the king murdered before her eyes.

In this way patriots cheerfully face immense peril without thought of applause or reward.

We have a great many heroines among the stout-hearted Scots. Read about the "White Rose of Scotland," who was associated with Perkin Warbeck; also Helen of Kirkconnell, who is immortalized by Wordsworth. Then there was Christian Grainger, who was in the castle where the Scottish regalia were kept when it was besieged by the insurgents. She was so loyal that she determined that the rebels should not get the crown even if they took the castle, so she managed to conceal the golden sceptre and the jewelled crown and the sword of state beneath her skirts and cloak, and in the confusion of the fighting she contrived to escape and deliver up her precious goods to their rightful keepers.

She managed to get them to Dunnottar Castle. But later the insurgents attacked that place too, and took the marischal prisoner. Still, the lieutenant, Ogilvy, protected the jewels, and when the troops besieged the castle, he smuggled the regalia away to a church, where they remained hidden for eight years.

Guarding your country by a deed of valour is not out of the power of quite a small child. Do you remember how the little Dutch boy saved his country from a dreadful flood? Parts of Holland lie below the sea-level, and so people build walls and banks to keep out the water. This little boy was, just as you might be, simply walking home from school, but he saw that the water was coming through the bank, and that the sea waves were washing the hole larger every moment. What could a little child do to save the whole country? There was no one near to help him, but he quickly stuffed his coat into the hole, and thrust his arm in to fill the gap, and there he held it all the long, dark hours of the night. Was it not brave and good of him never to leave off trying? His friends came to find him next morning, cold and weak, but also a conquering hero, for, had he not acted so quickly, and stayed there so courageously, all the crops would have been ruined, the houses flooded, and no one would have been able to live.

And then there is the story of how Agoustina of Saragossa bravely took her husband's place when he was killed by the enemy's shot during the famous siege. She fired his gun, and turned the tide of the battle at a critical moment, so helping to save her town. You can read about it in Charlotte Yonge's "Book of Golden Deeds."

The girls of the nation have the moulding of the men of the future. This great Empire is entrusted to their care, and what it will be in the future is just what the girls try to make it. Girls have great power and influence, and can serve their country even better than men can, by forming the minds and characters of the children.

Helping police

Girl Guides can be of special use in assisting the police in towns. In the first place, every Guide ought to know where the fixed police points are – that is, where a constable is always stationed, apart from the policemen on their beats. She ought to know where to find the fire alarm; where the nearest fire brigade station is, and the nearest hospital or ambulance station, and chemist.

On seeing an accident, if you cannot help at it you should run and inform the nearest policeman, and ask him how you can help him – whether you can call a doctor, a cab, and so on. If you hear a policeman's whistle sounding, run and offer to help him; it is your duty, as he is a king's servant.

If you find a lost child or lost dog, or any lost property, you should take them at once to the police station.

Sir H. Poland, K.C., had his watch snatched by a pickpocket the other day. The thief darted away down the street; but a small boy jumped on to a bike and followed him, crying, "Stop thief!" till he was caught – with the watch on him.

Not only can boys help the police, but girls also. Within the last few months I have noticed many cases of girls going to the assistance of constables who were in difficulties with violent men. In each case the girl got the policeman's whistle and blew it for him until assistance arrived. These heroines were Miss Edith Harris at Southampton, Miss Bessie Matthews in Clerkenwell, Mrs. Langley at Brentford, Frances Wright, and Dorothy Chambers.

Hints to instructors

Read up thrilling incidents in the history of our Colonies, and let the Guides each choose a part, and act scenes or tableaux of the decisive events.

INDEX

'4 Adventurers, The' (Harding) 379–384

Abdul Kerim 150
Abdullahi, Khalifa 336–341
Abdurrahman, Amir of Afghanistan 183
Aberdeen 419
aborigines 221
Abyssinia 329
academy 28
Acadie 71
Achilles 98
Adam 249–250
Adam, Edwin 411, 428
Adams, John 33
Adams, J.Q. 425
"Advancement of Learning" (Bacon) 73
Afghanistan 186–187, 196
Afghan war 34, 183, 187–188
Africa 34, 40, 85, 95, 99, 135, 142, 145, 150, 183, 190–191, 200, 265, 325–338, 371–377
African negroes 221, 233–235
Afrikander policy 180
Agoustina of Saragossa 470
agriculture 131, 201, 218, 239–240
Ajit Singh 462
Akbar Khan 187
Alaric I, King of Visigoths 133
Albert Edward, Prince of Wales 217
Albert, George Frederick Ernest, Duke of Cornwall and York 189
Albert of Saxe-Coburg and Gotha, Prince Consort 205
Alexander the Great 80
Alexandra, Princess of Wales 254
Alfred the Great 287–288
Alice, Princess of the United Kingdom 205–206

Allingham, Phillip 267
Almond, Hely Hutchinson 27, 122
Alston, J. Carfrae 402, 407, 411
Alston, J. Carfrae, Mrs. 402
Alston, William A. 411
ambulance classes 414–414, 419, 420, 422
American school system 31
American War of Independence 146, 201
Ampleforth College 140
ancient history 322–324
Anula 247–249
Arabia 393
archery 119
Aristotle 57, 100
Army Council 320
Arnold, Thomas 49, 56, 57, 59
Arthur, Prince, Duke of Connaught and Strathearn 271
Art of Teaching, The (Salmon) 39
Ashburner, Francis J. 262
Asia 186
Asia Minor 112
Assiento contract 81
Assyria 322
Astaire, Fred 268
athletic games 62–65, 74–75, 98–99, 122, 126, 131–132
Atkins, J.B. 280
Atkinson, F. 50
Attila the Hun 133
Augustus, Roman emperor 70, 80
Australasia 34, 40, 189, 265
Australia 32, 38, 44, 75, 78, 79, 81, 85, 135, 140–141, 142, 145, 146, 181–182, 189, 198–199, 220–221, 237, 244–246, 293, 304, 309, 311, 312, 313, 319, 320, 448, 450, 466, 467
Austral negroes 221

INDEX

Bacon, Francis 73
Baden-Powell, Agnes 44, 465–470
Baden-Powell, Robert 120; *Indian Memories* 44, 455–464; Patriotism 447–454; scout movement 27–28, 43
Bainsford, Mr. 443
Baker, T.W. 435
Balance of Power 274–275
Baldrey, Sergeant 167
Balfour, Arthur, Earl of Balfour 276, 311–313
Ballantyne, R.M. 43, 331, 345, 358, 362, 367, 379, 385, 390, 395
Bamford, T. W. 27, 33
Barnett, Richard C. 166
Barton, Edmund 182
Bass, George 199
Baxter's Second Innings (Drummond) 403
B.B.C. Northern Orchestra 267
Beale, Dorothea 142, 145
Beatrice, Princess of the United Kingdom 156
Bechuanaland 326, 327
Bechuanas 371
Beckett, C.E. 166
Beechey, Vincent 115
Begg, F. Faithfull 304, 305–307
Belsey, F.F. 421
Bengal 185, 196, 216, 309–310
Benin River 363
Berlin-Rome-Tokio Axis 330
Best, Geoffrey 26
Bevin, Ernest 269
Bewes, Reginald A. 404
Bible 99
Bickerstaff, Alfred L. 411
"Big Steamers" (Kipling) 266
Birmingham Education League 31
Bismarck, Otto von 25
Black, Adam Elliot 411
black Africans 38
blackfellows 244–246
Blakeney, Edward P. 414
Blakeney, John Edward 414, 424
Blanch, M.D. 40
Bland, Gordon 307
Blaquiere, Dora de 390–394
Bloomfield, Anne 39
Blyton, Enid: *Modern Teaching* 42; *Pictorial Knowledge* 42; *Teacher's Treasury, The* 42, 284, 286, 296; *Union Jack, The* 42, 284, 286, 296–303

Boadicea, Queen of the Iceni tribe 468
boarding schools 27
Board of Education 42, 322–324
Boer Camp 142–144, 145
Boer Republics 180–181, 191–192
Boer War 118, 157–175
Bonomi, Luigi 155–156
Booer, W.J. 421
Book of Common Prayer 99
"Book of Golden Deeds" (Yonge) 470
Booth, Mr. 280
'Bound in Benin' (Manson) 345–357
Bowley, J. 438
Boxers 189
Boyd, Kelly 43
Boyler, H.W. 331–344
Boys' Brigade 44, 254, 402–447
Boys' Brigade Bulletin, The 425
Boys' Brigade Gazette, The (magazine): battalion jottings 418–424; battalion secretaries 428; Boys' Brigade portraits 429–430; "boys' room" 444–446; company contributions 432–433; council dinner and conference at Sheffield 414–417; council meeting at Sheffield 406–414; district battalions 418; head-quarters' fund 430–431; head-quarters notes 402–404; officers wanted 404–406; parade addresses 433–435; public meeting and demonstration in Exeter Hall 417–418; public meeting at Falkirk 443–444; public meeting at Kirkcaldy 439–441; public meeting at Nottingham 435–439; public meeting at Thurso 441–443; work abroad 424–428
Boys' Brigade Scripture Union Card, The 403
Boy Scouts 44, 461–462
Boys of the Empire, The (youth magazine) 43, 331, 345, 358, 362, 367, 379, 385, 390, 395
Boys' Own Annual 43, 331, 345, 358, 362, 367, 379, 385, 390, 395
Boys' Own Paper (*BOP*) 42–43, 150, 157, 331, 345, 358, 362, 367, 379, 385, 390, 395, 416
Brabazon, Reginald, Lord Meath 39–40, 118, 251, 253, 256, 258, 260, 265, 269, 271, 304, 309, 311
Bradfield College 118, 126, 140
Brahminism 217, 218
Brahmins 217

INDEX

branch schools 29
Brett. Edward 43, 331, 345, 358, 362, 367, 379, 385, 390, 395
Brewill, Captain 423
Bridges, Frederick 421
"Brigade as a Field of Work for Young Men, The" (Drummond) 429
Bright, John 179
Britain, Battle of 330
Britannia 263–264, 265, 287, 288, 294, 295, 451
British Battles on Land and Sea (Grant) 34
British Boy Scouts (BBS) 43
British Columbia 71, 201, 226–229
British Empire 26, 27
British Empire and Its History, The (Hawke) 35
British Empire Club 304, 309, 311
British Empire League 41, 304–308, 309, 311
British Empire, The (Meiklejohn) 184
British Empire, The (Pollard) 35, 304, 309, 311
British India 34
British South Africa Company 182, 328
Brooke, James, Rajah of Sarawak 101
Broun-Ramsay, James, Lord Dalhousie 77, 186
Bruce, James 72
Bryce Commission 32
Brydon, William 187
Buddhism 218
Bull Dance 263
Bull, John 102, 115
Bulwer-Lytton, Edward Robert, Lord Lytton 182, 184
Burmah (Burma) 71, 112, 188, 218, 448, 466
Burmans 218
Busby, Richard 59–60
Butterworth, George 284, 286, 296
Buxton, Thomas Fowell 87
Byron, Allegra 72
Byron, George G., Lord Byron 56, 71

Cabot, John 201
cadet battalions 253–255
cadet corps 26, 40, 106–109, 118–119, 253–255
Cæsar, Julius 322
Cambridge University Press 35
Campbell, Colin 177, 197

Campbell, William 443
Camp fire yarn. No. 57 (Baden-Powell) 465–470
Canada 32, 44, 71, 75–76, 78, 135, 146, 179–180, 184, 190, 200–202, 237–238, 262, 265, 293, 304, 309, 311, 313, 319, 320, 405, 443, 448, 466
Canada Club 306
cannibals 235–236
Canning, George 54, 176, 177
Cape Colony 83–84, 168, 180, 182, 190, 191–192, 200, 220, 240, 328
careers 101–102
Carlyle, Thomas 73
Carter, E.H. 42, 325–330
Cartier, Jacques 201
Cassell & Company 34, 150, 157
Castle, Kathryn 37
Caswell, H.W. 435
Cato the Elder 73
Cavagnari, Louis 187
Cavendish, Thomas 70
Cavendish, William, Marquess of Hartington 117
Central Asia 112, 183
Cetewayo, King of Zulus 193
Ceylon 142–144, 145, 185, 195, 218, 219, 247–249, 319
Chamberlain, Joseph 173
Chambers New Geographical Reader, The (geographical reader) 37, 38, 216–221
Champlain, Samuel de 200
Chancellor, Richard 70
Chancellor, Valerie 37
Channel Islands 263
Chapman, Dr. 423
Chapman, Samuel 266
character 26, 42, 57–68, 76–77, 95–97, 100, 126–127, 131–133, 203, 209, 211, 279, 280, 359–361, 455–464
charity schools 26
Charles II, King of Scotland, England and Ireland 190, 201
Charles I, King of England, Scotland, and Ireland 292
Chartered Company of South Africa 171
Charterhouse School 26, 28, 140
Cheltenham College 108
Cheltenham Examiner (newspaper) 261
Cheltenham Ladies' College 28, 142, 145
Cheltenham Ladies' College Magazine, The 28, 260–264

473

INDEX

Chiffney, Clement 363–366
Child Villiers, Margaret Elizabeth Leigh, Dowager Countess of Jersey 311, 313
Chillon College 140
China 80, 156, 177, 188–189, 216, 229, 318, 330, 370–371
Chorlton, S.W. 435
Christ Church College 94
Christianity 36, 43, 49, 99, 104, 272–275, 337
Chuma, James 376, 377
Chums (youth magazine) 43, 331, 345, 358, 362, 367, 379, 385, 390, 395, 416
church attendance 416–417
Churchill, Winston 106, 330
Church Lads' Brigade 116, 254
Church Missionary Society 413
Church of England 29, 140, 413
Cicero 73
"Citizen Reader, The" (Foster) 307
citizenship 28, 31, 33, 35–36, 39, 145–149, 198, 203, 209, 211, 275, 307
Clarendon Commission 26
Clarendon Press 35, 195
Clarkson, Thomas 81, 92
class 26
Clifton College 108
Clive, Robert 30, 37, 40, 71, 200, 284, 286
clothing 391–394
coal 239
Cobden, Richard 179
Cole, Arthur U. 414
Coleman, E.E. 423, 438
Collar, G. 38
Colley, George 170, 180
Collie, R.J. 280
Collier, W.F. 35
Collins' Wide World Geography Reader (Collins) 38, 237–241
Collins, William 237–241
Colonial Conference of 1902 94
colonial expansion 184–194
Colonial Office 314, 319
Colonies 70, 77, 86–87, 148, 184–196, 200, 212–213, 263, 448–450, 466–468; *see also* individual countries
Colossians, Letter to 273
Columbus, Christopher 74
commerce 129
Commonwealth Bill of 1891 182
Commonwealth Day 251, 253, 256, 258, 260, 265, 269, 271

compulsory education 32, 278
Comrie, Peter 259
Comyn, Cicely 49
Congo 43
Connell, Mr. 442, 443
Connor, F.H.B. 166
Connor, W. 428
conscription 116
Constitutional History of England (Stubbs) 36
Convention of London (1881) 170
Convention of London (1884) 170–171, 174
Cook, James 30, 198, 199
Cook, Joseph 311, 313
Cook, Walter 428
Cooper, Anthony A., Lord Shaftesbury 68
Cooper, Fenimore 262–263
Coper, Ashley 201
Copley, John S., Lord Lyndhurst 82
copper 221, 239
'Corps, The' (*The Harrovian*) 106–109
Counsell, Miss 263
Country dances 285
courage 60
Cowper, H.E. 27
Cox, A.E. Mrs 265
cricket 64, 65, 74–75, 120
Croad, Hector 117
Cromwell, Oliver 134, 177, 195
Cronjé, Pieter Arnoldus "Piet" 175
Crook, C. 38
Cunning, M.E.D. 140
Curzon, George 80, 183
Cyprus 112, 320

Daily Mail 33
dame schools 29
dance 41, 263, 284–285
Danes, Richard 34, 150, 157–175
daughter nations 293–294
'David Livingstone' (*Young England*) 367–378
Davies, J. Glyn 422
Davis, John 70
Davis, Percy 309–310
Davys, George 30
Dawson, E.C.: 'Froth' 358–361; *Lion-Hearted* 332, 346, 359, 362, 368, 380, 385, 391, 396; *Missionary Heroines in India* 332, 346, 359, 362, 368, 380, 385, 391, 396
'Deeds that Won the Empire' (Fitchett) 452

INDEX

Devereux, Robert, Earl of Essex 214
Devonshire Regiment 164
Dhyan Singh 462–463
Diamond Jubilee 33, 40
diamonds 239, 327
Dick, Thomas 370
Differences Between Liberal and Conservative Imperialism (Drage) 94
Dingaan's Day 180
diplomatist 101–102
Disarmament Conference, 329
Disraelian rhetoric 33
Dixon, J.A. 423, 424, 435, 436, 438
Dodd, Catherine 33
Dods, Marcus 403
Dolman, D.H. 435
Dominions 42, 104, 126, 140, 182, 185, 188, 192, 263, 265, 304, 309, 311, 312, 313, 315, 319, 466, 467; *see also* individual countries
Dost Mohammed 186, 187
Douglas, Catherine 469
Douglas, Dr. 305, 307
Dover College 119
Downes, Graham 258, 259
Doyle, Arthur Conan 43, 331, 345, 358, 362, 367, 379, 385, 390, 395
Drage, Geoffrey: *Differences Between Liberal and Conservative Imperialism;* 94; *Eton and the Empire* 94–105; *Grievance of British Subjects in the Transvaal, The* 94; *Real Causes of the War; The* 94
Drake, Francis 70–71, 72, 211, 213–214, 449
drill 39–40, 118–119, 251–255, 402, 412, 420, 422, 423, 451
Drummond, Henry: *Baxter's Second Innings* 403; "Brigade as a Field of Work for Young Men, The" 429; portraits 429–430; "Tropical Africa" 429
Duane, Patrick 43
Dublin 419
Dulwich College 53, 69, 89
Dutch African Republic 169, 220
Dutch East India Company 168
'Duties and Privileges of Imperial Citizenship, The' (Hemingway) 145–149
Duty and Discipline Movement (DDM) 40, 251, 253, 256–257, 258, 260, 265, 269, 271

'Duty and Discipline Movement, The' (*The Times*) 256–257

"Early Days of Christianity" (Farrar) 416
East Africa 448, 450, 466, 468
East India Company 71, 178, 184, 185–186, 196, 197, 328
East Indies 265, 318
Eclipse or Empire? (Gray) 126
Eden, George, Lord Auckland 186
Edinburgh 419
Edinburgh Chamber of Commerce 258
education: class-based nature of 26–28; curriculum 26; development of British system 25–39; elementary schools 31, 35, 118, 198, 203, 209, 211, 251; grammar schools 28–29; imperial education 27, 32–42, 53, 69–88, 89, 304, 314–321; 'monotorial' system of teaching 29–30; preparatory schools 26, 28, 33, 49–52; profession 100; public schools 26–28, 53–68, 97–105, 140–141; use of school readers 27, 33, 35–38, 137, 198–250; vocational instruction and 25, 26, 30, 32; working class 27, 29–32, 35–36, 38, 42
Education Act 29, 32
Education Committee of Edinburgh Town Council 258
Edward III, King of England and Lord of Ireland 289–290
Edward, Prince of Wales 254
Edward VII, King of the United Kingdom of Great Britain and Ireland and the British Dominions 189, 314
Edward V, King of England and Lord of Ireland 290–291
Egypt 112, 158, 174, 183, 318, 322, 328, 333, 339, 343–344, 402
Eichholz, Dr. 253, 280
Elementary Code 31, 32
Elementary Education Act 31–32
elementary schools 31, 35, 118, 198, 203, 209, 211, 251
Elizabethan era 70–71
Elizabeth I, Queen of England and Ireland 70, 72, 95, 198, 200, 203, 209, 211–212, 214, 291
El Obeid 155
Empire: advancement of 468–470; Colonies of 70, 77, 86–87, 148, 184–196, 200, 212–213, 263, 448–450,

475

INDEX

466–468; defence of 450–451; Dominions of 42, 104, 126, 140, 182, 185, 188, 192, 263, 265, 304, 309, 311, 312, 313, 315, 319, 466, 467; Eton College and 94–105; growth of 198–202, 449–450, 465–468; imperial citizenship 28, 31, 35–36, 145–149; imperial education 27, 32–42, 53, 69–88, 89, 304, 314–321; in juvenile magazines for young boys and girls 42–44, 331–411; League of Nations and 271–275; place in educational curriculum 25–26, 32–42; public school tour 140–141; role of scout movement 28, 43, 120, 402, 447; training of gentlemen for 26, 53–68; training of imperial administrators for 26–28, 54, 55, 66; youth organisations 28, 43–44, 120, 254, 402–447, 462, 465–470; *see also* British Empire League; Empire Day; Empire Day Movement (EDM); individual countries; League of Empire; Victoria League

'Empire and the League of Nations, The' (Norwood) 28, 271–275

Empire Day 28, 39–40, 251, 253, 256, 258–270, 271, 272, 302

'Empire Day in Cheltenham' (*The Cheltenham Ladies' College Magazine*) 260–264

Empire Day Movement (EDM) 251, 253, 256, 258, 260, 265, 269, 271

Empire tours 140–141

Endowed Schools Act 29

engineering profession 100

England 29, 31, 33, 36–37, 40–41, 50, 53–68, 71–82, 84–85, 90–96, 110, 115–118, 128–133, 136, 145–146, 148–149, 174, 184–185, 203–208, 212, 214–215, 263, 273, 281, 286–295, 297, 299–302, 305, 313, 318, 319, 372, 374, 375, 448–450

England and Her Colonies (Froude) 36

English constitutio 94, 129

"English Flag, The" (Kipling) 79

English Folk Dance Society 41, 284, 286, 296

English history 30, 36–37, 66, 70–71, 81, 91, 176–178, 195–197, 203–208, 318

English language 63–64, 80, 220

Eton and the Empire (Drage) 94–105

Eton College 26, 27, 53, 55, 56, 66, 67, 69, 72, 75, 89, 94–95, 97–103, 105, 108, 117–118, 119, 140

Eton College Chronicle 28

Eton College Rifle Volunteer Corp (E.C.R.V.) 111

Evans, Celia 42

Eve 249–250

Expansion of England, The (Seeley) 36, 71

Fadden, Cyrus 349–355

fairness 64

Falconer, Harry 399–411

Faraday, Michael 79

Faraz Pasha 150, 153–154

Farmer, J.H. 435

Farrar, Frederic W. 416

Federal (LOE publication) 304, 309, 311

Felkin, Dr. 333

Fellows, Bruce 113

Fernald, Frank 426

Fernald, T.F. 426

Ferozeshah, Battle of 186

Fettes College 27

Field Batteries of Artillery 135, 162, 167

Field, H. 307

Fifoot, T.R. 422

Fiji Islands 320

Finch, R.J. 38, 222–232

Findlay, John 33

'first English colonies, or the work of Raleigh and his friends, The' (school reader) 211–215

Fish, A.H. 426

Fisher, A. Hugh 320

Fisher, Herbert 32

Fitchett, W.H. 452

Fitzpatrick, T.H. 435

Fitzroy, Almeric W. 276

Fitzroy Report 41, 276–283

FitzRoy, Robert 181

Fitzwygram, John 29, 30

Fletcher, Charles 34–35, 195–197

Fletcher, Percy 267

Flinders, Martin 199

folk songs 41

Folk Song Society 284, 286, 296

football 64, 75

Forrester, Henry 443

Forster, W.E. 31

Foster, H. Arnold 307

Fotheringham, T.F. 427

476

INDEX

founding principles 149
Four Freedoms 330
Fox, Charles James 102
Fox, Malcolm 254
France 117, 146, 184, 188, 274–275, 323, 330
Frederick the Great 274
Freeman, E.A. 36
Freeman Murray 309
Frere, Bartle 180
Fritchie, Barbara 469
Frobisher, Martin 70, 449
froth 359–361
'Froth' (Dawson) 358–361
Froude, J.A. 36, 91–92, 180
Fry, C.B. 64

Gaikwar of Baroda (Mahratta chief) 186
Gaiseric, King of the Vandals 133
Gama, Vasco da 74
Ganges Canal 188
Ganges River 56, 262, 387
Gardiner, Samuel Rawson: *Outline of English History, An* 30, 176; *School Atlas of English History, A* 176; *Student's History of England, A* 34, 176–178
Gardner, Alexander 462–464
Gardner, Edward 376
Garrod, Lieutenant 458
Gascoyne-Cecil, Robert, Lord Salisbury 254
Gear, Gillian 29
Gebel Nuba 155
Gem (youth magazine) 43, 331, 345, 358, 362, 367, 379, 385, 390, 395
Genge, C.J. 166
gentlemen 53–68
geographical readers: *Chambers New Geographical Reader, The* 37, 38, 216–221; *Collins' Wide World Geography Reader* 38, 233–236, 237–241; *Instructive Stories from English History, Holborn Series Historical Reader* 37; *Kingsway Book of Geography Stories* 38, 222–232; *Round the Globe* 38, 242–250; use in elementary education 35–38
geography 30, 31, 32–38, 78, 148, 314–321
George III, King of Great Britain and Ireland 30, 196, 292–293

George V, King of the United Kingdom and the British Dominions 269–270, 272
Germany 25, 113, 182, 189, 329, 330
Gibbon, Edward 131
Gibraltar 112, 184, 320
Gilbert, Humphrey 70–71, 212
Gillespie, Sheriff 441
Girl Guides 44, 462, 465–470
'Girl in the Bush, A' (Storer) 395–411
Girl's Own Paper (*GOP*) 43–44, 331, 345, 358, 362, 367, 379, 385, 390, 395
Gladstone, William E. 180
Glasgow 419–420
Glasgow University 371
Glenalmond College 27, 119, 140
Glendenning, F. 37
Glover, Frank 305, 307
goats 241
God: African knowledge of 37; character of young boys and 416; of Christianity 272–275, 337; faith in 76, 81, 83, 91–93, 99, 105, 204, 288, 368, 388–389; fear of 77–78; of History 127; of Mohammedan 217; in national life 89–93, 128, 134, 149, 290; serving state and 73, 301; of Sikhs 186
Godsal, Philip T. 111
'God Save the Queen' (patriotic song) 40
Godson, G.R. 87
gold 171, 189, 199, 239
Gold Coast 319, 448, 466
Golden Jubilee 33
Golding, Mrs. 262
Goldstrom, J.M. 30
Gordon, Charles G. 36, 39, 40, 77, 150–152, 155–156, 185, 332–333, 335–336
Gordon-Lennox, Charles, Duke of Richmond 156
Gordon, Lewis, Marquis of Huntly 156
Gorman, Dan 39
Gough, Hugh 186
government 94–95, 103–104
Gower, John 324–357
Graham, Robert 469
Grainger, Percy 284, 286, 296
grammar schools 28–29
Grant, James: *British Battles on Land and Sea* 34; *Illustrated History of India* 34, 150, 157; *Illustrated History of the War in the Soudan* 34, 150, 157; 'last day of Khartoum, The' 150–156

477

INDEX

Gray, H.B.: *Eclipse or Empire?* 126; 'Parents of England's Sons, To the' (Gray) 126–137; *Public Schools and the Empire, The* 126
Gray, Thomas 56
Great Mogul 177
Great Trek 191
Greece 98, 132, 133, 318, 322
Greek language 87
Green, J.R. 36, 416
Grenfell, Francis 339
Grenville, Richard 212, 214
Greswell, W.P. 83
Greyfriars stories 43
Grey, Henry G., Earl Grey 181
Grievance of British Subjects in the Transvaal, The (Drage) 94
Grieve, David G. 428
Griquas 220
Grond Wet (Fundamental Law) 169
Guiana 195, 214, 319, 448, 466
Guild of Play 284
Guinea 190
Gunning, Robert H. 111, 166
Gurkhas 186, 197, 467
Gützlaff, Karl 370
Gwynne; L.H. 423
Gwynne, L.H. 435

Haileybury College 27, 41
half-castes 220
Ham 169
Hambro, Norman 166
Hamed Ibn Hussein 341–343
Hamilton, Charles (aka Frank Richards) 43, 331, 345, 358, 362, 367, 379, 385, 390, 395
Hamilton, George 86
Hamilton-Gordon, John, Earl of Aberdeen 156
Hammersley, Frederick 166
Handbook of Suggestions (Board of Education) 322–324
Hansal, Martin 151
Hardinge, Henry 82
Hardingham, B.G. 38, 242–250
Harding, Robert 379–384
Harmsworth, Alfred 43, 331, 345, 358, 362, 367, 379, 385, 390, 395
Harris, John C. 426
Harrovian, The 106–109
Harrow History Prize 33, 49

Harrow School 26, 27, 53, 55, 66, 67, 68, 69, 72, 74, 85, 89, 106–109, 117–118, 119, 140
Hart, Arthur 411
Harun, Sultan 333
Hassan 229–232
Hastings, Dick 380–384
Hastings, Warren 37, 71, 200
Havelock, Henry 66, 77, 177, 197, 204
Hawke, Edward 35
Hawkins, Richard 449
Hay, J. Douglas 414–415
Hayward, Frank 33, 40
Hazara expedition 112
Heathorn, Stephen 36, 37
Heath Stubbs, Councillor 304, 307, 308
Heelas, N. 435
Hein Fung, Emperor of China 156
Helweg, Marianne 268
Hemingway, Phyllis D. 145–149
Henderson, Ebenezer 428
Henderson, J.A. 443
Hennings, Helen 28
Henry VIII, King of England 117
Henry VII, King of England 201
Henry V, King of England 290
Henty, G.A. 33, 43, 331, 345, 358, 362, 367, 379, 385, 390, 395
Herbartians 33
Herbart, Johann 33, 40
Herbert, George, Lord Carnarvon 180
Herbert, Robert 87
Herbert, Sidney 262, 263
Herbertson, A.J. 35
hereditary physical deterioration 277
'Heroes of Pioneering' (Sanderson) 452
high schools 28
Hill, J.R. 383, 417
Hill, Rowland 207
Hindus 187, 216–218, 229, 262, 386–389
Hindustan 187
'Hindu Women' (*The Girl's Own Paper*) 385–389
Historical Association 32
"Historical Geography of the British Colonies" (Lucas) 78
Histories (Martens and Carter) 42, 325–330
history 29–36, 38–39, 42, 148, 317, 322–324
History of the British Empire (Collier) 35
History of the English People (Green) 36

478

INDEX

History of the Norman Conquest (Freeman) 36
Hitler, Adolph 330
Hittites 169
Hivites 169
Hogg, David 370
Holkar (Mahratta chief) 186
Holland 469
Holland, Henry, Lord Knutsford, 86
Holmes, Oliver Wendell 414
Holy Land 402
Homer 98
Hong Kong 71, 188, 318, 319, 320
honour 57, 58–62
Honourable Artillery Company of London 117
hooliganism 116
Hope, John, Lord Hopetoun 182
Horace 369
Horniblow, Edmund 38, 233–236
Hottentots 220
Housing Acts 279
Howard, Charles, Lord Howard 214
How Girls Can Help to Build Up the Empire (Baden-Powell) 44, 465
Hudson Bay Company 190
Hulse, John 53, 69, 89
Hume, Edward 370, 377
Hunter, D.A. 424
Hunter, James S. 428
hunting 222–226
Hurt, J.S. 30
Hussars 158
Hutchison, Clark 259

Illustrated History of India (Grant) 34, 150, 157
Illustrated History of the Boer War (Danes) 34, 157–175
Illustrated History of the War in the Soudan (Grant) 34, 150, 157
imperial administrators 27, 36, 54, 55, 66, 67, 71, 83, 122
'Imperial Aspects of Education, The' (Welldon) 69–88
imperial attitude 318–319
Imperial British East Africa Company 191
imperial citizenship 28, 31, 35–36, 145–149
Imperial Conference of 1911 94
Imperial Economic Committee 314

imperial education 27, 32–42, 53, 69–88, 89, 304, 314–321
Imperial Federation League 41, 304, 306, 309, 311
imperialism 28, 32–36, 43–44, 94, 182, 275
imperial parliament 126
Imperial Shipping Committee 314
Imperial Union of Teachers 41, 304, 309, 311
India 34, 37, 40, 64, 66, 71, 75–76, 78, 80–81, 112, 135, 142, 145, 146, 158, 174, 176–178, 182–183, 185–186, 188, 196, 200, 216–219, 265, 293, 319, 320, 328, 380–384, 386–389, 391–394, 448, 450, 455–464, 466
Indian Civil Service 27
Indian cuisine 44
Indian famine of 1876–1878 184
Indian Memories (Baden-Powell) 44, 455–464
Indian Mutiny 37, 66, 176–178, 183, 186, 196–197, 203–205
industrial schools 29
'Infantry Drill, 1889' (drill book) 422
inferior races 148
influence 58, 60, 62
Inghram, F.H. 428
Inglis, J.A. 428
Instructive Stories from English History, Holborn Series Historical Reader (school reader) 37, 203–208
intellectual education 63
internationalism 42
International Labour Office 329
Ireland 30–31, 40, 90, 263, 319, 412–413, 456–457
Irish Municipal Bill 82
iron 239
Isazai expedition 112
Isle of Man 263
Ismail, Abdullah Bey 155
Italy 113, 318, 329, 330

Jackson, J.W. 428
Jaffrey, Mr. 443
Jamaica 319
James I, King of England and Ireland 70, 214–215, 469
Jameson, Leander S. 171
Jameson Raid 171, 181
Japan 54, 64, 67, 68, 80, 188, 329, 330

479

INDEX

'Jerusalem' (patriotic song) 40
jingoism 359–360
Johannesburgers 171–172
John Murray Publishers 35
John of Gaunt 273
Johnson, H.C. 111
Johnson, Samuel 29
Jones, Annie 142–144, 145
Jones, E. 421
Jones, Edward 428
Joubert, Piet 167, 174
journalism 33
Journal of Education 40
Ju-Ju man 355–357
justice 59–60

Kaffirs 38, 220, 242–244
Katz, Michael 25–26
Keatinge, M.W. 39
Kelly, Mr. 442–443
Kennedy, E.J. 414–416
Kernahan, Miss 262
Kerr, Mr. 443
Khartoum 150–156, 335–336
Kidston, William 420
Kimmins, G.T. 41, 284, 286–295
King's College 53, 69, 89
King's Royal Rifle Corps 110, 111, 112, 114, 140
King's Royal Rifles 158, 161, 162, 164–165, 167
Kingsway Book of Geography Stories (Finch) 38, 222–232
Kipling, Rudyard 33, 185; "Big Steamers" 266; "English Flag, The" 79; *Recessional* 264; *School History of England, A* 34–35, 195–197
Kitchener, Herbert, Lord Kitchener 122, 151, 152
Klickmann, Flora 331, 345, 358, 362, 367, 379, 385, 390, 395
Knighton, William 386
Koran 217
Korea 80
Kruger, Paul 159, 171, 174
Krupp (German corporation) 116

Ladies Empire Club 304, 309, 311
Lads' Drill Association 39
'Lads' Drill Association' (*Volunteer Service Gazette*) 253–255
Ladybarn Company 414

Laidlaw, David 419
Lake Bangweolo 376
Lake Nyasa 326, 375
Lake Tanganyika 376
Lamb, Stewart 259
Lambton, John G., Lord Durham; 179
Lammie, John 411
Lancashire Regiment 117
Lands and Life (Horniblow) 38, 233–236
Lang, John 452
language 32, 63–64, 80, 87
Lankester, Herbert 412, 413
La Salle, René-Robert Cavelier, Sieur de 201
'last day of Khartoum, The' (Grant) 150–156
Latham, Mr. 421
Latin language 87
Laurier, Wilfrid 180, 181
law 103
Lawrence, Captain 422
Lawrence, Henry Montgomery 77, 177
Lawrence, John 177, 197
Lawrence, Lieutenant 422
Lawrence, Thomas Edward 77
lawyers 102
League of Empire 35, 41, 304, 309–310, 311
League of Nations 40, 42, 273–275, 323, 328–330
League of Nations Union (LNU) 42
Lehna Singh 462
Leicester Regiment 158, 160
Leinster-Mackay, Donald 26
letters 102
Levy, Louis 268
liberty 103
Library of Useful Stories 34
"Liebelei" (Schnitzler) 268
Liebmann, J.A. 83–84
"Life of John Sterling" (Carlyle) 73
"Life of Livingstone" (Hume) 370
Life of Lord Beaconsfield (Froude) 91–92
"Life of Wilberforce, The" (Wilberforce and Wilberforce) 81
Limpopo 171
Lines Written Beneath an Elm in the Churchyard at Harrow (Byron) 56
Lion-Hearted (Dawson) 332, 346, 359, 362, 368, 380, 385, 391, 396
lions 219, 372
Liverpool 420

INDEX

Livingstone, Agnes, Mrs. 369
Livingstone, Charles 370
Livingstone, David 34, 36, 37, 77, 284, 286, 325–327, 367–378
Livingstone, Mary Moffat 372, 375
Llyod, Dr. 113
Lobengula, King of Matabeleland 191
Loch, Mr. 281
Lock Adams, Frederick 166
London Battalions 413
London Missionary Society 43, 331, 345, 358, 362, 367, 370, 371, 379, 385, 390, 395
London School Board 117
London School of Economics 314
London Sunday School Union 43, 331, 345, 358, 362, 367, 379, 385, 390, 395
Longman Publishing 35
Lord, Frewen, Mrs: 'Saint Paul's Cathedral' 452; 'Westminster Abbey' 452
Lorettonianism 27
Lorettonian, The (magazine) 122–125
Loretto School 27, 122
Louis, Prince of Hesse and by Rhine 205
Louis XIV, King of France 274, 323
loyalty 94–95
Lubbock, John, Lord Avebury 41
Lucas, Charles 78
Lucas, M.P. 307
lucifer match 208
Lucknow, relief of 66, 177–178, 203–204
Lupton, Frank 336–337
Lyon, John 72
Lyons, E.W. 428
Lyttelton, Edward 41

Macaulay, Rose 170
Macaulay, Thomas Babington, Lord Macaulay 56
Macdonald, Claude 56
Macdonald, John 180
Macdonald, W.J. 440–441
Mackay, R. J. 259
Mackenzie, John 35
Mackinder, H.J.: 'Man-Power as a Measure of National and Imperial Strength' 314; 'Teaching of Geography from an Imperial Point of View and the Use Which Could and Should be Made of Visual Instruction, The' 314–321
MacMahon, Patrice de 169

Macmillan, A. 441
Macmillan, Harold 251, 253, 256, 258, 260, 265, 269, 271
Macmillan Publishers Ltd. 35, 37
Madeley, Helen 42
Magna Carta 148
Magnet, The (youth magazine) 43, 331, 345, 358, 362, 367, 379, 385, 390, 395
Mahdi 150, 155, 185, 335–338
Mahomet, Jacoob 151–152
Mahrattas 186, 217
Maiwand, Battle of 187
Majuba Hill 158, 161, 168, 170, 180
Makepeace, J.F. 423, 438
Malays 220
Malta 184, 320
Manchester 414
Manchester Guardian (newspaper) 280
Manchester School 96, 179
Manchuria 329
Mangan, John 27, 122
manliness 43, 116, 447
'Man-Power as a Measure of National and Imperial Strength' (Mackinder) 314
Manson, A. 345–357
Manyuema 376
Maoris 34, 189, 199, 399, 467
Marlborough College 28, 108, 115, 117–118, 140, 251, 256, 258, 260, 265, 269, 271
Marlborough Corps 108
Marris, Isabel 257
Marsden, H.S. 111
Marshall, Elizabeth Ord 41
Martens, H. 42, 325–330
Mary of Teck, Queen of the United Kingdom and the British Dominions 272
Mashonaland 191, 327
Masque of the Children of the Empire, The (Kimmins) 41, 286–295
Matabeleland 191, 327
Matabeles 171, 191, 456
Matopo Hills 328
Mauritius 319
Maxwell. J.T. 423
McLea, Miss 260, 261
McLellan, Mrs. 262
medical profession 100
Mehtab Singh 452–453
Meiklejohn, J.M.D.: *British Empire, The* (Meiklejohn) 184; *School History of England, A* 184–194

481

INDEX

Meiklejohn, M.J.C. 184–194
Mellors, Robert 435, 438
Melrose, Andrew 43, 331, 345, 358, 362, 367, 379, 385, 390, 395
'Memoriam, In: William Joseph Myers 1858–1899' (in *Eton College Chronicle*) 110–114
Merchiston Castle School 27
Merrilees, Mr. 443
Methodist Reformation 92
Meyer, Lucas 159, 160, 167
Middlesex Regiment 106
militaristic culture 42, 43, 115–121
military drill 118–119, 254, 402
military profession 99–100, 120
'Military Training' (Way) 115–121
Millar, Ernest A. 421
Mill, John Stuart 179
Mills, Mr. 424–425
Milner, Alfred 173, 175
Milton, John 71, 73, 80, 92–93, 96, 117
Miranzai expedition 112
Missionary Heroines in India (Dawson) 332, 346, 359, 362, 368, 380, 385, 391, 396
M'Kay, William 442
M'Neill, John 428
Modern Teaching (Blyton) 42
Moffat, Robert 371, 372
Mohammed Ahmed 341
Mohammedans 216–217, 220, 317, 332, 337
Mohammed, prophet of Islam 217, 337
Molehabangwe, Mebalwe 371
Molesworth, Councillor 307
Möller, Benhardt 158, 167, 174
'monotorial' system 29–30
Moore, Edward Cecil, Lord Mayor 311
Moore, E.G. 435
moral instruction 26, 31
Morley, John 360
Morris dances 284–285
'Morris Dances' (Sharp) 284–285
Morrison, Mary 396–411
Morrison, Phobe 396, 398–399
Mother Kangaroo 244–245
Mozambique 375
Mundella Act 32
Murphy, Shirley 283
Murray, Freeman 304, 308
Murray, Mungo 373
Murray, William, Marquess of Tullibardine 122
muscular Christianity 43, 49

music: Myers interest in 113; school singing 99
Mussolini, Benito 330
M'Vicker, William 412–413
Myers, Charles 113
Myers, Dudley 113
Myers, Miss 113
Myers, W.H. 113
Myers, William Joseph 110–114

Napoleon I, Emperor of the French, General 275, 323
Napoleon III, Emperor of the French 117, 275
Natal 174, 180, 191, 193, 220, 240, 327
Natalian volunteers 158–159
Natal Mounted Carbineers 160
Natal Mounted Police 160
National and English Review (magazine) 314
national citizenship 35–36, 198, 203, 209, 211
national duty 92–93, 103–105, 147
National Education League 31
national faith 91–92
nationality 90–91
national life 89–93, 127–137
'National Life, The' (Welldon) 89–93
national morality 92
National Peace Scouts 43
national schools 29–30
National Service League (NSL) 39, 195
National Society for Promoting the Education of the Poor in the Principles of the Established Church 29
national virtues 127–128
Nelson, Horatio 36, 57, 75, 163, 450
Nepaul 186
Never-Never Land 244–246
New Brunswick 180, 190
Newcastle Commission 26
Newfoundland 70, 180, 201, 212
New Guinea 182, 235–236, 448, 466
Newham, W. Henry 428, 435, 436, 438
new imperialism 25, 33–36
New Poor Law 31
Newport 422
New South Wales 81, 179, 189, 199
New York Herald (newspaper) 376
New Zealand 32, 44, 71, 142, 145, 179, 181–182, 198–199, 293, 304, 309, 311, 312, 319, 320, 448, 466, 467

INDEX

Nicholl, William 428
Nicholson, Dr. 307
Nicholson, John 197, 452–453
Niger 190–191
Nigeria 183, 448, 466
Nisbet, James 34
nobility 67
Non-Conformists 29
Nore mutiny 75
North Borneo 320, 448, 466
North-East Passage 70
North London 420–421
North-West Passage 70, 212
Norwood, Cyril 28, 251, 253, 256, 258, 260, 265, 269, 271–274
Nottingham 422–423
Nova Scotia 180, 190
Nusri Pasha 154

obedience 57–58, 65, 94–95
Ode on a Distant Prospect of Eton College (Gray) 56
officer class 27
Ohrwalder, Joseph 338
Old Man Kangaroo 244–245
Oliver, A.T. 435
Ontario 190
open door principle 188
opium 188
Orange Free State 169, 175, 181, 191–192, 325
Orange River 325
O'Rell, Max 83
Oriental Steam Navigation Company Limited 380
Orinoco 214
Ormsby-Gore, W. 311
Orsini Plot 117
Osborne, Ken 42
Osborne. W.A. 117
Osborn, Samuel 411, 412
Osman Wad Ahmed 339
ostrich farms 241
Oswell, William Cotton 373
Oundle School 140
Our Empire Past and Present (Brabazon [Lord Meath]) 40
Outlanders 171–172, 174, 182
Outline of English History, An (Gardiner) 30, 176
Outram, James 66, 177
overcrowding 278, 282–283

Overrell, Councillor 305, 307
Oxford University 35, 55, 66

Palestine 318, 322
Pall Mall Gazette 33
Palmer, Sidney 363–366
Panama 113
'Parents of England's Sons, To the' (Gray) 126–137
Parker, Gilbert 41
Parkes, Henry 181–182
Parkin, George 41, 85–87
parochialism 132–133
Parr, J.W. 140
Parsees 217
Paterson, William 266
patriotic books 452
patriotic songs 451
patriotism 42, 77–78, 90, 94–95, 119, 126, 132–133, 147, 258–259, 275, 447–454, 468
Patriotism (Baden-Powell) 447–454
'Patriotism Plea' (*The Scotsman*) 258–259
patriots 468–470
Paul, Saint 273
Peace of Amiens 185
Peace of Versailles 75
peace-time conscription 39
Pearson, V.W. 414
Pechell, Mark 111, 166
Peel, Jonathan 117
Penago, Rosti 152, 155
penny dreadfuls 42–43
penny postage 207
Persia 112, 217, 322
Peters, Charles 43, 331, 345, 358, 362, 367, 379, 385, 390, 395
Philip II, King of Spain 323
physical deterioration 41, 276–283
Pictorial Knowledge (Blyton) 42
piety 94–95
Pioneer, The (newspaper) 380–381
Pitt, William, the Elder, Lord Chatham 94, 102
Pitt, William, the Younger 195
Plain and Short History of England for Children (Davys) 30
Ploszajska, Tesea 37
Pluck (youth magazine) 43, 331, 345, 358, 362, 367, 379, 385, 390, 395
Plymouth 423–424
Poland 329

INDEX

police 470
political attitude 129–130
Pollard, A.F. 35, 304, 309, 311
Pollock, George 187
Porter, Bernard 25
Porter, C.B. 435
Poulter, D.F.O. 423
Preparatory School Rifle Association 52
preparatory schools 26, 28, 33, 49–52
Preston Cecilian Choir 267
Pretorius, Marthinus W. 169
Prince Edward's Island 180
privilleges 146–147
Prowse, Daniel Woodley 84–85
Prussia 274–275
public elementary schools 277–278
Public Health Acts 279
'Public School Boys Empire Tour' (*The Times Educational Supplement*) 140–141
public schools: schoolboy life at 97–105; tour to Australia 140–141; training of gentlemen 26, 53–68; training of imperial administrators 26–28, 54, 55, 66
Public Schools Act 26
Public Schools and the Empire, The (Gray) 126
Punch (magazine) 360
punishment 59–60
Punjab 71, 186, 196
'Purchase of Outfits for India and the Colonies, On the' (Blaquiere) 390–394
Puritan Reformation 92
Purvis, J. 468

Quebec 190, 200
Queen's College, 126
Queensland 71

Radley College 140
Rae, W. Shaw 362–366
ragged schools 29
railways 207
Raleigh, Walter 71, 211–215, 449
Ramadan 332–333
Rand mines 172, 182, 239
Rani Jindan, regent of the Sikh Empire 462
Ranjit Singh 464
reading 416
Real Causes of the War; The (Drage) 94
Recessional (Kipling) 264
Reformation 71, 274

Reitz, Francis W. 174
religious instruction 26
Religious Tract Society (RTS) 42–43, 331
religious vocation 99, 104–105
Rennie, J.C. 443
Report of the Inter-Departmental Committee on Physical Deterioration, The (Fitzroy Report) 41, 276–283
Repton School 119, 140
Revenge, The (Tennyson) 214
Revival of Learning 71
Reynolds, Captain 422
Reynolds, George P. 411, 416–417
Rhodes, Cecil 76, 86, 172, 173, 181, 191, 284, 286, 296, 327–328
Rhodesia 171, 182, 191, 239, 325–328
Richard Coeur de Lion 289
Richard II (Shakespeare) 273
Richards, Councillor 305, 307
Richards, Jeffrey 43
Ridge, Charles 426–427
Riel, Louis 190
rifle corps 26, 106–109, 111–112, 119–120
rifle ranges 119–120
River Congo 326
Roberts, Frederick S., Lord Roberts 41, 52, 116, 117–118, 158, 166, 187
Robertson, Charles Grant 49
Robertson, James D. 428
Robespierre, Maximilien 360
Robson, J.A. 428
Rogers, Ginger 268
Roman Empire 133, 322, 323
Romans 468
Romilly, Samuel 81
Roosevelt, Franklin D. 330
Rorke's Drift 162
Rorke's Drift, defence of 206–207
Rose Hill Preparatory School 28
Rossall School 115, 117–118, 119
Round the Globe (Hardingham) 38, 242–250
Rouse, Parke 452
Rowntree, Mr. 280
Royal Colonial Institute 53, 69, 89, 179
Royal Dublin Fusiliers 158, 161, 162, 166
Royal Empire Society 35
Royal Geographical Society 32
Royal Irish Fusiliers 158, 161, 164–166
Royal Military Academy Sandhurst 51, 111
Royal Military Academy Woolwich 51
Royal Naval College Osborne 51

INDEX

Royal Niger Company 191
Ruddiman, Thomas 369
'Rudiments of Latin' (Ruddiman) 369
Rudsworth, F.E. 435
rugby 122
Rugby School 26, 49, 55, 56, 57, 108
Rumgay, Miss 266
Runjit Singh 186
Rupert of the Rhine, Prince 190
Russell, Baker 460
Russell, H.H. 426
Russell, John 181
Russia 96, 113, 183, 188, 203, 330
Russian Empire 186

Sadler, Michael 314
Said Abdullah 151–152
Saint Andrew's Ambulance Association 414–415
Saint Ann's School 309
Saint John's Ambulance Association 414
'Saint Paul's Cathedral' (Lord) 452
Saint Peter's 332, 346, 359, 362, 368, 380, 385, 391, 396
Salmon, Edward 195; *Art of Teaching, The* 39; *Story of the Empire, The* 34, 179–183
Sanderson, Edgar 452
Sand River Convention 168–169
Sandwith, Colonel 428
Schæffer, Colonel 340
Schnitzler, Arthur 268
School Atlas of English History, A (Gardiner) 176
School Board for London 251
school drill 39–40, 251–255
'School Drill' (*The Globe*) 251–252
School Empire Tour Committee 140
School History of England, A (Kipling and Fletcher) 34–35, 195–197
School History of England, A (Meiklejohn and Meiklejohn) 184–194
school readers: 'first English colonies, or the work of Raleigh and his friends, The' 211–215; *Instructive Stories from English History, Holborn Series Historical Reader* 37, 203–208; Twenty-second story. – the growth of the Empire 198–202; use in elementary education 27, 33, 35–38, 137, 198–250; *Young Briton's History Reader, The* 37, 209–210
school singing 99

science 63
Scindiah (Mahratta chief) 186
Scotland 27, 28, 31–32, 263, 319, 469
Scottish Football Union 122
Scottish Horse 122
Scottish Provincial Committee 320
Scottish Yeomanry 122–125
'Scottish Yeomanry in May, With the' (*The Lorettonian*) 122–125
Scott, Walter 150, 157, 175
scout movement 28, 43, 44, 120, 402, 447
Sebituane, Chief of the Makololo 373
Sechelé, Chief of the Bakwain. 371
secondary education 32
Second Reform Act 35
Sedbergh School 140
Seeley, John 33, 36, 71, 74, 77
Sekukuni (native chief) 180
self-adulation 127–128
self-denial 96
selfishness 96
self-respect 96
Sepoy army 176–177
Shah Sujah 186
Shakespeare, William 71, 80, 96, 273
Sharp, Cecil 41, 284–285, 286, 296
Sharp, Granville 210
Shaw, R.R. 414
Sheffield 406–417, 424
Sheil, Richard Lalor 82–83
Shemeld, W,H. 421
Shepstone, Theophilus 180
Sher Ali, Amir of Afghanistan 187
Sherston, John 166
Shiré River 375
"Short History of the English People" (Green) 416
Short History of the Expansion of the British Empire (Woodward) 35
Shrewsbury School 26
Shuttleworth, James Kay 30
Sidney, Philip 36
Sierra Leone 319
Sikhs 186, 196, 197, 462, 467
Sikokuni (native chief) 169
Sillar, R.L. 49, 51
silver 239
Singapore 195, 320, 328
Singhalese 218
Slatin, Rudolf Carl von 332–344
slavery 36, 37, 168, 188
slave trade 81–82, 92, 209–210
slum population 280–282

485

Smith, Adam 179
Smith, Donald, Lord Strathcona 41
Smith, Ethel 260, 261, 262
Smith, Irving 404
Smith, John 449
Smith, Michelle 44
Smith, Peter 162
Smith, Vincent 261
Smith, William A. 44, 423, 424, 441–442, 443
Sobraon, Battle of 186
Social Arrows (Brabazon) 251, 253, 256, 258, 260, 265, 269, 271
Somaliland 320, 448, 466, 468
songs 451
Soudan (Sudan) 96, 112, 157, 183, 448, 466, 468
South Africa 40, 44, 71, 78, 79, 83–84, 110, 112, 150, 157–175, 180–181, 191–193, 220, 237–241, 293, 304, 309, 311, 319, 325–328, 448, 449, 466
South African Republic 169–175
South African War 28, 33, 41, 106, 115, 122–125, 142, 145, 185, 276, 304, 309, 311, 467
South America 195, 214
Southern Nigeria 319
South London 421
South, Robert 59–60
Spain 95, 113, 211, 214, 215, 323
Sparto-Christian ideal 122
Spicer, Howard 43, 331, 345, 358, 362, 367, 379, 385, 390, 395
Springhall, John 44
Standard I 31
Standard IV 31, 40
standards 31, 32–33
Standard V 40
Standard VI 31, 33, 40
Standard VII 31
Standard VIII 40
Stanhope, James 86
Stanley, Arthur P. (Dean Stanley) 59
Stanley, Henry 34, 327, 376–377
Stark, Ralph 443
state schools 35, 38
statesmen 102
St. Cyprian's Preparatory School: district and school 50; outcome 52; play and recreations 51–52; Principal 51; work of school 51
Stead, W.T. 33
Steyn, Marthinus T. 174, 175

Stoneman, Leonard E. 411, 412, 428
Storer, H.C. 395–411
Storrar, Major 441
'Story of Captain Cook, The' (Lang) 452
Story of the Empire, The (Salmon) 34, 179–183
Stowe School 140
Straits Settlements 319, 448, 466
Stretcher Drill 414
Stubbs, Mrs. 304–305
Stubbs, William 36
Student's History of England, A (Gardiner) 34, 176–178
Sunday schools 29
Survey of the British Empire (Herbertson) 35
Susi, Abdullah 376, 377
Symons, William Penn 159–161, 163–165, 167, 174
Syria 393

Taché, Etienne 179
"Taffy and the Welshman" (nursery rhyme) 333
Tait, Major 441
Talana Hill 157–168
Talleyrand, Charles Maurice de 72
Tasmania 189, 448, 466
Taunton Commission 26
Taylor, John 166
Taylor, Mr. 443
Taylor, Robert 113
Taylor, Robert, Mrs. 113
Teacher's Treasury, The (Blyton) 42, 284, 286, 296
'Teaching of Geography from an Imperial Point of View and the Use Which Could and Should be Made of Visual Instruction, The' (Mackinder) 314–321
telegraph 207–208
Temple, Henry John, Lord Palmerston 78, 374
tenement housing 278, 282–283
Tennyson, Alfred 54, 117, 214
Thackeray, William Makepeace 62
Thebaw, King of Burma 188
'The Duty and Discipline Movement' (*The Times*) 256–257
Thesiger, Frederic A., Lord Chelmsford 193
Third French Republic 25
Third Reform Act 35
Thomas, A. Garrod 422

INDEX

Thomson, Edward Deas 181
Thornton, A.P. 28
Thornton, H.E. 435
three Rs 31
Thring, Edward 56, 315
'Through Peril to Fortune' (Rae) 362–366
Thucydides 80
Thuggism 188
Thursfield, T. W. 304
tin 239
Tom Brown's Schooldays (Hughes) 56
trade profession 100–101
'Training of the English Gentleman in the Public Schools, The' (Welldon) 53–68
Transvaal 84, 94, 122, 123, 159–160, 167–175, 180, 181, 191–193, 239, 325
Transvaal Dutch 171
'Travels of Captain John Smith' (Rouse) 452
Treaty of Paris 201
Treaty of Ulundi 112
Treaty of Utrecht 274
Treaty of Versailles 328
Treaty of Waitangi 34
Trinidad 319
Trinity College 27
"Tropical Africa" (Drummond) 429
T'saka, King of Zulus 193
Turkey 112, 393
Twenty-second story. – the growth of the Empire (school reader) 198–202

Uganda 183, 448, 466, 468
Ujiji 327, 376
Ulundi, Battle of 193
Union Jack 40, 96, 101, 448, 466, 467
Union Jack (Dods) 403
Union Jack, The (Blyton) 42, 284, 286, 296–303
Union Jack, The (Henty) 43, 331, 345, 358, 362, 367, 379, 385, 390, 395
Union Jack (youth magazine) 43, 331, 345, 358, 362, 367, 379, 385, 390, 395
Union of South Africa 328
United Empire 34
United Empire (journal) 179
United States 75–76, 78, 80, 118, 126, 146, 323, 328, 330, 425–427, 443, 449
universities 53–68
University of Cambridge 54, 55, 66
University of Edinburgh 184
Uppingham School 56, 119
urbanization 281–283

Vandeleur, Mrs. 113
Vaughan Williams, Ralph 284, 286, 296
veld 242–244
Verne, Jules 43, 331, 345, 358, 362, 367, 379, 385, 390, 395, 416
Victoria Cross 37, 204–205
Victoria Falls 326, 374
Victoria League 41, 261, 304, 309, 311–313
Victorian era 71–72
Victoria, Queen of the United Kingdom of Great Britain and Ireland 27, 30, 33, 34, 39, 53, 69, 70, 71, 72, 89, 178, 179, 182–183, 188, 190, 196, 197, 200, 205, 207–208, 210, 218, 261, 293, 311, 320, 325, 326
Victoria University of Manchester 33
Vienna Congress 275
vineyards 241
Virgil 70, 369
Virginia Company 71
'Visit to a Boer Camp, A' (Jones) 142–144
Visual Instruction Committee 314, 319–321
vocational instruction 26, 30, 32
Volunteer Cadet Corps 119
Volunteer Corps 117

Wad del Nejumi, Abdel Rahman 339
Wales 30, 31, 263, 281
Walker, Dougald 266
Warbeck, Perkin 469
Warburton, William 77
Ward, Georgina E., Lady Dudley 320
War Office 253
Warre, Edmond 26, 27
"Watches Carnival, The" (Fletcher) 267
Waterfield, Mrs. 262
Waters, R. 423
Way, J. P 115–121
Wayland, William A. 268
Wedderburn, Mr. 113
Wei-hai-wei 320
Weldon, George A. 166
Welldon, J.E.C.: as honorary chaplain to Queen Victoria 27, 53; 'Imperial Aspects of Education, The' 69–88; 'National Life, The' 89–93; 'Training of the English Gentleman in the Public Schools, The' 53–68
Wellesley, Arthur, Duke of Wellington 36, 56, 73, 77, 158, 450

INDEX

Wellesley, Richard, Marquis of Wellington 56, 72
Wellington School 108
Wentworth, William 181
Wesley, John 81
West Indies 81, 85, 113, 184, 195, 265, 309, 318, 448, 466
West London 421–422
'Westminster Abbey' (Lord) 452
Westminster School 26, 59
Weston, Drake 381, 383–384
Whately, Richard 81
White, D.G. 140
White, George 174
Whittier, John Greenleaf 469
Whittingstall, Herbert O.F. 113
Whitworth, Joseph 116
Wilberforce, William 81, 92
Wilkes, Lewis Vaughan 49–52
Williams, Eric 36
Williams, H. 422
William the Norman 288
Willoughby, Dr. 423
Willoughby, Hugh 70
Winchester College 26, 72, 99, 108, 117–118, 126, 140
Windly, Dr. 436
Wingate, F.R. 316–341, 344
Wolf Cubs 462
Wolfe, James 40, 71, 201, 284, 286
Wolley-Dod, C. 111
Wolseley, Garnet 180, 185
womanhood 43–44
'Wonderful Escape, A' (Boyler) 331–344
Woodburn, Mrs. 259

Wood, Evelyn 170
Woods, Frank 423, 435
Woodward, W.H. 35
working class education 27, 29–32, 35–36, 38, 42
working class youth 276–283
W.R. Chambers Publishers 35
Wright, Captain 423
Wyer, Otho 305, 307

Yates, R.P. 305, 307
Yeandle, P. 33, 37
Yonge, Charlotte 470
young boys 42–43, 254, 402–446
Young Briton's History Reader, The (school reader) 37, 209–210
Young England (youth magazine) 43, 331, 345, 358, 362, 367, 379, 385, 390, 395
young girls 28, 43–44, 278, 462, 465–470
Young, Mr. 426
youth organisations: Boys' Brigade 44, 254, 402–447; Girl Guides 44, 462, 465–470; scout movement 28, 43, 44, 120, 402, 447
Yule, James H. 164

Zambesi River 326, 373, 374
Zanzibar 327, 375–376
Zeki Belal 341–342
Zulu Campaign of 1879 112
Zulus 157, 162, 169, 180, 191, 193, 206–207
Zulu War 169
Zurbuchen, Dr. 332

9781138495043